ESSENTIALS OF
SOCIOLOGY

third edition

ESSENTIALS OF
SOCIOLOGY

third edition

Anthony Giddens
LONDON SCHOOL OF ECONOMICS

Mitchell Duneier
CITY UNIVERSITY OF NEW YORK
GRADUATE CENTER

PRINCETON UNIVERSITY

Richard P. Appelbaum
UNIVERSITY OF CALIFORNIA,
SANTA BARBARA

Deborah Carr
RUTGERS UNIVERSITY

W. W. NORTON & COMPANY, INC.
New York • London

W. W. NORTON & COMPANY has been independent since its founding in 1923, when William Warder Norton and Mary D. Herter Norton first published lectures delivered at the People's Institute, the adult education division of New York City's Cooper Union. The firm soon expanded its program beyond the Institute, publishing books by celebrated academics from America and abroad. By midcentury, the two major pillars of Norton's publishing program—trade books and college texts—were firmly established. In the 1950s, the Norton family transferred control of the company to its employees, and today—with a staff of four hundred and a comparable number of trade, college, and professional titles published each year—W. W. Norton & Company stands as the largest and oldest publishing house owned wholly by its employees.

Editor: Karl Bakeman
Editorial assistant: Rebecca Charney
Project editor: Kate Feighery
Senior production manager, College: Benjamin Reynolds
Art direction and design: Hope Miller Goodell
Information graphics design: Kiss Me I'm Polish LLC, New York
Photo research: Stephanie Romeo/Julie Tesser
E-media editor: Eileen Connell
Associate e-media editor: Laura Musich
Marketing manager: Natasha Zabohonski
Composition: TexTech/Jouve
Page layout: Brad Walrod/KenozaType
Manufacturing: Courier—Kendallville, IN

Library of Congress Cataloging-in-Publication Data
Essentials of sociology / Anthony Giddens ... [et al.]. – 3rd ed.
    p. cm.
Includes bibliographical references and index
ISBN **978-0-393-93237-9** (pbk.)
1. Sociology. I. Giddens, Anthony.
HM585.G52 2010
301—dc22

                              2010008147

W. W. Norton & Company, Inc., 500 Fifth Avenue, New York, N.Y. 10110
W. W. Norton & Company, Ltd., Castle House, 75/76 Wells Street, London W1T 3QT
wwnorton.com

3 4 5 6 7 8 9 0

contents

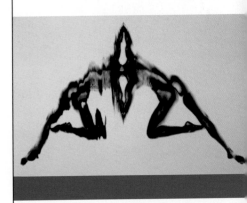

Contents xi

CHAPTER 15 Urbanization, Population, and the Environment 430

CHAPTER 16 Globalization in a Changing World 466

preface

We believe that sociology plays an essential role in modern intellectual culture and occupies a central place within the social sciences. We have aimed to write a book that merges classic sociological theories with up-to-the-minute social issues that interest sociologists today. We also believe that sociologists must use rigorous research methods in order to study and understand human behavior. We highlight findings from ethnographic studies to document the hows and whys of social behavior, and also present current statistical data to document important social trends. We aim to present material in a "fair and balanced" way. Although each of the authors has his or her own perspective on social theories, methods, and social policy, we have worked hard to ensure that our treatment is unbiased and non-partisan. We strive to present the most complete picture of sociology possible. Given the vast array of topics encompassed by sociology, however, we made difficult choices about what are the most essential topics in sociology today. We hope readers are engaged, intrigued, and occasionally inspired by the ideas presented in this book.

ABOUT THE ESSENTIALS EDITION

Essentials of Sociology is based on the Seventh Edition of our best-selling text, *Introduction to Sociology*. We created the Essentials edition for instructors and students who are looking for a briefer book that could fit into a compressed academic schedule. We have reduced the length of the book by roughly one-third, and we reduced the number of chapters from 20 to 16. We cut selected topics to focus the chapters on the core ideas of sociology, while still retaining the themes that have made the text a successful teaching tool.

MAJOR THEMES

The book is constructed around four basic themes that give the book its character. The newest theme is **applying sociology to everyday life**. Sociological thinking enables self-understanding, which in turn can be focused back on an improved understanding of the social world. Studying sociology can be a liberating experience: it expands our sympathies and imagination, opens up new perspectives on the sources of our own behavior, and creates an awareness of cultural settings different from our own. Sociological ideas challenge dogma, teach appreciation of cultural variety, and allow us insight into the working of social institutions. At a more practical level, the text shows how sociological concepts are used everyday by American workers (Making Sociology Work), and we show our social group members affect our daily experiences—as revealed in the new "D.I.Y. Sociology" quizzes.

Our second theme is **inequalities**. Throughout the text, we highlight that important resources—whether education, health, income, or social support—are not fairly or evenly distributed to all individuals. We highlight the ways that gender, race, social class, and age shape our daily life in the United States. We also pay keen attention to global inequalities, and reveal how differences in economic and even natural resources throughout the globe powerfully influence even very personal experiences—including health and personal relationships.

A third theme of the book is that of **social and historical context**. Sociology was born of the transformations that wrenched the industrializing social order of the West away from the ways of life characteristic of earlier societies. The pace of social change has continued to accelerate, and it is possible that we stand on the threshold of transitions as significant as those that occurred in the late eighteenth and nineteenth centuries. Sociology has prime responsibility for charting the transformations of the past and for grasping the major lines of development taking place today. Yet our understanding of the past also contributes to our understanding of institutions in the present and future.

The fourth fundamental theme of the book is **globalization**. For far too long, sociology has been dominated by the view that societies can be studied as independent entities. But even in the past, societies never really existed in isolation. In current times, we can see a clear acceleration in processes of global integration. This is obvious, for example, in the expansion of international trade across the world. The emphasis on globalization also connects closely with the weight given to the interdependence of the industrialized and developing worlds today.

Despite these interconnections, however, societies have their own distinctive attributes, traditions, and experiences. Sociology cannot be taught solely by understanding the institutions of any one particular society. While we have slanted the discussion toward the United States, we have also balanced it with a rich variety of materials drawn from other regions—especially those undergoing rapid social change such as the Middle East, Asia, Africa, and Eastern Europe. The book also includes much more material on developing countries than has been usual in introductory texts.

All of the chapters in the book have been updated and revised to reflect the most recent available data. Additionally, five chapters have received special attention: Chapter 4 (Social Interaction and Everyday Life) now begins with a vignette revealing how a bar employee enacts Erving Goffman's concept of "civil inattention." It includes new material on how technology, ranging from iPods to email, is reshaping the very ways that individuals communicate and interact with one another. Chapter 12 (Education and Religion) includes rich and controversial new information on the struggles that many students face in today's educational system, including the achievement gap between white males and all other students. Chapter 13 (Politics and Economic Life) provides new information on transnational corporations and outsourcing of jobs.

Chapter 14 (The Sociology of the Body: Health, Illness and Sexuality) has expanded its focus on the body and reveals the important ways that both excessively high and excessively low body weight create psychological and physical health problems for individuals, and also reflect sweeping macrosocial changes in food production and social no-0p9rms. Chapter 15 (Urbanization, Population, and Environment) now begins with a new section on China's rise as an industrial power and its effect on its population and environment The chapter also describes the distinctive characteristics (and problems) facing urban, rural, and suburban residents in the United States.

ORGANIZATION

There is very little abstract discussion of basic sociological concepts at the beginning of this book. Instead, concepts are explained when they are introduced in the relevant chapters, and we have sought throughout to illustrate them by means of concrete examples. While these are usually taken from sociological research, we have also used material from other sources (such as newspaper or popular magazine articles). We have tried to keep the writing style as simple and direct as possible, while endeavoring to make the book lively and full of surprises.

The chapters follow a sequence designed to help achieve a progressive mastery of the different fields of sociology, but we have taken care to ensure that the book can be used flexibly and is easy to adapt to the needs of individual courses. Chapters can be skipped or studied in a different order without much loss. Each has been written as a fairly autonomous unit, with cross-referencing to other chapters at relevant points.

STUDY AIDS

In the third edition of *Essentials of Sociology*, we have expanded the pedagogical program. Each chapter features:

NEW: "D.I.Y. Sociology" These short quizzes allow students to think about their own beliefs and behaviors, and to compare their answers with the United States as a whole, as well as with members of specific subgroups, such as members of one's birth cohort.

"Making Sociology Work" features These short features, which are integrated throughout the text and called out with an icon, provide students with scenarios from the work world and ask them to apply sociological concepts to each situation.

"Concept Checks" Every chapter in *Essentials of Sociology* includes several review quizzes embedded throughout the chapter, which are designed to help students prepare for a test or confirm for themselves that they comprehend the major topics in the book. Each "Concept Check" has at least three questions that range from reading comprehension to more advanced critical thinking skills.

End-of-Chapter Study Guide These help students prepare for exams and directs them to additional resources on the free student web site, StudySpace (wwnorton.com/studyspace).

ACKNOWLEDGMENTS

Many individuals offered us helpful comments and advice on particular chapters, and, in some cases, large parts of the text. They helped us see issues in a different light, clarified some difficult points, and allowed us to take advantage of their specialist knowledge in their respective fields. We are deeply indebted to them. Special thanks go to Joe Conti and Neha Gondal, who worked assiduously to help us update data in all chapters, and contributed significantly to editing as well; and Dmitry Khodyakov, who wrote thought-provoking Concept Check questions for each chapter.

We would like to thank the many readers of the text who have written with comments, criticisms, and suggestions for improvements. We have adopted many of their recommendations in this new edition.

Shannon Anderson, Roanoke College
Sheila Bluhm-Morley, Calvin College
Mary Burns, Michigan State University
Ernestos Bustillos, Pasadena City College
Carol Caronna, Towson University
Cedric DeLeon, Providence College
Kara Dillard, Kansas State University
Kathleen Fitzgerald, Columbia College
Lori Fowler, Tarrant County College
Adrianne Frech, The Ohio State University
Susan Friedman, California State University, Los Angeles
Greg Fulkerson, North Carolina State University
Clennis High, Houston Community College
Jenni Holsinger, Whitworth College
Aaron Howell, University of Cincinnati
Jeanne Humble, Bluegrass Community and Technical College
Abdy Javadzadeh, Florida International University
Tony Juge, Pasadena City College
Thomas Linneman, College of William & Mary
Jose Lopez, Pasadena City College
Barbara Miller, Pasadena City College
Juanita Ortiz, University of Oklahoma
Mari Plikuhn, Purdue University
Adrian Rapp, Lone Star College – North Harris
Jesse Rude, University of California, Davis
Jarron Saint Onge, University of Houston
Steven Severins, Kellogg Community College
Emily Tanner-Smith, Vanderbilt University
Mike Wehrman, University of Cincinnati
Lisa Weltman, Mott Community College
Cindy Whitney, Kansas State University
J. D. Wolfe, Indiana University
Laurie Woods, Belmont University

We have many others to thank as well. Jodi Beder did a marvelous job of copyediting the new edition. We are also extremely grateful to project editor Kate Feighery, who managed the countless details involved in creating the book. Editorial assistant Becky Charney skillfully tracked all the moving parts that go into publishing this complicated project. Production manager Ben Reynolds did impressive work guiding the book through production, so that it came out on time and in beautiful shape. We also thank Eileen Connell, our e-media editor, and Laura Musich, our associate e-media editor, for developing all of the useful supplements that accompany the book. Julie Tesser showed unusual flair and originality in the photo selections illustrating the book. Agnieszka Gasparska and the entire team of designers at Kiss Me I'm Polish managed to digest a huge amount of data to create the clever new infographics throughout *Essentials of Sociology*. Finally, Hope Miller Goodell earns our special thanks for creating the elegant new design for the third edition.

We are also grateful to our editors at Norton, Steve Dunn, Melea Seward, and Karl Bakeman, who have made important substantive and creative contributions to the book's chapters, and have ensured that we have referenced the very latest research. We also would like to register our thanks to a number of current and former graduate students—many of whom are now tenured professors at prestigious universities—whose contributions over the years have proved invaluable: Wendy Carter, Audrey Devin-Eller, Neil Gross, Blackhawk Hancock, Paul LePore, Alair MacLean, Ann Meier, Susan Munkres, Josh Rossol, Sharmila Rudrappa, Christopher Wildeman, David Yamane and Katherina Zippel.

Anthony Giddens
Mitchell Duneier
Richard Appelbaum
Deborah Carr

ESSENTIALS OF
SOCIOLOGY

third edition

Sociology: Theory and Method

THE BIG QUESTIONS

WHAT IS THE "SOCIOLOGICAL IMAGINATION"?

Learn what sociology covers as a field and how everyday topics like love and romance are shaped by social and historical forces.

Recognize that sociology is more than just acquiring knowledge; it also involves developing a sociological imagination and a global perspective, and understanding social change.

WHAT THEORIES DO SOCIOLOGISTS USE?

Learn about the development of sociology as a field. Be able to name some of the leading social theorists and the concepts they contributed to sociology. Learn the different theoretical approaches modern sociologists bring to the field.

WHAT KINDS OF QUESTIONS CAN SOCIOLOGISTS ANSWER?

Be able to describe the different types of questions sociologists address in their research—factual, theoretical, comparative, and developmental.

WHAT ARE THE SEVEN STEPS OF THE RESEARCH PROCESS?

Learn the steps of the research process and be able to complete the process yourself.

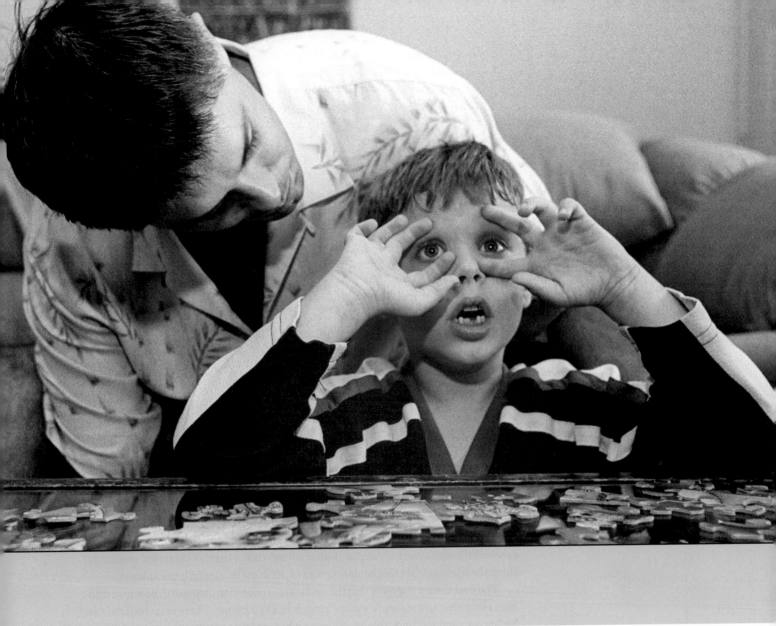

WHAT RESEARCH METHODS DO SOCIOLOGISTS USE?

Familiarize yourself with the methods available to sociological researchers, and know the advantages and disadvantages of each. See how researchers use multiple methods in a real study.

WHAT ETHICAL DILEMMAS DO SOCIOLOGISTS FACE?

Recognize the ethical problems researchers may face, and possible solutions to these dilemmas

HOW DOES THE "SOCIOLOGICAL IMAGINATION" AFFECT YOUR LIFE?

Understand how adopting a sociological perspective allows us to develop a richer understanding of ourselves, our significant others, and the world.

sociology • The study of human groups and societies, giving particular emphasis to analysis of the industrialized world. Sociology is one of a group of social sciences, which include anthropology, economics, political science, and human geography. The divisions between the various social sciences are not clear-cut, and all share a certain range of common interests, concepts, and methods.

Sociology is the scientific study of human social life, groups, and societies. It is a dazzling and compelling enterprise, as its subject matter is our own behavior as social beings. The scope of sociological study is extremely wide, ranging from the analysis of how people establish social connections with one another in interactions, to the investigation of global social processes such as the rise of Islamic fundamentalism.

Sociology teaches us that what we regard as natural, inevitable, good, or true may not be such, and that the "givens" of our life—including things we assume to be genetic or biological—are strongly influenced by historical and social forces. Understanding the subtle yet complex and profound ways in which our individual lives reflect the contexts of our social experience is basic to the sociological outlook. A brief example will provide an initial taste of the nature and objectives of sociology.

Have you ever known or heard of somebody with autism? In the past few decades, in the United States, and in many other developed nations, the incidence of autism—a profound developmental disorder—has increased rapidly, so much so that it appears as if we are in the midst of an autism "epidemic." People with autism often show less interpersonal ease and competence in routine social interaction. They don't make normal eye contact, they have trouble taking turns in conversation, and they have difficulty establishing social solidarity by smiling in response to others. Although no one knows for sure, different studies today suggest that as many as 1 in 150 children born in the United States today will be diagnosed with autism, or a related disorder.

Why would the incidence of autism have risen so rapidly? Since autism is a medical condition, some people are surprised that adopting a sociological perspective can help us understand its causes and thus help us design social policies that will stem its rise. No one knows what causes autism and no one knows what lies behind the rapid increase in cases. The search for a cause has produced hundreds of social and biological studies that have identified countless social and environmental factors and a host of possible genes as potentially related to the disease. In general, three theories compete for attention. What is important about these theories is that none of them argue that genetic influences can fully explain either autism risk or the rise in rates of autism. All three theories indicate that social aspects of life must be carefully considered.

The first theory suggests that the epidemic is related to changes in how practitioners recognize and measure autism's signs and symptoms. There is no medical test for autism, and methods for determining whether someone is autistic depend upon complicated criteria that require doctors to recognize particular social and interactional cues. In recent years, cues that were not formerly diagnosed as autism are now increasingly receiving this label. It is therefore plausible that the number of people with the characteristics we associate with autism has remained the same, but that the increasing number of documented cases is driven, in part, by diagnostic changes and increasingly aggressive surveillance and screening policies. If this theory is correct, it means that there has been no increase in the actual incidence of autism characteristics, just an increase in the diagnosis and treatment of children with autism.

The second theory proposes that the epidemic is fueled by increasing levels of toxic chemicals in the environment. This theory also suggests that further environmental changes could lead to more and more cases of autism. We know, for example, that many developmental disorders are caused by exposures to lead or the other base metals found in pesticides used in residential communities—such as on private golf courses—or new metals used in high-tech industrial sectors. Economic development and the pollution it causes may lead to a whole array of unanticipated health outcomes. The third theory is that the epidemic is being brought on by the increasing number of older men who are fathering children. This is because a father's age at the time of conception may be associated with an offspring's risk of developmental disorders like autism. As more men remain in school until older ages, and postpone marrying and having children, one might expect that the number of children with autism will increase in future generations.

To make sense of the autism epidemic, we need a strategy for identifying its causes. This is where thinking like a sociologist can make a difference. Sociologists Peter Bearman and Marissa King have begun to tackle the causes of the epidemic by assembling an unusual data set that allows them to distinguish what part of the epidemic is caused by diagnostic processes, genetic and/or family characteristics, and environmental change. By looking at data for every child born in California from 1992 to 2007, they have been able to show that almost one third of the autism epidemic is caused by changes in what doctors identify as "autism." This means, of course, that two out of every three cases of autism may be associated with other factors, perhaps other social factors, but perhaps environmental and/or genetic factors.

These researchers also have shown that the communities where autism cases appear to arise from diagnostic processes are very different from those where they do not. They differ in ways that make sociological sense. Treatment for autism is costly, and most school districts cannot afford the high level of care required for these students. Not surprisingly then, the ways that students are diagnosed varies with the level of wealth in a particularly community. Sociologists will not necessarily find the cure for autism, but their work is pointing the way for other scientists to narrow down the causes.

WHAT IS THE "SOCIOLOGICAL IMAGINATION"?

When we learn to think sociologically, as autism researcher Peter Bearman did, we can also better understand the most personal aspects of our own lives. For instance, have you ever been in love? Almost certainly you have. Most people who are in their teens or older know what being in love is like. Love and romance provide some of the most intense feelings we ever experience. Why do people fall in love? The answer may seem obvious: Love expresses a mutual physical and personal attachment between two individuals. These days, we might not all think that love is "forever"; but falling in love, we might agree, is an experience arising from universal human emotions. It seems natural for a couple in love to want personal and sexual fulfillment in their relationship, perhaps through marriage.

Yet this pattern whereby love leads to marriage is in fact very unusual. Romantic love is not an experience all people across the world have—and where it does happen, it is rarely connected to marriage. The idea of romantic love did not become widespread until fairly recently in our society, and it has never even existed in many other cultures.

Only in modern times have love and sexuality become closely connected. In the Middle Ages and for centuries afterward, men and women married mainly to keep property in the hands of the family or to raise children to work the family farm—or, in the case of royalty, to seal political alliances. Spouses may have become close companions after marriage, but not before. People sometimes had sexual affairs outside

What is the origin of romantic love? Originally, romantic love was limited to affairs for medieval aristocrats such as Tristan and Isolde, the subjects of a thirteenth-century court romance who inspired poems, operas, and films.

marriage, but these inspired few of the emotions we associate with love today. Romantic love was regarded as a weakness at best and a kind of sickness at worst.

Romantic love developed in courtly circles as a characteristic of extramarital sexual adventures by members of the aristocracy. Until about two centuries ago, it was confined to such circles and kept separate from marriage. Relations between husband and wife among aristocratic groups were often cool and distant. Each spouse had his or her own bedroom and servants; they may rarely have seen each other in private. Sexual compatibility was not considered relevant to marriage. Among both rich and poor, the decision of whom to marry was made by one's immediate and extended family; the individuals concerned had little or no say in the matter.

This remains true in many non-Western countries today. (Social scientists typically define "Western" countries as economically rich nations including most in North America and Europe, as well as Japan and Australia.) For example, in Afghanistan under the rule of the Taliban, men were prohibited from speaking to women they were not related or married to, and marriages were arranged by parents. If a girl and boy were seen by authorities to be speaking with one another, they would be whipped and left seriously injured, if not dead. The Taliban government saw romantic love as so offensive that it outlawed music and films. Like many in the non-Western world, the Taliban believed Afghanistan was being inundated by Hollywood movies and American pop music and videos, which are filled with sexual images.

Neither romantic love, then, nor its association with marriage can be understood as a natural or universal feature of human life. Rather, such love has been shaped by social and historical influences. These are the influences sociologists study.

Most of us see the world in terms of the familiar features of our own lives. Sociology demonstrates the need for a much broader view of our nature and our actions. It teaches that what we regard as "natural" in our lives is strongly influenced by historical and social forces. Understanding the subtle yet profoundly complex ways in which our individual lives reflect the contexts of our social experience is basic to the sociological outlook.

sociological imagination ● The application of imaginative thought to the asking and answering of sociological questions. Someone using the sociological imagination "thinks himself away" from the familiar routines of daily life.

Learning to think sociologically means cultivating the **sociological imagination**. As sociologists, we need to imagine, for example, what the experience of sex and marriage is like for people who consider the ideals of romantic love to be alien or absurd. Sociology is not just a routine process of acquiring knowledge; it requires breaking free from the immediacy of personal circumstances and putting things in a wider context. It requires what the American sociologist C. Wright Mills (1959), in a famous phrase, called the sociological imagination.

The sociological imagination requires us, above all, to "think ourselves away" from our daily routines in order to look at them anew. Consider the simple act of drinking a cup of coffee. What might the sociological point of view illuminate about such apparently uninteresting behavior? An enormous amount. First, coffee possesses symbolic value as part of our daily social activities (see "Globalization and Everyday Life: The Sociology of Coffee" on pp. 8–9). Often the ritual associated with coffee drinking is much more important than the act itself. Two people who arrange to meet for coffee are probably more interested in getting together and chatting than in what they actually drink. Drinking and eating in all societies, in fact, promote social interaction and the enactment of rituals—rich subject matter for sociological study.

Second, coffee contains caffeine, a drug that stimulates the brain. In Western culture, coffee addicts are not regarded as drug users. Like alcohol, coffee is a socially acceptable drug, whereas marijuana, for instance, is not. Yet some societies tolerate the consumption of marijuana or even cocaine but frown on coffee and alcohol. Sociologists are interested in why these contrasts exist.

Third, an individual who drinks a cup of coffee is participating in a complicated set of social and economic relationships stretching across the world. The production and distribution of coffee require continuous transactions among people who may be thousands of miles away from the coffee drinker. Studying such global transactions is an important task of sociology because many aspects of our lives are now affected by worldwide social influences and communications.

Finally, the act of sipping a cup of coffee presumes a process of past social and economic development. Widespread consumption of coffee—along with other now-familiar items of Western diets like tea, bananas, potatoes, and white sugar—began only in the late 1800s under Western colonial expansion. Virtually all the coffee we drink today comes from areas (South America and Africa) that were colonized by Europeans; it is in no sense a "natural" part of the Western diet.

STUDYING SOCIOLOGY

The sociological imagination allows us to see that many behaviors or feelings that we view as private and individualized actually reflect larger social issues. Try applying this sort of outlook to your own life. Consider, for instance, why you are attending college right now. You may think that you worked hard in high school, or that you have decided to go to college so that you have the academic credential required to find a good job, yet other larger social forces also may have played a role (see "D.I.Y." box on p. 11). Many students who work hard in high school cannot attend college, because their parents cannot afford to send them. Others have their schooling interrupted by large-scale events like wars or economic depressions. The notion that we need college to find a good job also is shaped by social context; in past eras when most people worked in agricultural rather than professional jobs, college attendance was rare—rather than an expected rite of passage.

Although we are all influenced by the social contexts in which we find ourselves, none of us is simply determined in his or her behavior by those contexts. We possess and create our own individuality. It is the goal of sociology to investigate the connections between what society makes of us and what we make of ourselves. Our activities both structure—give shape to—the social world around us and at the same time are structured by that social world.

Social structure is an important concept in sociology. It refers to the fact that the social contexts of our lives do not just consist of random assortments of events or actions; they are structured, or patterned, in distinct ways. There are regularities in the ways we behave and in the relationships we have with one another. But social structure is not like a physical structure, such as a building, which exists independently of human actions. Human societies are always in the process of **structuration**. They are reconstructed at every moment by the very "building blocks" that compose them—human beings like you.

"How would you like me to answer that question? As a member of my ethnic group, educational class, income group, or religious category?"

structuration ● The two-way process by which we shape our social world through our individual actions and by which we are reshaped by society.

DEVELOPING A GLOBAL PERSPECTIVE

As we just saw in our discussions of the sociological dimensions of drinking a cup of coffee, all our local actions—the ways in which we relate to one another in face-to-face contexts—form part of larger social settings that extend around the globe. These connections between the local and the global are quite new in human history. They have accelerated over the past thirty or forty years as a result of the dramatic advances

The Sociology of Coffee

The world drinks about 2.25 billion cups [of coffee] per day—the United States alone drinks one fifth of this. Coffee drinking is a cultural fixture that says as much about us as it does about the bean itself. Basically a habit-forming stimulant, coffee is nonetheless associated with relaxation and sociability. In a society that combines buzzing overstimulation with soul-aching meaninglessness, coffee and its associated rituals are, for many of us, the lubricants that make it possible to go on.

Perhaps for this reason coffee occupies a distinctive niche in our cultural landscape. Along with alcohol, it is the only beverage to engender public houses devoted to its consumption. . . . Uniquely, though, coffee is welcome in almost any situation, from the car to the boardroom, from the breakfast table to the public park, alone or in company of any kind. Since its adoption as a beverage, coffee has been offered as an antipode to alcohol—more so even than abstinence, perhaps in recognition of a human need for joyfully mood-altering substances and the convivial social interactions that go along with them.

Only a handful of consumer goods have fueled the passions of the public as much as coffee. . . . [C]offee has inspired impassioned struggles on the battlefields of economics, human rights, politics, and religion, since its use first spread. Coffee may be a drink for sharing, but as a commodity it invites protectionism, oppression, and destruction. Its steamy past implicates the otherwise noble bean in early colonialism, various revolutions, the

emergence of the bourgeoisie, international development, technological hubris, crushing global debt, and more. These forces, in turn, have shaped the way coffee has been incorporated into our culture and economy. Colonialism, for example, served as the primary reason

in communications, information technology, and transportation. The development of jet planes, large, speedy container ships, and other means of rapid travel has meant that people and goods can be continuously transported across the world. And our worldwide system of satellite communication, established only some thirty years ago, has made it possible for people to get in touch with each other instantaneously.

American society is influenced every moment of the day by globalization, the growth of world interdependence—a social phenomenon that will be discussed throughout this book. Globalization should not be thought of simply as the development of worldwide networks—social and economic systems that are remote from our individual concerns. It is a local phenomenon, too. For example, only a few years ago, for and vehicle of coffee's expansion throughout the globe; colonial powers dictated where coffee went and where it did not and established trading relationships that continue to this day.

The story of coffee also reveals how (and why) we interact with a plethora of other commodities, legal or not. Surprising similarities exist, for example, between coffee's early history and the current controversy over marijuana. Today's national debate over the merits of marijuana, although young by comparison, is the modern version of the strife surrounding coffee in other ages. The social acceptability of each has been affected by religious and political opinion, conflicting health claims, institutionalized cultural norms, and the monied interests of government and private industry. The evolution of coffee's social acceptability highlights the delicate dance of interests and "truths" that governs the ways in which we structure our societies.

Coffee is consumed with great fervor in rich countries such as the United States, yet is grown with few exceptions in the poorest parts of the globe. In fact, it is the second most valuable item of legal international trade (after petroleum), and the largest food import of the United States by value. It is the principal source of foreign exchange for dozens of countries around the world. The coffee in your cup is an immediate, tangible connection with the rural poor in some of the most destitute parts of the planet. It is a physical link across space and cultures from one end of the human experience to the other.

The coffee trading system that has evolved to bring all this about is an intricate knot of economics, politics, and sheer power—a bizarre arena trod . . . by some of the world's largest transnational corporations, by enormous governments, and by vast trading cartels. The trip coffee takes from the crop to your cup turns out not to be so straightforward after all, but rather a turbulent and unpredictable ride through the waves and eddies of international commodity dynamics, where the product itself becomes secondary to the wash of money and power.

Source: Dicum and Luttinger 1999.

when they dined out at restaurants, most Americans had few culinary choices. In many U.S. towns and cities today, a single street might feature Italian, Mexican, Japanese, Thai, Ethiopian, and other types of restaurants next door to each other. In turn, the dietary decisions we make are consequential for food producers who might live on the other side of the world.

Do college students today have a global perspective? By at least one measure, the answer is yes. According to an annual survey of more than 263,710 first-year college students, a record 49.7 percent of all students who entered U.S. colleges in 2005 reported that they had "participated in organized demonstrations" concerned with social, political, and economic issues during the previous year. This was the highest percentage since the University of California, Los Angeles (UCLA) survey began asking the question in 1966 (Sax et al. 2001). The demonstrations these students participated in were concerned with a wide range of issues, including the growing power of global institutions such as the World Trade Organization and the World Bank, the production of clothing in overseas sweatshops, global warming, and the right of workers to be paid a living wage (Meatto 2000). Concern with these issues reflects an awareness that globalization has a direct effect on our daily, private lives.

A global perspective not only allows us to become more aware of the ways that we are connected to people in other societies; it also makes us more aware of the many problems the world faces at the beginning of the twenty-first century. The global perspective opens our eyes to the fact that our interdependence with other societies means that our actions have consequences for others and that the world's problems have consequences for us.

UNDERSTANDING SOCIAL CHANGE

The changes in human ways of life in the last two hundred years, such as globalization, have been far-reaching. We have become accustomed, for example, to the fact that most of the population lives in towns and cities rather than in small agricultural communities. But this was never the case until the middle of the nineteenth century. For most of human history, the vast majority of people had to produce their own food and shelter and lived in tiny groups or in small village communities. Even at the height of the most developed traditional civilizations—such as ancient Rome or pre-industrial China—less than 10 percent of the population lived in urban areas; everyone else was engaged in food production in a rural setting. Today, in most of the industrialized societies, these proportions have become almost completely reversed. By 2050, nearly 70 percent of the world population is expected to live in urban areas. In more developed regions, including Europe, North America, Australia, New Zealand, and Japan, an estimated 86 percent will live in urban areas (United Nations 2008a).

These sweeping social transformations have radically altered, and continue to alter, the most personal and intimate side of our daily existence. To extend a previous example, the spread of ideals of romantic love was strongly conditioned by the transition from a rural to an urban, industrialized society. As people moved into urban areas and began to work in industrial production, marriage was no longer prompted mainly by economic motives—by the need to control the inheritance of land and to work the land as a family unit. "Arranged" marriages—fixed through the negotiations of parents and relatives—became less and less common. Individuals began to initiate marriage relationships on the bases of emotional attraction and personal fulfillment. The idea of "falling in love" as a precondition for marriage was formed in this context.

Sociology was founded by thinkers who sought to understand the initial impact of transformations that accompanied industrialization in the West. Although our world today is radically different from that of former ages, the original goal of sociologists remains: to understand our world and what future it is likely to hold for us. ✓

CONCEPT CHECKS ✓

1. How does sociology help us understand the causes of autism?

2. What is the sociological imagination, according to C. Wright Mills?

3. How does the concept of social structure help sociologists better understand social phenomena?

4. What is globalization? How might it affect the lives of college students today?

DO-IT-YOURSELF SOCIOLOGY

Are you the "typical" college student? Young adults today often take it for granted that they will attend college, and that their classmates will come from backgrounds very much like their own. Sociologists recognize that whether and why one attends college and what one's college experience is like are powerfully shaped by social and historical factors. How "typical" are you? (To find the answer, flip the page.)

Are you . . .

    male?

    female?

Are you . . .

    white?

    African American?

    Native American?

    Asian/Asian American?

    Latino?

    Other race or multiracial?

Did you apply to 3 or more colleges?

What was your average grade in high school?

    A– to A+

    B– to B+

    C– to C+

    D

How would you describe your political orientation?

    Liberal

    Middle of the road

    Conservative

What is your family's income?

What personal objectives do you rate as "very important or essential"?

    Being very well off financially

    Developing a meaningful philosophy of life

    Keeping up to date on political affairs

TURN PAGE →

Proportion of College Freshman Who. . . . →

	1970	1990	2007
Are male	52.1	46.9	45.2
Are female	47.9	53.1	54.8

Are:

	1970	1990	2007
white	90.9	80.7	76.5
African American	7.5	12.1	10.5
Native American	.9	1.3	2.2
Asian/Asian American	.6	3.8	8.6
Latino	.6	2.2	7.3
Other race or multiracial	2.3	3.5	10.9

	1970	1990	2007
Applied to 3 or more colleges.	NA	42.9	56.5

Had an average grade in high school of:

	1970	1990	2007
A– to A+	19.6	29.4	45.9
B– to B+	62.5	57.0	49.0
C– to C+	17.7	13.4	5.0
D	.3	.2	.1

Describe their political orientation as:

	1970	1990	2007
Liberal	35.7	24.6	29.3
Middle of the road	54.4	51.7	43.4
Conservative	17.3	20.6	23.1

	1970	1990	2007
Median family income	$12,800	$46,600	$78,200

Rated this personal objective as "very important or essential":

	1970	1990	2007
Being very well off financially	36.2	72.3	74.4
Developing a meaningful philosophy of life	79.1	45.9	49.2
Keeping up to date on political affairs	57.2	46.6	37.2

Source: HERI 2008.

WHAT THEORIES DO SOCIOLOGISTS USE?

Sociologists do more than collect facts; they also want to know why things happen. For instance, we know that industrialization has had a major influence on the emergence of modern societies. But what are the origins and preconditions of industrialization? Why is industrialization associated with changes in ways of criminal punishment or in family and marriage systems? To respond to such questions, we must construct explanatory theories.

THEORIES AND THEORETICAL APPROACHES

Theories involve constructing abstract interpretations that can be used to explain a wide variety of situations. Of course, factual research and theories can never completely be separated. Sociologists aiming to document facts must begin their studies with a theory that they will evaluate. Theory helps researchers to identify and frame a factual question, yet facts are needed to evaluate the strength of a theory. Conversely, once facts have been obtained, sociologists must use theory to interpret and make sense of these facts.

Theoretical thinking also must respond to general problems posed by the study of human social life, including issues that are philosophical in nature. For example, based on their theoretical and methodological orientations, sociologists hold very different beliefs about whether sociology should be modeled on the natural sciences.

EARLY THEORISTS

Humans have always been curious about why we behave as we do, but for thousands of years our attempts to understand ourselves relied on ways of thinking passed down from generation to generation, often expressed in religious rather than scientific terms. The systematic scientific study of human behavior is a relatively recent development, dating back to the late 1700s and early 1800s. The sweeping changes ushered in by the French Revolution of 1789 and the emergence of the Industrial Revolution in Europe formed the backdrop for the development of sociology. These major historical events shattered traditional ways of life, and forced thinkers to develop new understandings of both the social and natural worlds.

A key development was the use of science instead of religion to understand the world. The types of questions these nineteenth-century thinkers sought to answer are the very same questions sociologists try to answer today. What is human nature? How and why do societies change?

AUGUSTE COMTE

Many scholars contributed to early sociological thinking, yet particular credit is given to the French philosopher Auguste Comte (1798–1857), if only because he invented the word *sociology.* Comte originally used the term *social physics,* but some of his intellectual rivals at the time were also making use of that term. Comte wanted to distinguish his own views from theirs, so he introduced sociology to describe the subject he wished to establish.

Auguste Comte (1798–1857)

Comte believed that this new field could produce a knowledge of society based on scientific evidence. He regarded sociology as the last science to be developed—following physics, chemistry, and biology—but as the most significant and complex of all the sciences. Sociology, he believed, should contribute to the welfare of humanity by using science to understand, predict, and control human behavior. Late in his career, Comte drew up ambitious plans for the reconstruction of both French society in particular and human societies in general, based on scientific knowledge.

ÉMILE DURKHEIM

Émile Durkheim (1858–1917)

social facts • According to Émile Durkheim, the aspects of social life that shape our actions as individuals. Durkheim believed that social facts could be studied scientifically.

organic solidarity • According to Émile Durkheim, the social cohesion that results from the various parts of a society functioning as an integrated whole.

social constraint • The conditioning influence on our behavior of the groups and societies of which we are members. Social constraint was regarded by Émile Durkheim as one of the distinctive properties of social facts.

anomie • A concept first brought into wide usage in sociology by Durkheim, referring to a situation in which social norms lose their hold over individual behavior.

Another French scholar, Émile Durkheim (1858–1917), has had a much more lasting effect on modern sociology than Comte. Although he drew on aspects of Comte's work, Durkheim thought that many of his predecessor's ideas were too speculative and vague and that Comte had not successfully established a scientific basis for studying human behavior. To become a science, according to Durkheim, sociology must study **social facts**, aspects of social life that shape our actions as individuals, such as the state of the economy or the influence of religion. Durkheim believed that we must study social life with the same objectivity as scientists study the natural world. His famous first principle of sociology was "Study social facts as things!" By this he meant that social life can be analyzed as rigorously as objects or events in nature.

Like a biologist studying the human body, Durkheim saw society as a set of independent parts, each of which could be studied separately. A body consists of specialized parts, each of which contributes to sustaining the continuing life of the organism. These necessarily work in harmony with one another; if they do not, the life of the organism is under threat. So it is, according to Durkheim, with society. For a society to function and persist over time, its specialized institutions (such as the political system, religion, the family, and the educational system) must work in harmony with each other and function as an integrated whole. Durkheim referred to this social cohesion as "**organic solidarity**." He argued that the continuation of a society thus depends on cooperation, which in turn presumes a consensus, or agreement, among its members over basic values and customs.

Another major theme pursued by Durkheim, and by many others since, is that the society exerts **social constraint** over the actions of its members. Durkheim argued that society is far more than the sum of individual acts; when we analyze social structures, we are studying characteristics that have "solidity" comparable to structures in the physical world. Social structure, according to Durkheim, constrains our activities in a parallel way, setting limits on what we can do as individuals. It is "external" to us, just as the walls of the room are.

One of Durkheim's most influential studies was concerned with the analysis of suicide (Durkheim 1966; orig. 1897). Suicide may appear to be a purely personal act, the outcome of extreme personal unhappiness. Durkheim showed, however, that social factors exert a fundamental influence on suicidal behavior—**anomie**, a feeling of aimlessness or despair provoked by modern social life, being one of these influences. Suicide rates show regular patterns from year to year, he argued, and these patterns must be explained sociologically. According to Durkheim, changes in the modern world are so rapid and intense that they give rise to major social difficulties, which he linked to anomie. Traditional moral controls and standards, which were supplied by religion in earlier times, are largely broken down by modern social development; and this leaves individuals in many societies feeling that their daily lives lack meaning. Many critiques of Durkheim's study can be raised, but it remains a classic work that is relevant to sociology today.

KARL MARX

The ideas of the German philosopher Karl Marx (1818–1883) contrast sharply with those of Comte and Durkheim, but like them, he sought to explain the societal changes that took place during the Industrial Revolution. When he was a young man, Marx's political activities brought him into conflict with the German authorities; after a brief stay in France, he settled permanently in exile in Great Britain. Marx's viewpoint was founded on what he called the **materialist conception of history**. According to this view, it is not the ideas or values human beings hold that are the main sources of social change, as Durkheim claimed. Rather, social change is prompted primarily by economic influences. The conflicts between classes—the rich versus the poor—provide the motivation for historical development. In Marx's words, "All human history thus far is the history of class struggles."

Though he wrote about many historical periods, Marx concentrated on change in modern times. For him, the most important changes were bound up with the development of capitalism. **Capitalism** is a system of production that contrasts radically with previous economic systems in history; it involves the production of goods and services sold to a wide range of consumers. Those who own capital, or factories, machines, and large sums of money, form a ruling class. The mass of the population make up the working class, or wage workers who do not own the means of their livelihood but must find employment provided by the owners of capital. Capitalism is thus a class system in which conflict between classes is a common occurrence because it is in the interests of the ruling class to exploit the working class and in the interests of the workers to seek to overcome that exploitation.

Marx predicted that in the future capitalism will be supplanted by a society in which there are no classes—no divisions between rich and poor. He didn't mean that all inequalities would disappear. Rather, societies will no longer be split into a small class that monopolizes economic and political power and the large mass of people who benefit little from the wealth their work creates. The economic system will come under communal ownership, and a more equal society than we know at present will be established.

Marx's work had a far-reaching effect in the twentieth century. Through most of the century, until the fall of Soviet communism in the early 1990s, more than a third of the earth's population lived in societies whose governments claimed to derive their inspiration from Marx's ideas. In addition, many sociologists have been influenced by Marx's ideas about class inequalities.

Karl Marx (1818–1883)

materialist conception of history • The view developed by Marx, according to which material, or economic, factors have a prime role in determining historical change.

capitalism • An economic system based on the private ownership of wealth, which is invested and reinvested in order to produce profit.

MAX WEBER

Like Marx, Max Weber (pronounced "VA-ber"; 1864–1920) cannot be labeled simply a sociologist; his interests and concerns ranged across many areas. Born in Germany, where he spent most of his academic career, Weber was educated in a range of fields. Like other thinkers of his time, Weber sought to understand social change. He was influenced by Marx but was also strongly critical of some of Marx's views. He rejected the materialist conception of history and saw class conflict as less significant than did Marx. In Weber's view, economic factors are important, but ideas and values have just as much effect on social change.

Some of Weber's most influential writings compared the leading religious systems in China and India with those of the West; Weber concluded that certain aspects of Christian beliefs strongly influenced the rise of capitalism. He argued that the capitalist outlook of Western societies did not emerge only from economic changes, as Marx had argued. In Weber's view, cultural ideas and values help shape society and affect our individual actions.

Max Weber (1864–1920)

> **Table 1.1 | Interpreting Modern Development**
>
> DURKHEIM
> 1. The main dynamic of modern development is the **division of labor** as a basis for social cohesion and **organic solidarity.**
> 2. Durkheim believed that sociology must study **social facts** as things, just as science would analyze the natural world. His study of suicide led him to stress the important influence of social factors, qualities of a society external to the individual, on a person's actions. Durkheim argued that society exerts **social constraint** over our actions.
>
> MARX
> 1. The main dynamic of modern development is the expansion of **capitalism**. Rather than being cohesive, society is divided by class differences.
> 2. Marx believed that we must study the divisions within a society that are derived from the economic inequalities of capitalism.
>
> WEBER
> 1. The main dynamic of modern development is the **rationalization** of social and economic life.
> 2. Weber focused on why Western societies developed so differently from other societies. He also emphasized the importance of cultural ideas and values on social change.

One of the most influential aspects of Weber's work was his study of bureaucracy. A bureaucracy is a large organization that is divided into jobs based on specific functions and staffed by officials ranked according to a hierarchy. Industrial firms, government organizations, hospitals, and schools are examples of bureaucracies. Bureaucracy makes it possible for these large organizations to run efficiently, but at the same time it poses problems for effective democratic participation in modern societies. Bureaucracy involves the rule of experts, whose decisions are made without much consultation with those whose lives are affected by those decisions.

Weber's contributions range over many other areas, including the study of the development of cities, systems of law, types of economy, and the nature of classes. He also wrote about the overall character of sociology itself. According to Weber, humans are thinking, reasoning beings; we attach meaning and significance to most of what we do; and any discipline that deals with human behavior must acknowledge this.

NEGLECTED FOUNDERS

Durkheim, Marx, and Weber are widely acknowledged as foundational figures in sociology, yet other important thinkers from the same period also made valuable contributions to sociological thought. Very few women or members of racial minorities were given the opportunity to become professional sociologists during the "classical" period of the late nineteenth and early twentieth centuries. Their contributions deserve the attention of sociologists today.

HARRIET MARTINEAU

Harriet Martineau (1802–1876)

Harriet Martineau (1802–1876) was born and educated in England. She was the author of more than fifty books and numerous essays. Martineau is now credited with introducing sociology to England through her translation of Comte's founding treatise of the field, *Positive Philosophy* (Rossi 1973). She also conducted a firsthand systematic study of American society during her extensive travels throughout the United States in the 1830s, which is the subject of her book *Society in America*. Martineau is significant to sociologists today for several reasons. First, she argued that when one studies a society, one must focus on all its aspects, including key political, religious, and social institutions. Second, she insisted that an analysis of a society must include an understanding of women's lives. Third, she was the first to turn a sociological eye on previously ignored issues such as marriage, children, domestic and religious life, and race relations. As she wrote, "The nursery, the boudoir, and the kitchen are all excellent schools in which to learn the morals and manners of a people" (2009; orig. 1837). Finally, she argued that sociologists should do more than just observe, they should also act in ways to benefit a society. Martineau herself was an active proponent of both women's rights and the emancipation of slaves.

W. E. B. DU BOIS

W. E. B. Du Bois (1868–1963) was the first African American to earn a doctorate at Harvard University. Du Bois made many contributions to sociology. Perhaps most important is the concept of "double consciousness," which is a way of talking about identity through the lens of the particular experiences of African Americans. He argued that American society lets African Americans see themselves only through the eyes of others: "It is a particular sensation, this double consciousness, this sense of always measuring one's soul by the tape of a world that looks on in amused contempt and pity. One ever feels his two-ness—an American, a Negro, two souls, two thoughts, two unreconciled strivings, two warring ideals in one dark body, whose dogged strength alone keeps it from being torn asunder" (1903). Du Bois made a persuasive claim that one's sense of self and one's identity are greatly influenced by historical experiences and social circumstances—in the case of African Americans, the effect of slavery and, after emancipation, segregation and prejudice. Throughout his career, Du Bois focused on race relations in the United States; as he said in an often-repeated quote, "the problem of the twentieth century is the problem of the color line." His influence on sociology today is evidenced by continued interest in the questions that he raised, particularly his concern that sociology must explain "the contact of diverse races of men." Du Bois was also the first social researcher to trace the problems faced by African Americans to their social and economic underpinnings, a connection that most sociologists now widely accept. Finally, Du Bois became known for connecting social analysis to social reform. He was one of the founding members of the National Association for the Advancement of Colored People (NAACP) and a long-time advocate for the collective struggle of African Americans. Later in his life, Du Bois became disenchanted by the lack of progress in American race relations. He moved to the African nation of Ghana in 1961, when he was invited by the nation's president, Kwame Nkrumah, to direct the *Encyclopedia Africana,* a government publication that DuBois had long been interested in. He died in Ghana in 1963.

W. E. B. Du Bois (1868–1963)

MODERN THEORETICAL APPROACHES

The origins of sociology were mainly European, yet the subject is now firmly established worldwide—with some of the most important developments having taken place in the United States.

SYMBOLIC INTERACTIONISM

The work of George Herbert Mead (1863–1931), a philosopher teaching at the University of Chicago, had an important influence on the development of sociological thought,

symbolic interactionism ●
A theoretical approach in sociology developed by George Herbert Mead, which emphasizes the role of symbols and language as core elements of all human interaction.

symbol ● One item used to stand for or represent another—as in the case of a flag, which symbolizes a nation.

in particular through a perspective called **symbolic interactionism**. Mead placed great importance on the study of language in analyzing the social world. He reasoned that language allows us to become self-conscious beings—aware of our own individuality. The key element in this process is the **symbol**, something that stands for something else. For example, the word *tree* is a symbol that represents the object tree. Once we have mastered such a concept, Mead argued, we can think of a tree even if none is visible; we have learned to think of the object symbolically. Symbolic thought frees us from being limited in our experience to what we actually see, hear, or feel.

Unlike animals, according to Mead, human beings live in a richly symbolic universe. This applies even to our very sense of self. Each of us is a self-conscious being because we learn to look at ourselves as if from the outside—we see ourselves as others see us. When a child begins to use "I" to refer to that object (herself) whom others call "you," she is exhibiting the beginnings of self-consciousness.

Virtually all interactions between individuals involve an exchange of symbols, according to symbolic interactionists. When we interact with others, we constantly look for clues to what type of behavior is appropriate in the context and how to interpret what others are doing and saying. Symbolic interactionism directs our attention to the detail of interpersonal interaction and how that detail is used to make sense of what others say and do. For instance, suppose two people are out on a date for the first time. Each is likely to spend a good part of the evening sizing the other up and assessing how the relationship is likely to develop, if at all. Both individuals are careful about their own behavior, making every effort to present themselves in a favorable light; but, knowing this, both are likely to be looking for aspects of the other's behavior that would reveal his or her true beliefs and traits. A complex and subtle process of symbolic interpretation shapes the interaction between the two.

FUNCTIONALISM

Symbolic interactionism is open to the criticism that it concentrates too much on things that are small in scope. Symbolic interactionists have found difficulty in dealing with larger-scale structures and processes—the very thing that a rival tradition of thought, **functionalism**, tends to emphasize. Functionalist thinking in sociology was originally pioneered by Comte, who saw it as closely bound up with his overall view of the field.

To study the function of a social activity is to analyze the contribution that the activity makes to the continuation of the society as a whole. The best way to understand this idea is by analogy to the human body, a comparison Comte, Durkheim, and other functionalist authors made. To study an organ such as the heart, we need to show how it relates to other parts of the body. When we learn how the heart pumps blood around the body, we then understand that the heart plays a vital role in the continuation of the life of the organism. Similarly, analyzing the function of some aspect of society, such as religion, means showing the part it plays in the continued existence and health of a society. Functionalism emphasizes the importance of moral consensus in maintaining order and stability in society. Moral consensus exists when most people in a society share the same values. Functionalists regard order and balance as the normal state of society—this social equilibrium is grounded in the existence of a moral consensus among the members of society.

Functionalism became prominent in sociology in the mid-twentieth century through the writings of Talcott Parsons and Robert K. Merton, each of whom saw functionalist analysis as providing the key to the development of sociological theory and research. Merton's version of functionalism has been particularly influential.

Merton distinguished between manifest and latent functions. **Manifest functions** are those known to, and intended by, the participants in a specific type of social activity. **Latent functions** are consequences of that activity of which participants are unaware. To illustrate this distinction, Merton used the example of a rain dance performed by the Hopi tribe of Arizona and New Mexico. The Hopi believe that the ceremony will bring the rain they need for their crops (manifest function). This is why they organize and participate in it. But using Durkheim's theory of religion, Merton argued that the rain dance also has the effect of promoting the cohesion of the Hopi society (latent function). A major part of sociological explanation, according to Merton, consists in uncovering the latent functions of social activities and institutions.

For much of the twentieth century, functionalist thought was considered the leading theoretical tradition in sociology, particularly in the United States. In recent years, its popularity has declined as its limitations have become apparent. While this was not true of Merton, many functionalist thinkers (Talcott Parsons is an example) unduly stressed factors leading to social cohesion at the expense of those producing division and conflict. In addition, many critics argue that functional analysis attributes to societies qualities they do not have. Functionalists often wrote as though societies have "needs" and "purposes," even though these concepts make sense only when applied to individual human beings. Figure 1.1 shows how functionalism relates to other theoretical approaches in sociology.

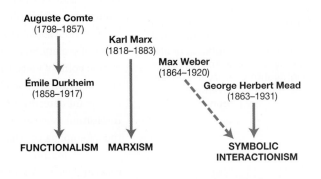

Figure 1.1 | Theoretical Approaches in Sociology

The solid lines indicate direct influence; the dotted line, an indirect connection. Mead is not indebted to Weber, but Weber's views—stressing the meaningful, purposive nature of human action—have affinities with the themes of symbolic interactionism.

Auguste Comte (1798–1857) → Émile Durkheim (1858–1917) → FUNCTIONALISM

Karl Marx (1818–1883) → MARXISM

Max Weber (1864–1920) ⇢ SYMBOLIC INTERACTIONISM

George Herbert Mead (1863–1931) → SYMBOLIC INTERACTIONISM

MARXISM AND CLASS CONFLICT

A third influential approach is **Marxism**. Marxists, of course, trace their views back to the writings of Karl Marx. But numerous interpretations of Marx's major ideas are possible, and there are today schools of Marxist thought that take very different theoretical positions.

In all of its versions, Marxism differs from non-Marxist perspectives in that its adherents see it as a combination of sociological analysis and political reform. Marxism is supposed to generate a program of radical political change. Moreover, Marxists lay more emphasis on conflict, class divisions, power, and ideology than many non-Marxist sociologists, especially most of those influenced by functionalism. The concepts of **power** and a closely associated notion, **ideology**, are of great importance to Marxist sociologists and to sociology in general. Power refers to the capability of individuals or groups to make their own concerns or interests count, even when others resist. Power sometimes involves the direct use of force but is almost always accompanied by the development of ideas (ideologies), which are used to justify the actions of the powerful. Power, ideology, and conflict are always closely connected. Many conflicts are about power, because of the rewards it can bring. Those who hold most power may depend mainly on the influence of ideology to retain their dominance but are usually able also to use force if necessary.

manifest functions • The functions of a particular social activity that are known to and intended by the individuals involved in the activity.

latent functions • Functional consequences that are not intended or recognized by the members of a social system in which they occur.

Marxism • A body of thought deriving its main elements from Karl Marx's ideas.

power • The ability of individuals or the members of a group to achieve aims or further the interests they hold. Power is a pervasive element in all human relationships. Many conflicts in society are struggles over power, because how much power an individual or group is able to achieve governs how far they are able to put their wishes into practice.

ideology • Shared ideas or beliefs that serve to justify the interests of dominant groups. Ideologies are found in all societies in which there are systematic and ingrained inequalities between groups. The concept of ideology connects closely with that of power, since ideological systems serve to legitimize the power that groups hold.

FEMINISM AND FEMINIST THEORY

feminist theory • A sociological perspective that emphasizes the centrality of gender in analyzing the social world and particularly the experiences of women. There are many strands of feminist theory, but they all share the intention to explain gender inequalities in society and to work to overcome them.

Feminist theory is one of the most prominent areas of contemporary sociology. This is a notable development because issues of gender are nearly absent in the work of the major figures who established the discipline. The success of feminism's entry into sociology required a fundamental—and often contested—shift in the discipline's approach.

Many feminist theorists brought their experiences in the women's movement of the 1960s and 1970s to their work as sociologists. Like Marxism, **feminism** makes a link between sociological theory and political reform. Feminist sociologists often have been advocates for political and social action to remedy the inequalities between women and men in both the public and private spheres.

feminism • Advocacy of the rights of women to be equal with men in all spheres of life. Feminism dates from the late eighteenth century in Europe, and feminist movements exist in most countries today.

Feminist sociologists argue that women's lives and experiences are central to the study of society. Sociology, like most academic disciplines, historically has presumed a male point of view. Driven by a concern with women's subordination in American society, feminist sociologists highlight gender relations and gender inequality as important determinants of social life in terms of both social interaction and social institutions such as the family, the workplace, and the educational system. Feminist theory emphasizes that gender differences are not natural, but socially constructed.

Today, feminist sociology often encompasses a focus on the intersection of gender, race, and class. A feminist approach to the study of inequality has influenced new academic fields, like gay and lesbian studies.

POSTMODERN THEORY

Postmodernists claim that the very foundation upon which classic social thought is based has collapsed. Early thinkers were inspired by the idea that history unfolds sequentially and leads to progress. Adherents of **postmodernism** counter that there are no longer any "grand narratives," or metanarratives—overall conceptions of history or society—that make any sense (Lyotard 1985). Some go so far as to argue there is no such thing as history. The postmodern world is not destined, as Marx hoped, to be a socialist one. Instead, it is one dominated by the new media, which "take us out" of our past. Postmodern society is highly pluralistic and diverse. In countless films, videos, TV programs, and Web sites, images circulate around the world. We are exposed to many ideas and values, but these have little connection with the history of places where we live, or with our own personal histories. The world is constantly in flux.

postmodernism • The belief that society is no longer governed by history or progress. Postmodern society is highly pluralistic and diverse, with no "grand narrative" guiding its development.

One of the important theorists of postmodernism is the French philosopher and sociologist Jean Baudrillard, who believes that the electronic media have destroyed our relationship to our past and created a chaotic, empty world. Baudrillard was strongly influenced by Marxism in his early years. However, he argues, the spread of electronic communication and the mass media have reversed the Marxist theorem that economic forces shape society. Rather, social life is influenced above all by signs and images.

In a media-dominated age, Baudrillard says, meaning is created by the flow of images, as in TV programs. Much of our world has become a sort of make-believe universe in which we are responding to media images rather than to real persons or places. Thus when Diana, Princess of Wales, died in 1997, there was an enormous outpouring of grief, not only in Great Britain but all over the world. Yet were people mourning a real person? Baudrillard would say not. Diana existed for most people only through the media. Her death was more like an event in a television drama than a real event, in the way in which people experienced it. Baudrillard speaks of "the dissolution of life into TV."

New York City's Times Square serves as the backdrop for live television programs such as ESPN's *SportsCenter* and *Dick Clark's New Year's Rockin' Eve with Ryan Seacrest.* Covered with advertisements and constantly in flux, it epitomizes Baudrillard's theories of postmodern society.

THEORETICAL THINKING IN SOCIOLOGY

We have described five theoretical approaches, which refer to broad orientations to the subject matter of sociology. Yet theoretical approaches are distinct from theories. Theories are more narrowly focused and represent attempts to explain particular social conditions or events. They are usually formed as part of the research process and in turn suggest problems to be investigated by researchers. An example would be Durkheim's theory of suicide, referred to earlier in this chapter.

Sometimes theories are set out very precisely and are even occasionally expressed in mathematical form—although this is more common in other social sciences (especially economics) than in sociology. Some theories, by contrast, have a much broader scope. Sociologists do not share a unified position on whether theories should be specific, wide-ranging, or somewhere in between. Robert K. Merton (1957), for example, argues forcefully that sociologists should concentrate their attention on what he calls *middle-range theories.* Middle-range theories are specific enough to be tested directly by empirical research, yet are sufficiently general to cover a range of different phenomena.

Relative deprivation theory is an example of a middle-range theory. It holds that how people evaluate their circumstances depends on whom they compare themselves to.

Feelings of deprivation do not necessarily correspond to the absolute level of material deprivation one experiences. A family living in a small home in a poor area, where everyone is in more or less similar circumstances, is likely to feel less deprived than a family living in a similar house in a neighborhood where the majority of the other homes are much larger and neighbors are wealthier.

Assessing theories, and especially theoretical approaches, in sociology is a challenging and formidable task. The fact that there is not a single theoretical approach that dominates the field of sociology might be viewed as a limitation. But this is not the case at all: The jostling of rival theoretical approaches and theories reveals the vitality of the sociological enterprise. This variety rescues us from dogma or narrow-mindedness. Human behavior is complex, and no single theoretical perspective could adequately cover all of its aspects. Diversity in theoretical thinking provides a rich source of ideas that can be drawn on in research, and stimulates the imaginative capacities so essential to progress in sociological work.

LEVELS OF ANALYSIS: MICROSOCIOLOGY AND MACROSOCIOLOGY

microsociology • The study of human behavior in contexts of face-to-face interaction.

macrosociology • The study of large-scale groups, organizations, or social systems.

One important distinction among the different theoretical perspectives we have discussed in this chapter involves the level of analysis each is directed at. The study of everyday behavior in situations of face-to-face interaction is usually called **microsociology**. **Macrosociology**, by contrast, is the analysis of large-scale social systems, like the political system or the economic order. It also includes the analysis of long-term processes of change, such as the development of industrialism. At first glance, it might seem as though micro and macro perspectives are distinct from one another. In fact, the two are closely connected (Giddens 1984; Knorr-Cetina and Cicourel 1981).

Macro analysis is essential if we are to understand the institutional background of daily life. The ways in which people live their everyday lives are shaped by the broader institutional framework. For example, because of societal-level technological developments, we have many ways of maintaining friendships today. We may choose to send an e-mail or text message, communicate via Facebook, or call on our cell phone, yet we also may choose to fly thousands of miles to spend the weekend with a friend.

Micro studies, in turn, are necessary for illuminating broad institutional patterns. Face-to-face interaction is clearly the main basis of all forms of social organization, no matter how large scale. Suppose we are interested in understanding how business corporations function. We could analyze the face-to-face interactions of directors in the boardroom, staff working in their offices, or workers on the factory floor. We would not build up a picture of the whole corporation in this way, since some of its business is transacted through printed materials, letters, the telephone, and computers. Yet we could certainly contribute significantly to understanding how the organization works.

In later chapters, we will see further examples of how interaction in micro contexts affects larger social processes, and how macro systems in turn influence more confined settings of social life. ✓

CONCEPT CHECKS ✓

1. What role does theory play in sociological research?

2. According to Émile Durkheim, what makes sociology a social science? Why?

3. According to Karl Marx, what are the differences between the two classes that make up a capitalist society?

4. What are the differences between symbolic interactionist and functionalist approaches to the analysis of society?

5. How are macro and micro analyses of society connected?

WHAT KINDS OF QUESTIONS CAN SOCIOLOGISTS ANSWER?

Can we really study human social life in a scientific way? To answer this question, we must first define the word "science."

Science is the use of *systematic methods of* **empirical investigation**, *the analysis of data, theoretical thinking, and the logical assessment of arguments*, to develop a body of knowledge about a particular subject matter. Sociology is a scientific endeavor, according to this definition. It involves systematic methods of empirical investigation, the analysis of data, and the assessment of theories in the light of evidence and logical argument.

High-quality sociological research goes beyond surface-level descriptions of ordinary life; rather, it helps us understand our social lives in a new way. Sociologists are interested in the same questions that other people worry about and debate. Why is there racism and sexism? How can mass starvation exist in a world that is far wealthier than it has ever been before? How will the Internet affect our lives? However, sociologists often develop answers that run counter to our commonsense beliefs—and that generate further questions.

Good sociological work also tries to make the questions as precise as possible and seeks to gather factual evidence before coming to conclusions. Some of the questions that sociologists ask in their research studies are largely **factual**, or empirical, **questions**.

Factual information about one society, of course, will not always tell us whether we are dealing with an unusual case or a general set of influences. For this reason, sociologists often want to ask **comparative questions**, relating one social context within a society to another or contrasting examples drawn from different societies. A typical comparative question might be: How much do patterns of criminal behavior and law enforcement vary between the United States and Canada? Similarly, **developmental questions** ask whether patterns in a given society have shifted over time: How is the past different from the present?

Yet sociologists are interested in more than just answering factual questions, however important and interesting they may be. To obtain an understanding of human behavior, sociologists also pose broader **theoretical questions** that encompass a wide array of specific phenomena (Table 1.2). For example, a factual question may ask: To what extent do expected earnings affect one's choice of an occupation? By contrast, a theoretical question may ask: To what extent does the maximization of rewards affect human decision-making?

Sociologists do not to attain theoretical or factual knowledge simply for its own sake, however. Social scientists agree that personal values should not be permitted to bias conclusions, but at the same time research should pose questions that are relevant to real-world concerns. In this chapter, we look further into such issues by asking whether it is possible to produce objective knowledge. First, we examine the steps involved in sociological research. We then compare the most widely used research methods as we consider some actual investigations. As we shall see, there are often significant differences between the way research should ideally be carried out and real-world studies. ✓

science • The disciplined marshaling of empirical data, combined with theoretical approaches and theories that illuminate or explain those data. Scientific activity combines the creation of new modes of thought with the careful testing of hypotheses and ideas. One major feature that helps distinguish science from other idea systems (such as religion) is the assumption that all scientific ideas are open to criticism and revision.

empirical investigation • Factual inquiry carried out in any area of sociological study.

factual questions • Questions that raise issues concerning matters of fact (rather than theoretical or moral issues).

comparative questions • Questions concerned with drawing comparisons between different human societies for the purposes of sociological theory or research.

developmental questions • Questions that sociologists pose when looking at the origins and path of development of social institutions from the past to the present.

theoretical questions • Questions posed by sociologists when seeking to explain a particular range of observed events. The asking of theoretical questions is crucial to allowing us to generalize about the nature of social life.

CONCEPT CHECKS ✓

1. Why is sociology considered to be science?

2. What are the differences between comparative and developmental questions?

Table 1.2 | A Sociologist's Line of Questioning

FACTUAL QUESTION	What happened?	During the 1980s, there was an increase in the proportion of women in their thirties bearing children for the first time.
COMPARATIVE QUESTION	Did this happen everywhere?	Was this a global phenomenon or did it occur just in the United States or only in a certain region of the United States?
DEVELOPMENTAL QUESTION	Has this happened over time?	What have been the patterns of childbearing over time?
THEORETICAL QUESTION	What underlies this phenomenon?	Why are more women now waiting until their thirties to bear children? What factors would we look at to explain this change?

WHAT ARE THE SEVEN STEPS OF THE RESEARCH PROCESS?

The research process begins with the definition of a research question, and ends with the dissemination of the study findings. Although researchers do not necessarily follow all seven steps in the order set forth here, these steps serve as a model for how to conduct a sociological study. Conducting research is a bit like cooking. New researchers, like novice cooks, may follow the "recipe" to a tee. Experienced cooks often don't work from recipes at all, yet they might cook better than those who do—relying on the skills and insights they've acquired through years of hands-on experience.

1. DEFINE THE RESEARCH PROBLEM

All research starts from a research problem. Often, researchers strive to uncover a fact: What proportion of the population attends weekly religious services? Are people today really disaffected with big government? How far does the economic position of women lag behind that of men?

The best sociological research, however, begins with problems that are also puzzles. A puzzle is not just a lack of information, but a gap in our understanding. The most intriguing and influential sociological research correctly identifies and solves important puzzles.

Rather than simply answering the question "What is happening?" skilled researchers contribute to our understanding by asking "Why is this phenomenon happening?" We might ask, for example, why does religious service attendance change over the life course? Or, what accounts for the decline in the proportion of the population voting in presidential elections throughout the twentieth century? Why are women underrepresented in science and technology jobs?

Research does not take place in a vacuum. A sociologist may discover puzzles by reading the work of other researchers in books and professional journals or by being aware of emerging trends in society. For example, over recent years, an increasing number of public health programs have sought to treat the mentally ill while they continue to live in the community rather than confining them in asylums. Sociologists might be prompted to ask, what has given rise to this shift in attitudes toward the mentally ill? What are the likely consequences both for the patients themselves and for the rest of the community?

hypothesis • An idea or a guess about a given state of affairs, put forward as a basis for empirical testing.

data • factual information used as a basis for reasoning, discussion, or calculation. Social science data often refer to individuals' responses to survey questions.

2. REVIEW THE EVIDENCE

Once a research problem is identified, the next step is to review the available evidence; it's possible that other researchers have already satisfactorily clarified the problem. If not, the sociologist will need to sift through whatever related research does exist to see how useful it is for his or her purposes. What have others found? If their findings conflict with one another, what accounts for the conflict? What aspects of the problem has their research left unanalyzed? Have they looked only at small segments of the population, such as one age group, gender, or region? Drawing on others' ideas helps the sociologist clarify the issues that might be raised and the methods that might be used in the research.

3. MAKE THE PROBLEM PRECISE

A third stage involves working out a clear formulation of the research problem. If relevant literature already exists, the researcher may have a good idea of how to approach the problem. Hunches about the nature of the problem can sometimes be turned into definite **hypotheses**—educated guesses about what is going on—at this stage. A hypothesis must be formulated in such a way that the factual material gathered will provide evidence either supporting or disproving it.

4. WORK OUT A DESIGN

The researcher must then decide how to collect the research material or **data**. Many different research methods exist, and researchers should choose the method (or methods) that are best suited to the study's overall objectives and topic. For some purposes, a survey (in which

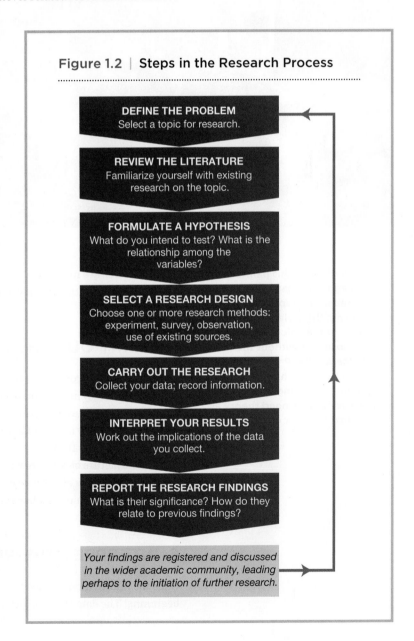

Figure 1.2 | Steps in the Research Process

DEFINE THE PROBLEM
Select a topic for research.

REVIEW THE LITERATURE
Familiarize yourself with existing research on the topic.

FORMULATE A HYPOTHESIS
What do you intend to test? What is the relationship among the variables?

SELECT A RESEARCH DESIGN
Choose one or more research methods: experiment, survey, observation, use of existing sources.

CARRY OUT THE RESEARCH
Collect your data; record information.

INTERPRET YOUR RESULTS
Work out the implications of the data you collect.

REPORT THE RESEARCH FINDINGS
What is their significance? How do they relate to previous findings?

Your findings are registered and discussed in the wider academic community, leading perhaps to the initiation of further research.

In looking at this painting by Brueghel, we can observe the number of people, what each is doing, the style of the buildings, or the colors the painter chose. But without the title, *Netherlandish Proverbs*, these facts tell us nothing about the picture's meaning. In the same way, sociologists need theory as a context for their observations.

questionnaires are normally used) might be suitable. In other circumstances, interviews or an observational study might be appropriate.

5. CARRY OUT THE RESEARCH

Researchers then proceed to carry out the plan developed in step 4. However, practical difficulties may arise, forcing the researcher to rethink his or her initial strategy. Potential subjects may not agree to answer questionnaires or participate in interviews. A business firm may not give a researcher access to its records. Yet omitting such persons or institutions from the study could bias the results, creating an inaccurate or incomplete picture of social reality. For example, it would be difficult for a researcher to answer questions about how corporations have complied with affirmative action programs if companies that have not complied do not want to be studied.

6. INTERPRET THE RESULTS

Once the information has been gathered, the researcher's work is not over—it is just beginning! The data must be analyzed, trends tracked, and hypotheses tested. Most importantly, researchers must interpret their results in such a way that they tell a clear story, and that they directly address the research puzzle outlined in step 1.

7. REPORT THE FINDINGS

The research report, usually published as a book or an article in a scholarly journal, provides an account of the research question, methods, findings, and the implications of the findings for social theory, public policy, or practice. This is a final stage only in terms of addressing the original research puzzle. In their written reports, most social scientists pose questions that remain unanswered, and suggest new questions that might be explored in future studies. Each individual study contributes to the larger, collective process of understanding the human condition. ✓

> ## CONCEPT CHECKS ✓
> 1. What are the seven steps of the research process?

WHAT RESEARCH METHODS DO SOCIOLOGISTS USE?

Table 1.3 | Three of the Main Methods Used in Sociological Research

RESEARCH METHOD	STRENGTHS	LIMITATIONS
Ethnography	Usually generates richer and more in-depth information than other methods.	Can be used to study only relatively small groups or communities.
	Ethnography can provide a broader understanding of social processes.	Findings might apply only to groups or communities studied; not easy to generalize on the basis of a single fieldwork study.
Surveys	Make possible the efficient collection of data on large numbers of individuals.	Material gathered may be superficial; if questionnaire is highly standardized, important differences among respondents' viewpoints may be glossed over.
	Allow for precise comparisons to be made among the answers of respondents.	Responses may be what people profess to believe rather than what they actually believe.
Experiments	Influence of specific variables can be controlled by the investigator.	Many aspects of social life cannot be brought into the laboratory.
	Are usually easier for subsequent researchers to repeat.	Responses of those studied may be affected by the experimental situation.

ETHNOGRAPHY

ethnography • The firsthand study of people using participant observation or interviewing.

An investigator using **ethnography** (firsthand studies of people using **participant observation** or interviewing) socializes or works or lives with members of a group, organization, or community and perhaps participates directly in its activities. An ethnographer cannot secretly infiltrate the groups she studies, but must explain and justify her presence to its members. She must gain the cooperation of the community and sustain it over a period of time, if any worthwhile results are to be achieved.

participant observation • A method of research widely used in sociology and anthropology, in which the researcher takes part in the activities of the group or community being studied. Also called *fieldwork*.

For a long while, research reports based on participant observation usually omitted any account of the hazards or problems that the researcher had to overcome, but more recently the published reminiscences and diaries of field workers have been more honest and open. The researcher may be frustrated because the members of the group refuse to talk frankly about themselves; direct queries may be welcomed in some contexts but met with a chilly silence in others. Some types of fieldwork may be emotionally isolating or even physically dangerous; for instance, a researcher studying a street gang might be seen as a police informer or might become unwittingly embroiled in conflicts with rival gangs.

In traditional works of ethnography, accounts were presented without very much information about the observer. It was believed that an ethnographer could present "objective" observations of the things they studied. More recently, ethnographers have been willing to talk and write about themselves and the nature of their connection to the people under study. For example, a researcher might discuss how her race, class, or gender affected the work, or how the status differences between observer and observed distorted the dialogue between them.

ADVANTAGES AND LIMITATIONS OF FIELDWORK

Where it is successful, ethnography provides rich information on the behavior of people in real-world settings. We may develop a better understanding not only of the group but of social processes that transcend the situation under study.

But fieldwork also has serious limitations. Only fairly small groups or communities can be studied. And much depends on the skill of the researcher in gaining the confidence of the individuals involved; without this skill, the research is unlikely to get off the ground at all. The reverse is also possible. A researcher may begin to identify so closely with the group that she loses the perspective of an objective observer. Or she may reach conclusions that are more about her own effects on the situation than she or her readers ever realize. Finally, the findings of field studies are seldom generalizable, meaning that researchers' conclusions may not hold true for other groups or settings.

SURVEYS

survey • A method of sociological research in which questionnaires are administered to the population being studied.

When conducting a **survey**, researchers ask subjects to provide answers to structured questionnaires. The researcher may administer the survey in person, or may mail it to a study participant who will then return the survey by mail. Survey results—especially those based on random samples of the larger population—often can be generalized to the population at large, yet this method provides less in-depth information than the highly descriptive nuanced slices of life obtained in fieldwork.

STANDARDIZED AND OPEN-ENDED QUESTIONS

Two types of questions are used in surveys. Some contain a standardized, or fixed-choice, set of questions, to which only a fixed range of responses is possible—for instance, *Yes/No/Don't know* or *Very likely/Likely/Unlikely/Very unlikely*. Such questions have the advantage that responses are easy to compare and count up because only a small number of categories are involved. However, the information they yield is limited, because they do not allow for subtleties of opinion or verbal expression.

Open-ended questions, by contrast, typically provide more detailed information because respondents may express their views in their own words. The researcher can probe more deeply into what the respondent thinks. The lack of standardization means that answers may be difficult to compare across respondents, however.

In surveys, all the items must be readily understandable to interviewers and interviewees alike. Questions are usually asked in a set order. Large national surveys are conducted regularly by government agencies and research organizations, with interviews carried out more or less simultaneously across the whole country. Those who conduct the interviews and those who analyze the data could not do their work effectively if they constantly had to be checking with each other about ambiguities in the questions or answers.

Survey researchers take care to ensure that respondents can easily understand both the questions and the response categories posed. For instance, a seemingly simple question like "What is your relationship status?" might baffle some people. It would be more appropriate to ask, "Are you single, married, separated, divorced, or widowed?" Many survey questions are "tried and true" measures that have been used successfully in numerous prior studies. Researchers developing new survey questions often conduct a pilot study to test out new items. A **pilot study** is a trial run in which a questionnaire is completed by a small number of people, and problematic questions are identified and revised.

SAMPLING

Often sociologists are interested in the characteristics of large numbers of individuals—for example, the political attitudes of the American population as a whole. It would be impossible to study all these people directly, so researchers' solution is to use **sampling**—they concentrate on a **sample**, or small proportion, of the overall group. One can usually be confident that results from a population sample can be generalized to the total population, as long as the sample was properly chosen. Studies of only two or three thousand voters, for instance, can give a very accurate indication of the attitudes and voting intentions of the entire population. But to achieve such accuracy, a sample must be **representative**: The group of individuals studied must be typical of the population as a whole.

A single best procedure for ensuring that a sample is representative is **random sampling**, in which a sample is chosen so that every member of the population has an

---

Making Sociology Work
POLITICAL POLLSTER

On the night of the 2000 presidential election, each of the major television networks trumpeted that Al Gore had won Florida, and that he would be the forty-third president of the United States. When George W. Bush was officially declared the victor hours later, Dan Rather sheepishly acknowledged, "We were wrong to call it as early as we did" (Pennenberg 2004). What went wrong? The television networks were relying heavily on data from exit polls; exit poll workers wait outside polling places on election night and ask people face to face, as they exit the building, how they voted. As a sociologist trained in survey research, would you recommend the use of exit poll data for projecting the results of presidential elections? What are the advantages of using a random sampling technique as a way to measure the views and political positions of American voters?

---

pilot study • A trial run in survey research.

sampling • Studying a proportion of individuals or cases from a larger population as representative of that population as a whole.

sample • A small proportion of a larger population.

representative sample • A sample from a larger population that is statistically typical of that population.

random sampling • Sampling method in which a sample is chosen so that every member of the population has the same probability of being included

In Philip Zimbardo's make-believe jail, tension between students playing guards and students playing prisoners became dangerously real. From his experiment Zimbardo concluded that behavior in prisons is influenced more by the nature of the prison itself than the individual characteristics of those involved.

experiment • A research method in which variables can be analyzed in a controlled and systematic way, either in an artificial situation constructed by the researcher or in naturally occurring settings

comparative research • Research that compares one set of findings on one society with the same type of findings on other societies.

equal probability of being included. The most sophisticated way of obtaining a random sample is to assign each member of the population a number and then use a computer to generate a random numbers list, from which the sample is derived—for instance, by picking every tenth number.

EXPERIMENTS

An **experiment** enables a researcher to test a hypothesis under highly controlled conditions established by the investigator. Experiments are often used in the natural sciences and psychology, as they are considered the best method for ascertaining causality, or the influence of a particular factor on the study's outcome. In an experimental situation, the researcher directly controls the circumstances being studied. Because most experiments occur in laboratories, however, the scope of topics explored is quite restricted. We can bring only small groups of individuals into a laboratory setting, and in such experiments, people know that they are being studied and may behave unnaturally. Experiments also neglect the macrosocial context, such as historical or political influences.

Nevertheless, several experimental studies have made important contributions to sociological knowledge. One example is the ingenious experiment carried out by Philip Zimbardo (1972), who set up a make-believe prison, randomly assigning some student volunteers to the role of prison guards and others to the role of prisoners. His aim was to see how one's social role shaped one's attitudes and behavior. The results shocked the investigators. Students who played at being guards quickly assumed an authoritarian manner; they displayed genuine hostility toward the prisoners, ordering them around and verbally abusing and bullying them. The prisoners, by contrast, showed a mixture of apathy and rebelliousness—a response often noted among inmates in real prisons. These effects were so marked and the level of tension so high that the experiment had to be called off at an early stage. Zimbardo concluded that behavior in prisons is influenced more by the nature of the prison situation itself than by the individual characteristics of those involved.

COMPARATIVE RESEARCH

Comparative research is of central importance in sociology, because it enables researchers to document whether social behavior varies across time, place, and by one's social group memberships. For example, divorce rates rose rapidly in the United States after World War II, reaching a peak in the early 1980s, then declining slightly and leveling off in recent years. As many as one in three couples marrying today will divorce (U.S. Bureau of the Census 2005a)—a statistic that expresses profound changes taking place in the area of sexual relations and family life. Do these changes reflect specific features of American society? We can find out by comparing divorce rates in the United States with those of other countries. Although the U.S. rate is higher than in most other Western societies, the overall trends are similar. Virtually all Western countries have experienced steadily climbing divorce rates over the past half century.

HISTORICAL ANALYSIS

A key aspect of the "sociological imagination" is considering ways that historical context shapes individual lives. As such, we frequently need a time perspective to make sense of the material we collect about a particular problem.

Sociologists commonly want to investigate past events directly. Some periods of history can be studied retrospectively, when potential study participants or reporters are still alive—such as in the case of the Holocaust in Europe during World War II. Research in **oral history** means interviewing people about events they witnessed at some point earlier in their lives. This kind of research can stretch back in time at the most only some sixty or seventy years. For historical research on an earlier period, sociologists depend on the use of documents and written records, often held in special collections at libraries or the National Archives.

An interesting example of the use of historical documents is sociologist Anthony Ashworth's (1980) study of trench warfare during World War I. Ashworth was interested in the lives of men who had to endure being under constant fire, crammed in close proximity for weeks on end. He used a range of documentary sources: official histories of the war, including those written about different military divisions and battalions; official publications of the time; the notes and records kept informally by individual soldiers; and personal accounts of war experiences. He discovered that most soldiers formed their own ideas about how often they intended to engage in combat with the enemy and often effectively ignored the commands of their officers. For example, on Christmas Day, German and Allied soldiers suspended hostilities, and in one place the two sides even staged an informal soccer match. These insights were gleaned from using a rich and diverse array of sources.

Despite the distinctive strengths of ethnography, surveys, experiments, comparative research, and historical analysis, each method has limitations. Sociologists often combine several methods in a single piece of research, using each to supplement and check on the others. This process is known as **triangulation**. Laud Humphreys's classic *Tearoom Trade* (1970) study is an example of how researchers may use multiple methods to develop a deep understanding of social behavior. *Tearoom Trade* is an exploration of the phenomenon within the gay community involving the pursuit of impersonal homosexual sex in public restrooms. This study used surveys and observation to obtain fascinating glimpses into the secret lives of gay men. Yet, as we will see in the next section, it also revealed the important ethical challenges faced by sociologists. ✓

oral history • Interviews with people about events they witnessed or experienced at some point earlier in their lives.

triangulation • The use of multiple research methods as a way of producing more reliable empirical data than is available from any single method.

CONCEPT CHECKS

1. What are the main advantages and limitations of ethnography as a research method?

2. Contrast the two types of questions commonly used in surveys.

3. What is a random sample?

4. Discuss the main strengths of experiments.

5. What are the similarities and differences between comparative and historical research?

6. Why is it important to use triangulation in social research?

WHAT ETHICAL DILEMMAS DO SOCIOLOGISTS FACE?

In his groundbreaking study *Tearoom Trade*, Humphreys investigated "tearooms" or public restrooms where men would go to have sex with other men—often hiding their "secret" lives from their wives, children, and coworkers. Humphreys's study cast a new light on the struggles of men who were forced to keep their sexual proclivities secret. His book led to a deeper understanding of the consequences of the social stigma and legal persecution associated with gay lifestyles.

STATISTICAL TERMS

Research in sociology often makes use of statistical techniques in the analysis of findings. Some are highly sophisticated and complex, but those most often used are easy to understand. The most common are **measures of central tendency** (ways of calculating averages) and **correlation coefficients** (measures of the degree to which one variable relates consistently to another). There are three methods of calculating averages, each of which has certain advantages and shortcomings. Take as an example the amount of personal wealth (including all assets such as houses, cars, bank accounts, and investments) owned by thirteen individuals. Suppose the thirteen own the following amounts:

1.	$ 000 (zero)	8. $	80,000
2.	$ 5,000	9. $	100,000
3.	$ 10,000	10. $	150,000
4.	$ 20,000	11. $	200,000
5.	$ 40,000	12. $	400,000
6.	$ 40,000	13. $	10,000,000
7.	$ 40,000		

The **mean** corresponds to the average, arrived at by adding together the personal wealth of all 13 people and dividing the result by 13. The total is $11,085,000; dividing this by 13, we reach a mean of $852,692.31. This mean is often a useful calculation because it is based on the whole range of data provided. However, it can be misleading where one or a small number of cases are very different from the majority. In the above example, the mean is not in fact an appropriate measure of central tendency, because the presence of one very large figure, $10,000,000, skews the picture. One might get the impression when using the mean to summarize these data that most of the people own far more than they actually do. In such instances, one of two other measures may be used.

The **mode** is the figure that occurs most frequently in a given set of data. In our example, it is $40,000.

The problem with the mode is that it doesn't take into account the *overall distribution* of the data—that is, the range of figures covered. The most frequently occurring case in a set of figures is not necessarily representative of their distribution as a whole and thus may not be a useful average. In this case, $40,000 is too close to the lower end of the figures.

The third measure is the **median,** which is the middle of any set of figures; here, this would be the seventh figure, again $40,000. Our example gives an odd number of figures, thirteen. If there had been an even number—for instance, twelve—the median would be calculated by taking the mean of the two middle cases, figures 6 and 7. Like the mode, the median gives no idea of the actual *range* of the data measured.

Sometimes a researcher will use more than one measure of central tendency to avoid giving a deceptive picture of the average. More often, he will calculate the **standard deviation** for the data in question. This is a way of calculating the **degree of dispersal,** or the range, of a set of figures—which in this case goes from $0 to $10,000,000.

Correlation coefficients offer a useful way of expressing how closely connected two (or more) variables are. Where two variables correlate completely, we can speak of a perfect positive correlation, expressed as 1.0. Where no relation is found between two variables—they have no consistent connection at all—the coefficient is 0. A perfect negative correlation, expressed as -1.0, exists when two variables are in a completely inverse relation to one another. Perfect correlations are never found in the social sciences. Correlations of the order of 0.6 or more, whether positive or negative, are usually regarded as indicating a strong degree of connection between whatever variables are being analyzed. Positive correlations on this level might be found between, say, social class background and voting behavior.

However, his research also is held up as a cautionary example of the ethical dilemmas that researchers face. The key ethical questions that sociologists must ask are: (1) Does the research pose risks to the subjects that are greater than the risks they face in their everyday lives? (2) Do the scientific gains or "benefits" of the research balance out the "risks" to the subjects? These questions do not have easy answers, as Humphreys's work reveals.

Humphreys set out to understand what kinds of men came to the tearooms. In order to answer this question, he took on the role of a "lookout"—a person who loitered in the tearoom, and would let the others know if an intruder, such as a police officer, was nearby. This allowed him to observe the gay men's' activity. He could not easily ask questions or talk to the men in the tearoom, because of the norm of silence that prevailed. Humphreys also could not ask personal questions of men who wanted to remain anonymous.

Given his desire to learn more than his observations would allow, Humphreys's solution was to learn more about the men in the tearooms using survey methods. He would write down the license plate numbers of men who drove into the parking lot and then went into the restrooms for the purpose of engaging in sexual relations. Humphreys then gave those license plate numbers to a friend who worked at the Department of Motor Vehicles, securing the addresses of the men.

Months later, Washington University in St. Louis was conducting a door-to-door survey of sexual habits. Humphreys asked the principal investigators in that survey if he could add the names and addresses of his sample of tearoom participants. Humphreys then disguised himself as one of the investigators and went to interview these men at their homes, supposedly just to ask only the survey questions but actually also to learn more about their social backgrounds and lives. He found that most of these men were married and led very conventional lives.

Humphreys later acknowledged that he was less than truthful to those whose behavior he was studying. He didn't reveal his identity as a sociologist when observing the tearoom activities. People who came into the tearoom assumed he was there for the same reasons they were and that his presence could be accepted at face value. While he did not tell any direct lies while observing the tearoom, he also did not reveal the real reason for his presence there.

Was his behavior ethical? The study had many benefits, including moving forward scientific knowledge about gay men during a period when their behaviors were highly stigmatized. If Humphreys had been completely frank at every stage of the research, his study might not have gotten as far as it did. At the same time, however, the costs to the research subjects were potentially high.

The observational part of his study posed only modest risk: Humphreys did not collect information about the participants that would have identified them. What he knew about them was similar to what all the other people in the tearoom knew. His presence did not expose them to any more risk than they already encountered in their everyday lives.

The more problematic aspect of Humphreys's study was that he wrote down the license plate numbers of the people who came into the tearooms, obtained their home addresses from Department of Motor Vehicles, and visited their homes under the guise of conducting a survey for Washington University. Even though Humphreys did not reveal to the men's families anything about the activities he observed in the tearooms, and even though he took great pains to keep the data confidential, the knowledge he gained could have been damaging. Because the activity he was documenting was illegal at the time, police officers might have demanded that he release information about the

measures of central tendency • The ways of calculating averages.

correlation coefficient • A measure of the degree of correlation between variables.

mean • A statistical measure of central tendency, or average, based on dividing a total by the number of individual cases.

mode • The number that appears most often in a given set of data. This can sometimes be a helpful way of portraying central tendency.

median • The number that falls halfway in a range of numbers—a way of calculating central tendency that is sometimes more useful than calculating a mean.

standard deviation • A way of calculating the spread of a group of figures.

degree of dispersal • The range or distribution of a set of figures.

READING A TABLE

You will often come across tables in reading sociological literature. They sometimes look complex, but are easy to decipher if you follow a few basic steps, listed here; with practice, these will become automatic. (See Table 1.4 as an example.) Do not succumb to the temptation to skip over tables; they contain information in concentrated form, which can be read more quickly than would be possible if the same material were expressed in words. By becoming skilled in the interpretation of tables, you will also be able to check how far the conclusions a writer draws actually seem justified.

1. Read the title in full. Tables frequently have longish titles, which represent an attempt by the researcher to state accurately the nature of the information conveyed. The title of Table 1.4 gives first the subject of the data, second the fact that the table provides material for comparison, and third the fact that data are given only for a limited number of countries.

2. Look for explanatory comments, or notes, about the data. A note at the foot of Table 1.4 linked to the main column heading indicates that the data cover only licensed cars. This is important, because in some countries the proportion of vehicles properly licensed may be lower than in others. Notes may say how the material was collected or why it is displayed in a particular way. If the data have not been gathered by the researcher but are based on findings originally reported elsewhere, a source

will be included. The source sometimes gives you some insight into how reliable the information is likely to be, as well as showing where to find the original data. In our table, the source note makes clear that the data have been taken from more than one source.

3. Read the headings along the top and left-hand side of the table. (Sometimes tables are arranged with "headings" at the foot rather than the top.) These tell you what type of information is contained in each row and column. In reading the table, keep in mind each set of headings as you scan the figures. In our example, the headings on the left give the countries involved, whereas those at the top refer to the levels of car ownership and the years for which they are given.

4. Identify the units used; the figures in the body of the table may represent cases, percentages, averages, or other measures. Sometimes it may be helpful to convert the figures to a form more useful to you: If percentages are not provided, for example, it may be worth calculating them.

5. Consider the conclusions that might be reached from the information in the table. Most tables are discussed by the author, and what he or she has to say should of course be borne in mind. But you should also ask what further issues or questions could be suggested by the data.

men's identities. A less skilled investigator might have slipped up when interviewing the subjects' families. Humphreys could have lost his notes, which could then have been found later by someone else.

Humphreys was one of the first sociologists to study the lives of gay men. (However, researchers today still face challenges in studying the lives of gays and lesbians.) Humphreys's account was a humane treatment that went well beyond what little was known about gay men at that time. Although none of his research subjects suffered as a result of his book, Humphreys himself later said that if he were to do the study again, he would not trace license plates or go to people's homes. Instead, after gathering his data

Table 1.4 | Automobile Ownership: Comparisons of Several Selected Countries

Several interesting trends can be seen from the figures in this table. First, the level of car ownership varies considerably among different countries. The number of cars per 1,000 people is more than six times greater in the United States than in Brazil, for example. Second, there is a clear connection between car ownership ratios as a rough indicator of differences in prosperity. Third, in all the countries respresented, the rate of car ownership increased between 1971 and 2002, but in some the rate of increase was higher than others—probably indicating differences in the degree to which countries have successfully generated economic growth or are catching up.

NUMBER OF CARS PER 1,000 OF THE ADULT POPULATION[a]

Country	1971	1981	1984	1989	1993	1996	2001	2002
Brazil	12	78	84	98	96	79	95	116
Chile	19	45	56	67	94	110	133	NA
China	NA	NA	NA	5[c]	6	8	12[d]	16
Ireland	141	202	226	228	290	307	442	445
France	261	348	360	574	503	524	584	592
Greece	30	94	116	150	271	312	428	450
Italy	210	322	359	424	586	674	638	655
Japan	100	209	207	286	506	552	577	581
Sweden	291	348	445	445	445	450	497	500
United Kingdom	224	317	343	366	386	399	554	551
United States	448	536	540	607	747	767	785	789
West Germany[b]	247	385	312	479	470	528	583	588

[a] Includes all licensed cars.
[b] Germany as a whole after 1989.
[c] Data for 1990.
[d] Data for 2000.
NA, not applicable.

Sources: Baltic 21 Secretariat; World Bank 1999; International Monetary Fund 2005; International Road Federation 1987, p. 68; OECD 2005a; Statistical Office of the European Communities 1991; *The Economist* 1996; Toyota Corporation 2003; United Nations Economic Commission for Europe 2003; World Bank 2005.

---

in the public tearooms, he might try to get to know a subset of the people well enough to inform them of his goals for the study.

It is unlikely that Humphreys's mistakes will be repeated in the future. In recent years, the federal government has become increasingly strict with universities that make use of government grant money for research purposes. The National Science Foundation and the National Institutes of Health have strict requirements outlining how human subjects must be treated. In response to these requirements, American universities now have Institutional Review Boards (IRBs) that routinely review all research involving human subjects.

The result of these review procedures has been both positive and negative. On the positive side, researchers are more aware of ethical considerations than ever before. On the negative side, however, many sociologists are finding it increasingly difficult to get their work done when IRBs require them to secure informed consent from their research subjects before they are able to establish a rapport with the subjects. **Informed consent** means that study participants are given a broad description

informed consent ● The process whereby the study investigator informs potential participants about the risks and benefits involved in the research study. Informed consent must be obtained before an individual participates in a study.

debriefing ● Following a research study, the investigator will inform study participants about the true purpose of the study, and will reveal any deception that happened during the study.

CONCEPT CHECKS ✓

1. What ethical dilemmas did Humphreys's *Tearoom Trade* study pose?

2. Contrast informed consent and debriefing.

of the study prior to agreeing to participate. After reading this summary, they are free to opt out of the research. Another safeguard used to protect subjects is **debriefing**; after the research study ends, the investigator discusses with the subjects their concerns, and acknowledges whether strategies such as deception were used. Despite these safeguards, there will likely never be easy solutions to vexing problems posed by research ethics. ✓

HOW DOES THE "SOCIOLOGICAL IMAGINATION" AFFECT YOUR LIFE?

When we observe the world through the prism of the "sociological imagination," we are affected in several important ways. First, we develop a greater awareness and understanding of cultural differences. For example, a white social worker operating in an African American community won't gain the confidence of its members without having a sensitivity to the differences in social experience that separate white and black in the United States.

Second, we are better able to assess the results of public policy initiatives. Consider the large public-housing blocks built in many urban centers following World War II. The goal was to provide high-quality homes for low-income groups from slum areas and to offer shopping amenities and other civic services. However, research later showed that many people who had moved to the large apartment blocks felt isolated and unhappy. High-rise apartment blocks and shopping malls in poorer areas often became dilapidated and provided breeding grounds for muggings and other violent crimes.

Third, we may become more self-enlightened, and may develop wise insights into our own behaviors. Self-enlightened groups can benefit from sociological research by using the information gleaned to respond to government policies or form policy initiatives of their own. Self-help groups such as Alcoholics Anonymous (AA) and social movements like the environmental movement are examples of social groups that have directly sought practical reforms, with some success.

Fourth, developing a sociological eye toward social problems and developing rigorous research skills opens many career doors—as industrial consultants, urban planners, social workers, and personnel managers, among other jobs. An understanding of society also serves those working in law, journalism, business, and medicine.

In sum, sociology is a discipline in which we often set aside our personal views and biases to explore the influences that shape our lives and those of others. Sociology emerged as an intellectual endeavor along with the development of modern societies, and the study of such societies remains its principal concern. Sociology has major practical implications for people's lives. Learning to become a sociologist is an exciting academic pursuit! The best way to make sure it is exciting is to approach the subject in an imaginative way and to relate sociological ideas and findings to your own life. ✓

CONCEPT CHECKS ✓

1. Describe three ways that sociology can help us in our lives.

2. What skills and perspectives do sociologists bring to their work?

NEED HELP STUDYING?

⊚ wwnorton.com/studyspace

Visit StudySpace to access free review materials such as:

- Vocabulary Flashcards
- Diagnostic Review Quizzes
- Study Outlines

REVIEW QUESTIONS

1. What is the sociological imagination? Give an example of how it can be used. What are some things students of sociology can do to acquire a sociological imagination?
2. What are the main differences between the theories of Émile Durkheim, Karl Marx, and Max Weber?
3. What is symbolic interactionism? What are its strengths and weaknesses as a theoretical perspective?
4. What is functionalism? What were Robert Merton's contributions to functionalist theory?
5. What are the similarities and differences between Marxist and feminist theories?
6. What are the benefits and constraints of micro and macro approaches in sociology?
7. Is sociology a science? In what ways does it differ from the natural sciences?
8. Briefly describe the kinds of research questions sociologists ask and how they differ.
9. What are the seven basic steps of a sociological research project?
10. Why is it important to take precautions while doing research to protect human subjects?

THINKING SOCIOLOGICALLY EXERCISES

1. Healthy older Americans often encounter discriminatory treatment when younger people assume that they are feeble-minded and thus overlook them for jobs they are fully capable of doing. How would each of the popular theoretical perspectives—functionalism, class conflict theory, and symbolic interactionism—explain the dynamics of prejudice against the elderly?
2. Your text discusses the sociology of coffee, suggesting that coffee is more than a simple product designed to quench a person's thirst and to help fend off drowsiness. Mention and discuss four sociological features of coffee that clearly show its "sociological" nature.
3. Let's suppose the dropout rate in your local high school increased dramatically. Faced with such a serious problem, the school board offers you a $500,000 grant to do a study to explain the sudden increase. Following the recommended study procedures outlined in your text, explain how you would go about doing your research. What might be some of the hypotheses to test in your study? How would you prove or disprove them?
4. Explain in some detail the advantages and disadvantages of doing comparative or historical research. What will it yield that will be better than experimentation, surveys, and ethnographic fieldwork? What are its limitations compared with those approaches?

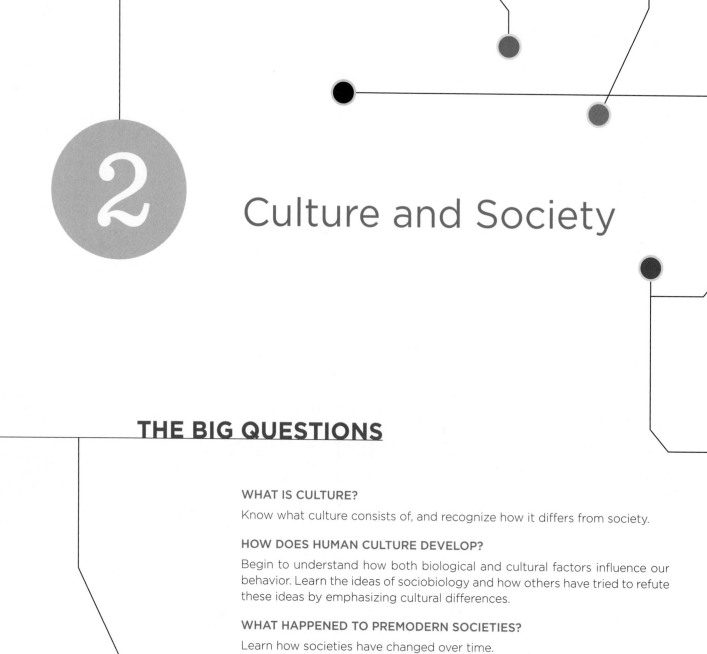

Culture and Society

2

THE BIG QUESTIONS

WHAT IS CULTURE?

Know what culture consists of, and recognize how it differs from society.

HOW DOES HUMAN CULTURE DEVELOP?

Begin to understand how both biological and cultural factors influence our behavior. Learn the ideas of sociobiology and how others have tried to refute these ideas by emphasizing cultural differences.

WHAT HAPPENED TO PREMODERN SOCIETIES?

Learn how societies have changed over time.

HOW HAS INDUSTRIALIZATION SHAPED MODERN SOCIETY?

Recognize the factors that changed premodern societies, particularly how industrialization and colonialism influenced global development. Know the differences between the First World, the Second World, and the developing world (Third World) and how they developed.

HOW DOES GLOBALIZATION AFFECT CONTEMPORARY CULTURE?

Recognize the effect of globalization on your life and the lives of people around the world. Think about the effect of a growing global culture.

In December 1996, the former French president Jacques Chirac was visiting France's new National Library, where he reportedly viewed for the first time a computer mouse. Chirac was amazed by the new technology (Cairncross 1997). The United States at that time ranked first among major countries in terms of Internet servers; France was not even among the top twenty-five (Starrs 1997).

France is no less modern than the United States. Why was it so reluctant to come online? Could it be that in 1996, as today, the Internet was dominated by the United States and was thus a powerful source for spreading American culture, along with the English language?

The unofficial language of the Internet is English, yet Internet users increasingly represent persons from throughout the globe. In 2000, nearly half of all Internet users worldwide were Americans (Nua.com 2000). Today, just over 14 percent of world Internet users are American (Internet World Stats 2009a). The Chinese are also going online in increasingly large numbers, with almost 300 million Internet users in 2009—over 1320 percent more than in 2000 (Internet World Stats 2009b). One study (published in French) concluded that 82 percent of all Web sites are in English—even though 94 percent of the world's population speaks some other language (Internet Society [ISOC] 1997; Wallraff 2000) and only about 29 percent of Internet users are native English speakers (Internet World Stats 2009c). The French are especially sensitive about the threat of American culture and the English language to their way of life. Many French people resent what they call American "cultural imperialism," seen as a form of conquest—one of values and attitudes—and including such unwelcome imports as McDonald's restaurants. McDonald's, their high golden arches a visible symbol of American cultural domination, have even been attacked and burned down in France.

France is not alone in resisting the inroads of American culture. As American culture spreads around the world through film, television, and the Internet, many people fear the erosion of their own cultures—even as they tune in to *Grey's Anatomy*, sip Coke or Pepsi, and download American music from the Web. Is modern technology an irresistible force that will eventually press the world's diverse cultures into a single mold? Or will it permit local cultures to flourish? These are some of the questions we explore in this chapter.

First, however, we look at what culture is and its role in encouraging conformity to shared ways of thinking and acting. We then consider the early development of human culture, emphasizing features that distinguish human behavior from that of other species. After assessing the role of biology in shaping human behavior, we examine the different aspects of culture that are essential for human society. This leads to a discussion of cultural diversity, examining the cultural variations not only across different societies but also within a single society such as the United States.

Cultural variations among human beings are linked to differing types of society, and we will compare and contrast the main forms of society found in history. The point of doing this is to tie together closely the two aspects of human social existence—the different cultural values and products that human beings have developed and the contrasting types of society in which such cultural development has occurred. Too often, culture is discussed separately from society as though the two were disconnected, whereas in fact, as we've already emphasized, they are closely intertwined. Throughout the chapter, we concentrate on how social change has affected cultural development. One instance of this is the effect of technology and globalization on the many cultures of the world, a topic we explore in the conclusion to this chapter.

WHAT IS CULTURE?

culture • The values, norms, and material goods characteristic of a given group. Like the concept of society, the notion of culture is widely used in sociology and the other social sciences (particularly anthropology). Culture is one of the most distinctive properties of human social association.

The sociological study of **culture** began with Émile Durkheim in the nineteenth century and soon became the basis of *anthropology*, a social science specifically focused on the study of cultural differences and similarities among the world's peoples. Early social scientists assumed that "primitive" cultures were inferior, lagging far behind modern European "civilization." However, sociologists and anthropologists now recognize that different cultures each have their own distinctive characteristics. The task of social science is to understand this cultural diversity, which is best done by avoiding value judgments.

DEFINING "CULTURE"

Culture consists of the values held by members of a particular group, the languages they speak, the symbols they revere, the norms they follow, and the material goods they create, from tools to clothing. Some elements of culture, especially the beliefs and expectations people have about each other and the world they inhabit, are a component of all social relations. **Values** are abstract ideals. For example, monogamy—being faithful to a single marriage partner—is a prominent value in most Western societies. In other cultures, on the other hand, a person may be permitted to have several wives or husbands simultaneously. **Norms** are widely agreed-upon principles or rules people are expected to observe; they represent the dos and don'ts of social life. Norms of behavior in marriage include, for example, how husbands and wives are supposed to behave toward their in-laws. In some societies, they are expected to develop a close relationship; in others, they keep a clear distance from each other.

Norms, like the values they reflect, vary widely across cultures. Among most Americans, for example, one norm calls for direct eye contact between persons engaged in conversation; completely averting one's eyes is usually interpreted as a sign of weakness or rudeness. Yet, among the Navajo, a cultural norm calls for averting one's eyes as a sign of respect. Direct eye contact, particularly between strangers, is considered rude because it violates a norm of politeness. When a Navajo and a Western tourist encounter one another for the first time, the Navajo's cultural norm calls for averting the eyes, while the tourist's cultural norm calls for direct eye contact. The result is likely to be a misunderstanding: The Navajo may see the tourist as impolite and vulgar, while the tourist may see the Navajo as disrespectful or deceptive. Such cultural misunderstandings may lead to unfair generalizations and stereotypes and even promote outright hostility. Values and norms work together to shape how members of a culture behave within their surroundings.

Finally, **material goods** refer to the physical objects that individuals in society create. These objects, in turn, influence how we live. They include the food we eat, the clothes we wear, the cars we drive to the houses we live in; the tools and technologies we use to make those goods, from sewing machines to computerized factories; and the towns and cities that we build as places in which to live and work. A central aspect of a society's material culture is technology.

Today material culture is rapidly becoming globalized, thanks in large part to modern information technology such as the computer, the cell phone, and the Internet. As noted at the beginning of this chapter, the United States has been in the forefront of this technological revolution, although most other industrial countries are rapidly catching up. In fact, it no longer makes sense to speak of an exclusively "U.S. technology" any more than it makes sense to speak of a U.S. car. The "world car," with parts manufactured across the planet in a global assembly line, embodies technology developed in Japan, the United States, and Europe.

When we use the term *culture* in daily conversation, we often think of "high culture"—like fine art, literature, classical music, ballet. For a sociological perspective, the concept includes these activities, but also many more. Culture refers to the ways of life of the individual members or groups within a society: their apparel, marriage customs and family life, patterns of work, religious ceremonies, and leisure pursuits. The concept also covers the goods they create and the goods that become meaningful for them—bows and arrows, plows, factories and machines, computers, books, dwellings. We should think of culture as a "design for living" or "tool kit" of practices, knowledge, and symbols acquired—as we shall see later—through learning rather than by **instinct** (Kluckhohn 1949; Swidler 1986).

Is it possible to describe an "American" culture? Although the United States is culturally diverse, we can identify several characteristics of a uniquely American culture. First, it reflects a particular range of values shared by many, if not all, Americans—such as the belief in the merits of individual achievement or in equality of opportunity. Second, these values are connected to specific norms: For example, it is usually expected

values • Ideas held by individuals or groups about what is desirable, proper, good, and bad. What individuals value is strongly influenced by the specific culture in which they happen to live.

norms • Rules of conduct that specify appropriate behavior in a given range of social situations. A norm either prescribes a given type of behavior or forbids it. All human groups follow definite norms, which are always backed by sanctions of one kind or another—varying from informal disapproval to physical punishment.

material goods • The physical objects that a society creates; these influence the ways in which people live.

instinct • A fixed pattern of behavior that has genetic origins and that appears in all normal animals within a given species.

A woman looks at a dish of worms during the Taipei Chinese Food Festival in Taiwan.

that people will work hard to achieve occupational success (Bellah et al. 1985; Parsons 1964). Third, it involves the use of material artifacts created mostly through modern industrial technology, such as cars, mass-produced food, clothing, and so forth.

Values and norms vary enormously across and even within cultures. Some cultures value individualism highly, whereas others place great emphasis on collectivism. A simple example makes this clear. Most pupils in the United States would be outraged to find another student cheating on an examination. In the United States, copying from someone else's paper goes against core values of individual achievement, equality of opportunity, hard work, and respect for the rules. Russian students, however, might be puzzled by this sense of outrage among their American peers. Helping each other pass an examination reflects the value Russians place on equality and on collective problem solving in the face of authority. Think of your own reaction to this example. What does it say about the values of your society?

Within a single society or community, values also may conflict: Some groups or individuals might value traditional religious beliefs, whereas others might favor progress and science. Some people might prefer material comfort and success, whereas others might favor simplicity and a quiet life. In our changing age—filled with the global movement of people, ideas, goods, and information—it is not surprising that we encounter instances of cultural values in conflict. Sociological research suggests that such conflicts foster a sense of frustration and isolation in American society (Bellah et al. 1985).

Norms, like the values they reflect, also change over time. For example, beginning in 1964, with the U.S. surgeon general's report "Smoking and Health," which presented definitive medical evidence linking smoking with a large number of serious health problems, the U.S. government waged a highly effective campaign to discourage people from smoking. A social norm favoring smoking—once associated with independence, sex appeal, and glamour—has given way to an equally strong antismoking social norm that depicts smoking as unhealthful, unattractive, and selfish. Today, the percentage of American adults who smoke is 20 percent, less than half the rate of 1964, when the surgeon general's report was issued (Centers for Disease Control 2007a).

Many of our everyday behaviors and habits are grounded in cultural norms. Movements, gestures, and expressions are strongly influenced by cultural factors. A clear example of this can be seen in the way people smile—particularly in public contexts—across different cultures.

Among the Inuit (Eskimos) of Greenland, for example, one does not find the strong tradition of public smiling that exists in many areas of western Europe and North America. This does not mean that the Inuit are cold or unfriendly; it is simply not their common practice to smile at or exchange pleasantries with strangers. As the service industry has expanded in Greenland in recent years, however, some employers have made efforts to instill smiling as a cultural value in the belief that smiling and expressing "polite" attitudes toward customers are essential to competitive business practices. Clients who are met with smiles and told to "Have a nice day" are more likely to become repeat customers. In many supermarkets in Greenland, shop assistants are now shown training videos on friendly service techniques; the staff at some have even been sent abroad on training courses. Initially these requirements were met with some discomfort by some staff, who found the style insincere and artificial. Over time, however, the idea of public smiling—at least in the workplace—has become more accepted.

CULTURE AND SOCIETY

"Culture" can be distinguished from "society," but these notions are closely connected. A **society** is a system of interrelationships that connects individuals together. No

society • A group of people who live in a particular territory, are subject to a common system of political authority, and are aware of having a distinct identity from other groups. Some societies, like hunting and gathering societies, are small, numbering no more than a few dozen people. Others are large, numbering millions—modern Chinese society, for instance, has a population of more than a billion people.

culture could exist without a society; and, equally, no society could exist without culture. Without culture, we would not be human at all, in the sense in which we usually understand that term. We would have no language in which to express ourselves, no sense of self-consciousness, and our ability to think or reason would be severely limited.

Culture also serves as a society's glue, because culture is an important source of conformity, providing ready-made ways of thinking and acting for its members. For example, when you say that you subscribe to a particular value, such as formal learning, you are probably voicing the beliefs that conform to those of your family members, friends, teachers, or others who are significant in your life.

Cultures differ, however, in how much they value conformity. Research based on surveys of more than 100,000 adults in over sixty countries shows that Japanese culture lies at one extreme in terms of valuing conformity (Hofstede 1997), while at the other extreme lies American culture, one of the least conformist, ranking among the world's highest in cherishing individualism.

American high school and college students often see themselves as especially nonconformist. The body piercers of today, like the hippies of the 1960s and the punks of the 1980s, sport distinctive clothing styles, haircuts, and other forms of bodily adornment. Yet how individualistic are they? Are young people with dyed hair or nose rings or studs in their tongues or tattoos really acting independently? Or are their styles perhaps as much the "uniforms" of their group as are navy blue suits among middle-aged business people? There is an aspect of conformity to their behavior—conformity to their own group.

Since some degree of conformity to norms is necessary for any society to exist, one of the key challenges for all cultures is to instill in people a willingness to conform. This is accomplished in two ways (Parsons 1964). First, individuals learn the norms of their culture. While this occurs throughout one's life, the most crucial learning occurs during childhood, and parents play a key role. When learning is successful, the

Members of a 1960s commune pose together for a group portrait *(left)*. Harajuku girls stroll down a street in Tokyo, Japan *(right)*. Though their distinctive styles set them apart from mainstream society, these people are not as nonconformist as they may think they are. Both subcultures pictured here conform to the norms of their respective social groups.

norms are so thoroughly internalized that they become unquestioned ways of thinking and acting; they come to appear "normal." (Note the similarity between the words *norm* and *normal*.)

When a person fails to learn and adequately conform to a culture's norms, a second way of instilling cultural conformity comes into play: social control. Social control often involves punishing rule breaking. Administration of punishment includes such informal behavior as rebuking friends for minor breaches of etiquette, gossiping behind their backs, or ostracizing them from the group. Official, formal forms of discipline might range from parking tickets to imprisonment (Foucault 1979). Durkheim, one of the founders of sociology (introduced in Chapter 1), argued that punishment serves not only to help guarantee conformity among those who would violate a culture's norms and values but also to vividly remind others what the norms and values are. ✓

CONCEPT CHECKS ✓

1. Describe the main elements of culture.
2. What role does culture play in society?

HOW DOES HUMAN CULTURE DEVELOP?

Human culture and human biology are closely intertwined. Understanding how culture is related to the physical evolution of the human species can help us better understand the central role that culture plays in shaping our lives.

EARLY HUMAN CULTURE: ADAPTATION TO PHYSICAL ENVIRONMENT

Scientists believe that the first humans evolved from apelike creatures on the African continent some four million years ago. Their conclusion is based on archaeological evidence and knowledge of the close similarities in blood chemistry and genetics between chimpanzees and humans. The first evidence of humanlike culture dates back only two million years. In these early cultures, humans fashioned stone tools, derived sustenance by hunting animals and gathering nuts and berries, harnessed the use of fire, and established a highly cooperative way of life. Because early humans planned their hunts, they must also have had some ability for abstract thought.

Culture enabled early humans to compensate for their physical limitations, such as lack of claws, sharp teeth, and running speed, relative to other animals (Deacon 1998). Culture freed humans from dependence on the instinctual and genetically determined set of responses to the environment characteristic of other species. The larger, more complex human brain permitted a greater degree of adaptive learning in dealing with major environmental changes such as the Ice Age. For example, humans figured out how to build fires and sew clothing for warmth. Through greater flexibility, humans were able to survive unpredictable challenges in their surroundings and shape the world with their ideas and their tools.

Yet early humans were closely tied to their physical environment, since they still lacked the technological ability to modify their immediate surroundings significantly (Bennett 1976; Harris 1975, 1978, 1980). Their ability to secure food and make clothing and shelter depended largely on the physical resources that were close at hand. Cultures in different environments varied widely as a result of adaptations by which people fashioned their cultures to be suitable to specific geographic and climatic conditions. For example, the cultures developed by desert dwellers, where water and food were scarce, differed significantly from the cultures that developed in rain forests, where such natural resources abounded. Human inventiveness spawned a rich tapestry of cultures around the world. As you will see at the conclusion of this chapter, however, modern technology and other forces of globalization pose both challenges and opportunities for future global cultural diversity.

NATURE OR NURTURE?

Because humans evolved as a part of the world of nature, it would seem logical to assume that human thinking and behavior are the result of biology and evolution. In fact, one of the oldest and most enduring controversies in the social sciences is the "nature/nurture" debate: Are we shaped by our biology or are we products of learning through life's experiences—that is, of nurture? Biologists and some psychologists emphasize biological factors in explaining human thinking and behavior. Sociologists, not surprisingly, stress the role of learning and culture. They are also likely to argue that because human beings are capable of making conscious choices, neither biology nor culture wholly determines human behavior.

The nature/nurture debate has raged for more than a century. In the 1930s and 1940s, many social scientists focused on biological factors, with some researchers seeking (unsuccessfully), for example, to prove that a person's physique determined his or her personality. In the 1960s and 1970s, scholars in different fields emphasized culture. For example, social psychologists argued that even the most severe forms of mental illness were the result of the labels that society attaches to unusual behavior rather than of biochemical processes (Scheff 1966). Today, partly because of new understandings in genetics and brain neurophysiology, the pendulum is again swinging toward the side of biology.

The resurgence of biological explanations for human behavior began in the 1970s, when the evolutionary biologist Edward O. Wilson published *Sociobiology: The New Synthesis* (1975). The term **sociobiology** refers to the application of biological principles to explain the social activities of animals, including human beings. Using studies of insects and other social creatures, Wilson argued that genes influence not only physical traits but behavior as well. In most species, for example, males are larger and more aggressive than females and tend to dominate the "weaker sex." Some suggest that genetic factors explain why, in all human societies that we know of, men tend to hold positions of greater authority than women.

One way in which sociobiologists have tried to illuminate the relations between the sexes is by means of the idea of "reproductive strategy." A reproductive strategy is a pattern of behavior, arrived at through evolutionary selection, that favors the chances of survival of offspring. The female body has a larger investment in its reproductive cells than the male—a fertilized egg takes nine months to develop. Thus, according to sociobiologists, women will not squander that investment and are not driven to have sexual relations with many partners; their overriding aim is the care and protection of children. Men, on the other hand, tend toward promiscuity. Their wish to have sex with many partners is sound strategy from the point of view of the species; to carry out their mission, which is to maximize the possibility of impregnation, they move from one partner to the next. In this way, it has been suggested, we can explain differences in sexual behavior and attitudes between men and women.

sociobiology • An approach that attempts to explain the behavior of both animals and human beings in terms of biological principles.

Sociobiologists do not argue that our genes determine 100 percent of our behavior. For example, they note that depending on the circumstances, men can choose to act in nonaggressive ways. Yet even though this argument would seem to open up the field of sociobiology to culture as an additional explanatory factor in describing human behavior, social scientists have roundly condemned sociobiology for claiming that a propensity for particular behaviors, such as violence, is somehow "genetically programmed" into our brains ("Seville Statement on Violence" 1990).

HOW NATURE AND NURTURE INTERACT

Most sociologists today would acknowledge a role for nature in determining attitudes and behavior, but with strong qualifications. For example, babies are born with the ability to recognize faces: Babies a few minutes old turn their heads in response to patterns that resemble human faces but not in response to other patterns (Cosmides and Tooby 1997; Johnson and Morton 1991). But it is a large leap to conclude that because babies are born with basic reflexes, the behavior of adults is governed by instincts, inborn, biologically fixed patterns of action found in all cultures.

Sociologists no longer pose the question as one of nature or nurture. Instead they ask how nature and nurture interact to produce human behavior. But their main concern is with how our different ways of thinking and acting are learned in interactions with family, friends, schools, television, and every other facet of the social environment. For example, sociologists argue that it's not an inborn biological disposition that makes American heterosexual males feel romantically attracted to a particular type of woman. Rather, it is the exposure they've had throughout their lives to tens of thousands of magazine ads, TV commercials, and film stars that emphasize specific cultural standards of female beauty.

Early child rearing is especially relevant to this kind of learning. Human babies have a large brain, requiring birth relatively early in their fetal development, before their heads have grown too large to pass through the birth canal. As a result, human babies are totally unequipped for survival on their own, compared with the young of other species, and must spend a number of years in the care of adults. This need, in turn, fosters a lengthy period of learning, during which the child is taught its society's culture.

Because humans think and act in so many different ways, sociologists do not believe that "biology is destiny." If biology were all-important, we would expect all cultures to be highly similar, if not identical. Yet this is hardly the case. For example, pork is forbidden to religious Jews and Muslims, but it is a dietary staple in China. This is not to say that human cultures have nothing in common. Surveys of thousands of different cultures have concluded that all known human cultures have such common characteristics as language, forms of emotional expression, rules that tell adults how to raise children or engage in sexual behavior, and even standards of beauty (Brown 1991). But there is enormous variety in exactly how these common characteristics play themselves out.

All cultures provide for childhood socialization, but what and how children are taught varies greatly from culture to culture. An American child learns the multiplication tables from a classroom teacher, while a child born in the forests of Borneo learns to hunt with older members of the tribe. All cultures have standards of beauty and ornamentation, but what is regarded as beautiful in one culture may be seen as ugly in another (Elias 1987; Elias and Dunning 1987; Foucault 1988).

CULTURAL DIVERSITY

The study of cultural differences highlights the importance of cultural learning as an influence on our behavior. Human behavior and practices—as well as beliefs—also vary widely from culture to culture and often contrast radically with what people from Western societies consider normal. For example, in the modern West, we regard the deliberate killing of infants or young children as one of the worst of all crimes. Yet in traditional Chinese culture, female children were sometimes strangled at birth because a daughter was regarded as a liability rather than an asset to the family. In the West, we eat oysters but we do not eat kittens or puppies, both of which are regarded as delicacies in some parts of the world. Westerners regard kissing as a normal part of sexual behavior, but in other cultures the practice is either unknown or regarded as disgusting. All these different kinds of behavior are aspects of broad cultural differences that distinguish societies from one another.

SUBCULTURES

Small societies tend to be culturally uniform, but industrialized societies are themselves culturally diverse or multicultural, involving numerous different **subcultures**. As you will discover in the discussion of global migration in Chapter 10, practices and social processes such as slavery, colonialism, war, migration, and contemporary globalization have led to populations dispersing across borders and settling in new areas. This, in turn, has led to the emergence of societies that are cultural composites, meaning that the population is made up of a number of groups from diverse cultural and linguistic backgrounds. In modern cities, many subcultural communities live side by side. For example, over ninety different cultural groups can be found in New York City today.

Subculture does not refer only to people from different cultural backgrounds, or who speak different languages, within a larger society. It can also refer to any segment of the population that is distinguishable from the rest of society by its cultural patterns. Examples might include Goths, computer hackers, hippies, Rastafarians, and fans of hip-hop. Some people might identify themselves clearly with a particular subculture, whereas others might move fluidly among a number of different ones.

Culture plays an important role in perpetuating the values and norms of a society, yet it also offers important opportunities for creativity and change. Subcultures and countercultures—groups that largely reject the prevailing values and norms of society—can promote views that represent alternatives to the dominant culture. Social movements or groups of people sharing common lifestyles are powerful forces of change within societies. In this way, subcultures allow freedom for people to express and act on their opinions, hopes, and beliefs.

U.S. schoolchildren are frequently taught that the United States is a vast melting pot, into which various subcultures are assimilated. **Assimilation** is the process by which different cultures are absorbed into a single mainstream culture. Although it is true that virtually all peoples living in the United States take on many common cultural characteristics, many groups strive to retain some subcultural identity. In fact, identification based on race or country of origin in the United States persists today, and is particularly strong among African Americans and immigrants from Asia, Mexico, and Latin America (Totti 1987).

Given the immense cultural diversity and number of subcultures in the United States, a more appropriate metaphor than the assimilationist "melting pot" might be the culturally diverse "salad bowl," in which all the various ingredients, though mixed together, retain some of their original flavor and integrity, contributing to the

subculture • Values and norms distinct from those of the majority, held by a group within a wider society.

assimilation • The acceptance of a minority group by a majority population, in which the new group takes on the values and norms of the dominant culture.

Reggae Music

When those knowledgeable about popular music listen to a song, they can often pick out the stylistic influences that helped shape it. Each musical style, after all, represents a unique way of combining rhythm, melody, harmony, and lyrics. And though it doesn't take a genius to notice the differences between grunge, hard rock, techno, and hip-hop, musicians often combine a number of styles in composing songs. Identifying the components of these combinations can be difficult. But for sociologists of culture, the effort is often rewarding. Different musical styles tend to emerge from different social groups, and studying how styles combine and fuse is a good way to chart the cultural contacts between groups.

Some sociologists of culture have turned their attention to reggae music because it exemplifies the process whereby contacts between social groups result in the creation of new musical forms. Reggae's roots can be traced to West Africa. In the seventeenth century, large numbers of West Africans were enslaved by the British and brought by ship to work in the sugarcane fields of the West Indies. Although the British attempted to prevent slaves from playing traditional African music, for fear it would serve as a rallying cry to revolt, the slaves managed to keep alive the tradition of African drumming, sometimes by integrating it with the European musical styles imposed by the slave owners. In Jamaica, the drumming

of one group of slaves, the Burru, was openly tolerated by slaveholders because it helped meter the pace of work. Slavery was finally abolished in Jamaica in 1834, but the tradition of Burru drumming continued, even as many Burru men migrated from rural areas to the slums of Kingston.

It was in these slums that a new religious cult began to emerge—one that would prove crucial for the development of reggae. In 1930, a man who took the title Haile Selassie (Power of the Trinity) was crowned emperor of the African country of Ethiopia. While opponents of

multiculturalism • The viewpoint according to which ethnic groups can exist separately and share equally in economic and political life.

richness of the salad as a whole. This viewpoint, termed **multiculturalism**, calls for respecting cultural diversity and promoting equality of different cultures. Adherents to multiculturalism acknowledge that certain central cultural values are shared by most people in a society but also that certain important differences deserve to be preserved (Anzaldua 1990).

CULTURAL IDENTITY AND ETHNOCENTRISM

Every culture displays its own unique patterns of behavior, which seem alien to people from other cultural backgrounds. If you have traveled abroad, you are probably familiar with the sensation that can result when you find yourself in a new culture. Aspects of daily life that you take for granted in your own culture may not be part of

European colonialism throughout the world cheered his accession to the throne, a number of people in the West Indies came to believe that Haile Selassie was a god, sent to earth to lead the oppressed of Africa to freedom. Haile Selassie's original name was Ras Tafari Makonnen, and the West Indians who worshiped him called themselves "Rastafarians." The Rastafarian cult soon merged with the Burru, and Rastafarian music came to combine Burru styles of drumming with biblical themes of oppression and liberation. In the 1950s, West Indian musicians began mixing Rastafarian rhythms and lyrics with elements of American jazz and black rhythm and blues. These combinations eventually developed into "ska" music, and then, in the late 1960s, into reggae, with its relatively slow beat, its emphasis on the bass, and its stories of urban deprivation and of the power of collective social consciousness. Many reggae artists, such as Bob Marley, became commercial successes, and by the 1970s, people the world over were listening to reggae music. In the 1980s, reggae was first fused with hip-hop (or rap) to produce new sounds, as can be heard today in the dance hall music of the Jamaican rapper Sean Paul.

The history of reggae is thus the history of contact between different social groups and of the meanings—political, spiritual, and personal—that those groups expressed through their music. Globalization has intensified these contacts. It is now possible for a young musician in Scandinavia, for example, to grow up listening to music produced by men and women in the ghettos of Los Angeles and to be deeply influenced as well by a mariachi performance broadcast live via satellite from Mexico City. If the number of contacts between groups is an important determinant of the pace of musical evolution, we can predict that a veritable profusion of new styles will flourish in the coming years as the process of globalization continues to unfold.

everyday life in other parts of the world. Everyday habits, customs, and behaviors that you take for granted in your own culture may not be part of everyday life in other parts of the world—even in countries that share the same language. The expression "culture shock" is an apt one! Often people feel disoriented when they become immersed in a new culture. This is because they have lost the familiar reference points that help them understand the world around them and have not yet learned how to navigate in the new culture.

A culture must be studied in terms of its own meanings and values—a key presupposition of sociology. Sociologists endeavor as far as possible to avoid **ethnocentrism**, which is judging other cultures in terms of the standards of one's own. Because human cultures vary so widely, it is not surprising that people belonging to one culture frequently find it difficult to understand the ideas or behavior of those from a different

ethnocentrism • The tendency to look at other cultures through the eyes of one's own culture, and thereby misrepresent them.

Papua New Guinean men in traditional clothing and face paint at the Sing-Sing Annual Cultural show. Beginning in 1964, tribes on the island gathered in Mt. Hagen City to compete with each other through singing and dancing. The event provides an important opportunity to celebrate cultural traditions.

cultural relativism • The practice of judging a society by its own standards.

culture. In studying and practicing sociology, we must remove our own cultural blinders in order to see the ways of life of different peoples in an unbiased light. The practice of judging a society by its own standards is called **cultural relativism**.

Applying cultural relativism—that is, suspending your own deeply held cultural beliefs and examining a situation according to the standards of another culture—can be fraught with uncertainty and challenge. Not only can it be hard to see things from a completely different point of view, but cultural relativism sometimes raises troubling issues. Consider, for example, the ritual acts of what opponents have called "genital mutilation" practiced in some societies. Young girls in certain African, Asian, and Middle Eastern cultures may undergo clitoridectomies. This is a painful cultural ritual in which the clitoris and sometimes all or part of the vaginal labia of young girls are removed with a knife or a sharpened stone and the two sides of the vulva are partly sewn together as a means of controlling the young woman's sexual activity and increasing the sexual pleasure of her male partner.

In cultures where clitoridectomies have been practiced for generations, they are regarded as a normal, even expected practice. A study of two thousand men and women in two Nigerian communities found that nine out of ten women interviewed had undergone clitoridectomies in childhood and that the large majority favored the procedure for their own daughters, primarily for cultural reasons; they would be viewed as social outcasts if they did not have the procedure. Yet a significant minority believed that the practice

DO-IT-YOURSELF SOCIOLOGY

D.I.Y.

How many of the following words or phrases can you identify? The United States is a melting pot, where many cultures live side-by-side. Americans often share in the cuisines, music, holiday traditions, and even language of cultures that are very different from their own family heritages. Yet even within a single ethnic or religious subculture, further subcultures exist, such as generational subcultures—where people born in the 1990s experience culture in very different ways than their parents or grandparents. Turn the page (or ask one of your classmates) to find out the answers.

1. bhangra
2. bocce
3. acupuncture
4. futon
5. tah deeg
6. pierogi
7. jumping the broom
8. chuppah
9. ushanka
10. sarape
11. djembe
12. sitar
13. LP
14. kaffeeklatsch
15. getting pinned

Spinach Pierogi

Bocce

TURN PAGE

Answers

1. **bhangra**: A type of music and dance that originated in the Punjab region of India, especially among Sikhs. American music fans may recognize bhangra melodies and rhythms from hip-hop artists including Beyonce and Beenie Man.

2. **bocce**: Bocce is a sport similar to bowling, although it takes place outside—usually on one's lawn or on a court made of stones or shells. The sport originated in Italy, and literally means "bowls."

3. **acupuncture**: A form of Chinese medicine that has grown in popularity in the United States over the past decade. It involves inserting fine needles into specific points on the body to relieve pain.

4. **futon**: A thick mattress with a cloth cover, used for sleeping. Although futons are common in college dorm rooms, they originated as beds in Japan.

5. **tah deeg**: A much-sought-after delicacy in Persian cooking; it is the crispy layer of browned rice at the bottom of a pan of cooked rice.

6. **pierogi**: A boiled dumpling of unleavened dough stuffed with ingredients such as potatos or cheese. Pierogis can be found at American grocery stores, but originally are from eastern European nations such as Poland.

7. **jumping the broom**: A common custom at African American wedding ceremonies. The bride and groom end their ceremony by jumping together or separately over a broom that is lying in front of the altar.

8. **chuppah**: A canopy traditionally used in Jewish weddings. It symbolizes the home the couple will build together.

9. **ushanka**: A fur cap with ear flaps that can be tied under the chin to protect the ears from the cold. The ushanka originates from Russia.

10. **sarape**: A colorful shawl or poncho worn in Mexico.

11. **djembe**: A large drum from West Africa. *Djembe* literally means "everyone gather together." American popular musicians Ben Harper, Paul Simon, and the Grateful Dead have added the djembe to their percussion lines.

12. **sitar**: A long-necked stringed instrument that is plucked. It is used primarily in music from India, Pakistan, and Bangladesh. Sitar music was widely introduced to the Western world when Ravi Shankar performed with the Beatles in the 1960s.

13. **LP**: a long-playing record, also known as a 33 1/3 rpm vinyl record. In the 1960s through the mid 1980s, this is how most people listened to recorded music. The LP has since given way to CDs and downloaded music stored in iPods.

14. **kaffeeklatsch**: An informal gathering of friends to drink coffee and chat, like on the television show *Friends*. This is a German word, although the idea is very familiar to Americans.

15. **getting pinned**. In the 1940s and 1950s, when a dating couple decided they wanted to be "exclusive," the boy would present the girl with a "pin"—typically earned for his athletic or academic achievements.

should be stopped (Ebomoyi 1987). Clitoridectomies are regarded with abhorrence by most people from other cultures and by a growing number of women in the cultures where they are practiced (El Dareer 1982; Johnson-Odim 1991; Lightfoot-Klein 1989).

These differences in views can result in a clash of cultural values, especially when people from cultures where clitoridectomies are common migrate to countries where the practice is actually illegal. France, for example, has a large North African immigrant population, among whom many mothers arrange for traditional clitoridectomies to be performed on their daughters. Some of these women have been tried and convicted under French law for mutilating their daughters. These African mothers have argued that they were only engaging in the same cultural practice that their own mothers had performed on them, that their grandmothers had performed on their mothers, and so on. They complain that the French are ethnocentric, judging traditional African rituals by French customs. Feminists from Africa and the Middle East, while themselves strongly opposed to clitoridectomies, have been critical of Europeans and Americans who sensationalize the practice by calling it backward or primitive, without seeking any understanding of the cultural and economic circumstances that sustain it (Accad 1991; Johnson-Odim 1991; Mohanty 1991). In this instance, globalization has led to a fundamental clash of cultural norms and values that has forced members of both cultures to confront some of their most deeply held beliefs. The role of the sociologist is to avoid knee-jerk responses and to examine complex questions carefully from as many different angles as possible.

CULTURAL UNIVERSALS

Amid the diversity of human behavior, several **cultural universals** prevail. For example, there is no known culture without a grammatically complex **language**. All cultures possess some recognizable form of family system, in which there are values and norms associated with the care of the children. The institution of **marriage** is a cultural universal, as are religious rituals and property rights. All cultures also practice some form of incest prohibition—the banning of sexual relations between close relatives, such as father and daughter, mother and son, and brother and sister. A variety of other cultural universals have been identified by anthropologists, including art, dancing, bodily adornment, games, gift giving, joking, and rules of hygiene.

Yet there are variations within each category. Consider, for example, the prohibition against incest. Incest is typically defined as sexual relations between members of the immediate family; but in some cultures "the family" has been expanded to include cousins, and others bearing the same family name. There have also been societies in which a small proportion of the population have been permitted to engage in incestuous practices. Within the ruling class of ancient Egypt, for instance, brothers and sisters were permitted to have sex with each other.

Among the cultural characteristics shared by all societies, two stand out in particular. All cultures incorporate ways of communicating and expressing meaning. All cultures also depend on material objects in daily life. In all cultures, language is the primary vehicle of meaning and communication. It is not the only such vehicle, however. Material culture itself carries meanings, as we shall show in what follows.

cultural universals • Values or modes of behavior shared by all human cultures.

language • The primary vehicle of meaning and communication in a society, language is a system of symbols that represent objects and abstract thoughts.

marriage • A socially approved sexual relationship between two individuals. Marriage almost always involves two persons of opposite sexes, but in some cultures, types of homosexual marriage are tolerated. Marriage normally forms the basis of a family of procreation—that is, it is expected that the married couple will produce and bring up children. Some societies permit polygamy, in which an individual may have several spouses at the same time.

LANGUAGE

Language is one of the best examples for demonstrating both the unity and the diversity of human culture, because there are no cultures without language, yet there are

Making Sociology Work
HEALTH-CARE PROVIDER

Health-care providers are well trained in anatomy and human physiology. They know how the human body functions and how to detect and treat illnesses. But more than ever, physicians, nurses, and physicians' assistants need a thorough understanding of culture if they hope to effectively treat their patients. That's why Betty Paulanka and Larry Purnell of the University of Delaware College of Health and Nursing Sciences wrote the *Guide to Culturally Competent Health Care* (2005). They believe it's essential reading if doctors and nurses want to address their patients' concerns. For example, the authors believe that practitioners should be trained to assess patients' facial expressions for cues to their pain as well as their receptiveness toward the practitioners' advice. In some cultures, patients will not tell doctors or nurses anything they think might disappoint them. "Many Asian patients don't like to answer, 'No,' so they answer, 'Yes,' to everything. And, in some cultures, people are taught to respect doctors, nurses and people in authority, so they won't complain to them, even if they're in pain," observe the authors. What are other ways that knowledge of cultural diversity may help health-care providers effectively care for their patients?

linguistic relativity hypothesis ● A hypothesis, based on the theories of Edward Sapir and Benjamin Lee Whorf, that perceptions are relative to language.

thousands of different languages spoken in the world. Anyone who has visited a foreign country armed with only a dictionary knows how difficult it is either to understand anything or to be understood. Although languages that have similar origins have words in common with one another—as do, for example, German and English—most of the world's major language groups have no words in common at all.

Language is involved in virtually all of our activities. In the form of ordinary talk or speech, it is the means by which we organize most of what we do. (We discuss the importance of talk and conversation in social life at some length in Chapter 4.) However, language is involved not just in mundane, everyday activities, but also in ceremony, religion, poetry, and many other spheres. One of the most distinctive features of human language is that it allows us to extend vastly the scope of our thought and experience. Using language, we can convey information about events remote in time or space and can discuss things we have never seen. We can develop abstract concepts, tell stories, and make jokes.

In the 1930s, the anthropological linguist Edward Sapir and his student Benjamin Lee Whorf advanced the **linguistic relativity hypothesis**, which argues that the language we use influences our perceptions of the world. That is because we are much more likely to be aware of things in the world if we have words for them (Haugen 1977; Malotki 1983; Witkowski and Brown 1982). Expert skiers or snowboarders, for example, uses terms such as *black ice, corn, powder,* and *packed powder* to describe different snow and ice conditions. Such terms enable them to more readily perceive potentially life-threatening situations that would escape the notice of a novice. In a sense, then, experienced winter athletes have a different perception of the world—or at least, a different perception of the alpine slopes—than do novices.

Language also helps give permanence to a culture and an identity to a people. Language outlives any particular speaker or writer, affording a sense of history and cultural continuity, a feeling of "who we are." In the beginning of this chapter, we argued that the English language is becoming increasingly global in its use, as a primary language of both business and the Internet. One of the central paradoxes of our time is that despite this globalization of the English language, local attachments to language persist, often out of cultural pride. For example, the French-speaking residents of the Canadian province of Quebec are so passionate about their linguistic heritage that they often refuse to speak English, the dominant language of Canada, and periodically seek political independence from the rest of Canada.

Languages—indeed, all symbols—are representations of reality. The symbols we use may signify things we imagine, such as mathematical formulas or fictitious creatures, or they may represent (i.e., "re-present," or make present again in our minds) things initially experienced through our senses. Human behavior is oriented toward the symbols we use to represent reality, rather than to the reality itself—and these symbols are determined within a particular culture. Because symbols are representations, their cultural meanings must be interpreted when they are used. When you see a four-footed furry animal, for example, you must determine which cultural symbol to attach to it. Do you decide to call it a dog, a wolf, or something else? If you determine it is a dog, what cultural meaning does that convey? In American culture, dogs are typically regarded as household pets and lavished with affection. Among the Akha of northern Thailand, dogs are seen as food and treated accordingly. The diversity of cultural meanings attached to the word *dog* thus requires an act of interpretation. In this way, we are freed, in a sense, from being directly tied to the physical world around us.

SPEECH AND WRITING

All societies use speech as a vehicle of language. However, there are other ways of "carrying," or expressing, language—most notably, writing. The invention of writing marked a major transition in human history. Writing first began as the drawing up of lists. Marks would be made on wood, clay, or stone to keep records about significant events, objects, or people. For example, a mark, or sometimes a picture, might be drawn to represent each tract of land possessed by a particular family or set of families (Gelb 1952). Writing began as a means of storing information and as such was closely linked to the administrative needs of early civilizations. A society that possesses writing can locate itself in time and space. Documents can be accumulated that record the past, and information can be gathered about present-day events and activities.

Writing is not just the transfer of speech to paper or some other durable material. It is a phenomenon of interest in its own right. Written documents or texts have qualities in some ways quite distinct from the spoken word. The impact of speech is always by definition limited to the particular contexts in which words are uttered. Ideas and experiences can be passed down through generations in cultures without writing, but only if they are regularly repeated and passed on by word of mouth. Texts, on the other hand, can endure for thousands of years, and through them people from past ages can in a certain sense address us directly. This is, of course, why documentary research is so important to historians. Through interpreting the texts that are left behind by past generations, historians can reconstruct what their lives were like.

SEMIOTICS AND MATERIAL CULTURE

The symbols expressed in speech and writing are the chief ways in which cultural meanings are formed and expressed. But they are not the only ways. Both material objects and aspects of behavior can be used to generate meanings. A **signifier** is any vehicle of meaning—any set of elements used to communicate. The sounds made in speech are signifiers, as are the marks made on paper or other materials in writing. Other signifiers, however, include dress, pictures or visual signs, modes of eating, forms of building or architecture, and many other material features of culture (Hawkes 1977). Styles of dress, for example, normally help signify differences between the sexes. In our culture, at least until relatively recently, women have worn skirts and men pants. In other cultures, this is reversed: women wear pants and men skirts (Leach 1976).

Semiotics—the analysis of verbal and nonverbal cultural meanings—opens up a fascinating field for both sociology and anthropology. Semiotic analysis can be very useful in comparing one culture with another. Semiotics allows us to contrast the ways in which different cultures are structured by looking at the cultural meanings of symbols. For example, the buildings in cities are not simply places in which people live and work. They often have a symbolic character. In traditional cities, the main temple or

signifier • Any vehicle of meaning and communication.

semiotics • The study of the ways in which linguistic and nonlinguistic phenomena can generate meaning.

Cologne Cathedral, built in the Middle Ages, stands at the center of Cologne, Germany, and towers over the city, symbolizing the central role Christianity played in medieval European life.

church was usually placed on high ground in or near the city center. It symbolized the all-powerful influence that religion was supposed to have over the lives of the people. In modern societies, by contrast, the skyscrapers of big business often occupy that symbolic position.

Of course, material culture is not simply symbolic; it is also vital for catering to physical needs—in the tools or technology used to acquire food, make weaponry, construct dwellings, and so forth. We have to study both the practical and the symbolic aspects of material culture in order to understand it completely.

CULTURE AND SOCIAL DEVELOPMENT

Cultural traits are closely related to overall patterns in the development of society. The level of material culture reached in a given society influences, although by no means completely determines, other aspects of cultural development. This is easy to see, for example, in the level of technology. Many aspects of culture characteristic of our lives today—cars, telephones, computers, running water, electric light—depend on technological innovations that have been made only very recently in human history.

The same is true at earlier phases of social development. Before the invention of the smelting of metal, for example, goods had to be made of organic or naturally occurring materials like wood or stone—a basic limitation on the artifacts that could be constructed. Variations in material culture provide the main means of distinguishing different forms of human society, but other factors are also influential. Writing is an example. As has been mentioned, not all human cultures have possessed writing—in fact, for most of human history, writing was unknown. The development of writing altered the scope of human cultural potentialities, making possible different forms of social organization than those that had previously existed.

We now turn to analyzing the main types of society that existed in the past and that are still found in the world. In the present day, we are accustomed to societies that contain millions of people, many of them living crowded together in urban areas. But for most of human history, the earth was much less densely populated than it is now, and it is only over the past hundred years or so that any societies have existed in which the majority of the population were city dwellers. To understand the forms of society that existed before modern industrialism, we have to call on the historical dimension of the sociological imagination. ✓

CONCEPT CHECKS ✓

1. Explain the nature/nurture debate.

2. Why do sociologists disagree with the claim that biology is destiny?

3. Give examples of subcultures that are typical of American society.

4. What is the difference between cultural ethnocentrism and cultural relativism?

5. Why is language considered to be a cultural universal?

6. What is the linguistic relativity hypothesis?

WHAT HAPPENED TO PREMODERN SOCIETIES?

Premodern societies can actually be grouped into three main categories: hunters and gatherers; larger agrarian or pastoral societies (involving agriculture or the tending of domesticated animals); and nonindustrial civilizations or traditional states. We shall look at the main characteristics of these societies in turn.

THE EARLIEST SOCIETIES: HUNTERS AND GATHERERS

For all but a tiny part of our existence on this planet, human beings have lived in hunting and gathering societies, small groups or tribes often numbering no more than thirty or forty people. Hunters and gatherers gain their livelihood from hunting, fishing, and gathering edible plants growing in the wild. Hunting and gathering cultures continue to exist in some parts of the world, such as in a few arid parts of Africa and the jungles of Brazil and New Guinea. Most such cultures, however, have been destroyed or absorbed by the spread of Western culture, and those that remain are unlikely to stay intact for much longer. Currently, less than a quarter of a million people in the world support themselves through hunting and gathering—only 0.004 percent of the world's population.

Compared with larger societies—particularly modern societies, such as the United States—most hunting and gathering groups were egalitarian. Thus there was little difference among members of the society in the number or kinds of material possessions—there were no divisions of rich and poor. The material goods they needed were limited to weapons for hunting, tools for digging and building, traps, and cooking utensils. Differences of position or rank tended to be limited to age and gender; men were almost always the hunters, while women gathered wild crops, cooked, and brought up the children.

The elders—the oldest and most experienced men in the community—usually had an important say in major decisions affecting the group. But just as there was little variation in wealth among members, differences of power were much less than in larger types of society. Hunting and gathering societies were usually participatory rather than competitive: All adult male members tended to assemble together when important decisions were to be made or crises were faced.

Hunters and gatherers moved about a good deal, but not in a completely erratic way. They had fixed territories, around which they migrated regularly from year to year. Because they were without animal or mechanical means of transport, they could take few goods or possessions with them. Many hunting and gathering communities did not have a stable membership; people often moved among different camps, or groups split up and joined others within the same overall territory.

Hunters and gatherers had little interest in developing material wealth beyond what was needed for their basic wants. Their main concerns were with religious values and ritual activities. Members participated regularly in elaborate ceremonials and often spent a great deal of time preparing the dress, masks, paintings, or other sacred objects used in such rituals.

Hunters and gatherers are not merely primitive peoples whose ways of life no longer hold any interest for us. Studying their cultures allows us to see more clearly that some of our institutions are far from being natural features of human life. We shouldn't idealize the circumstances in which hunters and gatherers lived, but the lack of major inequalities of wealth and power and the emphasis on cooperation rather than competition are instructive reminders that the world created by modern industrial civilization is not necessarily to be equated with progress.

PASTORAL AND AGRARIAN SOCIETIES

pastoral societies • Societies whose subsistence derives from the rearing of domesticated animals.

agrarian societies • Societies whose means of subsistence are based on agricultural production (crop growing).

About fifteen thousand years ago, some hunting and gathering groups turned to the raising of domesticated animals and the cultivation of fixed plots of land as their means of livelihood. **Pastoral societies** relied mainly on domesticated livestock, while **agrarian societies** grew crops (practiced agriculture). Some societies had mixed pastoral and agrarian economies.

Depending on the environment in which they lived, pastoralists reared animals such as cattle, sheep, goats, camels, or horses. Some pastoral societies still exist in the modern world, concentrated especially in areas of Africa, the Middle East, and Central Asia. They are usually found in regions of dense grasslands or in deserts or mountains, which are poor land for agriculture to be profitable.

At some point, hunting and gathering groups began to sow their own crops rather than simply collect those growing in the wild. This practice first developed as what is usually called *horticulture*, in which small gardens were cultivated by the use of simple hoes or digging instruments. Like pastoralism, horticulture provided for a more reliable supply of food than was possible from hunting and gathering and therefore could support larger communities. Because they were not on the move, people whose livelihood was horticulture could develop larger stocks of material possessions than people in either hunting and gathering or pastoral communities. Some peoples in the world still rely primarily on horticulture for their livelihood.

TRADITIONAL SOCIETIES OR CIVILIZATIONS

From about 6000 B.C.E. onward, we find evidence of societies larger than any that existed before and that contrast in distinct ways with earlier types. These societies were based on the development of cities, led to pronounced inequalities of wealth and power, and were ruled by kings or emperors. Because writing was used and science and art flourished, they are often called "civilizations."

The earliest civilizations developed in the Middle East, usually in fertile river areas. The Chinese Empire originated in about 1800 B.C.E., at which time powerful states were also in existence in what are now India and Pakistan.

Most traditional (premodern) civilizations were also empires: They achieved their size through the conquest and incorporation of other peoples (Kautsky 1982). This was true, for instance, of traditional Rome and China. At its height, in the first century C.E., the Roman Empire stretched from Britain in northwest Europe to beyond the Middle East. The Chinese Empire, which lasted for more than two thousand years, up to the threshold of the twentieth century, covered most of the massive region of eastern Asia now occupied by modern China. ✓

CONCEPT CHECKS ✓

1. Compare the two main types of premodern societies.

HOW HAS INDUSTRIALIZATION SHAPED MODERN SOCIETY?

What happened to destroy the forms of society that dominated the whole of history up to two centuries ago? The answer, in a word, is **industrialization**—the emergence of machine production, based on the use of inanimate power resources (such as steam or electricity). The industrialized, or modern, societies differ in several key respects from any previous type of social order, and their development has had consequences stretching far beyond their European origins.

industrialization • The emergence of machine production, based on the use of inanimate power resources (such as steam or electricity).

THE INDUSTRIALIZED SOCIETIES

Industrialization originated in eighteenth-century Britain as a result of the Industrial Revolution, a complex set of technological changes that affected the means by which people gained their livelihood. These changes included the invention of new machines (such as the spinning jenny for weaving yarn), the harnessing of power resources (especially water and steam) for production, and the use of science to improve production methods. Because discoveries and inventions in one field lead to more in others, the pace of technological innovation in **industrialized societies** is extremely rapid compared with that of traditional social systems.

In even the most advanced of traditional civilizations, most people were engaged in working on the land. The relatively low level of technological development did not permit more than a small minority to be freed from the chores of agricultural production. By contrast, a prime feature of industrialized societies today is that the large majority of the employed population work in factories, offices, or shops rather than in agriculture. And over 90 percent of people live in towns and cities, where most jobs are to be found and new job opportunities created. The largest cities are vastly greater in size than the urban settlements found in traditional civilizations. In the cities, social life becomes more impersonal and anonymous than before, and many of

industrialized societies • Highly developed nation-states in which the majority of the population work in factories or offices rather than in agriculture, and most people live in urban areas.

Over 90 percent of the people who live in industrial societies live in cities or towns. Life in these cities can be anonymous and dominated by day-to-day encounters with strangers.

our day-to-day encounters are with strangers rather than with individuals known to us. Large-scale organizations, such as business corporations or government agencies, come to influence the lives of virtually everyone.

A further feature of modern societies concerns their political systems, which are more developed and intensive than forms of government in traditional states. In traditional civilizations, the political authorities (monarchs and emperors) had little direct influence on the customs and habits of most of their subjects, who lived in fairly self-contained local villages. With industrialization, transportation and communications became much more rapid, making for a more integrated "national" community.

The industrialized societies were the first nation-states to come into existence. **Nation-states** are political communities with clearly delimited borders dividing them from each other, rather than the vague frontier areas that used to separate traditional states. Nation-state governments have extensive powers over many aspects of citizens' lives, framing laws that apply to all those living within their borders. The United States is a nation-state, as are virtually all other societies in the world today.

The application of industrial technology has been by no means limited to peaceful processes of economic development. From the earliest phases of industrialization, modern production processes have been put to military use, and this has radically altered ways of waging war, creating weaponry and modes of military organization much more advanced than those of nonindustrial cultures. Together, superior economic strength, political cohesion, and military superiority account for the seemingly irresistible spread of Western ways of life across the world over the past two centuries.

nation-state • A particular type of state, characteristic of the modern world, in which a government has sovereign power within a defined territorial area, and the population are citizens who know themselves to be part of a single nation. Nation-states are closely associated with the rise of nationalism, although nationalist loyalties do not always conform to the boundaries of specific states. Nation-states developed as part of an emerging nation-state system, originating in Europe; in current times, they span the whole globe.

GLOBAL DEVELOPMENT

From the seventeenth to the early twentieth centuries, the Western countries established colonies in numerous areas previously occupied by traditional societies, using their superior military strength where necessary. Although virtually all these colonies have now attained their independence, **colonialism** was central to shaping the social map of the globe as we know it today. In some regions, such as North America, Australia, and New Zealand, which were only thinly populated by hunting and gathering or pastoral communities, Europeans became the majority population. In other areas, including much of Asia, Africa, and South America, the local populations remained in the majority.

Societies of the first of these two types, including the United States, have become industrialized. Those in the second category are mostly at a much lower level of industrial development and are often referred to as less developed societies, or the **developing world**. Such societies include China, India, most of the African countries (such as Nigeria, Ghana, and Algeria), and those in South America (e.g., Brazil, Peru, and Venezuela). Because many of these societies are situated south of the United States and Europe, they are sometimes referred to collectively as the South, and contrasted to the wealthier, industrialized North.

colonialism • The process whereby Western nations established their rule in parts of the world away from their home territories.

developing world • The less-developed societies, in which industrial production is either virtually nonexistent or only developed to a limited degree. The majority of the world's population live in less-developed countries.

THE DEVELOPING WORLD

The large majority of less developed societies are in areas that underwent colonial rule in Asia, Africa, and South America. A few colonized areas gained independence early, such as Haiti, which became the first autonomous black republic in January 1804.

The Spanish colonies in South America acquired their freedom in 1810, while Brazil broke away from Portuguese rule in 1822.

Some countries that were never ruled from Europe were nonetheless strongly influenced by colonial relationships, the most notable example being China. By force of arms, China was compelled from the seventeenth century on to enter into trading agreements with European powers, by which the Europeans were allocated the government of certain areas, including major seaports. Hong Kong was the last of these. Most nations in the developing world have become independent states only since World War II—often following bloody anticolonial struggles. Examples include India, which shortly after achieving self-rule split into India and Pakistan, a range of other Asian countries (like Myanmar, Malaysia, and Singapore), and countries in Africa (including Kenya, Nigeria, the Democratic Republic of Congo, Tanzania, and Algeria).

Women waiting in line for food in Calcutta, India. Why does poverty disproportionately affect women around the world?

Although they may include peoples living in traditional fashion, developing countries are very different from earlier forms of traditional society. Their political systems are modeled on systems first established in the societies of the West—that is to say, they are nation-states. Most of the population still live in rural areas, but many of these societies are experiencing a rapid process of city development. Although agriculture remains the main economic activity, crops are now often produced for sale in world markets rather than for local consumption. Developing countries are not merely societies that have "lagged behind" the more industrialized areas. They have in large part been created by contact with Western industrialism, which has undermined the earlier, more traditional systems that were in place.

Conditions in the more impoverished of these societies have deteriorated rather than improved over the past few years. There are nearly 1.4 billion people living on less than $1.25 per day, and an additional 1.2 billion people live on less than $2 per day (World Bank 2008c). Together, nearly 40 percent of the world's population faces the reality of extreme poverty on a daily basis. About a fourth of the world's poor live in South Asia, in countries such as India, Myanmar, and Cambodia. China, on the other hand has made great strides, reducing by three-fourths the number of people living in poverty since 1981 (World Bank 2008a). About half of the population in sub-Saharan Africa lives on less than $1.25 a day, and the impoverished population has doubled since 1981 (World Bank 2008a). A substantial proportion of those in extreme poverty, however, live on the doorstep of the United States—in Central and South America.

Once more, the existence of global poverty shouldn't be seen as remote from the concerns of Americans. Whereas in previous generations the majority of immigrants into the United States came from the European countries, most now come from poor, developing societies. Recent years have seen waves of Hispanic immigrants, nearly all from Latin America. Some U.S. cities near the entry points of much of this immigration, such as Los Angeles and Miami, are bursting with new immigrants and also maintain trading connections with developing countries.

In most developing societies, poverty tends to be at its worst in rural areas. Malnutrition, lack of education, low life expectancy, and substandard housing are generally most severe in the countryside. Many of the poor are to be found in areas where arable land is scarce, agricultural productivity low, and drought or floods common. Women are usually more disadvantaged than men. They encounter cultural, social, and economic problems that even the most underprivileged men do not. For instance, they often work longer hours and, when they are paid at all, earn lower wages. (See Chapter 9 for a lengthier discussion of gender inequality.)

The poor in developing countries live in conditions almost unimaginable to Americans. Many have no permanent dwellings apart from shelters made of cartons or loose pieces of wood. Most have no running water, sewer systems, or electricity. Nonetheless, millions of poor people also live in the United States, and there are connections between poverty in America and global poverty. Almost half of the people living in poverty in the United States immigrated from the global South. This is true of the descendants of the black slaves brought over by force centuries ago; and it is true of more recent, and willing, immigrants who have arrived from Latin America, Asia, and elsewhere.

THE NEWLY INDUSTRIALIZING ECONOMIES

newly industrializing economies (NIEs) • Developing countries that over the past two or three decades have begun to develop a strong industrial base, such as Singapore and Hong Kong.

Although the majority of developing countries lag well behind societies of the West, some have now successfully embarked on a process of industrialization. These are sometimes referred to as **newly industrializing economies (NIEs)**, and they include Brazil, Mexico, Hong Kong, South Korea, Singapore, and Taiwan. The rates of economic growth of the most successful NIEs, such as those in East Asia, are several times those of the Western industrial economies. No developing country figured among the top thirty exporters in the world in 1968, but twenty-five years later South Korea was in the top fifteen.

The East Asian NIEs have shown the most sustained levels of economic prosperity. They are investing abroad as well as promoting growth at home. South Korea's production of steel has doubled in the last decade, and its shipbuilding and electronics industries are among the world's leaders. Singapore is becoming the major financial and commercial center of Southeast Asia. Taiwan is an important player in the manufacturing and electronics industries. All these changes in the NIEs have directly affected the United States, whose share of global steel production, for example, has dropped significantly since the 1970s. ✓

CONCEPT CHECKS ✓

1. What does the concept of industrialization mean?

2. How has industrialization hurt traditional social systems?

3. Why are many African and South American societies classified as part of the developing world?

HOW DOES GLOBALIZATION AFFECT CONTEMPORARY CULTURE?

In Chapter 1 we noted that the chief focus of sociology historically has been the study of the industrialized societies. As sociologists, can we thus safely ignore the developing world, leaving this as the domain of anthropology? We certainly cannot. The industrialized and the developing societies have developed in interconnection with one another and are today more closely related than ever before. Those of us living in the industrialized societies depend on many raw materials and manufactured products coming from developing countries to sustain our lives. Conversely, the economies of most developing states depend on trading networks that bind them to the industrialized countries. We can fully understand the industrialized order only against the backdrop of societies in the developing world—in which, in fact, by far the greater proportion of the world's population lives.

As the world rapidly moves toward a single, unified economy, businesses and people move about the globe in increasing numbers in search of new markets and economic opportunities. As a result, the cultural map of the world changes: Networks of peoples span national borders and even continents, providing cultural connections between their birthplaces and their adoptive countries (Appadurai 1986). A handful of languages come to dominate, and in some cases replace, the thousands of different languages that were once spoken on the planet.

It is increasingly impossible for cultures to exist as islands. There are few, if any, places on earth so remote as to escape radio, television, air travel—and the throngs of tourists this technology brings—or the computer. A generation ago, there were still tribes whose way of life was completely untouched by the rest of the world. Today, these peoples use machetes and other tools made in the United States or Japan, wear T-shirts and shorts manufactured in garment factories in the Dominican Republic or Guatemala, and take medicine manufactured in Germany or Switzerland to combat diseases contracted through contact with outsiders. These people also have their stories broadcast to people around the world through satellite television and the Internet. Within a generation or two at the most, all the world's once-isolated cultures will be touched and transformed by global culture, despite their persistent efforts to preserve their age-old ways of life.

The forces that produce a global culture are discussed throughout this book. These include

- Television, which brings U.S. culture (through networks such as MTV and shows such as *The Simpsons*) into homes throughout the world daily, while also adapting a Swedish cultural product (*Expedition: Robinson*) for a U.S. audience in the form of *Big Brother* and *Survivor*
- The emergence of a unified global economy, with business whose factories, management structures, and markets often span continents and countries
- "Global citizens," such as managers of large corporations, who may spend as much time crisscrossing the globe as they do at home, identifying with a global, cosmopolitan culture rather than with their own nation's
- A host of international organizations, including United Nations agencies, regional trade and mutual defense associations, multinational banks and other global financial institutions, international labor and health organizations, and global tariff and trade agreements, that are creating a global political, legal, and military framework
- Electronic communications (telephone, fax, e-mail, and the Internet), which make instantaneous communication with almost any part of the planet an integral part of daily life in the business world

DOES THE INTERNET PROMOTE A GLOBAL CULTURE?

Many believe that the rapid growth of the Internet around the world will hasten the spread of a global culture—one resembling the cultures of Europe and North America, currently home to nearly three-quarters of all Internet users (Global Map 2.1). Belief in such values as equality between men and women, the right to speak freely, democratic participation in government, and the pursuit of pleasure through consumption are readily diffused throughout the world over the Internet. Moreover, Internet technology itself would seem to foster such values: Global communication, seemingly unlimited (and uncensored) information, and instant gratification are all characteristics of the new technology.

Yet it may be premature to conclude that the Internet will sweep aside traditional cultures, replacing them with radically new cultural values. As the Internet spreads around the world, evidence shows that it is in many ways compatible with traditional cultural values as well, perhaps even a means of strengthening them.

Consider, for example, the Middle Eastern country of Kuwait, a traditional Islamic culture that has recently experienced strong American and European influences. Kuwait, an oil-rich country on the Persian Gulf, has one of the highest average per-person incomes in the world. The government provides free public education through the university level, resulting in high rates of literacy and education for both men and women. Kuwaiti television frequently carries NFL football and other U.S.

Global Map 2.1 | The Exploding Internet, 2008

Internet traffic is growing by about 50 percent annually, with video and music streaming rising fastest. At the same time, the web is becoming divided along language lines. By 2012, Asian web surfers, including about 490 million Chinese, will outnumber North Americans by 3 to 1, and Indians will become the third-largest group online. Tomorrow's web will probably be dominated by a mixture of the English, Mandarin, Hindi, Portuguese, and Russian languages.

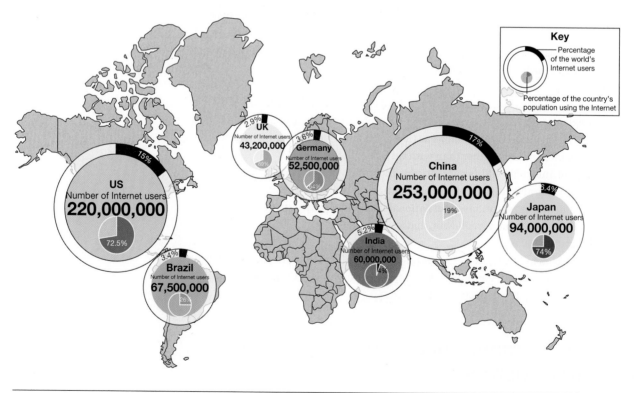

Source: Barras 2009.

Using the Internet to connect with the world around them is common among young people across cultures. Above, an Iranian woman films a protest with her mobile phone to upload online.

programming, although broadcasts are regularly interrupted for the traditional Muslim calls to prayer. Half of Kuwait's approximately two million people are under twenty-five years old, and like their youthful counterparts in Europe and North America, many surf the Internet for new ideas, information, and consumer products.

Although Kuwait is in many respects a modern country, Kuwaiti law treats men and women differently. Legally, women have equal access to education and employment, yet they are barred from voting or running for political office. Cultural norms treating men and women differently have just as powerful an influence on daily life as formal laws. Women are generally expected to wear traditional clothing that leaves only the face and hands visible, and are forbidden to leave home at night or to be seen in public at any time with a man who is not a spouse or relative.

Deborah Wheeler (1998) spent a year studying the effect of the Internet on Kuwaiti culture. The Internet is increasingly popular in Kuwait; half of all Internet users in Middle Eastern Arab countries live in this tiny country. The new communications technologies are clearly enabling men and women to talk with each other in a society where such communications outside of marriage are extremely limited. Wheeler also notes that ironically men and women are segregated in the Internet cafés. Furthermore, she finds that Kuwaitis are extremely reluctant to voice strong opinions or political views online. With the exception of discussing conservative Islamic religious beliefs, which are freely disseminated over the Internet, Kuwaitis are remarkably inhibited online.

Wheeler concludes that Kuwaiti culture, which is hundreds of years old, is not likely to be easily transformed by simple exposure to different beliefs and values on the Internet. The fact that a few young people are participating in global chat rooms does not mean that Kuwaiti culture is adopting the sexual attitudes of the United States or even the form of everyday relations found between men and women in the West. The culture that eventually emerges as a result of the new technologies will not be the same as American culture; it will be uniquely Kuwaiti.

GLOBALIZATION AND LOCAL CULTURES

The world has become a single *social system* as a result of the growing interdependence, both social and economic, that now affects virtually everyone. But it would be a mistake to think of this increasing interdependence, or globalization, of the world's societies simply as the growth of world unity. The globalizing of social relations should be understood primarily as the reordering of time and distance in social life. Our lives, in other words, are increasingly and quickly influenced by events happening far away from our everyday activities.

Globalizing processes have brought many benefits to Americans: A much greater variety of goods and foodstuffs is available than ever before. At the same time, the fact that we are all now caught up in a much wider world has helped create some of the most serious problems American society faces, such as the threat of terrorism.

The influence of a growing global culture has provoked numerous reactions at the local level. Many local cultures remain strong or are experiencing a rejuvenation, partly as a response to the diffusion of global culture. Such a response grows out of the concern that a global culture, dominated by North American and European cultural values, will corrupt the local culture. For example, the Taliban, an Islamic movement that controls most of Afghanistan, historically has sought to impose traditional, tribal values throughout the country. Through its governmental "Ministry for Ordering What Is Right and Forbidding What Is Wrong," the Taliban banned music, closed movie theaters, abolished the use of alcohol, and required men to grow full beards. Women were ordered to cover their entire bodies with burkas, tentlike garments with a woven screen over the eyes, out of which to see; they were forbidden to work outside their homes, or even to be seen in public with men who were not their spouses or relations. Violations of these rules were severely punished, sometimes by death. The rise of the Taliban can be understood at least partly as a rejection of the spread of Western culture.

nationalism • A set of beliefs and symbols expressing identification with a national community.

The resurgence of local cultures is sometimes seen throughout the world in the rise of **nationalism**, a sense of identification with one's people that is expressed through a common set of strongly held beliefs. Sometimes these include the belief that the people of a particular nation have historical or God-given rights that supersede those of other people. Nationalism can be strongly political, involving attempts to assert the power of a nation based on a shared ethnic or racial identity over people of a different ethnicity or race. The world of the twenty-first century may well witness responses to globalization that celebrate ethnocentric nationalist beliefs, promoting intolerance and hatred rather than a celebration of diversity.

HOW GLOBALIZATION AND CULTURE AFFECT YOU

New nationalisms, cultural identities, and religious practices are constantly being forged throughout the world. When you socialize with students from the same cultural background or celebrate traditional holidays with your friends and family, you are sustaining your culture. The very technology that helps foster globalization also supports local cultures: The Internet enables you to communicate with others who share your cultural identity, even when they are dispersed around the world. Those who share a passion for a particular type of music can stay up all night in Internet chat rooms with like-minded people; if you are studying abroad you can stay connected with communities back home by logging on to the Web site of your hometown newspaper (Wallraff 2000). A casual search of the Web reveals thousands of pages devoted to different cultures and subcultures.

Although sociologists do not yet fully understand these processes, they often conclude that despite the powerful forces of globalization operating in the world today, local cultures remain strong and indeed flourish. But it is still too soon to tell whether and how globalization will transform our world, whether it will result in the homogenization of the world's diverse cultures, the flourishing of many individual cultures, or both. ✓

CONCEPT CHECKS ✓

1. How does global culture influence local cultures?

NEED HELP STUDYING?

 wwnorton.com/studyspace

Visit StudySpace to access free review materials such as:

- Vocabulary Flashcards
- Diagnostic Review Quizzes
- Study Outlines

REVIEW QUESTIONS

1. What are the main elements of a culture? Give an example of each element from your own cultural group.
2. How does culture instill a willingness to conform among its members?
3. How do sociologists address the nature/nurture debate?
4. Compare and contrast assimilationist and multicultural models of cultural integration.
5. Compare and contrast ethnocentrism and cultural relativism. Which stance do sociologists strive to adopt and what are the difficulties associated with that position?
6. What are the three main categories of premodern societies? List some of the characteristics of each.
7. Describe some of the changes brought about by industrialization.
8. What forces produce global culture?
9. What challenges and opportunities does globalization pose for cultural diversity?

THINKING SOCIOLOGICALLY EXERCISES

1. Mention at least two cultural traits that you would claim are universals; mention two others you would claim are culturally specific traits. Locate and use case study materials from different societies you are familiar with to show the differences between universal and specific cultural traits. Are the cultural universals you have discussed derivatives of human instincts? Explain your answer fully.
2. What does it mean to be ethnocentric? How is ethnocentrism dangerous in conducting social research? How is ethnocentrism problematic among nonresearchers in their everyday lives?

3

Socialization, the Life Course, and Aging

THE BIG QUESTIONS

HOW ARE CHILDREN SOCIALIZED?
Learn about socialization (including gender socialization), and know the most important agents of socialization.

WHAT ARE THE FIVE MAJOR STAGES OF THE LIFE COURSE?
Learn the various stages of the life course, and see the similarities and differences among different cultures.

HOW DO PEOPLE AGE?
Understand that aging is a combination of biological, psychological, and social processes. Consider the various theories of aging, particularly those that focus on how society shapes the social roles of older people and that emphasize aspects of age stratification.

WHAT ARE THE CHALLENGES OF AGING IN THE UNITED STATES?
Evaluate the experience of growing old in the United States. Identify the physical, emotional, and financial challenges faced by older adults.

At the start of J. K. Rowling's first Harry Potter adventure, *Harry Potter and the Sorcerer's Stone*, the shrewd wizard Albus Dumbledore leaves Harry, a newly orphaned infant, at the doorstep of Harry's nonmagician (or "muggle") uncle and aunt's house. Harry has already shown himself to have unique powers, but Dumbledore is concerned that if left in the wizarding world, Harry won't mature healthily. "It would be enough to turn any boy's head," he says. "Famous before he can walk and talk! Famous for something he won't even remember! Can't you see how much better off he'll be, growing up away from all that until he's ready to take it?" (Rowling 1998).

The Harry Potter novels, each of which follows Harry through a single year of his life, are based on the premise that there is no adventure greater than that of growing up. Although Harry attends the Hogwarts School of Witchcraft and Wizardry, it's still a school, because everyone, even a young wizard with limitless power, needs help developing a set of values. We all pass through important life stages: the passage from childhood to adolescence, and then to adulthood. So, for example, like many children, Harry plays sports and develops a crush on a pretty classmate. Rowling loves to use the paranormal to help us see the enchanting complexities behind the fundamentals of everyday life. In her universe, owls unerringly deliver letters; is this really any stranger than the postal system or e-mail? The function of children's stories is to make the process of growing up more understandable, whether they're set in a fairy-tale universe, our own world, or—as with the innovation of the Harry Potter series—both.

Socialization is the process whereby an innocent child becomes a self-aware, knowledgeable person, skilled in the ways of the culture into which he or she was born. Socialization among the young allows for the more general phenomenon of **social reproduction**—the process whereby societies have structural continuity over time. During the course of socialization, especially in the early years of life, children learn the ways of their elders, thereby carrying on their values, norms, and social practices. All societies have characteristics that endure over long stretches of time, even though their members change as individuals are born and die. American society, for example, has many distinctive social and cultural characteristics that have persisted for generations—such as the fact that English is the main language spoken.

Socialization connects the different generations to one another (Turnbull 1983). The birth of a child alters the lives of those who are responsible for its upbringing—who themselves therefore undergo new learning experiences. Parenting usually ties the activities of adults to children for the remainder of their lives. Older people still remain parents when they become grandparents, thus forging another set of relationships that bond the generations. Although the process of cultural learning is much more intense in infancy and early childhood than later, learning and adjustment go on through the whole life course.

In the sections to follow, we continue the theme of "nature interacting with nurture," introduced in the previous chapter. We first describe the process of human development from infancy to early childhood. We compare different theoretical interpretations of how and why children develop as they do, and how gender identities develop. We move on to discuss the main groups and social contexts that influence socialization throughout the life course. Finally, we focus on one distinctive stage of the life course: old age. We discuss the special problems and resources of older adults, who now make up the most rapidly growing age group in the United States and the developed world.

HOW ARE CHILDREN SOCIALIZED?

THEORIES OF CHILD DEVELOPMENT

One of the most distinctive features of human beings, compared with other animals, is self-awareness—the awareness that one has an identity distinct and separate from others. During the first months of life, the infant possesses little or no understanding of differences between human beings and material objects in the environment, and has no awareness of self. Children begin to use concepts such as "I," "me," and "you" around age two or after. They gradually come to understand that others have distinct identities, consciousness, and needs separate from their own.

The problem of the emergence of self is much debated, in part, because the most prominent theories about child development emphasize different aspects of socialization. The American philosopher and sociologist George Herbert Mead gives attention

socialization • The social processes through which we develop an awareness of social norms and values and achieve a distinct sense of self. Although socialization processes are particularly significant in infancy and childhood, they continue to some degree throughout life. None of us are immune from the reactions of others around us, which influence and modify our behavior at all phases of our life course.

social reproduction • The process whereby societies have structural continuity over time. Social reproduction is an important pathway through which parents transmit or produce values, norms, and social practices among their children.

mainly to how children learn to use the concepts of "I" and "me." Jean Piaget, the Swiss student of child behavior, focused on **cognition**—the ways in which children learn to think about themselves and their environment.

G. H. MEAD AND THE DEVELOPMENT OF SELF

Because Mead's ideas form the main basis of a general tradition of theoretical thinking, *symbolic interactionism*, they have had a very broad impact in sociology. Symbolic interactionism emphasizes that interaction between human beings takes place through symbols and the interpretation of meanings (see Chapter 1). Mead's work also provides an account of the main phases of child development, giving particular attention to the emergence of a sense of self.

According to Mead, infants and young children develop as social beings by imitating the actions of those around them. Play is one way in which this takes place; small children often imitate what adults do. A small child will make mud pies, having seen an adult cooking, or dig with a spoon, having observed someone gardening. Children's play evolves from simple imitation to more complicated games in which a child of four or five years old will act out an adult role. Mead called this "taking the role of the other"—learning what it is like to be in the shoes of another person. At this stage, children acquire a developed sense of self; that is, they develop an understanding of themselves as separate agents—as a "me"—by seeing themselves through the eyes of others.

We achieve self-awareness, according to Mead, when we learn to distinguish the "me" from the "I." The "I" is the unsocialized infant, a bundle of spontaneous wants and desires. The "me," as Mead used the term, is the **social self**. Individuals develop **self-consciousness**, Mead argued, by coming to see themselves as others see them. A further stage of child development, according to Mead, occurs when the child is about eight or nine years old. This is the age at which children tend to take part in organized games, rather than unsystematic play. It is at this period that children begin to understand the overall values and morality according to which social life is conducted. To learn organized games, children must understand the rules of play and notions of fairness and equal participation. Children at this stage learn to grasp what Mead termed the **generalized other**—the general values and moral rules of the culture in which they are developing.

JEAN PIAGET AND THE STAGES OF COGNITIVE DEVELOPMENT

Piaget emphasized the child's active capability to make sense of the world. Children do not passively soak up information, but instead select and interpret what they see, hear, and feel in the world around them. Piaget described several distinct stages of cognitive development during which children learn to think about themselves and their environment. Each stage involves the acquisition of new skills and depends on the successful completion of the preceding one.

Piaget called the first stage, which lasts from birth up to about age two, the **sensorimotor stage**, because infants learn mainly by touching objects, manipulating them, and physically exploring their environment. Until about age four months or so, infants cannot differentiate themselves from their environment. Objects are not differentiated from persons, and the infant is unaware that anything exists outside her range of vision. Infants gradually learn to distinguish people from objects, coming to see that both have an existence independent of their immediate perceptions. The main

Using their toy wheelbarrows to help their father with the gardening, these boys are, according to Mead, "taking on the role of the other" and achieving an understanding of themselves as separate social agents.

cognition • Human thought processes involving perception, reasoning, and remembering.

social self • The basis of self-consciousness in human individuals, according to the theory of G. H. Mead. The social self is the identity conferred upon an individual by the reactions of others. A person achieves self-consciousness by becoming aware of this social identity.

self-consciousness • Awareness of one's distinct social identity as a person separate from others. Human beings are not born with self-consciousness but acquire an awareness of self as a result of early socialization. The learning of language is of vital importance to the processes by which the child learns to become a self-conscious being.

generalized other • A concept in the theory of George Herbert Mead, according to which the individual takes over the general values of a given group or society during the socialization process.

sensorimotor stage • According to Jean Piaget, a stage of human cognitive development in which the child's awareness of its environment is dominated by perception and touch.

preoperational stage • According to Jean Piaget, a stage of human cognitive development, in which the child has advanced sufficiently to master basic modes of logical thought.

egocentric • According to Jean Piaget, the characteristic quality of a child during the early years of her life. Egocentric thinking involves understanding objects and events in the environment solely in terms of the child's own position.

concrete operational stage • A stage of human cognitive development, as formulated by Jean Piaget, in which the child's thinking is based primarily on physical perception of the world. In this phase, the child is not yet capable of dealing with abstract concepts or hypothetical situations.

formal operational stage • According to Jean Piaget, a stage of human cognitive development at which the growing child becomes capable of handling abstract concepts and hypothetical situations.

agents of socialization • Groups or social contexts within which processes of socialization take place.

accomplishment of this stage is that by its close children understand their environment to have distinct and stable properties.

The next phase, called the **preoperational stage**, is the one to which Piaget devoted the bulk of his research. This stage lasts from age two to seven. Children acquire a mastery of language and an ability to use words to represent objects and images in a symbolic fashion. A four-year-old might use a sweeping hand, for example, to represent the concept "airplane." Piaget termed the stage "preoperational" because children are not yet able to use their developing mental capabilities systematically. Children in this stage are **egocentric**. As Piaget used it, this concept does not refer to selfishness, but to the tendency of the child to interpret the world exclusively in terms of his own position. A child during this period does not understand, for instance, that others see objects from a different perspective from his own. Holding a book upright, the child may ask about a picture in it, not realizing that the other person sitting opposite can only see the back of the book.

Children at the preoperational stage cannot hold connected conversations with others. In egocentric speech, what the child says is more or less unrelated to what the other speaker said. Children talk together, but not to one another in the same sense that adults do. During this phase of development, children have no general understanding of categories of thought that adults tend to take for granted: concepts such as causality, speed, weight, or number.

A third period, the **concrete operational stage**, lasts from age seven to eleven. During this phase, children master abstract, logical notions. They are able to handle ideas such as causality without much difficulty. They become capable of carrying out the mathematical operations of multiplying, dividing, and subtracting. Children by this stage are much less egocentric. In the preoperational stage, if a girl is asked "How many sisters do you have?" she may correctly answer one. But if asked "How many sisters does your sister have?" she will probably answer none, because she cannot see herself from the point of view of her sister. The concrete operational child is able to answer such a question with ease.

The years from eleven to fifteen cover what Piaget called the **formal operational stage**. During adolescence, the developing child becomes able to grasp highly abstract and hypothetical ideas. When faced with a problem, children at this stage are able to review all the possible ways of solving it and go through them theoretically in order to reach a solution.

According to Piaget, the first three stages of development are universal; but not all adults reach the formal operational stage. The development of formal operational thought depends in part on processes of schooling. Adults of limited educational attainment tend to continue to think in more concrete terms and retain large traces of egocentrism.

AGENTS OF SOCIALIZATION

Agents of socialization are groups or social contexts in which significant processes of socialization occur. Primary socialization occurs in infancy and childhood and is the most intense period of cultural learning. It is the time when children learn language and basic behavioral patterns that form the foundation for later learning. The family is the main agent of socialization during this phase. Secondary socialization takes place later in childhood and into maturity. In this phase, schools, peer groups, social organizations (such as sports teams), the media, and eventually the workplace become socializing forces for individuals. Social interactions in these contexts help people learn the values, norms, and beliefs that make up the patterns of their culture.

THE FAMILY

Since family systems vary widely, the range of family contacts that the infant experiences is by no means standard across cultures. The mother everywhere is commonly the most important individual in the child's early life, but the nature of the relationships established between mothers and their children is influenced by the form and regularity of their contact.

In modern societies, most early socialization occurs within a small-scale or **nuclear family** context. Most American children spend their early years within a domestic unit containing mother, father, and perhaps one or two other children. In many other cultures, by contrast, aunts, uncles, and grandparents are often part of a single household and serve as caretakers even for very young infants. Yet even within American society family contexts vary widely. Some children are brought up in single-parent households; some are cared for by one biological and one non-biological parent figure (for example, a divorced parent and a stepparent). A high proportion of mothers are now employed outside the home and return to their paid work relatively soon after the births of their children. In spite of these variations, the family typically remains the major agency of socialization from infancy to adolescence and beyond—in a sequence of development connecting the generations.

In most traditional societies, the family into which a person was born largely determined the individual's social position for the rest of his or her life. In modern societies, social position is not inherited at birth in this way, yet the region and social class of the family into which an individual is born affects patterns of socialization. Children pick up ways of behaving from their parents or others in their neighborhood or community.

Patterns of child rearing and discipline, together with contrasting values and expectations, are found in different sectors of large-scale societies. It is easy to understand the influence of different types of family background if we think of what life is like, say, for a child growing up in a poor black family living in a run-down city neighborhood compared to one born into an affluent white family living in an all-white suburb (Kohn 1977).

Of course, few if any children simply take over unquestioningly the outlook of their parents. This is especially true in the modern world, in which change is so pervasive. Moreover, the very existence of a range of socializing agents in modern societies leads to many divergences between the outlooks of children, adolescents, and the parental generation.

nuclear family • A family group consisting of an adult or adult couple and their dependent children.

SCHOOLS

Another important socializing agent is the school. Schooling is a formal process: Students pursue a definite curriculum of subjects. Yet schools are agents of socialization in more subtle respects. Students are expected to be punctual, to be quiet in class, to obey their teachers, and to observe rules of school discipline. How teachers react to their students, in turn, affects the students' views and expectations of themselves. These expectations also become linked to later job experience when students leave school. Peer groups are often formed at school, and the system of keeping children in classes according to age reinforces their impact.

peer group • A friendship group composed of individuals of similar age and social status.

age-grades • The system found in small traditional cultures by which people belonging to a similar age group are categorized together and hold similar rights and obligations.

Another socializing agency is the **peer group**. Peer groups consist of individuals of a similar age. In some cultures, particularly small traditional societies, peer groups are formalized as **age-grades** (normally confined to males). There are often specific ceremonies or rites that mark the transition of men from one age-grade to another. A typical set of age-grades consists of childhood, junior warriorhood, senior warriorhood, junior elderhood, and senior elderhood. Men move through these grades not as individuals, but as whole groups.

The family's importance in socialization is obvious because the experience of the infant and young child is shaped more or less exclusively within it. It is less apparent, especially to those of us living in Western societies, how significant peer groups are. Yet even without formal age-grades, children over four or five usually spend a great deal of time in the company of friends the same age. Given the high proportion of women now in the workforce whose young children play together in day-care centers, peer relations are even more important today than before (Corsaro 1997; Harris 1998).

Peer relations are likely to have a significant effect beyond childhood and adolescence. Informal groups of people of similar ages, at work and in other situations, are usually of enduring importance in shaping individuals' attitudes and behavior.

THE MASS MEDIA

Newspapers and periodicals flourished in the West from the early 1800s onward, but they were confined to a fairly small readership. It was not until a century later that such printed materials became part of the daily experience of millions of people, influencing their attitudes and opinions. The spread of mass media involving printed documents was soon accompanied by electronic communication—radio, television, records, and videos. American children spend the equivalent of almost a hundred schooldays per year watching television.

Much research has been done to assess the effects of television programs on the audiences they reach, particularly children. Perhaps the most commonly researched topic is the impact of television on propensities to crime and violence.

The most extensive studies are those carried out by George Gerbner and his collaborators. In 1967, Gerbner founded the Cultural Indicators Project to study the effects of television violence on society. His research team has analyzed samples of prime-time and weekend daytime TV for all the major American networks each year since 1967. Violence is defined as physical force directed against the self or others, in which physical harm or death occurs. A recent study investigating the depiction of violence during prime time on six major networks in the United State finds the season beginning 2005 to be one of the most violent in recent history. Between 1998 and 2006, violence during the 8 P.M. family slot increased by 45 percent, 9 P.M. by 92 percent, and 10 P.M. by 167 percent. On average prime-time TV contains 4.4 violent episodes per hour (Parents Television Council 2006). In addition, the study finds that violent scenes increasingly include a sexual element. Children's programs show even higher levels of violence, although killing is less commonly portrayed. Cartoons depict the highest number of violent acts and episodes of any type of television program.

In recent years researchers have become interested in studying the ways that video games (and especially, violent video games) affect children. In his book *Video Kids* (1991), Eugene Provenzo analyzes the effect of Nintendo. There are currently some 134 million Nintendo, Microsoft, and Sony games in the United States, and many more in other countries (NPD 2009). A sizeable proportion are owned and operated by children.

Video games have become a key part of the culture and experience of childhood today. Studies have indicated that playing video games might have a positive effect on children's social and intellectual development.

Video games, Provenzo concludes, have become a key part of the culture and experience of childhood and adolescence today. But is this a potentially harmful trend?

It is doubtful that a child's involvement with Nintendo harms her achievement at school. While at time increased video game use and decreased school performance go hand in hand, it is unlikely that video games cause a decline in school performance. For example, where strong pressures deflect students from an interest in their schoolwork, absorption with TV or video pursuits will tend to reinforce these attitudes. Video games and TV then can become a refuge from a disliked school environment.

It is also possible that video games can act to develop skills that might be relevant both to formal education and to wider participation in a society that depends increasingly on electronic communication. The sound and look of video games has been a major influence on the development of rave music, rockers like Trent Reznor of Nine Inch Nails, and even films like *The Matrix, Lara Croft: Tomb Raider*, and *Max Payne*. Patricia Greenfield (1993) has argued that "video games are the first example of a computer technology that is having a socializing effect on the next generation on a mass scale, and even on a world-wide basis."

WORK

Across all cultures, work is an important setting within which socialization processes operate, although it is only in industrial societies that large numbers of people go out to work—that is, go each day to places of work separate from the home. In traditional communities many people farmed the land close to where they lived or had workshops in their dwellings. "Work" in such communities was not as clearly distinct from other activities as it is for most members of the workforce in the modern West. In the industrialized countries, going out to work for the first time ordinarily marks a much greater transition in an individual's life than entering work in traditional societies. The work environment often poses unfamiliar demands, perhaps calling for major adjustments in the person's outlook or behavior.

SOCIAL ROLES

social roles • Socially defined expectations of an individual in a given status, or social position.

self-identity • The ongoing process of self-development and definition of our personal identity through which we formulate a unique sense of ourselves and our relationship to the world around us.

Through the process of socialization, individuals learn about **social roles**—socially defined expectations that a person in a given social position follows. The social role of doctor, for example, encompasses a set of behaviors that should be enacted by all individual doctors, regardless of their personal opinions or outlooks. Because all doctors share this role, it is possible to speak in general terms about the professional role behavior of doctors, irrespective of the specific individuals who occupy that position.

Some sociologists, particularly those associated with the functionalist school, regard social roles as fixed and relatively unchanging parts of a society's culture. According to this view, individuals learn the expectations that surround social positions in their particular culture and perform those roles largely as they have been defined. Social roles do not involve negotiation or creativity. Rather, they prescribe, contain, and direct an individual's behavior. Through socialization, individuals internalize social roles and learn how to carry them out.

This view, however, is mistaken. It suggests that individuals simply take on roles, rather than creating or negotiating them. Yet socialization is a process in which humans can exercise agency; they are not simply passive subjects waiting to be instructed or programmed. Individuals come to understand and assume social roles through an ongoing process of social interaction.

IDENTITY

The cultural settings in which we are born and mature to adulthood influence our behavior, but that does not mean that humans are robbed of individuality or free will. Some sociologists do tend to write about socialization as though this was the case. But such a view is fundamentally flawed—socialization is also at the origin of our very individuality and freedom. In the course of socialization each of us develops a sense of identity and the capacity for independent thought and action.

Identity is a multifaceted concept—it relates to the understandings people hold about who they are and what is meaningful to them. Some of the main sources of identity include gender, sexual orientation, nationality or ethnicity, and social class. Sociologists typically speak of two types of identity: social identity and self-identity (or personal identity). These concepts are analytically distinct but are closely related to one another. Social identity refers to the characteristics that other people attribute to an individual. These can be seen as markers that indicate who the individual is. At the same time, they place that individual in relation to other individuals who share the same attributes. Examples of social identities might include student, mother, lawyer, Catholic, homeless, Asian, dyslexic, married, and so forth. Nearly all individuals have social identities comprising more than one attribute. A person could simultaneously be a mother, an engineer, a Muslim, and a city council member. Multiple social identities reflect the many dimensions of people's lives. Although this plurality of social identities can be a potential source of conflict for people, most individuals organize meaning and experience in their lives around a primary identity that is fairly continuous across time and place.

If social identities mark ways in which individuals are the same as others, self-identity (or personal identity) sets us apart as distinct individuals. **Self-identity** refers to the process of self-development through which we formulate a unique sense of ourselves and our relationship to the world around us. The notion of self-identity draws heavily on the work of symbolic interactionists. The individual's constant negotiation

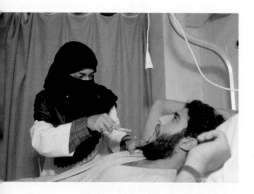

People often exhibit multiple social identities simultaneously, sometimes seemingly conflicting ones. Focusing on her primary identity as a medical professional in this context, a male patient at King Fahd Military Medical Complex in Saudi Arabia allows a doctor who is also a Muslim woman to examine him.

with the outside world helps create and shape his or her sense of self. Though the cultural and social environment is a factor in shaping self-identity, individual agency and choice are of central importance.

If at one time people's identities were largely informed by their membership in broad social groups, bound by class or nationality, they are now more multifaceted and less stable. Individuals have become more socially and geographically mobile due to processes including urban growth and industrialization. This has freed people from the tightly knit, relatively homogeneous communities of the past in which patterns were passed down in a fixed way across generations. It has created the space for other sources of personal meaning, such as gender and sexual orientation, to play a greater role in people's sense of identity.

In today's world, we have unprecedented opportunities to create our own identities. We are our own best resources in defining who we are, where we have come from, and where we are going. Now that the traditional signposts of identity have become less essential, the social world confronts us with a dizzying array of choices about who to be, how to live, and what to do, without offering much guidance about which selections to make. The decisions we make in our everyday lives—about what to wear, how to behave, and how to spend our time—help make us who we are. Through our capacity as self-conscious, self-aware human beings, we constantly create and re-create our identities.

GENDER SOCIALIZATION

Agents of socialization play an important role in how children learn gender roles. Let's now turn to the study of gender socialization, the learning of gender roles through social factors such as the family and the media.

REACTIONS OF PARENTS AND ADULTS

Many studies have been carried out on the degree to which gender differences are the result of social influences. Studies of mother–infant interaction show differences in the treatment of boys and girls even when parents believe their reactions to both are the same. Adults asked to assess the personality of a baby give different answers according to whether they believe the child to be a girl or a boy. In one experiment, five young mothers were observed in interaction with a six-month-old called Beth. They tended to smile at her often and offer her dolls to play with. She was seen as "sweet," having a "soft cry." The reaction of a second group of mothers to a child the same age, named Adam, was noticeably different. The baby was likely to be offered a train or other "male" toys to play with. Beth and Adam were actually the same child, dressed in different clothes (Will et al. 1976).

GENDER LEARNING

Gender learning by infants is almost certainly unconscious. Before a child can accurately label itself as either a boy or a girl, it receives a range of preverbal cues. For instance, male and female adults usually handle infants differently. The cosmetics women use contain scents different from those the baby might learn to associate with males. Systematic differences in dress, hairstyle, and so on provide visual cues for the infant in the learning process. By age two, children have a partial understanding of what gender is. They know whether they are boys or girls, and they can usually

In her "Pink & Blue" project, photographer JeongMee Yoon records girls' obsession with the color pink. What are the implications of the gender-typed packaging and color-coding that we see in children's toys and clothing?

categorize others accurately. Not until five or six, however, does a child know that everyone has gender, and that sex differences between girls and boys are anatomically based.

The toys, picture books, and television programs with which young children come into contact all tend to emphasize differences between male and female attributes. Toy stores and mail-order catalogs usually categorize their products by gender. Even toys that seem neutral in terms of gender are not always so in practice. For example, toy kittens and rabbits are recommended for girls, whereas lions and tigers are seen as more appropriate for boys.

Vanda Lucia Zammuner (1986) studied the toy preferences of boys and girls aged between seven and ten in Italy and Holland. On average, the Italian children chose gender-differentiated (versus gender-neutral) toys to play with more often than the Dutch children—a finding that conformed to expectations, because Italian culture tends to hold a more traditional view of gender divisions than does Dutch society. As in other studies, girls from both societies chose gender-neutral or boys' toys to play with far more than boys chose girls' toys.

STORYBOOKS AND TELEVISION

Over thirty years ago, Lenore Weitzman and her colleagues (1972) systematically analyzed gender roles in some of the most widely used preschool children's books. They found that images of males outnumbered females by a ratio of 11 to 1; including animals with gender identities, the ratio was 95 to 1. The activities of males and females also differed. The males engaged in adventurous pursuits and outdoor activities demanding independence and strength. When girls did appear, they were portrayed as passive and confined mostly to indoor activities. Girls cooked and cleaned for the males or awaited their return. Much the same was true of the adult men and women represented in the storybooks. Women who were not wives and mothers were imaginary creatures like witches or fairy godmothers. There was not a single woman in all the books analyzed who held an occupation outside the home. By contrast, the men were depicted as fighters, policemen, judges, and kings.

More recent research suggests that things have changed somewhat but that the large bulk of children's literature remains much the same (Davies 1991). Fairy tales, for example, embody traditional attitudes toward gender and the sorts of aims and ambitions girls and boys are expected to have. "Some day my prince will come"—in versions of fairy tales from several centuries ago, this usually implied that a girl from a poor family might dream of wealth and fortune. Today, its meaning has become more closely tied to the ideals of romantic love. Even the contemporary *Twilight* series enchants teenage girls with the romantic tale of high school student Bella Swann meeting her soul mate (and vampire) Edward Cullen.

Although there are some notable exceptions, analyses of television programs designed for children conform to the findings about children's books. Studies of the most frequently watched cartoons show that most of the leading figures are male and that males dominate the active pursuits. Similar images are found in the commercials that appear throughout the programs. Gender socialization is very powerful, and gender-typed expectations are fulfilled and reproduced in everyday life (Bourdieu 1990; Lorber 1994). ✓

CONCEPT CHECKS ✓

1. What is social reproduction? What are some specific ways that the four main agents of socialization contribute to social reproduction?

2. According to Mead, how does a child develop a social self?

3. What are the four stages of cognitive development according to Piaget?

4. Compare and contrast social roles and social identities.

5. How do the media contribute to gender role socialization?

WHAT ARE THE FIVE MAJOR STAGES OF THE LIFE COURSE?

life course • The various transitions and stages people experience during their lives.

The transitions that individuals pass through during their lives seem at first glance to be biologically fixed—from childhood to adulthood and eventually to death. But the stages of the human **life course** are social as well as biological in nature. They are influenced by culture and by the material circumstances of people's lives. For example, in the modern West, death is usually thought of in relation to old age, because most people enjoy a life span of seventy-five or more. In traditional societies of the past, however, more people died at younger ages than survived to old age.

CHILDHOOD

To people living in modern societies, childhood is a clear and distinct stage of life. Children are different from babies or toddlers; childhood is the stage between infancy and adolescence. Yet the concept of childhood, like so many other aspects of social life today, has come into being only over the past two or three centuries. In earlier societies, the young moved directly from a lengthy infancy into working roles within the community. French historian Philippe Ariès (1965) argued that "childhood," conceived of as a separate phase of development, did not exist in medieval times. In the paintings of medieval Europe, children are portrayed as little adults, with mature faces and the same style of dress as their elders. Children took part in the same work and play activities as adults, rather than in the childhood games we now take for granted.

Up until the twentieth century, in the United States and most other Western countries, children were put to work at what now seems a very young age. There are countries in the world today, in fact, where young children are engaged in full-time work, sometimes in physically demanding circumstances (for example, in coal mines). The ideas that children have distinctive rights and that the use of child labor is morally wrong are quite recent developments.

Because of the prolonged period of childhood that we recognize today, societies now are in some respects more child centered than traditional ones. But a child-centered society, it must be emphasized, is not one in which all children experience love and care from parents or other adults. The physical and sexual abuse of children is a not uncommon feature of family life in present-day society, although the full extent of such abuse has only recently come to light.

It seems possible that as a result of changes currently occurring in modern societies, the separate character of childhood is diminishing once more. Some observers have suggested that children now grow up too fast—even small children may watch the same television programs as adults, thereby becoming much more familiar early on with the adult world than did preceding generations.

This *Madonna and Child*, painted in the thirteenth century by Duccio da Buoninsegna, depicts the infant Jesus with a mature face. Until recently, children in Western society were viewed as little adults.

THE TEENAGER

The idea of the "teenager," so familiar to us today, also didn't exist until recently. The biological changes involved in puberty (the point at which a person becomes capable of adult sexual activity and reproduction) are universal. Yet in many cultures, these physical changes do not produce the degree of emotional turmoil and uncertainty often found among teens in modern societies. In cultures that celebrate "rites of passage" or distinct ceremonials that signal a person's transition to adulthood, the process of psychosexual development generally seems easier to negotiate. Adolescents in such societies have less to "unlearn" because the pace of change is slower. There is a time when children in Western societies are required to be children no longer: to put away their toys and break with childish pursuits. In traditional cultures, where children are already working alongside adults, this process of unlearning is normally much less jarring.

In Western societies, teenagers are betwixt and between: Pop culture promotes sexy clothing among teens, yet frowns upon teenage sexual activity. Teens may wish to go to work and earn money as adults do, but are legally required to stay in school. Teenagers in the West live in between childhood and adulthood, growing up in a society subject to continuous change.

YOUNG ADULTHOOD

Young adulthood is a stage of exploration, often before one settles on a permanent job, spouse, or home. This stage of personal and sexual development is unique to modern societies (Goldscheider and Waite 1991). Particularly among more affluent groups, people in their early twenties are taking the time to travel and explore sexual, political, and religious affiliations. The importance of this postponement of the responsibilities of full adulthood is likely to grow, given the extended period of education many people now undergo.

MIDLIFE OR "MIDDLE AGE"

Most young adults in the West today can look forward to a life stretching right through to old age. In premodern times, few could anticipate such a future with much confidence. Death through sickness or injury was much more frequent among all age groups than it is today, and women in particular were at great risk because of the high rate of mortality in childbirth.

On the other hand, some of the strains we experience now were less pronounced in previous times. People usually maintained a closer connection with their parents and other kin than in today's more mobile populations, and the routines of work they followed were the same as those of their forebears. In current times, major uncertainties must be resolved in marriage, family life, and other social contexts. We have to "make" our own lives more than people did in the past. The creation of romantic ties, for instance, now depends on individual initiative and selection, rather than being fixed by parents. This represents greater freedom for the individual, but the responsibility can also impose difficulties.

Keeping a forward-looking outlook in middle age has taken on a particular importance in modern societies. Most people do not expect to be doing the same thing all their lives, as was the case for the majority in traditional cultures. For example, women who spent their early adulthood raising a family and whose children have left home may feel free to pursue new personal goals, while men who stayed at financially stable jobs while supporting their young families may choose to pursue their earlier career dreams. Midlife is a turning point where men and women often make choices that prepare them for the second half of life.

Japanese and American Teenagers

Studies comparing socialization in different cultural settings show some interesting contrasts. For example, the idea of the teen years as an extended period of transition between childhood and adulthood emerged in America before it did in Japan. In fact, the Japanese term *cheenayja* is an adaptation of the American *teenager*. In premodern Japan, the movement from childhood to adulthood occurred in an instant, because it happened as part of an age-grade system. A child would become an adult when he or she participated in a special rite. Japanese boys became adults at some point between ages eleven and sixteen, depending on their social rank. The parallel ceremony at which girls were recognized as women occurred at the "kami" age, the age at which they began to wear their hair up rather than down.

Just as in most other nonmodern societies, including those of medieval Europe, young people in Japan knew who they would be and what they would be doing when they became adults. The teenage years weren't a time to experiment. Japanese children were schooled to follow closely the ways of their parents, to whom they owed strict obedience; family norms emphasizing the duties of children toward their parents were very strong.

Such norms have endured to the present day, but they have also come under strain with the high pace of industrial development in contemporary Japan. So are Japanese teenagers now just like American ones? Merry White, a sociologist at Boston University, attempted to answer this question. White (1993) interviewed one hundred teens in each culture over a period of three years,

trying to gain an in-depth view of their attitudes toward sexuality, school, friendship, and parents. She found big differences between the Japanese and American teenagers, but also came up with unexpected conclusions about both. In neither culture are most teenagers the rebels she expected to find. Instead, she found a fairly high degree of conformity to wider cultural ideas and an expressed respect for parents in both countries.

What the adults say of their teenage offspring in Japan and the United States is much the same: "Why don't you listen more to what I say?" "When I was your age . . ." The Japanese and American teens also echo each other in some ways: "Do you like me?" "What should I aim for in my life?" "We're cool, but they aren't." Pop music, films, and videos figure large in the experience of both—as does at least a surface sexual knowledgeability,

LATER LIFE OR "OLD AGE"

In traditional societies, older people were normally accorded a great deal of respect. Among cultures that included age-grades, the elders usually had a say over matters of importance to the community. Within families, the authority of both men and women typically increased with age. In industrialized societies, by contrast, older people tend to lack authority within both the family and the wider social community. Having retired from the labor force, they may be poorer than ever before in their lives. At the same time, there has been a great increase in the proportion of the population over age since from an early age in both cultures sexual information, including warnings about sexual disease, is widespread.

The Japanese teenagers, however, come out well ahead of the Americans in terms of school achievements: 95 percent of Japanese teenagers reach a level in academic tests met by only the top 5 percent of young Americans. And while both express respect for parents, the Japanese teenagers remain much closer to theirs than do most of the American teenagers.

The Japanese teenagers are certainly interested in sex but placed it at the bottom of a list of priorities White presented them with; the Americans put it at the top. Teenagers in Japan are nonetheless sexually very active, probably even more so than their American counterparts. Two thirds of Japanese girls are sexually active by age fifteen. White reports that they are, by Western standards, amazingly forthcoming about their sexual fantasies and practices; nearly 90 percent of the Japanese girls reported that they masturbate twice or more a week.

The Japanese separate clearly three areas of sexuality that are more mixed up for the American teenagers: physical passion, socially approved pairing or marriage, and romantic fantasies. "Love marriages," in which two people establish a relationship on the basis of emotional and sexual attraction, are now common in Japan. However, they are often the result of an initial introduction of suitable partners arranged by parents, followed by falling in love prior to marriage. Even the most sexually experienced

young person in Japan may continue to prefer to have a mature adult arrange an appropriate marriage.

Japanese teenagers often stress that love should grow in marriage, rather than being the basis of choosing a partner in the first place. The sexual activity of young girls tends to involve several older boys and not be bound up with dating. White quotes as typical of young, unmarried Japanese women a respondent who was in her early twenties when interviewed. She first had sexual intercourse at fifteen—like three quarters of her friends—and since had accumulated many "sex friends." These were not *boifurends* (boyfriends), a relationship that implies emotional attachment. She said, "I do it [have sex] because it is fun. However, marriage is a totally different story, you know. Marriage should be more realistic and practical" (White 1993).

sixty-five. In 1900, only one in thirty people in the United States was over sixty-five. Today, one in eight is over sixty-five and this proportion is projected to rise to one in five by the year 2050 (U.S. Bureau of the Census 2009a & 2009b). The same trend is found in all the industrially advanced countries.

Surviving until the life course stage of "elder" in a traditional culture often marked the pinnacle of the status an individual could achieve. In modern societies, retirement tends to bring the opposite consequences. No longer living with their children and often having retired from paid work, some older people may find it difficult to make the final period of their life rewarding. It used to be thought that those who successfully cope with old age do so by turning to their inner resources, becoming less interested in the material rewards that social life has to offer. Although this may often be true, it seems likely that in a society in which many are physically healthy in old age, an outward-looking view will become more and more prevalent. Those in retirement might find renewal in what has been called the "third age," in which a new phase of education begins (see also Chapter 12 on lifelong learning). ✓

CONCEPT CHECKS

1. What are the five stages of the life course, and what are some defining features of each stage?

HOW DO PEOPLE AGE?

Of all the life course stages that sociologists study, older adults are the group of greatest interest to policy makers. Why? Older adults, or individuals aged sixty-five and older, are the most rapidly growing segment of the U.S. population; as such, they will create new challenges for American society. In 2008, 39 million Americans were sixty-five or older, including 5.7 million over eighty-five years old (U.S. Bureau of the Census 2009a). Growing old can be a fulfilling and rewarding experience, or it can be filled with physical distress and social isolation. For most older Americans, the experience of aging lies somewhere in between.

In this section, we delve into the meaning of being old and look at the ways in which people adapt to growing old, at least in the eyes of sociologists.

THE MEANINGS OF "AGE"

aging • The combination of biological, psychological, and social processes that affect people as they grow older.

What does it mean to age? **Aging** can be defined as the combination of biological, psychological, and social processes that affect people as they grow older (Abeles and Riley 1987; Atchley 2000; Riley et al. 1988). These three processes suggest the metaphor of three different, although interrelated, developmental "clocks": (1) a biological one, which refers to the physical body; (2) a psychological one, which refers to the mind and mental capabilities; and (3) a social one, which refers to cultural norms, values, and role expectations having to do with age. Our notions about the meaning of age are rapidly changing, both because recent research is dispelling many myths about aging and because advances in nutrition and health have enabled many people to live longer, healthier lives than ever before.

GROWING OLD: TRENDS AND COMPETING SOCIOLOGICAL EXPLANATIONS

social gerontologists • Those who study aging and the elderly.

Social gerontologists, or social scientists who study aging, have offered a number of theories regarding the nature of aging in U.S. society. Some of the earliest theories emphasized individual adaptation to changing social roles as a person grows older. Later theories focused on how society shapes the social roles of older adults, often in inequitable ways, and emphasized various aspects of age stratification. The most recent theories have been more multifaceted, focusing on the ways in which older persons actively create their lives within specific institutional contexts (Hendricks 1992).

DO-IT-YOURSELF SOCIOLOGY

D.I.Y.

Do you feel like an adult? If yes, what was the exact moment when you felt like a "grown-up"? If no, why not? Your answer to this question may very well mirror the attitudes of most Americans, who have well-defined ideas about what it takes to be an adult. For each of the events listed below, check off those that you've already completed. Then, turn the page to find out whether the average American would view you as a bonafide "adult."

___ Become financially independent

___ Leave parents' home

___ Complete formal education

___ Work full-time

___ Able to support a family

___ Get married

___ Have a child

TURN PAGE →

THE FIRST GENERATION OF THEORIES: FUNCTIONALISM

The earliest theories of aging reflected the functionalist approach that was dominant in sociology during the 1950s and 1960s. They emphasized how individuals adjusted to changing social roles as they aged and how those roles were useful to society. The earliest theories often assumed that aging brings with it physical and psychological decline and that changing social roles have to take this decline into account (Hendricks 1992).

Talcott Parsons, one of the most influential functionalist theorists of the 1950s, argued that U.S. society needs to find roles for older persons consistent with advanced age. He expressed concern that the United States, with its emphasis on youth and its avoidance of death, had failed to provide roles that adequately drew on the potential wisdom and maturity of its older citizens. Moreover, given the graying of U.S. society that was evident even in Parsons's time, he argued that this failure could well lead to older people's becoming discouraged and alienated from society. To achieve a "healthy maturity," Parsons (1960) argued, older adults need to adjust psychologically to their changed circumstances, while society needs to redefine the social roles of older persons. Their former roles (such as work) have to be abandoned, while new forms of productive activity (such as volunteer service) need to be identified.

	Percent who say this transition is "Important" for someone to be considered an adult	Percent who believe transition should occur by age:			
		<20	20-24	25-29	30+
Become financially independent	97%	34%	52%	12%	2%
Leave parents' home	82%	29%	55%	15%	1%
Complete education	97%	25%	52%	19%	3%
Work full-time	96%	32%	52%	15%	1%
Able to support a family	94%	6%	36%	44%	13%
Get married	55%	2%	29%	48%	21%
Have a child	52%	2%	20%	54%	24%

Source: General Social Survey (GSS, March 2002), as reported Furstenberg et al. (2003).

disengagement theory •
A functionalist theory of aging that holds that it is functional for society to remove people from their traditional roles when they become elderly, thereby freeing up those roles for others.

Parsons's ideas set the foundation for **disengagement theory**, the notion that it is functional for society to remove people from their traditional roles when they become older, thereby freeing up those roles for others (Cumming and Henry 1961; Estes et al. 1992). According to this perspective, given the increasing frailty, illness, and dependency of older people, it becomes increasingly dysfunctional for them to occupy traditional social roles they are no longer capable of adequately fulfilling. Older adults, therefore, should retire from their jobs, pull back from civic life, and eventually withdraw from other activities as well. Disengagement is assumed to be functional for the larger society because it opens up roles formerly filled by older individuals for younger people, who presumably will carry them out with fresh energy and new skills. Disengagement is also assumed to be functional for older persons because it enables them to take on less taxing roles consistent with their advancing age and declining health.

Although there is some intuitive appeal to disengagement theory, the idea that older people should completely disengage from the larger society is based on the outdated stereotype that old age involves frailty and dependence. As a result, no sooner did the theory appear than these very assumptions were challenged, often by some of the theory's original proponents (Cumming 1963, 1975; Hendricks 1992; Henry 1965; Hochschild 1975; Maddox 1965, 1970). These challenges gave rise to another functionalist theory of aging, which drew conclusions quite opposite to those of disengagement theory: activity theory.

According to **activity theory**, older people who are busy and engaged, leading fulfilling and productive lives, can be functional for society. Activity theory regards aging as a normal part of human development and argues that older people can best serve society, as well as themselves, by remaining active as long as possible. Although there may come a time in most peoples' lives when disengagement will best serve their interests as well as society's, activity theory argues that an active individual is much more likely to remain healthy, alert, and socially useful. In this view, people should remain engaged in their work and other social roles as long as they are capable of doing so. If a time comes when a particular role becomes too difficult or taxing, then other roles can be sought—for example, volunteer work in the community.

Activity theory finds support in research showing that continued activity well into old age is associated with enhanced mental and physical health (Birren and Bengston 1988; Rowe and Kahn 1987; Schaie 1983). For example, there is some evidence that continued part- or full-time employment is associated with higher morale and happiness, possibly because of the expanded friendship networks that result from continued work (Bosse et al. 1987; Conner et al. 1985; Mor-Barak et al. 1992; Riddick 1985; Soumerai and Avorn 1983).

Critics of functionalist theories of aging argue that these theories emphasize the need for older adults to adapt to existing conditions, either by disengaging from socially useful roles or by actively pursuing them, but that they do not question whether or not the circumstances faced by older persons are fair. In reaction, another group of theories arose—those growing out of the social conflict tradition.

Making Sociology Work
EMPLOYMENT POLICY SPECIALIST

On September 1, 2006, Helmut Panke, the sixty-year-old chief executive of BMW, was forced to step down from his position. Panke was widely regarded as one of the most successful auto chief executives in Europe. In just four years with the company, he expanded the German automaker into China, earned record profits, and diversified the product line with sharp new vehicles that appealed to younger car buyers. Why was Panke forced to step down, given this stellar record? BMW company policy mandated that its workers retire at age sixty, to open up jobs for younger workers. Some advocates of mandatory retirement say that older workers simply can't keep up with new technology and that car buyers are drawn by the new and modern. Others—Panke included—view the policy as ageist and based on dated assumptions about older adults. How could sociological theories and research on aging inform the corporate policy makers at BMW? How might a knowledge of disengagement theory and activity theory shape employment policy?

activity theory •
A functionalist theory of aging which holds that busy, engaged people are more likely to lead fulfilling and productive lives.

THE SECOND GENERATION OF THEORIES: SOCIAL CONFLICT

Unlike their predecessors, whose emphasis was on how well older individuals could be integrated into the larger society, the second generation of theorists focused on sources of social conflict between older persons and society (Hendricks 1992). According to this view, many of the problems of aging—such as poverty, inadequate health care, and lack of high-quality, affordable nursing homes—are systematically produced by the routine operation of social institutions. A capitalist society, the reasoning goes, favors those who are most economically powerful. Although there are certainly some older people who have made it and are set for life, many have not—and these people must fight to get even a meager share of society's scarce resources.

Conflict theories of aging flourished during the 1980s, when a shrinking job base and cutbacks in federal spending threatened to pit different social groups against each other in the competition for scarce resources. Older individuals were seen as competing with the young for increasingly scarce jobs and dwindling federal dollars. Conflict theorists further pointed out that even among persons in later life, those who fared worst were women, low-income people, and minorities, in a cumulating spiral

conflict theories of aging •
Arguments that emphasize the ways in which the larger social structure helps to shape the opportunities available to the elderly. Unequal opportunities are seen as creating the potential for conflict.

of social conflict (Atchley 2000; Estes 1986, 1991; Estes et al. 1982, 1984; Hendricks 1992; Hendricks and Hendricks 1986; McKinlay 1975).

THE THIRD GENERATION OF THEORIES: SELF-CONCEPT AND AGING

The most recent theories reject what they regard as the one-sided emphases of both functionalism and conflict theory. They view older adults as playing an active role in determining their own physical and mental well-being, rather than as merely adapting to the larger society (functionalism) or as victims of the stratification system (social conflict). Circumstances such as family, work, and one's living situation are important sources of one's self-concept, which in turn affects one's life satisfaction. Older persons are seen as playing a significant role in shaping those circumstances (Dannefer 1989; Hendricks 1992; Schaie and Hendricks 2000).

These recent theories also emphasize the increasing diversity among older adults, showing how people age differently, depending on their social class, family status, physical health, and level of social integration (Nelson and Dannefer 1992). Many provide detailed ethnographic accounts of what it means to grow old in U.S. society, with concrete illustrations from older peoples' lives (Gubrium 1986, 1991, 1993; Gubrium and Sankar 1994). ✓

> ## CONCEPT CHECKS ✓
>
> 1. What factors or processes should we keep in mind when studying aging or the meaning of being old? Why?
>
> 2. Summarize the three theoretical frameworks used to describe the nature of aging in U.S. society.
>
> 3. What are the main criticisms of functionalism and conflict theory?

WHAT ARE THE CHALLENGES OF AGING IN THE UNITED STATES?

Older individuals make up a highly diverse category about whom few broad generalizations can be made. For one thing, the aged population reflects the diversity of U.S. society that we've made note of elsewhere in this textbook: They are rich, poor, and in between; they belong to all racial and ethnic groups; they live alone and in families of various sorts; they vary in their political values and preferences; and they are gay and lesbian as well as heterosexual. Furthermore, like other Americans, they are diverse with respect to health: Although some suffer from mental and physical disabilities, most lead active, independent lives.

Race has a powerful influence on the lives of older persons. Whites, on average, live five years longer than African Americans, largely because blacks have much greater odds of dying in infancy, childhood, and young adulthood. Blacks also have much higher rates of poverty and, therefore, are more likely to suffer from inadequate health care compared to whites. As a result, a much higher percentage of whites have survived past age sixty-five compared to other racial groups. The combined effect of race and sex is substantial—white women live, on average, twelve years longer than black men.

Currently, 4.5 million or 11.5 percent of the age 65+ population in the United States is foreign born. In California, New York, Hawaii, and other states that receive large numbers of immigrants, as much as one fifth of the population ages sixty-five and older was born outside the United States (U.S. Bureau of the Census 2009c). Most older immigrants either do not speak English well or do not speak it at all. Integrating older immigrants into U.S. society poses special challenges: Some are highly educated, but most are not. Many require special education and training programs. Most lack a retirement

Figure 3.1 | **Growth of the Elderly Population by Age Group, 1900–2050 (number and percent)**

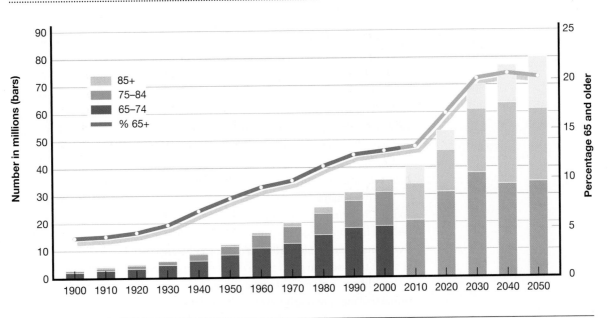

Source: U.S. Bureau of the Census 1996.

income, so that they must depend on their families or public assistance for support. Among those who arrived in the United States during the 1980s, 22 percent were living in poverty in 2003, over twice the rate of older people born in this country (U.S. Bureau of the Census 2005b). In 2003, 570,000 (15.4 percent) foreign-born elders were living below the poverty level in the United States (U.S. Bureau of the Census 2005c).

Finally, as people live to increasingly older ages, they are diverse in terms of age itself. It is useful to distinguish among different age categories of the 65+ population, such as the **young old** (ages sixty-five to seventy-four), the **old old** (ages seventy-five to eighty-four), and the **oldest old** (age eighty-five and older) (Figure 3.1). The young old are most likely to be economically independent, healthy, active, and engaged; the oldest old—the fastest-growing segment of the age 65+ population—are most likely to encounter difficulties such as poor health, financial insecurity, isolation, and loneliness. These differences are not necessarily due only to the effects of aging; they also reflect cohort differences. The young-old came of age during the post–World War II period of strong economic growth and benefited as a result: They are more likely to be educated; to have acquired wealth in the form of a home, savings, or investments; and to have had many years of stable employment. These advantages are much less likely to be enjoyed by the oldest old, partly because their education and careers began at an earlier time, when economic conditions were not so favorable (Treas 1995).

What is the experience of growing old in the United States? Although older persons do face some special challenges, most older people lead relatively healthy, satisfying lives. Still, one national survey found a substantial discrepancy between what most Americans under sixty-five thought life would be like when they passed that milestone and the actual experiences of those who had. We will next examine some of the common problems that older adults confront (see Chapter 7 for a discussion of poverty among older Americans), and we point out the factors that put older persons at risk for these problems.

young old • Sociological term for persons aged sixty-five to seventy-four.

old old • Sociological term for persons aged seventy-five to eighty-four.

oldest old • Sociological term for persons aged eighty-five and older.

SOCIAL ISOLATION

One common stereotype about older adults is that they are socially isolated. This is not true of the majority of older people, however: Four out of five older people have living children, and the vast majority of them can rely on their children for support if necessary (American Association of Retired Persons [AARP] 1997). More than nine out of ten adult children believe that maintaining parental contact is important to them, including the provision of financial support if it is needed (Finley et al. 1988). The reverse is also true: Many studies have found that older parents continue to provide support for their adult children, particularly during times of difficulty such as divorce. Most older parents and adult children report feeling that the amount of support they receive from the other is fair. Being geographically distant from family members does not seem to be a problem either. Among older adults who do not live with their child, approximately three-quarters live within a 35-minute drive of at least one, and half have two children within this range (Lin and Rogerson 1995).

Future generations may suffer more from social isolation than do older people today. Changing patterns of family structure, including increases in divorce and a decline in remarriage, may mean that an increasing proportion of older people will live alone (Goldscheider 1990). A majority of such people will likely be women, given the fact that women on average outlive men. Among people over fifty-five, there are only eighty-two men for every one hundred women; for those eighty-five or older, the number of men per one hundred women drops to forty-six (U.S. Bureau of the Census 2009d). Partly because of the dearth of older men, only 57 percent of all women aged sixty-five to seventy-four are married, compared with 78 percent of men in that age range. Among those eight-five and over, only 15 percent of all women are married; the rate for men is 60 percent (Federal Interagency Forum on Aging-Related Statistics 2008). Women are also more likely than men to be widowed. In 2002, 31 percent of women and only 9 percent of men aged fifty-five and over were widowed (Smith 2003).

The fact that women outlive men means that older women are more likely to experience problems of isolation and loneliness. These problems are compounded by cultural values that make growing old gracefully easier for men than for women. In U.S. culture, youth and beauty are viewed as especially desirable qualities for women. Older men, on the other hand, are more likely to be valued for their material success: Graying at the temples is a sign of distinction for a man, rather than a call for a visit to the hairdresser. As a result, older divorced or widowed men are much more likely to find a mate than older women who are living alone because the pool of eligible mates for older men is more likely to include potential partners who are many years younger.

PREJUDICE

ageism • Discrimination or prejudice against a person on the grounds of age.

Discrimination on the basis of age is now against federal law. Nonetheless, prejudices based on false stereotypes are common. **Ageism** is prejudice and/or discrimination based on age. Like all prejudices, it is fueled in part by stereotypes. Older adults are frequently seen as perpetually lonely, sad, infirm, forgetful, dependent, senile, old-fashioned, inflexible, and embittered.

There are a number of reasons for such prejudice. The previously mentioned American obsession with youthfulness, reflected in popular entertainment and advertising, leads many younger people to disparage their elders, frequently dismissing them as irrelevant. The new information technology reinforces these prejudices because youthfulness and computer abilities seem to go hand in hand. In the fast-paced world of MTV, the Web, and dot-com businesses that seem to flourish and perish overnight, young people may come to view the older as anachronistic or incompetent.

In one study (Levin 1988), college students were shown a photograph of the same man at ages twenty-five, fifty-two, and seventy-three and were asked to rate him in terms of a variety of personality characteristics. The ratings were significantly more negative for the man depicted at age seventy-three. When he looked old in his photograph, the students were more likely to perceive him negatively, even though they knew absolutely nothing about him. The mere fact of his being older was sufficient to trigger a negative cultural stereotype. Widely shared cultural stereotypes of grumpy old men can lead to private opinions that are hurtful to older people.

ELDER ABUSE

It is very difficult for scholars to accurately measure elder abuse, because the concept comprises diverse types of abuse–including emotional, physical, and financial. Because of the stigma and embarrassment associated with such mistreatment, abuse is typically underreported by both older adults and their caregivers. Worldwide, it is estimated that between 4 and 6 percent of persons age 65+ experience some form of abuse at home (Hood 2002). Nationwide it is estimated that between one and two million Americans over sixty-five have been injured, exploited, or otherwise mistreated. Yet, experts estimate that only one in twenty-five abuse cases are reported (National Center on Elder Abuse 2005). One random sample survey among two thousand noninstitutionalized older people in the Boston area found that only about 2 percent had experienced physical violence, although these figures may be somewhat low because abuse rates may be higher among those who are unable to respond to surveys. Older adults also may be reluctant or embarrassed to report mistreatment (Pillemer and Finkelhor 1988).

It is widely believed that abuse results from the anger and resentment that adult children feel when confronted with the need to care for their infirm parents (King 1984; Steinmetz 1983). Most studies, however, have found this to be a false stereotype. More than half of the abuse reported in the above-mentioned Boston study was perpetrated by a spouse; only a quarter of the cases occurred at the hands of an adult child (Pillemer and Finkelhor 1988). Furthermore, in cases in which a child abused an aged parent, it was found that he or she was more likely to be financially dependent on the parent, rather than the reverse. The child may feel resentment about being dependent, whereas the parent may be unwilling to terminate the abusive relationship because he or she feels obligated to help the child (Pillemer 1985).

HEALTH PROBLEMS

The prevalence of chronic disabilities among the older population has declined in recent years (Manton et al. 1993), and most aged people rate their health as reasonably good and free of major disabilities. Still, older people obviously suffer from more health problems than most younger people, and health difficulties often increase with advancing age. In 2004, persons age sixty-five and older accounted for over a third of all U.S. health-care expenditures (U.S. Department of Health and Human Services 2007). Chronic health problems are very common among older adults. In 2007, more than half of all noninstitutionalized persons ages sixty-five and older reported having at least some problems with hypertension, slightly less than half reported suffering from arthritis, about a third have heart disease; and more than 20 percent have experienced some type of cancer (Federal Interagency Forum on Aging-Related Statistics 2008).

In 2004, nearly three quarters of noninstitutionalized people over sixty-five considered their health to be "good" or "good to excellent"; nearly two out of three people aged eighty-five or older reported the same (Federal Interagency Forum on Aging-Related Statistics 2008). It is not surprising that the percentage of people needing help with daily activities increases with age: Whereas only about one in ten people between the ages of sixty-five and seventy-five report needing daily assistance, the figure rises to one in five for people between seventy-five and seventy-nine and to one in three for people between eighty and eighty-four. Half of all people over eighty-five require assistance (Federal Interagency Forum on Aging-Related Statistics 2008).

Paradoxically, there is some evidence that the fastest-growing group of the aged population, the oldest old (those eighty-five and older), tend to enjoy relative robustness, which partially accounts for their having reached their advanced age. This is possibly one of the reasons that health care costs for a person who dies at ninety are about a third of those for a person who dies at seventy (Angier 1995). Unlike many other Americans, persons age 65+ are fortunate in having access to public health insurance (Medicare) and, therefore, medical services. The United States, however, stands virtually alone among the industrialized nations in failing to provide adequately for the complete health care of its most senior citizens, as well as younger persons (Hendricks and Hatch 1993). Although nearly 46 million Americans lacked health insurance in 2007 (15.3 percent of the population), less than 2 percent of older adults lacked coverage due to Medicare (DeNavas-Walt et al. 2008). About 94 percent of the 65+ population is covered to some extent by Medicare. But because this program covers about half of the total health care expenses of the individuals age 65+, nearly two out of three older people supplement Medicare with their own private insurance (DeNavas-Walt et al. 2008; Federal Interagency Forum on Aging-Related Statistics 2008). The rising costs of private insurance, unfortunately, have made this option impossible for a growing number of older adults. Between 1997 and 2007, the number of older adults with out-of-pocket health care expenses increased from roughly 83 to over 98 percent. Despite Medicare, today older persons still spend on average over one fifth of their income on health care (DeNavas-Walt et al. 2008; Federal Interagency Forum on Aging-Related Statistics 2004a). At present, the rising costs of Medicare have made it a candidate for federal budget cuts.

When older adults become physically unable to care for themselves, they may move into assisted living facilities or nursing homes. Only about 1 percent of people between age sixty-five and seventy-four are in a nursing home, a figure that rises to about 3.6 percent among people seventy-five to eighty-four, and to almost 14 percent for those over eighty-five (Federal Interagency Forum on Aging-Related Statistics 2008). Medicaid, the government program that provides health insurance for the poor, covers long-term supervision and nursing costs, although only when most of one's assets (except for one's home) have been used up. About 7 percent of older people in nursing homes receive assistance from Medicaid (Federal Interagency Forum on Aging-Related Statistics 2004a). Because the average (median) cost of a nursing home is now over $74,000 a year (Genworth 2009), the nonpoor older who require such institutionalization may find that their lifetime savings will be quickly depleted. Nursing homes have long had a reputation for austerity and loneliness. However, the quality of most has improved in recent years, both because federal programs such as Medicaid help cover the cost of care and because of federal quality regulations. Still, living for many years in a nursing home was cited as a concern about growing old by over half of respondents, according to a recent national survey.

Even if the problems of social isolation, prejudice, physical abuse, and health declines affect only a relatively small proportion of all older persons, the raw numbers of people facing these challenges will increase as the large baby boom cohort enters into old age. The baby boom cohort refers to the 75 million people born between 1946 and 1964 in the United

CONCEPT CHECKS ✓

1. Contrast the young old, old old, and oldest old.

2. Describe four common problems that older Americans often confront.

3. What characteristics differentiate those older adults who are emotionally and physically well from those who face great distress in later life?

States; the oldest boomers turned sixty in 2006. This large population will provide unforeseen challenges for government-funded programs such as Social Security and Medicare, while reinventing the very meaning of *old age*. The baby boom cohort is more educated than any generation that has come before it; American society will no doubt benefit by incorporating rather than isolating future cohorts of older adults, by drawing on their considerable reserves of experience and talents. ✓

NEED HELP STUDYING?

 wwnorton.com/studyspace

Visit StudySpace to access free review materials such as:

- Vocabulary Flashcards
- Diagnostic Review Quizzes
- Study Outlines

REVIEW QUESTIONS

1. Define socialization and describe how it contributes to social reproduction.
2. The authors explain that what differentiates humans from other species is self-awareness. Briefly contrast Mead's and Piaget's theories of childhood development.
3. What are the agents of socialization? In your opinion, what is the most important or influential agent of socialization and why?
4. Define social roles and give an example of a social role that pertains to your own life.
5. What is the difference between personal and social identity? List some of the sources of both personal and social identity.
6. Describe how people learn gender roles and elaborate on the roles of the family and the media in this learning process.
7. What are the stages of the life course? Describe how they vary culturally and historically.
8. How do sociologists define aging? Discuss each of the processes that sociologists include when they study aging.
9. Discuss theories of self-concept and aging. Give an example of this theoretical perspective.

THINKING SOCIOLOGICALLY EXERCISES

1. Concisely review how an individual becomes a social person according to each of the two leading theorists discussed in this chapter: G. H. Mead and Jean Piaget. Which of these two theories seems most appropriate and correct to you? Explain why.
2. Using alcoholic beverages is one of many things we do as a result of socialization. Suggest how the family, peers, schools, and mass media help to establish the desire to consume alcoholic drinks. Of the preceding, which force is the most persuasive? Explain.

Social Interaction and Everyday Life in the Age of the Internet

THE BIG QUESTIONS

WHAT IS SOCIAL INTERACTION?

Familiarize yourself with the study of everyday life. Know the various forms of nonverbal communication.

HOW DO WE MANAGE IMPRESSIONS IN DAILY LIFE?

Learn about the ways you carefully choose to present yourself to others in daily interactions.

WHAT RULES GUIDE HOW WE COMMUNICATE WITH OTHERS?

Learn the research process of ethnomethodology, the study of our conversations, and how we make sense of each other.

HOW DO TIME AND SPACE AFFECT OUR INTERACTIONS?

Understand that interaction is situated, that it occurs in a particular place and for a particular length of time. See that the way we organize our social actions is not unique by learning how other cultures organize their social lives.

HOW DO THE RULES OF SOCIAL INTERACTION AFFECT YOUR LIFE?

See how face-to-face interactions and broader features of society are closely related.

Matt Kehoe is a waiter at the Spotted Pig, an upscale pub in New York City, where he has worked for the past five years. Every day, he takes the subway from his home in Brooklyn to his job in the city. In his subway car, he is surrounded by hundreds of people who are almost always strangers. After he walks a few blocks from the subway exit to the Spotted Pig, Matt enters a place where he knows dozens of people at any time: coworkers, customers who come to eat and drink, and current and former employees who hang out at the bar when they are off work.

The movement from a social context where most of the people around him are strangers to one where they are known implies a dramatic shift in social interaction, yet there are commonalities. In both the pub and the subway car personal space is limited. For example, in the subway car, bodies touch as commuters squeeze into seats next to others. In the restaurant, tables, chairs, and stools are all located closely together, with little room in between.

Elbow to elbow with people from the time he gets on the subway in the morning until the times he gets home from work, it is almost impossible for Matt to move anywhere in these physical spaces without potentially making eye contact—on the train with a stranger, in the pub with an acquaintance. But like many urban residents, Matt makes an effort to maintain his sense of personal space by creating some semblance of solitude. On the subway, he wears an iPod and reads his text messages, which makes it possible for him to go into "his own zone" and "extend his personal space" (Goffman 1971) generally ignoring the people around him. At times when he does inadvertently make eye contact with strangers, he quickly shifts his gaze—an action that sociologists call a norm of everyday life.

In the restaurant, it would be socially inappropriate for Matt to continue wearing the iPod because he is expected to be working and interacting with others. Yet, even here there is an appropriate balance between eye contact and looking away. He will greet certain patrons and fellow workers the first time he sees them, but afterward it is usually understood that they will go about their own business without acknowledging one another in the way they did earlier.

When passersby—either strangers or intimates—quickly glance at each other and then look away again, they demonstrate what Erving Goffman (1967, 1971) calls the **civil inattention** we require of each other in many situations. Civil inattention is not the same as merely ignoring another person. Each individual indicates recognition of the other person's presence but avoids any gesture that might be taken as too intrusive. Can you think of examples of civil inattention in your own life? Perhaps when you are walking down the hall of a dormitory or trying to decide where to sit in the cafeteria or simply walking across campus? Civil inattention to others is something we engage in more or less unconsciously, but it is of fundamental importance to the existence of social life, which must proceed efficiently and, sometimes among total strangers, without fear.

The best way to see the importance of civil inattention is by thinking of examples where it doesn't apply. When a person stares fixedly at another, allowing her face openly to express a particular emotion, it is frequently with a romantic partner, family member, or close friend. Strangers or chance acquaintances, whether encountered on the street, at work, or at a party, virtually never hold the gaze of another in this way. To do so may be taken as an indication of hostile intent. It is only where two groups are strongly antagonistic to one another that strangers might indulge in such a practice.

Even friends in close conversation need to be careful about how they look at one another. Each individual demonstrates attention and involvement in the conversation by regularly looking at the eyes of the other, but not staring into them. To look too intently might be taken as a sign of mistrust about, or at least failure to understand, what the other is saying. Yet if each party does not engage the eyes of the other at all, he is likely to be thought evasive or socially awkward.

civil inattention • The process whereby individuals in the same physical setting demonstrate to one another that they are aware of each other's presence.

WHAT IS SOCIAL INTERACTION?

microsociology • The study of human behavior in contexts of face-to-face interaction.

social interaction • The process by which we act and react to those around us.

Erving Goffman, the first to develop the concept of civil inattention, was a sociologist who created a new field of study called **microsociology** or **social interaction**. Goffman believed that sociologists needed to concern themselves with seemingly trivial aspects of everyday social behavior. Passing someone on the street or exchanging a few words with a friend are unremarkable activities, things we do countless times a day without giving them any thought. Goffman argued that the study of such apparently insignificant forms of social interaction is of major importance in sociology and, far from being uninteresting, is one of the most absorbing of all areas of sociological investigation. There are three reasons for this.

First, our ordinary routines give structure and form to what we do. We can learn a great deal about ourselves as social beings, and about social life itself, from studying them. Our lives are organized around the repetition of similar patterns of behavior from day to day, week to week, month to month, and year to year. Think of what you did yesterday, for example, and the day before that. If they were both weekdays, you probably woke up at about the same time each day (an important routine in itself). You may have gone off to class fairly early in the morning, making a journey from home to school that you make virtually every weekday. You perhaps met some friends for lunch, returning to classes or private study in the afternoon. Later, you retraced your steps back home, possibly going out later in the evening with other friends.

Of course, the routines we follow are not identical from day to day, and our patterns of activity on weekends usually contrast with those on weekdays. And if we make a major change in our life, like leaving college to take up a job, alterations in our daily routines are usually necessary; but then we establish a new and fairly regular set of habits again.

Second, the study of everyday life reveals to us how humans can act creatively to shape reality. Although social behavior is guided to some extent by forces such as roles, norms, and shared expectations, individuals perceive reality differently according to their backgrounds, interests, and motivations. Because individuals are capable of creative action, they continuously shape reality through the decisions and actions they take. In other words, reality is not fixed or static—it is created through human interactions.

Third, studying social interaction in everyday life sheds light on larger social systems and institutions. All large-scale social systems, in fact, depend on the patterns of social interaction we engage in daily. This is easy to demonstrate. Consider the case of two strangers passing on the street. Such an event may seem to have little direct relevance to large-scale, more permanent forms of social organization. But when we take into account many such interactions, they are no longer irrelevant. In modern societies, most people live in towns and cities and constantly interact with others whom they do not know personally. Civil inattention is one among other mechanisms that give public life, with its bustling crowds and fleeting, impersonal contacts, the character it has.

When we published the first edition of this book, the study of face-to-face communication was a well-settled territory. Over the past decade or so, however, social interaction has undergone a major transformation due to the rise of the Internet. In this chapter, we will review the traditional findings of the field, but we will also ask how these findings must be modified in the light of the rise of e-mail, Internet chatting, and social networking sites like Facebook. We will first learn about the nonverbal cues (facial expressions and bodily gestures) all of us use when interacting with each other. We then move on to analyze everyday speech—how we use language to communicate to others the meanings we wish to get across. Finally, we focus on the ways in which our lives are structured by daily routines, paying particular attention to how we coordinate our actions across space and time.

Walking along a crowded city street, one engages in civil inattention. Though the people in the photo above can hear the phone conversations these men are having, they make no indication of their awareness.

NONVERBAL COMMUNICATION

Social interaction requires many forms of **nonverbal communication**—the exchange of information and meaning through facial expressions, gestures, and movements of the body. Nonverbal communication, sometimes referred to as "body language," often

nonverbal communication •
Communication between individuals based on facial expression or bodily gestures rather than on language.

alters or expands on what is said with words. In some cases, our body language may convey a message that is discrepant with our words.

FACE, GESTURES, AND EMOTION

One major aspect of communication is the facial expression of emotion. Paul Ekman and his colleagues have developed what they call the Facial Action Coding System (FACS) for describing movements of the facial muscles that give rise to particular expressions (Ekman and Friesen 1978). By this means, they have tried to inject some precision into an area notoriously open to inconsistent or contradictory interpretations—for there is little agreement about how emotions are to be identified and classified. Charles Darwin, one of the originators of evolutionary theory, claimed that basic modes of emotional expression are the same in all human beings. Although some have disputed the claim, Ekman's research among people from widely different cultural backgrounds seems to confirm Darwin's view. Ekman and W. V. Friesen carried out a study of an isolated community in New Guinea, whose members had previously had virtually no contact with outsiders. When they were shown pictures of facial expressions conveying six

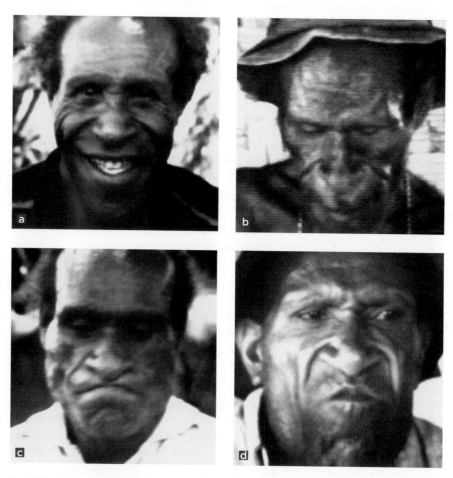

Paul Ekman's photographs of facial expressions from a tribesman in an isolated community in New Guinea helped to test the idea that basic modes of emotional expression are the same among all people. Here the instructions were to show how your face would look if you were a person in a story and (a) your friend had come and you were happy, (b) your child had died, (c) you were angry and about to fight, and (d) you saw a dead pig that had been lying there a long time.

emotions, the New Guineans identified the same emotions (happiness, sadness, anger, disgust, fear, surprise) we would.

According to Ekman, the results of his own and similar studies of different peoples support the view that the facial expression of emotion and its interpretation are innate in human beings. He acknowledges that his evidence does not conclusively demonstrate this, and it may be that widely shared cultural learning experiences are involved; however, his conclusions are supported by other types of research. I. Eibl-Eibesfeldt (1972) studied six children born deaf and blind to see to what extent their facial expressions were the same as those of sighted and hearing individuals in particular emotional situations. He found that the children smiled when engaged in obviously pleasurable activities, raised their eyebrows in surprise when sniffing at an object with an unaccustomed smell, and frowned when repeatedly offered a disliked object. Because the children could not have seen other people behaving in these ways, it seems that these responses must be innately determined.

There are no gestures or bodily postures that have been shown to characterize all, or even most, cultures. In some societies, for instance, people nod when they mean no, the opposite of Anglo-American practice. Gestures Americans tend to use a great deal, such as pointing, seem not to exist among certain peoples (Bull 1983). Similarly, a straightened forefinger placed in the center of the cheek and rotated is used in parts of Italy as a gesture of praise but appears to be unknown elsewhere.

Like facial expressions, gestures and bodily posture are continually used to fill out utterances as well as to convey meanings when nothing is actually said. All three can be used to joke, show irony, or show skepticism. The nonverbal impressions that we convey inadvertently often indicate that what we say is not quite what we really mean. Blushing is perhaps the most obvious example, but innumerable other subtle indicators can be picked up by other people. Genuine facial expressions tend to evaporate after four or five seconds. A smile that lasts longer could indicate deceit. An expression of surprise that lasts too long may indicate deliberate sarcasm—to show that the individual is not in fact surprised after all.

On the Internet, it is very difficult to capture dimensions of emotion that are only present with facial expression. At first, the need that Internet users felt to approximate facial gestures resulted in at least two common faces:

:) or :-)

As time passed, a need for greater subtlety resulted in other widely understood variations, such as this winking smiley face:

;-)

which means that a comment is meant to be taken with a grain of salt.

E-mail may have once been devoid of facial expression, but today the average e-mail user expects to insert different emotions into a message. The strong need human beings feel to communicate with their faces has also led to other innovations, like the webcam (Web camera), which has become a relatively inexpensive and widely used technology. But in general, people who communicate over the Internet or even the telephone lack the benefit of seeing the faces of their conversational partners as they speak. This void is felt even more strongly in text-messaging, which lacks faces and voices, and sometimes relies on cryptic abbreviations that may not be recognized by the other texter!

How might this matter? On the telephone, an individual person will frequently talk longer for a stretch of time than she would in face-to-face conversation. Unable to see the face of a conversational partner, she can't as readily adjust what she says in response to a sense that her partner already "gets it" or thinks she is going down an unproductive (or silly) path. Yet, the telephone maintains at least some immediacy of feedback that e-mail lacks. This is why in e-mail disputes people who are unable to make mutual adjustments in response to verbal or facial cues will end up saying much more—communicated in the form of long messages—than they would need to say in spoken conversation.

Which is better? Would you prefer to make your point in e-mail or in person? Using sociological insights like these might make you prefer electronic communication at some times and face-to-face communication at others. For example, if you are dealing with a powerful person and want to get your thoughts across, you may want to avoid a situation where he can signal with facial gestures that your idea is silly and thus inhibit you from making all your points. The power to signal with facial gestures is one of the things that people do to control the flow of a conversation. On the other hand, face-to-face communication gives you an opportunity to try out an idea on someone more powerful than yourself without going too far down the road if he is actually unreceptive. ✓

CONCEPT CHECKS ✓

1. What is microsociology?

2. What are three reasons why it is important to study daily social interaction?

3. What is nonverbal communication?

4. Describe several ways that individuals communicate their emotions to one another?

5. How do e-mail and in-person communication differ?

social role • The expected behavior of a person occupying a particular social position. The idea of social role originally comes from the theater, referring to the parts that actors play in a stage production. In every society, individuals play a number of social roles.

status • The social honor or prestige that a particular group is accorded by other members of a society. Status groups normally display distinct styles of life—patterns of behavior that the members of a group follow. Status privilege may be positive or negative. Pariah status groups are regarded with disdain or treated as outcasts by the majority of the population.

social position • The social identity an individual has in a given group or society. Social positions may be general in nature (those associated with gender roles) or may be more specific (occupational positions).

impression management • Preparing for the presentation of one's social role.

HOW DO WE MANAGE IMPRESSIONS IN DAILY LIFE?

IMPRESSION MANAGEMENT ("STRIKING A POSE")

Goffman and other writers on social interaction often use notions from drama and theater in their analyses. The concept of **social role**, for example, originated in a theatrical setting. Roles are socially defined expectations that a person in a given **status** (or **social position**) follows. To be a teacher is to hold a specific position; the teacher's role consists of acting in specified ways toward her pupils. Goffman sees social life as though played out by actors on a stage—or on many stages, because how we act depends on the roles we are playing at a particular time. People are sensitive to how they are seen by others and use many forms of **impression management** to compel others to react to them in the ways they wish. Although we may sometimes do this in a calculated way, usually it is among the things we do without conscious attention. When someone attends a business meeting, he wears a suit and is on his best behavior; that evening, when going to a club, he may first work out, and then wear "sexy" garments. This is impression management, or more colloquially, "striking a pose."

A central insight of sociology since Goffman has been that a crucial aspect of social interaction is that every human being possesses a self that is forever fragile and vulnerable to embarrassment or even humiliation. People are intensely attuned to what others think of them and how they are being viewed. Seeking approval and respect,

DO-IT-YOURSELF SOCIOLOGY

D.I.Y.

An important debate among sociologists is whether online communication will replace face-to-face communication as the main way that humans interact. The very way that we engage with one another online has changed drastically in recent decades, and college students today can barely remember life before the Internet. Are you a "typical" Internet user? How do your online interactions differ from those of your parents or grandparents? Please answer the questions below and flip the page to see how you stack up relative to your peers, and to older generations.

Do you . . .

	YES	NO
1. "Go online" or use the Internet?		
2. Send instant messages?		
3. Use social networking sites?		
4. Read blogs?		
5. Create a blog?		
6. Use e-mail?		
7. Get news online?		
8. Play games online?		
9. Visit a virtual world?		

TURN PAGE ⇨

they want to "save face" at every turn. In social interactions, human beings tend to collaborate with others to make sure that the encounter ends without embarrassment for anyone. As a stage, social life has many players, and they must collaborate together to make each scene work.

Think of examples from your own life when you had a choice of whether to collaborate with another person. If you go to a club and someone approaches you who you don't want to meet, you will likely try to end the interaction in a way that is least embarrassing to the other person. It is highly unlikely that you would simply tell the person "Get lost!" rather than help him save face. This is because there is a norm of collaboration by which human beings try to move through life without embarrassing or humiliating others. When this collaboration does not occur, the interaction is notable for the participants.

The "pose" that we adopt depends a great deal on our social role, but no particular role implies any particular presentation of self. A person's demeanor can be different depending on the social context. For instance, as a "student" you have a certain status and are expected to act a certain way when you are around your professors. Some pupils will enact the self-presentation of the dutiful student, while others will enact

Percentage who:	Year of Birth			
	1990–1995	1977–1990	1965–1976	1946–1954
Currently use the Internet	93	87	82	79
Send instant messages	68	59	55	43
Use social networking sites	65	67	36	20
Read blogs	49	43	34	27
Create a blog	18	20	10	6
Use e-mail	73	94	93	90
Get news online	63	74	76	70
Visit a virtual world	10	2	3	1

Source: Pew 2009a.

an uncaring or apathetic pose. In many poor minority schools, students afraid of being accused of "acting white" will adopt a more oppositional stance. Yet, the appearance may not give an accurate sense of what is going on inside. A student who takes on the demeanor of the "street" may be studying just as hard as someone who appears to act in accordance with old-fashioned propriety.

FOCUSED AND UNFOCUSED INTERACTION

unfocused interaction •
Interaction occurring among people present in a particular setting but not engaged in direct face-to-face communication.

In many social situations, we engage in what Goffman calls *unfocused interaction* with others. **Unfocused interaction** takes place whenever individuals exhibit mutual awareness of one another's presence but do not engage in direct communication or conversation. This is usually the case anywhere large numbers of people are assembled, as on a busy street, in a theater crowd, or at a party. When people are in the presence of others, even if they do not directly talk to them, they continually communicate non-verbally through their posture and facial and physical gestures.

Focused interaction occurs when individuals directly attend to what others say or do. Except when someone is standing alone, say at a party, all interaction involves both focused and unfocused exchanges. Goffman calls an instance of focused interaction an **encounter**, and much of our day-to-day life consists of encounters with other people—family, friends, colleagues—frequently occurring against the background of unfocused interaction with others present on the scene. Small talk, seminar discussions, games, and routine face-to-face contacts (with ticket clerks, waiters, shop assistants, and so forth) are all examples of encounters.

Encounters always need "openings," which indicate that civil inattention is being discarded. When strangers meet and begin to talk at a party, the moment of ceasing civil inattention is always risky because misunderstandings can easily occur about the nature of the encounter being established (Goffman 1971). Hence the making of eye contact may first be ambiguous and tentative. A person can then act as though she had made no direct move if the overture is not accepted. In focused interaction, each person communicates as much by facial expression and gesture as by the words actually exchanged.

Goffman distinguishes between the expressions individuals "give" and those they "give off." The first are the words and facial expressions people use to produce certain impressions on others. The second are the clues that others may spot to check their sincerity or truthfulness. For instance, a restaurant owner listens with a polite smile to the statements of customers about how much they enjoyed their meals. At the same time, he is noting how pleased they seemed to be while eating the food, whether a lot was left over, and the tone of voice they use to express their satisfaction.

Think about how Goffman's concepts of focused and unfocused interaction, developed mainly to explain face-to-face social encounters, would apply to our current age. Can you think of a way in which unfocused interaction occurs in instant messaging, Facebook, Twitter, or Web sites that have a chat forum? In some of these small online

focused interaction • Interaction between individuals engaged in a common activity or in direct conversation with one another.

encounter • A meeting between two or more people in a situation of face-to-face interaction. Our daily lives can be seen as a series of different encounters strung out across the course of the day. In modern societies, many of these encounters are with strangers rather than people we know.

Identify examples of focused and unfocused interaction in this photograph by Jeff Wall. What are some of the messages these individuals give off?

communities, everyone can have a mutual awareness of who else is on line, without being in direct contact with them. In some of these programs, people are constantly broadcasting elements of what they are doing or their current situation through status messages.

These status messages make it possible for people in unfocused interaction to have even more control over how they are perceived than people who are merely in one another's presence. Instead of revealing their facial expressions or posture, which they may be unconscious of, people can consciously choose what message or "tweet" they wish to broadcast.

AUDIENCE SEGREGATION

Although people cooperate to help one another "save face," they also endeavor individually to preserve their own dignity, autonomy, and respect. One of the ways that people do this is by arranging for "audience segregation" in their lives. In each of their roles they act somewhat differently, and they endeavor to keep the roles both distinct and separate from each other. This means that they can have multiple selves. Frequently these selves are consistent, but sometimes they are not. People find it very stressful when boundaries break down, or when they cannot reconcile their role in one part of life with their role in another. For example, someone may have two friends who do not like one another. Rather than choose between them, she will spend time with both friends, but never mention to either friend that she is close with the other. Or, some people live very different lives at home and at work. For example, due to discrimination against gays and lesbians, someone who appears "straight" at work may be comfortably gay at home. Like all people who engage in audience segregation, they show a different face to different people, striking a different pose in each context.

"MY WORST E-MAIL DISASTER": IMPRESSION MANAGEMENT IN THE INTERNET AGE

The concept of "audience segregation" helps to understand some of the dilemmas of electronic communication. Many people are very sensitive about having things sent to their business e-mail address that they don't want their coworkers or supervisors to know about. Thus, they maintain different addresses for home ("back region") and office ("front region"), a practice that is increasingly important because many companies have policies against sending personal e-mails from a company's computer. In 2007, employees of PNC Bank in New Jersey discovered the hard way how important it is to maintain such boundaries. Heidi Arace was fired in 2007 after forwarding a picture of a bare-breasted woman attached to Hilary Clinton's face.

Or consider the social situation of a copied message. You write a message to a friend asking her whether she prefers to go to the early show or the late show. You also tell your friend that you have a new boyfriend who you hope she will like. She replies and copies the other people who are thinking of going to the movie, many of whom you never intended to tell about the new romance. Suddenly, the audience segregation you had imagined has broken down.

In recent years, undergraduate students have posted pictures of themselves drinking at parties, or even naked, only to discover that future employers have found these and other postings on the Web before making a hiring decision. Some of these items remain on the Internet long after anyone would normally remember the situation that gave rise to them.

Stacy Snyder was an aspiring teacher who was about to graduate from Millersville University's School of Education in 2006 when a campus official discovered a photograph on her MySpace page that showed Snyder sipping from a plastic cup and wearing a pirate hat. The photo's caption read "Drunken Pirate." Although Snyder was of legal drinking age, school administrators labeled her conduct unprofessional and refused to give her a teaching certificate. How is this refusal an example of impression management?

Disasters like these, and ones far worse, occur frequently in the age of e-mail. One of the most troublesome of breakdowns occurs due to "autofill," the tool on e-mail that fills in the rest of an address. Here is one common story:

> My worst e-mail disaster was not too long ago when I composed an e-mail using my work e-mail (MS Outlook) asking my friend Krista for a link to a porn site. My e-mail was something like "Yo Krista! where's the link to that porn site? I need to forward it to Jenny!"
>
> Anyone who uses MS Outlook knows that it has this autofill feature for the "To:" field, and instead of selecting "Krista," I selected "Kirsten," who's a coworker!
>
> I had no idea I sent it to the wrong person until Kirsten e-mailed me back, asking if the e-mail I just sent her was meant for her or "someone else"!
>
> I still can't look Kirsten in the eye. And I never send personal e-mail using my work e-mail account. EVER. ✓

WHAT RULES GUIDE HOW WE COMMUNICATE WITH OTHERS?

We can make sense of what is said in conversation only if we know the social context, which does not appear in the words themselves. Take the following conversation (Heritage 1985):

> A: I have a fourteen-year-old son.
> B: Well, that's all right.
> A: I also have a dog.
> B: Oh, I'm sorry.

What do you think is happening here? What is the relation between the speakers? What if you were told that this is a conversation between a prospective tenant and a landlord? The conversation then becomes sensible: Some landlords accept children but don't permit their tenants to keep pets. Yet if we don't know the social context, the responses of individual B seem to bear no relation to the statements of A. Part of the sense is in the words, and part is in the way in which the meaning emerges from the social context.

SHARED UNDERSTANDINGS

The most inconsequential forms of daily talk presume complicated, shared knowledge brought into play by those speaking. In fact, our small talk is so complex that it has so far proved impossible to program even the most sophisticated computers to converse with human beings. The words used in ordinary talk do not always have precise meanings, and we "fix" what we want to say through the unstated assumptions that back it up. If Maria asks Tom, "What did you do yesterday?" the words in the question themselves suggest no obvious answer. A day is a long time, and it would be logical for Tom to answer, "Well, at 7:16, I woke up. At 7:18, I got out of bed, went to the bathroom, and started to brush my teeth. At 7:19, I turned on the shower. . . ." We understand the type of response the question calls for by knowing Maria, what sort of activities she and Tom consider relevant, and what Tom usually does on a particular day of the week, among other things.

ETHNOMETHODOLOGY

ethnomethodology • The study of how people make sense of what others say and do in the course of day-to-day social interaction. Ethnomethodology is concerned with the "ethnomethods" by which people sustain meaningful exchanges with one another.

Ethnomethodology is the study of the "ethnomethods"—the folk, or lay, methods—people use to make sense of what others do and particularly of what they say. We all apply these methods, normally without having to give any conscious attention to them. This field was created by Harold Garfinkel, who after Goffman was the most important figure in the study of micro interaction.

Garfinkel argued that in order to understand the way people use context to make sense of the world, sociologists need to study the "background expectancies" with which we organize ordinary conversations. He highlighted these in some experiments he undertook with student volunteers (1963). The students were asked to engage a friend or relative in conversation and to insist that casual remarks or general comments be actively pursued to make their meaning precise. If someone said "Have a nice day," the student was to respond "Nice in what sense, exactly?" "Which part of the day do you mean?" and so forth. One of the exchanges that resulted ran as follows. S is the friend, E, the student volunteer (Garfinkel 1963):

> S: How are you?
>
> E: How am I in regard to what? My health, my finances, my school work, my peace of mind, my . . . ?
>
> S: (red in the face and suddenly out of control): Look! I was just trying to be polite. Frankly, I don't give a damn how you are.

Why do people get so upset when apparently minor conventions of talk are not followed? The answer is that the stability and meaningfulness of our daily social lives depend on the sharing of unstated cultural assumptions about what is said and why. If we weren't able to take these for granted, meaningful communication would be impossible. Any question or contribution to a conversation would have to be followed by a massive "search procedure" of the sort Garfinkel's subjects were told to initiate, and interaction would simply break down. What seem at first sight to be unimportant conventions of talk, therefore, turn out to be fundamental to the very fabric of social life, which is why their breach is so serious.

SOCIAL RULES AND TALK

Although we routinely use nonverbal cues in our own behavior and in making sense of the behavior of others, much of our interaction is done through talk—casual verbal exchange—carried on in informal conversations with others. Sociologists have always accepted that language is fundamental to social life. However, an approach has been developed that is specifically concerned with how people use language in the ordinary contexts of everyday life.

INTERACTIONAL VANDALISM

We have already seen that conversations are one of the main ways in which our daily lives are maintained in a stable and coherent manner. We feel most comfortable when the tacit conventions of small talk are adhered to; when they are breached, we can feel threatened, confused, and insecure. In most everyday talk, conversants are carefully attuned to the cues they get from others—such as changes in intonation, slight pauses, or gestures—to facilitate conversation smoothly. By being mutually aware, conversants "cooperate" in opening and closing interactions and in taking turns to speak. Interactions in which one party is conversationally "uncooperative," however, can give rise to tensions.

Garfinkel's students created tense situations by intentionally undermining conversational rules as part of a sociological experiment. But what about situations in the real world in which people make trouble through their conversational practices? One study investigated verbal interchanges between pedestrians and street people in New York City to understand why such interactions are often seen as problematic by passersby. The researchers used a technique called **conversation analysis** to compare a selection of street interchanges with samples of everyday talk. Conversation analysis is a methodology that examines all facets of a conversation for meaning—from the smallest filler words (such as "um" and "ah") to the precise timing of interchanges (including pauses, interruptions, and overlaps).

The study looked at interactions between black men—many of whom were homeless, alcoholic, or drug addicted—and white women who passed by them on the street. The men often try to initiate conversations with passing women by calling out to them, paying them compliments, or asking them questions. But something "goes wrong" in these conversations, because the women rarely respond as they would in a normal interaction. Even though the men's comments are rarely hostile in tone, the women tend to quicken their step and stare fixedly ahead (Duneier and Molotch 1999).

The term **interactional vandalism** describes cases like these in which a subordinate person breaks the tacit rules of everyday interaction that are of value to the more powerful. The men on the street often do conform to everyday forms of speech in their interactions with one another, local shopkeepers, the police, relatives, and acquaintances. But when they choose to, they subvert the tacit conventions for everyday talk in a way that leaves passersby disoriented. Even more than physical assaults or vulgar verbal abuse, interactional vandalism leaves victims unable to articulate what has happened.

This study of interactional vandalism provides another example of the two-way links between micro-level interactions and forces that operate on the macro level. To the men on the street, the white women who ignore their attempts at conversation appear distant, cold, and bereft of sympathy—legitimate targets for such interactions. The women, meanwhile, may often take the men's behavior as proof that they are indeed dangerous and best avoided. Interactional vandalism is closely tied up with overarching class, gender, and racial structures. The fear and anxiety generated in such mundane interactions help constitute the outside statuses and forces that, in turn, influence the interactions themselves. Interactional vandalism is part of a self-reinforcing system of mutual suspicion and incivility.

conversation analysis • The empirical study of conversations, employing techniques drawn from ethnomethodology. Conversation analysis examines details of naturally occurring conversations to reveal the organizational principles of talk and its role in the production and reproduction of social order.

interactional vandalism • The deliberate subversion of the tacit rules of conversation.

Making Sociology Work
RESTAURATEUR

Restaurant owners know that food alone does not make for a five-star dining experience. Rather, customers are looking to enjoy a physical space and to interact with restaurant workers who make them feel good about themselves and their evening out. Whether it's the gregarious young wait staff, mechanical jungle animals, and simulated rainstorm in the tree-filled Rainforest Café, or the elegant European-style service at one of New York's venerable French restaurants, restaurateurs know that image is everything. But even the most beautiful setting and delicious meal can be ruined if diners are exposed to squabbles among restaurant workers or get a glimpse into an unsanitary kitchen. How might the writings of Erving Goffman guide the decisions made by the professionals who design, manage, and work at eating establishments? How can wait staff and food-preparation workers ensure that diners enjoy their experience in the restaurant's front region?

How do background expectancies influence our conversations? Try Garfinkel's experiment yourself and see how your friends and relatives react.

How might interactional vandalism play out on the Internet? Can we think of ways in which less powerful people engaged in electronic communications undermine the taken-for-granted rules of interaction that are of value to the more powerful? The very existence of the Internet creates spaces in which less powerful people can make their superiors accountable in ways they never were before. Think of all the blogs in which workers talk anonymously about their bosses, or the common situations in which workers forward rude messages from their boss to other employees. Because of the Internet, powerful people are less able to segregate their audiences—treating some people poorly behind the scenes and treating others very nicely in public.

RESPONSE CRIES

Some kinds of utterances are not talk but consist of muttered exclamations, or what Goffman (1981) has called **response cries**. Consider Lucy, who exclaims, "Oops!" after knocking over a glass of water. "Oops!" seems to be merely an uninteresting reflex response to a mishap, rather like blinking your eye when a person moves a hand sharply toward your face. It is not a reflex, however, as shown by the fact that people do not usually make the exclamation when alone. "Oops!" is normally directed toward others present. The exclamation demonstrates to witnesses that the lapse is only minor and momentary, not something that should cast doubt on Lucy's command of her actions.

"Oops!" is used only in situations of minor failure, rather than in major accidents or calamities—which also demonstrates that the exclamation is part of our controlled management of the details of social life. This may all sound very contrived and exaggerated. Why bother to analyze such an inconsequential utterance in this detail? Surely we don't pay as much attention to what we say as this example suggests? Of course we don't—on a conscious level. The crucial point, however, is that we take for granted an immensely complicated, continuous control of our appearance and actions. In situations of interaction, we are never expected just to be present on the scene. Others expect, as we expect of them, that we will display what Goffman calls "controlled alertness." A fundamental part of being human is continually demonstrating to others our competence in the routines of daily life.

PERSONAL SPACE

There are cultural differences in the definition of **personal space**. In Western culture, people usually maintain a distance of at least three feet when engaged in focused interaction with others; when standing side by side, they may stand closer together. In the Middle East, people often stand closer to each other than is thought acceptable in the West. Westerners visiting that part of the world are likely to find themselves disconcerted by this unexpected physical proximity.

Edward T. Hall (1969, 1973), who has worked extensively on nonverbal communication, distinguishes four zones of personal space. *Intimate distance*, of up to one and a half feet, is reserved for very few social contacts. Only those involved in relationships in which regular bodily touching is permitted, such as lovers or parents and children, operate within this zone of private space. *Personal distance*, from one and a half to four feet, is the normal spacing for encounters with friends and close acquaintances. Some intimacy of contact is permitted, but this tends to be strictly limited. *Social distance*, from four to twelve feet, is the zone usually maintained in formal settings such as interviews. The fourth zone is that of *public distance*, beyond twelve feet, preserved by those who are performing to an audience.

response cries • Seemingly involuntary exclamations individuals make when, for example, being taken by surprise, dropping something inadvertently, or expressing pleasure.

personal space • The physical space individuals maintain between themselves and others.

In ordinary interaction, the most fraught zones are those of intimate and personal distance. If these zones are invaded, people try to recapture their space. We may stare at the intruder as if to say, "Move away!" or elbow her aside. When people are forced into proximity closer than they deem desirable, they might create a kind of physical boundary: A reader at a crowded library desk might physically demarcate a private space by stacking books around its edges (Hall 1969, 1973). ✓

CONCEPT CHECKS

1. What is interactional vandalism?
2. Give an example of response cries.
3. What are the four zones of personal space?

HOW DO TIME AND SPACE AFFECT OUR INTERACTIONS?

Understanding how activities are distributed in time and space is fundamental to analyzing encounters and to understanding social life in general. All interaction is situated—it occurs in a particular place and has a specific duration in time. Our actions over the course of a day tend to be "zoned" in time as well as in space. Thus, for example, most people spend a zone—say, from 9:00 A.M. to 5:00 P.M.—of their daily time working. Their weekly time is also zoned: They are likely to work on weekdays and spend weekends at home, altering the pattern of their activities on the weekend days. As we move through the temporal zones of the day, we are also often moving across space as well: To get to work, we may take a bus from one area of a city to another or perhaps commute in from the suburbs. When we analyze the contexts of social interaction, therefore, it is often useful to look at people's movements across **time-space**.

The concept of **regionalization** will help us understand how social life is zoned in time-space. Take the example of a private house. A modern house is regionalized into rooms, hallways, and floors (if there is more than one story). These spaces are not just physically separate areas but are zoned in time as well. The living rooms and kitchen are used most in the daylight hours, the bedrooms at night. The interaction that occurs in these regions is bound by both spatial and temporal divisions. Some areas of the house form back regions, with "performances" taking place in the others. At times, the whole house can become a back region. Once again, this idea is beautifully captured by Goffman (1973):

> On a Sunday morning, a whole household can use the wall around its domestic establishment to conceal a relaxing slovenliness in dress and civil endeavor, extending to all rooms the informality that is usually restricted to kitchen and bedrooms. So, too, in American middle-class neighborhoods, on afternoons the line between children's playground and home may be defined as backstage by mothers, who pass along it wearing jeans, loafers, and a minimum of make-up. . . .

time-space • When and where events occur.

regionalization • The division of social life into different regional settings or zones.

CLOCK TIME

In modern societies, the zoning of our activities is strongly influenced by **clock time**. Without clocks and the precise timing of activities, and their resulting coordination

clock time • Time as measured by the clock, in terms of hours, minutes, and seconds. Before the invention of clocks, time reckoning was based on events in the natural world, such as the rising and setting of the sun.

Online Interaction in China

Just over ten percent of China's population uses the Internet (Fallows 2007). These estimated 137 million Internet users make China second only to the United States in terms of sheer numbers of users. Chinese Internet users are expected to outnumber the online population of the United States within a few years. Even so, there are big differences in who is going online in each country. Currently only 20 percent of people living in Chinese cities use the Internet, most of whom are men under the age of 30. In contrast, in the United States over 70 percent of urban dwellers use the Internet; men and women use the Internet in about equal numbers, and only about a third are younger than 30 years old (Fallows 2007).

As more and more Chinese people start to use the Internet, big changes are expected. The Internet offers opportunities for communication between people who speak different languages. Because the Internet offers a common written system, it is possible for speakers of the multitude of Chinese dialects to communicate with each other. Tools that translate the text on web pages from one language to another can facilitate cross-cultural communication. Such tools make global cyberspace available to Chinese Internet users, while English speakers can gain access to the quickly developing Chinese cyberspace. The rapid growth of Chinese Internet users, however, may reshape all of cyberspace. The dominant language of the Internet is currently English. As more and more Chinese come online and more and more Web pages are written in Chinese, English speakers will have to share cyberspace with Chinese speakers.

The experience of being online in China may be similar to how Internet users interact online in other parts of the world. For instance, Chinese college students, just like their U.S. counterparts, have been drawn to social networking sites. Sites like Xiaonei.com are the Chinese equivalent of Facebook.com and have a similar look and features, such as personal profile pages, blogs, the ability to add friends, photo hosting, groups, and event sharing. Xiaonei.com was recently purchased by a competing social networking site, 5Q.com, in a deal financed in part by a former executive at Amazon.com. The combined social network has over a million participants (Chen 2006). Considering that students make up about a third of China's Internet users, social networking sites are playing an important role in bringing together China's online community. It is also a highly sought-after venue for advertising to the next generation of highly educated Chinese who are poised to take the lead in China's continued transformation into a market economy.

China's rapid economic growth is also taking place in cyberspace, a new frontier for generating profit. Multiplayer online games, such as World of Warcraft and Lineage II, have generated large markets for buying and selling—with real money—virtual currency and other commodities that provide advantages while playing the game. In China, "factories," often called "gold farms,"

across space, industrialized societies could not exist (Mumford 1973). The measuring of time by clocks is today standardized across the globe, making possible the complex international transport systems and communications we now depend on. World standard time was first introduced in 1884 at a conference of nations held in Washington, DC. The globe was then partitioned into twenty-four time zones, one hour apart, and an exact beginning of the universal day was fixed.

Today, virtually all social institutions schedule their activities precisely across the day and week. The greater the number of people and resources involved, the more precise the scheduling must be. Eviatar Zerubavel (1979, 1982) demonstrated this in his study of the temporal structure of a large modern hospital. A hospital must operate on a twenty-four-hour basis, and coordinating the staff and resources is a highly complex matter. For instance, the nurses work for one time period in ward A, another have emerged that hire young people to play massively multiplayer games, exploiting aspects of the game to "farm" valuable items, such as currency, magic spells, equipment, and even whole characters, which are then sold online to players in other parts of the world.

Graduate student researcher at the University of California, San Diego, Ge Jin has found that "China is currently the world factory of virtual commodities" (Jin 2006). Large gold farms are far from virtual: they include dormitories and actual meals, along with alternating 12-hour shifts at the same computer in "mining operations" that run around the clock. Gold farmers receive modest pay, but some farmers are willing to work for free as long as they have a place to live and can play games for free. Gold farms are sometimes referred to as "sweatshops." Jin noted that "gold farms reflect China's current role in global economy, which is mainly a source of cheap labor. The gold farmers are being exploited by farm owners and international brokers. . . . Sitting in front of a computer and killing monsters for 10 hours a day can be detrimental to their health" (Jin 2006).

Still, many gold farmers, who are mostly men in their early 20s, do not have better alternatives, facing unemployment or far worse jobs if they were to leave. At the same time, some of these young men enjoy their work, which they may have played as a hobby before becoming a "professional." Jin concluded that "the game world can be a space of empowerment and com-

pensation for them. In contrast to their impoverished real lives, their virtual lives give them access to power, status and wealth which they can hardly imagine in real life. . . . This is a paradox that the term 'sweatshop' cannot convey: in the gold farms exploitation is entangled with empowerment and productivity is entangled with pleasure" (Jin 2006).

View a short documentary on gold farming by Jin at http://youtube.com/watch?v=ho5Yxe6UVv4

time period in ward B, and so on, and are also called on to alternate between day- and night-shift work. Nurses, doctors, and other staff, plus the resources they need, must be integrated together both in time and in space.

SOCIAL LIFE AND THE ORDERING OF SPACE AND TIME

The Internet is another example of how closely forms of social life are bound up with our control of space and time. The Internet makes it possible for us to interact with people we never see or meet, in any corner of the world. Such technological change rearranges space—we can interact with anyone without moving from our chair. It also alters our experience of time, because communication on the electronic highway is almost immediate. We are so used to being able to switch on the TV and watch the news or make a phone call or send an e-mail message to a friend in another state that it is hard for us to imagine what life would be like otherwise.

THE COMPULSION OF PROXIMITY

In modern societies, we are constantly interacting with others whom we may never see or meet. Almost all of our everyday transactions, such as buying groceries or making a bank deposit, bring us into contact—but indirect contact—with people who may live thousands of miles away. The banking system, for example, is international. Any money you deposit is a small part of the financial investments the bank makes worldwide.

Some people are concerned that the rapid advances in communications technology such as e-mail, the Internet, and e-commerce will only increase this tendency toward indirect interactions. Our society is becoming "devoiced," some claim, as the capabilities of technology grow ever greater. According to this view, as the pace of life accelerates, people are increasingly isolating themselves; we now interact more with our televisions and computers than with our neighbors or members of the community.

Now that e-mail, instant messages, electronic discussion groups, and chat rooms have become facts of life for many people in industrialized countries, it is important to ask, what is the nature of these interactions and what new complexities are emerging from them? One study conducted at Stanford University found that about 20 percent of Internet users use the medium to communicate with people that they do not know (Nie et al. 2004). Another study conducted on 170,000 school-age children found that 50 percent of high school students and 25 percent of those in grades 5 through 8 communicate with strangers on the Internet (National Assessment Center 2006). At the same time, the study found that Internet use reduces face-to-face socializing, TV watching, and sleep. Some researchers conclude that the substitution of e-mail for face-to-face

Cultural norms frequently dictate the acceptable boundaries of personal space. In the Middle East, for example, people frequently stand closer to each other than is common in the West.

communication has led to a weakening of social ties and a disruption of techniques used in personal dialogue for avoiding conflict. Further, online communication seems to allow more room for misinterpretation, confusion, and abuse than more traditional forms of communication (Friedman and Currall 2003). Others counter, however, that social relations continue to thrive even in the face of frequent online communication (Wellman 2008).

Many Internet enthusiasts disagree. They argue that online communication has many inherent advantages that cannot be claimed by more traditional forms of interaction such as the telephone and face-to-face meetings. The human voice, for example, may be far superior in terms of expressing emotion and subtleties of meaning, but it can also convey information about the speaker's age, gender, ethnicity, or social position—information that could be used to the speaker's disadvantage. Electronic communication, it is noted, masks all these identifying markers and ensures that attention focuses strictly on the content of the message. This can be a great advantage for women or other traditionally disadvantaged groups whose opinions are sometimes devalued in other settings (Pascoe 2000). Electronic interaction is often presented as liberating and empowering because people can create their own online identities and speak more freely than they would elsewhere.

Who is right in this debate? How far can electronic communication substitute for face-to-face interaction? Sociologists Deirdre Boden and Harvey Molotch (1994) argue that there is no substitute for face-to-face interaction. They argue further that humans have a true need for personal interaction, which they call the "**compulsion of proximity**." People put themselves out to attend meetings, Boden and Molotch suggest, because situations of copresence provide much richer information about how other people think and feel, and about their sincerity, than any form of electronic communication. Only by actually being in the presence of people who make decisions affecting us in important ways do we feel able to learn what is going on and confident that we can impress them with our own views and our own sincerity. ✓

compulsion of proximity • People's need to interact with others in their presence.

CONCEPT CHECKS ✓

1. How does time structure human life?

2. Is face-to-face interaction, or copresence, an important aspect of human action? Why or why not?

HOW DO THE RULES OF SOCIAL INTERACTION AFFECT YOUR LIFE?

As we saw in Chapter 1, microsociology, the study of everyday behavior in situations of face-to-face interaction, and macrosociology, the study of the broader features of society like race, class, or gender hierarchies, are closely connected. We now examine a social encounter that you may experience frequently—walking down a crowded city sidewalk—to illustrate this point. The ways that you may interact with others on the street are likely shaped by your gender and race.

WOMEN AND MEN IN PUBLIC

Take, for example, a situation that may seem micro on its face: A woman walking down the street is verbally harassed by a group of men. In a study published as *Passing By:*

How has electronic communication transformed social interaction? Why do Molotch and Boden argue that proximity between people matters?

Gender and Public Harassment, Carol Brooks Gardner (1995) found that in various settings, most famously the edges of construction sites, these types of unwanted interaction occur as something women frequently experience as abusive.

Although the harassment of a single woman might be analyzed in microsociological terms by looking at a single interaction, it is not fruitful to view it that simply. Such harassment is typical of street talk involving men and women who are strangers (Gardner 1995). And these kinds of interactions cannot be understood without also looking at the larger background of gender hierarchy in the United States. In this way we can see how microanalysis and macroanalysis are connected. For example, Gardner linked the harassment of women by men to the larger system of gender inequality, represented by male privilege in public spaces, women's physical vulnerability, and the omnipresent threat of rape.

BLACKS AND WHITES IN PUBLIC

Have you ever crossed to the other side of the street when you felt threatened by someone behind you or someone coming toward you? One sociologist who tried to understand simple interactions of this kind is Elijah Anderson.

Anderson began by describing social interaction on the streets of two adjacent urban neighborhoods. In his book *Streetwise: Race, Class, and Change in an Urban Community* (1990), Anderson noted that studying everyday life sheds light on how social order is created by the individual building blocks of infinite micro-level interactions. He was particularly interested in understanding interactions when at least one party was viewed as threatening. Anderson showed that the ways many blacks and whites interact on the streets of a northern city had a great deal to do with the structure of racial stereotypes, which is itself linked to the economic structure of society. In this way, he showed the link between micro interactions and the larger macro structures of society.

Anderson began by recalling Erving Goffman's description of how social roles and statuses come into existence in particular contexts or locations: "When an individual enters the presence of others, they commonly seek to acquire information about him or bring into play information already possessed. Information about the individual helps to define the situation, enabling others to know in advance what he will expect of them and they may expect of him" (Anderson 1990).

Following Goffman's lead, Anderson asked, what types of behavioral cues and signs make up the vocabulary of public interaction? He concluded that the people most likely to pass inspection are those who do not fall into commonly accepted stereotypes of dangerous persons: "children readily pass inspection, while women and white men do so more slowly, black women, black men, and black male teenagers most slowly of all." In showing that interactional tensions derive from outside statuses such as race, class, and gender, Anderson shows that we cannot develop a full understanding of the situation by looking at the micro interactions themselves. This is how he makes the link between micro interactions and macro processes.

Anderson argues that people are streetwise when they develop skills such as "the art of avoidance" to deal with their felt vulnerability to violence and crime. According to Anderson, whites who are not streetwise do not recognize the difference between different kinds of black men (e.g., middle-class youths vs. gang members). They may also not know how to alter the number of paces to walk behind a suspicious

CONCEPT CHECKS ✓

1. How would sociologists explain the street harassment that women often experience?

2. How would sociologist Elijah Anderson define "streetwise"?

person or how to bypass bad blocks at various times of day. In these ways, social science research can help you to understand how a very ordinary behavior—navigating one's way through the city streets—reveals important lessons about the nature of social interaction today. ✓

NEED HELP STUDYING?

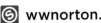 **wwnorton.com/studyspace**

Visit StudySpace to access free review materials such as:

- Vocabulary Flashcards
- Diagnostic Review Quizzes
- Study Outlines

REVIEW QUESTIONS

1. Why is it important to study microsociology?
2. According to Goffman, why do people cooperate in impression management?
3. Briefly define "social role" and provide an example from your own life that illustrates how social roles change in different contexts.
4. How can the desire for audience segregation be frustrated by e-mail communication?
5. Why are shared meanings a central concern of ethnomethodology?
6. What is conversation analysis?
7. How is the Internet reshaping our "compulsion of proximity"?
8. What does it mean to say that social life is "zoned in time-space," and how is that changing because of the Internet?
9. Why is it important to link microsociological analysis to macrosociological analysis? Give an example.

THINKING SOCIOLOGICALLY EXERCISES

1. Identify the elements important to the dramaturgical perspective. This chapter shows how the theory might be used to understand interactions between customers and service providers, for example. How would you apply the theory to account for a plumber's visit to a client's home?
2. Smoking cigarettes is a pervasive habit found in many parts of the world and a habit that could be explained by both microsociological and macrosociological forces. Give an example of each that would be relevant to explain the proliferation of smoking. How might your suggested micro- and macro-level analyses be linked?

5 Groups, Networks, and Organizations

THE BIG QUESTIONS

WHAT ARE SOCIAL GROUPS?

Learn the variety and characteristics of groups, as well as the effect of groups on an individual's behavior.

HOW DO WE BENEFIT FROM SOCIAL NETWORKS?

Understand the importance of social networks and the advantages they confer on some people.

HOW DO ORGANIZATIONS FUNCTION?

Know how to define an organization and understand how organizations developed over the last two centuries. Learn Max Weber's theory of organizations and view of bureaucracy.

IS BUREAUCRACY AN OUTDATED MODEL?

Familiarize yourself with some of the alternatives to bureaucracy that have developed in other societies or in recent times. Think about the influence of technology on how organizations operate.

HOW DO GROUPS AND ORGANIZATIONS AFFECT YOUR LIFE?

Learn how social capital enables people to accomplish their goals and expand their influence.

The U.S. Military Academy—West Point—is very hard to get into. More than fifty thousand high school students make inquiries about applying to the academy, of which perhaps twelve thousand are sufficiently qualified to actually apply. Another four thousand are nominated by their congressional representative or U.S. senator or by the White House. Yet among all of these, barely two thousand pass the physical fitness test, and only twelve hundred are finally admitted. Many of these are top students: Their "median grade point average is 3.5; 14 percent are Eagle Scouts, 20 percent are class presidents, 60 percent are varsity team captains" (Lipsky 2003a).

From Reception Day, students' first day at West Point, the academy emphasizes conformity to group norms. The first-year "plebes," as they are called, say good-bye to their civilian life, giving up all aspects of their former identity to the army:

At R-Day [Reception Day] you surrender your old self in stages. You've already left behind family and control over your environment. In the fluorescent Thayer hallways, you hand over your belongings, then file to the treasurers' office to give up your cash; any sum greater than forty dollars gets banked. . . . "No talking," a cadre announces. "Do not move, do not smile. Hands will remain cupped at all times. You need to look at anything, look at my wall." Unless you had an unlucky home life, this is the first time anybody has spoken to you this way. The candidates are just blank eyes now, mouths so tight the lips appear to be hiding. . . . Now the army demands your clothing. In their dressing room, male candidates tuck on black gym shorts and white T-shirts with a speed that suggests grade events. "You *must* put on a jockstrap," a TAC-NGO commands. "Let's go—move with a purpose. . . ." Then the academy takes custody of your actual skin. "If you have," the sergeant booms, "any tattoo, brand, or body piercing, regardless of whether it is visible while wearing a uniform, you must declare it at this time to the registration desk at my rear. . . ." Then the army takes your hair. . . . Now you're shorn of everything. You look, act, dress like everyone beside you, maybe for the first time in your life. (Lipsky 2003a)

David Lipsky was a writer for *Rolling Stone* magazine in 1998. He specialized in stories about youth culture—young people in colleges and universities, the media, TV actors, movie stars—when he was asked to write an article on the West Point class of 2002. Lipsky had been raised in a liberal family and held a dim view of the military profession. Although he initially was resistant to taking the assignment, once the academy gave him unrestricted access to the cadets he immersed himself in the project, and wound up staying the full four years. In his words, he wanted "to find out what kind of men and women would subject themselves to the intense discipline of West Point" (Lipsky 2003a).

What he found was "a place where everyone tried their hardest. A place where everybody—or at least most people—looked out for each other. . . . Of all the young people I'd met, the West Point cadets—although they are grand, epic complainers—were the happiest" (Lipsky 2003a). Part of the reason, Lipsky concluded, was the military value system, one that emphasized self-sacrifice, discipline, honor, respect, and loyalty: "One of the efficient byproducts of plebe-year stress is what's called *unit cohesion*, the bonds that cadets form. In battle, what often drives soldiers isn't simply courage but a complicated version of crisis loyalty, the desire not to let down their friends." West Point cohesion is so strong that cadets seldom betray one another, even when they know that rules are being broken.

Military discipline depends on such values as group loyalty and conformity. After all, some day a soldier's life may depend on such values. And the strict training regimen of military academies such as West Point is designed to foster these values—to create uniform ways of thinking and acting among young people raised in a culture that presumably emphasizes the very opposite. "We are a culture that stresses individually pleasing yourself. What surprised me, getting to know the officers and getting to know the cadets who love the army, is that often the best way to please yourself individually is to live that other way. We're group animals. There's a part of us that really responds to meeting challenges together" (Lipsky 2003b).

In this chapter we examine the ways in which all of us—not just cadets at West Point—are group animals. We will consider different kinds of groups, the ways group size affects our behavior in groups, and the nature of leadership. We will see how group norms promote conformity, often to disastrous ends. We also examine the role played by organizations in American society, the major theories of modern organizations, and the ways in which organizations are changing in the modern world. The increased effect of technology on organizations and the prominence of the Internet in our group life is also explored. The chapter concludes by discussing the debate over declines in social capital and social engagement in the United States today.

WHAT ARE SOCIAL GROUPS?

Nearly all of our important interactions occur through some type of social group. You and your roommate make up a social group, as do the members of your introductory sociology class. A **social group** is a collection of people who share a common identity and regularly interact with one another on the basis of shared expectations concerning behavior. People who belong to the same social group identify with each other, expect each other to conform to certain ways of thinking and acting, and recognize the boundaries that separate them from other groups or people.

social group • A collection of people who regularly interact with one another on the basis of shared expectations concerning behavior and who share a sense of common identity.

GROUPS: VARIETY AND CHARACTERISTICS

Every day nearly all of us participate in groups and group activities. We hang out with groups of friends, study with classmates, eat dinner with family members, play team sports, and go online to find new friends or people who share our interests (Aldrich and Marsden 1988).

However, just being in each other's company does not make a collection of individuals a social group. People milling around in crowds or strolling on a beach are said to make up a social aggregate. A **social aggregate** is a simple collection of people who happen to be together in a particular place but do not significantly interact or identify with each other. People waiting together at a bus station, for example, may be conscious of one another's presence, but they are unlikely to think of themselves as a "we"—the group waiting for the next bus to Poughkeepsie or Des Moines. By the same token, people may comprise a **social category**, sharing a common characteristic

social aggregate • A collection of people who happen to be together in a particular place but do not significantly interact or identify with one another.

social category • People who share a common characteristic (such as gender or occupation) but do not necessarily interact or identify with one another.

What makes the people on the left a social aggregate and the people on the right a social group?

(such as gender or occupation), without necessarily interacting or identifying with one another. The sense of belonging to a common social group is missing.

IN-GROUPS AND OUT-GROUPS

in-group • A group toward which one feels particular loyalty and respect—the group to which "we" belong.

out-group • A group toward which one feels antagonism and contempt—"those people."

In-groups are groups toward which one feels particular loyalty and respect—the groups that "we" belong to. **Out-groups**, on the other hand, are groups toward which one feels antagonism and contempt—"those people." The "sense of belonging" among members of the in-group is sometimes strengthened by the group's scorning the members of other groups (Sartre 1965; orig. 1948). Creating a sense of belonging in this way is especially true of racist groups, which promote their identity as "superior" by hating "inferior" groups. Jews, Catholics, African Americans, immigrants, and gay people historically have been the targets of such hatred in the United States.

Most people occasionally use in-group–out-group imagery to trumpet what they believe to be their group's strengths vis-à-vis some other group's presumed weaknesses. For example, members of a fraternity or a sorority may bolster their feelings of superiority—in academics, sports, or campus image—by ridiculing the members of a different house. Similarly, a church may hold up its "truths" as the only ones, while native-born Americans may accuse immigrants—always outsiders upon arriving in a new country—as ruining the country for "real Americans."

PRIMARY AND SECONDARY GROUPS

primary group • A group that is characterized by intense emotional ties, face-to-face interaction, intimacy, and a strong, enduring sense of commitment.

Our lives and personalities are molded by our earliest experiences in **primary groups**—namely, our families, our peers, and our friends. Primary groups are small groups characterized by face-to-face interaction, intimacy, and a strong, enduring sense of commitment. There is also often an experience of unity, a merging of the self with the group into one personal "we." Sociologist Charles Horton Cooley (1864–1929) termed such groups "primary" because he believed that they were the basic form of association, exerting a long-lasting influence on the development of our social selves (Cooley 1964; orig. 1902).

secondary group • A group characterized by its large size and by impersonal, fleeting relationships.

Secondary groups, by contrast, are large, impersonal, and often involve fleeting relationships. Secondary groups seldom involve intense emotional ties, powerful commitments to the group itself, or a feeling of unity. We seldom feel we can "be ourselves" in a secondary group; rather, we are often playing a particular role, such as employee or student. Cooley argued that while people belong to primary groups mainly because such groups are inherently fulfilling, people join secondary groups to achieve some specific goal: to earn a living, get a college degree, or compete in sports. Examples of secondary groups include business organizations, schools, work groups, athletic clubs, and governmental bodies. Secondary groups may become primary groups for some of their members. For example, when coworkers begin to socialize after hours, they create bonds of friendship that constitute a primary group.

For most of human history, nearly all interactions took place within primary groups. This pattern began to change with the emergence of larger, agrarian societies, which included such secondary groups as those based on governmental roles or occupation. Some early sociologists, such as Cooley, worried about a loss of intimacy as more and more interactions revolved around large impersonal organizations. However, what Cooley saw as the growing anonymity of modern life may also offer an increasing tolerance of individual differences. Primary groups, which often enforce strict conformity to group standards (Durkheim 1964; orig. 1893; Simmel 1955), can be stifling. Secondary groups, by contrast, are more likely than primary groups to be concerned with accomplishing a task, rather than with enforcing conformity to group standards of behavior.

REFERENCE GROUPS

We often judge ourselves by how we think we appear to others, which Cooley termed the "looking-glass self." Robert K. Merton (1968; orig. 1938) elaborated on Cooley's concept by discussing reference groups as a standard by which we evaluate ourselves. A **reference group** is a group that provides a standard for judging one's own attitudes or behaviors (see also Hyman and Singer 1968). The family, peers, classmates, and coworkers are crucial reference groups. However, you do not have to belong to a group for it to be your reference group. For example, young people living thousands of miles away from the bright lights of Hollywood may still compare their looks and fashion choices with their favorite celebrity. Although most of us seldom interact socially with such reference groups as these, we may take pride in identifying with them, and even imitate the ways of those people who do belong to them. This is why it is critical for children—minority children in particular, whose groups are often represented in the media using negative stereotypes—to be exposed to reference groups that will shape their lives for the better.

reference group • A group that provides a standard for judging one's attitudes or behaviors.

THE EFFECTS OF SIZE

Another significant way in which groups differ has to do with their size. Sociological interest in group size can be traced to the German sociologist Georg Simmel (1858–1918), who studied and theorized about the impact of small groups on people's behavior. Since Simmel's time, small-group researchers have conducted a number of laboratory experiments to examine the effects of size on both the quality of interaction in the group and the effectiveness of the group in accomplishing certain tasks (Bales 1953, 1970; Hare et al. 1965; Homans 1950; Mills 1967).

Advertising creates a set of imaginary reference groups meant to influence consumers' buying habits by presenting unlikely—often impossible—ideals to which consumers aspire.

Figure 5.1 | Dyads

The larger the number of people, the greater the possible number of relationships. Note that this figure illustrates only dyads; if triads and more complex coalitions were to be included, the numbers would be still greater (four people yield ten possibilities).

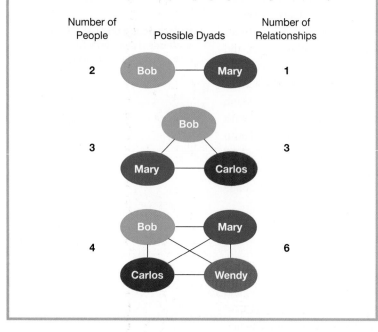

Number of People | Possible Dyads | Number of Relationships

2 — Bob — Mary — 1

3 — Bob, Mary, Carlos — 3

4 — Bob, Mary, Carlos, Wendy — 6

dyad • A group consisting of two persons.

triad • A group consisting of three persons.

DYADS

The simplest group, which Simmel (1955) called a **dyad**, consists of two persons. Simmel reasoned that dyads, which involve both intimacy and conflict, are likely to be simultaneously intense and unstable. To survive, they require the full attention and cooperation of both parties. If one person withdraws from the dyad, it vanishes. Dyads are typically the source of our most elementary social bonds, often constituting the group in which we are most likely to share our deepest secrets. But dyads can be very fragile. That is why, Simmel believed, a variety of cultural and legal supports for marriage are found in societies where marriage is regarded as an important source of social stability.

TRIADS

Triads, or three-person groups, are more stable than dyads according to Simmel, since the third person relieves some of the pressure on the other two to always get along and energize the relationship. In a triad, one person can temporarily withdraw attention from the relationship without necessarily threatening it. In addition, if two of the members have a disagreement, the third can play the role of mediator, as when you try to patch up a falling-out between two of your friends. Yet triads are not without potential problems. Alliances (sometimes termed "coalitions") may form between two members of a triad, enabling them to gang up on the third and thereby destabilize the group.

LARGER GROUPS

Simmel identified an important aspect of groups: As group size increases, their intensity decreases, while their stability and exclusivity increase. Larger groups have less intense interactions, simply because a larger number of potential smaller group relationships exist as outlets for individuals who are not getting along with other members of the group. In a dyad, only a single relationship between two people is possible; in a triad, three different two-person relationships can occur. In a ten-person group, the number of possible two-person relationships explodes to forty-five! When one relationship doesn't work out to your liking, you can easily move on to another, as you probably often do at large parties.

Large groups also tend to be more stable than smaller ones because the withdrawal of some members usually does not threaten the group's survival. A marriage or love relationship falls apart if one person leaves, whereas an athletic team or drama club routinely survives—though it may sometimes temporarily suffer from—the loss of its graduating seniors. Larger groups also tend to be more exclusive, since it is easier for their members to limit their social relationships to the group itself and avoid relationships with nonmembers.

Beyond a certain size, perhaps a dozen people, groups tend to develop a formal structure. Formal leadership roles may arise, such as president or secretary, and official rules may be developed to govern what the group does. We discuss formal organizations later in this chapter.

TYPES OF LEADERSHIP

A **leader** is a person who is able to influence the behavior of other members of a group. All groups have leaders, even if the leader is not formally recognized as such. Some leaders are especially effective in motivating group members, inspiring them to achievements that might not ordinarily be accomplished. Such **transformational leaders** go beyond the merely routine, instilling in the members of their group a sense of mission or higher purpose and thereby changing the nature of the group itself (Burns 1978; Kanter 1983). They can also be a vital inspiration for social change in the world. For example, Nelson Mandela, the South African leader who spent twenty-seven years in prison, successfully led his African National Congress (ANC) party into overthrowing South Africa's system of *apartheid*, or racial segregation. He was later elected president—leader—of the entire country.

Most leaders are not as visionary as Mandela, however. Leaders who simply get the job done are termed **transactional leaders.** They are concerned with accomplishing the group's tasks, getting group members to do their jobs, and ensuring that the group achieves its goals. Transactional leadership is routine leadership. For example, the teacher who simply gets through the lesson plan each day—rather than making the classroom a place where students explore new ways of thinking and behaving—is exercising transactional leadership.

leader • A person who is able to influence the behavior of other members of a group.

transformational leader • A leader who is able to instill in the members of a group a sense of mission or higher purpose, thereby changing the nature of the group itself.

transactional leader • A leader who is concerned with accomplishing the group's tasks, getting group members to do their jobs, and making certain that the group achieves its goals.

CONFORMITY

Pressures to conform to the latest styles are especially strong among teenagers and young adults, among whom the need for group acceptance is often acute. While wearing navel rings or the latest style of jeans—or rigidly conforming to the military code of West Point—may seem relatively harmless, conformity to group pressure can also lead to extremely destructive behavior, such as drug abuse, or even murder. For this reason, sociologists and social psychologists have long sought to understand why most people tend to go along with others, and under what circumstances they do not.

GOING ALONG WITH THE GROUP: ASCH'S RESEARCH

More than fifty years ago, psychologist Solomon Asch (1952) conducted some of the most influential studies of conformity to group pressures. In one of his classic

Would you define Nelson Mandela as a transformational leader? Why?

Figure 5.2 | The Asch Task

In the Asch task, participants were shown a standard line (left) and then three comparison lines. Their task was simply to say which of the three lines matched the standard. When confederates gave false answers first, one third of participants conformed by also giving the wrong answer.

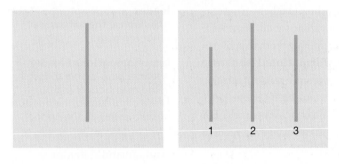

experiments, Asch asked individual subjects to decide which of three lines of different length most closely matched the length of a fourth line. The differences were obvious; subjects had no difficulty in making the correct match. Asch then arranged a version of the experiment in which the subjects were asked to make the matches in a group setting, with each person calling out the answer in turn. In this setting, all but one of the subjects were actually Asch's secret accomplices, and these accomplices all practiced a deception on that one true subject. Each accomplice picked a line as a match that was clearly unequal to the fourth line. The unwitting subject, one of the last to call out an answer, felt enormous group pressure to make the same error. Amazingly, at least half of the times the experiment was conducted, one third of these subjects gave the same wrong answer as the others in the group. They sometimes stammered and fidgeted when doing so, but they nonetheless yielded to the unspoken pressure to conform to the group's decision. Asch's experiments clearly showed that many people are willing to go along with the group consensus, even if they believe it is incorrect.

OBEDIENCE TO AUTHORITY: MILGRAM'S RESEARCH

Another classic study of conformity was conducted by Stanley Milgram (1963). Milgram wanted to see how far a person would go when ordered by a scientist to give another person increasingly powerful electric shocks. He did so by setting up an experiment that he told the subjects was about memorizing pairs of words. In reality, it was about obedience to authority.

The male subjects who volunteered for the study were supposedly randomly divided into "teachers" and "learners." In fact, the learners were actually Milgram's confederates. The teacher was told to read pairs of words from a list that the learner was to memorize. Whenever the learner made a mistake, the teacher was to give him an electric shock by flipping a switch on a fake but official-looking machine. The control board on the machine indicated shock levels ranging from "15 volts—slight shock" to "450 volts—danger, severe shock." For each mistake, the voltage of the shock was to be increased, until it eventually reached the highest level. As the experiment progressed, the learner began to scream out in pain for the teacher to stop delivering shocks. Milgram's assistant, who was administering the experiment, exercised his authority as a scientist and ordered the teacher to continue administering shocks if the teacher tried to quit. (In reality, the learner, who was usually carefully concealed from the teacher by a screen, never received any electric shocks, and his "screams" had actually been prerecorded on a tape.)

The teacher was confronted with a major moral decision: Should he obey the scientist and go along with the experiment, even if it meant injuring another human being? Much to Milgram's surprise, over half the subjects in the study kept on administering electric shocks. They continued even until the maximum voltage was reached and the learner's screams had subsided into an eerie silence as he presumably died of a heart attack. How could ordinary people so easily conform to orders that would turn them into possible accomplices to murder?

The answer, Milgram found, was deceptively simple: ordinary citizens will conform to orders given by someone in a position of power or authority—even if those orders have horrible consequences. From this, we can learn something about Nazi atrocities during World War II, which were Milgram's original concern. Many ordinary Germans who participated in the mass execution of Jews in Nazi concentration camps did so on the grounds that they were "just following orders." Milgram's research has sobering implications for anyone who thinks that only "others" will always knuckle under to authority, but "not me" (Zimbardo et al. 1977).

GROUPTHINK AND GROUP PRESSURES TO CONFORM: JANIS'S RESEARCH

The pressure to conform to group opinions may occasionally lead to bad decisions, rather than creative new solutions to problems. Irving L. Janis (1972, 1989; Janis and Mann 1977) called this phenomenon **groupthink**, a process by which the members of a group ignore those ideas, suggestions, and plans of action that go against the group consensus. Groupthink may embarrass potential dissenters into conforming, and may also produce a shift in perceptions so that alternative possibilities are ruled out without being seriously considered. Groupthink may facilitate reaching a quick consensus, but the consensus may also be ill chosen. It may even be downright dangerous.

groupthink • A process by which the members of a group ignore ways of thinking and plans of action that go against the group consensus.

Janis engaged in historical research to see if groupthink had characterized U.S. foreign policy decisions. He examined several critical decisions, including that behind the infamous Bay of Pigs invasion of Cuba in 1961. John F. Kennedy, then the newly elected president, inherited a plan from the previous administration to help Cuban exiles liberate Cuba from the Communist government of Fidel Castro. The plan called for U.S. supplies and air cover to assist an invasion by an ill-prepared army of exiles at Cuba's Bay of Pigs. Although a number of Kennedy's top advisers were certain that the plan was fatally flawed, they refrained from bucking the emerging consensus to carry it out. As history now shows, the invasion was a disaster. The army of exiles, after parachuting into a swamp nowhere near their intended drop zone, was immediately defeated, and Kennedy suffered a great deal of public embarrassment.

Kennedy's advisers were smart, strong willed, and well educated. How could they have failed to voice their concerns about the proposed invasion? Janis identified a

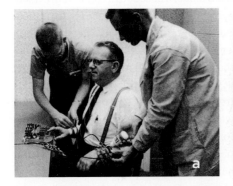  

(a) The Milgram experiment required participants to "shock" the confederate learner (seated). The research participant (left) helped apply the electrodes that would be used to shock the learner. (b) An obedient participant shocks the learner in the "touch" condition. Fewer than one third obeyed the experimenter in this condition. (c) After the experiment, all of the participants were introduced to the confederate learner so they could see he was not actually harmed.

CONCEPT CHECKS ✓

1. What is the difference between social aggregates and social groups? Give examples that illustrate this difference.

2. Describe the main characteristics of primary and secondary groups.

3. When groups become large, why does their intensity decrease but their stability increase?

4. What is groupthink? How can it be used to explain why some decisions made by a group can lead to negative consequences?

number of possible reasons. First, the advisers were hesitant to disagree with the president lest they lose his favor. Second, they also did not want to diminish group harmony in a crisis situation where teamwork was all-important. Third, they faced intense time pressures and had little opportunity to consult outside experts who might have offered radically different perspectives. All these circumstances contributed to a single-minded pursuit of the president's initial ideas, rather than an effort to generate effective alternatives. To avoid groupthink, the group must ensure the full and open expression of all opinions, even strong dissent. ✓

HOW DO WE BENEFIT FROM SOCIAL NETWORKS?

network • A set of informal and formal social ties that links people to each other.

"Who you know is often as important as what you know." This adage expresses the value of having "good connections." Sociologists refer to such connections as **networks**—all the direct and indirect connections that link a person or a group with other people or groups. Your personal networks thus include people you know directly (such as your friends) as well as people you know indirectly (such as your friends' friends). The groups and organizations you belong to also may be networked. For example, all the chapters of Gamma Phi Beta or Hillel are linked, thus connecting members to like-minded individuals throughout the United States and the world.

Networks serve us in many ways. You are likely to rely on your networks for a broad range of contacts, from obtaining access to your congressperson or senator to finding a date for Saturday night. Sociologist Mark Granovetter (1973) demonstrated that there can be enormous strength in weak ties, particularly among higher socioeconomic groups. Upper-level professional and managerial employees are likely to hear about new jobs through connections such as distant relatives or remote acquaintances. Such weak ties can be of great benefit because relatives or acquaintances tend to have very different sets of connections from one's closer friends, whose social contacts are likely to be similar to one's own. Among lower socioeconomic groups, Granovetter argued, weak ties are not necessarily bridges to other networks and so do not really widen one's opportunities (see also Knoke 1990; Marsden and Lin 1982; Wellman et al. 1988). After graduation from college, you may rely on good grades and a strong résumé to find a job. But it may prove beneficial if it happens that your second cousin went to school with a top person in the organization where you are seeking work.

Most people rely on their personal networks to gain advantages, but not everyone has equal access to powerful networks. Some sociologists argue, for example, that women's business, professional, and political networks are fewer and weaker than men's, so that women's power in these spheres is reduced (Brass 1985). Yet as more and more women move up into higher-level occupational and political positions, the resulting networks can foster further advancement. One study found that women are more likely to be hired or promoted into job levels that already have a high proportion of women (Cohen et al. 1998).

THE INTERNET AS SOCIAL NETWORK

Our opportunities to belong to and access social networks have skyrocketed in recent years, due to the Internet. Until the early 1990s, when the World Wide Web was developed, there were few Internet users outside of university and scientific communities. By 2008, however, an estimated 251.3 million Americans were using the Internet (Internet World Stats 2009a), and on any given day in the United States, an average of 181 million people are online (Pew 2009b). With such rapid communication and global reach, it is now possible to radically extend one's personal networks. The Internet is especially useful for networking with like-minded people on specific issues, such as politics, business, hobbies, or romance (Southwick 1996; Wellman et al. 1996). It also enables people who might otherwise lack contact with others to become part of global networks. For example, shut-ins can join chat rooms to share common interests, people in small rural communities can now engage in "distance learning" through courses that are offered on the Web, and long-lost high school friends can reconnect via Facebook.

The Internet fosters the creation of new relationships, often without the emotional and social baggage or constraints that go along with face-to-face encounters. In the absence of the usual physical and social cues, such as skin color or residential address, people can get together electronically on the basis of shared interests rather than similar social characteristics. Such factors as social position, wealth, race, ethnicity, gender, and physical disability are less likely to cloud the social interaction (Coate 1994; Jones 1995; Kollock and Smith 1996). In fact, new technologies like Twitter allow people from all walks of life to catch glimpses into the lives of celebrities (as well as non-celebs) by subscribing to their "tweets" or regular reports of their thoughts and activities.

One limitation of Internet-based social networks is that not everyone has equal access to the Internet. Lower income persons and ethnic minorities are less likely than wealthier persons and whites to have Internet access. However, the "digital divide" has narrowed in recent years, and cyberspace is among the most egalitarian planes of social interaction (Nielsen Media Research 2001a, 2001b; Pew Research 2005). In the words of one recent study that tracked Internet use among different socioeconomic groups, "The Internet was, at first, an elitist country club reserved only for individuals with select financial abilities and technical skills. . . . Now, nearly every socioeconomic group is aggressively adopting the Web" (Nielsen Media Research 2001b). This pattern is not limited to the United States; rates of Internet use are creeping up throughout the world, enabling individuals to connect with anyone in the world who shares their interests. ✓

CONCEPT CHECKS ✓

1. According to Granovetter, what are the benefits of weak ties? Why?

2. How do men's and women's weak ties differ?

HOW DO ORGANIZATIONS FUNCTION?

People frequently band together to pursue activities that they could not otherwise accomplish by themselves. A principal means for accomplishing such cooperative actions is the **organization**, a group with an identifiable membership that engages

organization • A large group of individuals with a definite set of authority relations. Many types of organizations exist in industrialized societies, influencing most aspects of our lives. While not all organizations are bureaucratic, there are close links between the development of organizations and bureaucratic tendencies.

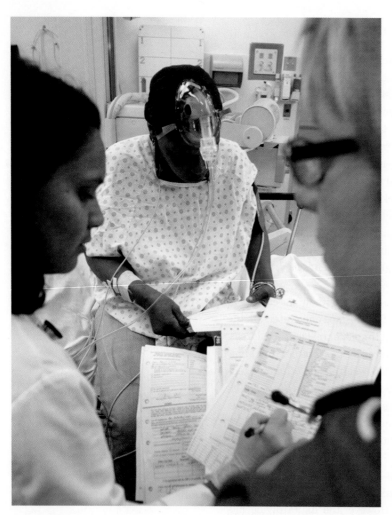

A woman suffering from severe asthma fills out paperwork in an emergency room at San Francisco General Hospital. Modern hospitals are complex organizations with impersonal structures and procedures—but they are designed for a personal outcome.

in concerted collective actions to achieve a common purpose (Aldrich and Marsden 1988). An organization can be a small primary group, but it is more likely to be a larger, secondary one: Universities, religious bodies, and business corporations are all examples of organizations. Such organizations are a central feature of all societies, and their study is a core concern of sociology today.

Organizations tend to be highly formal in modern industrial and postindustrial societies. A **formal organization** is rationally designed to achieve its objectives, often by means of explicit rules, regulations, and procedures. As Max Weber (1979; orig. 1921) first recognized almost a century ago, there has been a long-term trend in Europe and North America toward formal organizations. This rise of formality in organizations is in part the result of the fact that formality is often a requirement for legal standing. For a college or university to be legally accredited, for example, it must satisfy explicit written standards governing everything from grading policy to faculty performance to fire safety. Today, formal organizations are the dominant form of organization throughout the entire world.

It is easy to see why organizations are so important to us today. In the premodern world, families, close relatives, and neighbors provided for most needs—food, the instruction of children, work, and leisure-time activities. In modern times, the mass of the population is much more interdependent than was ever the case before. Many of our requirements are supplied by people we never meet and who indeed might live many thousands of miles away. A substantial amount of coordination of activities and resources—which organizations provide—is needed in such circumstances. A downside, however, is that organizations take things out of our own hands and put them under the control of officials or experts over whom we have little influence. For instance, we are all required to do certain things the government tells us to do—pay taxes, abide by laws, go off to fight wars—or face punishment.

THEORIES OF ORGANIZATIONS

Max Weber developed the first systematic interpretation of the rise of modern organizations. Organizations, he argued, are ways of coordinating the activities of human beings, or the goods they produce, in a stable manner across space and time. Weber emphasized that the development of organizations depends on the control of information, and he stressed the central importance of writing in this process: An organization needs written rules for its functioning and files in which its "memory" is stored. Weber saw organizations as strongly hierarchical, with power tending to be concentrated at the top. Was Weber right? If he was, it matters a great deal to us all. For Weber detected

formal organization • Means by which a group is rationally designed to achieve its objectives, often using explicit rules, regulations, and procedures.

a clash as well as a connection between modern organizations and democracy that he believed had far-reaching consequences for social life.

BUREAUCRACY

All large-scale organizations, according to Weber, tend to be bureaucratic in nature. The word *bureaucracy* was coined by Monsieur de Gournay in 1745, who combined the word *bureau*, meaning both an office and a writing table, with the suffix *cracy*, derived from the Greek verb meaning "to rule." **Bureaucracy** is thus the rule of officials. The term was first applied only to government officials, but it gradually was extended to refer to large organizations in general. Perceptions of "bureaucracy" range from highly negative—fraught with red tape, inefficiency, and wastefulness—to quite positive—a model of carefulness, precision, and effective administration.

Weber's account of bureaucracy steers between these two extremes. He argued that the expansion of bureaucracy is inevitable in modern societies; bureaucratic authority is the only way of coping with the administrative requirements of large-scale social systems. Yet he also conceded that bureaucracy exhibits a number of major failings that have important implications for the nature of modern social life.

To study the origins and nature of the expansion of bureaucratic organizations, Weber constructed an ideal type of bureaucracy. (*Ideal* here refers not to what is most desirable, but to a pure form of bureaucratic organization. An **ideal type** is an abstract description constructed by accentuating certain features of real cases so as to pinpoint their most essential characteristics.) Weber (1979; orig. 1921) listed several characteristics of the ideal type of bureaucracy:

1. **A clear-cut hierarchy of authority, such that tasks in the organization are distributed as "official duties."** Each higher office controls and supervises the one below it in the hierarchy, thus making coordinated decision making possible.

2. **Written rules govern the conduct of officials at all levels of the organization.** The higher the office, the more the rules tend to encompass a wide variety of cases and demand flexibility in their interpretation.

3. **Officials are full time and salaried.** Each job in the hierarchy has a definite and fixed salary attached to it. Promotion is possible on the basis of capability, seniority, or a mixture of the two.

4. **There is a separation between the tasks of an official within the organization and his life outside.**

5. **No members of the organization own the material resources with which they operate.** The development of bureaucracy, according to Weber, separates workers from the control of their means of production; officials do not own the offices they work in, the desks they sit at, or the office machinery they use.

Weber believed that the more an organization approaches the ideal type of bureaucracy, the more effective it will be in pursuing the objectives for which it was established. Yet he recognized that bureaucracy could be inefficient and accepted that many bureaucratic jobs are dull, offering little opportunity for the exercise of creative capabilities. While Weber feared that the bureaucratization of society could have negative consequences, he concluded that bureaucratic routine and the authority of officialdom over our lives are prices we pay for the technical effectiveness of bureaucratic

bureaucracy • A type of organization marked by a clear hierarchy of authority and the existence of written rules of procedure and staffed by full-time, salaried officials.

ideal type • A "pure type," constructed by emphasizing certain traits of a social item that do not necessarily exist in reality. An example is Max Weber's ideal type of bureaucratic organization.

organizations. Since Weber's time, the bureaucratization of society has become more widespread. Critics of this development who share Weber's initial concerns have questioned whether the efficiency of rational organizations comes at a price greater than Weber could have imagined. The most prominent of these critiques refers to "the McDonaldization of society," discussed later in this chapter.

FORMAL AND INFORMAL RELATIONS WITHIN BUREAUCRACIES

formal relations • Relations that exist in groups and organizations, laid down by the norms, or rules, of the official system of authority.

Weber's analysis of bureaucracy gave prime place to **formal relations** within organizations, the relations between people as stated in the rules of the organization. Weber had little to say about the informal connections and small-group relations that may exist in all organizations. But in bureaucracies, informal ways of doing things often allow for a flexibility that couldn't otherwise be achieved.

informal networks • Relations that exist in groups and organizations developed on the basis of personal connections; ways of doing things that depart from formally recognized modes of procedure.

Informal networks tend to develop at all levels of organizations. At the very top, personal ties and connections may be more important than the formal situations in which decisions are supposed to be made. For example, meetings of boards of directors and shareholders supposedly determine the policies of business corporations. In practice, a few members of the board often really run the corporation, making their decisions informally and expecting the board to approve them. Informal networks of this sort can also stretch across different corporations. Business leaders from different firms frequently consult one another in an informal way and may belong to the same clubs and leisure-time associations.

John Meyer and Brian Rowan (1977) argue that formal rules and procedures in organizations are usually quite distant from the practices actually adopted by the organizations' members. Formal rules, in their view, are often "myths" that people profess to follow but that have little substance in reality. They serve to legitimate—to justify—ways in which tasks are carried out, even while these ways may diverge greatly from how things are supposed to be done, according to the rules.

Deciding how far informal procedures generally help or hinder the effectiveness of organizations is not a simple matter. Systems that resemble Weber's ideal type tend to give rise to a forest of unofficial ways of doing things. This is partly because the flexibility that is lacking ends up being achieved by unofficial tinkering with formal rules. For those in dull jobs, informal procedures often also help to create a more satisfying work environment. Informal connections between officials in higher positions may be effective in ways that aid the organization as a whole. On the other hand, these officials may be more concerned about advancing or protecting their own interests than furthering those of the overall organization.

THE DYSFUNCTIONS OF BUREAUCRACY

Robert Merton (1957), a functionalist scholar, observed that several elements inherent in bureaucracy could lead to harmful consequences for the smooth functioning of the bureaucracy itself—or "dysfunctions of bureaucracy." Merton noted that bureaucrats are trained to rely strictly on written rules and procedures. They are not encouraged to be flexible, to use their own judgment in making decisions, or to seek creative solutions; bureaucracy is about managing cases according to a set of objective criteria.

Merton also noted that adherence to the bureaucratic rules could eventually take precedence over the underlying organizational goals. Moreover, bureaucracies often do not adequately address cases that need special treatment and consideration. Because so much emphasis is placed on the correct procedure, it is possible to lose sight of the big picture. A bureaucrat responsible for processing insurance claims, for example, might refuse to compensate a policyholder for legitimate damages, citing the absence of a form, or a form being completed incorrectly.

BUREAUCRACY AND DEMOCRACY

The diminishing of democracy with the advance of modern forms of organization was another problem that worried Weber a great deal (see also Chapter 13). What especially disturbed him was the prospect of rule by faceless bureaucrats. How can democracy be anything other than a meaningless slogan in the face of the increasing power bureaucratic organizations are wielding over us? After all, Weber reasoned, bureaucracies are necessarily specialized and hierarchical. Those near the bottom of the organization inevitably find themselves reduced to carrying out mundane tasks and have no power over what they do; power passes to those at the top. Weber's student Robert Michels (1967) invented a phrase that has since become famous, to refer to this loss of power: In large-scale organizations, and more generally a society dominated by organizations, he argued, there is an "**iron law of oligarchy**." **Oligarchy** means rule by the few. According to Michels, the flow of power toward the top is simply an inevitable part of an increasingly bureaucratized world—hence the term *iron law*.

Was Michels right? It surely is correct to say that large-scale organizations involve the centralizing of power. Yet there is good reason to suppose that the iron law of oligarchy is not quite as hard and fast as Michels claimed. Unequal power is not just a function of size. In modest-sized groups there can be very marked differences of power. In a small business, for instance, where the activities of employees are directly visible to the directors, much tighter control might be exerted than in offices in larger organizations. Further, in many modern organizations power is also quite often openly delegated downward from superiors to subordinates. In many large companies, corporate heads are so busy coordinating different departments, coping with crises, and analyzing budget and forecast figures that they have little time for original thinking. Many corporate leaders frankly admit that for the most part they simply accept the conclusions given to them.

iron law of oligarchy • A term coined by Weber's student Robert Michels meaning that large organizations tend toward centralization of power, making democracy difficult.

oligarchy • Rule by a small minority within an organization or society.

GENDER AND ORGANIZATIONS

Until some two decades ago, organizational studies did not devote very much attention to the question of gender. The rise of feminist scholarship in the 1970s, however, led to examinations of gender relations in all the main institutions in society, including organizations and bureaucracy. Feminist sociologists not only focused on the imbalance of gender roles within organizations, they also explored the ways in which modern organizations themselves had developed in a specifically gendered way.

Feminists have argued that the emergence of the modern organization and the bureaucratic career depended on a particular gender configuration. They point to two main ways in which gender is embedded in the very structure of modern organizations. First, bureaucracies are characterized by occupational gender segregation. As women began to enter the labor market in greater numbers, they tended to be segregated into categories of occupations that were low paying and involved routine work. These positions were subordinate to those occupied by men and did not provide opportunities for women to be promoted. Women were used as a source of cheap, reliable labor but were not granted the same opportunities as men to build careers.

Second, the idea of a bureaucratic career was in fact a male career in which women played a crucial supporting role. In the workplace, women performed the

Brenda Barnes, CEO of Sara Lee, at the company's headquarters in Chicago. Sara Lee is the largest U.S. corporation headed by a woman. As women climb the corporate ladder, will they change the methods as well as the face of management?

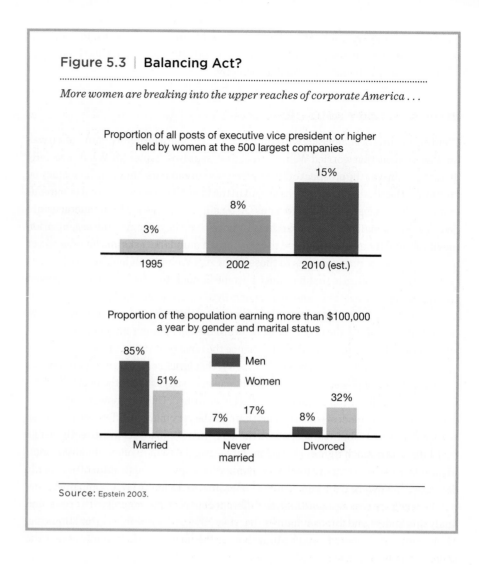

Figure 5.3 | Balancing Act?

More women are breaking into the upper reaches of corporate America . . .

Proportion of all posts of executive vice president or higher
held by women at the 500 largest companies

- 3% — 1995
- 8% — 2002
- 15% — 2010 (est.)

Proportion of the population earning more than $100,000
a year by gender and marital status

■ Men
■ Women

- Married: 85% (Men), 51% (Women)
- Never married: 7% (Men), 17% (Women)
- Divorced: 8% (Men), 32% (Women)

Source: Epstein 2003.

routine tasks—as clerks, secretaries, and office managers—thereby freeing up men to advance their careers. Men could concentrate on obtaining promotions or landing big accounts because the female support staff handled much of the busywork. In the domestic sphere, women also supported the bureaucratic career by caring for the home, the children, and the man's day-to-day well-being. Women serviced the needs of the male bureaucrat by allowing him to work long hours, travel, and focus solely on his work without concern about personal or domestic issues.

As a result of these two tendencies, early feminist writers argued, modern organizations have developed as male-dominated preserves in which women are excluded from power, denied opportunities to advance their careers, and victimized on the basis of their gender through sexual harassment and discrimination. Although most early feminist analysis focused on a common set of concerns—unequal pay, discrimination, and the male hold on power—there was no consensus about the best approach to take in working for women's equality. ✓

CONCEPT CHECKS ✓

1. What role do organizations play in contemporary society?

2. What does the term *bureaucracy* mean?

3. Describe five characteristics of an ideal type of bureaucracy.

4. According to Merton, what are some of the drawbacks of bureaucracies?

5. Explain how modern organizations have developed in a gendered way.

IS BUREAUCRACY AN OUTDATED MODEL?

For quite a long while in the development of Western societies, Weber's model held well. In government, hospital administration, universities, and business organizations, bureaucracy seemed to be dominant. Although informal social groups always develop in bureaucratic settings and tend to function effectively in the workplace, it seemed as though the future might be just what Weber had anticipated: constantly increasing bureaucratization.

Bureaucracies still exist aplenty in the West, but Weber's idea that a clear hierarchy of authority, with power and knowledge concentrated at the top, is the only way to run a large organization is starting to look archaic. Numerous organizations are overhauling themselves to become less, rather than more, hierarchical. Traditional bureaucratic structures are now believed to stifle innovation and creativity in cutting-edge industries. Departing from rigid vertical command structures, many organizations are turning to "horizontal," collaborative models in order to become more flexible and responsive to fluctuating markets. In this section we shall examine some of the main forces behind these shifts, including globalization and the growth of information technology, and consider some of the ways in which modern organizations are reinventing themselves in the light of the changing circumstances.

THE TRANSFORMATION OF MANAGEMENT

Traditional Western forms of management are hierarchical and authoritarian, whereas corporations in Japan, for example, typically focus on management-worker relations and try to ensure that employees at all levels feel a personal attachment to the company. The Japanese emphasis on teamwork, consensus-building approaches, and broad-based employee participation has been demonstrated to yield more productive and competitive workers. As a result, in the 1980s, many Western organizations began to introduce new management techniques in order to rival the productivity and competitiveness of their Japanese counterparts.

Two popular branches of management theory—human resource management and the corporate culture approach—have since been adopted by Western organizations. **Human resource management** is a style of management that regards a company's workforce as vital to its economic competitiveness: If the employees are not completely dedicated to the firm and its product, the firm will never be a leader in its field. To generate employee enthusiasm and commitment, the entire organizational culture must be retooled so that workers feel they have an investment in the workplace and in the work process.

The second management trend—creating a distinctive **corporate culture**—is closely related to human resource management. To promote loyalty to the company and pride in its work, the company's management works with employees to build an organizational culture involving rituals, events, or traditions unique to that company. These cultural activities are designed to draw all members of the firm—from the most senior managers to the newest employee—together so that they make common cause with each other and strengthen group solidarity. Company picnics, casual Fridays (days on which employees can dress down), and company-sponsored community service projects are examples of techniques for building a corporate culture.

human resource management • A style of management that regards a company's workforce as vital to its economic competitiveness.

corporate culture • An organizational culture involving rituals, events, or traditions that are unique to a specific company.

Social Networks and Music Taste

Are our music choices a matter of personal taste or an example of conforming behavior? We tend to think of the music that we listen to as an intensely personal choice made independently of the people around us and that reflects our individual personalities. How much, however, do our social networks determine our most personal of decisions like our aesthetic tastes?

Social scientists Matthew Salganik, Peter Dodds, and Duncan Watts (2006) conducted research to test the effects of the influence of social networks on musical choices. To do so, they created an artificial cultural market on a Web site named Music Lab. Over 14,000 participants registered with the site and were asked to listen to music by bands that they were unfamiliar with and then rate the songs. If they liked the music, they could download songs. The researchers first divided their sample into two groups. The control group was unable to use the Web site to see what other participants were listening to. The second group, the "social influence" group, was able to see what other participants on the Web site were listening to as well as downloading. The social

influence group was further divided into eight "worlds," and participants could only see the rankings and number of downloads of people in their world.

The researchers found that in the social influence groups, the most popular songs were more popular than those in the control group—that is, when participants knew what songs were favored by others, they were more likely to favor those songs themselves. And the most popular song in each world was also different, providing further evidence of the importance of group influence. This suggests that the determinants of popularity in music were based on the listener's social "world." That is, the "intrinsic" quality of the music mattered less than the number of people in each world who were listening to the song, giving it high ratings, and downloading it. The authors of the study described the effect of social networks as a "cumulative advantage" where "if one object happens to be slightly more popular than another at just the right point, it will tend to become more popular still. As a result, even tiny, random fluctuations can blow up, generating potentially

TECHNOLOGY AND MODERN ORGANIZATIONS

information technology •
Forms of technology based on information processing and requiring microelectronic circuitry.

The development of **information technology**—computers and electronic communication media such as the Internet—is another factor currently influencing organizational structures (Attaran 2004; Bresnahan et al. 2002; Castells 2000, 2001; Kanter 1991; Kobrin 1997; Zuboff 1988). Since data can be processed instantaneously in any part of the world linked to a computer-based communications system, there is no need for physical proximity between those involved. As a result, the introduction of new technology has allowed many companies to reengineer their organizational structure.

Telecommuting is an example of how large organizations have become more decentralized as the more routine tasks disappear, reinforcing the tendency toward smaller, more flexible types of enterprises (Burris 1998). A good deal of office work, for instance, can be carried out by telecommuters who use the Internet and other mobile technologies, such as cell phones, to do their work at home or somewhere other than their employer's primary office. Worldwide there are an estimated 137 million workers who telework (Telework Coalition 2004). According to the International Telework Association and Council (ITAC) (2009), in 2008 approximately 34 million workers enormous long-run differences among even indistinguishable competitors—a phenomenon that is similar in some ways to the famous 'butterfly effect' from chaos theory" (Watts 2007). Their study revealed the impact of our social networks, which are now increasingly virtual networks, on our music decisions.

Studying how consumers make decisions is a part of a much deeper sociological tradition that is concerned with conformity, propaganda, and the question of how leaders have persuaded whole populations to take part in horrific deeds. The Holocaust, which claimed the lives of more than six million Jews and others, left many social scientists searching to understand how, why, and under what conditions ordinary people will conform to authority. Many students who have seen or read about Milgram's experiments or the Stanford Prison experiments (both discussed in this chapter) tend to think that they would not conform to the demands of an authority figure the way the study participants did.

Yet, the music market study reveals how social environments impact our behavior and how we all, at times,

conform to the movements of larger social groups even in something as personal as the music that we like. How do you think social influence effects your own, presumably personal, decisions?

in the United States telecommuted at least one day per month. Of these, nearly half were "contract commuters" who work on contract, are self-employed, or are business owners, and the remaining were "employee telecommuters" who work from home for their employers (ITAC 2009). Of the 34 million, 24.2 million telecommuted at least one day a week—and 13.5 million of these telecommuted everyday. Nearly 90 percent of this work was performed at home. Telecommuters in the United States are typically males from the Northeast and West who have college degrees and work in professional or managerial positions (Davis and Polonko 2001).

One rationale for why telecommuting increases productivity is that it eliminates time spent by workers commuting to and from the office, permitting greater concentration of energy on work-related tasks (Hartig et al. 2003). However, there are repercussions from these new work arrangements. First, the employees lose the human side of work; computer terminals are not an attractive substitute for face-to-face interaction with colleagues and friends at work. The flexibility of telework creates new types of stress stemming from isolation, distraction, and conflicting demands of work and home responsibilities (Ammons and Markham 2004; Raghuram and Wiesenfeld 2004). In addition, female telecommuters face more stress resulting from greater housework

Barbara Magnoni telecommutes from her Manhattan apartment. She finds that working from home requires stern self-discipline and an ability to tune out her spouse, children, and pets. For the more sociable or emotionally needy, it can feel like house arrest, especially if the phone hasn't rung in a while.

and child-care responsibilities (Ammons and Markham 2004; Olson 1989; Olson and Primps 1984). Nearly 59 percent of telecommuters say that they work longer hours because they are working at home, though employers view this increased productivity as a primary benefit of telecommuting (ITAC 2004). On the other hand, management cannot easily monitor the activities of employees not under direct supervision (Dimitrova 2003; Kling 1996). While this may create problems for employers, it allows employees greater flexibility in managing their nonwork roles, thus contributing to increased worker satisfaction (Davis and Polonko 2001). Telecommuting also creates new possibilities for older and disabled workers to remain independent, productive, and socially connected (Bouma et al. 2004; Bricout 2004).

The growth of telecommuting is effecting profound changes in many social realms. It is restructuring business management practices and authority hierarchies within businesses (Illegems and Verbeke 2004; Spinks and Wood 1996) as well as contributing to new trends in housing and residential development that prioritize spatial and technological requirements for telework in homes, which are built at increasing distances from city centers (Hartig et al. 2003).

The experiences of telecommuters are reminders that negative consequences can result from the implementation of information technology to reorder organizations. While computerization has resulted in a reduction in hierarchy, it has created a two-tiered occupational structure composed of technical "experts" and less-skilled production or clerical workers. In these restructured organizations, jobs are redefined based more on technical skill than rank or position. For expert professionals, traditional bureaucratic constraints are relaxed to allow for creativity and flexibility, but other workers have limited autonomy (Burris 1993). Although professionals benefit more from this expanded autonomy, computerization makes production and service workers more visible and vulnerable to supervision (Wellman et al. 1996; Zuboff 1988).

Granted, the computerization of the workplace does have some positive effects. It has made some mundane tasks associated with clerical jobs more interesting and flexible. And, as in the case of telecommuting, computerization can contribute to greater flexibility for workers to manage both their personal and professional lives. But in the large majority of workplaces, computerization benefits only those professionals who possess the knowledge and expertise about how to gain from it (Kling 1996).

THE "McDONALDIZATION" OF SOCIETY

Not everyone agrees that our society and its organizations are moving away from the Weberian view of rigid, orderly bureaucracies. The idea that we are witnessing a process of debureaucratization, they argue, is overstated.

In a contribution to the debate over debureaucratization, George Ritzer (1993) has developed a vivid metaphor to express his view of the transformations taking place in industrialized societies. He argues that although some tendencies toward debureaucratization have indeed emerged, on the whole what we are witnessing is the "McDonaldization" of society. According to Ritzer, McDonaldization is "the process by which the principles of the fast-food restaurants are coming to dominate more and more sectors of American society as well as the rest of the world." Ritzer uses the four guiding principles for McDonald's restaurants—efficiency, calculability, uniformity, and control through automation—to show that our society is becoming ever more rationalized with time.

If you have ever visited McDonald's restaurants in two different locations, you will have noticed that there are very few differences between them. The interior decoration may vary slightly and the language spoken will most likely differ from country to country, but the layout, the menu, the procedure for ordering, the staff uniforms, the tables, the packaging, and the "service with a smile" are virtually identical. The McDonald's system is deliberately constructed to maximize efficiency and minimize human responsibility and involvement in the process. Except for certain key tasks such as taking orders and pushing the start and stop buttons on cooking equipment, the restaurants' functions are highly automated and largely run themselves.

Ritzer argues that society as a whole is moving toward this highly standardized and regulated model for getting things done. Ritzer, like Weber before him, is fearful of the harmful effects of bureaucratization on the human spirit and creativity. He argues that McDonaldization is making social life more homogeneous, more rigid, and less personal. ✓

CONCEPT CHECKS ✓

1. How has the Japanese model influenced the Western approach to management?

2. Explain how the development of information technology has changed the ways people live and work.

3. According to George Ritzer, what are the four guiding principles used in McDonald's restaurants?

HOW DO GROUPS AND ORGANIZATIONS AFFECT YOUR LIFE?

SOCIAL CAPITAL: THE TIES THAT BIND

Most people join organizations to gain connections and increase their influence. The time and energy invested in an organization can yield valuable rewards. Parents who belong to the PTA, for example, are more likely to be able to influence school policy than those who do not belong. The members know whom to call, what to say, and how to exert pressure on school officials.

social capital • The social knowledge and connections that enable people to accomplish their goals and extend their influence.

Sociologists call these benefits of organizational membership **social capital**, the social knowledge and connections that enable people to accomplish their goals and extend their influence (Coleman 1988, 1990; Loury 1987; Putnam 1993, 1995, 2000). Social capital is a broad concept, and encompasses useful social networks, a sense of mutual obligation and trustworthiness, an understanding of the norms that govern effective behavior, and other social resources that enable people to act effectively. College students often become active in the student government or the campus newspaper partly because they hope to learn social skills and make connections that will pay off when they graduate. They may, for example, get to interact with professors, administrators, or even successful alumni, who then will go to bat for them when they are looking for a job or applying to graduate school.

Differences in social capital mirror larger social inequalities. In general, men have more capital than women, whites more than nonwhites, the wealthy more than the poor. Differences in social capital can also be found among countries. According to the World Bank (2001), countries with high levels of social capital, where businesspeople can effectively develop the "networks of trust" that foster healthy economies, are more likely to experience economic growth.

Robert Putnam (2000), a political scientist and author of the famous book *Bowling Alone*, distinguishes two types of social capital: *bridging*, which is outward looking and inclusive, and *bonding*, which is inward looking and exclusive. Bridging social capital unifies people across social cleavages, as exemplified by interfaith religious organizations, or the civil rights movement, which brought blacks and whites together in the struggle for racial equality. Bonding social capital reinforces exclusive identities and homogeneous groups; it can be found in ethnic fraternal organizations, church-based women's reading groups, and elite country clubs.

People who actively belong to organizations are more likely to feel connected; they feel engaged, able to somehow make a difference. Democracy flourishes when social capital is strong. Historically, declines in organizational membership, neighborliness, and trust in organizations and corporations have been paralleled by a decline in democratic participation and trust in the government.

Although scholars have bemoaned the fact that political involvement, club membership, and other forms of social and civic engagement that bind Americans to one another eroded significantly in the late twentieth and early twenty-first centuries, the high levels of voter turnout and especially youthful voter turnout in the 2008 election provide a glimmer of optimism. In the 2008 election, 62 percent of eligible voters went to the polls. This is the highest level of voter turnout since 1968. Even more telling, however, is the stark increase in the turnout of youthful voters. The proportion of

DO-IT-YOURSELF SOCIOLOGY

D.I.Y.

How socially engaged are you? Robert Putnam and others have bemoaned the fact that Americans are "bowling alone," and that civic engagement is dead. Yet optimists point to the record-breaking turn-out of youthful voters in the 2008 presidential election as an indication of public engagement. Check off each of the activities that you've done, and then flip the page to discover your civic engagement profile.

	YES	NO
1. Are you an active member of at least one voluntary group or association?		
2. Are you a regular volunteer for a nonpolitical group?		
3. In the past year, have you tried to resolve a problem in your community?		
4. In the past year, have you run, walked, or biked for charity?		
5. In the past year, have you done something else to raise money for charity?		
6. Do you regularly vote in elections?		
7. Do you try to persuade others to vote a particular way?		
8. Do you display a campaign button or sign?		
9. Did you donate money to a political candidate or campaign in the last year?		
10. Do you regularly volunteer for political causes?		

In the past year, have you . . .

	YES	NO
11. contacted a public official?		
12. contacted the print media to express your opinion?		
13. contacted the broadcast media to express your opinion?		
14. protested (e.g., a march or demonstration)?		
15. signed an e-mail petition?		
16. boycotted a product or company?		
17. "buycotted" (i.e., bought a product because you support the company's values)?		
18. canvassed, or gone door-to-door for a political or social cause?		

TURN PAGE

Look below to see what proportion of 15–25-year-olds answered "yes" to each question in 2006.

————————————————————————————————————→

1. Are you an active member of at least one voluntary group or association?	20%
2. Are you a regular volunteer for a nonpolitical group?	19%
3. In the past year, have you tried to resolve a problem in your community?	19%
4. In the past year, have you run, walked, or biked for charity?	18%
5. In the past year, have you done something else to raise money for charity?	24%
6. Do you regularly vote in elections?	26%
7. Do you try to persuade others to vote a particular way?	35%
8. Do you display a campaign button or sign?	23%
9. Did you donate money to a political candidate or campaign in the last year?	7%
10. Do you regularly volunteer for political causes?	2%

In the past year, have you . . .

————————————————————————————————————→

11. contacted a public official?	11%
12. contacted the print media to express your opinion?	7%
13. contacted the broadcast media to express your opinion?	9%
14. protested (e.g., a march or demonstration)?	11%
15. signed an e-mail petition?	16%
16. boycotted a product or company?	30%
17. buycotted (i.e., bought a product because you support the company's values)?	29%
18. canvassed, or gone door-to-door for a political or social cause?	3%

If you answered "yes" to more than 10 activities, you are among the 7 percent of American youth who are "hyper-engaged." If you answered "yes" to zero activities, you are in the 17% of young people classified as "highly disengaged."

If you answered "yes" to 2 items in questions 1–5, then you are among the 17 percent of young people who are "civic specialists."

If you answered "yes" to 2 items in questions 6–10, then you are among the 12 percent of young people who are "electoral specialists."

If you answered "yes" to 2 items each in sections 1–5 and 6–10, you are among the 13 percent of young people who are "dual activists."

Source: Lopez, et. al. 2006.

persons ages 18–29 who voted in the 2008 presidential election topped 52%—compared with turnout rates of 37% in 1996, 41% in 2000, and 48% in 2004 (Nonprofit Voter Engagement Network 2009).

Other indicators of social participation do not tell such an encouraging story. Attendance at public meetings concerning education or civic affairs has dropped sharply since the 1970s, and three out of four Americans today tell pollsters that they either "never" trust the government or do so only "sometimes" (Putnam 1995). However, trust in the U.S. government ebbs and flows, as the world around us changes. For instance, following the terrorist attacks of September 11, 2001, researchers witnessed a resurgence of trust, with those saying that they trust the government some of the time doubling to nearly 60 percent (Pew 2002). Although since then, trust has declined to 46 percent, this is still significantly higher than in previous decades. This level of trust has remained relatively stable: In a more recent poll, about 42 percent of Americans said they have a "great deal" or "fair amount" of trust in the federal government to handle international problems (Gallup 2008).

Research on membership in organizations such as the Sierra Club (with 1.3 million members), the National Organization for Women (NOW) (with half a million members), and the American Association of Retired Persons (AARP, with 40 million members) is even more discouraging. The vast majority of these organizations' members simply pay their annual dues and receive a newsletter. Very few members actively participate, failing to develop the social capital Putnam regards as an important underpinning of democracy. Many of the most popular organizations today, such as twelve-step programs or weight loss groups, emphasize personal growth and health rather than collective goals to benefit society as a whole.

There are undoubtedly many reasons for these declines. For one, women, who were traditionally active in voluntary organizations, are more likely to hold a job than ever before. Furthermore, the commuting that results from flight to the suburbs uses up time and energy that might have been available for civic activities. But the principal source of declining civic participation, according to Putnam, is simple: television. The many hours Americans spend at home alone watching TV has replaced social engagement in the community.

However, there are reasons to speculate that voluntarism and social participation may increase in the coming decade. President Barack Obama, elected in November 2008, has named public service as an important goal of his "Blueprint for America." Proposed programs such as Senior Corps, which promotes community service among retired older adults, and programs to encourage public service among high school students may create a new culture of civic engagement. Sociologists also speculate that the economic recession may increase a spirit of community-mindedness, especially among young people. Applications to programs such as the Peace Corps and Teach for America, as well as applications to divinity schools and public policy programs, increased during the recession of 2008–2009 (Zernike 2009). ✓

> ## CONCEPT CHECKS ✓
> 1. What is social capital?
> 2. Describe the difference between bridging social capital and bonding social capital.

CONCLUSION

You now know better how the groups and organizations you belong to influence your life. The primary groups of your earliest years were crucial in shaping your sense of self—a sense that changed very slowly thereafter. Throughout life, groups also instill in their members norms and values that enable and enrich social life.

Although groups remain central in our lives, group affiliation in the United States is rapidly changing. As you have seen in this chapter, conventional groups appear to be losing ground in our daily life. For example, today's college students are less likely to join civic groups and organizations than were their parents, a decline that may well signal a lower commitment to their communities. Some sociologists worry that this signals a weakening of society itself, which could bring about social instability. Yet others argue that group life is being redefined, as young people belong to virtual groups and communities, via networking Web sites like Facebook.

The global economy and information technology are redefining group life in many diverse ways. For instance, your parents are likely to spend much of their careers in a handful of long-lasting, bureaucratic organizations; you are much more likely to be part of a larger number of networked, "flexible" ones. As we just noted, many of your group affiliations will be created through the Internet or through other forms of communication that today can barely be envisioned. It will become increasingly easy to connect with like-minded people anywhere, creating geographically dispersed groups that span the planet—and whose members may never meet each other face-to-face.

How will these trends affect the quality of your social relationships? For nearly all of human history, most people interacted exclusively with others who were close at hand. The Industrial Revolution, which facilitated the rise of large, impersonal bureaucracies where people knew one another only casually if at all, changed social interaction. Today, the information revolution is once again changing human interaction. Tomorrow's groups and organizations could provide a renewed sense of communication and social intimacy—or they could spell further isolation and social distance.

NEED HELP STUDYING?

 wwnorton.com/studyspace

Visit StudySpace to access free review materials such as:

- Vocabulary Flashcards
- Diagnostic Review Quizzes
- Study Outlines

REVIEW QUESTIONS

1. What is a social group? How is it different from a social aggregate or a social category?
2. Discuss how membership in different types of groups contributes to feelings of belonging in a social group.
3. Briefly explain Stanley Milgram's experiment and the importance of his findings.

4. What are weak ties? What is the strength of weak ties according to Mark Granovetter?
5. How has the Internet changed social networks? What are some of the advantages and disadvantages of the Internet in facilitating access to social networks?
6. What is an organization? Why, according to Max Weber, are formal organizations so pervasive in modern society?
7. How does Weber define an ideal-type bureaucracy?
8. What does Ritzer mean by the "McDonaldization of society"?
9. Why is organizational membership considered a form of social capital? What is the relationship between social capital and inequality?

THINKING SOCIOLOGICALLY EXERCISES

1. According to Georg Simmel, what are the primary differences between dyads and triads? Explain, according to his theory, how the addition of a child would alter the relationship between a husband and wife. Does the theory fit this situation?
2. The advent of computers and the computerization of the workplace may change our organizations and relationships with coworkers. Explain how you see modern organizations changing with the adaptation of newer information technologies.

6

Conformity, Deviance, and Crime

THE BIG QUESTIONS

WHAT IS DEVIANT BEHAVIOR?

Learn how sociologists define deviance and how it is closely related to social power and social class. See the ways in which conformity is encouraged.

WHY DO PEOPLE COMMIT DEVIANT ACTS?

Know the leading sociological, psychological, and biological theories of deviance and how each is useful in understanding crime.

HOW DO WE DOCUMENT CRIME?

Recognize the usefulness and limitations of crime statistics. Learn some important differences between men and women related to crime. Familiarize yourself with some of the varieties of crime.

WHOSE LIVES ARE AFFECTED BY CRIME?

Understand why members of some social groups are more likely to commit or be the victims of crime.

HOW CAN CRIME BE REDUCED?

Consider the ways in which individuals and governments can address crime.

HOW DO CRIME AND DEVIANCE AFFECT YOUR LIFE?

Understand the costs and functions of crime and deviance.

Willie is a street vendor who lives and works on a street in New York City. He earns money by taking magazines out of recycled trash and reselling them to passersby. Willie has lived on a corner for about six years, ever since he was released from serving a prison sentence for committing a robbery. He is just one of approximately six hundred thousand people released from prison every year—about sixteen hundred per day (Mauer 2004).

In 2008, the number of prisoners held in federal, state, and county facilities exceeded 2.3 million people (U.S. Department of Justice 2008a). The U.S. rate of incarceration is five to eight times higher than Canada and the countries of Western Europe (Garland 2002). The United States has less than 5 percent of the world's population, but almost a quarter of the world's prisoners (Liptak 2008). The high rate of imprisonment in the United States in recent decades in due in part to "three strikes" laws, which became very popular in the 1990s. These laws require state courts to hand down mandatory and often lengthy prison sentences to persons who have been convicted of a serious criminal offense three or more times.

This dramatic increase in incarceration has had a major effect on the African American and Latino populations in particular. According to Marc Mauer (2004), a leading scholar of incarceration, "In 1997, the state-wide population of Maryland, Illinois, North Carolina, South Carolina, and Louisiana was two thirds or more white, but prison growth since 1985 was 80% non-white. . . . In New York, where the state's adult minority population is less than 31.7%, nine out of ten new prisoners are from an ethnic or racial minority."

The effect of the criminal justice system is clear in the lives of people like Willie. While they are in prison, they are not part of the labor force, and thus are not counted in the rates of unemployment reported by the government. As a result, estimates of unemployment among some subgroups, such as African American men, may be understated. At the same time, incarceration increases the long-term chances of unemployment for men like Willie once they are released from prison (Western and Beckett 1999).

Although the United States currently imprisons more than two million people at the state and local level, it has failed to make adequate preparations for their release (Gonnerman 2004). After leaving prison, Willie went directly to the streets. He didn't have a job or a home. People he knew from prison were already living on this corner and he heard he could find them there.

Willie is a man whom many people would define as a "deviant." We all know who deviants are, or so we tend to think. Deviants are those individuals who do not live by the rules that the majority of us follow. Some do so by choice, others are incapable of following the rules because they lack the resources to do so. Sometimes they're violent criminals, drug addicts, or down-and-outs, who don't fit in with what most people would define as normal standards of acceptability. These are the cases that seem easy to identify. Yet things are not quite as they appear—a lesson sociology often teaches us, for it encourages us to look beyond the obvious. The notion of the deviant, as we shall see, is actually not an easy one to define.

We have learned in previous chapters that social life is governed by rules or norms. Our activities and relationships would collapse into chaos if we didn't stick to rules that define some kinds of behavior as proper in particular contexts and others as inappropriate. As we learned earlier in discussing the concept of culture, **norms** are clearly defined and established principles or rules people are expected to observe; they represent the dos and don'ts of society. Orderly behavior on the highway, for example, would be impossible if drivers didn't observe the rule of driving on the right. No deviants here, you might think, except perhaps for the drunken or reckless driver. If you did think this, you would be incorrect. When we drive, most of us are not merely deviants but criminals. For most drivers regularly drive at well above the legal speed limits, while others type instant messages—assuming there isn't a police car in sight. In such cases, breaking the law is normal behavior!

We are all rule breakers as well as conformists. We are all also rule creators. Most American drivers may break the law on the freeways, but in fact they've evolved informal rules that are superimposed on the legal rules. When the legal speed limit on the highway is 65 mph, most drivers don't go above 75 or so, and they drive slower when driving through urban areas.

In most European countries, the legal speed limits are higher than in the United States—between 65 and 70 mph, depending on the country. Drivers there break the law most of the time just as they do in the United States, but their informal rules about proper driving produce higher speeds than in America. People regularly drive at 80–90 mph. Conventional rules about what is and isn't reckless driving also vary. Americans who drive in the south of Italy, for example, where drivers break other traffic rules as well, are apt to find the experience a hair-raising one.

norms • Rules of conduct that specify appropriate behavior in a given range of social situations. A norm either prescribes a given type of behavior or forbids it. All human groups follow definite norms, which are always backed by sanctions of one kind or another—varying from informal disapproval to physical punishment.

When we begin the study of deviant behavior, we must consider which rules people are observing and which they are breaking. Nobody breaks all rules, just as no one conforms to all rules. Even an individual who might seem far removed from mainstream society, such as Willie, is likely to be following many rules of the groups and society of which he is a member.

For example, when Willie had enough money for a meal, he would go to a small Chinese restaurant around the corner from where he lived. He would sit and eat his egg rolls, chow mein, and egg drop soup with the same manners as other diners. In this restaurant, he hardly appeared deviant. When Willie was out on the street, he followed the rules of the other street vendors who survive on the street. In the world of street vendors, he appeared as a conformist most of the time. Indeed, some "deviant" groups such as the homeless have strict codes of social behavior for those who live among them. Those who deviate from these informal codes of behavior may be ostracized or expelled from the group and be forced to go elsewhere (Duneier 1999). Thus, even deviants are conformists at times.

Willie's life is just one example of what happens to people who spend time in the American criminal justice system. Because prisons and jails make little accommodation for people after release, many former prisoners are unable to find homes or jobs in the formal economy. Working on the street is hardly a long-term solution for men like Willie, and after six years of "staying clean" on Sixth Avenue he was rearrested for another drug offense. This is very common: Almost two thirds of all persons leaving prison will be recidivists, meaning that they will commit at least one serious crime after their release (Mauer 2004).

WHAT IS DEVIANT BEHAVIOR?

The study of deviant behavior is one of the most intriguing yet complex areas of sociology. It teaches us that none of us is quite as normal as we might like to think. It also helps us see that people whose behavior might appear incomprehensible or odd can be seen as rational beings when we understand why they act as they do.

The study of deviance, like other fields of sociology, directs our attention to *social power*, which encompasses gender, race, and social class. When we look at deviance from or conformity to social rules or norms, we always have to bear in mind the question, *Whose rules*? As we shall see, social norms are strongly influenced by divisions of power and class.

WHAT IS DEVIANCE?

Deviance may be defined as nonconformity to a given set of norms that are accepted by a significant number of people in a community or society. No society, as has already been stressed, can be divided up in a simple way between those who deviate from norms and those who conform to them. Most of us on some occasions violate generally accepted rules of behavior. Although a large share of all deviant behavior (such as committing assault or murder) is also criminal

deviance ● Modes of action that do not conform to the norms or values held by most members of a group or society. What is regarded as deviant is as variable as the norms and values that distinguish different cultures and subcultures from one another. Forms of behavior that are highly esteemed by one group are regarded negatively by others.

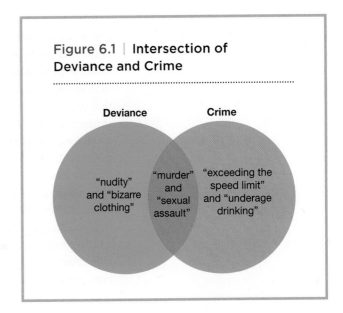

Figure 6.1 | Intersection of Deviance and Crime

Deviance

"nudity" and "bizarre clothing"

"murder" and "sexual assault"

Crime

"exceeding the speed limit" and "underage drinking"

Computer hacker Kevin Mitnick was arrested in 1995 and later convicted of stealing millions of dollars worth of software from a number of technology companies. His release from prison in 2000 was conditioned on the understanding that he would refrain from using computers or speaking publicly about technology issues.

deviant subculture ● A subculture whose members hold values that differ substantially from those of the majority.

and violates the law, many deviant behaviors—ranging from bizarre fashion choices to joining a religions cult—are not criminal. By the same token, many behaviors that are technically "crimes," such as underage drinking or exceeding the speed limit, are not considered deviant because they are quite normative (see Figure 6.1). Sociologists tend to focus much of their research on behaviors that are both criminal *and* deviant, as such behaviors have importance for the safety and well-being of our nation.

Although most of us associate the word "deviant" with behaviors that we view as dangerous or unsavory, assessments of deviance are truly in the eye of the beholder, as our next example will illustrate. Kevin Mitnick has been described as the "world's most celebrated computer hacker." To the world's estimated hundred thousand computer hackers, Mitnick is a pioneering genius whose five-year imprisonment in a U.S. penitentiary was unjust and unwarranted—proof of how misunderstood computer hacking has become with the spread of information technology. To U.S. authorities and high-tech corporations, Mitnick is one of the world's most dangerous men. A recent survey by the U.S. Secret Service and Carnegie Mellon University found that hackers are responsible for 26 percent of computer crime (E-Crime Watch 2007). Mitnick was captured by the FBI in 1995 and later convicted of downloading source code and stealing software allegedly worth millions of dollars from companies such as Motorola and Sun Microsystems. As a condition of his release from prison in January 2000, Mitnick was restricted from using any communications technology other than a landline telephone. He successfully fought this legal decision, and gained access to the Internet. He now runs his own computer security consultancy.

Over the past decade or so, hackers have been gradually transformed from a little-noticed population of computer enthusiasts to a much-reviled group of deviants who are believed to threaten the very stability of the information age. Yet, according to Mitnick and others in the hacker community, such depictions could not be further from the truth. Hackers are quick to point out that most of their activities are not criminal. Rather, they are primarily interested in exploring the edges of computer technology, trying to uncover loopholes and to discover how far it is possible to penetrate into other computer systems. Once flaws have been discovered, the "hacker ethic" demands that the information be shared publicly. Many hackers have even served as consultants for large corporations and government agencies, helping them to defend their systems against outside intrusion.

Deviance does not refer only to individual behavior; it concerns the activities of groups as well. Heaven's Gate was a religious group whose beliefs and practices were different from those of the majority of Americans. The cult was established in the early 1970s when Marshall Herff Applewhite made his way around the West and Midwest of the United States preaching his beliefs, ultimately advertising on the Internet his belief that civilization was doomed and that the only way people could be saved was to kill themselves so their souls could be rescued by a UFO. On March 26, 1997, thirty-nine members of the cult followed his advice in a mass suicide at a wealthy estate in Rancho Santa Fe, California.

The Heaven's Gate cult represents an example of a **deviant subculture**. They were able to survive fairly easily within the wider society, supporting themselves by running a Web site business and recruiting new members by sending e-mail messages to people they thought might be interested in their beliefs. They had plenty of money and lived together in an expensive home in a wealthy California suburb. Their position is distinct from that of another deviant subculture that we discussed in the introduction to this chapter: the homeless.

NORMS AND SANCTIONS

We most often follow social norms because, as a result of socialization, we are accustomed to doing so. Individuals become committed to social norms through interactions with people who obey the law and mainstream values. Through these interactions, we learn self-control. The more numerous and frequent our interactions, the fewer opportunities we have to deviate from conventional norms. And, over time, the longer that we interact in ways that are conventional, the more we have to lose by not conforming (Gottfredson and Hirschi 1990).

All social norms are accompanied by sanctions that promote conformity and protect against nonconformity. A **sanction** is any reaction from others to the behavior of an individual or group that is meant to ensure that the person or group complies with a given norm. Sanctions may be positive (the offering of rewards for conformity) or negative (punishment for behavior that does not conform). They can also be formal or informal. Formal sanctions are applied by a specific body of people or an agency to ensure that a particular set of norms is followed. Informal sanctions are less organized and more spontaneous reactions to nonconformity, such as when a student is teasingly accused by friends of working too hard or being a nerd if he decides to spend an evening studying rather than going to a party.

The main types of formal sanctions in modern societies are those represented by the courts and prisons. The police, of course, are the agency charged with bringing offenders to trial and possible imprisonment. **Laws** are norms defined by governments as principles that their citizens must follow; sanctions are used against people who do not conform to them. Where there are laws, there are also **crimes**, since crime can most simply be defined as any type of behavior that breaks a law.

It is important to recognize, however, that the law is only a guide to the kinds of norms that prevail in a society. Oftentimes, subcultures invent their own dos and don'ts. For example, the street people that Willie lived among created their own norms for determining where each of them could set up the magazines to sell on the sidewalk. Other homeless vendors didn't set up in Willie's spot because that would have shown "disrespect." This example further illustrates that even members of so-called deviant groups usually live in accordance with some norms. What makes them deviant subcultures is that these norms are at odds with the norms of the mainstream of society. ✓

sanction • A mode of reward or punishment that reinforces socially expected forms of behavior.

law • A rule of behavior established by a political authority and backed by state power.

crime • Any action that contravenes the laws established by a political authority. Although we may think of criminals as a distinct subsection of the population, there are few people who have not broken the law in one way or another during their lives. While laws are formulated by state authorities, it is not unknown for those authorities to engage in criminal behavior in certain situations.

CONCEPT CHECKS

1. How do sociologists define deviance?

2. Is all crime deviant? Is all deviance criminal? Why?

3. Contrast positive and negative sanctions.

WHY DO PEOPLE COMMIT DEVIANT ACTS?

Answers to the question "Why are people deviant?" vary widely, depending on one's academic discipline, and even, within sociology, one's theoretical approach. We will briefly review biological and psychological explanations for deviance, and will then turn to the four sociological approaches that have been developed to interpret and analyze deviance: functionalist theories, reinforcement theories, conflict theories, and interactionist theories.

THE BIOLOGICAL VIEW OF DEVIANCE

Some of the first attempts to explain crime emphasized biological factors. The Italian criminologist Cesare Lombroso, working in the 1870s, believed that criminal types could be identified by the shape of the skull. He accepted that social learning could influence the development of criminal behavior, but he regarded most criminals as biologically degenerate or defective. Lombroso's ideas were later thoroughly discredited, but similar views have repeatedly been suggested.

Another theory distinguished three main types of human physique and claimed that one type was directly associated with delinquency. Muscular, active types (mesomorphs) were considered more likely to become delinquent than those of thin physique (ectomorphs) or more fleshy people (endomorphs) (Glueck and Glueck 1956; Sheldon et al. 1949).

Most biological theories have been widely criticized on methodological grounds. Even if there were a correlation between body type and delinquency, this would not necessarily reveal that one's body type "causes" criminal behavior. For instance, people who engage in criminal activities may need to develop more muscular physiques in order to protect themselves on the streets. Moreover, nearly all studies in this field have been restricted to delinquents in reform schools, and it may be that the tougher, athletic-looking delinquents are more liable to be sent to such schools than fragile-looking, skinny ones.

More recent, methodologically rigorous research has sought to rekindle the argument that deviance has a biological or genetic basis. In a study of New Zealand children, researchers investigated whether a child's propensity for aggression was linked to biological factors present at birth (Moffitt 1996). Rather than viewing biology as deterministic, this new breed of research emphasizes that biological factors, when combined with certain social factors such as one's home environment, could lead to social situations involving crime. This perspective, which emphasizes *gene-environment interaction*, reasons that one's genes may "select" or draw a person into a particular behavior, such as aggression. Yet at the same time, the social environment may strengthen or weaken the link between genetics and deviant behavior. For instance, even if a baby was born with a genetic predisposition for alcoholism, that baby would not likely become a problem drinker if his or her social environment provided few opportunities to drink.

THE PSYCHOLOGICAL VIEW OF DEVIANCE

Like biological interpretations, psychological theories of crime associate criminality with particular types of personality. Some have suggested that in a minority of individuals, an amoral, or psychopathic, personality develops. **Psychopaths** are withdrawn, emotionless characters who delight in violence for its own sake.

Individuals with psychopathic traits do sometimes commit violent crimes, but there are major problems with the concept of the psychopath. It isn't at all clear that psychopathic traits are inevitably criminal. Nearly all studies of people said to possess these characteristics have been of convicted prisoners, and their personalities inevitably tend to be presented negatively. If we describe the same traits positively, the personality type sounds quite different, and there seems no reason why people of this sort should be inherently criminal. Should we be looking for psychopathic individuals for a research study, we might place the following ad (Widom and Newman 1985):

psychopath • A specific personality type; such individuals lack the moral sense and concern for others held by most normal people.

Such people might be explorers, spies, gamblers, or just bored with the routines of day-to-day life. They might be prepared to contemplate criminal adventures but could be just as likely to look for challenges in socially respectable ways.

Psychological theories of criminality can at best explain only some aspects of crime. While some criminals may possess personality characteristics distinct from the remainder of the population, it is highly improbable that the majority of criminals do. There are all kinds of crimes, and it is implausible that those who commit them share some specific psychological characteristics. Some crimes are carried out by lone individuals, whereas others are the work of organized groups. It is not likely that the psychological makeup of people who are loners will have much in common with that of the members of a close-knit gang. Observational studies also can't discount the possibility that becoming involved with criminal groups influences people's outlooks, rather than that the outlooks actually produce criminal behavior in the first place.

Both biological and psychological approaches to criminality presume that deviance is a sign of something "wrong" with the individual rather than with society. They see crime and deviance as caused by factors outside an individual's control, embedded either in the body or in the mind. These early approaches to criminology came under great criticism from later generations of scholars, who argued that any satisfactory account of the nature of crime must be sociological, for what crime is depends on the social institutions of a society.

SOCIOLOGICAL PERSPECTIVES ON DEVIANCE

Contemporary sociological thinking about crime emphasize that definitions of conformity and deviance vary based on one's social context. Modern societies contain many different subcultures, and behavior that conforms to the norms of one particular subculture may be regarded as deviant outside it; for instance, there may be strong pressure on a member of a boys' gang to prove himself by stealing a car. Moreover, there are wide divergences of wealth and power in society that greatly influence opportunities open to different groups. Theft and burglary, not surprisingly, are carried out mainly by people from the poorer segments of the population; embezzling and tax evasion are by definition limited to persons in positions of some affluence.

FUNCTIONALIST THEORIES

Functionalist theories see crime and deviance resulting from structural tensions and a lack of moral regulation within society. If the aspirations held by individuals and groups in society do not coincide with available rewards, this disparity between desires and fulfillment will be felt in the deviant motivations of some of its members.

CRIME AND ANOMIE: DURKHEIM AND MERTON

anomie • A concept first brought into wide usage in sociology by Durkheim, referring to a situation in which social norms lose their hold over individual behavior.

As we saw in Chapter 1, the notion of **anomie** was first introduced by Émile Durkheim, who suggested that in modern societies traditional norms become undermined without being replaced by new ones. Anomie exists when there are no clear standards to guide behavior in a given area of social life. Under such circumstances, Durkheim believed, people feel disoriented and anxious; anomie is therefore one of the social factors influencing dispositions to suicide.

Durkheim saw crime and deviance as social facts; he believed both of them to be inevitable and necessary elements in modern societies. According to Durkheim, people in the modern age are less constrained by social expectations than they were in traditional societies. Because there is more room for individual choice in the modern world, nonconformity is inevitable. Durkheim recognized that no society would ever be in complete consensus about the norms and values that govern it.

Deviance is also necessary for society, according to Durkheim; it fulfills two important functions. First, deviance has an adaptive function. By introducing new ideas and challenges into society, deviance is an innovative force. It brings about change. Second, deviance promotes boundary maintenance between "good" and "bad" behaviors in society. A criminal act can ultimately enhance group solidarity and clarify social norms. Deviance can also contribute to the stability of society. In his classic essay on prostitution, functionalist theorist Kingsley Davis (1937) wrote that prostitution may be illegal, yet it is functional for society because it allows married men to fulfill their sexual urges with a new partner, without threatening their marriages. By contrast, a married man who forms an emotional attachment with a woman with whom he is having a "legal" though clandestine relationship can threaten both his and her marriages. Prostitution, Davis argued, indirectly contributes to the stability of the family.

Early functionalist perspectives on crime and deviance were influential in shifting attention from individual explanations to social forces. Durkheim's notion of anomie was drawn on by American sociologist Robert K. Merton (1957), who constructed a highly influential theory of deviance that located the source of crime within the very structure of American society.

Merton modified the concept of anomie to refer to the strain put on individuals' behavior when accepted norms conflict with social reality. In American society—and to some degree in other industrial societies—generally held values emphasize material success, and the means of achieving success are supposed to be self-discipline and hard work. Accordingly, it is believed that people who work hard can succeed no matter what their starting point in life. This idea is not in fact valid, because most of the disadvantaged have very few conventional opportunities for advancement, such as high-quality education. Yet those who do not "succeed" find themselves condemned for their apparent inability to make material progress. In this situation, there is great pressure to try to get ahead by any means, legitimate or illegitimate. According to Merton, then, deviance is a by-product of economic inequalities.

Merton identifies five possible reactions to the tensions between socially endorsed values and the limited means of achieving them (see Figure 6.2). *Conformists* accept both societal values and the conventional means of realizing them, whether or not they meet with success. The majority of the population falls into this category. *Innovators* accept socially approved values but

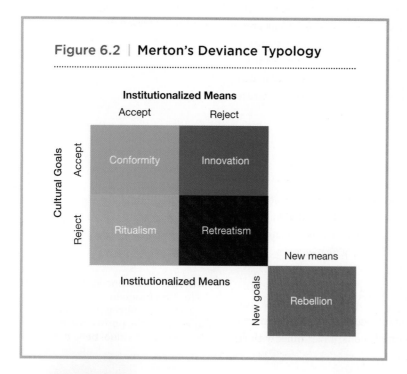

Figure 6.2 | Merton's Deviance Typology

Institutionalized Means

Accept   Reject

Cultural Goals

Accept: Conformity | Innovation

Reject: Ritualism | Retreatism

Institutionalized Means

New means

New goals: Rebellion

use illegitimate or illegal means to follow them. Criminals who acquire wealth through illegal activities exemplify this type.

Ritualists conform to socially accepted standards although they have lost sight of the values behind these standards. They follow rules for their own sake without a broader end in view, in a compulsive way. A ritualist might dedicate herself to a boring job, even though it has no career prospects and provides few rewards. *Retreatists* have abandoned the competitive outlook altogether, thus rejecting both the dominant values and the approved means of achieving them. An example would be the members of a self-supporting commune. Finally, *rebels* reject both the existing values and the means of pursuing them, but wish actively to substitute new values and reconstruct the social system. The members of radical political and religious groups, such as the Heaven's Gate cult, fall into this category.

Merton's writings addressed one of the main puzzles in the study of criminology: At a time when society as a whole is becoming more affluent, why do crime rates continue to rise? By emphasizing the contrast between rising aspirations and persistent inequalities, Merton points to a sense of relative deprivation as an important element in deviant behavior.

SUBCULTURAL EXPLANATIONS

Later researchers located deviance in terms of subcultural groups that adopt norms that encourage or reward criminal behavior. Like Merton, Albert Cohen saw the contradictions within American society as the main cause of crime. However, Cohen saw the responses occurring collectively, through subcultures, while Merton emphasized individual responses. In *Delinquent* Boys (1955), Cohen argued that boys in the lower working class who are frustrated with their positions in life often join together in

Members of an El Salvadoran gang flash signs and display their tattoos. The gangs, called *maras*, began in Los Angeles in the 1980s to protect themselves from established street gangs after their working-class families fled civil war in Central America. How might Cohen, Cloward, and Ohlin explain the emergence of the *maras*?

delinquent subcultures, such as gangs. These subcultures reject middle-class values and replace them with norms that celebrate defiance, such as delinquency and other acts of nonconformity.

Richard A. Cloward and Lloyd E. Ohlin (1960) argued further that such gangs arise in subcultural communities where the chances of achieving success legitimately are slim, such as among deprived ethnic minorities. Recent research by sociologists has examined the validity of claims that immediate material deprivation and lack of opportunity can lead people to commit crimes. A survey of homeless youth in Canada, for instance, shows a strong correlation between hunger, lack of shelter, and unemployment, on the one hand, and theft, prostitution, and even violent crime on the other (Hagan and McCarthy 1992).

Functionalist theories rightly emphasize connections between conformity and deviance in different social contexts. We should be cautious, however, about the idea that people in poorer communities, like Willie, aspire to the same level of success as more affluent people. Most tend to adjust their aspirations to what they see as the reality of their situation. Merton, Cohen, and Cloward and Ohlin can all be criticized for presuming that middle-class values have been accepted throughout society. It would also be wrong to suppose that a mismatch of aspirations and opportunities is confined to the less privileged. There are pressures toward criminal activity among other groups too, as indicated by the so-called white-collar crimes of embezzlement, fraud, and tax evasion.

REINFORCEMENT THEORIES

Sociologists studying crime and deviance in the reinforcement tradition focus on deviance as a behavior that we learn, just as we learn conventional behavior. Reinforcement theories are based on the assumption that individuals learn through rewards and punishments; we engage in behaviors that we find rewarding, and either avoid or stop performing a behavior that is punished. The more we're rewarded for a behavior, the more likely we are to incorporate that behavior into our repertoire. "Rewards" and "punishments" are far-ranging, and may be financial (such as a speeding ticket), or social (such as being rejected by one's friends and family). *Opportunity costs,* the benefits we lose or forgo by seizing another opportunity, also matter. For instance, a young person who chooses to commit a petty crime may risk being expelled from school; that is, the opportunity to get a high school diploma may be lost if one commits crimes. Opportunity costs vary widely based on one's social class, though, and persons with the lowest opportunity costs have the least to lose by committing a deviant act. A high school senior who has been accepted to a prestigious college has much more to lose upon expulsion than would a classmate who has no clear-cut plans for what to do after high school.

The rewards and costs associated with committing deviant acts also may be social—such as the "reward" of acceptance by peers, or the "cost" of being shunned by one's social group. Differential association and control theory emphasize social relationships as an influence on deviant behavior. *Differential* association holds that we learn deviant behaviors from those significant others with whom we spend the greatest amount of time, while *control theory* proposes that deviance occurs when an individual's bonds to conventional society are inadequate.

LEARNED DEVIANCE: DIFFERENTIAL ASSOCIATION

One of the earliest writers to suggest that deviance is learned through interaction with others was Edwin H. Sutherland. In 1949, Sutherland advanced a notion that was

According to interactionists, it's not the act of smoking marijuana that makes one a deviant, but the way others react to marijuana smoking.

to influence much of the later interactionist work: He linked crime to what he called **differential association**. Differential association theory argues that we learn deviant behavior in precisely the same way we learn about conventional behavior: from our contacts with primary groups, such as peers, family members, and coworkers. The term "differential" refers to the ratio of deviant to conventional social contacts. We become deviant when exposed to a higher level of deviant persons and influences, compared to conventional influences. In a society that contains a variety of subcultures, some individuals have greater exposure to social environments that encourage illegal activities, whereas others do not.

Differential association can be used to assess Willie's life. Before Willie went to prison, he lived in New York City's Penn Station with a group of homeless men. From this group, he learned how to target and rob restaurant delivery boys, whom he learned were unlikely to report the crime to the police because many of them were illegal immigrants from Mexico and China. Willie would not have known these facts unless he had learned them from associating with others who were already the carriers of criminal norms.

differential association • An interpretation of the development of criminal behavior proposed by Edwin H. Sutherland, according to whom criminal behavior is learned through association with others who regularly engage in crime.

CONTROL THEORY

Control theory posits that crime occurs as a result of an imbalance between impulses toward criminal activity and the social or physical controls that deter it. Core assumptions are that people act rationally and that, given the opportunity, everyone would engage in deviant acts. Many types of crime, it is argued, are a result of "situational decisions"—a person sees an opportunity and is motivated to act.

One of the best-known control theorists, Travis Hirschi, has argued that humans are fundamentally selfish beings who make calculated decisions about whether or not to engage in criminal activity by weighing the potential benefits and risks of doing so. In *Causes of Delinquency* (1969), Hirschi claimed that there are four types of bonds that link people to society and law-abiding behavior: attachment, commitment, involvement, and belief.

Attachment refers to emotional and social ties to persons who accept conventional norms, such as a peer group of students who value good grades and hard work. *Commitment* refers to the rewards obtained by participating in conventional activities and pursuits. For example, a school dropout has little to lose by being arrested, while a dedicated student may lose his or her chance of going to college. *Involvement* refers

control theory • A theory that views crime as the outcome of an imbalance between impulses toward criminal activity and controls that deter it. Control theorists hold that criminals are rational beings who will act to maximize their own reward unless they are rendered unable to do so through either social or physical controls.

to one's participation in conventional activities, such as paid employment, school, or community activities. The time spent in conventional activities means time *not* spent in deviant activities. Finally, *beliefs* involve values that are consistent with conventional tenets of society.

When sufficiently strong, these four elements help to maintain social control and conformity by rendering people unfree to break rules. If these bonds with society are weak, however, delinquency and deviance may result. Hirschi's approach suggests that delinquents are often individuals whose low levels of self-control are a result of inadequate socialization at home or at school (Gottfredson and Hirschi 1990).

CONFLICT THEORY

conflict theory • Argument that deviance is deliberately chosen and often political in nature.

Like reinforcement theorists, adherents to **conflict theory** seek to identify why people commit crime. Rather than drawing on notions of reward maximization, however, conflict theorists draw on elements of Marxist thought to argue that deviance is deliberately chosen and often political in nature. Conflict theorists reject the idea that deviance is "determined" by factors such as biology, personality, anomie, social disorganization, or labels. Rather, individuals purposively engage in deviant behavior in response to the inequalities of the capitalist system. Members of countercultural groups regarded as deviant—such as supporters of the black power or gay liberation movements—are engaging in political acts that challenge the social order.

new criminology • A branch of criminological thought, prominent in Great Britain in the 1970s, that regarded deviance as deliberately chosen and often political in nature. The new criminologists argued that crime and deviance could only be understood in the context of power and inequality within society.

Theorists of the **new criminology** frame their analysis of crime and deviance in terms of the structure of society and the preservation of power among the ruling class. For example, they argue that laws are tools used by the powerful to maintain their own privileged positions. They reject the idea that laws are neutral and are applied evenly across the population. Instead, they claim that as inequalities increase between the ruling class and the working class, law becomes an ever more important instrument for the powerful to maintain order. This dynamic can be seen in the workings of the criminal justice system, which has become increasingly oppressive toward working-class "offenders," or in tax legislation that disproportionately favors the wealthy. This power imbalance is not restricted to the creation of laws, however. The powerful also break laws, but are rarely caught. These crimes on the whole are much more significant than the everyday crime and delinquency that attracts the most attention. But fearful of the implications of pursuing white-collar criminals, law enforcement instead focuses its efforts on less powerful members of society, such as prostitutes, drug users, and petty thieves (Chambliss 1988; Pearce 1976).

Studies by Chambliss, Pearce, and others associated with the new criminology have played an important role in widening the debate about crime and deviance to include questions of social justice, power, and politics. They emphasize that crime occurs at all levels of society and must be understood in the context of inequalities and competing interests between social groups.

SYMBOLIC INTERACTIONIST APPROACHES

LABELING THEORY

labeling theory • An approach to the study of deviance that suggests that people become "deviant" because certain labels are attached to their behavior by political authorities and others.

Symbolic interactionists have made important contributions to our understanding of criminality, exemplified by their development of labeling theory. One of the earliest works based on **labeling theory** is Howard S. Becker's (1963) study of marijuana smokers. In the early 1960s, marijuana use was a marginal activity carried on by subcultures rather than the lifestyle choice—that is, an activity accepted by many in the mainstream of society—it is today (Hathaway 1997). Becker found that becoming a marijuana smoker depended on one's acceptance into the subculture, close association with experienced users, and one's attitudes toward nonusers. Labeling theorists like Becker interpret deviance not as a set of characteristics of individuals or groups, but as a process of interaction between deviants and nondeviants. In other words, it is not the act of marijuana smoking that makes one a deviant, but the way others react to marijuana smoking that makes it deviant. While other sociological perspectives are focused on why people are deviant, labeling theorists seek to understand why some people become tagged with a deviant label.

In short, persons with the greatest social and economic power tend to place labels on those with less social power. Further, the labels that create categories of deviance thus express the power structure of society. The rules in terms of which deviance is defined are framed by the wealthy for the poor, by men for women, by older people for younger people, and by ethnic majorities for minority groups. For example, many children wander into other people's gardens, steal fruit, or play truant. In an affluent neighborhood, these might be regarded by parents, teachers, and police alike as relatively innocent pastimes of childhood. In poor areas, they might be seen as evidence of tendencies toward juvenile delinquency.

Once a child is labeled a delinquent, he is stigmatized as a deviant and is likely to be considered untrustworthy by teachers and prospective employers. He then relapses into further criminal behavior, widening the gulf with orthodox social conventions. Edwin Lemert (1972) called the initial act of rule breaking **primary deviance**. **Secondary deviance** occurs when the individual comes to accept the label and sees himself as deviant. The "self-fulfilling prophecy" may occur, where the labeled person begins to behave in such a way that perpetuates the deviant behavior. Research has shown that how we think of ourselves and how we believe others perceive us influences our propensity for committing crime. One study examining self-appraisals of a random national sample of young men showed that such appraisals are strongly tied to levels of criminality (Matsueda 1992).

Labeling theory is important because it begins from the assumption that no act is intrinsically deviant. Rather, to be "deviant," one must be labeled as such. In the case of criminal activity, definitions of criminality are established by the powerful through the formulation of laws and their interpretation by police, courts, and correctional institutions. Critics of labeling theory have sometimes argued that certain acts such as murder, rape, and robbery are consistently prohibited across virtually all cultures. This view is surely incorrect. Even within our own culture, killing is not always regarded as murder; in times of war, killing of the enemy is positively approved. And until recently the laws in most U.S. states did not recognize sexual intercourse forced on a woman by her husband as rape.

We can more convincingly criticize labeling theory on other grounds. First, in emphasizing the active process of labeling, labeling theorists neglect the processes that lead to acts defined as deviant. Labeling certain activities as deviant is not completely arbitrary; differences in socialization, attitudes, and opportunities influence how far people engage in behavior likely to be labeled deviant. For instance, children from deprived backgrounds are on average more likely to steal from shops than are richer children. It is not the labeling that leads them to steal in the first place so much as the background from which they come.

Second, it is not clear whether labeling actually does have the effect of increasing deviant conduct. Delinquent behavior tends to increase following a conviction, but is this the result of the labeling itself? Other factors, such as increased interaction with other delinquents or learning about new criminal opportunities, may be involved.

primary deviance • According to Edwin Lemert, the actions that cause others to label one as a deviant.

secondary deviance • According to Edwin Lemert, following the act of primary deviance, secondary deviation occurs when an individual accepts the label of deviant and acts accordingly.

THEORETICAL CONCLUSIONS

The contributions of the sociological theories of crime are twofold. First, these theories correctly emphasize the continuities between criminal and "respectable" behavior. The contexts in which particular types of activity are seen as criminal and punishable by law vary widely. Second, all agree that context is important in criminal activities. Whether someone engages in a criminal act or comes to be regarded as a criminal is influenced fundamentally by social learning and social surroundings.

The way in which crime is understood directly affects the policies developed to combat it. For example, if crime is seen as the product of deprivation or social disorganization, policies might be aimed at reducing poverty and strengthening social services. If criminality is seen as voluntaristic, or freely chosen by individuals, attempts to counter it will take a different form. Now let's look directly at the nature of the criminal activities occurring in modern societies, paying particular attention to crime in the United States. ✓

CONCEPT CHECKS ✓

1. What are the main similarities and differences between biological and psychological views of deviance?

2. How do Merton's and Durkheim's definitions of anomie differ?

3. According to subcultural explanations, how does criminal behavior get transmitted from one group to another?

4. What is the core idea behind differential association theory?

5. What are two criticisms of labeling theory?

6. What are the root causes of crime, according to conflict theorists?

HOW DO WE DOCUMENT CRIME?

How dangerous are our streets compared with yesteryear? Is American society more violent than other societies? You should be able to use the sociological skills you have developed already to answer these questions.

In Chapter 1, for example, we learned something about how to interpret statistics. Crime statistics are a constant focus of attention on television and in the newspapers. Most TV and newspaper reporting is based on official statistics on crime, collected by the police and published by the government. Most of these reports are based on two sources: Uniform Crime Reports (UCR) and victimization studies. Each has its own limitations, and offers only a partial portrait of crime in American life.

Uniform Crime Reports (UCR) document contain official data on crime that is reported to law enforcement agencies across the country who then provide the data to the Federal Bureau of Investigation (FBI). UCR focus on "index crimes," which include serious crimes such as murder and non-negligent manslaughter, robbery, forcible rape, aggravated assault, burglary, larceny/theft, motor vehicle theft, and arson. Critics of UCR note that they do not accurately reflect crime rates because they include only those crimes reported to law enforcement agencies. Further, the index crimes do not include less serious crimes, or crimes reported to other agencies such as the IRS. Some argue that by excluding crimes that are traditionally committed by middle-class persons, such as fraud and embezzlement, UCR reify the belief that crime is an activity of the poor and ethnic minorities.

Because the UCR program focuses narrowly on crimes reported to the police, criminologists also rely on self-reports provided by the crime victims themselves. This second source of data is essential, as some criminologists think that about half of all serious crimes, such as robbery with violence, are not reported. The proportion

Uniform Crime Reports (UCR) • Documents that contain official data on crime that is reported to law enforcement agencies who then provide the data to the FBI.

of less serious crimes, especially small thefts, that don't come to the attention of the police is even higher. Since 1973, the Bureau of the Census has been interviewing households across the country to find out how many members were the victims of particular crimes over the previous six months. This procedure, which is called the National Crime Victimization Survey, has confirmed that the overall rate of crime is higher than the reported crime index. For instance, in 2004, only 50 percent of violent crimes were reported, including only 36 percent of rapes, 61 percent of robberies, 45 percent of simple assaults, and 53 percent of burglaries. Auto theft is the crime most frequently reported to the police (85 percent) (Catalano 2005).

Public concern in the United States tends to focus on crimes of violence—murder, assault, and rape—even though only about 12.4 percent of all crimes are violent (Figure 6.3). In general, whether indexed by police statistics or by the National Crime Victimization Survey, violent crime, burglary, and car theft are more common in cities than in the suburbs surrounding them, and they are more common in the suburbs than in smaller towns.

In the 1990s, there was a drop in the overall crime rate throughout the United States to its lowest levels since 1973, when the victimization survey was first used. Rates of violent crime in particular dropped substantially, murders by 31 percent and robberies by 32 percent. There is no one prevailing explanation among sociologists for this decline, although many politicians would like to take credit for it. Aggressive new efforts by local police to stop the use of guns certainly contributed to the decrease in homicides, but other social factors were also at work. Key among these were the declining market for crack cocaine and the stigmatization of crack among young urban dwellers, and the booming economy of the 1990s, which provided job opportunities for those who may have been enticed to work in the drug trade (Butterfield 1998).

One reason often given for the relatively high rates of violent crime in the United States is the widespread availability of handguns and other firearms. This is relevant but does not provide a complete answer. Switzerland has very low rates of violent crime, yet firearms are easily accessible. All Swiss males are members of the citizen army and keep weapons in their homes, including rifles, revolvers, and sometimes other automatic weapons, plus ammunition; nor are gun licenses difficult to obtain.

The most likely explanation for the high level of violent crime in the United States is a combination of the availability of firearms, the general influence of the "frontier tradition," and the subcultures of violence in the large cities. Violence by frontiersmen and vigilantes is an honored part of American history. Some of the first established immigrant areas in the cities developed their own informal modes of neighborhood control, backed by violence or the threat of violence. Similarly, young people in African American and Hispanic communities today have developed subcultures of manliness and honor associated with rituals of violence, and some belong to gangs whose everyday life is one of drug dealing, territory protection, and violence.

Although reports of horrific crimes regularly kick off evening news reports, in reality, most crimes are mundane and happen quietly, behind closed doors. Most assaults and homicides bear little resemblance to the murderous, random acts of gunmen or the carefully planned homicides given most prominence in the media. Murders generally happen in the context of family and other interpersonal relationships; the victim usually knows his or her murderer. ✓

CONCEPT CHECKS ✓

1. What are the main sources of crime data in the United States?

2. Contrast Uniform Crime Reports and the National Crime Victimization Survey.

3. Describe crime trends in the 1970s through today.

4. How would sociologists explain the high rate of violent crime in the United States?

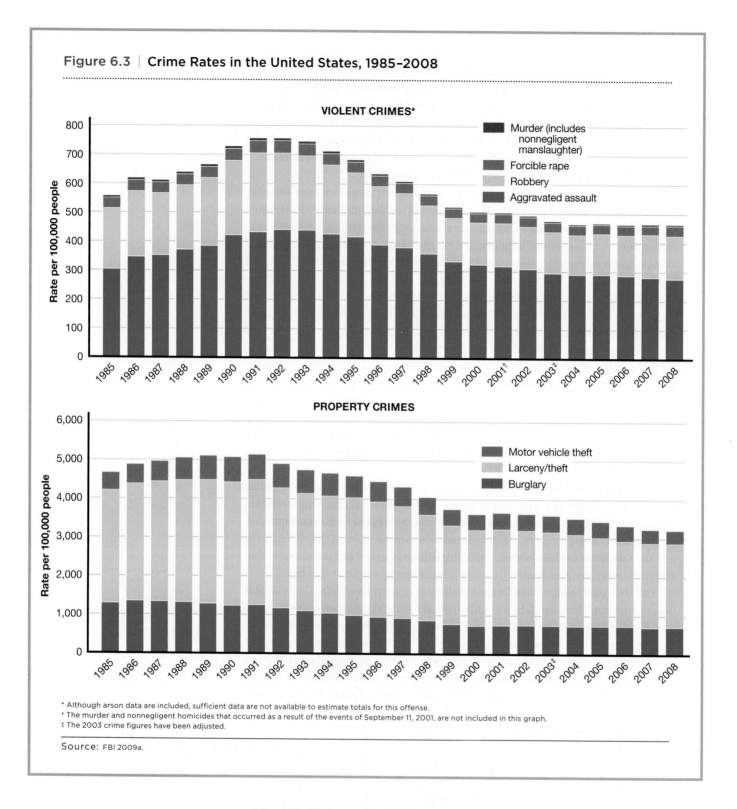

Figure 6.3 | **Crime Rates in the United States, 1985–2008**

VIOLENT CRIMES*

- Murder (includes nonnegligent manslaughter)
- Forcible rape
- Robbery
- Aggravated assault

Rate per 100,000 people

PROPERTY CRIMES

- Motor vehicle theft
- Larceny/theft
- Burglary

Rate per 100,000 people

* Although arson data are included, sufficient data are not available to estimate totals for this offense.
† The murder and nonnegligent homicides that occurred as a result of the events of September 11, 2001, are not included in this graph.
‡ The 2003 crime figures have been adjusted.

Source: FBI 2009a.

WHOSE LIVES ARE AFFECTED BY CRIME?

Are some individuals or groups more likely to commit crimes or to become the victims of crime? (See "D.I.Y." box on p. 163.) Criminologists say yes—research and crime statistics show that crime and victimization are not random occurrences across the population. Men, young persons, and African Americans are more likely than women, older persons, and whites to be both crime victims and perpetrators. Young African American men face a triple disadvantage in the United States (see Figure 6.4). For example, the rate of murder among black male teenagers is over six times the rate for their white counterparts, though this disparity has been declining in recent years.

The likelihood of someone becoming a victim of crime is closely linked to other social factors including where he or she lives. Areas suffering from greater material deprivation generally have higher crime rates. Individuals living in inner-city neighborhoods run a much greater risk of becoming victims of crime than do residents of more affluent suburban areas. That ethnic minorities are concentrated disproportionately in inner-city regions appears to be a significant factor in their higher rates of victimization.

GENDER AND CRIME

Like other areas of sociology, criminological studies have traditionally ignored half the population. Feminists have been correct in criticizing criminology for being a male-dominated discipline in which women are largely invisible in both theoretical considerations and empirical studies. Since the 1970s, many important feminist works have drawn attention to the way in which criminal transgressions by women occur in different contexts from those by men, and to how women's experiences with the criminal justice system are influenced by certain gendered assumptions about appropriate male and female roles. Feminists have also played a critical role in highlighting the prevalence of violence against women, both at home and in public.

MALE AND FEMALE CRIME RATES

The statistics on gender and crime are startling. In 2007, an overwhelming 86.4 percent of people in jail were adult men (Bureau of Justice Statistics 2008b). Men drastically outnumber women in prison, not only in the United States but in all industrialized countries. Adult women made up only 12.6 percent of the prison population in 2008.

Men and women also vary in the types of crimes they commit; women rarely engage in violent crime and instead tend to commit less serious offenses. Petty thefts like shoplifting and public order offenses such as public drunkenness and prostitution are typical female crimes.

A controversial argument set forth in the 1950s proposes, however, that the gender gap may be less vast then statistics suggest. Otto Pollak (1950) argued that women's crimes may go undetected or unreported, or may be treated more leniently by (male) police officers, who adopt a "chivalrous" attitude toward them. A number of empirical studies have been undertaken to test the chivalry thesis, but the results remain inconclusive.

Recent research by feminist scholars does reveal that violence is not exclusively a characteristic of male criminality. By studying girl gangs, female terrorists, and women prisoners, scholars

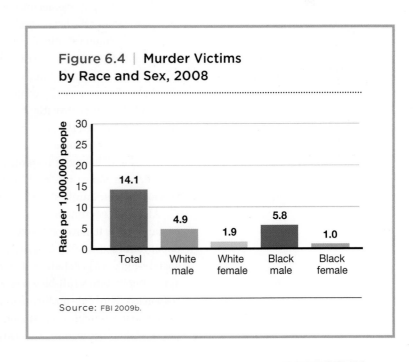

Figure 6.4 | **Murder Victims by Race and Sex, 2008**

Rate per 1,000,000 people

Total: 14.1
White male: 4.9
White female: 1.9
Black male: 5.8
Black female: 1.0

Source: FBI 2009b.

have demonstrated that women are much less likely than men to participate in violent crime but are not always inhibited from taking part in violent episodes. Why, then, are female rates of criminality so much lower than those of men?

There is some evidence that female lawbreakers quite often escape coming before the courts because they are able to persuade the police or other authorities to see their actions in a particular light. They invoke what has been called the "gender contract"—the implicit contract between men and women whereby to be a woman is to be erratic and impulsive on the one hand and in need of protection on the other (Worrall 1990). Yet differential treatment could hardly account for the vast difference between male and female rates of crime.

The reasons are almost certainly the same as those that explain gender differences in other spheres. "Male crimes" remain "male" because of differences in socialization and because men's activities and involvements are still more nondomestic than those of most women. Further, control theory also may offer insights. Because women are usually the primary caregiver to their children and other relatives, they may have attachments and commitments that prevent them from committing deviant acts. Imprisonment would have very high and undesirable costs both to women and their kin.

As the boundaries between men's and women's social roles increasingly blur, however, criminologists have predicted that gender equality would reduce or eliminate the differences in criminality between men and women. Whether the variations between female and male crime rates will one day disappear we still cannot say with any certainty.

YOUTH AND CRIME

Popular fear about crime centers on offenses such as theft, burglary, assault, and rape—street crimes that are largely seen as the domain of young working-class males. Media coverage of rising crime rates often focuses on moral breakdown among young people and highlights such issues as vandalism, school truancy, and drug use to illustrate the increasing permissiveness in society. This equation of youth with criminal activity is not a new one, according to some sociologists. Young people are often taken as an indicator of the health and welfare of society itself.

Official crime statistics do reveal high rates of offense among young people. About 34 percent of all offenders arrested for criminal offenses in 2007 were under the age of twenty-one (Federal Bureau of Investigation 2007a). For both males and females, the share of arrests peaks around age eighteen or nineteen and declines thereafter (Federal Bureau of Investigation 2005a). Control theory has been used to explain this pattern, called the *age-crime curve*. As young people gradually transition into adulthood, they acquire the very social attachments and commitments that make "conventional" behavior rewarding. As they marry, have children, find jobs, and set up their own homes, the "cost" of deviance is high; rational actors would not want to risk losing their families and homes and thus avoid deviant acts.

Although criminologists have demonstrated persuasively that most youthful deviants go on to have perfectly happy, healthy, law-abiding lives, widespread panic about youth criminality persist. Importantly, these panics may not accurately reflect social reality. An isolated event involving young people and crime can be transformed symbolically into a full-blown crisis of childhood, demanding tough law-and-order responses. The high-profile mass murders at Columbine High School and Virginia Tech provide examples of how moral outrage can deflect attention from larger societal issues. Columbine was a watershed event in media portrayals of youth crime, and some

DO-IT-YOURSELF SOCIOLOGY

D.I.Y.

What Is Your Risk of Becoming a Crime Victim?

Although evening news reports suggest that crime happens randomly, with innocent bystanders being grazed by flying bullets, sociological research documents that important social, economic, and geographic factors affect both one's chances of being a perpetrator and of being a victim of crime. These factors are not deterministic, but they do help us understand differences in one's risk of being affected by crime. What is your risk of being a crime victim? On average, the following characteristics affect one's overall chances of being victimized, although risk factors vary by type of crime.

How likely are you to be a victim of a crime? Answer these 10 questions and compare your answers with the risk factors reported on the next page.

1. What is your gender? _____
2. What is your race or ethnicity? _____
3. Do you live in a poor, middle-class, or wealthy neighborhood? _____
4. Have you been a victim of a crime in the past? _____
5. Do you live in the South? _____
6. How often do you drink alcohol? _____
7. How old are you? _____
8. How much is your annual income? _____
9. What is your marital status? _____
10. What is your job? _____

TURN PAGE →

have speculated that it led to "copycat" school killings in high schools in Arkansas, Kentucky, California, and elsewhere. Even though the number of murders committed on school and university grounds has been declining over the past half century, attention to these mass murders has led many to think that all youth are potential violent threats. The perpetrators of the Columbine killings were labeled "monsters" and "animals"; less attention was paid to how easily they were able to obtain the weapons they used to commit these murders.

Similar caution can be expressed about the popular view of drug use by teenagers. Every year, the Department of Health and Human Services conducts the National

Increase Chances of Crime Victimization?	Decrease Chances of Crime Victimization?
Male	Female
African American or Native American	White or Asian
Reside in poor neighborhood	Reside in middle-class neighborhood
Reside in a neighborhood with a high crime rate	Reside in a neighborhood with a low crime rate
Having been a victim in the past	No prior victimizations
Reside in the South	Reside in the non-South
High levels of alcohol use	Low to moderate levels of alcohol use
Teenager or young adult	Mature adult
Low household income	Moderate to high income
Divorced or separated	Currently married
Work as law enforcement officer, security guard, or taxicab driver	Work as college professor

Source: U.S. Bureau of Justice Statistics 2008c.

Survey of Drug Use and Health about drug use habits. In 2007 it surveyed nearly sixty-eight thousand noninstitutionalized individuals over the age of twelve and found that 51.1 percent of respondents between the ages of twelve and seventeen had reported being current drinkers of alcohol and 23.3 percent had participated in binge drinking at least once in the 30 days prior to the survey. Similarly, about 24.2 percent had smoked a cigarette, while 8 percent had used an illicit drug in the last month (U.S. Department of Health and Human Services 2007b).

Trends in drug use have shifted away from hard drugs such as heroin and toward combinations of substances such as amphetamines, prescription drugs like OxyContin, alcohol, and the drug ecstasy. Ecstasy in particular has become a lifestyle drug associated with the rave and club subcultures, rather than the basis of an expensive, addictive habit. The war on drugs, some have argued, criminalizes large segments of the youth population who are generally law abiding (Muncie 1999).

Taking illegal drugs, like other forms of socially deviant behavior, is often defined in racial, class, and cultural terms; different drugs come to be associated with different groups and behaviors. When crack cocaine appeared in the 1980s, it was quickly defined by the media as the drug of choice for black, inner-city kids who listened to hip-hop. Perhaps as a result, jail sentences for crack possession were set at higher levels than sentences for possession of cocaine, which was associated more with white and suburban users. Ecstasy has, until recently, had similar white and middle- or upper-class associations.

CRIMES OF THE POWERFUL

It is plain enough that there are connections between crime and poverty. But it would be a mistake to assume that crime is concentrated among the poor. Crimes carried out by people in positions of power and wealth can have farther-reaching consequences than the often petty crimes of the poor.

The term **white-collar crime**, first introduced by Edwin Sutherland (1949), refers to crime typically carried out by people in the more affluent sectors of society. This category of criminal activity includes tax fraud, antitrust violations, illegal sales practices, securities and land fraud, embezzlement, the manufacture or sale of dangerous products, and illegal environmental pollution, as well as straightforward theft. The distribution of white-collar crimes is even harder to measure than that of other types of crime; most do not appear in the official statistics at all.

Efforts to detect white-collar crime are ordinarily limited, and it is only on rare occasions that those who are caught go to jail. Although the authorities regard white-collar crime in a more tolerant light than crimes of the less privileged, it has been calculated that the amount of money involved in white-collar crime in the United States is forty times greater than the amount involved in crimes against property, such as robberies, burglaries, larceny, forgeries, and car thefts (President's Commission on Organized Crime 1986). Some forms of white-collar crime, moreover, affect more people than lower-class criminality. An embezzler might rob thousands—or today, via computer fraud, millions—of people.

white-collar crime • Criminal activities carried out by those in white-collar, or professional, jobs.

CORPORATE CRIME

Corporate crime refers to the types of offenses that are committed by large corporations in society. Pollution, product mislabeling, and violations of health and safety regulations affect much larger numbers of people than does petty criminality. Both quantitative and qualitative studies of corporate crime have concluded that a large number of corporations do not adhere to the legal regulations that apply to them (Slapper and Tombs 1999). Corporate crime is not confined to a few bad apples but is instead pervasive and widespread. Studies have revealed six types of violations linked to large corporations: administrative (paperwork or noncompliance), environmental (pollution, permits violations), financial (tax violations, illegal payments), labor (working conditions, hiring practices), manufacturing (product safety, labeling), and unfair trade practices (anticompetition, false advertising).

corporate crime • Offenses committed by large corporations in society. Examples of corporate crime include pollution, false advertising, and violations of health and safety regulations.

Sometimes there are obvious victims, as in environmental disasters such as the 1984 spill at the Bhopal chemical plant in India and the health dangers posed to women by silicone breast implants. But very often victims of corporate crime do not see themselves as such. This is because in "traditional" crimes the proximity between victim and offender is much closer—it is difficult not to realize that you have been mugged! In the case of corporate crime, greater distances in time and space mean that victims may not realize they have been victimized or may not know how to seek redress for the crime.

The effects of corporate crime are often experienced unevenly within society. Those who are disadvantaged by other types of socioeconomic inequalities tend to suffer disproportionately. For example, safety and health risks in the workplace tend to be concentrated most heavily in low-paying occupations. Many of the risks from health care products and pharmaceuticals have had a greater impact on women than

One of the most high profile white collar criminals in recent memory is Bernie Madoff, a financier who choreographed a $50 million Ponzi scheme to defraud thousands of people and organizations.

on men, as is the case with contraceptives or fertility treatments with harmful side effects (Slapper and Tombs 1999).

ORGANIZED CRIME

organized crime • Criminal activities carried out by organizations established as businesses.

Organized crime refers to forms of activity that have some of the characteristics of orthodox business but that are illegal. Organized crime embraces illegal gambling, drug dealing, prostitution, large-scale theft, and protection rackets, among other activities. In *End of Millennium* (1998), Manuel Castells argues that the activities of organized crime groups are becoming increasingly international in scope. The coordination of criminal activities across borders—with the help of new information technologies—is becoming a central feature of the new global economy. Involved in activities ranging from the narcotics trade to counterfeiting to smuggling immigrants and human organs, organized crime groups are now operating in flexible international networks rather than within their own territorial realms.

According to Castells, criminal groups set up strategic alliances with each other. The international narcotics trade, weapons trafficking, the sale of nuclear material, and money laundering have all become linked across borders and crime groups. The flexible nature of this networked crime makes it relatively easy for crime groups to evade the reach of law enforcement initiatives.

Despite numerous campaigns by the government and the police, the narcotics trade is one of the most rapidly expanding international criminal industries, having an annual growth rate of more than 10 percent in the 1980s and early 1990s and an extremely high level of profit. The United Nations Office on Drugs and Crime (2005) has estimated that in 2004 the global trade in illegal drugs was worth $322 billion—more than the global trade in coffee, grains, or meat. Heroin networks stretch across Asia, particularly South Asia, and are also located in North Africa, the Middle East, and Latin America. Supply lines also pass through Vancouver and other parts of Canada; from here drugs are commonly supplied to the United States. ✓

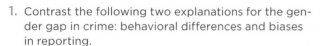

CONCEPT CHECKS ✓

1. Contrast the following two explanations for the gender gap in crime: behavioral differences and biases in reporting.

2. What is the age-crime curve, and what factors have contributed to this pattern?

3. What are some of the consequences of white-collar crime?

4. Give one example of an activity classified as organized crime.

HOW CAN CRIME BE REDUCED?

Despite the limitations of official crime statistics, they do provide laypersons with a snapshot of criminal activity in their neighborhoods. However, citizens often perceive themselves to be at greater risk of falling victim to crime than crime statistics would predict. Residents of inner-city areas have more reason to be concerned about crime than people living in other settings. Regardless of whether these fears are accurate, both individuals and governments feel strongly that crime and victimization must be curtailed. In fact, one of the central tasks of social policy in modern states has been controlling crime and delinquency. Which policies and practices are most effective? And why?

ARE PRISONS THE ANSWER?

According to police statistics, rates of violent crime have declined since 1990. Ironically, however, many people in the United States continue to view crime as their most serious social concern (Lacayo 1994). Surveys show that Americans favor tougher prison sentences for all but relatively minor crimes. The price of imprisonment, however, is enormous: In 2008 it cost an average of $25,895 to keep a prisoner in the federal prison system for one year (U.S. Courts 2008). Some argue that this is not money well spent: Even if the prison system were expanded, it wouldn't reduce the level of serious crime a great deal. Only about a fifth of all serious crimes result in an arrest—and this is of crimes known to the police, an underestimate of the true rate of crime. And no more than half of arrests for serious crimes result in a conviction. Even so, America's prisons are so overcrowded (Figure 6.5) that the average convict only serves a third of his sentence.

The United States already locks up more people (nearly all men) per capita than any other country. More than 2.3 million people are presently incarcerated in American prisons (U.S. Bureau of Justice Statistics 2008c; McDonough 2005; Slevin 2005). More than one quarter of African American men are either in prison or otherwise under the control of the penal system. Some 57 percent of individuals imprisoned in the United States are serving sentences for nonviolent drug-related crimes.

Support for *capital punishment* (the death penalty) also is high in the United States. In 2008, approximately 63 percent of adults surveyed said that they believed in capital punishment; 30 percent opposed it (Harris Poll 2008). This represents a significant shift from 1965, when 38 percent of those surveyed supported the death penalty and 47 percent were opposed. However, given the choice between the death penalty and life imprisonment, the share of those supporting the death penalty falls to 50 percent (ABC News/Washington Post Poll 2006). The number of individuals awaiting execution has climbed steadily since 1977, when the

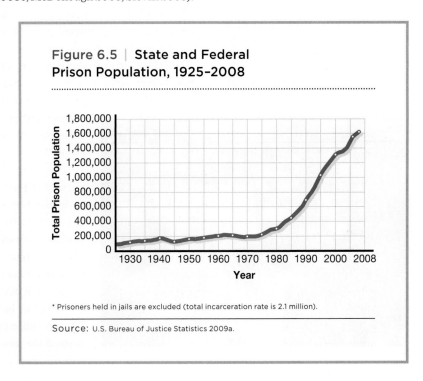

Figure 6.5 | **State and Federal Prison Population, 1925–2008**

* Prisoners held in jails are excluded (total incarceration rate is 2.1 million).

Source: U.S. Bureau of Justice Statistics 2009a.

Supreme Court upheld state capital punishment laws. Since that time there have been 1,168 executions in the United States (Death Penalty Information Center 2009). Two thirds of these executions have taken place in five states: Texas (439), Virginia (103), Oklahoma (90), Missouri (67), and Florida (67). At the end of 2008, a total of 3,309 prisoners were held on death row (Death Penalty Information Center 2009b). The group was 98.5 percent men, 42 percent white, and 45 percent black. In 2008 a total of 37 prisoners were executed in ten states, and all were men.

While we might suppose that imprisoning large numbers of people or stiffening sentences would deter individuals from committing crimes, there is little evidence to support this. In fact, sociological studies have demonstrated that prisons can easily become schools for crime. Instead of preventing people from committing crimes, prisons often actually make them more hardened criminals. This pattern is consistent with the key theme of differential association theory, discussed earlier; deviance is learned by deviant peers. The more harsh and oppressive prison conditions are, the more likely inmates are to be brutalized by the experience. Yet if prisons were made into attractive and pleasant places to live, would they have a deterrent effect?

Although prisons do keep some dangerous men (and a tiny minority of dangerous women) off the streets, evidence suggests that we need to find other means to deter crime. A sociological interpretation of crime makes clear that there are no quick fixes. The causes of crime, especially crimes of violence, are bound up with structural conditions of American society, including widespread poverty, the condition of the inner cities, and the deteriorating life circumstances of many young men.

THE MARK OF A CRIMINAL RECORD

An experiment by sociologist Devah Pager (2003) showed the long-term consequences of prison on the lives of felons. Pager had pairs of young black and white men apply for real entry-level job openings throughout the city of Milwaukee. The applicant pairs were matched by appearance, interpersonal style, and, most important, by all job-related characteristics such as education level and prior work experience. In addition to varying the race of the applicant pairs, Pager also had applicants alternate presenting themselves to employers as having criminal records. One member of each of the applicant pairs would check the box "yes" on the applicant form in answer to the question, "Have you ever been convicted of a crime?" The pair alternated each week which young man would play the role of the ex-offender. The experimental design allowed Pager to make the applicant pairs identical on all job-relevant characteristics so that she could know for sure that any differences she saw were the result of discrimination against felons, rather than other qualifications or weaknesses of the applicant.

Pager's study revealed some striking findings. First, whites were much preferred over blacks, and nonoffenders were much preferred over ex-offenders. Whites with a felony conviction were half as likely to be considered by employers as equally qualified nonoffenders. For blacks the effects were even larger: Black ex-offenders were only one-third as likely to receive a call back compared to nonoffenders. Even more surprising was the comparison of these two effects: Blacks with no criminal history fared no better than did whites with a felony conviction. These results suggest that being a black male in America today is about the same as being a convicted criminal, at least in the

How do factors such as a criminal record affect an individual's ability to get a job? Elton Luckey looks at a list of potential employers at a job fair for ex-convicts in Dallas, Texas. Police said more than 5,000 people attended the event, which was co-sponsored by churches and advocacy groups for former inmates.

Figure 6.6

INCARCERATION RATES AROUND THE WORLD

Number of people in prison per 100,000 population

0 100 300 500 700 1,000

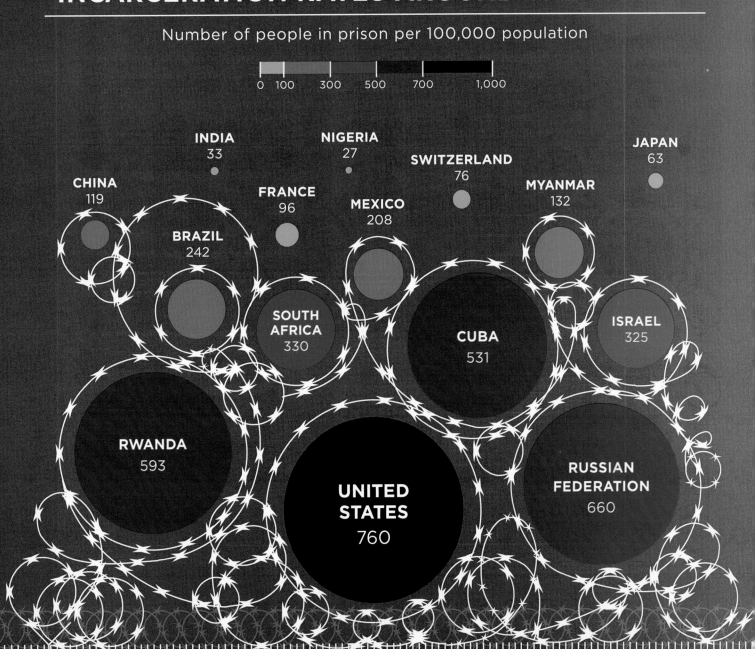

INDIA
33

NIGERIA
27

SWITZERLAND
76

JAPAN
63

CHINA
119

FRANCE
96

MEXICO
208

MYANMAR
132

BRAZIL
242

SOUTH
AFRICA
330

CUBA
531

ISRAEL
325

RWANDA
593

UNITED
STATES
760

RUSSIAN
FEDERATION
660

WHO'S IN PRISON IN THE UNITED STATES?

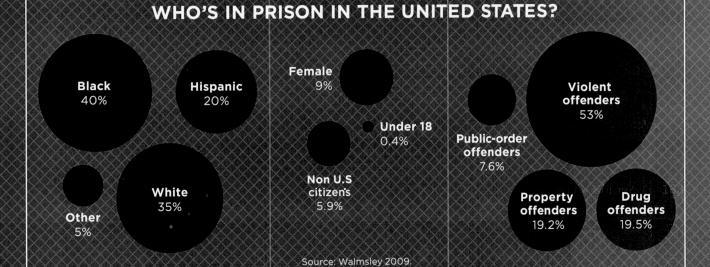

Black
40%

Hispanic
20%

Female
9%

Under 18
0.4%

Violent
offenders
53%

Public-order
offenders
7.6%

White
35%

Non U.S
citizens
5.9%

Property
offenders
19.2%

Drug
offenders
19.5%

Other
5%

Source: Walmsley 2009.

Drug Trafficking

How easy would it have been for you to purchase marijuana in high school? How easy would it be to do so today? Lamentable as it may seem to some, most young people in the United States have relatively easy access to illegal drugs. According to the National Survey on Drug Use and Health, nearly 11 percent of those between ages twelve and seventeen have used illegal drugs in the last month; less than 1 percent have tried heroin. Almost 53 percent of those aged eighteen to twenty-five have tried marijuana at least once, and nearly 2 percent have tried heroin (U.S. Department of Health and Human Services 2005a).

What factors determine the availability of illegal drugs in your community? The level of police enforcement is important, of course, as is the extent of local demand. But no less important is the existence of networks of traffickers able to transport the drugs from the countries in which they are grown to your hometown. These networks have been able to flourish in part because of globalization.

While the cultivation of marijuana in the United States represents a major illicit industry, almost all of the world's coca plants and opium poppies are grown in the developing world. The U.S. government spends billions of dollars each year to assist developing nations with eradication efforts and also devotes significant resources to stopping

the flow of drugs past U.S. borders. In 1995, the federal government spent more than $8.2 billion on the "war on drugs"; between 1981 and 1996 the government spent a total of $65 billion (Bertram et al. 1996). By 2005, the annual federal budget for the war on drugs had climbed to $12.4 billion, but this figure excludes the costs of incarceration as well as military involvement (Office of National Drug Control Policy 2005). It also excludes funds spent by state governments to wage the war on drugs, estimated to be an additional $30 billion (Drug-WarFacts.org 2005). Despite this massive expenditure, there is little evidence that eradication or interdiction

eyes of Milwaukee employers. For those who believe that race no longer represents a major barrier to opportunity, these results represent a powerful challenge. Being a black felon is a particularly tough obstacle to overcome.

POLICING

Some sociologists and criminologists have suggested that visible policing techniques, such as patrolling the streets, are reassuring for the public. Such activities are consistent with the perception that the police are actively engaged in controlling crime, efforts have significantly decreased the supply of illegal drugs in the United States. Why have these efforts failed?

One answer is that the profit is simply too great. Farmers struggling to scratch out a living for themselves in Bolivia or Peru, members of the Colombian drug cartels, and low-level street dealers in the United States all receive substantial monetary rewards for their illegal activities. These rewards create a strong incentive to devise ways around antidrug efforts and to run the risk of getting caught.

Another answer—one discussed at a summit attended by leaders of the eight major industrial powers—is that drug traffickers have been able to take advantage of globalization. First, in their attempts to evade the authorities, traffickers make use of all the communications technologies that are available in a global age. As one commentator put it, drug traffickers "now use sophisticated technology, such as signal interceptors, to plot radar and avoid monitoring . . . [and] they can use faxes, computers and cellular phones to coordinate their activities and make their business run smoothly" (Chepesiuk 1998). Second, the globalization of the financial sector has helped create an infrastructure in which large sums of money can be moved around the world electronically in a matter of seconds, making it relatively easy to "launder" drug money (i.e., to make it appear to have come from

a legitimate business venture). Third, recent changes in government policy designed to allow the freer flow of persons and legitimate goods across international borders have increased the opportunities for smuggling.

At the same time, globalization may create new opportunities for governments to work together to combat drug trafficking. Indeed, world leaders have called for greater international cooperation in narcotics enforcement, stressing the need for information sharing and coordinated enforcement efforts.

investigating offenses, and supporting the criminal justice system. But sociologists also suggest that we need to reassess the role of policing in the early twenty-first century. Although maintaining law and order, interacting with citizens, and providing services are part of contemporary policing, they represent only a fraction of what the police actually do. Policing, sociologists argue, is now less about controlling crime and more about detecting and managing risks. Most of all, it is about communicating knowledge about risk to other institutions in society that demand that information (Ericson and Haggerty 1997).

According to this view police are first and foremost "knowledge workers." As such, the vast majority of police time is spent on activities aimed at processing information,

Nearly every day, the evening news recounts a story of a brutal crime committed by an offender who is out on parole. Among the most startling was the April 2006 murder of a Roman Catholic nun, Sister Karen Klimczak, sixty-two. At the time of her murder, Klimczak had lived for sixteen years in a rectory that she had converted into Bissonette House, a halfway house for recently released convicts. Her upstate New York community was shocked when she was murdered by Craig Lunch, a convicted car thief who moved into Bissonette after being paroled from a medium-security prison. Such high-visibility stories draw attention away from the fact that many released convicts do resume law-abiding and successful lives after their release from jail. But reintegrating into society can be difficult, and ex-convicts' readjustment often depends on the assistance they receive from parole officers. Parole officers monitor the living arrangements, daily activities, and personal needs of ex-convicts and help them find and maintain jobs, and reestablish secure relationships with members of their family. However, parole officers often face uphill battles as they try to help their clients establish normal lives. The work of sociologist Devah Pager demonstrates just how difficult it is for parolees to find work. Drawing on the work of Pager and others, how would you try to assist your clients most effectively if you were a parole officer?

drafting reports, or communicating data. The "simple" case of an automobile accident in Ontario, Canada, illustrates this point. A police officer is called to the scene of an automobile accident involving two vehicles. No one has been killed, but there are minor injuries and one of the drivers is drunk. The investigation takes one hour; the drunk driver is charged with the impaired operation of a motor vehicle causing bodily harm and with operating a motor vehicle with excess alcohol. The driver's license is automatically suspended for twelve hours.

Following this routine investigation, the officer spends three hours writing up sixteen separate reports documenting the incident. The officer is required to provide information for the provincial motor registry about the vehicle and people involved; the automobile industry must be informed about the vehicles involved in the accident; the insurance companies need information about the case; the public health system requires details on any injuries; the criminal courts require police information for the prosecution; and the police administration needs reports on the incident for internal records and national databases.

This example reveals how the police are a key node in a complicated information circuit of institutions that are all in the business of risk management. With the help of new forms of technology, police work is increasingly about mapping and predicting risk within the population.

This emphasis on information collection and processing can be frustrating for police, especially those who entered the force because they wanted to interact with people—not paper files and computers. Many police officers see a vast distinction between "real" police work—such as investigating crimes—and the "donkey work" of reports and paper trails; they do not see the point of the extensive documentation that is required.

CRIME AND COMMUNITY

Preventing crime and reducing fear of crime are both important paths to rebuilding strong communities. One of the most significant innovations in criminology in recent years has been the discovery that the decay of day-to-day civility relates directly to criminality. Although sociologists and criminologists in earlier decades focused almost exclusively on serious crime—robbery, assault, and other violent crime—they have since discovered that minor crimes and public disorder have a powerful effect on neighborhoods. When asked to describe their problems, residents of troubled neighborhoods mention seemingly minor concerns such as abandoned cars, graffiti, prostitution, youth gangs, and similar phenomena.

People act on their anxieties about these issues: They move out of these neighborhoods (if they can afford to), they buy heavy locks for their doors and bars for their windows, they abandon public places like parks, and they even avoid healthy behaviors like jogging and walking because of fear. As they withdraw physically, they also withdraw from roles of mutual support with fellow citizens, thereby relinquishing the social controls that formerly helped to maintain civility within the community.

The recognition that even seemingly small acts of crime and disorder can threaten a neighborhood is based on the *broken windows theory* (Wilson and Kelling 1982). This sociological theory evolved from an innovative study conducted by the social psychologist Philip Zimbardo. He abandoned cars without license plates and with their hoods up in two entirely different social settings, the wealthy community of Palo Alto, California, and a poor neighborhood in the Bronx, New York. In both places, both cars were vandalized once passersby, regardless of class or race, sensed that the cars were abandoned and that "no one cared" (Zimbardo 1969). Any sign of social disorder in a community, even one unrepaired broken window, is a sign that no one cares. Breaking more windows—that is, committing more serious crimes—is a rational response by criminals to this situation of social disorder. Minor acts of deviance can lead to a spiral of crime and social decay.

In the late 1980s and 1990s, the broken windows theory served as the basis for new policing strategies that aggressively focused on minor crimes such as traffic violations and drinking or using drugs in public. Studies have shown that proactive policing directed at maintaining public order can have a positive effect on reducing more serious crimes such as robbery (Sampson and Cohen 1988). However, one flaw of the broken windows theory is that the police are left to identify "social disorder" however they wish. Without a systematic definition of disorder, the police are authorized to see almost anything as a sign of disorder and anyone as a threat. In fact, as crime rates fell throughout the 1990s, the number of complaints of police abuse and harassment went up, particularly by young, urban, black men who fit the "profile" of a potential criminal. In response to these limitations, criminologists and policy makers have developed alternative strategies to crime prevention, including community policing, target hardening, and shaming.

COMMUNITY POLICING

One idea that has grown in popularity in recent years is that the police should work closely with citizens to improve local community standards and civil behavior, using education, persuasion, and counseling instead of incarceration.

Community policing implies not only drawing in citizens themselves, but changing the characteristic outlook of police forces. A renewed emphasis on crime prevention rather than law enforcement can go hand in hand with the reintegration of policing with the community. The isolation of the police from those they are supposed to serve often produces a siege mentality, since the police have little regular contact with ordinary citizens.

community policing •
A renewed emphasis on crime prevention rather than law enforcement to reintegrate policing within the community.

In order to work, partnerships among government agencies, the criminal justice system, local associations, and community organizations have to be inclusive—all economic and ethnic groups must be involved (Kelling and Coles 1997). Government and business can act together to help repair urban decay. One model is the creation of business improvement districts providing tax breaks for corporations that participate in strategic planning and offer investment in designated areas. To be successful, such schemes demand a long-term commitment to social objectives.

Emphasizing these strategies does not mean denying the links between unemployment, poverty, and crime. Rather, the struggle against these social problems should be coordinated with community-based approaches to crime prevention.

These approaches can in fact contribute directly and indirectly to furthering social justice. Where social order has decayed along with public services, other opportunities, such as new jobs, decline as well. Improving the quality of life in a neighborhood can revive them.

TARGET HARDENING

target hardening • Practical measures used to limit a criminal's ability to commit crime, such as community policing and use of house alarms.

Community policing is just one strategy that falls under a larger set of strategies that criminologists call **target hardening**. Consistent with the core notions of control theory, this practice makes it more difficult for criminals to commit crimes by minimizing their opportunities to do. Rather than changing the criminal, the best policy is to take practical measures to control the criminal's ability to commit crime, by promoting the use of crime-deterring technologies and practices like community policing, private security services, car alarms, house alarms, guard dogs, and even gated communities.

Target-hardening techniques have gained favor among politicians in recent years and appear to have been successful in some contexts in curtailing crime. But criticisms of such an approach can also be made. These tactics do not address the underlying causes of crime but instead are aimed at protecting and defending certain elements of society from its reach. There is another unintended consequence of such policies: As popular crime targets are "hardened," patterns of crime may simply shift from one domain to another. Target hardening approaches run the risk of displacing criminal offenses from better protected areas to more vulnerable ones. Neighborhoods that are poor or lacking in social cohesion may well experience a growth in crime and delinquency as target hardening in affluent regions increases.

SHAMING AS PUNISHMENT

shaming • A way of punishing criminal and deviant behavior based on rituals of public disapproval rather than incarceration. The goal of shaming is to maintain the ties of the offender to the community.

In recent years, **shaming**, a form of punishing criminal and deviant behavior that attempts to maintain the ties of the offender to the community, has grown in popularity as an alternative to incarceration. According to some criminologists, the fear of being shamed within one's community is an important deterrent to crime. As a result, the public's formal disapproval could achieve the same deterrent effect as incarceration, without the high costs of building and maintaining prisons.

Criminologist John Braithwaite (1996) has described two types of shaming: reintegrative and stigmatizing. *Stigmatizing shaming* is the process whereby a criminal is labeled as a threat to society and is treated as an outcast. The labeling process has potentially damaging consequences, as we learned earlier in this chapter. A negative label may trigger others' efforts to marginalize the individual, perhaps leading to future criminal behavior and higher crime rates. *Reintegrative shaming*, by contrast, involves rather than marginalizes the offender. People central to the criminal's immediate community—such as family members, employers and coworkers, and friends—are brought into court to state their condemnation of the offender's behavior. At the same time, these people accept responsibility for reintegrating the offender back into their community. The goal is to rebuild the social bonds of the individual to the community as a means of deterring future criminal conduct.

Japan, with one of the lowest crime rates in the world, has been quite successful in implementing this approach. The process is largely based on a voluntary network of over five hundred thousand local crime prevention associations dedicated to facilitating reintegration into the community and on a criminal justice system that is encouraged to be lenient for this purpose. As a result, in Japan only 5 percent of persons convicted for a crime serve time in prison, as compared to 30 percent in the

United States. Though reintegrative shaming is not a standard practice in the American criminal justice system, it is a familiar practice in other social institutions such as the family. A parent may express disapproval of a child's naughty behavior and try to make the child feel ashamed of her conduct, but the parent may also reassure the child that she is a loved member of the family.

Could reintegrative shaming succeed in the United States? Skeptics say these tactics are soft on crime, that Americans are too individualistic to participate in community-based policing, and that high-crime areas are less community oriented. However, community networks have been successful in working with the police in preventing crime. These social bonds could also be fostered to increase the power of shame and reintegrate offenders into local networks of community involvement. ✓

CONCEPT CHECKS ✓

1. How does imprisonment affect the life chances of ex-cons?

2. Why has the U.S. prison population grown so steeply over the past three decades?

3. What are the primary tasks that police officers do each day?

4. Name at least two specific ways that community members can combat local crime.

HOW DO CRIME AND DEVIANCE AFFECT YOUR LIFE?

THE COSTS OF CRIME

Crime can take a toll on the financial and emotional well-being of even those people whose only contact with the criminal justice system is watching reruns of *Law and Order*. As we learned earlier in the chapter, corporate crime can affect everything from the quality of the food we eat to the safety of the cars we drive and the cleanliness of the air we breathe. Even those of us who live in safe and quiet neighborhoods may find our lives touched by the criminal acts of corporations, in the form of air pollution or tainted foods or medicines.

Our lives also are affected by the high fiscal costs of street crime. Maintaining local, state, and national criminal justice systems is costly—and growing costlier by the minute. As we learned earlier in this chapter, the number of people behind bars in the United States has climbed steadily in the past decade due in part to policies like the "three strikes" laws. State governments are having a difficult time finding enough money to house, feed, and provide medical care to these growing numbers of inmates. In 1987, the states spent a total of $10.6 billion of their general funds on corrections. In 2006, by contrast, they spent more than $69 billion (U.S. Bureau of Justice Statistics 2008d). Adjusted for inflation, the increase was 127 percent, while over the same time period spending on higher education rose just 21 percent (Pew Center on the States 2008).

Lawmakers have few options for footing this large bill. Tax hikes are one option, but that would mean higher income taxes, property taxes, and sales taxes for everyone. In the absence of tax hikes, lawmakers may find themselves forced to cut back on other important social programs that benefit most Americans, including transportation, education, and health care (Pew Center on the States 2008). Corrections now take up about 6.8 percent of state funds, and if this proportion increases, it could touch the lives of Americans using the many other state programs that compete for valuable tax dollars.

THE FUNCTIONS OF DEVIANCE

The deviant acts of others also affect our personal behaviors in powerful ways. As noted earlier, deviants help us to understand what is considered "right" and "wrong" among our peers, friends, and community members. Most of us try very hard to avoid the sanctions that result from doing "wrong," and we make our daily choices accordingly. For example, most of us don't want to be socially ostracized, so we may choose clothes, hobbies, romantic partners, and even our future career paths so that we fit in with peers. To be considered "deviant" often means being treated as a social outcast.

At a more serious level, though, most of us know what the punishments are for even minor violations, such as speeding or running a red light. By learning about the fees and punishments levied on those who break the rules, most of us will behave in accordance with the law—to avoid a fate like suspension of a driver's license or spending a night in jail. Public punishments, whether locking horse thieves into "stocks" in town squares and making an adulteress wear a scarlet letter "A" around her neck in the colonial United States, or publicizing the names and addresses of registered sex offenders in the contemporary United States, are designed not only to punish the "guilty" but also to prevent others from behaving in a similar way. These public humiliations affect us, because they make us rethink whether it's really worthwhile to try to get away with a crime.

NEED HELP STUDYING?

 wwnorton.com/studyspace

....

Visit StudySpace to access free review materials such as:

- Vocabulary Flashcards
- Diagnostic Review Quizzes
- Study Outlines

REVIEW QUESTIONS

1. How does deviance lead to increased levels of social solidarity according to Émile Durkheim? Give a contemporary example that illustrates these theories.
2. What are sanctions and what are the various forms that they take? Give an example of each type of sanction.
3. How do sociological theories differ from biological and psychological explanations of deviance?
4. Discuss Merton's five possible reactions to tensions produced by anomie. Why is he considered a functionalist?
5. Compare and contrast interactionist and conflict theories of deviance. What theory is most convincing to you?
6. What is broken windows theory and its policy trajectory? What are some critiques of this theory?
7. What are the main sources of data on crime in the United States? What are some methodological concerns about the measurement of crime? How are these issues illustrated in the rates of rape in the United States?

8. Compare theories that are used to explain the difference in crime rates between men and women.
9. How do crimes committed by powerful groups complicate theories of crime that link it to impoverished social conditions?
10. What are some current methods of reducing crime? Are they effective? If you were a policy maker in the criminal justice system, what strategies would you employ?

THINKING SOCIOLOGICALLY EXERCISES

1. Briefly summarize several leading theories explaining crime and deviance presented in this chapter: differential association, anomie, labeling, conflict, and control theories. Which theory appeals to you? Explain why.
2. Explain how differences in power and social influence can play a significant role in defining and sanctioning deviant behavior.

Stratification, Class, and Inequality

THE BIG QUESTIONS

WHAT IS SOCIAL STRATIFICATION?
Learn about social stratification and how social background affects one's life chances. Become acquainted with the most influential theories of stratification.

HOW IS SOCIAL CLASS DEFINED IN THE UNITED STATES?
Understand the social causes and consequences of social class in U.S. society.

WHAT ARE THE CAUSES AND CONSEQUENCES OF SOCIAL INEQUALITY IN THE UNITED STATES?
Recognize why and how the gap between rich and poor has increased in recent decades. Understand social mobility, and think about your own mobility.

HOW DOES POVERTY AFFECT INDIVIDUALS?
Learn about poverty in the United States today, explanations for why it exists, and means for combating it. Learn how people become marginalized in a society and the forms that this marginalization takes.

HOW DOES SOCIAL INEQUALITY AFFECT YOUR LIFE?
Learn how changes in the American economy have led to growing inequalities since the 1970s.

Kate and Ellen were joking with Robert about having found him a date for the dance. I did not catch the name of the girl they were making fun of, but they told him he could go with that "big, fat, blond girl." This inspired Robert to start making jokes about the trouble he would have wrapping his arms around the girl and to laugh about how she would roll over him (Milner 2004).

T his high school conversation was recorded as part of a study of teenage behavior by sociologist Murray Milner. Milner wanted to find out why American teenagers are so status conscious—why it is so important to look good and be popular that high school students routinely spend large amounts of money on clothing and other consumer goods, while ruthlessly putting down anyone who in their view doesn't make the grade.

Milner's book *Freaks, Geeks, and Cool Kids: American Teenagers, Schools, and the Culture of Consumption* is based on interviews with hundreds of college students about their high school experiences as well as detailed observations of a single high school over a three-year period. He sets out to answer some questions about behaviors that have troubled American teenagers for a half century or more:

> Why are many teenagers obsessed with who sits with them at lunch, the brand of clothes they wear, what parties they are invited to, the privacy of their bedrooms, who is dating or hooking up with whom, what is the latest popular music? Why have alcohol, drug use, and casual sex become so widespread? . . . Why are teenagers frequently mean and even cruel to one another?

The answer, Milner argues, has to do with teenage power, or rather the lack of it. Teenagers have little economic or political power. Stuck somewhere between childhood and adulthood, they spend most of their days in class, where their teachers rule. After school, their parents have the final say (or at least think they should). Teenagers respond by creating social worlds in which their ability to evaluate one another—usually by standards very different from those of their parents or teachers—provides them with a sense of power.

Milner calls such power "status power." Sociologists define **status** as the prestige that goes along with one's social position. Status power derives from the ability to increase one's own prestige, often at the expense of others. This ability depends in large part on the basis of one's social location—in this case, in the high school pecking order. Whom you date is important, because the people you hang out with have a big influence on your social status. Putting others down helps make sure that the in-crowd is a small, exclusive club. Dressing like the in-crowd, or having the latest model iPhone or other consumer gadget, is another important marker of status. In fact, consumerism in general is a key source of status power. As Milner (2004) notes, "Consumerism in high schools is not only about clothes, but also a broader array of expensive items, such as the limousine to go to the prom or the hotel suite that is rented for the all-night party afterward, or where you will fly to for spring break."

In this chapter we examine the relationship between social status, economic position, and inequality in society.

status ● The social honor or prestige that a particular group is accorded by other members of a society. Status groups normally display distinct styles of life—patterns of behavior that the members of a group follow. Status privilege may be positive or negative. Pariah status groups are regarded with disdain or treated as outcasts by the majority of the population.

How do students derive status from the products they buy and the clothes they wear? Do you know students who increase their prestige at the expense of others?

Sociologists speak of **social stratification** to describe inequalities among individuals and groups within human societies. Often we think of stratification in terms of assets or property, but it can also occur on the basis of other attributes, such as gender, age, religious affiliation, or military rank. The three key aspects of social stratification are class, status, and power (Weber 1947). Although they frequently overlap, this is not always the case. The "rich and famous" often enjoy high status; their wealth often provides political influence and sometimes direct access to political power. Yet there are exceptions. Drug lords, for example, may be wealthy and powerful, yet they usually enjoy low status. In this chapter, we focus on stratification in terms of inequalities based on wealth and income, status, and power. In later chapters, we will look at the ways in which gender (Chapter 9), race and ethnicity (Chapter 10), and age (Chapter 14) all play a role in stratification.

social stratification • The existence of structured inequalities between groups in society, in terms of their access to material or symbolic rewards. While all societies involve some forms of stratification, only with the development of state-based systems did wide differences in wealth and power arise. The most distinctive form of stratification in modern societies is class divisions.

WHAT IS SOCIAL STRATIFICATION?

All socially stratified systems share three characteristics:

1. **The rankings apply to social categories of people who share a common characteristic, such as gender or ethnicity.** Women may be ranked differently from men, wealthy people differently from the poor. This does not mean that individuals from a particular category cannot change their rank; however, it does mean that the category continues to exist even if individuals move out of it and into another category.
2. **People's life experiences and opportunities depend heavily on how their social category is ranked.** Being male or female, black or white, upper class or working class makes a big difference in terms of your life chances—often as big a difference as personal effort or good fortune.
3. **The ranks of different social categories tend to change very slowly over time.** In U.S. society, for example, only in the last forty years have women begun to achieve economic equality with men (see Chapter 9). Similarly, only since the 1970s have significant numbers of African Americans begun to obtain economic and political equality with whites—even though slavery was abolished nearly a century and a half ago and discrimination declared illegal in the 1950s and 1960s (see Chapter 10).

As you saw in Chapter 2, stratified societies have changed throughout human history. The earliest human societies, which were based on hunting and gathering, had very little social stratification—mainly because there were few resources to be divided up. The development of agriculture produced considerably more wealth and, as a result, a great increase in stratification. Social stratification in agricultural societies came to resemble a pyramid, with a large number of people at the bottom and a successively smaller number of people as one moves toward the top. Today, advanced industrial societies are extremely complex; their stratification is more likely to resemble a teardrop, with a large number of people in the middle and lower-middle ranks (the so-called middle class), a slightly smaller number of people at the bottom, and very few people as one moves toward the top.

But before turning to stratification in modern societies, let's first review the three basic systems of stratification: slavery, caste, and class.

SLAVERY

slavery • A form of social stratification in which some people are owned by others as their property.

Slavery is an extreme form of inequality, in which certain people are owned as property by others. Historically, sometimes slaves have been deprived of almost all rights by law, as was the case on Southern plantations in the United States. In other societies, their position was more akin to that of servants. For example, in the ancient Greek city-state of Athens, some slaves occupied positions of great responsibility. They were excluded from political positions and from the military but were accepted in most other types of occupation. Some were literate and worked as government administrators; many were trained in craft skills. For the less fortunate, however, their days began and ended in hard labor in the mines.

Systems of slave labor have tended to be unstable, because slaves have historically fought back against their subjection. Slavery also is not economically efficient, as it requires constant supervision, and often involves severe punishment, which impedes worker productivity. Moreover, from about the eighteenth century on, many people in Europe and America came to see slavery as morally wrong. Today, slavery is illegal in every country of the world, but it still exists in some places. Recent research has documented that people are taken by force and held against their will—from enslaved brick makers in Pakistan to sex slaves in Thailand and domestic slaves in France. Slavery remains a significant human rights violation in the world today (Bales 1999).

CASTE SYSTEMS

caste system • A social system in which one's social status is given for life.

caste society • A society in which different social levels are closed, so that all individuals must remain at the social level of their birth throughout life.

endogamy • The forbidding of marriage or sexual relations outside one's social group.

A **caste system** is a social system in which one's social status is given for life. In **caste societies**, therefore, different social levels are closed, so that all individuals must remain at the social level of their birth throughout life. Everyone's social status is based on personal characteristics—such as perceived race or ethnicity (often based on such physical characteristics as skin color), parental religion, or parental caste—that are accidents of birth and are therefore believed to be unchangeable. Caste societies can be seen as a special type of class society—in which class position is ascribed at birth, rather than achieved through personal accomplishment. In caste systems, intimate contact with members of other castes is strongly discouraged. Such "purity" of a caste is often maintained by rules of **endogamy**, marriage within one's social group as required by custom or law.

Before modern times, caste systems were found throughout the world. In modern times, caste systems have typically been found in agricultural societies that have not yet developed industrial capitalist economies, such as rural India or South Africa prior to the end of white rule in 1992. The Indian caste system, for example, reflects Hindu religious beliefs and is more than two thousand years old. According to Hindu beliefs, there are four major castes, each roughly associated with broad occupational groupings. Below the four castes are those known as the "untouchables" or *Dalits* (oppressed people), who—as their name suggests—are to be avoided at all costs. Untouchables are limited to the worst jobs in society such as removing human waste, and they often resort to begging and searching in garbage for their food. India made it illegal to discriminate on the basis of caste in 1949, but aspects of the caste system remain in full force today, particularly in rural areas.

The few remaining caste systems in the world are being challenged further by globalization. For example, as India's modern capitalist economy brings people of different castes together, whether in the same workplace, airplane, or restaurant, it is increasingly difficult to maintain the rigid barriers required to sustain the caste system.

CLASS

The concept of **class** is most important for analyzing stratification in industrialized societies like the United States. Everyone has heard of class, but most people in everyday talk use the word in a vague way. As employed in sociology, it has some precision.

A social class is a large group of people who occupy a similar economic position in the wider society. The concept of life chances, introduced by Max Weber, is the best way to understand what class means. Your **life chances** are the opportunities you have for achieving economic prosperity. A person from a humble background, for example, has less chance of ending up wealthy than someone from a more prosperous one. And the best chance an individual has of being wealthy is to start off as wealthy in the first place.

Women from the Dalit caste (formally known as Untouchables) earn a living as sewage scavengers in the slums of Ranchi, India. They are paid between 30 and 100 rupees (65 cents–$2.25) per house per month for retrieving human waste from residential dry latrines and emptying the buckets into nearby gutters and streams.

America, it is always said, is the land of opportunity. For some, this is so. There are many examples of people who have risen from humble means to positions of great wealth and power. And yet there are more cases of people who have not, including a disproportionate share of women and members of minority groups. The idea of life chances is important because it emphasizes that although class is an important influence on what happens in our lives, it is not completely determining. Class divisions affect which neighborhoods we live in, what lifestyles we follow, and even which sexual or marriage partners we choose (Mare 1991; Massey 1996). Yet they don't fix people for life in specific social positions, as the older systems of stratification did. A person born into a caste position has no opportunity of escaping from it; the same isn't true of class.

Class systems differ from slavery and castes in four main respects:

1. **Class systems are fluid.** Unlike the other types of strata, classes are not established by legal or religious provisions. The boundaries between classes are never clear-cut. There are no formal restrictions on intermarriage between people from different classes.
2. **Class positions are in some part achieved.** An individual's class is not simply assigned at birth, as is the case in the other types of stratification systems. Social mobility—movement upward and downward in the class structure—is relatively common.
3. **Class is economically based.** Classes depend on inequalities in the possession of material resources. In the other types of stratification systems, non-economic factors (such as race in the former South African caste system) are generally most important.
4. **Class systems are large scale and impersonal.** In the other types of stratification systems, inequalities are expressed primarily in personal relationships

class • Although it is one of the most frequently used concepts in sociology, there is no clear agreement about how the term should be defined. Most sociologists use the term to refer to socioeconomic variations between groups of individuals that create variations in their material prosperity and power.

life chances • A term introduced by Max Weber to signify a person's opportunities for achieving economic prosperity.

of duty or obligation—between slave and master or lower- and higher-caste individuals. Class systems, by contrast, operate mainly through large-scale, impersonal associations such as pay or working conditions.

ARE CLASS BOUNDARIES WEAKENING?

Stratification scholars currently grapple with two important debates about the declining importance of social class. First, they ask whether caste systems will give way to class systems, against the backdrop of globalization. Second, scholars wonder whether inequality is declining in class-based societies, due in part to educational expansion and other social policies.

To address the first question, there is some evidence that globalization will hasten the end of legally sanctioned caste systems throughout the world. Most official caste systems have already given way to class-based ones in industrial capitalist societies; Modern industrial production requires that people move about freely, work at whatever jobs they are suited or able to do, and change jobs frequently according to economic conditions. The rigid restrictions found in caste systems interfere with this necessary freedom. Nonetheless, elements of caste persist even in advanced industrial societies. For example, some Indian immigrants to the United States seek to arrange traditional marriages for their children along caste lines, while the relatively small number of intermarriages between blacks and whites in the United States suggests the strength of racial barriers.

To address the second question, some evidence suggests that, at least until recently, mature capitalist societies have been increasingly open to movement between classes, thereby reducing the level of inequality. For example, studies of European countries, the United States, and Canada suggested that inequality peaked in these places before World War II, declined through the 1950s, and remained roughly the same through the 1970s (Berger 1986; Nielsen 1994). Lowered postwar inequality was due in part to economic expansion in industrial societies, which created opportunities for people at the bottom to move up, and because of government health insurance, welfare, and other programs aimed at reducing inequality. As you will see later in this chapter and in Chapter 14 (where we discuss the changing nature of the American economy), however, this trend has reversed: Inequality has actually been increasing in the United States since the 1970s.

THEORIES OF STRATIFICATION IN MODERN SOCIETIES

The most influential theoretical approaches to studying stratification are those developed by Karl Marx and Max Weber. Most subsequent theories of stratification are heavily indebted to their ideas.

MARX: MEANS OF PRODUCTION AND THE ANALYSIS OF CLASS

means of production • The means whereby the production of material goods is carried on in a society, including not just technology but the social relations between producers.

capitalists • People who own companies, land, or stocks (shares) and use these to generate economic returns.

For Marx, the term *class* refers to people who stand in a common relationship to the **means of production**—the means by which they gain a livelihood. In modern societies, the two main classes are those who own the means of production—industrialists, or **capitalists**—and those who earn their living by selling their labor to them, the working class. The relationship between classes, according to Marx, is an exploitative one. In the course of the working day, Marx reasoned, workers produce more than is actually needed by employers to repay the cost of hiring them. This **surplus value** is the source of profit, which capitalists are able to put to their own use. A group of workers in a clothing factory, say, might be able to produce a hundred suits a day. Selling half the suits provides enough income for the manufacturer to pay the workers' wages. Income from the sale of the remainder of the garments is taken as profit.

Marx believed that the maturing of industrial capitalism would bring about an increasing gap between the wealth of the minority and the poverty of the mass of the population. In his view, the wages of the working class could never rise far above subsistence level, while wealth would pile up in the hands of those owning capital. In addition, laborers would daily face work that is physically wearing and mentally tedious, as is the situation in many factories. At the lowest levels of society, particularly among those frequently or permanently unemployed, there would develop an "accumulation of misery, agony of labor, slavery, ignorance, brutality, moral degradation" (1977; orig. 1864).

Marx was right about the persistence of poverty in industrialized countries and in anticipating that large inequalities of wealth and income would continue. He was wrong in supposing that the income of most of the population would remain extremely low. Most people in Western countries today are much better off materially than were comparable groups in Marx's day.

WEBER: CLASS AND STATUS

There are two main differences between Weber's theory and that of Marx. First, according to Weber, class divisions derive not only from control or lack of control of the means of production but from economic differences that have nothing directly to do with property. Such resources include especially people's skills and credentials, or qualifications. Those in managerial or professional occupations earn more and enjoy more favorable conditions at work, for example, than people in blue-collar jobs. The qualifications they possess, such as degrees, diplomas, and the skills they have acquired, make them more "marketable" than others without such qualifications.

Second, Weber distinguished another aspect of stratification besides class, which he called "status." According to Weber, status refers to differences between groups in the social honor, or prestige, they are accorded by others. Status distinctions can vary independent of class divisions. Social honor may be either positive or negative. For instance, doctors and lawyers have high prestige in American society. **Pariah groups**, on the other hand, are negatively privileged status groups, subject to discrimination that prevents them from taking advantage of opportunities open to others. Possession of wealth normally tends to confer high status, but there are exceptions to this principle, such as Hollywood starlets who earn high salaries but lack the education or refinement typically associated with "status." Importantly, status depends on people's subjective evaluations of social differences, whereas class is an objective measure.

Weber's writings on stratification are important because they show that other dimensions of stratification besides class strongly influence people's lives. Most sociologists hold that Weber's scheme offers a more flexible and sophisticated basis for analyzing stratification than that provided by Marx.

DAVIS AND MOORE: THE FUNCTIONS OF STRATIFICATION

Kingsley Davis and Wilbert E. Moore (1945) provided a functionalist explanation of stratification, arguing that it has beneficial consequences for society. They claimed

surplus value • The value of a worker's labor power, in Marxist theory, left over when an employer has repaid the cost of hiring the worker.

pariah groups • Groups who suffer from negative status discrimination—they are looked down on by most other members of society. The Jews, for example, have been a pariah group throughout much of European history.

that certain positions or roles in society, such as brain surgeons, are functionally more important than others, and these positions require special skills for their performance. However, only a limited number of individuals in any society have the talents or experience appropriate to these positions. To attract the most qualified people, rewards need to be offered, such as money, power, and prestige. Davis and Moore determined that since the benefits of different positions in any society must be unequal, then all societies must be stratified. They concluded that social stratification and social inequality are functional because they ensure that the most qualified people, attracted by the rewards bestowed by society, fill the roles that are most important to a smoothly functioning society.

Davis and Moore's theory suggests that a person's social position is based solely on his innate talents and efforts. Not surprisingly, their theory has been met with criticism by other sociologists. As we have seen, the United States is not entirely a meritocratic society. Those at the top tend to have unequal access to economic and cultural resources, such as the highest quality education, which help the upper classes transmit their privileged status from one generation to the next. For those without access to these resources, even those with superior talents, social inequality serves as a barrier to reaching their full potential. ✓

CONCEPT CHECKS ✓

1. What are the three shared characteristics of socially stratified systems?

2. What is one example of a caste system in the world today?

3. How is the concept of class different from that of caste?

4. According to Karl Marx, what are the two main classes and how do they relate to one another?

5. What are the two main differences between Max Weber's and Karl Marx's theories of social stratification?

6. How does social stratification contribute to the functioning of society? What is wrong with this argument?

HOW IS SOCIAL CLASS DEFINED IN THE UNITED STATES?

Social class in the United States typically is defined by some combination of one's income, wealth, educational attainment, and occupational status. In this section, we describe each of these attributes, and describe how they are distributed throughout the U.S. population. We also compare and contrast the five major social class groups in the United States.

INCOME

income • Payment, usually derived from wages, salaries, or investments.

Income refers to wages and salaries earned from paid occupations, plus unearned money (or interest) from investments. One of the most significant changes occurring in Western countries over the past century has been the rising real income of the majority of the working population. (*Real income* is income excluding rises owing to inflation, to provide a fixed standard of comparison from year to year.) The majority of the population today is vastly more affluent than any peoples have previously been in human history.

Nevertheless, income distribution is unequal, and reveals a clear case of the "haves" and "have-nots." In 2007, the top 5 percent of households in the United States received 21.2 percent of total income; the top 20 percent obtained 49.7 percent; and the bottom

20 percent received only 3.4 percent (Figure 7.2) (U.S. Bureau of the Census 2008a). Between 1977 and 2006, income inequality increased dramatically. The average household earnings (calculated at 2006 dollars), meaning the combined incomes of all persons living in a single household, of the bottom 20 percent of people in the United States rose by almost 15 percent (U.S. Bureau of the Census 2007a). During the same period, the richest 20 percent saw their incomes grow by 60 percent, while for the richest 5 percent of the population, income rose by more than 85 percent. And despite the growth of the economy and millions of new jobs, these trends continued throughout the 1990s and into the new century, leading some observers to deem the United States a "two-tiered society" (Freeman 1999). However, recent estimates indicate that income inequality has been declining. Income inequality decreased between 2006 and 2007, as measured by shares of aggregate household income by quintiles. The share of aggregate income received by households in the top fifth of the income distribution declined, while the shares for the third and fourth quintiles increased (U.S. Bureau of the Census 2008a).

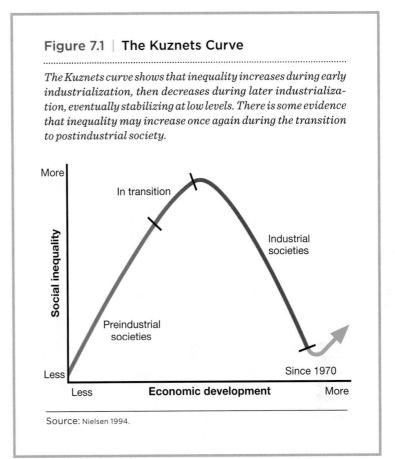

Figure 7.1 | The Kuznets Curve

The Kuznets curve shows that inequality increases during early industrialization, then decreases during later industrialization, eventually stabilizing at low levels. There is some evidence that inequality may increase once again during the transition to postindustrial society.

Source: Nielsen 1994.

WEALTH

Wealth refers to all assets individuals own: cash, savings and checking accounts, investments in stocks, bonds, real estate properties, and so on. While most people earn their income from their work, the wealthy often derive the bulk of theirs from interest on their investments, some of them inherited. Some scholars argue that wealth—not income—is the real indicator of social class.

Net financial assets are far lower for minority groups than for whites (Oliver and Shapiro 1995). Between 1983 and 2007, the median net financial assets of white Americans rose from $19,900 to $170,400 (Figure 7.3). Most African Americans began to accumulate net financial assets only in the 1990s; by 2000, the median net worth was $6,166. For Hispanic households, median net financial worth grew from effectively zero in 1998 to surpass African Americans, with a median net worth of $27,800 in 2007 (Survey of Consumer Finances 2009).

What are some of the reasons for the racial disparity in wealth? Do blacks simply have less money with which to purchase assets? To some degree, the answer is yes. The old adage "It takes money to make money" is a fact of life for those who start with little or no wealth. Since whites historically have enjoyed higher incomes and levels of wealth than blacks, whites are able to accrue even more wealth, which they then are able to pass on to their children (Conley 1999). In fact, economists estimate that more than half the wealth that one accumulates in a lifetime can be traced to a person's progenitors. But family advantages are not the only factors. Oliver and Shapiro (1995) argued that it is easier for whites to obtain assets even when they have fewer resources than blacks, because discrimination plays a major role in the racial gap in

wealth • Money and material possessions held by an individual or group.

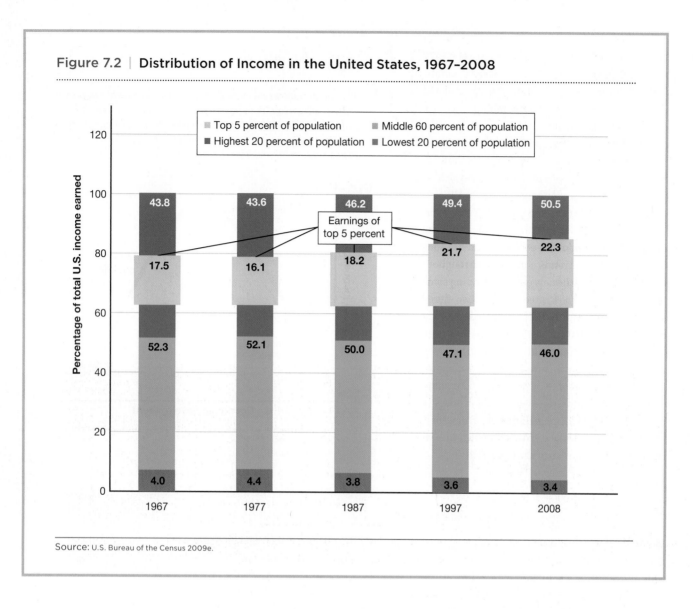

Figure 7.2 | Distribution of Income in the United States, 1967–2008

Source: U.S. Bureau of the Census 2009e.

home ownership. Blacks are rejected for mortgages 60 percent more often than whites, even when they have the same qualifications and creditworthiness. When blacks do receive mortgages, they are more likely to take subprime mortgage loans, which charge on average 2 percent more in interest. In 2006, 30.3 percent of blacks took out subprime home loans, compared to 24 percent of Hispanics and 17.7 percent of whites.

Research shows that subprime loans are offered by only a few lenders; but those lenders focus on minority communities, whereas the prime lenders are unable or unwilling to lend in those communities (Avery and Canner 2005). These issues are particularly important because home ownership constitutes American families' primary means for accumulating wealth. The potentially harmful consequences of subprime lending became evident in the late 2000s, however. Beginning in late 2006, a sharp rise in the number of subprime mortgage defaults and foreclosures caused more than one hundred subprime mortgage lenders to fail or file for bankruptcy. In the process, many Americans lost their homes and were thrown into personal bankruptcy.

Figure 7.3

SOCIAL INEQUALITY IN THE U.S.

Median net worth of American families based on various social factors

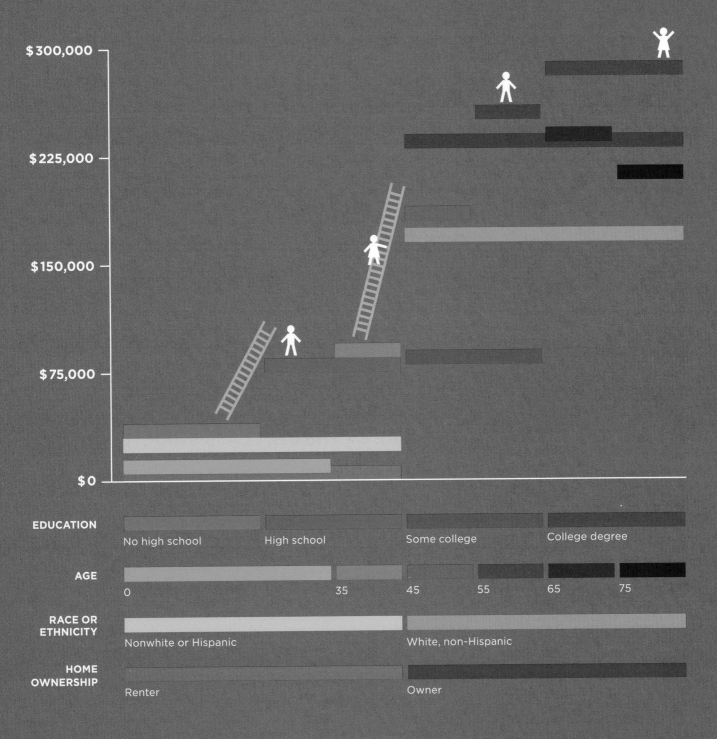

$300,000

$225,000

$150,000

$75,000

$0

EDUCATION
No high school   High school   Some college   College degree

AGE
0   35   45   55   65   75

RACE OR ETHNICITY
Nonwhite or Hispanic   White, non-Hispanic

HOME OWNERSHIP
Renter   Owner

MEDIAN NET WORTH BY PERCENTILE

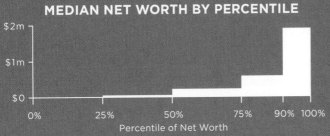

$2m

$1m

$0

0%   25%   50%   75% 90% 100%

Percentile of Net Worth

Source: U.S. Federal Reserve Board 2009.

EDUCATION

Sociologists also believe that *education*, or the number of years of schooling a person has completed, is an important dimension of social stratification. The value of a college education has increased significantly in the past twenty years as a result of the increased demand for and wages paid to educated workers in the more technology- and information-based economy (Danziger and Gottschalk 1995). Education is one of the strongest predictors of one's occupation, income, and wealth later in life. As we will see later in this chapter, how much education one receives is often influenced by the social class of one's parents.

Racial differences in levels of education persist, and this explains in part why racial differences in income and wealth also persist. In 2007, of those age 25 and older, 87 percent of whites, 80 percent of blacks, and 85.5 percent of Asian Americans had completed high school, whereas only 60 percent of Latinos had at least a high school degree (U.S. Bureau of the Census 2007b).

OCCUPATION

status • The social honor or prestige that a particular group is accorded by other members of society. Status groups normally display distinct styles of life—patterns of behavior that the members of a group follow. Status privilege may be positive or negative.

Status refers to the prestige that goes along with one's social position. In the United States and other industrialized societies, occupation is an important indicator of one's social standing. Occupational status depends heavily on one's level of educational attainment. In fact, in studies where persons are asked to rate jobs in terms of how "prestigious" they are, the occupations that are ranked most highly are those requiring the most education (Treiman 1977). To read more about occupational prestige, see the D.I.Y box on page 191.

A PICTURE OF THE U.S. CLASS STRUCTURE

Although money cannot buy everything, one's class position can make an enormous difference in terms of lifestyle. Most sociologists identify social classes in terms of wealth and income, noting how social class makes a difference in terms of consumption, education, health, and access to political power. The purpose of the following discussion is to describe broad class differences in the United States. Bear in mind that there are no sharply defined boundaries between the classes.

THE UPPER CLASS

upper class • A social class broadly composed of the more affluent members of society, especially those who have inherited wealth, own businesses, or hold large numbers of stocks (shares).

The **upper class** consists of the very wealthiest Americans—those households earning more than $297,000 or approximately 5 percent of all American households (U.S. Bureau of the Census 2007c). Most Americans in the upper class are wealthy but not superrich. They are likely to own a large suburban home as well as a town house or a vacation home, to drive expensive automobiles, to fly first class to vacations abroad, to educate their children in private schools and colleges, and to have their desires attended to by a staff of servants. Their wealth stems in large part from their substantial investments, from stocks and bonds to real estate, and the interest income derived from those investments. They are politically influential at the national, state, and local levels. The upper class includes people who acquired their wealth in a variety ways—the heads of major corporations, people who have made large amounts of money through investments or real estate, those fortunate enough to have inherited

DO-IT-YOURSELF SOCIOLOGY

D.I.Y.

Occupations can be ranked on the basis of their prestige. Please rank order the following sixteen jobs on an imaginary "ladder of social standing," where (1) is the most prestigious, and (16) the least prestigious. Flip the page to see whether your perceptions match up with those of other Americans, and people throughout the world.

Occupation	Rank (1 = most prestigious; 16 = least prestigious)
Accountant	_____
Cab driver	_____
Carpenter	_____
Classical musician	_____
Electrical engineer	_____
Garbage collector	_____
Journalist	_____
Physician	_____
Police officer	_____
Real estate agent	_____
Registered nurse	_____
Secretary	_____
Shoe shiner	_____
Social worker	_____
Sociologist	_____
Waiter or waitress	_____

TURN PAGE →

great wealth from their parents, a few highly successful celebrities and professional athletes, and a handful of others.

At the very top of this group are people who have accumulated vast fortunes permitting them to enjoy a lifestyle unimaginable to most Americans. The superrich are highly self-conscious of their unique and privileged social class position; some give generously to such worthy causes as the fine arts, hospitals, and charities. Their homes are often lavish and sometimes filled with collections of fine art. Their common class identity is strengthened by such things as being listed in the social register or having attended the same exclusive private secondary schools (to which they also send their

Social stratification researchers have designed the Standard International Occupational Prestige Scale to rank-order occupations. In the United States and across 55 different nations, individuals of all social classes were asked to rank-order more than 100 jobs. Cross-national comparisons show that there is very high agreement in prestige rankings. Occupations ranked most highly are those requiring the most education (Treiman 1977). According to researchers, this is how the sixteen jobs listed on the preceding page were ranked by evaluators:

1. Physician
2. Electrical engineer
3. Sociologist
4. Accountant
5. Registered nurse
6. Classical musician
7. Police officer
8. Journalist
9. Social worker
10. Secretary
11. Real estate agent
12. Carpenter
13. Cab driver
14. Waiter or waitress
15. Garbage collector
16. Shoe shiner

children). They sit on the same corporate boards of directors and belong to the same private clubs. They contribute large sums of money to their favorite politicians and are likely to be on a first-name basis with members of Congress and perhaps even with the president (Domhoff 1998).

The turn of this century saw extraordinary opportunities for the accumulation of such wealth. Globalization is one reason. Those entrepreneurs who are able to invest globally often prosper, both by selling products to foreign consumers and by making profits cheaply by using low-wage labor in developing countries. The information revolution is another reason for the accumulation of wealth. Before the dot-com bubble finally burst in 2001, young entrepreneurs with startup high-tech companies such as Yahoo! or eBay made legendary fortunes. As a consequence, the number of superrich Americans has exploded in recent years. At the end of World War II, there were only thirteen thousand people worth a million dollars or more in the United States. In 2008, there were 6.7 million millionaires households in the United States, the lowest level since 2003 (Spectrem Group 2009) as well as 371 billionaires (Forbes 2009)—reflecting the sweeping global economic downturn that begin in 2008. The 400 richest Americans are worth more than $1.57 trillion dollars—equal to approximately one ninth the gross domestic product of the United States and only slightly less than the gross domestic product of Mexico (Forbes 2009). There are billionaires outside the United States as well. The collective net worth of the world's 793 billionaires was $2.4 trillion in 2008 (Forbes 2009), approximately 80 percent of the gross domestic product of India.

Unlike "old-money" families such as the Rockefellers or the Vanderbilts, who accumulated their wealth in earlier generations and thus are viewed as a sort of American aristocracy, this "new wealth" often consists of upstart entrepreneurs such as Microsoft's Bill Gates, whose net worth was estimated by Forbes (2009) at $40 billion.

THE MIDDLE CLASS

When Americans are asked to identify their social class, the majority claim to be middle class. The reason is partly the American cultural belief that the United States is relatively free of class distinctions. Few people want to be identified as being too rich or too poor. Most Americans seem to think that others are not very different from their immediate family, friends, and coworkers (Kelley and Evans 1995; Simpson et al. 1988; Vanneman and Cannon 1987). Since people rarely interact with those outside of their social class, they tend to see themselves as like "most other people," who they then regard as being "middle class" (Kelley and Evans 1995).

The **middle class** is a catchall for a diverse group of occupations, lifestyles, and people who earn stable and sometimes substantial incomes at primarily white-collar jobs. It grew throughout much of the first three quarters of the twentieth century, then shrank during most of the last quarter century. During the late 1990s, however, economic growth halted this decline. Whether this trend will continue depends on whether or not the economy expands or contracts during the next several years. Currently, the middle class includes slightly more than half of all American households. While the middle class was once largely white, today it is increasingly diverse, both racially and culturally, including African Americans, Asian Americans, and Latinos.

The American middle class can be subdivided into two groups: the upper middle class and the lower middle class.

middle class ● A social class composed broadly of those working in white-collar and lower managerial occupations.

THE UPPER MIDDLE CLASS

The *upper middle class* consists of highly educated professionals (for example, doctors, lawyers, engineers, and professors), mid-level corporate managers, people who own or manage small businesses and retail shops, and some large-farm owners. Household incomes range quite widely, from about $120,000 to perhaps $300,000. The lower end of the income category would include college professors, for example, while the higher end would include corporate managers and small business owners. The upper middle class includes approximately 20 percent of all American households (U.S. Bureau of the Census 2007d). Its members are likely to be college educated (as are their children) with advanced degrees. Their jobs are secure and provide retirement and health benefits. They own comfortable homes, drive expensive late-model cars, have some savings and investments, and are often active in local politics and civic organizations. However, they tend not to enjoy the same high-end luxuries, social connections, or extravagancies as members of the upper class.

THE LOWER MIDDLE CLASS

The *lower middle class* consists of trained office workers (for example, secretaries and bookkeepers), elementary and high school teachers, nurses, salespeople, police officers, firefighters, and others who provide skilled services. This group, which includes about 40 percent of American households, is the most varied of the social class strata, and

Income Inequality in the Global Economy

Although many economists, politicians, and business-people have sung the praises of globalization, there is reason to approach such claims cautiously. Globalization may well be increasing economic inequality in the world's advanced industrial societies. Although the U.S. economy has been growing consistently since the end of the recession of 1982–1983, the gap between the wages of high-skilled and low-skilled workers also has been increasing. In 1979, college graduates taking entry-level positions earned on average 37 percent more than those without college degrees. By 2005, the differential had grown to 104 percent (U.S. Bureau of the Census 2007k). Although this growing "wage premium" has encouraged more Americans to go to college—such that nearly 29 percent of the American workforce had college degrees in 2005, compared with 18 percent in 1979 (*Business Week* 1997; U.S. Bureau of the Census 2007k)—it has also helped widen the gap between the wealthiest and the poorest workers.

As an analyst for the U.S. Department of Labor (1997) put it, "it is by now almost a platitude . . . that wage inequality has increased quite sharply since the late 1970s, for both men and women."

Although few studies have directly implicated globalization as a cause of this growing inequality, there is reason to view it as an indirect causal factor. It is true that whereas countries such as the United States, Canada, and

may include college educated persons with relatively modest earnings such as public elementary school teachers, as well as quite highly paid persons with high school diplomas only, such as skilled craftsmen (e.g., plumbers) and civil servants with many years of seniority. Household incomes in this group range from about $48,000 to $122,000 (U.S. Bureau of the Census 2007d). Members of the lower middle class may own a modest house, although many live in rental units. Their automobiles may be late models, but not the more expensive ones. Almost all have a high school education, and some have college degrees. They want their children to attend college, although this usually requires work-study programs and student loans. They are rarely politically active beyond exercising their right to vote.

THE WORKING CLASS

working class • A social class broadly composed of people working in blue-collar, or manual, occupations.

The **working class**, about 20 percent of all American households, includes primarily blue-collar and pink-collar laborers (for example, factory workers, mechanics, clerical the United Kingdom have witnessed a growth in earnings inequality since the late 1970s, countries like Germany, Japan, and France—which have, presumably, been equally affected by the forces of globalization—have seen either a decline or little change in inequality. At the same time, many of the factors that sociologists see as causes of inequality are clearly linked to globalization. First, in some cases, U.S. companies that manufacture in the United States lowered wages to compete with other U.S. firms that manufacture their products overseas, especially in the developing world. Second, globalization has encouraged immigration to the United States. Immigrants—many of whom are relegated to low-wage work—increase the competition for jobs among those in the low-wage labor pool, lowering wages somewhat in this segment of the labor market. Third, globalization has undermined the strength of U.S. labor unions. A number of studies have shown that when firms that used to do the bulk of their manufacturing in one region begin to spread their manufacturing base out across countries and continents, it becomes increasingly difficult for unions to organize workers and negotiate with management. But strong unions decrease earnings inequality through their commitment to raising wages.

Of course, globalization is not the only cause of inequality. Many researchers, for example, blame increasing inequality on the spectacular growth of high-tech industries, which employ mostly well-paid, white-collar workers and offer little in the way of traditional blue-collar employment. Still, it seems safe to conclude that globalization is not without its role in the growing stratification of American society.

aids, sales clerks, restaurant and hotel workers). Household incomes range from perhaps $28,777 to $48,223 (U.S. Bureau of the Census 2007d), and at least two household members work to make ends meet. Family income is just enough to pay the rent or the mortgage, to put food on the table, and perhaps to save for a summer vacation. The working class includes factory workers, mechanics, office workers, sales clerks, restaurant and hotel workers, and others who earn a modest weekly paycheck at a job that involves little control over the size of their income or working conditions. As you will see later in this chapter, many blue-collar jobs in the United States are threatened by economic globalization, and so members of the working class today are likely to feel insecure about their own and their family's future.

The working class is racially and ethnically diverse. While older members of the working class may own a home that was bought a number of years ago, younger members are likely to rent. The home or apartment is likely to be in a lower-income suburb or a city neighborhood. The household car, a lower-priced model, is unlikely to be new. Children who graduate from high school are unlikely to go to college and will attempt to get a job immediately instead. Most members of the working class are not likely to be politically active even in their own community, although they may vote in some elections.

THE LOWER CLASS

lower class • A social class comprised of those who work part time or not at all and whose household income is typically low.

The **lower class**, roughly 15 percent of American households, includes those who work part time or not at all; household income is typically lower than $28,777 (U.S. Bureau of the Census 2007d). Most lower-class individuals are found in cities, although some live in rural areas and earn a little money as farmers or part-time workers. Some manage to find employment in semiskilled or unskilled manufacturing or service jobs, ranging from making clothing in sweatshops to cleaning houses. Their jobs, when they can find them, are dead-end jobs, since years of work are unlikely to lead to promotion or substantially higher income. Their work is probably part time and highly unstable, without benefits such as medical insurance, disability, or social security. Even if they are fortunate enough to find a full-time job, there are no guarantees that it will be around next month or even next week. Many people in the lower class live in poverty. Very few own their own homes. Most of the lower class rent, and some are homeless. If they own a car at all, it is likely to be a used car. A higher percentage of the lower class is nonwhite than is true of other social classes. Its members do not participate in politics, and they seldom vote.

THE "UNDERCLASS"

underclass • A class of individuals situated at the bottom of the class system, often composed of people from ethnic minority backgrounds.

In the lower class, some sociologists have recently identified a group they call the **underclass** because they are "beneath" the class system in that they lack access to the world of work and mainstream patterns of behavior. Located in the highest-poverty neighborhoods of the inner city, the underclass is sometimes called the "new urban poor."

Table 7.1 | How Has an Increase in Income Inequality Affected American Households during the Last Thirty-Two Years?

INCOME CATEGORY	ACTUAL 2006 MEAN INCOME ($)[a]	2006 INCOME IF INEQUALITY HAD NOT CHANGED FROM 1974 ($)[b]	DIFFERENCE: HOW MUCH POORER OR RICHER ($)
Lowest fifth	11,352	12,052	–700
Second fifth	28,777	29,954	–1,177
Middle fifth	48,223	48,272	–49
Fourth fifth	76,329	69,717	+6,612
Highest fifth	168,170	123,519	+44,651
Top 5 percent	297,405	187,749	+109,656

Sources: (a) U.S. Bureau of the Census 2007d; (b) calculations based on historical mission rate change of 333.05 percent between January 1974 and December 2006.

The underclass includes many African Americans who have been trapped for more than one generation in a cycle of poverty from which there is little possibility of escape (Wacquant 1993, 1996; Wacquant and Wilson 1993; Wilson 1996). These are the poorest of the poor. Their numbers have grown rapidly over the past quarter century and today include unskilled and unemployed men, young single mothers and their children on welfare, teenagers from welfare-dependent families, and many of the homeless. They live in poor neighborhoods troubled by drugs, gangs, and high levels of violence. They are the truly disadvantaged, people with extremely difficult lives who have little realistic hope of ever making it out of poverty.

In recent years, some sociologists have argued that members of the underclass perpetuate their own inequality because the difficult conditions they face have made them "ill suited to the requirements of the formally rational sector of the economy" (Wacquant 2002). Although these scholars see the sources of such behavior in the social structure, they believe the culture of the underclass has taken on a life of its own, serving as both cause and effect. Such claims have generated considerable controversy, inspiring a number of studies that have taken issues with this viewpoint. Those who stand on the other side argue that although urban poverty is an immobile stratum, it is not simply a "defeated" and disconnected class, as theorists of the underclass believe. Thus, studies of fast-food workers and homeless street vendors have argued that the separations between the urban poor and the rest of society are not as great as scholars of the underclass believe (Newman 2000; Duneier 1999). ✓

> ## CONCEPT CHECKS ✓
>
> 1. Name at least three components of social class. How do blacks and whites differ along these components?
>
> 2. What are the major social class groups in the United States today? Describe at least two ways (other than their income) that these groups differ from one another.

WHAT ARE THE CAUSES AND CONSEQUENCES OF SOCIAL INEQUALITY IN THE UNITED STATES?

A GROWING GAP BETWEEN RICH AND POOR

The United States prides itself on being a nation of equals. Indeed, except for the Great Depression of the 1930s, inequality declined throughout much of the twentieth century, reaching its lowest levels during the 1960s and early 1970s. But during the past quarter century inequality has started to increase once again. The rich have gotten much, much richer. Middle-class incomes have stagnated. The poor have grown in number and the gap between rich and poor in the United States is the largest since the Census Bureau started measuring it in 1947 (U.S. Bureau of the Census 2000a) and the largest in the industrial world (Figure 7.4). One statistical analysis of income and poverty among industrial nations found that the United States had the most unequal distribution of household income among all twenty-one industrial countries studied (Sweden had the most equal) (Smeeding 2000).

Figure 7.4 | Income Inequality in Selected Industrialized Countries: Ratio of Richest 20 Percent to Poorest 20 Percent for 2008

For the last ten years, the richest fifth of all Americans were on average nine times richer than the poorest fifth, one of the highest ratios in the industrialized world. In Japan, at the other extreme, the ratio was about 3.4 to 1.

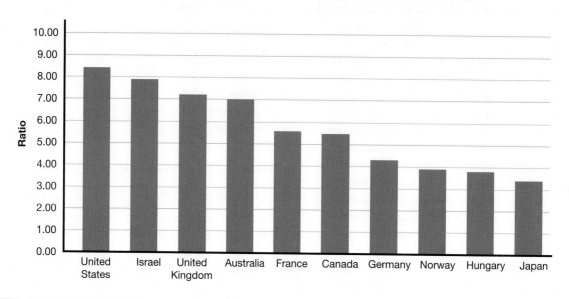

Source: UNDP 2009.

ETHNIC MINORITIES VERSUS WHITE AMERICANS

There are substantial differences in income based on race and ethnicity, since minorities in the United States are more likely to hold the lowest-paying jobs. Black and Latino household income, for example, averages between two thirds and three quarters that of whites (Figure 7.5). For blacks, this is a slight improvement over previous years, as a growing number of blacks have gone to college and moved into middle-class occupations. For Latinos, however, the situation has worsened, as recent immigrants from rural areas in Mexico and Central America find themselves working at low-wage jobs (U.S. Bureau of the Census 2001).

Oliver and Shapiro (1995) found that the "wealth gap" between blacks and whites is even greater than the income gap. While blacks on average earned two thirds as much as whites, their net worth was only one tenth as much. More recent data show that the wealth gap has decreased only slightly. In 2007, whites had a median net worth of $170,400, compared with $27,800 for non-white or Hispanics (Survey of Consumer Finances 2009). Oliver and Shapiro also found that when blacks attained educational or occupational levels comparable to whites, the wealth gap still did not disappear.

Oliver and Shapiro (1995) argued that blacks in the United States have encountered many barriers to acquiring wealth throughout history. After the Civil War ended slavery in 1865, legal discrimination (such as mandatory segregation in the South and separate schools) tied the vast majority of blacks to the lowest rungs of the economic ladder. Racial discrimination was made illegal by the Civil Rights Act of 1964; nonetheless, discrimination has remained, and although some blacks have moved into middle-class occupations, many have remained poor or in low-wage jobs where the opportunities for accumulating wealth are nonexistent. Less wealth means less social and cultural capital: fewer dollars to invest in schooling for one's children, a business, or the stock market—investments that in the long run would create greater wealth for future investments.

SOCIAL MOBILITY

Social mobility refers to the upward or downward movement of individuals and groups between different class positions as a result of changes in occupation, wealth, or income. There are two ways of studying social mobility. First, we can look at people's own careers—how far they move up or down the socioeconomic scale in the course of their working lives. This is called **intragenerational mobility**. Alternatively, we can analyze where children are on the scale compared with their parents or grandparents. Mobility across the generations is called **intergenerational mobility**. Sociologists have long studied both types of mobility, with increasingly sophisticated methods. Unfortunately, with the exception of some recent studies, much of this research has been limited to male mobility, particularly of white males. We look at some of the research in this section.

social mobility • Movement of individuals or groups between different social positions.

intragenerational mobility • Movement up or down a social stratification hierarchy within the course of a personal career.

intergenerational mobility • Movement up or down a social stratification hierarchy from one generation to another.

Figure 7.5 | Black and Latino Household Income Compared to Whites'

Since the mid-1980s, the gap between black and white household income has narrowed, although blacks still earn, on average, only two thirds as much as whites earn. In 1972, the average black income was 57 percent of white income; by 2006, the gap had dropped slightly to 65 percent (the average household income in 2006 was $42,454 for blacks and $68,603 for whites). Latino households today are roughly the same relative to white households as they were in 1972: In that year Latino household income averaged 74 percent, whereas in 2006 it averaged 70 percent (the average household income in 2006 for Latinos was $50,574). While black households experienced steady gains over the period, Latino households experienced a worsening condition relative to white households until the 1990s. The economic growth at that time improved the relative situation of both blacks and Latinos, although some of these gains have been lost since 2000.

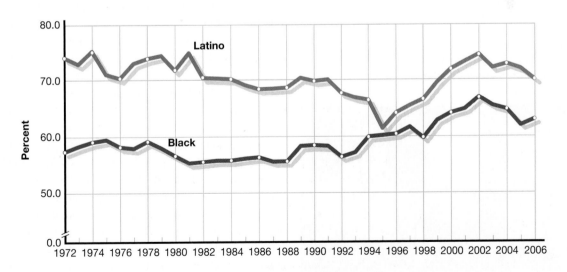

Source: U.S. Bureau of the Census 2007d.

Over the last two decades Tony Barbagallo has collected around $3.6 million in stock options from companies he has worked for. Despite his good fortune, he is surprised that, like most other Americans, he worries about matters as varied as the soaring cost of health care, the high price of college, and the pressure to save more money for retirement.

OPPORTUNITIES FOR MOBILITY: WHO GETS AHEAD?

Is it possible for a young person from a working class background to transcend class roots, and become an upper-class professional? If yes, how? Sociologists have sought to answer this question by trying to understand which social factors are most influential in determining an individual's status or position in society.

In a classic study of intergenerational mobility in the United States, the sociologists Peter Blau and Otis Dudley Duncan (1967) found that long-range intergenerational mobility, that is, from working class to upper-middle class, was rare. Why? Blau and Duncan concluded that the key factor behind occupational status was educational attainment. But a child's education is influenced by family social status; this, in turn, affects the child's social position later in life. Sociologists William Sewell and Robert Hauser (1980) later confirmed Blau and Duncan's conclusions. They added to the argument by claiming that the connection between family background and educational attainment occurs because parents, teachers, and friends influence the educational and career aspirations of the child and that these aspirations then become an important influence on the schooling and careers obtained throughout the child's life.

The former governor of Florida, Jeb Bush, shares a joke with former president George W. Bush, his brother, and his father, former president George H. W. Bush. How would Bourdieu explain the vertical mobility of the Bush family?

French sociologist Pierre Bourdieu (1984, 1988) has also been a major figure in examining the importance of family background to social status, but his emphasis is on the cultural advantages that parents can provide to their children. Bourdieu argued that among the factors responsible for social status, the most important is the transmission of cultural capital, or the cultural advantages that coming from a "good home" confers. Wealthier families are able to afford to send their children to better schools, an economic advantage that benefits the children's social status as adults. Parents from the upper and middle classes are mostly highly educated themselves and tend to be more involved in their children's education—reading to them, helping with homework, purchasing books and learning materials, and encouraging their progress. Bourdieu noted that working-class parents are concerned about their children's education, but they lack the economic and cultural capital to make a difference.

Although Bourdieu focused on social status in France, the socioeconomic order in the United States is similar. Those who already hold positions of wealth and power can ensure their children have the best available education, and this will often lead them into the best jobs. Studies consistently show that the large majority of people who have "made money" did so on the basis of inheriting or being given at least a modest amount initially—which they then used to make more. In U.S. society, it's better to start at the top than at the bottom (Jaher 1973; Rubinstein 1986; Duncan et al. 1998).

DOWNWARD MOBILITY

Downward mobility is less common than upward mobility; nevertheless, about 20 percent of men in the United States are downwardly mobile intergenerationally, although most of this movement is short range. A person with **short-range downward mobility** moves from one job to another that is similar in pay and prestige; for example, from a routine office job to semiskilled blue-collar work. Downward intragenerational mobility, also a common occurrence, is often associated with psychological problems and anxieties. Some people are simply unable to sustain the lifestyle into which they were born. But another source of downward mobility among individuals arises through no fault of their own. During the late 1980s and early 1990s, and again in the late 2000s, corporate America was flooded with instances in which middle-aged men lost their jobs because of company mergers, takeovers, or bankruptcies. These executives either had difficulty finding new jobs or could only find jobs that paid less than their previous jobs. ✓

downward mobility • Social mobility in which individuals' wealth, income, or status is lower than what they or their parents once had.

short-range downward mobility • Social mobility that occurs when an individual moves from one position in the class structure to another of nearly equal status.

CONCEPT CHECKS ✓

1. What are two pieces of statistical evidence used to support the claim that the gap between the rich and the poor is growing in the United States?

2. How would you explain the wealth gap between blacks and whites in the United States today?

3. Contrast intragenerational and intergenerational mobility.

4. According to classic studies of mobility in the United States, how does family background affect one's social class in adulthood?

5. According to Pierre Bourdieu, how does the family contribute to the transmission of social class from generation to generation?

6. Describe at least three reasons for downward mobility.

HOW DOES POVERTY AFFECT INDIVIDUALS?

At the bottom of the class system in the United States are the millions of people who live in poverty. Many do not maintain a proper diet and live in miserable conditions; their average life expectancy is lower than that of the majority of the population. In addition, the number of individuals and families who have become homeless has increased greatly over the past twenty years.

In defining poverty, a distinction is usually made between absolute and relative poverty. **Absolute poverty** means that a person or family simply can't get enough to eat. People living in absolute poverty are undernourished and, in situations of famine, may actually starve to death. Absolute poverty is common in the poorer developing countries.

absolute poverty • The minimal requirements necessary to sustain a healthy existence.

relative poverty • Poverty defined according to the living standards of the majority in any given society.

poverty line • An official government measure to define those living in poverty in the United States.

In the industrial countries, **relative poverty** is essentially a measure of inequality. It means being poor as compared with the standards of living of the majority. It is reasonable to call a person poor in the United States if he lacks the basic resources needed to maintain a decent standard of housing and healthy living conditions.

MEASURING POVERTY

When President Lyndon B. Johnson began his War on Poverty in 1964, around 36 million Americans lived in poverty. In 2007, this number sat at 37.3 million people, or roughly 12.5 percent of the population (DeNavas-Walt et al. 2008). This proportion greatly exceeds that of most other advanced industrial nations. In the mid-1990s, for example, when the U.S. poverty rate was around 14 percent, France's was 10 percent, Canada's and Germany's 7 percent (Smeeding et al. 2000).

What does it mean to be poor in the world's richest nation? The U.S. government calculates the **poverty line** as an income equal to three times the cost of a nutritionally adequate diet—a strict no-frills budget that assumes a nutritionally adequate diet could be purchased in 1999 for only $3.86 per day for each member, along with about $7.72 on all other items (including rent and utilities, clothing, medical expenses, and transportation). For a family of four in 2009, that works out to an annual cash income of $27,570 (Federal Register 2009).

How realistic is this formula? Some critics believe it overestimates the amount of poverty. They point out that the current standard fails to take into account non-cash forms of income available to the poor, such as food stamps, Medicare, Medicaid, and public housing subsidies, as well as "under the table" pay obtained from work at odd jobs that is concealed from the government. Other critics counter that the government's formula greatly underestimates the amount of poverty, because it overemphasizes the proportion of a family budget spent on food and severely underestimates the share spent on housing. According to some estimates, poor families today may spend as much as three-quarters of their income on housing alone (Dolbeare 1995; Joint Center for Housing Studies of Harvard University 2005).

The official U.S. poverty rate is the highest among the major advanced industrial nations, more than three times that of such European countries as Sweden or Norway (Smeeding et al. 2000). The largest concentrations of poverty in the United States are found in the South and the Southwest, in inner cities, and in rural areas. Among the poor, 15.6 million Americans (or 5.2 percent of the country) live in extreme poverty: Their incomes are only half of the official poverty level, meaning that they live at near-starvation levels (DeNavas-Walt et al. 2008).

Making Sociology Work
SCHOOL GUIDANCE COUNSELOR

High school guidance counselors can play a pivotal role in helping teens formulate and work toward their future educational and career goals. But as much as guidance counselors would like to believe that every student can achieve his or her dreams, they also recognize that some students face particularly difficult obstacles. Students from poor families often have to work for pay after school, giving up valuable after-school activities and study time. Other high school students are the first in their family to dream of going to college, and they're not sure of the best classes to take or whether to take the SAT. Guidance counselors at the largest inner-city schools face a further burden; they often can't make time for their many students. The American School Counselor Association recommends a ratio of one counselor for every 250 students. According to the National Center for Education Statistics, however, the national average is one counselor for every 315 students, and in many large schools the ratio can be as low as one counselor for every 600 students, if there are any counselors at all. Sociologists like Blau, Duncan, Hauser, Sewell, and Bourdieu have described the ways that social background and environment can shape one's future. Drawing on this sociological research, if you were a high school guidance counselor, what kind of advice would you offer to your students? Would you give different types of assistance and advice to students from upper-, middle-, working-, and lower-class and underclass backgrounds? Why?

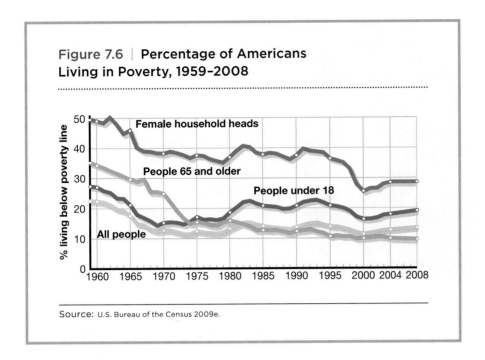

Figure 7.6 | Percentage of Americans Living in Poverty, 1959–2008

Female household heads

People 65 and older

People under 18

All people

Source: U.S. Bureau of the Census 2009e.

WHO ARE THE POOR?

Most Americans think of the poor as people who are unemployed or on welfare. Surveys repeatedly show that the majority of Americans regard the poor as responsible for their plight and are antagonistic to those who live on "government handouts." For example, a Gallup poll (1998) found that 55 percent of the public believed that lack of effort by the poor was the principal reason for poverty. Nearly two thirds believed that government assistance programs reduced incentives to work. Yet these views are out of line with the realities of poverty. The poor are as diverse as other groups.

THE WORKING POOR

Many Americans are the **working poor**—that is, people who work but whose earnings are not high enough to lift them above poverty. The federal minimum wage, the legal floor for wages in the United States, was first set in 1938 at $0.25 an hour. As of July 24, 2009, the minimum wage was $7.25 per hour, although individual states can set higher minimum wages than the federal standard. Fifteen have chosen to do so; the highest is in the state of Washington, at $8.55 per hour. Although the federal minimum wage has increased over the years, since 1965 it has failed to keep up with inflation.

About one third of those officially living in poverty are actually working. In 2007, there were an estimated 7.5 million working poor (2.5 percent of population) (U.S. Bureau of Labor Statistics 2009a). Of those working poor, 4.4 million usually worked full-time and another 2.5 million usually worked part-time. Most poor people, contrary to popular belief, do not receive welfare payments, because they earn too much to qualify for welfare. Only 5 percent of all low-income families with a full-time, full-year worker receive welfare benefits, and over half rely on public health insurance rather than employer-sponsored insurance. The working poor are disproportionately nonwhite and immigrant (Urban Institute 2005). Qualitative research on low-wage fast-food workers further reveals that many working poor lack adequate education, do not have health insurance to cover medical costs, and are trying to support families on poverty-level wages (Newman 2000).

working poor • People who work, but whose earnings are not enough to lift them above the poverty line.

What does Katherine Newman's research reveal about the working poor? What obstacles must they overcome to make ends meet?

POVERTY, RACE, AND ETHNICITY

Poverty rates in the United States are much higher among most minority groups than among whites, even though more than two thirds of the poor are white. As Figure 7.7 shows, blacks and Latinos continue to earn around two thirds of what whites earn in the United States, while experiencing three times the poverty rate whites experience. This is because they often work at the lowest-paying jobs and because of racial discrimination. Asian Americans have the highest income of any group, but their poverty rate is slightly less than one and a half times that of whites, reflecting the recent influx of relatively poor Asian immigrant groups.

Latinos have somewhat higher incomes than blacks, although their poverty rate is comparable. Nonetheless, the number of blacks living in poverty has declined considerably in recent years. In 1959, 55.1 percent of blacks were living in poverty; by 2007, that figure had dropped to 24.5 percent. A similar pattern holds for Latinos: Poverty grew steadily between 1972 and 1994, peaking at 30.7 percent of the Latino population. By 2007, however, the poverty rate for Latinos had fallen to 21.5 percent (DeNavas-Walt et al. 2008). This is mainly because the economic expansion of the 1990s created new job opportunities (DeNavas-Walt et al. 2005).

THE FEMINIZATION OF POVERTY

feminization of poverty •
An increase in the proportion of the poor who are female.

Much of the growth in poverty is associated with the **feminization of poverty**, an increase in the proportion of the poor who are female. Growing rates of divorce, separation, and single-parent families have placed women at particular disadvantage, since it is extremely difficult for unskilled or semiskilled, low-income, poorly educated women to raise children by themselves while they also hold down a job that could raise them out of poverty. As a result, in 2007 28.3 percent of all single-parent families headed by women were poor, compared to only 4.9 percent of married couples with children (DeNavas-Walt et al. 2008).

The feminization of poverty is particularly acute among families headed by Latino women (Figure 7.8). Although the rate declined by almost 30 percent since its peak in the mid-1980s (64 percent in 1985), 42.5 percent of all female-headed Latino families lived in poverty in 2006. An almost identical percentage (43.6 percent) of female-headed African American families also live in poverty; both considerably higher than either white (30.2 percent) or Asian (24.1 percent) female-headed households (U.S. Bureau of the Census 2007e).

A single woman attempting to raise children alone is caught in a vicious circle. If she has a job, she must find someone to take care of her children, since she cannot afford to hire a babysitter or pay for day care. From her standpoint, she will take in more money if she accepts welfare payments from the government and tries to find illegal part-time jobs that pay cash not reported to the government rather than find a regular full-time job paying minimum wage. Even though welfare will not get her out of poverty, if she finds a regular job she will lose her welfare altogether, and she and her family may even be worse off economically.

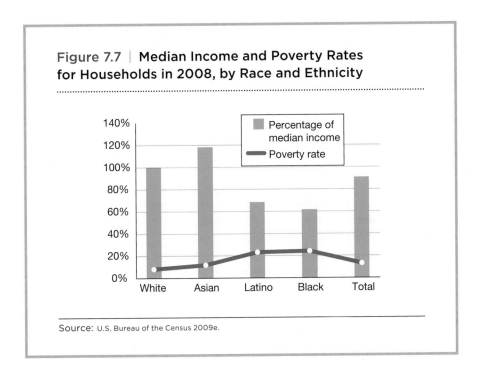

Figure 7.7 | Median Income and Poverty Rates for Households in 2008, by Race and Ethnicity

Source: U.S. Bureau of the Census 2009e.

CHILDREN IN POVERTY

Given the high rates of poverty among families headed by single women, it follows that children are the principal victims of poverty in the United States. Child poverty rates (defined as poverty among people under eighteen) in the United States are by far the highest in the industrial world. Nonetheless, the child poverty rate has varied considerably over the last forty years, declining when the economy expands or the government increases spending on antipoverty programs and rising when the economy slows and government antipoverty spending falls. The child poverty rate declined from 27.3 percent of all children in 1959 to 14.4 percent in 1973—a period associated with both economic growth and the War on Poverty declared by the Johnson administration (1963–1969). During the late 1970s and 1980s, as economic growth slowed and cutbacks were made in government antipoverty programs, child poverty grew, exceeding 20 percent during much of the period. The economic expansion of the 1990s saw a drop in child poverty rates, and in 2002 the rate had fallen to 16.3 percent, a twenty-year low (U.S. Bureau of the Census 2003a). Yet, child poverty again reached 18 percent in 2007, and is still increasing (DeNavas-Walt et al. 2008).

The statistics are significantly higher for racial minorities and children of single mothers. Of those children under the age of eighteen who were living in poverty in 2007, 9.7 percent

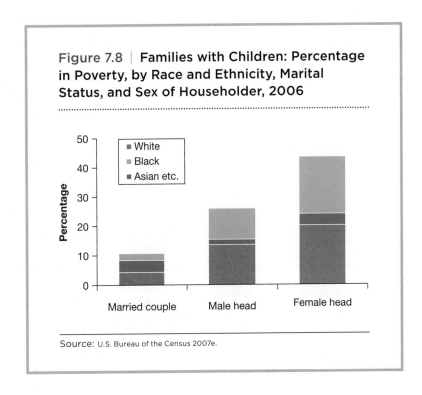

Figure 7.8 | Families with Children: Percentage in Poverty, by Race and Ethnicity, Marital Status, and Sex of Householder, 2006

Source: U.S. Bureau of the Census 2007e.

were white, 33.6 percent were black, 11.3 percent were Asian, and 28.3 percent were Hispanic; 28.4 percent lived in a single-mother household (DeNavas-Walt et al. 2008).

THE ELDERLY IN POVERTY

Although relatively few persons age sixty-five and older live in poverty, some of the very poorest people are elderly, particularly among minorities. Among whites, only 7.4 percent of the elderly reported poverty-level incomes in 2007, compared with 23.3 percent of blacks, 11.2 percent of Asians, and 17.1 percent of Hispanics (DeNavas-Walt et al. 2008).

Because older people have for the most part retired from paid work, their income is based primarily on **Social Security** and private retirement programs. Social Security and **Medicare** have been especially important in lifting many elderly people out of poverty. Yet people who depend solely on these two programs for income and health-care coverage are likely to live modestly at best. Social Security accounts for only about 40 percent of the income of the typical retiree; most of the remainder comes from investments and private pension funds, and sometimes earnings. Low-income households in particular are likely to rely heavily on Social Security, which accounts for as much as three quarters of all income for retirees living on less than $10,000 a year (Atchley 2000). Yet even the combination of Social Security and private pensions results in modest retirement incomes for most people (Krueger 1995).

Social Security • A government program that provides economic assistance to persons faced with unemployment, disability, or old age.

Medicare • A program under the U.S. Social Security Administration that reimburses hospitals and physicians for medical care provided to qualifying people over sixty-five years old.

EXPLAINING POVERTY: THE SOCIOLOGICAL DEBATE

Explanations of poverty can be grouped under two main headings: theories that see poor individuals as responsible for their status and theories that view poverty as produced and reproduced by structural forces in society. These competing approaches are sometimes described as "blame the victim" and "blame the system" theories, respectively. We shall briefly examine each in turn.

There is a long history of attitudes that hold the poor responsible for their own disadvantaged positions. Early efforts to address the effects of poverty, such as the poorhouses of the nineteenth century, were grounded in a belief that poverty was the result of an inadequacy or pathology of individuals. The poor were seen as those who were unable—due to lack of skills, moral or physical weakness, absence of motivation, or below-average ability—to succeed in society. Social standing was taken as a reflection of a person's talent and effort; those who deserved to succeed did so, while others less capable were doomed to fail. The existence of winners and losers was regarded as a fact of life.

Such outlooks enjoyed a renaissance, beginning in the 1970s and 1980s, as the political emphasis on individual ambition rewarded those who "succeeded" in society and held those who did not responsible for the circumstances in which they found themselves. Often explanations for poverty were sought in the lifestyles of poor people, along with the attitudes and outlooks they supposedly espoused. Oscar Lewis (1968) set forth one of the most influential of such theories, arguing that a **culture of poverty** exists among many poor people. According to Lewis, poverty is not a result of individual inadequacies, but is a result of a larger social and cultural milieu into which poor children are socialized. The culture of poverty is transmitted across generations because young people from an early age see little point in aspiring to something more. Instead, they resign themselves fatalistically to a life of impoverishment.

culture of poverty • The thesis, popularized by Oscar Lewis, that poverty is not a result of individual inadequacies but is instead the outcome of a larger social and cultural atmosphere into which successive generations of children are socialized. The culture of poverty refers to the values, beliefs, lifestyles, habits, and traditions that are common among people living under conditions of material deprivation.

The culture of poverty thesis has been taken further by the American sociologist Charles Murray. According to Murray, individuals who are poor through "no fault of their own"—such as widows or widowers, orphans, or the disabled—fall into a different category from those who are part of the **dependency culture**. By this term, Murray refers to poor people who rely on government welfare provision rather than entering the labor market. He argues that the growth of the welfare state has created a subculture that undermines personal ambition and the capacity for self-help. Rather than orienting themselves toward the future and striving to achieve a better life, those dependent on welfare are content to accept handouts. Welfare, he argues, has eroded people's incentive to work (Murray 1984).

A second approach to explaining poverty emphasizes larger social processes that produce conditions of poverty that are difficult for individuals to overcome. According to such a view, structural forces within society—factors like class, gender, ethnicity, occupational position, education attainment, and so forth—shape the way in which resources are distributed (Wilson 1996). Writers who advocate structural explanations for poverty argue that the lack of ambition among the poor that is often taken for the dependency culture is in fact a consequence of their constrained situations, not a cause of it. Reducing poverty is not a matter of changing individual outlooks, they claim, but instead requires policy measures aimed at distributing income and resources more equally throughout society. Child-care subsidies, a minimum hourly wage, and guaranteed income levels for families are examples of policy measures that have sought to redress persistent social inequalities.

Both theories have enjoyed broad support, and social scientists consistently encourage variations of each view in public debates about poverty. Critics of the culture of poverty view accuse its advocates of "individualizing" poverty and blaming the poor for circumstances largely beyond their control. They see the poor as victims, not as freeloaders who are abusing the system. Yet we should be cautious about accepting uncritically the arguments of those who see the causes of poverty as lying exclusively in the structure of society itself. Such an approach implies that the poor simply passively accept the difficult situations in which they find themselves.

dependency culture • A term popularized by Charles Murray to describe individuals who rely on state welfare provision rather than entering the labor market. The dependency culture is seen as the outcome of the "paternalistic" welfare state that undermines individual ambition and people's capacity for self-help.

SOCIAL EXCLUSION

What are the social processes that lead to a large number of people's being marginalized in society? The idea of **social exclusion** refers to new sources of inequality—ways in which individuals may become cut off from involvement in the wider society. It is a broader concept than that of the underclass and has the advantage that it emphasizes processes—mechanisms of exclusion. Social exclusion can take a number of forms—it may occur in isolated rural communities cut off from many services and opportunities or in inner-city neighborhoods marked by high crime rates and substandard housing. Exclusion and inclusion may be seen in economic terms, political terms, and social terms.

The concept of social exclusion raises the question of agency. After all, the word *exclusion* implies that someone or something is being shut out by another. Certainly in some instances, individuals are excluded through decisions that lie outside their own control. Insurance companies might reject an application for a policy on the basis of an applicant's personal history and background. An employee laid off later in life may be refused further jobs on the basis of his or her age.

But social exclusion can also result from people excluding themselves from aspects of mainstream society. Individuals can choose to drop out of education, to

social exclusion • The outcome of multiple deprivations that prevent individuals or groups from participating fully in the economic, social, and political life of the society in which they live.

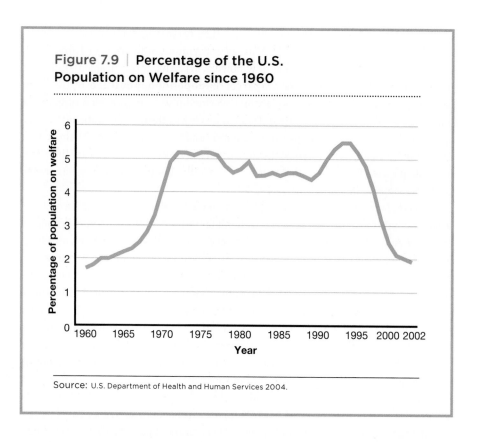

Figure 7.9 | Percentage of the U.S. Population on Welfare since 1960

Source: U.S. Department of Health and Human Services 2004.

turn down a job opportunity and become economically inactive, or to abstain from voting in political elections. In considering the phenomenon of social exclusion, we must once again be conscious of the interaction between human agency and responsibility on the one hand and the role of social forces in shaping people's circumstances on the other hand.

THE HOMELESS

homeless • People who have no place to sleep and either stay in free shelters or sleep in public places not meant for habitation.

No discussion of social exclusion is complete without reference to the people who are traditionally seen as at the very bottom of the social hierarchy: the **homeless**. The growing problem of homelessness is one of the most distressing signs of changes in the American stratification system. The homeless are a common sight in nearly every U.S. city and town and are increasingly found in rural areas as well. Two generations ago, the homeless were mainly elderly, alcoholic men who were found on the skid rows of the largest metropolitan areas. Today they are primarily young single men, often of working age. The fastest-growing group of homeless, however, consists of families with children, who make up as much as a third of those currently homeless (National Law Center on Homelessness and Poverty 2009). Approximately 42 percent of those children are under the age of five. In 2004, the National Law Center on Homelessness and Poverty estimated that 41 percent of homeless persons are single men and 14 percent are single women. Equal shares of the homeless population are black and white (40 percent), while 11 percent are Hispanic and 8 percent are Native American. Very few homeless are Latino or Asian American immigrants, possibly because these groups enjoy close-knit family and community ties that provide a measure of security against homelessness (Waxman and Hinderliter 1996). The National Coalition of Homeless Veterans estimates that there are nearly 200,000 homeless veterans on the streets on any given day (NCVH 2007)

Because it is extremely difficult to count people who do not have a stable residence (Appelbaum 1990), estimates of the number of homeless vary widely. The most recent estimate is that there are 664,414 persons living in emergency shelters, transitional housing, and on the streets on any given night, while 124,135 are chronically homeless in the United States (U.S. Department of Housing & Human Services 2009).

There are many reasons why people become homeless. About two thirds reported having a problem with alcohol at some point during their life, another two thirds reported having a problem with drugs at some point, and nearly 60 percent have experienced a mental health problem. (National Law Center on Homelessness and Poverty 2004). One reason for the widespread incidence of such problems among the homeless is that many public mental hospitals have closed their doors. The number of beds in state mental hospitals has declined by as many as half a million since the early 1960s, leaving many mentally ill people with no institutional alternative to a life on the streets or in homeless shelters. Such problems are compounded by the fact that many homeless people lack family, relatives, or other social networks to provide support.

The rising cost of housing is another factor, particularly in light of the increased poverty noted elsewhere in this chapter. Declining incomes at the bottom, along with rising rents, create an affordability gap between the cost of housing and what poor people can pay in rents (Dreier and Appelbaum 1992). The median share of income that renters spend on rent is 29 percent. It is estimated that nearly a third of all households spend 30 percent or more of their incomes on housing, and 13 percent spend 50 percent of their income on housing (Joint Center for Housing Studies of Harvard University 2005). The burden of paying rent is extremely difficult for low-income families whose heads work for minimum wage or slightly higher. Paying so much in terms of rent leaves them barely a paycheck away from a missed rental payment and eventual eviction (National Low Income Housing Coalition [NLIHC] 2000). ✓

CONCEPT CHECKS ✓

1. What is the poverty line, and how does the U.S. government calculate this statistic?

2. Describe the demographic characteristics of the poor in the United States.

3. Why are women and children at a high risk of becoming impoverished in the United States today?

4. Contrast the culture of poverty argument and structural explanations for poverty.

5. Describe the concept of social exclusion.

6. Describe the demographic characteristics of the homeless population in the United States today.

7. What are the main reasons people become homeless?

The people who are at the greatest risk of becoming homeless are those who work in jobs that have low wages, live in poverty, and also struggle with personal troubles such as mental illness, alcoholism, and family problems.

HOW DOES SOCIAL INEQUALITY AFFECT YOUR LIFE?

Throughout this chapter, we have shown how changes in the American economy affect social stratification, emphasizing the importance of both globalization and changes in information technology. We have pointed out that the global spread of an industrial capitalist economy, driven in part by the information revolution, has helped to break down closed caste systems around the world and replace them with more open class systems. The degree to which this process will result in greater equality in countries undergoing capitalist development will be explored in the next chapter.

What do these changes hold in store for you? On the one hand, new jobs are opening up, particularly in high-technology fields that require special training and skills and pay high wages. A flood of new products are flowing into the United States, many made with cheap labor that has lowered their costs. This has enabled consumers such as yourselves to buy everything from computers to automobiles to athletic shoes at costs lower than you otherwise would have paid, thereby contributing to a rising standard of living.

But these benefits come with potentially significant costs. Given high levels of job loss in the recent recession and American's demands for low-cost products, you may find yourselves competing for jobs with workers in other countries who work for lower wages. This has already been the case for the manufacturing jobs that once provided the economic foundation for the working class and segments of the middle class. Companies that once produced in the United States—from automobiles to apparel to electronics—now use factories around the world, taking advantage of labor costs that are a fraction of those in the United States. Will the same hold true for other, more highly skilled jobs—jobs in the information economy itself? Many jobs that require the use of computers—from graphic design to software engineering—can be done by anyone with a high-speed computer connection, anywhere in the world. The global spread of dot-com companies will open up vastly expanded job opportunities for those with the necessary skills and training—but it will also open up equally expanded global competition for those jobs.

Partly as a result of these forces, inequality has increased in the United States since the early 1970s, resulting in a growing gap between rich and poor. The global economy has permitted the accumulation of vast fortunes at the same time that it has contributed to declining wages, economic hardship, and poverty in the United States. Although the working class is especially vulnerable to these changes, the middle class is not exempt: A growing number of middle-class households experienced downward mobility from the late 1970s through the mid-1990s, until a decade of economic growth benefited all segments of American society. Yet the economic recession that began in 2008 has further contributed to the downward mobility of middle-class Americans, and has left many recent college graduates with high levels of debt and few prospects for rewarding employment. Although it is always hazardous to try to predict the future, global economic integration will likely continue to increase for the foreseeable future. How this will affect your jobs and careers—and stratification in the United States—is much more difficult to foresee. ✓

CONCEPT CHECKS ✓

1. How has globalization affected the life chances of young adults in the United States today?

NEED HELP STUDYING?

⊚ **wwnorton.com/studyspace**

Visit StudySpace to access free review materials such as:

- Vocabulary Flashcards
- Diagnostic Review Quizzes
- Study Outlines

REVIEW QUESTIONS

1. What are the differences between income and wealth?
2. What is the basis of Karl Marx's theory of class?
3. What are two consequences of globalization for the United States?
4. According to William Sewell and Robert Hauser, how does family background influence one's educational attainment?
5. What is the difference between intragenerational mobility and intergenerational mobility?
6. What is the "feminization of poverty"?
7. How does Charles Murray explain the cause of the underclass in inner cities?
8. What is the relationship between social exclusion and crime?
9. How is a caste system different from a class system?
10. What are some social and demographic characteristics of the homeless population?

THINKING SOCIOLOGICALLY EXERCISES

1. If you were doing your own study of status differences in your community, how would you measure people's social class? Base your answer on the textbook's discussion of these matters to explain why you would take the particular measurement approach you've chosen. What would be its value(s) and shortcoming(s) compared with adopting alternative measurement procedures?
2. Using occupation and occupational change as your mobility criteria, view the social mobility within your family for three generations. As you discuss the differences in jobs between your paternal grandfather, your father, and yourself, apply all these terms correctly: vertical and horizontal mobility, upward and downward mobility, intragenerational and intergenerational mobility. Explain fully why you think people in your family have moved up, moved down, or remained at the same status level.

8

Global Inequality

THE BIG QUESTIONS

WHAT IS GLOBAL INEQUALITY?
Understand the systematic differences in wealth and power between countries.

WHAT IS DAILY LIFE LIKE IN RICH VERSUS POOR COUNTRIES?
Recognize the impact of different economic standards of living on people throughout the world.

CAN POOR COUNTRIES BECOME RICH?
Analyze the success of the newly industrializing economies.

HOW DO SOCIOLOGICAL THEORIES EXPLAIN GLOBAL INEQUALITY?
Learn several sociological theories explaining why some societies are wealthier than others, as well as how global inequality can be overcome.

HOW DOES GLOBAL INEQUALITY AFFECT YOUR LIFE?
Understand how global economic inequality affects the daily life of you and your peers.

The past quarter century has seen the appearance of more global billionaires than ever before in history. Despite the recent global economic downturn, in 2009 there were 793 billionaires worldwide, down from 1,125 in 2008—with 373 falling off the list (355 due to declining fortunes and 18 who died), 3 who regained their positions as billionaires, and 38 newcomers. These billionaires included 371 Americans, 32 Russians, 24 Indians, 28 Chinese, and 12 Spaniards, as well as billionaires from Cyprus, Oman, Romania, Serbia, and other nations (Forbes 2009). Their combined assets in 2009 were estimated at $2.4 trillion—greater than the total gross national income of all but the top seven economies of the world (calculated from World Bank 2008a). The success of the United States' high-technology economy, coupled with the financial crisis that struck Asia in the late 1990s, propelled the United States to lay claim to over half the world's billionaires.

As of 2009, the wealthiest person in the world was Microsoft Corporation's founder Bill Gates, with a net worth of $40 billion in that year—down from $63 billion in 2000, due to the decline in the stock market. Gates, whose fortune is based largely on ownership of his company's stock, would seem the personification of American

The billionaire Carlos Slim is an example of the many superrich who accumulated tremendous wealth through investment in technology and telecommunications.

entrepreneurialism: a computer nerd turned capitalist whose software provides the operating system for nearly all personal computers. During the late 1990s, Gates was the first person in history to have a net worth in excess of $100 billion. Even with the declining value of Microsoft stock, Gates has been ranked number one in wealth in the world for thirteen years in a row.

Gates is followed on the billionaire list by the financier Warren Buffett, at $37 billion. Buffet is an investor and CEO of Berkshire Hathaway Inc., which owns companies such as Geico Direct Auto Insurance, Dairy Queen, and See's Candies. In 2003, Buffet became an adviser to California's governor, Arnold Schwarzenegger.

The third richest person in the world is also Latin America's richest man. Carlos Slim Helu owns a diverse array of investments in retail, banking, and insurance but made his way to the top of the list based on his investment in two Mexican telecommunication companies as well as significant shares of American-based MCI, which was recently bought out by Verizon. His net worth is $35 billion. Fourth on the list is Lawrence Ellison of Oracle Corporation, with a net worth of $22.5 billion. Ingvar Kamprad, owner of IKEA, came in fifth. His investments have established his worth at $22 billion (Forbes 2009).

Among the twenty-eight richest people on the 2009 list, fourteen are from the United States, eight are from Europe, two from India, two were from Hong Kong, and one each from Canada, Mexico, and Saudi Arabia (Forbes 2009). If Bill Gates typifies the American high-tech entrepreneur, Hong Kong's Li Ka-shing—who is number sixteen on the list and East Asia's richest man—is the hero in a rags-to-riches story that characterizes the success of many Asian businessmen. Li (his surname) began his career by making plastic flowers; in 2009, his $16.2 billion in personal wealth derived from a wide range of real estate and other investments throughout Asia.

Globalization—the increased economic, political, and social interconnectedness of the world—has produced opportunities for unthinkable wealth. Yet at the same time it has produced widespread poverty and suffering. Consider, for example, Wirat Tasago, a twenty-four-year-old garment worker in Bangkok, Thailand. Tasago—along with more than a million other Thai garment workers, most of whom are women—labors from 8 A.M. until 11 P.M. or even later six days a week, earning little more than $3 an hour (Dahlburg 1995). Millions of workers such as Tasago are being drawn into the global labor force, many working in oppressive conditions that would be unacceptable, if not unimaginable, under U.S. labor laws. And these are the fortunate ones: Those who remain outside the global economy are frequently even worse off.

In the previous chapter we examined the American class structure, noting vast differences between individuals' income, wealth, jobs, and quality of life. The same is true in the world as a whole: Just as we can speak of rich or poor individuals within a country, so we can talk about rich or poor countries in the world system. A country's position in the global economy affects how its people live, work, and even die. In this chapter, we look closely at differences in wealth and power between countries in the late twentieth and early twenty-first centuries. We examine how differences in economic standards of living affect people throughout the world. We then turn to the newly industrializing economies of the world to understand which countries are improving their fortunes and why. This will lead us to a discussion of different theories that attempt to explain why global inequality exists and what can be done about it. We conclude by speculating on the future of economic inequality in a global world.

WHAT IS GLOBAL INEQUALITY?

Global inequality refers to the systematic differences in wealth and power that exist between countries. These differences exist alongside differences within countries: Even the wealthiest countries today have growing numbers of poor people, while less wealthy nations are producing many of the world's superrich. Sociology's challenge is not merely to identify all such differences, but to explain why they occur—and how they might be overcome.

global inequality • The systematic differences in wealth and power between countries.

One simple way to classify countries in terms of global inequality is to compare the wealth produced by each country per average citizen. This approach measures the value of a country's yearly output of goods and services produced by its total population and then divides that total by the number of people in the country. The resulting measure is termed the *per person gross national income* (GNI), a measure of the country's yearly output of goods and services per person. The World Bank, an international lending organization that provides loans for development projects in poorer countries, uses this measure to classify countries as high income (an annual per person GNI of $11,906 or more, in 2008 dollars), upper middle income ($3,856–11,905), lower middle income ($976–3,855), or low income (under $975) (World Bank 2008b). This system of classification will help us better understand why living standards vary so widely between countries.

Figure 8.1 shows how the World Bank (2009a) divides 208 countries and economies (such as the West Bank and Gaza, Taiwan, and Macau), containing over six billion people, into the three economic classes. The figure shows that while nearly 40 percent of the world's population lives in low-income countries, less than 16 percent lives in high-income countries. Bear in mind that this classification is based on average income for each country; therefore, it masks income inequality within each country. Such differences can be significant, although we do not focus on them in this chapter. For example, the World Bank classifies India as a low-income country because its per person GNI in 2007 was only $950. Yet despite widespread poverty, India also boasts a large and growing middle class. China, on the other hand, was reclassified in 1999 from low to middle income because its GNI per capita in that year was $780 (at that time the World Bank's lower limit for a lower-middle-income country was $736). Yet even though its average income grew to $2,310 in 2007, placing China squarely in the world's lower-middle-class status, it nonetheless has hundreds of millions of people living in poverty.

Comparing countries on the basis of economic output alone may be misleading in another way, since gross national income includes only goods and services that are produced for cash sale. Many people in low-income countries are farmers or herders who produce for their own families or for barter, involving noncash transactions. The value of their crops and animals is not taken into account in the statistics. Further, economic output is not the sole indicator of a country's worth: Poor countries are no less rich in history, culture, and traditions than their wealthier neighbors, but the lives of their people are much harsher.

HIGH-INCOME COUNTRIES

High-income countries are generally those that were the first to industrialize, a process that began in England some two hundred fifty years ago and then spread to Europe, the United States, and Canada. In the 1970s, Japan joined the ranks of high-income, industrialized nations, while Singapore, Hong Kong, and Taiwan moved into this category only within the last decade or so. The reasons for the success of these Asian latecomers to industrialization are much debated by sociologists and economists; we will look at them later in the chapter.

High-income countries are home to 16 percent of the world's population, or just more than a billion people, yet they lay claim to over 75 percent of the world's annual output of wealth (derived from World Bank 2007a). High-income countries offer adequate housing and food, drinkable water, and other comforts unknown in many parts of the world. Although these countries often have large numbers of poor people, most of their inhabitants enjoy a standard of living unimaginable by the majority of the world's people.

MIDDLE-INCOME COUNTRIES

The *middle-income countries* are located primarily in East and Southeast Asia and also include the oil-rich countries of the Middle East and North Africa, the Americas (Mexico, Central America, Cuba and other countries in the Caribbean, and South America), and the once-communist republics that formerly made up the Soviet Union and its Eastern European allies (Global Map 8.1). Most of these countries began to industrialize relatively late in the twentieth century and therefore are not yet as industrially developed (nor as wealthy) as the high-income countries. The countries that once comprised the Soviet Union, on the other hand, are highly industrialized, although their living standards have eroded during the past two decades as a result of the collapse of communism and the move to capitalist economies. In Russia, for example, the wages of ordinary people dropped by nearly a third between 1998 and 1999, while retirement pensions dropped by nearly half. Millions of people, many of them elderly, suddenly found themselves destitute (CIA 2000). Since then, the Russian economy has recovered somewhat, with foreign investment gradually increasing and the energy market booming.

In 2007, middle-income countries were home to 64.4 percent of the world's population (4.25 billion people) but accounted for only 23.4 percent of the wealth produced in that year. Although many people in these countries are substantially better off than their neighbors in low-income countries, most do not enjoy anything resembling the standard of living common in high-income countries. The ranks of the world's middle-income countries expanded between 1999 and 2000, at least according to the World Bank's system of classification, when China—with 1.3 billion people (22 percent of the world's population)—was reclassified from low- to middle-income because of its economic growth. Today, China's per capita GNI is $2,370, which is well above the lower limit ($976) defined by the World Bank for lower-middle-income countries. Nonetheless, a majority of China's population is low income by World Bank standards.

LOW-INCOME COUNTRIES

Finally, the *low-income countries* include much of eastern, western, and sub-Saharan Africa; Vietnam, Cambodia, Indonesia, and a few other East Asian countries; India, Nepal, Bangladesh, and Pakistan in South Asia; East and Central European countries such as Georgia and Ukraine; and Haiti and Nicaragua in the Western Hemisphere. These countries have mostly agricultural economies and have only recently begun to industrialize. Scholars debate the reasons for their late industrialization and widespread poverty, as we will see later in this chapter.

In 2007, the low-income countries accounted for over 19.6 percent of the world's population (1.3 billion people) yet produced only 1.4 percent of the world's yearly output

Figure 8.1

GLOBAL INEQUALITY

Comparing Quality of Life Among Countries

	LOW-INCOME COUNTRIES	MEDIUM-INCOME COUNTRIES	HIGH-INCOME COUNTRIES	WORLD
GROSS NATIONAL INCOME PER CAPITA (Current U.S. $)	$524	 $3,260	 $39,345	 $8,613
TOTAL POPULATION	973 million	4,651 million	1,069 million	6,692 million
ANNUAL POPULATION GROWTH	+ 2.1%	+ 1.1%	+ 0.7%	+ 1.2%
LIFE EXPECTANCY AT BIRTH	59 59 years	69 69 years	79 79 years	69 69 years
FERTILITY RATE	4 births per woman	2.4 births per woman	1.8 births per woman	2.5 births per woman
MORTALITY RATE	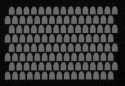 120 per 1,000	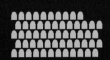 58 per 1,000	7 per 1,000	68 per 1,000

Source: World Bank 2009b.

of wealth (World Bank 2007a). Moreover, this inequality is increasing. Fertility rates are much higher in low-income countries than elsewhere, with large families providing additional farm labor or otherwise contributing to family income. (In wealthy industrial societies, where children are more likely to be in school than on the farm, the economic benefit of large families declines, so people tend to have fewer children.) Because of this, the populations of low-income countries grew more than twice as fast as those of high-income countries between 1990 and 2005.

In many of these low-income countries, people struggle with poverty, malnutrition, and even starvation. Most people live in rural areas, although this is rapidly changing: Hundreds of millions of people are moving to huge, densely populated cities, where they live either in dilapidated housing or on the open streets (see Chapter 15).

GROWING GLOBAL INEQUALITY: THE RICH GET RICHER, THE POOR GET POORER

During the last thirty years, the overall standard of living in the world has risen slowly. The average global citizen is today better off than ever before. Illiteracy rates are down, infant mortality and malnutrition are less common, people are living longer, average income is higher, and poverty is down. Since these figures are overall averages, however, they hide the substantial differences between countries: Many of these gains have been in the high- and middle-income countries, while living standards in many of the

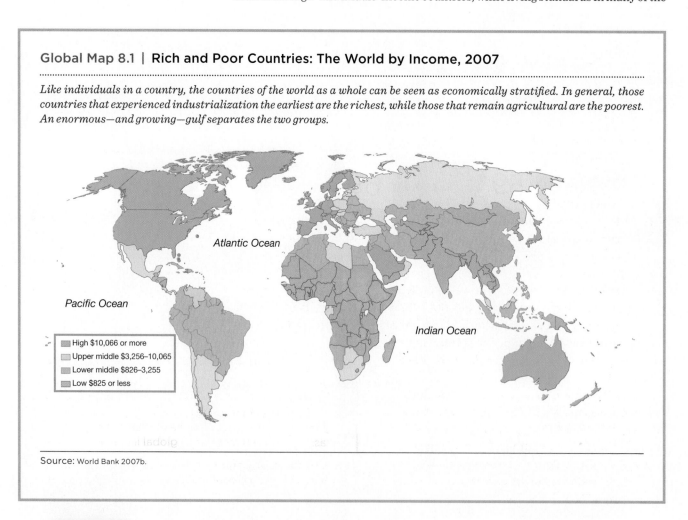

Global Map 8.1 | Rich and Poor Countries: The World by Income, 2007

Like individuals in a country, the countries of the world as a whole can be seen as economically stratified. In general, those countries that experienced industrialization the earliest are the richest, while those that remain agricultural are the poorest. An enormous—and growing—gulf separates the two groups.

Atlantic Ocean

Pacific Ocean

Indian Ocean

High $10,066 or more
Upper middle $3,256–10,065
Lower middle $826–3,255
Low $825 or less

Source: World Bank 2007b.

Figure 8.2 | **GNI per Person in Low-, Middle-, and High-Income Countries, 1983–2008**

Despite overall growth in the global economy, the gap between rich and poor countries has not declined in recent years. Between 1983 and 2008, per-person gross national income (GNI) in low-income countries increased an average of 2.9 percent a year, far less than in high-income countries (6.5 percent). As a consequence, the average person in a high-income country earned roughly sixty-three times as much as the average person in a low-income country. Average per-person GNI in middle-income countries split the difference and increased by an average 4.3 percent.

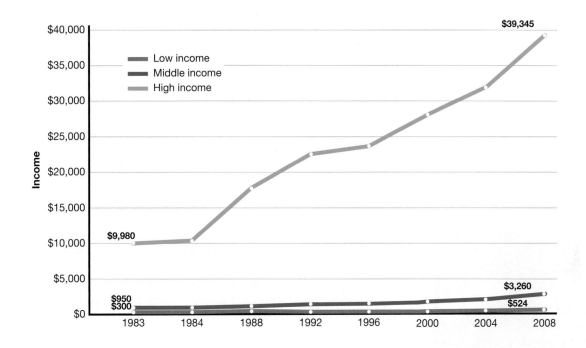

Source: World Bank 2009c.

poorest countries have declined. Overall, the gap between rich and poor countries has widened over the last two decades.

Between 1988 and 2006, average per person GNI increased by 105.4 percent in high-income countries and by 75.7 percent in low-income countries, widening the global gap between rich and poor (Figure 8.2). But most of the growth in low-income per capita income has been since 2000, when it was $380 per person (it was $370 in 1988, declined to a low of $310 in 1993–1994, and then gradually increased back to 1970s levels of income per capita by 2000). But by 2007, per capita income in low-income countries had jumped to $574 (current dollars). The per capita GNI of middle-income countries has grown steadily, more than doubling in the twenty-year period between 1994 and 2007.

In 2007, the average person in a typical high-income country earned $37,572 (per capita) based on current U.S. dollars, 65 times as much as the $574 earned by his or her counterpart in a low-income country (World Bank 2007a). About half of the world's population is estimated to live on less than $2 a day (Global Issues 2006). ✓

CONCEPT CHECKS ✓

1. Explain how the World Bank measures global inequality, and discuss some of the problems associated with measuring global inequality.

2. Compare and contrast high-income, middle-income, and low-income countries.

WHAT IS DAILY LIFE LIKE IN RICH VERSUS POOR COUNTRIES?

An enormous gulf in living standards separates most people in rich countries from their counterparts in poor ones (Harvard Magazine 2000). Wealth and poverty make life different in a host of ways. For instance, about one third of the world's poor are undernourished, and almost all are illiterate and lack access to even primary-school education. The world is no longer predominantly rural. Over half of the world's population now lives in urban areas. And by 2050, urban areas will house 70 percent of the world's population (United Nations 2007a). More than 40 percent of all urban residents in developing countries live in slums (United Nations Food and Agriculture Organization [UN FAO] 2004). Many of the poor come from racial, ethnic, or religious groups that differ from the dominant groups of their countries, and their poverty is at least in part the result of discrimination (Narayan 1999).

Here we look at differences between high- and low-income countries in terms of health and nutrition.

HEALTH

Nkonge Mata (left), a 10-year-old displaced Congolese boy, sits in a clinic run by the medical charity Medecins Sans Frontieres (Doctors without Borders) in the remote town of Dubie in Congo's southeastern Katanga province. The world's greatest concentrations of hunger are in central and sub-Saharan Africa. The majority of deaths of children under the age of five are the result of being hungry.

People in high-income countries are far healthier than their counterparts in low-income countries. Low-income countries generally suffer from inadequate health facilities, and their hospitals and clinics seldom serve the poorest people. People living in low-income countries also lack proper sanitation, drink polluted water, and run a much greater risk of contracting infectious diseases. They are more likely to suffer malnutrition, starvation, and famine. All of these factors contribute to physical weakness and poor health, making people in low-income countries susceptible to illness and disease. There is growing evidence that the high rates of HIV/AIDS infection found in many African countries are due in part to the weakened health of impoverished people (Stillwagon 2001).

Because of poor health conditions, people in low-income countries are more likely to die in infancy and less likely to survive until old age than people in high-income countries. Infants are thirteen times more likely to die at birth in low-income countries than they are in high-income countries, and—if they survive the first year of life—they are likely to live on average twenty years fewer. Children often die of illnesses that are readily treated in wealthier countries, such as measles or diarrhea. In some parts of the world, such as sub-Saharan Africa, a child is more likely to die before the age of five than to enter secondary school (World Bank 2005). Still, conditions have improved in low- and middle-income countries: Between 1980 and 2007, for example, the infant mortality rate dropped from 97 (per thousand live births) to 80 in low-income countries and from 60 to 35 in middle-income countries (World Bank 2007a). For the poorest of the poor countries, AIDS and growing poverty have contributed to the increase in infant mortality in recent years.

During the past three decades, some improvements have occurred in most of the middle-income countries of the world as well as in some of the low-income countries. Throughout the world, infant mortality has been cut in half, and average life expectancy has increased by ten years or more because of the wider availability of modern medical technology, improved sanitation, and rising incomes.

HUNGER, MALNUTRITION, AND FAMINE

Hunger, malnutrition, and famine are major global sources of poor health. These problems are nothing new. What seems to be new is their pervasiveness—the fact that so many people in the world today appear to be on the brink of starvation. A recent study by the United Nations Food and Agriculture Organization (UN FAO 2009) estimates that 1.02 billion people go hungry every day, most of them in developing countries. The program defines "hunger" as a diet of 1,800 or fewer calories a day—or 300 calories less than the 2,100 deemed sufficient for active adults.

According to the U.N. Children's Fund, in 2008 nearly 200 million children under age five in poor countries were stunted by a lack of nutrients in their food. More than 90 percent of those children live in Africa and Asia, and more than a third of all deaths in that age group are linked to undernutrition (UNICEF 2009). Close to 17 million babies are born with low birth weight stemming from the inadequate nutrition of their mothers (UNWFP 2004). Yet more than three quarters of all malnourished children under the age of five in the world's low- and middle-income countries live in countries that actually produce a food surplus (Lappe et al. 1998).

Most famine and hunger today are the result of a combination of natural and social forces. Drought alone affects an estimated 100 million people in the world today. In countries such as Sudan, Ethiopia, Eritrea, Indonesia, Afghanistan, Sierra Leone, Guinea, and Tajikistan, the combination of drought and internal warfare has wrecked food production, resulting in starvation and death for millions of people. The role of conflict and warfare in creating hunger is on the increase: Conflict and economic problems were cited as the main cause of 35 percent of food shortages between 1992 and 2003, compared to 15 percent in the period between 1986 and 1991 (UN FAO 2005). In Latin America and the Caribbean, 53 million people (11 percent of the population) are malnourished—and even higher numbers are malnourished in Asia (525 million, 17 percent) and sub-Saharan Africa (180 million, 33 percent) (UNWFP 2001).

The AIDS epidemic has also contributed to the problem of food shortages and hunger, killing many working-age adults. One recent study by the United Nations Food and Agricultural Organization (UN FAO) predicts that HIV/AIDS–caused deaths in the ten African countries most afflicted by the epidemic will reduce the labor force by 26 percent by the year 2020. Of the estimated 33 million people worldwide infected with HIV, 95 percent live in developing countries, and 68 percent of new infections are in sub-Saharan Africa (UNAIDS 2007a). 2.1 million people died from AIDS in 2007. According to the FAO (UN FAO 2001), the epidemic can be devastating to nutrition, food security, and agricultural production, affecting "the entire society's ability to maintain and reproduce itself."

Making Sociology Work
PROGRAM OFFICER FOR CHARITABLE FOUNDATION

In July 2006, Warren Buffett made the stunning announcement that he would give away most of his $40 billion fortune to the world's largest charitable organization, the Bill and Melinda Gates Foundation. Buffett is chairman and chief executive of Omaha, Nebraska–based Berkshire Hathaway Inc. and the second-richest man in the world. Buffett's gift, estimated at roughly $30 billion, could more than double the size of the Gates Foundation, which already commands a $29 billion endowment. Bill Gates (the only person whose wealth outstrips Buffett's) and his wife, Melinda, have given nearly $26 billion to the foundation. The Gates Foundation, founded in 1994, has focused much of its efforts on global health, backing the development, testing, manufacturing, and delivery of vaccines for diseases such as malaria, tuberculosis, and acute diarrhea that kill millions of children in developing countries every year. As a program officer responsible for designing and implementing new initiatives at the Gates Foundation, how would you allocate the newly received funds? Drawing on sociological studies of health, hunger, malnutrition, and famine in low-income nations, what social problems would you earmark as high-priority initiatives? Why?

The countries affected by famine and starvation are for the most part too poor to pay for new technologies that would increase their food production. Nor can they afford to purchase sufficient food imports from elsewhere in the world. At the same time, paradoxically, as world hunger grows, food production continues to increase, often in the very countries experiencing hunger emergencies (UN FAO 2004). Between 1965 and 1999, for example, world production of grain doubled. Even allowing for the substantial world population increase over this period, the global production of grain per person was 15 percent higher in 1999 than it was thirty-four years earlier. This growth, however, is not evenly distributed around the world. In much of Africa, for example, food production per person declined in recent years. Surplus food produced in high-income countries such as the United States is seldom affordable to the countries that need it most. ✓

CONCEPT CHECKS ✓

1. Why do people who live in high-income countries have better health than those who live in low-income countries?

CAN POOR COUNTRIES BECOME RICH?

In the mid-1970s a number of low-income countries in East Asia were undergoing a process of industrialization that appeared to threaten the global economic dominance of the United States and Europe (Amsden 1989). This process had begun with Japan in the 1950s but quickly extended to the **newly industrializing economies (NIEs)**, that is, the rapidly growing economies of the world, particularly in East Asia but also in Latin America. The East Asian NIEs included Hong Kong in the 1960s and Taiwan, South Korea, and Singapore in the 1970s and 1980s. Other Asian countries began to follow in the 1980s and the early 1990s, most notably China, but also Malaysia, Thailand, and Indonesia. Today, most are middle income, and some—such as Hong Kong, South Korea, Taiwan, and Singapore—have moved up to the high-income category.

The low- and middle-income economies of the East Asian region as a whole averaged 7.7 percent growth a year during much of the 1980s and 1990s—a rate that is extraordinary by world standards (World Bank 2000–2001). By 1999, the gross domestic product per person in Singapore was virtually the same as that in the United States. China, the world's most populous country, has one of the most rapidly growing economies on the planet. At an average annual growth rate of 10 percent between 1980 and 1999, the Chinese economy doubled in size.

Economic growth in East Asia has been accompanied by important social problems. These have included the sometimes violent repression of labor and civil rights, terrible factory conditions, the exploitation of an increasingly female workforce, the exploitation of immigrant workers from impoverished neighboring countries, and widespread environmental degradation. Nonetheless, thanks to the sacrifices of past generations of workers, large numbers of people in these countries are prospering.

The economic success of the East Asian NIEs can be attributed to a combination of factors. Some of these factors are historical, including those stemming from world political and economic shifts. Some are cultural. Still others have to do with the ways these countries pursued economic growth. Sociologists cite five main reasons for the recent economic advances of the East Asian NIES. First, most were part of colonial situations that, while imposing many hardships, also helped to pave the way for economic

newly industrializing economies (NIEs) • Developing countries that over the past two or three decades have begun to develop a strong industrial base, such as Singapore and Hong Kong.

growth. For example, Hong Kong and Singapore were former British colonies; Britain encouraged industrial development, constructed roads and other transportation systems, built relatively efficient governmental bureaucracies, and actively developed both Hong Kong and Singapore as trading centers (Gold 1986; Cumings 1987).

Second, the East Asian region benefited from a long period of world economic growth. Between the 1950s and the mid-1970s, the growing economies of Europe and the United States provided a big market for the clothing, footwear, and electronics that were increasingly being made in East Asia, creating a "window of opportunity" for economic development (Henderson and Appelbaum 1992). Third, economic growth in this region took off at the high point of the cold war, when the United States and its allies, in erecting a defense against communist China, provided generous economic aid that fueled investment in such new technologies as transistors, semiconductors, and other electronics, contributing to the development of local industries (Mirza 1986; Cumings 1987, 1997; Deyo 1987; Evans 1987; Amsden 1989; Henderson 1989; Haggard 1990; Castells 1992). Fourth, many of the East Asian governments followed strong policies that favored economic growth—by keeping labor costs low, encouraging economic development through tax breaks and other economic policies, and offering free public education.

Finally, some argue that cultural traditions, including a shared Confucian philosophy, contributed to these economic advances. Scholars who view the rise of capitalism in Western Europe as a function of the Protestant belief in thrift, frugality, and hard

Hong Kong (pictured below), along with Taiwan, South Korea, and Singapore, have become some of the most rapidly growing economies on Earth.

work (Weber 1977; orig. 1904) have observed a similar process in Asian economic history. Confucianism, it is argued, inculcates respect for one's elders and superiors, education, hard work, and proven accomplishments as the key to advancement, as well as a willingness to sacrifice today to earn a greater reward tomorrow. As a result of these values, the Weberian argument goes, Asian workers and managers are highly loyal to their companies, submissive to authority, hard working, and success oriented. Workers and capitalists alike are said to be frugal. Instead of living lavishly, they are likely to reinvest their wealth in further economic growth (Berger 1986; Wong 1986; Berger and Hsiao 1988; Redding 1990; Helm 1992).

Whether the growth of these economies will continue is unclear. In 1997–1998, a combination of poor investment decisions, corruption, and world economic conditions brought these countries' economic expansion to an abrupt halt. Their stock markets collapsed, their currencies fell, and the entire global economy was threatened. The experience of Hong Kong was typical: After thirty-seven years of continuous growth, the economy stalled and its stock market lost more than half its value. Yet the "Asian meltdown," as the newspapers called it in early 1998, turned out to have been merely a blip in the region's recent growth. China in particular has been growing at a high rate and is today the world's fourth largest economy.

Recent social and cultural changes may undermine the influence of traditional values on Asian economic development. For example, thrift, a central Confucian cultural value, appears to be on the decline in Japan and the NIEs, as young people—raised in the booming prosperity of recent years—increasingly value conspicuous consumption over austerity and investment (Helm 1992). ✓

CONCEPT CHECKS ✓

1. What are the five factors that have facilitated the economic success of the newly industrialized East Asian economies?

2. What are potential obstacles to the continued economic success of the NIEs?

HOW DO SOCIOLOGICAL THEORIES EXPLAIN GLOBAL INEQUALITY?

What causes global inequality? How can it be overcome? In this section we will examine four different kinds of theories that have been advanced over the years to explain global inequality: market-oriented, dependency, world-systems, and state-centered theories. These theories each have strengths and weaknesses. One shortcoming of all of them is that they frequently give short shrift to the role of women in economic development. By drawing on all four theories together, however, we should be able to answer a key question facing the 85 percent of the world's population living outside high-income countries: How can they move up in the world economy?

MARKET-ORIENTED THEORIES

market-oriented theories • Theories about economic development that assume that the best possible economic consequences will result if individuals are free to make their own economic decisions, uninhibited by governmental constraint.

Forty years ago, the most influential theories of global inequality advanced by American economists and sociologists were **market-oriented theories**. These theories assume that the best possible economic consequences will result if individuals are free, uninhibited by any form of governmental constraint, to make their own economic decisions. Unrestricted capitalism, if allowed to develop fully, is said to be the avenue to economic growth. Government bureaucracy should not dictate which goods to produce, what prices to charge, or how much workers should be paid. According to market-oriented theorists, governmental direction of the economies of low-income countries results only in blockages to economic development. (Rostow 1961; Warren 1980; Berger 1986; Ranis and Mahmood 1992; Ranis 1996).

Market-oriented theories inspired U.S. government foreign-aid programs that attempted to spur economic development in low-income countries by providing money, expert advisers, and technology, paving the way for U.S. corporations to make investments in these countries. One of the most influential early proponents of such theories was W. W. Rostow, an economic adviser to former U.S. president John F. Kennedy, whose ideas helped shape U.S. foreign policy toward Latin America during the 1960s. Rostow's explanation is one version of a market-oriented approach, termed "modernization theory." **Modernization theory** argues that low-income societies can develop economically only if they give up their traditional ways and adopt modern economic institutions, technologies, and cultural values that emphasize savings and productive investment.

According to Rostow (1961), the traditional cultural values and social institutions of low-income countries impede their economic effectiveness. For example, many people in low-income countries, in Rostow's view, would rather consume today than invest for the future. But to modernization theorists, the problems in low-income countries run even deeper. The cultures of such countries, according to the theory, tend to support "fatalism"—a value system that views hardship and suffering as the unavoidable plight of life. Acceptance of one's lot in life thus discourages people from working hard to overcome their fate. In this view, then, a country's poverty is due largely to the cultural failings of the people themselves. Such failings are reinforced by government policies that set wages and control prices and generally interfere in the operation of the economy. How can low-income countries break out of their poverty? Rostow viewed economic growth as going through several stages, which he likened to the journey of an airplane:

modernization theory • A version of market-oriented development theory that argues that low-income societies develop economically only if they give up their traditional ways and adopt modern economic institutions, technologies, and cultural values that emphasize savings and productive investment.

1. **Traditional stage.** This is the stage just described. It is characterized by low rates of savings, the supposed lack of a work ethic, and a fatalistic value system. The airplane is not yet off the ground.

2. **Takeoff to economic growth.** This stage occurs when poor countries begin to jettison their traditional values and institutions and start to save and invest money for the future. Wealthy countries, such as the United States, can facilitate this growth by financing birth-control programs or providing low-cost loans for electrification, road and airport construction, and starting new industries.

3. **Drive to technological maturity.** According to Rostow, with the help of money and advice from high-income countries, the airplane of economic growth would taxi down the runway, pick up speed, and become airborne. The plane would slowly climb to cruising altitude, improving its technology, reinvesting its recently acquired wealth in new industries, and adopting the institutions and values of the high-income countries.

4. **High mass consumption.** Finally, the country would reach the phase of high mass consumption. Now people are able to enjoy the fruits of their labor by achieving a high standard of living. The airplane (country) cruises along on automatic pilot, having entered the ranks of high-income countries.

What Can You Do about Child Labor?

Does child labor still exist in the world today? According to the United Nations International Labor Organization, more than 250 million boys and girls between the ages of five and fourteen are working in developing countries, about one out of every four children in the world. Some 50 to 60 million children between the ages of five and eleven work under hazardous conditions. Child labor is found throughout the developing world—in Asia (61 percent of the children are engaged in labor), Africa (32 percent), and Latin America (7 percent). They are forced to work because of a combination of family poverty, lack of education, and traditional indifference among some people in many countries to the plight of those who are poor or who are ethnic minorities (ILO 2000; UNICEF 2000).

Two thirds of working children labor in agriculture, with the rest in manufacturing, wholesale and retail trade, restaurants and hotels, and a variety of services, including working as servants in wealthy households. At best, these children work for long hours with little pay and are therefore unable to go to school and develop the skills that might eventually enable them to escape their lives of poverty. Many, however, work at hazardous and exploitative jobs under slavelike conditions, suffering a variety of illnesses and injuries. The International Labor Organization provides a grisly summary: "wounds, broken or complete loss of body parts, burns and skin diseases, eye and hearing impairment, respiratory and gastro-intestinal illnesses, fever, headaches from excessive heat in the fields or factories" (ILO 2000).

A United Nations report provides several examples:

In Malaysia, children may work up to 17-hour days on rubber plantations, exposed to insect and snake bites. In the United Republic of Tanzania, they pick coffee, inhaling pesticides. In Portugal, children as young as 12 are subject to the heavy labor and myriad dangers of the construction industry. In Morocco, they hunch at looms for long hours and little pay, knotting the strands of luxury carpets for export. In the United States, children are exploited in garment industry sweatshops. In the Philippines, young boys dive in dangerous conditions to help set nets for deep-sea fishing.

Conditions in many factories are horrible:

Dust from the chemical powders and strong vapors in both the storeroom and the boiler room were obvious. . . . We found 250 children, mostly below 10 years of age, working in a long hall filling in a slotted frame with sticks. Row upon row of children, some barely five years old, were involved in the work. (UNICEF 1997)

One form of child labor that is close to slavery is *bonded labor.* In this system children as young as eight or nine are pledged by their parents to factory owners in exchange for small loans. These children are paid so little that they never manage to reduce the debt, condemning them to a lifetime of bondage. One recent case of bonded labor that attracted international attention was that of Iqbal Masih, a Pakistani child who, at age four, was sold into slavery by his father in order to borrow six hundred rupees (roughly $16) for the wedding of his firstborn son. For six years, Iqbal spent most of his time chained to a carpet-weaving loom, tying tiny knots for hours on end. After fleeing the factory at age ten, he began speaking to labor organizations and schools about his experience. Iqbal paid a bitter price for his outspokenness: At age thirteen, while riding his bicycle in his hometown, he was gunned down by agents believed to be working for the carpet industry (Bobak 1996).

Abolishing exploitative child labor will require countries around the world to enact strong child-labor laws and be willing to enforce them. International organizations, such as the United Nations' International Labor Organization (ILO), have outlined a set of standards for such laws to follow. In June 1999, the ILO adopted Convention 182, calling for the abolition of the "Worst Forms of Child Labor." These are defined as including:

- all forms of slavery or practices similar to slavery, such as the sale and trafficking of children, debt bondage and serfdom, and forced or compulsory labor, including forced or compulsory recruitment of children for use in armed conflict;
- the use, procuring, or offering of a child for prostitution, for the production of pornography, or for pornographic performances;
- the use, procuring, or offering of a child for illicit activities, in particular for the production and trafficking of drugs as defined in the relevant international treaties; and
- work that, by its nature or the circumstances in which it is carried out, is likely to harm the health, safety, or morals of children. (ILO 1999)

Countries must also provide free public education and require that children attend school full time (UNICEF 2000). But at least part of the responsibility for solving the problem lies with the global corporations that manufacture goods using child labor—and, ultimately, with the consumers who buy those goods. Here are two things that you can do right now:

1. **Check the label.** Mind what you are buying. Begin by looking at the label. When you purchase clothing, rugs, and other textiles, the label will tell you where it was made, if unionized labor was used, and, in a few cases, whether it is certified to be "sweatshop free." Avoid buying garments made in countries with known human rights abuses, such as Myanmar (Burma). If the product has a label indicating it was made with union labor, it is likely to be free from child labor. "Sweatshop free" labels, although still rare, are likely to become more common in coming years, as labor and consumer groups pressure the U.S. government to more closely

monitor imported goods. In one well-publicized campaign that grew out of Iqbal's tragic experience, Indian human rights activists developed the "Rugmark" label, which certifies that the carpet is free of child labor. The U.S. Department of Labor is also working toward a way of certifying goods that are sold in the United States to be "sweatshop free," although at this time there is no way to do so reliably: The millions of factories around the world involved in making consumer goods are too vast and dispersed to monitor.

2. **Join up.** Join (or start) an anti-sweatshop campaign at your own college or university. There is a national campaign, organized by United Students Against Sweatshops, to require schools to engage in "responsible purchasing" when they buy or sell clothing, athletic equipment, and other goods that carry the school logo. Schools are urged to sign agreements with all their vendors that require full disclosure of the names and locations of the factories where the goods are made, certifying that the goods are free from child labor and other forms of exploitation. School sales are a multibillion-dollar business, and if schools set a high standard, manufacturers will be forced to take notice.

In a global economy, you can choose what you buy, as well as influence others to make informed and ethical choices about the products they consume. Be a smart shopper—it can make a difference.

neoliberalism • The economic belief that free market forces, achieved by minimizing government restrictions on business, provide the only route to economic growth.

dependency theories • Marxist theories of economic development arguing that the poverty of low-income countries stems directly from their exploitation by wealthy countries and the multinational corporations that are based in wealthy countries.

colonialism • The process whereby Western nations established their rule in parts of the world away from their home territories.

Rostow's ideas remain influential. **Neoliberalism**, the prevailing view among economists today, argues that free-market forces, achieved by minimizing governmental restrictions on business, provide the only route to economic growth. Neoliberalism holds that global free trade will enable all countries of the world to prosper; eliminating governmental regulation is seen as necessary for economic growth to occur. Neoliberal economists therefore call for an end to restrictions on trade and often challenge minimum wage and other labor laws, as well as environmental restrictions on business.

Sociologists, on the other hand, question the extent to which moral, religious, and folk beliefs affect development (Davis 1987; So 1990). At the same time, they are interested in identifying local conditions that resist change, such as the belief in some cultures that business and trade lead to moral decay and social unrest.

DEPENDENCY THEORIES

During the 1960s, a number of theorists questioned market-oriented explanations of global inequality. Many of these critics were sociologists and economists from the low-income countries of Latin America and Africa who rejected the idea that their countries' economic underdevelopment was due to their own cultural or institutional failings. Instead, they built on the theories of Karl Marx, who argued that world capitalism would create a class of countries manipulated by more powerful countries just as capitalism within countries leads to the exploitation of workers. The **dependency theorists**, as they are called, argue that the poverty of low-income countries stems from their exploitation by wealthy countries and the multinational corporations that are based in wealthy countries. In their view, global capitalism locked their countries into a downward spiral of exploitation and poverty.

They argue that this exploitation began with **colonialism**, a political-economic system under which powerful countries establish, for their own profit, rule over weaker peoples or countries. Powerful nations have colonized other countries usually to procure the raw materials needed for their factories and to control markets for the products manufactured in those factories. Although colonialism typically involved European countries establishing colonies in North and South America, Africa, and Asia, some Asian countries (such as Japan) had colonies as well.

Colonialism ended throughout most of the world after World War II, yet the exploitation did not: Transnational corporations continued to reap enormous profits from their branches in low-income countries. According to dependency theory, these global companies, often with the support of the powerful banks and governments of rich countries, established factories in poor countries, using cheap labor and raw materials to maximize production costs without governmental interference. In turn,

Although Nigeria is the world's eighth largest producer of oil, the overwhelming majority of the profits generated in the energy trade go to oil companies and the military government, providing no benefit to the country's poverty-stricken inhabitants. These women are protesting Royal Dutch Shell's exploitation of Nigeria's oil and natural gas resources.

Female workers make Barbie dolls at a toy factory in the Guangdong province of China.

the low prices set for labor and raw materials prevented poor countries from accumulating the profit necessary to industrialize themselves. Local businesses that might compete with foreign corporations were prevented from doing so. In this view, poor countries are forced to borrow from rich countries, thus increasing their economic dependency.

Low-income countries are thus seen not as underdeveloped, but rather as misdeveloped (Emmanuel 1972; Amin 1974; Frank 1966, 1969a, 1969b, 1979; Prebisch 1967, 1971). Since dependency theorists believe that exploitation has kept their countries from achieving economic growth, they typically call for revolutionary changes that would push foreign corporations out of their countries altogether (Frank 1966, 1969a, 1969b).

Dependency theorists regard the exercise of political and military power as central to enforcing unequal economic relationships. According to this theory, whenever local leaders question such unequal arrangements, their voices are quickly suppressed. When people elect a government opposing these policies, that government is likely to be overthrown by the country's military, often backed by the armed forces of the industrialized countries themselves. Dependency theorists point to many examples: the role of the CIA in overthrowing the Marxist governments of Guatemala in 1954 and Chile in 1973 and in undermining support for the leftist government in Nicaragua in the 1980s. In the view of dependency theory, global economic inequality is thus backed up by force.

WORLD-SYSTEMS THEORY

During the last quarter century, sociologists have increasingly seen the world as a single (although often conflict-ridden) economic system. While dependency theories hold that individual countries are economically tied to one another, **world-systems theory** argues that the world capitalist economic system is not merely a collection of independent countries engaged in diplomatic and economic relations with one another but rather must be understood as a single unit. The world-systems approach is most closely identified with the work of Immanuel Wallerstein and his colleagues.

world-systems theory •
Pioneered by Immanuel Wallerstein, this theory emphasizes the interconnections among countries based on the expansion of a capitalist world economy. This economy is made up of core countries, semiperipheral countries, and peripheral countries.

Wallerstein showed that capitalism has long existed as a global economic system, beginning with the extension of markets and trade in Europe in the fifteenth and sixteenth centuries (Wallerstein 1974a, 1974b, 1979, 1990, 1996a, 1996b; Hopkins and Wallerstein 1996). The world system is seen as comprising four overlapping elements (Chase-Dunn 1989):

- a world market for goods and labor;
- the division of the population into different economic classes, particularly capitalists and workers;
- an international system of formal and informal political relations among the most powerful countries, whose competition with one another helps shape the world economy; and
- the carving up of the world into three unequal economic zones, with the wealthier zones exploiting the poorer ones.

World-systems theorists term these three economic zones "core," "periphery," and "semiperiphery." All countries in the world system are said to fall into one of the three categories. **Core countries** are the most advanced industrial countries, taking the lion's share of profits in the world economic system. These include Japan, the United States, and the countries of Western Europe. The **peripheral countries** comprise low-income, largely agricultural countries that are often manipulated by core countries for their own economic advantage. Examples of peripheral countries are found throughout Africa and to a lesser extent in Latin America and Asia. Natural resources, such as agricultural products, minerals, and other raw materials, flow from periphery to core—as do the profits. The core, in turn, sells finished goods to the periphery, also at a profit. World-systems theorists argue that core countries have made themselves wealthy with this unequal trade, while at the same time limiting the economic development of peripheral countries. Finally, the **semiperipheral countries** occupy an intermediate position: These are semi-industrialized, middle-income countries that extract profits from the more peripheral countries and in turn yield profits to the core countries. Examples of semiperipheral countries include Mexico in North America; Brazil, Argentina, and Chile in South America; and the newly industrializing economies of East Asia. The semiperiphery, though to some degree controlled by the core, is thus also able to exploit the periphery. Moreover, the greater economic success of the semiperiphery holds out to the periphery the promise of similar development. Although the world system tends to change very slowly, once-powerful countries eventually lose their economic power and others take their place.

An important offshoot of the world systems approach is a concept that emphasizes the global nature of economic activities. **Global commodity chains** are worldwide networks of labor and production processes yielding a finished product. These networks consist of all pivotal production activities that form a tightly interlocked "chain" extending from the raw materials needed to create the product to its final consumer (Gereffi 1995, 1996; Hopkins and Wallerstein 1996; Appelbaum and Christerson 1997).

The commodity-chain approach argues that manufacturing is becoming increasingly globalized. Manufactures accounted for approximately three quarters of the world's total economic growth during the 1990s. The sharpest growth has been among middle-income countries: Manufactures accounted for only 54 percent of these countries' exports in 1990, compared with 71 percent just eight years later. Yet the high rate of increase of manufactures as a share of world exports has since slowed (World

core countries • According to world-systems theory, the most advanced industrial countries, which take the lion's share of profits in the world economic system.

peripheral countries • Countries that have a marginal role in the world economy and are thus dependent on the core producing societies for their trading relationships.

semiperipheral countries • Countries that supply sources of labor and raw materials to the core industrial countries and the world economy but are not themselves fully industrialized societies.

global commodity chain • A worldwide network of labor and production processes yielding a finished product.

Trade Organization [WTO] 2008). China, which has moved from the ranks of low- to middle-income countries in part because of its role as an exporter of manufactured goods, partly accounts for this trend. The most profitable activities in the commodity chain—engineering, design, and advertising—are likely to be found in the core countries, while the least profitable activities, such as factory production, usually are found in peripheral countries.

Although manufacturing in the global commodity chain typically takes place in peripheral countries, an exception to this trend has developed. Low-wage, low-profit factories known as sweatshops are today reappearing in core countries, sometimes for the first time in half a century or more. A sweatshop is a small factory that has numerous violations of wage, health, and safety laws. In New York City and Los Angeles, for example, more than 100,000 workers labor in tiny garment factories that make many of the brands of clothing you can buy in major department stores. Many laborers work for less than minimum wage, in buildings described by government officials as firetraps.

STATE-CENTERED THEORIES

Some of the most recent explanations of successful economic development emphasize the role of state policy in promoting growth. Differing sharply from market-oriented theories, **state-centered theories** argue that appropriate government policies do not interfere with economic development but rather can play a key role in bringing it about. A large body of research now suggests that in some regions of the world, such as East Asia, successful economic development has been state led. Even the World Bank, long a strong proponent of free-market theories of development, has changed its thinking about the role of the state. In its 1997 report *The State in a Changing World*, the World Bank concludes that without an effective state, "sustainable development, both economic and social, is impossible" (World Bank 1997).

Strong governments contributed in various ways to economic growth in the East Asian NIEs during the 1980s and 1990s (Appelbaum and Henderson 1992; Amsden et al. 1994; Evans 1995; Cumings 1997; World Bank 1997):

state-centered theories • Development theories that argue that appropriate government policies do not interfere with economic development, but rather can play a key role in bringing it about.

1. **East Asian governments have sometimes aggressively acted to ensure political stability, while keeping labor costs low.** They have accomplished this by acts of repression, such as outlawing trade unions, banning strikes, jailing labor leaders, and, in general, silencing the voices of workers. The governments of Taiwan, South Korea, and Singapore in particular have engaged in such practices.

2. **East Asian governments have frequently sought to steer economic development in desired directions. Some examples include:** state agencies providing cheap loans and tax breaks to businesses that invest in industries favored by the government; and governments preventing businesses from investing their profits in other countries, forcing them to invest in economic growth at home.

3. **East Asian governments have often been heavily involved in social programs such as low-cost housing and universal education.** The world's largest public housing systems (outside of socialist or formerly socialist countries) have been in Hong Kong and Singapore, where government subsidies keep rents extremely low. As a result, workers don't require high wages to pay for their housing, so they can compete better with American and European workers in the emerging global labor market.

EVALUATING GLOBAL THEORIES OF INEQUALITY

Each of the four sets of theories of global inequality just discussed has its strengths and weaknesses. Together they enable us to better understand the causes and cures for global inequality.

1. **Market-oriented** theories recommend the adoption of modern capitalist institutions to promote economic development, as the recent example of East Asia attests. They further argue that countries can develop economically only if they open their borders to trade. But market-oriented theories also fail to take into account the various economic ties between poor countries and wealthy ones—ties that can impede economic growth under some conditions and enhance it under others. They tend to blame low-income countries themselves for their poverty rather than looking to the influence of outside factors, such as the business operations of more powerful nations. Market-oriented theories also ignore the ways government can work with the private sector to spur economic development. Finally, they fail to explain why some countries manage to take off economically while others remain grounded in poverty and underdevelopment.

2. **Dependency theories** address the market-oriented theories' neglect in considering poor countries' ties with wealthy countries by focusing on how wealthy nations have economically exploited poor ones. However, although dependency theories help to account for much of the economic backwardness in Latin America and Africa, they are unable to explain the occasional success stories among such low-income countries as Brazil, Argentina, and Mexico or the rapidly expanding economies of East Asia.

3. **World-systems** theory seeks to overcome the shortcomings of both market-oriented and dependency theories by analyzing the world economy as a whole. Within the world-systems framework, the concept of global commodity chains takes this notion one step further, focusing on global businesses and their activities rather than relationships between countries. World-systems theory is thus well suited to understanding the global economy at a time when businesses are increasingly free to set up operations anywhere, acquiring an economic importance that rivals that of many countries. Yet this is also a weakness of the commodity chains approach: It tends to emphasize the importance of business decisions over other factors, such as the role that both workers and governments play in shaping a country's economy (Amsden 1989; Deyo 1989; Evans 1995; Cumings 1997).

4. **State-centered theories** stress the governmental role in fostering economic growth. They thus offer a useful alternative to both the prevailing market-oriented theories, with their emphasis on states as economic hindrances, and dependency theories, which view states as allies of global business elites in exploiting poor countries. When combined with the other theories—particularly world-systems theory—state-centered theories can explain the radical changes now transforming the world economy. ✓

CONCEPT CHECKS ✓

1. Describe the main assumptions of market-oriented theories of global inequality.

2. Why are dependency theories of global inequalities often criticized?

3. Compare and contrast core, peripheral, and semiperipheral nations.

4. How have strong governments of some East Asian nations contributed to the economic development of that region?

Theories of global inequality often emphasize the role of values in economic development. Adherents to modernization theories argue that traditional societies hold attitudes that impede economic progress, while other scholars have speculated that adherence to Confucian beliefs has propelled Asian economies. How do nations vary in their beliefs about economic development and fate? How do your personal attitudes compare with those of persons in other nations? Indicate how strongly you agree or disagree with each attitude, and then turn the page to see how you (and residents of other nations) stack up.

Do you completely agree, mostly agree, mostly disagree, or completely disagree?

1. Most people are better off in a free market economy, even though some people are rich and some are poor.
2. Success in life is pretty much determined by forces outside our control.
3. It is the responsibility of the government to take care of very poor people who can't take care of themselves.

The Skeens in Pearland, Texas and the Castillo Balderas in Guadalajara, Mexico are both considered middle class families in their respective communities. Do you think they would have the same attitudes about capitalism and poverty?

TURN PAGE

This chart indicates the proportion of persons throughout the globe who "agree completely" or "agree mostly" with the statements on the previous page. Do you notice any patterns? Do attitudes appear to vary based on a nation's level of economic development? Or depending on whether Confucianism prevails? What trends do you find most interesting and why?

Proportion who agree "completely" or "mostly"

Nation	Free market opportunity better	Success determined by outside forces	Government should care for poor
U.S.	70	33	70
Canada	71	34	81
Brazil	65	58	90
Mexico	55	56	81
Great Britain	72	45	91
France	56	52	83
Germany	65	70	92
Russia	53	59	86
Ukraine	66	57	87
Turkey	60	68	86
Egypt	50	37	67
Palestinian territories	66	56	89
Israel	72	55	90
Pakistan	60	68	84
Bangladesh	81	80	93
Indonesia	45	52	93
China	75	65	90
India	76	80	92
Japan	49	47	59
South Korea	72	75	87
Ethiopia	47	35	86
Nigeria	79	63	86
Uganda	67	60	84

Source: Pew 2007.

HOW DOES GLOBAL INEQUALITY AFFECT YOUR LIFE?

Today the social and economic forces leading to a single global capitalist economy appear to be irresistible. What does rapid globalization mean for the future of global inequality? No sociologist knows for certain, but many possible scenarios exist. In one, our world might be dominated by large, global corporations, with workers everywhere competing with one another at a global wage. Such a scenario might predict falling wages for large numbers of people in today's high-income countries and rising wages for a few in low-income countries. There might be a general leveling out of average income around the world, although at a level much lower than that currently enjoyed in the United States and other industrialized nations. In this scenario, the polarization between the haves and the have-nots would grow, as the whole world would be increasingly divided into those who benefit from the global economy and those who do not. Such polarization could fuel conflict between ethnic groups and even nations, as those suffering from economic globalization would blame others for their plight (Hirst and Thompson 1992; Wagar 1992).

On the other hand, a global economy could mean greater opportunity for everyone, as the benefits of modern technology stimulate worldwide economic growth. According to this more optimistic scenario, the more successful East Asian NIEs, such as Hong Kong, Taiwan, South Korea, and Singapore, are only a sign of things to come. Other NIEs such as Malaysia and Thailand will soon follow, along with China, Indonesia, Vietnam, and other Asian countries. India, the world's second most populous country, already boasted a middle class of around 300 million people in 2007, about a third of its total population (David 2007).

A countervailing trend, however, is the technology gap that divides rich and poor countries, which today appears to be widening, making it even more difficult for poor countries to catch up. This gap is a result of the disparity in wealth between nations, but it also reinforces those disparities, widening the gap between rich and poor countries. Poor countries cannot easily afford modern technology—yet, in the absence of modern technology, they face major barriers to overcoming poverty. They are caught in a vicious downward spiral from which it is difficult to escape.

Jeffrey Sachs, director of the Center for International Development and professor of international trade at Harvard University, and a prominent adviser to many Eastern European and developing countries, claims that the world is divided into three classes: technology innovators, technology adopters, and the technologically disconnected (Sachs 2000). *Technology innovators* are those regions that provide nearly all of the world's technological inventions; they account for no more than 15 percent of the world's population. *Technology adopters* are those regions that are able to adopt technologies invented elsewhere, applying them to production and consumption; they account for 50 percent of the world's population. Finally, the *technologically disconnected* are those regions that neither innovate nor adopt technologies developed elsewhere; they account for 35 percent of the world's population. In fact, the Organization for Economic Cooperation and Development (OECD 2005b) reports that over half of the patents issued worldwide were concentrated inside just ten regions within the most advanced industrial nations.

Note that Sachs also speaks of regions rather than countries: In today's increasingly borderless world, technology use (or exclusion) does not always respect national frontiers. Technologically disconnected regions such as tropical sub-Saharan Africa or the Ganges valley states of India lack access to markets or major ocean trading routes.

They are caught in what Sachs terms a "poverty trap," plagued by "tropical infectious disease, low agricultural productivity and environmental degradation—all requiring technological solutions beyond their means" (2000).

What can be done to overcome the technological abyss that divides rich and poor countries? Sachs urges the governments of wealthy countries, along with international lending institutions, to provide loans and grants for scientific and technological development. Sachs notes that very little money is available to support research and development in poor countries. The World Bank, a major source of funding for development projects in poor countries, spends only $60 million a year supporting tropical, agricultural, or health research and development. By way of comparison, Pfizer—the world's largest pharmaceutical corporation in terms of market share—spends 141 times that much ($8.5 billion) for research and development for its own products (Pfizer 2007). From computers and the Internet to biotechnology, the "wealth of nations" increasingly depends on modern information technology. As long as major regions of the world remain technologically disconnected, it seems unlikely that global poverty will be eradicated.

In the most optimistic view, the republics of the former Soviet Union, as well as the formerly socialist countries of Eastern Europe, will eventually advance into the ranks of the high-income countries. Economic growth will spread to Latin America, Africa, and the rest of the world. Because capitalism requires that workers be mobile, the remaining caste societies around the world will be replaced by class-based societies. These societies will experience enhanced opportunities for upward mobility.

What is the future of global inequality? It is difficult to be entirely optimistic for now. Global economic growth has slowed, and many of the once promising economies of Asia now seem to be in trouble. It remains to be seen whether the countries of the world will learn from one another and work together to create better lives for their peoples. What is certain is that the past quarter century has witnessed a global economic transformation of unprecedented magnitude. The effects of this transformation in the next quarter century will leave few lives on the planet untouched. ✓

CONCEPT CHECKS ✓

1. What is the role of technology in deepening existing global inequalities?

NEED HELP STUDYING?

 wwnorton.com/studyspace

Visit StudySpace to access free review materials such as:

- Vocabulary Flashcards
- Diagnostic Review Quizzes
- Study Outlines

REVIEW QUESTIONS

1. How does the World Bank measure inequality between countries? Why might their approach be misleading?

2. In the last half of the twentieth century, the average overall standard of living improved. At the same time, the gap between rich and poor countries increased. What explains this situation?
3. Describe the social factors that contribute to famine and hunger.
4. Economic growth in East Asia can be attributed to a number of factors. Discuss three of these factors and some of the costs associated with rapid economic development.
5. What does modernization theory say countries need to do to get out of poverty?
6. How does dependency theory explain inequality and what, according to this view, is the solution?
7. What are the zones of the modern world system? How are they related?
8. What is a commodity chain and how does it help explain global inequality?
9. What do state-centered theories of development say the role of the state should be in fostering economic development? How does this compare to the ideas of modernization theory?
10. How does the use of technology relate to poverty on a global scale?

THINKING SOCIOLOGICALLY EXERCISES

1. Concisely review the four theories offered in this chapter that explain why there are gaps between nations' economic developments and resulting global inequality: market-oriented theory, dependency theory, world-systems theory, and state-centered theories. Briefly discuss the distinctive characteristics of each theory and how each differs from the others. Which theory do you feel offers the most explanatory power to addressing economic developmental gaps?
2. This chapter states that global economic inequality has personal relevance and importance to people in advanced, affluent economies. Briefly review this argument. Explain carefully whether you were persuaded by it or not.

9

Gender Inequality

THE BIG QUESTIONS

ARE GENDER DIFFERENCES DUE TO NATURE, NURTURE, OR BOTH?
Evaluate whether differences between women and men are the result of biological differences or social and cultural influences.

HOW DO GENDER INEQUALITIES AFFECT SOCIAL INSTITUTIONS?
Recognize that gender differences are a part of our social structure and create inequalities between women and men. Learn the forms these inequalities take in social institutions including the workplace, the family, the educational system, and the political system in the United States, and globally.

WHY ARE WOMEN THE TARGET OF VIOLENCE?
Learn about the specific ways that women are the target of physical and sexual violence in the United States and globally.

HOW DOES SOCIAL THEORY EXPLAIN GENDER INEQUALITY?
Think about various explanations for gender inequality. Learn some feminist theories about how to achieve gender equality.

WHAT ARE THE GLOBAL CONSEQUENCES OF GENDER INEQUALITY?
Learn how globalization has transformed ideas about women's rights.

Around midnight one cold night in December, a little before the end of the second shift, Andrea Ellington is standing by the soda machine in the workers' lounge, cleaning out her oversized pocketbook. She empties its contents, which begin with a gold plastic makeup bag, a wallet, and a bunch of monthly bills. "I gotta go wake my five-year-old daughter up at my mother's house," she says as she opens the makeup bag. "Then I go to the other babysitter and get my baby twins. Then I take them home and they've gotta try to go back to sleep. By the time my daughter gets back to sleep, it's time for her to get back up again" (interview by the authors).

An African American woman of twenty-three, Andrea Ellington has three children to support on a low-rung clerical salary of $30,000 per year. She has been working at a Chicago law firm for four years; she had taken the job believing that with hard work, she could someday advance enough to move her family out of public housing.

Most of the five hundred or so employees in the law office where she works are not attorneys but "support staff," who work in one of many departments at the center of the floors, surrounded by plush attorneys' offices on the perimeter. The Network Center where she types is solely a nighttime word-processing department, with shifts from 4 P.M. to midnight and midnight to 8 A.M. The people who work as word processors are all women. They sit at computer terminals in one of four clusters separated by gray partitions. Almost all of these women who work at night are also raising children. Most live far from the law firm's gleaming downtown building.

Balancing work and family demands creates both time pressures and financial strains. Raising three children on her modest income, Andrea lives from paycheck to paycheck. She seeks out extra work to help her get by with her everyday responsibilities, like food, rent, and clothing for her children. As a result of Andrea's persistence, her supervisor assigned her to work an extra eight hours of overtime per week, on Sundays. Andrea came to work for the first two Sundays and then began missing her weekend assignments when she couldn't find a babysitter for her three children. When her supervisor learned of the absences, she canceled the overtime.

Many people who encounter someone like Andrea Ellington might make certain assumptions about her life. They might assume, for example, that a disproportionate number of women become word processors because it is "natural" for women to have certain kinds of occupations, including secretarial jobs. They might also assume that mothers should be responsible for taking care of children. Finally, they might assume that Andrea's poverty and low-status position at work are a result of her natural abilities. It is the job of sociologists to analyze these assumptions and to adopt a much wider view of our society and people like Andrea. Sociology allows us to understand why women are likely to work in low-paying clerical jobs, why women are likely to spend more time on child care, and why women on the whole are less powerful in society than men. Explaining the differences and inequalities between women and men in a society is now one of the most central topics in sociology.

In this chapter, we will take a sociological approach to the exploration of gender differences and gender inequality. Gender is a way for society to divide people into two categories: "men" and "women." According to this socially created division, men and women have different identities and social roles. Men and women are expected to think and act in certain different ways. Gender also serves as a social status, since in almost all societies men's roles are valued more than are women's roles. Men and women are not only different, but also unequal in terms of power, prestige, and wealth. Despite the advances that many women have made in the United States and other Western societies, this remains true today. Sociologists are interested in explaining how society differentiates between women and men, and how these differences serve as the basis for social inequalities (Chafetz 1990). Some sociologists are also concerned with the ways in which women can achieve positions of equality in society.

We will first look at the origins of gender differences, assessing the debate over the role of biological versus social influences in the formation of gender roles. We will also look to other cultures for evidence on this debate. Then we will review the various forms of gender inequality that exist in American society and throughout the globe. In this section, we will focus on the prominent social institutions of the workplace, the family, the educational system, and the political system. Next, we will examine how and why women are so often the targets of sexual violence. We will review the various forms of feminism and assess prospects for future change toward a gender equal society. We will then analyze some theories of gender inequality and apply them to the circumstances of Andrea's life. We conclude the chapter by looking at the role of women around the world as we enter the twenty-first century.

ARE GENDER DIFFERENCES DUE TO NATURE, NURTURE, OR BOTH?

Are differences between boys and girls, men and women, due to nature, nurture, or some combination of the two? As we first noted in Chapter 2, scholars are divided about the degree to which inborn biological characteristics have an enduring impact on our gender identities as "feminine" or "masculine" and the social roles based on those identities. No one would argue that our behavior is purely instinctive or hard-wired. Yet scholars disagree in the extent to which they believe gender differences are the product of learning and socialization.

Before we review the relative influences of nature and nurture, we first need to make an important distinction between sex and gender. **Sex** refers to physical differences of the body, whereas **gender** concerns the psychological, social, and cultural differences between males and females. This distinction is fundamental, because many differences between males and females are not biological in origin.

sex • The biological and anatomical differences distinguishing females from males.

gender • Social expectations about behavior regarded as appropriate for the members of each sex. Gender refers not to the physical attributes distinguishing men and women but to socially formed traits of masculinity and femininity. The study of gender relations has become one of the most important areas of sociology in recent years.

THE ROLE OF BIOLOGY

How much are differences in the behavior of women and men the result of biological differences? Some researchers hold that innate differences of behavior between women and men appear in some form in all cultures and that the findings of sociobiology point strongly in this direction. Such researchers are likely to draw attention to the fact, for example, that in almost all cultures, men rather than women take part in hunting and warfare. Surely, they argue, this indicates that men possess biologically based tendencies toward aggression that women lack. In looking at the case of the word processors, they might point out that typing is a more passive occupation than being a bicycle messenger (an equivalent job category within the firm), which requires more physical strength and aggressiveness in traffic.

Many children's toys may promote gender stereotyping.

Making Sociology Work

PARENT

Parenting is often described as the world's toughest job but also one of the most rewarding. Parents aren't just responsible for feeding, clothing, and protecting their young children; parents know that how they raise their sons and daughters will have powerful consequences for their offsprings' experiences as young men and women. Sociologists argue further that parental socialization plays a critical role in one's gender identity; children learn from their parents (as well as from the media and educational system) how to behave in a way that is "male" or "female." Yet strict adherence to typically male or female behavioral expectations may create personal challenges. For instance, boys who are raised to be rowdy and rambunctious often face difficulties as they enter the structured realm of elementary school. Girls who are socialized to be quiet and unassertive may do well at school yet may be disadvantaged as they enter the competitive worlds of work or sports. Given the many ways that gender exposes individuals to inequality in politics, schools, and the workplace, and in terms of crime victimization, what kind of gender role messages would you impart to your children? Drawing on gender socialization literature, what social norms and expectations would you convey to your sons versus your daughters? Why?

Most sociologists are unconvinced by these arguments. The level of aggressiveness of men, they say, varies widely across cultures, and women are expected to be more passive or gentle in some cultures than in others (Elshtain 1981). Theories of "natural difference" are often grounded in data on animal behavior, critics point out, rather than in anthropological or historical evidence about human behavior, which reveals variation over time and place. In the majority of cultures, most women spend a significant part of their lives caring for children and therefore cannot readily take part in hunting or war.

The hypothesis that biological factors wholly determine behavior patterns in men and women is undermined, in part, by a lack of empirical evidence. Nearly a century of research fails to identify the physiological and biological origins of the complex social behaviors exhibited by human males and females (Connell 1987). Theories that see individuals as complying with some kind of innate predisposition neglect the vital role of social interaction in shaping human behavior.

What does the research show? Some studies show differences in hormonal makeup between the sexes, with the male sex hormone, testosterone, associated with the male propensity to violence (Rutter and Giller 1984). For instance, if male monkeys are castrated at birth, they become less aggressive; conversely, female monkeys given testosterone will become more aggressive than normal females. However, it has also been found that providing monkeys with opportunities to dominate others actually increases the testosterone level. Aggressive behavior may thus affect the production of the hormone, rather than the hormone's causing increased aggression—thus underscoring the importance of social context.

Another source of information comes from the experience of identical twins. Identical twins derive from a single egg and have exactly the same genetic makeup. In one particular case, one of a pair of identical male twins was seriously injured while being circumcised, and the decision was made to reconstruct his genitals as a female. He was thereafter raised as a girl. The twins at six years old demonstrated typical male and female traits as found in Western culture. The little girl enjoyed playing with other girls, helped with the housework, and wanted to get married when she grew up. The boy preferred the company of other boys, his favorite toys were cars and trucks, and he wanted to become a firefighter or police officer.

For some time, this case was treated as a conclusive demonstration of the overriding influence of social learning on gender differences. However, when the girl was a teenager, she was interviewed during a television program, and the interview showed that she felt some unease about her gender identity, even perhaps that she was "really" a boy after all. She had by then learned of her unusual background, and this knowledge may very well have been responsible for this altered perception of herself (Ryan 1985).

GENDER SOCIALIZATION

Another explanation for gender differences is **gender socialization**, or ways that individuals learn gender roles from socializing agents such as the family and the media (see also Chapter 4). Through contact with various agents of socialization, children gradually internalize the social norms and expectations that are seen to correspond with their sex. Gender differences are not biologically determined; they are culturally produced. According to this view, gender inequalities result because men and women are socialized into different roles.

People create gender through social interactions with others, such as family members, friends, and colleagues. This process begins at birth when doctors, nurses, and family members—the first to see an infant—assign the person to a gender category on the basis of physical characteristics. Babies are immediately dressed in a way that marks the sex category: "parents don't want to be constantly asked if their child is a boy or a girl" (Lorber 1994). Once the child is marked as male or female, everyone who interacts with the child will treat it in accordance with its gender. They do so on the basis of the society's assumptions, which lead people to treat women and men differently, even as opposites (Renzetti and Curran 1995).

THE SOCIAL CONSTRUCTION OF GENDER

In recent years, socialization and gender role theories have been criticized by a growing number of sociologists. Rather than seeing sex as biologically determined and gender as culturally learned, they argue that we should view both sex and gender as socially constructed products. Theorists who believe in the **social construction of gender** reject all biological bases for gender differences. Gender identities emerge, they argue, in relation to perceived sex differences in society and in turn help to shape those differences. For example, a society in which ideas of masculinity are characterized by physical strength and tough attitudes will encourage men to cultivate a specific body image and set of mannerisms (Connell 1987; Butler 1989; Scott and Morgan 1993).

GENDER IDENTITY IN EVERYDAY LIFE

Our conceptions of gender identity are formed so early in life that as adults we mainly take them for granted. Yet gender is more than learning to act like a girl or boy. Gender differences are something we live with every day. Some sociologists argue that we "do gender" in our daily interactions with others (West, Fenstermaker, and Zimmerman 1987); that means that we learn how to present ourselves as "male" or "female" through our choice of behaviors, fashion choices, hairstyle, and even tone of voice.

For instance, Jan Morris, the celebrated travel writer, used to be a man. As James Morris, she was a member of the British expedition, led by Sir Edmund Hillary, that successfully climbed Mount Everest. She was, in fact, a very "manly" man—a race car driver and an athlete. Yet she had always felt herself to be a woman in a male body. So she underwent a sex-change operation and has lived the rest of her life as a woman. Jan Morris had to learn how to do gender when she discovered how differently she was expected to behave as a woman, rather than as a man. As she says, there is "no aspect of existence" that is not gendered. But she did not notice this until she changed her sex.

It amuses me to consider, for instance, when I am taken out to lunch by one of my more urbane men friends, that not so many years ago

gender socialization • The learning of gender roles through social factors such as schooling, the media, and family.

social construction of gender • The learning of gender roles through socialization and interaction with others.

This photo (top), dated November 30, 1952, shows George Jorgensen before his sex change. After he was discharged from the U.S. Army he traveled to Copenhagen, Denmark, where he had a sex-change operation. After the operation he changed his name to Christine. Christine Jorgensen (bottom), returning from a nightclub engagement in Cuba in 1953.

th[e] waiter would have treated me as he is now treating him. Then he would have greeted me with respectful seriousness. Now he unfolds my napkin with a playful flourish, as if to humor me. Then he would have taken my order with grave concern, now he expects me to say something frivolous (and I do). (Morris 1974)

The subtle ways in which we do gender are so much a part of our lives that we don't notice them until they are missing or radically altered. Because gender is so pervasive in structuring social life, gender statuses must be clearly differentiated if society is to function in an orderly manner (Lorber 1994; West and Fenstermaker 1995).

FINDINGS FROM OTHER CULTURES

If gender differences were mostly the result of biology, then we could expect that gender roles would not vary much from culture to culture. However, one set of findings that helps show gender roles are in fact socially constructed comes from anthropologists, who have studied gender in other times and cultures.

NEW GUINEA

A *we'wha* (or berdache) of the Zuni people of New Mexico. Berdaches often behaved like persons of the opposite gender.

In her classic New Guinea study, *Sex and Temperament in Three Primitive Societies,* Margaret Mead (1963; orig. 1935) observed wide variability among gender role prescriptions—and such marked differences from those in the United States—that any claims to the universality of gender roles had to be rejected. Mead studied three separate tribes in New Guinea, which varied widely in their gender roles. In Arapesh society, both males and females generally had characteristics and behaviors that would typically be associated with the Western female role. Both sexes among the Arapesh were passive, gentle, unaggressive, and emotionally responsive to the needs of others. In contrast, Mead found that in another New Guinea group, the Mundugumor, both the males and females were characteristically aggressive, suspicious, and, from a Western observer's perspective, excessively cruel, especially toward children. In both cultures, however, men and women were expected to behave very similarly. In a third group, the Tchambuli tribe of New Guinea, gender roles of the males and females were almost exactly reversed from the roles traditionally assigned to males and females in Western society. Women "managed the business affairs of life" while "the men . . . painted, gossiped and had temper tantrums" (1972).

THE !KUNG

Another example can be found among the !Kung of the Kalahari desert. The !Kung do have specific gender roles, but it is very common for both men and women to engage in child care. Due to the non-confrontational parenting practices of the !Kung, who oppose violent conflict and physical punishment, children learn that aggressive behavior will not be tolerated by either men or women. Although the !Kung abide by the seeming traditional arrangement where "men hunt and women gather," the vast majority of its food actually comes from the gathering activities of women (see Draper, as cited in Renzetti and Curran 2000). Women return from their gathering expeditions armed not only with food for the community but also with valuable information for hunters.

DO-IT-YOURSELF SOCIOLOGY

D.I.Y.

How Masculine or Feminine Are You?

How well does each of these phrases describe you? Please rate each of these 20 terms on a scale of 1 to 7, where 1 means the word is "never or almost never true" in describing you, and 7 is "always or almost always true."

RATING 1–7

1. acts as a leader
2. affectionate
3. aggressive
4. cheerful
5. analytical
6. compassionate
7. competitive
8. eager to soothe hurt feelings
9. defends own beliefs
10. gentle
11. has leadership abilities
12. loves children
13. individualistic
14. loyal
15. makes decisions easily
16. soft-spoken
17. self-reliant
18. sympathetic
19. strong personality
20. understanding

TURN PAGE →

MULTIPLE GENDERS

The understanding that only two genders (i.e., male and female) exist is not universal. The Spaniards who came to both North and South America in the seventeenth century noticed men in the native tribes who had taken on the mannerisms of women, as well as women who occupied male roles.

Add up your scores on the odd-numbered terms. This is your Masculine Score. _____

Add up your scores on the even-numbered terms. This is your Feminine Score. _____

Subtract your Feminine Score from your Masculine Score. This is your Bem Score. _____

Compare your Bem score to the categories below to find out how you rate on the Bem Androgyny scale.

≤ -10	-9 to -5	-5 to +5	+5 to +10	≥ +20
Feminine	Nearly Feminine	Androgynous	Nearly Masculine	Masculine

Social scientist Sandra Bem considered an "androgynous" balance of traits to be psychologically desirable. She proposed that individuals who draw on traditionally masculine and feminine emotions and behaviors are well equipped to cope with life's challenges in a well-rounded way. Do you agree? Do you believe that the "masculine" and "feminine" traits listed on the previous page reflect nature, nurture, or a combination of the two?

_____

Source: Bem 1974.

A person occupying an opposite gender role is called a *berdache*. Roscoe (1991) has studied berdaches among the Zuni, a Native American tribe. Roscoe documented that berdaches are not necessarily homosexual; rather, some are heterosexual, some homosexual, and others sexually oriented toward other berdaches. He also found that the gendered behavior of berdaches varied across societies. In one society, both males and females had characteristics typically associated with the female role in the West. In another group, both males and females were aggressive. Yet in both cultures, men and women were expected to behave similarly. These findings demonstrate that culture—not biology—is at the root of gender differences ✓

CONCEPT CHECKS ✓

1. What is the difference between *sex* and *gender*?

2. How do both biology and gender socialization contribute to differences between men and women?

3. How can studies of gender in other cultures contribute to the argument that gender is socially constructed?

HOW DO GENDER INEQUALITIES AFFECT SOCIAL INSTITUTIONS?

Anthropologists and historians have found that most groups, collectives, and societies throughout history differentiate between women's and men's roles. Although there are considerable variations in the respective roles of women and men in different cultures, there are few instances of a society in which women are more powerful than men. Women everywhere typically are responsible for child rearing and the maintenance of the home, while political and military activities tend to be resoundingly male. Nowhere in the world do men have primary responsibility for the rearing of children. Conversely, there are few if any cultures in which women are charged with the main responsibility for the herding of large animals, the hunting of large game, deep-sea fishing, or plow agriculture (Brown 1977). Just because women and men perform different tasks or have different responsibilities in societies does not necessarily mean that women are unequal to men. However, if the work and activities of women and men are valued differently, then the division of labor between them can become the basis for unequal gender relations. In modern societies, the division of labor between the sexes has become less clear cut than it was in premodern cultures, but men still outnumber women in all spheres of power and influence.

Male dominance in a society is usually referred to as **patriarchy**. Although men are favored in almost all of the world's societies, the degree of patriarchy varies. In the United States, women have made tremendous progress, but several forms of gender inequality still exist. Yet throughout the world, many cultures exist where women suffer tremendous disadvantages relative to men.

Sociologists define **gender inequality** as the difference in the status, power, and prestige women and men have in groups, collectives, and societies. In thinking about gender inequality between men and women, we can ask the following questions: Do women and men have equal access to valued societal resources—for example, food, money, power, and time? Second, do women and men have similar life options? Third, are women's and men's roles and activities valued similarly? We will turn to look at the various forms of gender inequality in the workplace, in the home, in education systems, and in politics. As you read through this section, keep the above questions in mind.

patriarchy • The dominance of men over women. All known societies are patriarchal, although there are variations in the degree and nature of the power men exercise, as compared with women. One of the prime objectives of women's movements in modern societies is to combat existing patriarchal institutions.

gender inequality • The inequality between men and women in terms of wealth, income, and status.

WOMEN AND THE WORKPLACE

Rates of employment of women outside the home, for all classes, were quite low until well into the twentieth century in the United States. Even as late as 1910 in the United States, more than a third of gainfully employed women were maids or house servants. The female labor force consisted mainly of young, single women and children. When women or girls worked in factories or offices, employers often sent their wages straight home to their parents. When they married, they withdrew from the labor force.

Since the turn of the twentieth century, women's participation in the paid labor force has risen more or less continuously, especially in the past fifty years (see Figure 9.1). In 2008, 59.5 percent (72 million) of women age sixteen and older were in the labor force (U.S. Department of Labor 2008). In contrast, 38 percent of working-age women were in the labor force in 1960. An even greater change in the rate of labor force participation has occurred among married mothers of young children. In 1975, only 39 percent of married women with preschool-age children (under six years old) were

Figure 9.1 | Women's Participation in the Labor Force in the United States[a]

Women's labor force[b]
participation rates

Women as a percentage
of the total labor force

[a] Civilians age sixteen and over. [b] Labor force participants as a percentage of all civilian women age sixteen and over.

Source: U.S. Bureau of Labor Statistics 2009b.

in the labor force, yet this figure had increased to 63 percent by 2006 (U.S. Bureau of Labor Statistics 2007a).

How can we explain this increase? One force behind women's increased entry into the labor force was the increase in demand, since 1940, for clerical and service workers like Andrea, as the U.S. economy expanded and changed (Oppenheimer 1970). From 1940 until the mid- to late-1960s, labor force activity increased among women who were past their prime child-rearing years. During the 1970s and 1980s, as the marriage age rose, birth rates declined, and women's educational attainment increased, the growth in labor force participation spread to younger women. Many women now postpone family formation to complete their education and establish themselves in the labor force. Despite family obligations, today a majority of women of all educational levels now work outside the home during their child-rearing years (Spain and Bianchi 1996).

INEQUALITIES AT WORK

Until recently, women workers were overwhelmingly concentrated in routine, poorly paid occupations. The fate of the occupation of clerk (office worker) provides a good illustration. In 1850 in the United States, clerks held responsible positions, requiring accountancy skills and carrying managerial responsibilities; fewer than 1 percent were

Figure 9.2 | Women at Work

Of all jobs in a given occupation, the following shows the proportion held by women for each year (percentage).

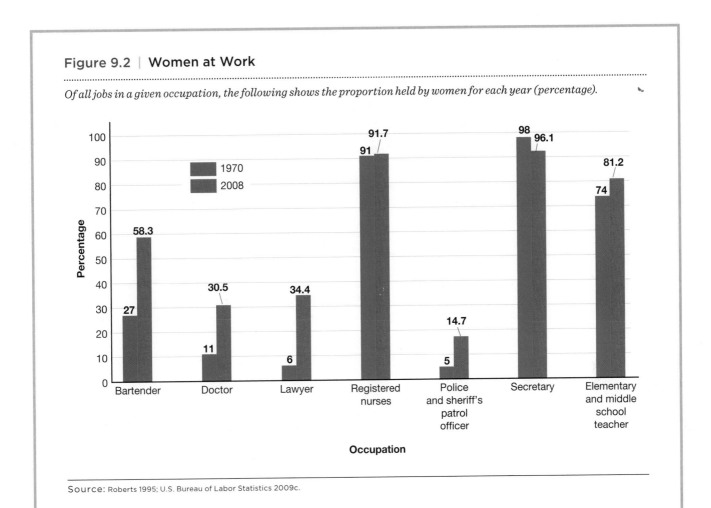

Source: Roberts 1995; U.S. Bureau of Labor Statistics 2009c.

women. The twentieth century saw a general mechanization of office work (starting with the introduction of the typewriter in the late nineteenth century), accompanied by a marked downgrading of the status of clerk—together with a related occupation, secretary—into a routine, low-paid occupation. Women filled these occupations as the pay and prestige of such jobs declined. Today, most secretaries and clerks are women. Once an occupation has become **gender typed**—once it is seen as mainly a "woman's job"—inertia sets in.

Women have recently made some inroads into occupations once defined as "men's jobs" (Figure 9.2). By the 1990s, women constituted a majority of workers in previously male-dominated professions such as accounting, journalism, psychology, public service, and bartending. In fields such as law, medicine, and engineering, their proportion has risen substantially since 1970. While women's employment in professional and managerial occupations has steadily increased, to be the largest occupational category for women (47.2 million or 39 percent in 2008), a considerable proportion are still employed in technical, sales, and administrative support occupations (39.9 million or 33 percent in 2008) (U.S. Department of Labor 2008).

Another important economic trend of the past thirty years has been the narrowing of the gender gap in earnings. Between 1970 and 2008, the ratio of women's to men's earnings among full-time, year-round workers increased from 62 to 80 percent. Moreover, this ratio increased among all races and ethnic groups. During the 1980s, women's hourly wages as a percentage of men's increased from 64 to 79 percent, weekly earnings rose from 64 to 71 percent, and among all workers (not just those working

gender typing • Designation of occupations as male or female, with "women's" occupations, such as secretarial and retail positions, having lower status and pay, and men's occupations, such as managerial and professional positions, having higher status and pay.

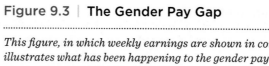

Figure 9.3 | The Gender Pay Gap

This figure, in which weekly earnings are shown in constant 2000 dollars, illustrates what has been happening to the gender pay gap over time. After narrowing gradually for years, it widened a little after 1993, when men's inflation-adjusted earnings were increasing slightly and women's were not. A ratio of 1.0 means earnings equity.

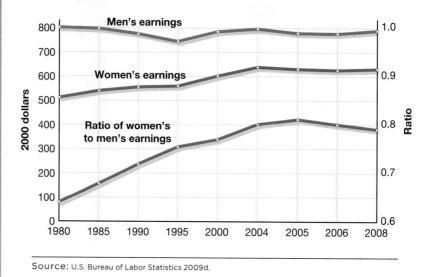

Source: U.S. Bureau of Labor Statistics 2009d.

full time) women's annual earnings increased from 46 to 61 percent of men's earnings (Spain and Bianchi 1996; U.S. Bureau of Labor Statistics 2005a). Despite the lessening of the gender gap in pay, men still earn substantially more than women (see Figure 9.3).

COMPARABLE WORTH

comparable worth • Policies that attempt to remedy the gender pay gap by adjusting pay so that those in female-dominated jobs are not paid less for equivalent work.

Comparable worth is a policy that compares pay levels of jobs held disproportionately by women with pay levels of jobs held disproportionately by men and tries to adjust pay so that the women and men who work in female-dominated jobs are not penalized. The policy presumes that jobs can be ranked objectively according to skill, effort, responsibility, and working conditions. After such a ranking, pay is adjusted so that equivalently ranked male- and female-dominated jobs receive equivalent pay (Hartmann et al. 1985).

Although comparable worth policies may help to reduce the gender gap in pay, only a handful of U.S. states have instituted comparable worth policies for public sector employees (Blum 1991). One reason that comparable worth policies have not been implemented is that it is very difficult to evaluate and ascertain which particular male- and female-dominated jobs are "comparable" with respect to skill, effort, responsibility, and working conditions (Stryker 1996). Substantial research shows that gender-neutral assessments of jobs and required job skills are very difficult (Steinberg 1990).

Opposition to comparable worth policies has been offered by both economists and feminists. Some economists worry that comparable worth is inflationary and will cause wage losses and unemployment for some (disproportionately women) because of benefits enacted for others. Feminists counter that comparable worth reinforces gender stereotyping rather than breaking down gender barriers at work (Blum 1991).

Although women are increasingly entering "traditionally male" jobs, their entry into such jobs is not necessarily accompanied by increases in pay—and increases in occupational mobility—due to the "glass ceiling." The **glass ceiling** is a promotion barrier that prevents a woman's upward mobility within an organization. The glass ceiling is particularly problematic for women who work in male-dominated occupations and the professions. Women's progress is blocked not by virtue of innate inability or lack of basic qualifications, but by not having the sponsorship of well-placed, powerful senior colleagues to articulate their value to the organization or profession (Alvarez et al. 1996). As a result, women tend to progress until mid-level management positions, but they do not, in proportionate numbers, move beyond mid-management ranks.

By contrast, men who work in female-dominated professions often enjoy a more rapid ascent up the hierarchy. The sociologist Christine Williams (1992) has observed that a **"glass escalator"** pushes these men to the top of their corporate ladders. Williams found that employers singled out male workers in traditionally female jobs, such as nurse, librarian, elementary school teacher, and social worker, and promoted them to top administrative jobs in disproportionately high numbers. "Often, despite their intentions, they face invisible pressures to move up in their professions," writes Williams (1992). These pressures may take positive forms, such as close mentoring and encouragement from supervisors, or they may be the result of prejudicial attitudes of those outside the profession, such as clients who prefer to work with male rather than female executives.

glass ceiling • A promotion barrier that prevents a woman's upward mobility within an organization.

glass escalator • The process by which men in traditionally female professions benefit from an unfair rapid rise within an organization.

ECONOMIC INEQUALITY IN GLOBAL PERSPECTIVE

The United States is not alone in having a history of gender inequality in the workplace. Across the globe, men outpace women in most workplace and economic indicators. Yet like in the United States, most nations have witnessed tremendous strides in women's economic progress in recent decades.

Factory worker in Changzhou, China, assembling parts for switchgears. What are the social consequences of women's changing economic roles around the world?

Women now make up more than 50 percent of the world's paid workforce in all regions except northern Africa, South Asia, and parts of the Middle East (International Labor Organization [ILO] 2006). Women around the world work in the lowest-wage jobs and are likely to make less than men doing similar work—although there is some evidence that the wage gap is slowly decreasing, at least in industrialized countries (ILO 1995). Because women throughout the world also perform housework and childcare at the end of the paid work, often dubbed the "second shift," women also work longer hours than men in most countries. A recent United Nations report found that women in the United States worked on average 25 minutes each day more than men—a difference that was considerably smaller than that in Austria (45 minutes) or Italy (103 minutes). Because of persistent discrimination, higher unemployment, and lower wages, women represent 60 percent of the world's 550 million working poor (ILO 2004a).

Women remain in the poorest-paying industrial and service-sector jobs in all countries, and in the less industrialized nations they are concentrated in the declining agricultural sector. The feminization of the global workforce has brought with it the increased exploitation of young, uneducated, largely rural women around the world. These women labor under conditions that are often unsafe and unhealthy, at low pay and with nonexistent job security.

Yet at the same time, even poor-paying factory jobs may enable some women to achieve a measure of economic independence and power. The International Labor Organization (2004a) found that while the gap between the number of men and women in the labor force has been decreasing in all regions of the world since 1993, this decrease has varied widely. Although women in the transitional economies and East Asia—where the number of women working per 100 men is 91 and 83, respectively—have nearly closed the gap, in other regions of the world such as the Middle East, North Africa, and South Asia, less than 40 percent of women work.

At the other end of the occupational spectrum, a recent study by the International Labor Organization concludes that women throughout the world still encounter a "glass ceiling" that restricts their movement into the top positions. Even though women have made progress in moving into managerial and professional positions, globally they still hold only 2 to 3 percent of the top corporate jobs, and those who do make it to the top typically earn less than men. In Japan, for example, women are especially likely to

Sociologist Christine Williams asserts than men in female-dominated professions, such as this elementary school teacher, are routinely promoted to top administrative positions and face constant pressure to advance.

face barriers to upper-level positions: When college-educated Japanese women interview for managerial jobs, they are typically assigned to noncareer secretarial work. As many as 40 percent of Japanese companies hire no women college graduates for management-level positions (French 2001a). On the other hand, in Australia, Canada, Thailand, and the United States women own more than 30 percent of all businesses (ILO 2003). Female participation in senior management has reached nearly 22 percent in the Netherlands, 21 percent in Canada, and over 36 percent in Hungary, although it remains low (13.6 percent) in the United States (ILO 2004b). In some developing countries, progress has been even greater: In Chile, for example, 27 percent of senior managers are women; in Singapore, 37 percent (ILO 2003).

SEXUAL HARASSMENT IN THE WORKPLACE

Economic disadvantage is just one challenge women workers face worldwide. Another pervasive yet poorly documented obstacle is sexual harassment. **Sexual harassment** is unwanted or repeated sexual advances, remarks, or behaviors that are offensive to the recipient and cause discomfort or interference with job performance. Power imbalances facilitate harassment; even though women can and do sexually harass subordinates, because men usually hold positions of authority, it is more common for men to harass women (Reskin and Padavic 1994).

sexual harassment • The making of unwanted sexual advances by one individual toward another, in which the first person persists even though it is clear that the other party is resistant.

The U.S. courts have identified two types of sexual harassment. One is the *quid pro quo*, in which a supervisor demands sexual acts from a worker as a job condition or promises work-related benefits in exchange for sexual acts. The other is the "hostile work environment," in which a pattern of sexual language, lewd posters, or sexual advances makes a worker so uncomfortable that it is difficult for her to do her job (Reskin and Padavic 1994).

Sociologists have observed that "the great majority of women who are abused by behavior that fits legal definitions of sexual harassment—and who are traumatized by the experience—do not label what has happened to them as sexual harassment" (Paludi and Barickman 1991).

Women's reluctance to report may be due to the following factors: (1) Many still do not recognize that sexual harassment is an actionable offense; (2) victims may be reluctant to come forward with complaints, fearing that they will not be believed, that their charges will not be taken seriously, or that they will be subject to reprisals; (3) it may be difficult to differentiate between harassment and joking on the job (Giuffre and Williams 1994).

THE FAMILY AND GENDER ISSUES

BALANCING WORK AND CHILD CARE

One of the major factors affecting women's careers is the male perception that for female employees, work comes second to having children. One study carried out in Britain (Homans 1987) investigated the views of managers interviewing female applicants for positions as technical staff in the health services. The researchers found that the interviewers always asked the women about whether or not they had, or intended to have, children (this is now illegal in the United States). They virtually never followed this practice with male applicants. When asked why, two themes ran through their answers: Women with children may require extra time off for school holidays or if a child falls sick, and responsibility for child care is a mother's problem rather than a parental one.

U.S. Marine Michael Mink discusses school behavior notes that came home in his sons' backpacks. Mink takes care of his five children while his wife, Angela, who is also a Marine, serves in Iraq. Like many families with two working parents, the Minks struggle to balance raising children and working full-time jobs.

Some managers thought their questions indicated an attitude of "caring" toward female employees. But most saw such a line of questioning as part of their task in assessing how far a female applicant would prove a reliable colleague. Women were seen as likely to interrupt their careers to care for young children, no matter how senior a position they might have reached. The few women in this study who held senior management positions were all without children, and several of those who planned to have children in the future said they intended to leave their jobs and would perhaps retrain for other positions subsequently.

How should we interpret these findings? Are women's job opportunities hampered mainly by male prejudices? Some managers expressed the view that women with children should not work, but should occupy themselves with child care and the home. Most, however, accepted the principle that women should have the same career opportunities as men. The bias in their attitudes had less to do with the workplace itself than with the domestic responsibilities of parenting. So long as most of the population take it for granted that parenting cannot be shared on an equal basis by both women and men, the problems facing women employees will persist. It will remain a fact of life, as one of the managers put it, that women are disadvantaged, compared with men, in their career opportunities.

HOUSEWORK

housework ● Unpaid work carried on in the home, usually by women; domestic chores such as cooking, cleaning, and shopping. Also called domestic labor.

Although there have been revolutionary changes in women's status in recent decades in the United States, including the entry of women into male-dominated professions, one area of work has lagged far behind: **housework**. Because of the increase of married women in the workforce and the resulting change in status, it was presumed that men would contribute more to housework. On the whole, this has not been the case. Although men now do more housework than they did three decades ago, a large gender gap persists. In 1976, women performed 26 hours of housework per week, although this number dropped to 16.5 hours by 2005. By contrast, men's housework has increased from 6 to 12 hours per week, between 1976 and 2005. However, this means that women still put in significantly more time than their spouses (Achen and Stafford 2005).

The UN estimates that women in the United States work 6 percent more than men, a majority of which is spent in non-market activities such as housework and making clothing and food for their families (UN 2003). These figures do not include time spent on child care, which if factored in would increase the gap. The UN has estimated that if all of the non-market work of women was accounted for, the official estimate of the size of the world economy would be $11 trillion higher (UN 1995).

Some sociologists have suggested that this phenomenon is best explained as a result of economic forces: Household work is exchanged for economic support. Because women earn less than men, they are more likely to remain economically dependent on their husbands and thus perform the bulk of the housework. Until the earnings gap is narrowed, women will likely remain in their dependent position.

EDUCATION AND UNEQUAL TREATMENT IN THE CLASSROOM

Sociologists have found that schools help foster gender differences in outlook and behavior. Studies document that teachers interact differently—and often inequitably—with their male and female students. These interactions differ in at least two ways: the frequency of teacher-student interactions and the content of those interactions. Both of the patterns are based on—and perpetuate—traditional assumptions about male and female behavior and traits.

One study showed that regardless of the sex of the teacher, male students interacted more with their teachers than female students did. Boys received more teacher attention and instructional time than girls did. This was due in part to the fact that boys were more demanding than girls (American Association of University Women 1992). Another study reported that boys were eight times more likely to call out answers in class, thus grabbing their teachers' attention. This research also showed that even when boys did not voluntarily participate in class, teachers were more likely to solicit information from them than from girls. However, when girls tried to bring attention to themselves by calling out in class without raising their hands, they were reprimanded (Sadker and Sadker 1994). Boys were also disadvantaged in several ways, however. Because of their rowdy behavior, they were more often scolded and punished than the girl students. Moreover, boys outnumber girls in special education programs by startling percentages.

This differential treatment of boys and girls perpetuates stereotypic gender-role behavior. Girls are trained to be quiet, well behaved, and to turn to others for answers, while boys are encouraged to be inquisitive, outspoken, active problem solvers.

GENDER INEQUALITY IN POLITICS

Women are playing an increasingly important role in U.S. politics, although they are still far from achieving full equality. Before 1993, there were only two women in the U.S. Senate (out of one hundred Senate members), and twenty-nine in the U.S. House of Representatives (out of 435). Less than a decade later—in 2001—there were a record thirteen women in the Senate and fifty-nine in the House. Currently, there are seventeen women senators and seventy-five representatives (U.S. House of Representatives 2009). Women in 2009 held 24.3 percent of all seats in state legislatures, five times as many as they held in 1969, but only six governorships (out of fifty) (NCSL 2009; ERGD 2009). The U.S. Supreme Court had its first woman justice appointed in 1981.

It was not until 1984 that a woman was nominated as the vice presidential candidate of either major party, neither of which has ever nominated a woman for the presidency. Women politicians are overwhelmingly affiliated with the Democratic party. In the U.S. Congress 85 percent of women are Democrats, and in state legislatures, over 70 percent of women legislators are Democrats (NCSL 2009, ERGD 2009).

Typically, the more local the political office, the more likely it is to be occupied by a woman. Men outnumber women in politics at all levels, but women are often elected members of city and county governing boards and as mayors. In most states, women are less likely to be found as representatives to state government than as representatives at the local level, but even women elected at the state level are more common than women representatives to Congress. The reason is partly that local politics is often part-time work, particularly in smaller cities and towns. Local politics can thus be good "women's work," offering low-pay, part-time employment, flexible hours, and the absence of a clear career path. The farther from home the political office, the more likely it is to be regarded as "man's work," providing a living wage, full-time employment, and a lifetime career.

GENDER AND POLITICS: GLOBAL PERSPECTIVE

Women play an increasing role in politics throughout the world. In Japan, for example, where women have traditionally faced significant barriers to achieving equality with men, five women were recently appointed to cabinet-level positions by Junichiro Koizumi, the reform-minded prime minister who took office in spring 2001—one in the key position of foreign minister (French 2001b). Yet of the 192 countries that belong to the United Nations, only twenty-four are presently headed by women. Since World War II, thirty-eight countries have been headed by women; the United States is not among them.

As of 2009, women made up only 18.4 percent of the combined membership of the national legislatures throughout the world. Only in Sweden (58 percent), Luxembourg (50 percent), Netherlands (44.4 percent), Slovenia (42.9 percent), and France (42.3 percent) do women make up a significant part of parliament; in the Arab states, the figure is only 9.1 percent (Women in National Parliaments [WNP] 2009). It is interesting that Rwanda, which rates very low on the UN's Human Development Index, is close to Sweden for the highest share of women in the lower house of the parliament. The U.S. Congress is 15.3 percent female, placing the United States seventy-first out of 188 countries for which data exist (WNP 2009).

The United Nations ranks countries according to a measure of "gender empowerment," which is based on such factors as seats in the national legislature held by women, female administrators and managers (as a percentage of total administrators and managers), female professional and technical workers (as a percentage of total professional and technical workers), and the ratio of women's to men's earned income. By this measure, the United States ranks eighteenth—behind the Scandinavian and other northern European countries and Canada and New Zealand. (see Figure 9.4). ✓

CONCEPT CHECKS ✓

1. Describe at least three examples of how gender inequalities emerge in the workplace. How would a sociologist explain these inequities?

2. What are signs of declining economic inequality between men and women from a global perspective?

3. How do inequalities in the home, especially with regard to housework and child care, reflect larger gender inequities in society?

4. Do you believe that girls or boys are more disadvantaged in the classroom? Why?

5. What are some important differences between men's and women's political participation in the United States?

6. What are some signs of progress in terms of women's political equality from a global perspective?

GENDER EMPOWERMENT AROUND THE WORLD

Figure 9.4

Ten Countries Ranked by Gender Empowerment Measure

 % of seats in parliament

 % of legislators, senior officials, & managers

 % of professional & technical workers

	Year women could vote	Income ratio*
1. SWEDEN	1919	0.67
2. NORWAY	1913	0.77
3. FINLAND	1906	0.73
7. AUSTRALIA	1902	0.70
9. GERMANY	1918	0.59
12. CANADA	1917	0.65
14. TRINIDAD & TOBAGO	1946	0.55
16. SINGAPORE	1947	0.53
18. UNITED STATES	1920	0.79
25. UNITED ARAB EMIRATES	2006	0.27

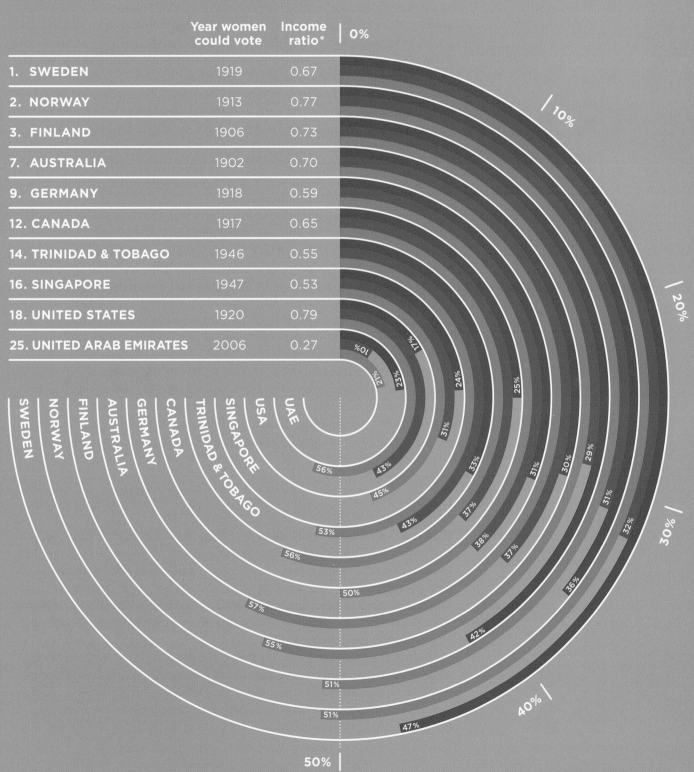

* Ratio of estimated female to male earned income
Source: UNDP 2009a.

WHY ARE WOMEN THE TARGET OF VIOLENCE?

Violence directed against women is found in many societies, including the United States. One out of three women has been beaten, coerced into sex, or abused in some other way—most often by someone she knows, including her husband or a male relative (United Nations Population Fund [UNFPA] 2005a). One in five worldwide will be a victim of rape or attempted rape in her lifetime (UNFPA 2005b). More women are injured as a result of beatings by spouses than by any other cause, a problem that is ignored by most governments (Human Rights Watch 1995). In India, an estimated twenty thousand brides were killed between 1990 and 1995—usually by being burned alive—for bringing an inadequate dowry to their husbands' families (Wagner-Wright 2006). In 2006 alone, there were an estimated roughly 7,500 deaths of women at the hands of husbands and relatives because the women brought an insufficient dowry, an increase of 8.4 percent from 2004. An additional 2,000 women committed suicide in dowry disputes (Zee News 2007). Between 100 and 140 million girls and women worldwide have been subjected to "genital mutilation"; an equal number are "missing," partly as the result of female infanticide in cultures where boys are more highly valued than girls (World Health Organization 2000).

The trafficking of women for forced prostitution, which has been called "the largest slave trade in history," appears to be a growing problem (UNFPA 2005b). The UNFPA (2005a) estimates that each year 800,000 people, 80 percent of whom are women and 50 percent of whom are under age 18, are moved across borders as a part of the worldwide sex trade. While victims of sex trafficking come from all regions of the world, more than a quarter (275,000 per year) come from the former Soviet Union and Eastern Europe, followed by Asia (250,000). War, displacement, and economic and social inequities between and within countries and the demand for low-wage labor and sex work drive this illicit trade in women.

In the United States, many scholars argue that the increased depiction of violence in movies, on television, and elsewhere in American popular culture contributes to a climate in which women are often victimized. The most common manifestation of violence against women is sexual assault, although stalking and sexual harassment increasingly are seen as a form of psychological (if not physical) violence as well.

RAPE

rape • The forcing of non-consensual vaginal, oral, or anal intercourse.

Rape can be sociologically defined as the forcing of nonconsensual vaginal, oral, or anal intercourse. As one researcher observed, between consensual sex and rape lies "a continuum of pressure, threat, coercion, and force" (Kelly 1987). Common to all forms of rape is the lack of consent: At least in principle, "no" means "no" when it comes to sexual relations in most courts of law in the United States. Virtually all rapes are committed by men against women, although men rape other men in prisons and other all-male institutional environments.

Rape is an act of violence, rather than a purely sexual act. It is often carefully planned rather than performed on the spur of the moment to satisfy some uncontrollable sexual desire. Many rapes involve beatings, knifings, and even murder. Even when rape leaves no physical wounds, it is a highly traumatic violation of a woman's person that leaves long-lasting psychological scars.

It is difficult to know with accuracy how many rapes actually occur, since most rapes go unreported. One comprehensive study of American sexual behavior found that 22 percent of the women surveyed reported having been forced into a sexual encounter. Yet the same study found that only 3 percent of the men admitted to having forced a woman into having sex, a discrepancy the study's authors attribute to different perceptions between men and women regarding what constitutes forced sex (Laumann et al. 1994). Based on its semiannual survey of nearly 100,000 Americans, the U.S. Department of Justice estimates that in 2007, there were 90,427 rapes committed on women. The total number of sexual assaults, attempted rapes, and rapes (204,370) was more than 21 percent lower than in 2002—part of an overall decrease in violent crimes since 1994. In fact, criminal victimizations, which include rape and sexual assault, are at their lowest point since 1973 (Catalano 2005).

Most rapes are committed by relatives (fathers or stepfathers, brothers, uncles), partners, or acquaintances. Among college students, most rapes are likely to be committed by boyfriends, former boyfriends, or classmates. The National College Women Sexual Victimization (NCWSV) study, a national survey of 4,446 women attending two- or four-year colleges or universities, presents a chilling picture of violence against women on campuses across the country (Fisher et al. 2000). The study, which was conducted during spring semester 1997, asked college women about their experience with rape, attempted rape, coerced sex, unwanted sexual contact, and stalking during the 1996–1997 school year. Overall, since the beginning of the school year, 1.7 percent had been the victim of a completed rape, and 1.1 percent of an attempted rape.

Moreover, fully a tenth of the female students surveyed had been raped prior to the study period (which began in the fall of 1996), and another tenth had been the victims of attempted rape. The study also found that for both completed and attempted rapes, nine out of ten offenders were known to the victim. Fifty-five percent of rape victims used physical force in an effort to thwart the rape, as did 69 percent of attempted rape victims.

The incidence of other forms of victimization reported in the study was substantially higher than that of rape. Nearly one out of six female students reported being the target of attempted or completed sexual coercion or unwanted sexual contact during the current academic year, half involving the use or threat of physical force. More than a third reported that they had experienced a threatened, attempted, or completed unwanted sexual assault at some time during their lives. And about one out of every eight reported having been stalked at some time during the current year, almost always by someone they knew—typically a former boyfriend or classmate. Stalking, it was reported, was emotionally traumatizing and in 15 percent of the incidents involved actual or threatened physical harm.

WHY ARE WOMEN SO OFTEN THE TARGETS OF SEXUAL VIOLENCE?

Some scholars claim that men are socialized to regard women as sex objects, to feel a sense of sexual entitlement, and to instill fear in women by dominating them (Brownmiller 1986). This socialization context, described as a "rape culture" by Susan Brownmiller (1986), may make men insensitive to the difference between consensual and nonconsensual sex and thus contribute to the high levels of victimization women reported to the NCWSV study (Griffin 1979; Dworkin 1981, 1987).

The fact that "acquaintance rapes" occur suggests that at least some men are likely to feel entitled to sexual access if they already know the woman. A survey of nearly 270,000 first-year college students reported that 55 percent of male students agreed with the statement "If two people really like each other, it's all right for them to have sex even if they've known each other only for a very short time." Only 31 percent of female students were in agreement, suggesting a rather large gender gap concerning notions of sexual entitlement (American Council on Education 2001). When a man goes out on a date with sexual conquest on his mind, he may force his attentions on an unwilling partner, overcoming her resistance through the use of alcohol, persistence, or both. While such an act may not be legally defined as rape, it would be experienced as such by many women. ✓

CONCEPT CHECKS ✓

1. How common is violence against women in the United States?

2. What proportion of sexual assaults are believed to go unreported?

3. Why are women more likely than men to be the targets of sexual violence?

HOW DOES SOCIAL THEORY EXPLAIN GENDER INEQUALITY?

Investigating and accounting for gender inequality has become a central concern of sociologists. Many theoretical perspectives have been advanced to explain men's enduring dominance over women—in the realm of economics, politics, the family, and elsewhere. In this section, we will review the main theoretical approaches to explaining the nature of gender inequality at the level of society.

FUNCTIONALIST APPROACHES

As we saw in Chapter 1, the functional approach sees society as a system of interlinked parts that, when in balance, operate smoothly to produce social solidarity. Thus, functionalist and functionalist-inspired perspectives on gender seek to show that gender differences contribute to social stability and integration. Though such views once commanded great support, they have been heavily criticized for neglecting social tensions at the expense of consensus and for promulgating a conservative view of the social world.

Talcott Parsons, a leading functionalist thinker, concerned himself with the role of the family in industrial societies (Parsons and Bales 1955). He was particularly interested in the socialization of children and believed that stable, supportive families are the key to successful socialization. In Parsons's view, the family operates most efficiently with a clear-cut sexual division of labor in which females act in *expressive* roles, providing care and security to children and offering them emotional support, and men perform *instrumental* roles—namely, being the breadwinner in the family. This complementary division of labor, springing from a biological distinction between the sexes, would ensure the solidarity of the family according to Parsons.

Feminists have sharply criticized claims of a biological basis to the sexual division of labor, arguing that there is nothing natural or inevitable about the allocation of tasks in society. Women are not prevented from pursuing occupations on the basis of any biological features; rather, humans are socialized into roles that are culturally expected of them. Parsons's notions of the "expressive" female have been attacked by feminists and other sociologists who see his views as condoning the subordination of women in the home. There is no basis to the belief that the "expressive" female is necessary for the smooth operation of the family—rather, it is a role that is promoted largely for the convenience of men.

In addition, cross-cultural and historical studies show that even though most societies distinguish between men's and women's roles, the degree to which they differentiate tasks as exclusively male or female and assign different tasks and responsibilities to women and men can vary greatly across time and place (Coltrane 1992). Thus, gender inequalities do not seem to be fixed or static.

FEMINIST APPROACHES

The feminist movement has given rise to a large body of theory that attempts to explain gender inequalities and set forth agendas for overcoming those inequalities. **Feminist theories** in relation to gender inequality contrast markedly with one another. Feminist writers are all concerned with women's unequal position in society, but their explanations for it vary substantially. Competing schools of feminism have sought to explain gender inequalities through a variety of deeply embedded social processes,

feminist theory • A sociological perspective that emphasizes the centrality of gender in analyzing the social world and particularly the uniqueness of the experience of women. There are many strands of feminist theory, but they all share the intention to explain gender inequalities in society and to work to overcome them.

Why would a functionalist agree that the division of labor between the homemaking wife and breadwinning husband in this Japanese household is ideal?

such as sexism, patriarchy, capitalism, and racism. In the following sections, we will look at the arguments behind three main feminist perspectives—liberal, radical, and black feminism.

LIBERAL FEMINISM

liberal feminism • Form of feminist theory that believes that gender inequality is produced by unequal access to civil rights and certain social resources, such as education and employment, based on sex. Liberal feminists tend to seek solutions through changes in legislation that ensure that the rights of individuals are protected.

Liberal feminism looks for explanations of gender inequalities in social and cultural attitudes. Unlike radical feminists, liberal feminists do not see women's subordination as part of a larger system or structure. Instead, they draw attention to many separate factors that contribute to inequalities between men and women. For example, liberal feminists are concerned with sexism and discrimination against women in the workplace, educational institutions, and the media. They tend to focus their energies on establishing and protecting equal opportunities for women through legislation and other democratic means. Legal advances such as the Equal Pay Act of 1963 and the Sex Discrimination Act of 1984 were actively supported by liberal feminists, who argued that enshrining equality in law is important to eliminating discrimination against women. Liberal feminists seek to work through the existing system to bring about reforms in a gradual way. In this respect, they are more moderate in their aims and methods than radical feminists, who call for an overthrow of the existing system.

While liberal feminists have contributed greatly to the advancement of women over the past century, critics charge that they are unsuccessful in dealing with the root cause of gender inequality and do not acknowledge the systemic nature of women's oppression in society. They say that by focusing on the independent deprivations that women suffer—sexism, discrimination, the "glass ceiling," unequal pay—liberal feminists draw only a partial picture of gender inequality. Radical feminists accuse liberal feminists of encouraging women to accept an unequal society and its competitive character.

radical feminism • Form of feminist theory that believes that gender inequality is the result of male domination in all aspects of social and economic life.

RADICAL FEMINISM

At the heart of **radical feminism** is the belief that men are responsible for and benefit from the exploitation of women. The analysis of patriarchy—the systematic domination of females by males—is of central concern to this branch of feminism. Patriarchy is viewed as a universal phenomenon that has existed across time and cultures. Radical feminists often concentrate on the family as one of the primary sources of women's oppression in society. They argue that men exploit women by relying on the free domestic labor that women provide in the home, and that as a group, men also deny women access to positions of power and influence in society.

Radical feminists differ in their interpretations of the basis of patriarchy, but most agree that it involves the appropriation of women's bodies and sexuality in some form. Because women are biologically able to give birth to children, they become dependent materially on men for protection and livelihood. This "biological inequality" is socially organized in the nuclear family. Other radical feminists point to male violence against women as central to male supremacy. According to such a view, domestic violence, rape, and sexual harassment are all part of the systematic oppression of women, rather than isolated cases with their own psychological or criminal roots.

Radical feminists believe that gender equality can only be attained by overthrowing the patriarchal order, because patriarchy is a systemic phenomenon. The use of patriarchy

Surrounded by minority women at the Houston Civic Center, Coretta Scott King speaks about the resolution on minority women's rights that won the support of the National Women's Conference in 1977. The minority resolution, proposed by representatives of many races, declared that minority women suffered discrimination based on both race and sex.

as a concept for explaining gender inequality has been popular with many feminist theorists. In asserting that "the personal is political," radical feminists have drawn widespread attention to the many linked dimensions of women's oppression.

Many objections can be raised, however, to radical feminist views. The main one, perhaps, is that the concept of patriarchy as it has been used is inadequate as a general explanation for women's oppression. Radical feminists have tended to claim that patriarchy has existed throughout history and across cultures—that it is a universal phenomenon. Critics argue, however, that such a conception of patriarchy does not leave room for historical or cultural variations. It also ignores the important influence that race, class, or ethnicity may have on the nature of women's subordination. In other words, it is not possible to see patriarchy as a universal phenomenon; doing so risks biological reductionism—attributing all the complexities of gender inequality to a simple distinction between men and women.

BLACK FEMINISM

Do the versions of feminism outlined above apply equally to the experiences of both white and nonwhite women? Many black feminists and feminists from developing countries claim they do not. They argue that ethnic divisions among women are not considered by the main feminist schools of thought, which are oriented to the dilemmas of white, predominantly middle-class women living in industrialized societies. It is not valid, they claim, to generalize theories about women's subordination as a whole from the experience of a specific group of women.

This dissatisfaction has led to the emergence of a **black feminism** that concentrates on the particular problems facing black women. The writings of African American feminists emphasize the influence of the powerful legacy of slavery, segregation, and the civil rights movement on gender inequalities in the black community. They point out that early black **suffragettes** supported the campaign for women's rights but realized that the question of race could not be ignored. Black feminists contend, therefore, that any theory of gender equality that does not take racism into account cannot be expected to explain black women's oppression adequately. Some also argue that black women are multiply disadvantaged on the basis of their color, their sex, and their class position. When these three factors interact, they reinforce and intensify each other (Brewer 1993). ✓

black feminism • A strand of feminist theory that highlights the multiple disadvantages of gender, class, and race that shape the experiences of nonwhite women. Black feminists reject the idea of a single, unified gender oppression that is experienced evenly by all women and argue that early feminist analysis reflected the specific concerns of white, middle-class women.

suffragettes • Members of early women's movements who pressed for equal voting rights for women and men.

CONCEPT CHECKS

1. Contrast functionalist and feminist approaches to understanding gender inequality.

2. What are the key ideas of liberal feminism? What are critiques of this perspective?

3. What are the key ideas of radical feminism? What are critiques of this perspective?

4. What are the key ideas of black feminism? What are critiques of this perspective?

WHAT ARE THE GLOBAL CONSEQUENCES OF GENDER INEQUALITY?

According to a Chinese saying, "Women hold up half the sky." In fact, as we have seen in this chapter, women typically hold up far more than half: Women have become a central part of the world's paid workforce, while at the same time maintaining their

The International Women's Movement

Do you have any interest in joining the women's movement? Every year countless American college students are inspired by feminism and enlist in the fight for such causes as reproductive rights, equal pay, or the preservation of welfare benefits for poor women. In today's increasingly globalized world, there is a good chance that those who become active in the U.S. women's movement will come into contact with women pursuing other feminist struggles overseas.

The women's movement, of course, is not simply an American or Western European phenomenon. In China, for example, women are working to secure "equal rights, employment, women's role in production, and women's participation in politics" (Zhang and Xu 1995). In South Africa, women played a pivotal role in the battle against apartheid and are fighting in the post-apartheid era to improve "the material conditions of the oppressed majority; those who have been denied access to education, decent homes, health facilities, and jobs" (Kemp et al. 1995). In Peru, activists have been working for decades to give women a greater "opportunity to participate in public life" (Blondet 1995), while "in Russia, women's protest was responsible for blocking the passage of legislation that the Russian parliament considered in 1992 that encouraged women to stay home and perform 'socially necessary labor'" (Basu 1995).

Although participants in women's movements have, for many years, cultivated ties to activists in other countries, the number and importance of such contacts has increased with globalization. A prime forum for the establishment of cross-national contacts has been the United Nation's Conference on Women, held four times between 1975 and 1995. Approximately fifty thousand people—of which more than two thirds were women—attended the last conference, held in Beijing, China, in 1995. Delegates from 181 nations were in attendance, along with representatives from thousands of nongovernmental organizations (UN Chronicle 1995).

traditional responsibilities for home and family. Although global gender inequalities may seem very far removed from your life, they have a direct effect on the daily lives of all the citizens of the globe.

China was the site of the 1995 United Nations' Fourth World Conference on Women, where some 35,000 people, representing 180 governments and 7,000 women's organizations, discussed the problems of women worldwide. The conference, held in the capital city of Beijing, grappled with a central problem women face the world over: What happens when a country's traditional cultural beliefs conflict with modern notions of women's rights? Globalization has not only brought factories and television to nearly every place on the planet, but has also exposed people throughout the world to ideas about equality and democracy. The modern women's movement has become a global champion of universal rights for women.

Seeking ways to "ensure women's equal access to economic resources including land, credit, science and technology, vocational training, information, communication and markets," conference participants spent ten days listening to presentations on the state of women worldwide, debating ways to improve their condition, and building professional and personal ties to one another. Mallika Dutt, one of the attendees, wrote in the journal *Feminist Studies* that "for most women from the United States, Beijing was an eye-opening, humbling, and transformative experience. U.S. women were startled by the sophisticated analysis and well-organized and powerful voices of women from other parts of the world" (1996). At the same time, according to Dutt, many of the conference participants left Beijing with a "sense of global solidarity, pride, and affirmation" (1996).

The Platform for Action finally agreed to by the conference participants called on the countries of the world to address such issues as:

- The persistent and increasing burden of poverty on women;
- Violence against women;
- The effects of armed or other kinds of conflict on women;
- Inequality between men and women in the sharing of power and decision-making;
- Stereotyping of women;
- Gender inequalities in the management of natural resources;
- Persistent discrimination against and violation of the rights of the girl child.

Must women's movements have an international orientation to be effective? Are women's interests essentially the same throughout the world? What might feminism mean to women in the developing world? These and many other questions are being hotly debated as the process of globalization continues apace.

The Beijing Women's Conference's final action platform was clear: When cultural traditions conflict with women's rights, women's rights should take precedence. The platform called for women's right to control their own reproduction and sexuality, as well as to inherit wealth and property—two rights that women are denied in many countries. It concluded that no society can truly hope to better the lives of its citizens until it fosters gender equality.

HOW GENDER INEQUALITY AFFECTS OUR LIVES

Five years after the Beijing conference, a special session of the United Nations General Assembly reaffirmed these principles, challenging the world's governments to realize the conference's goals. Noting that women occupied only 13 percent of parliament seats worldwide, the UN called for a global increase in women's political power. The Women's Environment and Development Organization, a New York–based women's advocacy group, was more specific in its statement to the UN: It pushed for equal representation of women in cabinet ministries and legislative bodies by 2005. The goal was set not only to benefit women, but to benefit society as a whole. In the view of the organization's executive director, increased women's representation would help shift a country's policies to "real-life concerns," as is seen in Scandinavia, where women are well represented in all levels of government: "Their commitment to the social safety net, to [an] expansive childcare system, to helping women and men balance work and family needs, I think, reflects women's experiences" (Hogan 2000).

Clearly that goal has not been met. Had it been, the UN Human Development Report (2005b) notes, there would be "14 million more girls in primary school today, 6 million of them in India and Pakistan and another 4 million in Sub-Saharan Africa. Trend projections are not encouraging. By 2015 the shortfall from the gender parity target will be equivalent to 6 million girls out of school, the majority of them in Sub-Saharan Africa."

The feminization of labor has altered the world economy. Will the feminization of politics do the same for global governance? The shift to a greater role for women in economics and politics may well signal a shift to greater equality for all people—not only for women but also for minority people, including sexual minorities—the world over. ✓

CONCEPT CHECKS ✓

1. The message emerging from the Beijing Women's Conference was that when cultural traditions conflict with women's rights, women's rights should take precedence. Do you agree with this? Why or why not?

NEED HELP STUDYING?

wwnorton.com/studyspace

Visit StudySpace to access free review materials such as:

- Vocabulary Flashcards
- Diagnostic Review Quizzes
- Study Outlines

REVIEW QUESTIONS

1. What have some theorists argued is the difference between sex and gender? What have been the critiques of those definitions?
2. What sort of evidence is brought to bear to explain differences between men and women based on biology? What are limitations of these theories?
3. What is the functionalist perspective on gender socialization? What are the critiques of this perspective?
4. What does it mean when sociologists say that we "do gender"? Describe some of the ways that you do gender in your daily life.

5. What do anthropological studies of gender and research on multiple genders tell us about the social construction of gender?
6. According to the authors, what explains the gender gap in pay? Compare and contrast economic and sociological explanations of this gender gap.
7. The authors show an increase of women in the workforce since the beginning of the twentieth century. Has this led to an equal distribution of domestic work?
8. The authors cite statistics that indicate high incidences of sexual violence on college campuses. How do sociologists explain the high incidence of sexual violence against women? Do these explanations make sense in the context of sexual violence on your campus?
9. What does gender equity look like in politics in the United States? What does this picture look like in comparison to other countries around the world and what can this tell us about global gender inequality?
10. Compare and contrast the main feminist theoretical approaches to gender inequality.

THINKING SOCIOLOGICALLY EXERCISES

1. What does cross-cultural evidence from tribal societies in New Guinea, Africa, and North America suggest about the differences in gender roles? Explain.
2. Why are minority women likely to think very differently about gender inequality than white women? Explain.

10

Ethnicity and Race

THE BIG QUESTIONS

WHAT ARE RACE AND ETHNICITY?
Learn the cultural bases of race and ethnicity and how racial and ethnic differences create sharp divisions in society. Learn the leading psychological theories and sociological interpretations of prejudice and discrimination.

HOW DO ETHNIC GROUPS COEXIST AND COMPETE?
Recognize the importance of the historical roots, particularly in the expansion of Western colonialism, of ethnic conflict. Understand the different models for a multiethnic society.

WHY DO ETHNIC GROUPS MIGRATE?
Understand global migration patterns and their impact.

HOW DO ETHNIC MINORITIES EXPERIENCE LIFE IN THE UNITED STATES?
Familiarize yourself with the history and social dimensions of ethnic relations in America.

HOW DOES RACIAL AND ETHNIC INEQUALITY AFFECT YOUR LIFE?
Learn the forms of inequality experienced by different racial and ethnic groups in the United States. Understand how the history of prejudice and discrimination against ethnic minorities has created conditions of hardship for many, while others have succeeded despite societal barriers.

Maureen, a forty-five-year-old black woman who was born in the Caribbean, came to England at the age of twelve with her family. She is the Social Services Manager for Home Care in Leicester, a city located ninety miles north of London. She has three brothers and ten nieces and nephews. All of her brothers have established families with white Englishwomen. She describes six of her nieces and nephews as "dual heritage." Yet she also believes that these children of multiracial heritage will be classified as "black" by those outside the family. Here she sums her view of one of her white sisters-in-law whom she respects: "I feel—she very much wants the child to have a black identity. So, every Sunday she would bring [my niece] up to my mum's house so that she knows her black family." Maureen and her other black Caribbean family members consider her niece to be "racially" black although she has a white birth mother. They recognize that in spite of having a white mother, this girl will be classified as black because of her physical appearance—demonstrating how "race," like ethnicity, is learned. Both are "socially constructed."

Sharon Dawkins (far right) is pictured with her daughters Aisha, Tanika, Rhea, and Imani (on her lap). She has been married to their father, a Jamaican-British man, for more than twenty years. She has participated in a longitudinal ethnography conducted by France Winddance Twine. Photograph by Michael Smyth.

In 2001, according to the U.K. census almost 50 percent of U.K.-born men who described their ethnic group as "Other Black" and almost 30 percent of "Black Caribbean" men were married to women outside their black ethnic group, in most cases white women (UK Statistics Authority 2001). The sociologist France Winddance Twine (2004) has found in her research among black-white multiracial families in the United States and the United Kingdom that some parents train their children to develop what she terms "racial literacy" skills in order to help them cope with racial hierarchies and to integrate multiple ethnic identities. Twine's research, as well as others, illustrates how difficult it is to pinpoint the conditions of racial and ethnic group membership for some individuals of multiracial heritage. In recent decades a number of sociologists have turned their attention to this problem of multiracial identity and racial classification schemes. They have argued that a "static measure of race" is not useful for individuals of multiracial heritage who may assert different identities in different social contexts (Harris 2003; Harris and Sim 2000; Goldstein and Morning 2000).

WHAT ARE RACE AND ETHNICITY?

In your daily life, you have no doubt used the terms *race* and *ethnicity* many times, but do you know what they mean? Defining and differentiating these terms is very difficult, however.

ethnicity • Cultural values and norms that distinguish the members of a given group from others. An ethnic group is one whose members share a distinct awareness of a common cultural identity, separating them from other groups. In virtually all societies, ethnic differences are associated with variations in power and material wealth. Where ethnic differences are also racial, such divisions are sometimes especially pronounced.

Ethnicity refers to cultural practices and outlooks of a given community that have emerged historically and tend to set people apart. Members of ethnic groups see themselves as culturally distinct from other groups in a society and are seen by those other groups to be so in return. Different characteristics may serve to distinguish ethnic groups from one another, but the most common are some combination of language, history, religious faith, and ancestry—real or imagined—and styles of dress or adornment. Ethnic differences are learned. Some examples of ethnic groups in the United States are Irish Americans, Jewish Americans, Italian Americans, Cuban Americans, and Japanese Americans.

The difference between race and ethnicity is not as clear-cut as some people think. Everything that has been said here about ethnicity would apply very well to Maureen's mixed-race nieces above. Their black relatives and white mother teach the children many cultural practices that people associate with being black—from how to braid their hair to how to respond to racism. So does this mean that race is really a kind of ethnicity?

In a way it is, but race has certain defining characteristics that make it different from ethnicity. At certain historical moments, ethnic differences take on two additional characteristics. First, some ethnic differences become the basis of stigmas that cannot be removed by conversion or assimilation. Second, these stigmas become the basis of extreme hierarchy.

race • Differences in human physical characteristics used to categorize large numbers of individuals.

Race, then, can be understood as a classification system that assigns individuals and groups to categories that are ranked or hierarchical. There really are no clear-cut "races," only a range of physical variations among human beings. Differences in physical type between groups of human beings arise from population inbreeding, which varies according to the degree of contact between different social or cultural groups. Human population groups are a continuum. The genetic diversity within populations that share visible physical traits is as great as the diversity between them. Racial distinctions are more than ways of describing human differences—they are also important factors in the reproduction of patterns of power and inequality within society.

The process by which understandings of race are used to classify individuals or groups of people is called **racialization**. Historically, racialization meant that certain groups of people came to be labeled as constituting distinct biological groups on the basis of naturally occurring physical features. From the fifteenth century onward, as Europeans came into increased contact with people from different regions of the world, they attempted to "racialize" non-European populations in opposition to the European "white race." In some instances this racialization took on codified institutional forms, as in the case of slavery in the former British, French, and Spanish colonies in the Americas, slavery in the United States, and the establishment of apartheid in South Africa after 1948. More commonly, however, everyday political, educational, legal, and other institutions become racialized through legislation. In the United States de facto racial segregation and racial hierarchies persisted even after state-sanctioned segregation was dismantled during the Civil Rights era of the late 1960s. Within a racialized system, an individual's social life and his or her life chances—including education, employment, incarceration, housing, health care, and legal representation—are all shaped and constrained by the racial assignments and racial hierarchies in that system.

In recent years, sociologists who study ethnicity in the United States have come to understand that the importance of ethnicity has declined in recent years, at least among whites. As a result, "ethnicity" now includes a choice of whether to be ethnic at all. More and more whites must also make a choice about which ethnicity to be, given high rates of ethnic intermarriage (Gans 1979; Waters 1990). By contrast, race is not always such a choice for nonwhites. One sociologist who has studied how many

racialization • The process by which understandings of race are used to classify individuals or groups of people. Racial distinctions are more than ways of describing human differences; they are also important factors in the reproduction of patterns of power and inequality.

Celebrating the Chinese New Year with performances and decorations is not just a picturesque event every year in Soho, but an important symbol of cultural continuity for London's Chinese community, and Chinese communities throughout the world.

racism • The attribution of characteristics of superiority or inferiority to a population sharing certain physically inherited characteristics. Racism is a form of prejudice focusing on physical variations between people. Racist attitudes became entrenched during the period of Western colonial expansion, but also rest on mechanisms of prejudice and discrimination found in human societies today.

institutional racism • Patterns of discrimination based on ethnicity that have become structured into existing social institutions.

Four schoolboys represent the "racial scale" in South Africa—black, Indian, half-caste, and white.

Americans think about their ancestry and backgrounds has written that "the social and political consequences of being Asian or Hispanic or black are not symbolic for the most part, or voluntary. They are real and often hurtful" (Waters 1990). Minority group status can have many negative consequences for its members. One such negative consequence is segregation (discussed later in this chapter).

Despite the increase in the number of people in the United States self-identifying as multiracial, many North Americans continue to believe, mistakenly, that race is a natural category and that human beings can be neatly separated into biologically distinct "races." This is a legacy of European colonialism and scientific racism. During the sixteenth century, Europeans began to classify animals, people, and the material culture that they collected as they explored the world. In 1735, Swedish botanist Carolus Linnaeus published what is recognized as the first version of a modern classification scheme of human populations. He grouped human beings into four basic categories—Europaeus, Americanus, Asiaticus, and Africanus. Linnaeus assumed that each subgroup had qualities of behavior or temperament that were innate and could not be altered. He acquired much of his data from the writings, descriptions, commentaries, and beliefs of plantation owners, missionaries, slave traders, explorers, and travelers. Thus his scientific data were shaped by the prejudices of Europeans and the power that they had over the people whom they conquered (Smedley 1993).

RACISM

Some see **racism** as a system of domination that operates in social processes and social institutions; others see it as operating in the individual consciousness. Racism can refer to explicit beliefs in racial supremacy such as the systems established in Nazi Germany, before the civil rights movement in the United States, and in South Africa under apartheid.

Yet many have argued that racism is more than simply the ideas held by a small number of bigoted individuals. Rather, racism is embedded in the very structure and operation of society. The idea of **institutional racism** suggests that racism pervades all of society's structures in a systematic manner. According to this view, institutions such as the police, the health-care industry, and the educational system all promote policies that favor certain groups while discriminating against others.

The concept of institutional racism was developed in the United States in the late 1960s by black power activists Stokely Carmichael and Charles Hamilton, who believed that white supremacy structured all social relations and that racism was the foundation of the very fabric of U.S. society, rather than merely representing the opinions of a small minority. The term was taken up by civil rights campaigners, and in subsequent years the existence of institutional racism came to be widely accepted and openly acknowledged in many settings including law enforcement and the media. A 1990s investigation into the practices of the Los Angeles Police Department, in light of the beating of Rodney King, found that institutional racism is pervasive within the police force and the criminal justice system. A similar case occurred more recently in New York City in 2006, when plainclothes New York City Police detectives shot and killed another unarmed man, 23-year-old Sean Bell—on the day Bell was to be married.

We see instances of institutional racism in Hollywood films, television broadcasting (negative or limited portrayals of racial and ethnic minorities in programming), and the international modeling industry (industry-wide bias against fashion models who appear to be of non-European ancestry and/or mixed race).

PSYCHOLOGICAL INTERPRETATIONS OF PREJUDICE AND DISCRIMINATION

Psychological theories can help us understand the nature of prejudiced and racist attitudes and also why ethnic differences matter so much to people.

PREJUDICE, DISCRIMINATION, AND RACISM

Prejudice, discrimination, and racism are related but distinctive concepts. **Prejudice** refers to opinions or attitudes held by members of one group toward another. A prejudiced person's preconceived views are often based on hearsay rather than on direct evidence, and are resistant to change even in the face of new information. People may harbor favorable prejudices about groups with which they identify and negative prejudices against others. Someone who is prejudiced against a particular group will refuse to give it a fair hearing.

Discrimination refers to actual behavior toward another group. It can be seen in activities that distribute rewards and benefits unequally based on membership in the dominant ethnic groups. It involves excluding or restricting members of specific groups, often defined by "race" or ethnicity, from opportunities that are available to other groups. Discrimination does not necessarily derive directly from prejudice. For example, white home buyers might steer away from purchasing properties in predominantly black neighborhoods, not because of attitudes of hostility they might feel toward African Americans, but because of worries about declining property values. Prejudiced attitudes in this case influence discrimination, but in an indirect fashion.

> **prejudice** ● The holding of preconceived ideas about an individual or group, ideas that are resistant to change even in the face of new information. Prejudice may be either positive or negative.

> **discrimination** ● Behavior that denies to the members of a particular group resources or rewards that can be obtained by others. Discrimination must be distinguished from prejudice: Individuals who are prejudiced against others may not engage in discriminatory practices against them; conversely, people may act in a discriminatory fashion toward a group even though they are not prejudiced against that group.

STEREOTYPES AND SCAPEGOATS

Prejudice operates mainly through the use of **stereotyping**, which means thinking in terms of fixed and inflexible categories. Stereotyping is often closely linked to the psychological mechanism of **displacement**, in which feelings of hostility or anger are directed against objects that are not the real origin of those feelings. People vent their antagonism against **scapegoats**, others who are blamed for problems that are not their fault. Scapegoating is common when two deprived ethnic groups come into competition with one another for economic rewards. People who direct racial attacks against African Americans, for example, are often in a similar economic position to them. They blame blacks for grievances whose real causes lie elsewhere. Scapegoating is normally directed against groups that are distinctive and relatively powerless, because they make an easy target.

> **stereotype** ● A fixed and inflexible category.

> **displacement** ● The transferring of ideas or emotions from their true source to another object.

> **scapegoat** ● An individual or group blamed for wrongs that were not of their doing.

MINORITY GROUPS

The term **minority group** as used in everyday life can be quite confusing. This is because the term refers to political power and is not simply a numerical distinction. There are many minorities in a statistical sense, such as people having red hair or weighing more than two hundred fifty pounds, but these are not minorities according to the sociological concept. In sociology, members of a minority group are disadvantaged as compared with the **dominant group** (a group possessing more wealth, power, and prestige) and have some sense of group solidarity, of belonging together. The

> **minority group** ● A group of people who are in a minority in a given society and who, because of their distinct physical or cultural characteristics, find themselves in situations of inequality within that society. Also known as ethnic minority.

> **dominant group** ● The opposite of a minority group; the dominant group possesses more wealth, power, and prestige in a society.

experience of being subject to prejudice and discrimination usually heightens feelings of common loyalty and interests.

Members of minority groups, such as Spanish speakers in the United States, often tend to see themselves as a people separated or distinct from the majority. Minority groups are sometimes, but not always, physically and socially isolated from the larger community. Although they tend to be concentrated in certain neighborhoods, cities, or regions of a country, their children may often intermarry with members of the dominant group. People who belong to minority groups sometimes (for example, Jews) actively promote endogamy (marriage within the group) in order to keep alive their cultural distinctiveness.

The idea of a "minority group" is more confusing today than ever before. Some groups that were once clearly identified as minorities, such as Asians and Jews, now have more resources, intermarry at greater rates, and experience less discrimination than they did when they were originally conceived of as minority groups. This highlights the fact that the concept of a minority group is really about disadvantage, rather than a numerical distinction. Perhaps in the future it would be more meaningful for sociologists to use the terms *dominant* and *disadvantaged* to avoid these misunderstandings, but these new terms would be fraught with their own problems! For now, sociologists continue to use the term *minority group*, so it is best for the student to be aware of its definitions and ambiguities as a concept. ✓

CONCEPT CHECKS

1. Explain the difference between ethnicity and race.
2. What does the term *racialization* refer to?
3. How does prejudice operate in society?
4. Why are Hispanics and African Americans considered to be minority groups in American society?

HOW DO ETHNIC GROUPS COEXIST AND COMPETE?

In an age of globalization and rapid social change, the rich benefits and complex challenges of ethnic diversity are confronting a growing number of states. International migration is accelerating with the further integration of the global economy; the movement and mixing of human populations seems sure to intensify in years to come. Meanwhile, ethnic tensions and conflicts continue to flare in societies around the world, threatening to lead to the disintegration of some multiethnic states and hinting at protracted violence in others. How can ethnic diversity be accommodated and the outbreak of ethnic conflict averted? Within multiethnic societies, what should be the relation between ethnic minority groups and the majority population? There are four primary models of ethnic integration that have been adopted by multiethnic societies in relation to these challenges: assimilation, the "melting pot," pluralism, and multiculturalism. These will be discussed shortly.

To fully analyze ethnic relations in current times, we must first take a historical and comparative perspective. It is impossible to understand ethnic divisions today without giving prime place to the impact of the expansion of Western colonialism on the rest of the world (Global Map 10.1). Global migratory movements resulting from colonialism helped to create ethnic divisions by placing different peoples in close proximity. We will now delve into this history in more detail.

Global Map 10.1 | Colonization and Ethnicity

This map shows the massive movement of peoples from Europe who colonized the Americas, South Africa, Australia, and New Zealand, resulting in the ethnic composition of populations there today. People from Africa were brought to the Americas to be slaves.

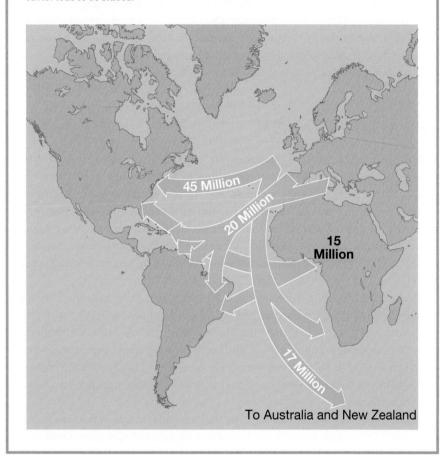

ETHNIC ANTAGONISM: A HISTORICAL PERSPECTIVE

From the fifteenth century onward, Europeans began to venture into previously uncharted seas and unexplored landmasses, pursuing the aims of exploration and trade but also conquering and subduing native peoples. They poured out by the millions from Europe to settle in these new areas. In the shape of the slave trade, they also occasioned a large-scale movement of people from Africa to the Americas.

These population flows formed the basis of the current ethnic composition of the United States, Canada, the countries of Central and South America, South Africa, Australia, and New Zealand. In all of these societies, the indigenous populations were decimated by disease, war, and genocide and subjected to European rule. They are now impoverished ethnic minorities. Since the Europeans were from diverse national and ethnic origins, they transplanted various ethnic hierarchies and divisions to their new homelands. At the height of the colonial era, in the nineteenth and early twentieth centuries, Europeans also ruled over native populations in many other regions: South Asia, East Asia, the South Pacific, and the Middle East.

For most of the period of European expansion, ethnocentric attitudes were rife among the colonists, many of whom were convinced that, as Christians, they were on a civilizing mission to the rest of the world. Europeans of all political persuasions believed themselves to be superior to the peoples they colonized and conquered. The early period of colonization coincided with the rise of scientific racism, and ever since then, the legacy of European colonization has generated ethnic divisions that have occupied a central place in regional and global conflicts. In particular, racist views distinguishing the descendants of Europeans from those of Africans became central to European racist attitudes.

THE RISE OF RACISM

Why has racism flourished? There are several reasons. The first reason for the rise of modern racism lies in the exploitative relations that Europeans established with the peoples they encountered and conquered. The slave trade could not have been carried on had Europeans not constructed a belief system that allowed them to justify their actions by convincing themselves that Africans belonged to an inferior, even subhuman race. Racism helped justify colonial rule over nonwhite peoples and denied them the rights of political participation that were being won by whites in their European homelands.

Second, an opposition between the colors white and black as cultural symbols was deeply rooted in European culture. White had long been associated with purity, black with evil (there is nothing natural about this symbolism; in some other cultures, it is reversed). The symbol of blackness held negative meanings before the West came into extensive contact with black peoples. These symbolic meanings tended to infuse the Europeans' reactions to blacks when they were first encountered on African shores.

A third important factor leading to modern racism was simply the invention and diffusion of the concept of race itself. Count Joseph Arthur de Gobineau (1816–1882), who is sometimes called the father of modern racism, proposed ideas that became influential in many circles. According to de Gobineau, three races exist: white, black, and yellow. The white race possesses superior intelligence, morality, and will power, and these inherited qualities underlie the spread of Western influence across the world. The blacks are the least capable, marked by an animal nature, a lack of morality, and emotional instability. The yellows were described as the "exact opposite" of blacks: restrained, discerning, and hard working, although not particularly creative.

ETHNIC CONFLICT

The most extreme and devastating form of group relations in human history involves **genocide**, the systematic, planned destruction of a particular group, on the grounds of group members' ethnicity, religion, culture, or political views. The most horrific recent instance of brutal destructiveness against such a group was the massacre of six million Jews in the German concentration camps during World War II. The Holocaust is not the only example of mass genocide in the twentieth century. Between 1915 and 1923 over a million Armenians were killed by the Ottoman Turkish government. In the late

A young girl joins members of the Ku Klux Klan at a demonstration against the Martin Luther King Day holiday in Pulaski, Tennessee.

genocide • The systematic, planned destruction of a racial, political, or cultural group.

1970s two million Cambodians died in the Khmer Rouge's killing fields. During the 1990s, in the African country of Rwanda, hundreds of thousands of the minority Tutsis were massacred by the dominant Hutu group. And in the former Yugoslavia, Bosnian and Kosovar Muslims were summarily executed by the Serb majority.

In other areas of the world, exploitation of minority groups has been an ugly part of many countries' histories. The separation of the minority from the majority has been institutionalized in the form of **segregation**, a practice whereby racial and ethnic groups are kept physically separate by law, thereby maintaining the superior position of the dominant group. For instance, in apartheid-era South Africa, laws forced blacks to live separately from whites and forbade sexual relations between races. In the United States, African Americans have also experienced legal forms of segregation. In 1967 the Supreme Court ruled in the case of *Loving v. Virginia* that the prohibition of interracial marriage violated the right to privacy. At that time racial intermarriage was still a crime in most southern states. Interracial marriage had been criminalized for much of the United States' history, in every state except Alaska and Hawaii. Economic and social segregation was enforced by laws, for instance those requiring blacks and whites to use separate public bathrooms. Even today, *de facto* segregated residential areas still exist in many cities, leading some to claim that an American system of apartheid has developed (Massey and Denton 1993).

segregation • The practices of keeping racial and ethnic groups physically separate, thereby maintaining the superior position of the dominant group.

MODELS OF ETHNIC INTEGRATION

For many years, the two most common positive models of political ethnic harmony in the United States were those of assimilation and the melting pot. **Assimilation** meant that new immigrant groups would assume the attitudes and language of the dominant white community. The idea of the **melting pot** was different—it meant merging different cultures and outlooks by stirring them all together. A newer model of ethnic relations is **pluralism**, in which ethnic cultures maintain their unique practices and communities, yet also participate in the larger society's economic and political life. A recent outgrowth of pluralism is **multiculturalism**, in which ethnic groups exist separately and equally. It does seem at least possible to create a society in which ethnic groups are separate but equal, as is demonstrated by Switzerland, where French, German, and Italian groups coexist in the same society. But this situation is unusual, and it seems unlikely that the United States could come close to mirroring this achievement in the near future.

assimilation • The acceptance of a minority group by a majority population, in which the new group takes on the values and norms of the dominant culture.

melting pot • The idea that ethnic differences can be combined to create new patterns of behavior drawing on diverse cultural sources.

pluralism • A model for ethnic relations in which all ethnic groups in a society retain their independent and separate identities, yet share equally in the rights and powers of citizenship.

multiculturalism • The viewpoint according to which ethnic groups can exist separately and share equally in economic and political life.

CONFLICT AND ECONOMIC POWER

Many commentators have argued that the best way to reduce ethnic conflicts such as those discussed earlier is to establish democracy and a free market. They argue that this would promote peace by giving everyone a say in running the country and by giving them access to the prosperity that comes from trading with others. In an influential book, *World on Fire: How Exporting Free Market Democracy Breeds Ethnic Hatred and Global Instability* (2003), Amy Chua, a professor at Yale University, contests this view.

Chua's starting point is that in many developing countries a small ethnic minority enjoys disproportionate economic power. One obvious example is the white minority that exploited the nonwhite ethnic groups in apartheid South Africa. Chua also observes that the massacre of Tutsis by Hutus in Rwanda in 1994 and the hatred felt by Serbs toward Croats in former Yugoslavia were also partly related to the economic

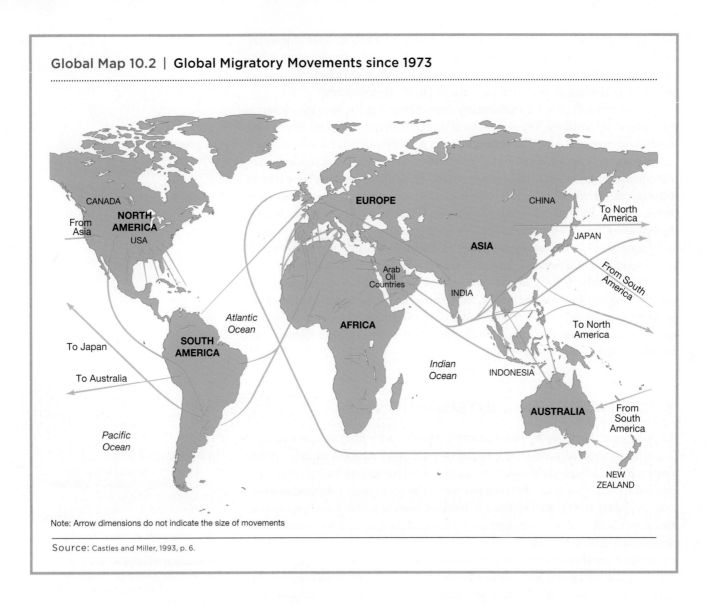

Note: Arrow dimensions do not indicate the size of movements

Source: Castles and Miller, 1993, p. 6.

CONCEPT CHECKS ✓

1. What are three reasons racism has flourished in the United States?

2. Compare and contrast three forms of ethnic conflicts.

3. What is the difference between assimilation and melting pot strategies of ethnic integration?

advantage enjoyed by the Tutsis and the Croats in their respective countries.

Chua's account shows us that although democracy and the market economy are in principle beneficent forces, they must be grounded in an effective system of law and civil society. Where they are not, as in many parts of the developing world, new and acute ethnic conflicts can emerge. ✓

WHY DO ETHNIC GROUPS MIGRATE?

Today floods of refugees and emigrants move restlessly across different regions of the globe, either trying to escape from conflicts or fleeing poverty in search of a better life. Often they reach a new country only to find they are resented by people who some

generations ago were immigrants themselves. Sometimes there are reversals, as has happened in Southern California and other areas of the United States along the Mexican border. Much of what is now California was once part of Mexico. Today, some Mexican Americans might say, the new waves of Mexican immigrants are reclaiming what used to be their heritage—except that most of the existing groups in California don't quite see things this way.

Jany Deng at the Arizona Lost Boys Center in Phoenix. Deng and eight other refugees escaped war in the Sudan and resettled in the United States.

MIGRATORY MOVEMENTS

Although migration is not a new phenomenon, it is one that seems to be accelerating as part of the process of global integration. Worldwide migration patterns can be seen as one reflection of the rapidly changing economic, political, and cultural ties among countries. It has been estimated that the world's migrant population in 1990 was more than eighty million people, twenty million of whom were refugees. By 2006, the number of migrants was estimated at one hundred ninety one million (ESRC 2007). This number appears likely to continue increasing in the twenty-first century, prompting some scholars to label this the "age of migration" (Castles and Miller 1993).

Immigration, the movement of people into a country to settle, and **emigration**, the process by which people leave a country to settle in another, combine to produce global migration patterns linking countries of origin and countries of destination. Migratory movements add to ethnic and cultural diversity in many societies and help

immigration • The movement of people into one country from another for the purpose of settlement.

emigration • The movement of people out of one country in order to settle in another.

to shape demographic, economic, and social dynamics. The intensification of global migration since World War II, and particularly over the last three decades, has transformed immigration into an important political issue in many countries. Rising immigration rates in many Western societies have challenged commonly held notions of national identity and have forced a reexamination of concepts of citizenship.

In examining recent trends in global migration, Stephen Castles and Mark Miller (1993) have identified four tendencies that they claim characterize migration patterns today and that are expected to persist in the coming years.

- ACCELERATION. Migration across borders is occurring in greater numbers than ever before.
- DIVERSIFICATION. Most countries now receive immigrants of many different types, in contrast with earlier times when particular forms of immigration, such as labor immigration or refugees, were predominant.
- GLOBALIZATION. Migration has become more global in nature, involving a greater number of countries as both senders and recipients (Global Map 10.2).
- FEMINIZATION. A growing number of migrants are women, making contemporary migration much less male dominated than in previous times. The increase in female migrants is closely related to changes in the global labor market, including the growing demand for domestic workers, the expansion of sex tourism and "trafficking" in women, and the "mail-order brides" phenomenon.

GLOBAL DIASPORAS

diaspora • The dispersal of an ethnic population from an original homeland into foreign areas, often in a forced manner or under traumatic circumstances.

Another way to understand global migration patterns is through the study of diasporas. The term **diaspora** refers to the dispersal of an ethnic population from an original homeland into foreign areas, often in a forced manner or under traumatic circumstances. References are often made to the Jewish and African diasporas to describe the way in which these populations have become redistributed across the globe as a result of slavery and genocide. Although members of a diaspora are by definition scattered apart geographically, they are held together by factors such as shared history, a collective memory of the original homeland, or a common ethnic identity that is nurtured and preserved. ✓

CONCEPT CHECKS ✓

1. According to Castles and Miller, which four trends characterize current and future migration?

2. What is diaspora? Explain the role diasporas play in preserving ethnic culture in contemporary societies.

HOW DO ETHNIC MINORITIES EXPERIENCE LIFE IN THE UNITED STATES?

We concentrate for the rest of the chapter on the origins and nature of ethnic diversity in the United States (see Figure 10.1)—and its consequences, which have often been highly contentious. More than most other societies in the world, this country is peopled almost entirely by immigrants. Only a tiny minority, less than 1 percent, of the population

Figure 10.1
RACIAL AND ETHNIC POPULATIONS IN THE U.S.

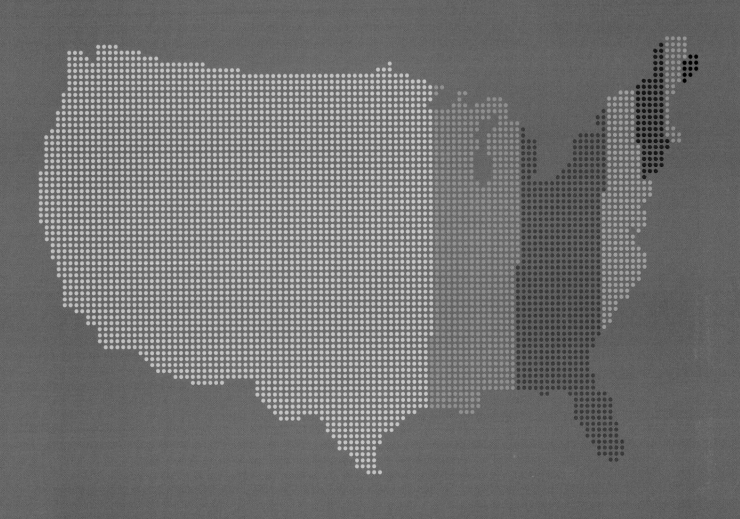

 65.9%
WHITE
(NON-HISPANIC)

198,420,355 people

 15.1%
HISPANIC
OR LATINO

45,432,158 people

 12.1%
AFRICAN
AMERICAN

36,397,922 people

 4.3%
ASIAN

13,000,306 people

 1.6%
TWO OR
MORE
RACES

4,794,461 people

 0.7%
AMERICAN
INDIAN AND
ALASKA
NATIVE

2,041,269 people

 0.1%
NATIVE
HAWAIIAN AND
OTHER PACIFIC
ISLANDER

413,294 people

 0.2%
SOME
OTHER RACE

737,938 people

Note: This map is not geographically representative of population distribution.
Source: U.S. Bureau of the Census 2008b.

today are Native Americans, those whom Christopher Columbus, erroneously supposing he had arrived in India, called Indians.

Before the American Revolution, British, French, and Dutch settlers established colonies in what is now the United States. Some descendants of the French colonists are still to be found in parts of Louisiana. Millions of slaves were brought over from Africa to North America. Huge waves of European, Asian, and Latin American immigrants have washed across the country at different periods since then. The United States is one of the most ethnically diverse countries on the face of the globe. In this section we will pay particular attention to the divisions that have separated whites and nonwhite minority groups, such as African Americans and Hispanic Americans. The emphasis is on *struggle*. Members of these groups have made repeated efforts to defend the integrity of their cultures and advance their social position in the face of persistent prejudice and discrimination from the wider social environment.

EARLY COLONIZATION

The first European colonists in what was to become the United States were actually of quite homogeneous background. At the time of the Declaration of Independence, the majority of the colonial population was of British descent, and almost everyone was Protestant. Settlers from outside the British Isles were at first admitted only with reluctance, but the desire for economic expansion meant having to attract immigrants from other areas. Most came from countries in northwest Europe, such as Holland, Germany, and Sweden; such migration into North America dates initially from around 1820. In the century following, about 33 million immigrants entered the United States. No migrant movement on such a scale had ever been documented, nor has such a migration occurred since.

The early waves of immigrants came mostly from the same countries of origin as the groups already established in the United States. They left Europe to escape economic hardship and religious and political oppression, and because of the opportunities to acquire land as the drive westward gained momentum. As a result of successive potato famines that had produced widespread starvation, 1.5 million people migrated from Ireland. The Irish were accustomed to a life of hardship and despair. In contrast to other immigrants from rural backgrounds, most Irish settled in urban industrial areas, where they sought work.

A major new influx of immigrants arrived in the 1880s and 1890s, this time mainly from southern and eastern Europe—the Austro-Hungarian Empire, Russia, and Italy. Each successive group of immigrants was subject to considerable discrimination on the part of people previously established in the country. Negative views of the Irish, for example, emphasized their supposedly low level of intelligence and drunken behavior. But as they were concentrated within the cities, the Irish Americans were able to organize to protect their interests and gained a strong influence over political life. The Italians and Polish, when they reached America, were in turn discriminated against by the Irish.

Asian immigrants first arrived in the United States in large numbers in the late nineteenth century, encouraged by employers who needed cheap labor in the developing industries of the West. Some two hundred thousand Chinese emigrated in this period. Most were men, who came with the idea of saving money to send back to their families in China, anticipating that they would also later return there. Bitter conflicts broke out between white workers and the Chinese when employment opportunities

Throughout our nation's history, Americans' attitudes toward different racial and ethnic groups have shifted drastically. People's willingness to interact socially with members of different racial and ethnic groups also has changed dramatically over the last century.

For each of the ethnic groups listed below, please indicate on a scale from 1 to 7 how much closeness you find acceptable between you and members of that group: 1 = as close relatives by marriage; 2 = as your close personal friends; 3 = as neighbors on the same street; 4 = as coworkers in your occupation; 5 = as citizens in your country; 6 = as only visitors in your country; 7 = you would exclude them from your country.

RANK

1. Africans
2. African Americans
3. Americans (White)
4. Arabs
5. British
6. Canadians
7. Chinese
8. Cubans
9. Dominicans
10. Dutch
11. Filipinos
12. French
13. Germans
14. Greeks
15. Haitians
16. Indians (Asians)
17. Indians (Native Americans)
18. Irish
19. Italians
20. Jamaicans
21. Japanese
22. Jews
23. Koreans
24. Mexicans
25. Muslims
26. Other Latinos (exc. Mexicans, Puerto Ricans, and Dominicans)
27. Polish
28. Puerto Ricans
29. Russians
30. Vietnamese

TURN PAGE

In 1926, sociologist Emory Bogardus designed the Bogardus Social Distance scale, as a way to measure students' attitudes towards different racial and ethnic groups. His study has been replicated many times, with the overall "mean" level of social distance declining from 2.14 in 1926, to 2.08 in 1956, and 1.93 in 1977. In late September and early October of 2001, the study was replicated once again, among a sample of roughly 3,000 students from 22 colleges and universities throughout the United States. Look below to see how your responses compare (Parillo and Donaghue 2005). How do you think these rank orderings would differ if the study were conducted in 1980? 1960? 1940? 2010? What social or historical forces might have affected study participants' responses?

	Average Closeness Score in 2001	Rank Order (2001) 1 = Most close
1. Africans	1.43	13
2. African Americans	1.33	9
3. Americans (White)	1.07	1
4. Arabs	1.94	30
5. British	1.23	4
6. Canadians	1.20	3
7. Chinese	1.47	17
8. Cubans	1.53	23
9. Dominicans	1.51	21
10. Dutch	1.35	10
11. Filipinos	1.46	16
12. French	1.28	6
13. Germans	1.33	8
14. Greeks	1.33	7
15. Haitians	1.63	27
16. Indians (Asians)	1.60	26
17. Indians (Native Americans)	1.40	12
18. Irish	1.23	5
19. Italians	1.15	2
20. Jamaicans	1.49	19
21. Japanese	1.52	22
22. Jews	1.38	11
23. Koreans	1.54	24
24. Mexicans	1.55	25
25. Muslims	1.88	29
26. Other Latinos	1.45	15
27. Polish	1.45	14
28. Puerto Ricans	1.47	18
29. Russians	1.50	20
30. Vietnamese	1.69	28

Sources: Bogardus 1967; Parillo and Donaghue 2005.

diminished. The Chinese Exclusion Act, passed in 1882, cut down further immigration to a trickle until after World War II.

Japanese immigrants began to arrive not long after the ending of Chinese immigration. They were also subject to great hostility from whites. Opposition to Japanese immigration intensified in the early part of the twentieth century, leading to strict limits, or *quotas*, being placed on the numbers allowed to enter the United States.

Most immigrant groups in the early twentieth century settled in urban areas and engaged in the developing industrial economy. They also tended to cluster in ethnic neighborhoods of their own. Chinatowns, Little Italys, and other clearly defined areas became features of most large cities. The very size of the influx provoked backlash from the Anglo-Saxon segment of the population. One result was the new immigration quotas of the 1920s, which restricted immigration from southern and eastern Europe. Many immigrants found the conditions of life in their new land little better and sometimes worse than the areas from which they originated.

This nineteenth-century cartoon, *Where the Blame Lies*, offers an unflattering portrait of new immigrants and characterizes the discrimination that many new immigrants faced after arriving in the United States.

AFRICAN AMERICANS IN THE UNITED STATES

By 1780, there were nearly 4 million slaves in the American South. Since there was little incentive for them to work, physical punishment was often resorted to. Slaves had virtually no rights in law whatsoever. But they did not passively accept the conditions their masters imposed on them. The struggles of slaves against their oppressive conditions sometimes took the form of direct opposition or disobedience

Immigrant America

If globalization is understood as the emergence of new patterns of interconnection among the world's peoples and cultures, then surely one of the most significant aspects of globalization is the changing racial and ethnic composition of Western societies. In the United States, shifting patterns of immigration since the end of World War II have altered the demographic structure of many regions, affecting social and cultural life in ways that can hardly be overstated. Although the United States has always been a nation of immigrants (with the obvious exception of Native Americans), most of those who arrived here prior to the early 1960s were European.

Throughout the nineteenth and early twentieth centuries, vast numbers of people from Ireland, Italy, Germany, Russia, and other European countries flocked to America in search of a new life, giving a distinctive European bent to American culture. (Of course, until 1808, another significant group of immigrants—Africans—came not because America was a land of opportunity, but because they had been enslaved.) In part because of changes in immigration policy, however, most of those admitted since 1965 have been Asian or Hispanic. In the years 2000 to 2003, for example, of the approximately 4.5 million immigrants who were legally admitted to the United States, almost 1.2 million came from Asia and nearly 2.6 million were from Latin America (U.S. Bureau of the Census 2003b).

There are also an estimated 7 to 11 million illegal immigrants living in the United States, about 70 percent of whom are Mexican (CNN 2003; National Immigration Forum 2006). Thus, as of 2003, more than 53 percent of U.S. residents who were foreign born were from Latin America, and 25 percent were from Asia (U.S. Bureau of the Census 2003b). In contrast, in 1900 almost 85 percent of the foreign born were European (Duignan and Gann 1998).

Most of these new immigrants have settled in six "port-of-entry" states: California, New York, Texas, Illinois, New Jersey, and Massachusetts. These states are attractive to new immigrants not necessarily because

to orders, and occasionally outright rebellion (although collective slave revolts were more common in the Caribbean than in the United States). On a more subtle level, their response took the form of a cultural creativity—a mixing of aspects of African cultures, Christian ideals, and cultural threads woven from their new environments.

of the job opportunities they afford, but because they house large immigrant communities into which newcomers are welcomed (Frey and Liaw 1998). As the flow of Asian and Hispanic immigration continues, and as some nonimmigrants respond by moving to regions of the country with smaller immigrant populations, the percentage of residents of port-of-entry states who are white will continue to drop. California was approximately 52 percent white in 1996; in 2004 this number had dropped to 44.5 percent, and by 2010, it is expected to fall to 40 percent (Maharidge 1996; U.S. Bureau of the Census 2005d). "Other states will follow," Dale Maharidge writes in the book *The Coming White Minority* (1996), "Texas sometime around 2015, and in later years Arizona, New York, Nevada, New Jersey, and Maryland. By 2050 the nation will be almost half nonwhite."

The effect of these demographic changes on everyday social life has been profound. Residents of California's urban centers, for example, fully expect street scenes to be multiethnic in character and would be shocked to visit a state like Wisconsin, where the vast majority of public interactions take place between whites. In some California communities, store and street signs are printed in Spanish or Chinese or Vietnamese, as well as in English. Interracial marriages are on the rise, ethnic restaurants have proliferated, and the schools are filled with nonwhite children. In fact, nonwhites make up two thirds of the undergraduate population at the University of California at Berkeley, where Asian students are on the verge of predominating.

Unfortunately, these changes have exacerbated social tensions. Many white Californians have retreated into prosperous suburban enclaves and have grown resentful of immigrants and nonwhites. Because rates of voter turnout are higher for whites than for other racial groups in the state and because whites control a significant share of the state's wealth, they have managed to pass a number of laws that seek to preserve opportunities for the "coming white minority." Proposition 187, for example, passed in 1994, denied vital public services to illegal immigrants. More recently, the regents of the University of California, in a highly controversial move, decided to abolish affirmative action for the entire nine-campus state university system. Were these decisions based on solid economic and philosophical rationales—the perception that California taxpayers were shouldering too much of the economic burden of illegal immigration or the sense that affirmative action constitutes "reverse discrimination" against whites—or were they motivated principally by *xenophobia*, the fear of immigrants and other persons different from oneself? Whatever the answer, there can be little doubt that immigration—an important aspect of globalization—is changing the face of American society.

Some of the art forms they developed, as in music—for example, the invention of jazz—were genuinely new.

Feelings of hostility toward blacks on the part of the white population were in some respects more strongly developed in states where slavery had never been known than in the South itself. Moral rejection of slavery seems to have been confined to a few more educated groups. The main factors underlying the Civil War were political and economic; most northern leaders were more interested in sustaining the Union than in abolishing slavery, although this was the eventual outcome of the conflict. The formal abolition of slavery changed the real conditions of life for African Americans in the South relatively little. The "black codes"—laws limiting the rights of blacks—placed restrictions on the behavior of the former slaves and punished their transgressions in much the same way as under slavery. Acts were also passed legalizing segregation of blacks from whites in public places. One kind of slavery was thus replaced by another, based on social, political, and economic discrimination.

INTERNAL MIGRATION FROM SOUTH TO NORTH

Industrial development in the North, combined with the mechanization of agriculture in the South, produced a progressive movement of African Americans northward from the turn of the century on. In 1900, more than 90 percent of African Americans lived in the South, mostly in rural areas. Today, less than half of the black population remains in the South; three quarters now live in northern urban areas. African Americans used to be farm laborers and domestic servants, but over a period of little more than two generations, they have become mainly urban, industrial, and service-economy workers. But African Americans have not become assimilated into the wider society in the way in which the successive groups of white immigrants were. They have for the most part been unable to break free from the conditions of neighborhood segregation and poverty that other immigrants faced on arrival. Together with those of Anglo-Saxon origin, African Americans have lived in the United States far longer than most other immigrant groups. What was a transitional experience for most of the later, white immigrants has become a seemingly permanent experience for blacks. In the majority of cities, both South and North, blacks and whites live in separate neighborhoods and are educated in different schools. It has been estimated that 80 percent of either blacks or whites would have to move in order to desegregate housing fully in the average American city.

Martin Luther King, Jr. addresses a large crowd at a civil rights march on Washington in 1963. Born in 1929, King was a Baptist minister, civil rights leader, and winner of the 1964 Nobel Peace Prize. He was assassinated by James Earl Ray in 1968.

THE CIVIL RIGHTS MOVEMENT

Struggles by minority groups to achieve equal rights and opportunities have for a long while been a part of the United States. In contrast to other racial and ethnic minorities, blacks and Native Americans have largely been denied opportunities for self-advancement. The National Association for the Advancement of Colored People (NAACP) and the National Urban League, founded in 1909 and 1910 respectively, fought for black civil rights, but began to have some real effect only after World War II, when the NAACP instituted a campaign against segregated public education. This struggle came to a head when the organization sued five school boards, challenging the concept of separate but equal schooling that then prevailed. In 1954, in *Brown v. Board of Education of Topeka, Kansas*, the U.S. Supreme Court unanimously decided that "separate educational facilities are inherently unequal."

This decision became the platform for struggles for civil rights from the 1950s through the 1970s. The strength of the resistance from many whites persuaded black leaders that mass militancy was necessary to give civil rights any real substance. In 1955, a black woman, Rosa Parks, was arrested in Montgomery, Alabama, for declining to give up her seat on a bus to a white man. As a result, almost the entire African American population of the city, led by a Baptist minister, Martin Luther King, Jr., boycotted the transportation system for 381 days. Eventually the city was forced to abolish segregation in public transportation.

Further boycotts and sit-ins followed, with the object of desegregating other public facilities. The marches and demonstrations began to achieve a mass following of blacks and white sympathizers. In 1963, a quarter of a million civil rights supporters staged a march on Washington and cheered as King announced, "We will not be satisfied until justice rolls down like the waters and righteousness like a mighty stream." In 1964, the Civil Rights Act was passed by Congress and signed into law by President Lyndon B. Johnson, comprehensively banning discrimination in public facilities, education, employment, and any agency receiving government funds. Further bills in following years were aimed at ensuring that African Americans became fully registered voters and outlawed discrimination in housing.

How successful has the civil rights movement been? On one hand, a substantial black middle class has emerged over the last three to four decades. And many African Americans—such as President Barack Obama, the writer Toni Morrison, the literary scholar Henry Louis Gates, media mogul Oprah Winfrey, and rap star Jay-Z—have achieved positions of power and influence in the wider society. On the other hand, a large number of African Americans, making up an underclass, live trapped in the ghettos. Scholars have debated whether the existence of the black underclass has resulted primarily from economic disadvantage or dependency on the welfare system. We will examine the forms of inequality that African Americans and other minority groups continue to experience later in this chapter.

LATINOS IN THE UNITED STATES

The wars of conquest that created the boundaries of the contemporary United States were not only directed against the Native American population but also against Mexico. The territory that later became California, Nevada, Arizona, New Mexico, and Utah—along with a quarter of a million Mexicans—was taken by the United States in 1848 as a result of the American war with Mexico. The terms *Mexican American* and *Chicano* include the descendants of these people, together with subsequent immigrants from Mexico. The term *Latino* refers to anyone from Spanish-speaking regions living in the United States. The words *Latino* and *Hispanic* are often used interchangeably.

The three main groups of Latinos in the United States are Mexican Americans (around 29.2 million), Puerto Ricans (4.1 million), and Cubans (1.6 million). An additional 10.5 million Spanish-speaking residents are from countries in Central and South America and other Hispanic or Latino regions (U.S. Bureau of the Census 2007g). The Latino population, as mentioned earlier, is increasing at an extraordinary rate—by 53 percent between 1980 and 1990, 58 percent between 1990 and 2000, and almost 20 percent from 2002 to 2007—mainly as a result of the large-scale flow of new immigrants from across the Mexican border (U.S. Bureau of the Census 2007g). Latino residents now outnumber African Americans.

MEXICAN AMERICANS

Mexican Americans continue to reside mainly in California, Texas, and the remaining southwestern states, although there are substantial groups in the Midwest and in northern cities. The majority of Mexican immigrants have come to the United States to work at low-paying jobs. In the post–World War II period up to the early 1960s, Mexican workers were admitted without much restriction. This was succeeded by a phase in which numbers were limited and efforts made to deport those who had entered illegally. Illegal immigrants today continue to flood across the border. Large numbers are intercepted and sent back each year by immigration officials, but most simply try again, and it is estimated that four times as many escape officials as are stopped.

Since Mexico is a relatively poor country existing alongside the much wealthier United States, it seems unlikely that this flow of people northward will diminish in the near future. Undocumented immigrants can be employed more cheaply than native-born Americans, and they are prepared to perform jobs that most of the rest of the population would not accept. Legislation was passed by Congress in 1986 making it possible for illegal immigrants who had lived in the United States for at least five years to claim legal residence.

Many Mexican Americans resist assimilation into the dominant English-speaking culture and, in common with other ethnic groups, have increasingly begun to display pride in their own cultural identity within the United States.

PUERTO RICANS AND CUBANS

Puerto Rico was acquired by the United States through war, and Puerto Ricans have been American citizens since 1917. The island is poor, and many of its inhabitants have migrated to the mainland United States to improve their conditions of life. Puerto Ricans originally settled in New York City, but since the 1960s, they have moved elsewhere. A reverse migration of Puerto Ricans began in the 1970s; more have left the mainland than have arrived over the past three decades. One of the most important issues facing Puerto Rican activists is the political destiny of their homeland. Puerto Rico is at present a commonwealth of the United States. As such, Puerto Ricans residing on the island are U.S. citizens, yet they do not pay federal income tax, nor can they vote for the president of the United States. For years, Puerto Ricans have been divided about whether the island should retain its present status, opt for independence, or attempt to become the fifty-first state of the Union.

A third Latino group in the United States, the Cubans, differs from the two others in key respects. Half a million Cubans fled communism following the rise of Fidel Castro in 1959, and the majority settled in Florida. Unlike other Latino immigrants, they were mainly educated people from white-collar and professional backgrounds. They have managed to thrive within the United States, many finding positions comparable to those they abandoned in Cuba. As a group, Cubans have the highest family income of all Latinos.

A further wave of Cuban immigrants, from less affluent origins, arrived in 1980. Lacking the qualifications held by the first wave, these people tend to live in circumstances closer to the rest of the Latino communities in the United States. Both sets of Cuban immigrants are mainly political refugees rather than economic migrants. The later immigrants to a large extent have become the "working class" for the earlier immigrants. They are paid low wages, but Cuban employers tend to take them on in preference to other ethnic groups. In Miami, nearly one third of all businesses are owned by Cubans, and 75 percent of the labor force in construction is Cuban.

THE ASIAN CONNECTION

About 4.4 percent of the population of the United States is of Asian origin—13.2 million people (U.S. Bureau of the Census 2007h). Chinese, Japanese, and Filipinos (immigrants from the Philippines) form the largest groups, but now there are also significant numbers of Asian Indians, Pakistanis, Koreans, and Vietnamese living in America.

In this 1942 photo, young Japanese Americans wait for baggage inspection upon arrival at a World War II Assembly Center in Turlock, California. From here they were transported to one of several internment camps for Japanese Americans.

And as a result of the war in Vietnam, some 350,000 refugees from that country entered the United States in the 1970s.

Most of the early Chinese immigrants settled in California, where they were employed mainly in heavy industries such as mining and railroad construction. The retreat of the Chinese into distinct Chinatowns was not primarily their choice, but was made necessary by the hostility they faced.

The early Japanese immigrants also settled in California and the other Pacific states. During World War II, following the attack on Pearl Harbor by Japan, all Japanese Americans in the United States were made to report to "relocation centers," which were effectively concentration camps, surrounded by barbed wire and gun turrets. In spite of the fact that most of these people were American citizens, they were compelled to live in the hastily established camps for the duration of the war. Paradoxically, this situation eventually led to their greater integration within the wider society, since, following the war, Japanese Americans did not return to the separate neighborhoods in which they had previously lived. They have become extremely successful in reaching high levels of education and income, marginally outstripping whites. The rate of intermarriage of Japanese Americans with whites is now nearly 50 percent.

Following the passing of a new immigration act in 1965, large-scale immigration of Asians into the United States again took place. Foreign-born Chinese Americans today outnumber those brought up in the United States. The newly arrived Chinese have avoided the Chinatowns in which the long-established Chinese have tended to remain, mostly moving into other neighborhoods. ✓

CONCEPT CHECKS ✓

1. According to Figure 10.1, which group is the largest ethnic minority in American society?

2. How did the civil rights movement help minority groups achieve equal rights and opportunities?

HOW DOES RACIAL AND ETHNIC INEQUALITY AFFECT YOUR LIFE?

Since the civil rights movement of the 1960s, has real progress been made in eliminating racial disparities in life chances? Is racial and ethnic inequality primarily the result of a person's racial or ethnic background or does it reflect a person's class position? In other words, is a black American, for example, more likely to live in poverty because of racial discrimination or because of the lower-class status that many blacks hold? In this section, we will first examine the facts: how racial and ethnic inequality is reflected in terms of educational and occupational attainment, income, health, residential segregation, and political power. We will then look at the divergent social statuses found within the largest racial and ethnic groups. We will conclude by looking at how sociologists have sought to explain racial inequality.

EDUCATIONAL ATTAINMENT

Differences between blacks and whites in levels of educational attainment have decreased, but these seem more the result of long-established trends rather than the direct outcome of the struggles of the 1960s. After steadily improving their levels of educational attainment for the last fifty years, young African Americans are for the first time close to whites in terms of finishing high school. The number of blacks over

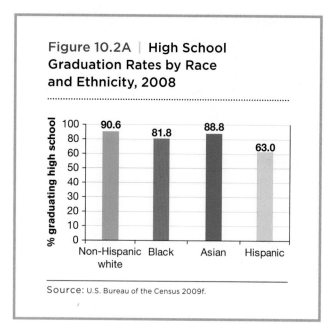

Figure 10.2A | High School Graduation Rates by Race and Ethnicity, 2008

% graduating high school

Non-Hispanic white: 90.6
Black: 81.8
Asian: 88.8
Hispanic: 63.0

Source: U.S. Bureau of the Census 2009f.

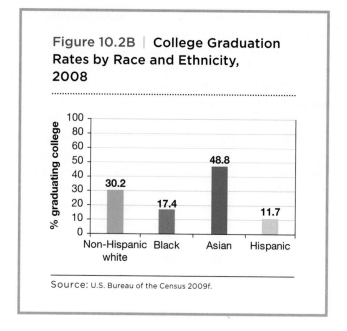

Figure 10.2B | College Graduation Rates by Race and Ethnicity, 2008

% graduating college

Non-Hispanic white: 30.2
Black: 17.4
Asian: 48.8
Hispanic: 11.7

Source: U.S. Bureau of the Census 2009f.

the age of twenty-five with high school degrees has increased from about 20 percent in 1960 to 80.1 percent in 2007 (U.S. Bureau of the Census 2007i). By contrast, almost 87 percent of whites have completed high school (Figure 10.2a). Some analysts see this development as a hopeful sign and an indicator that young blacks need not live a life of hopelessness and despair. But not all signs have been positive. While more blacks are attending college now than in the 1960s, a much higher proportion of whites than blacks graduate from college today. In today's global economy and job market, which value college degrees, the result is a wide disparity in incomes between whites and blacks (see Figure 10.3).

Another negative trend with potentially far-reaching consequences is the large gap in educational attainment between Latinos and both whites and blacks. Hispanics have by far the highest high school dropout rate of any group in the United States. While rates of college attendance and success in graduation have gradually improved for other groups, the rate for Hispanics has held relatively steady since the mid-1980s (Figure 10.2b). Only 12.4 percent hold a college degree (U.S. Bureau of the Census 2008c). It is possible that these poor results can be attributed to the large number of poorly educated immigrants from Latin America who have come to the United States in the last two decades. Many of these immigrants have poor English language skills and their children encounter difficulties in schools. One study found, however, that even among Mexican Americans whose families have lived in the United States for three generations or more, there has been a decline in educational attainment (Bean et al. 1994). For these Hispanics with low levels of education and poor language skills, living in the United States has been "the American nightmare, not the American dream" (Holmes 1997).

EMPLOYMENT AND INCOME

As a result of the increase in educational attainment, blacks now hold a slightly higher proportion of managerial and professional jobs than in 1960, though still not in proportion to their overall numbers. In 2006, out of the approximately 50.4 million managerial

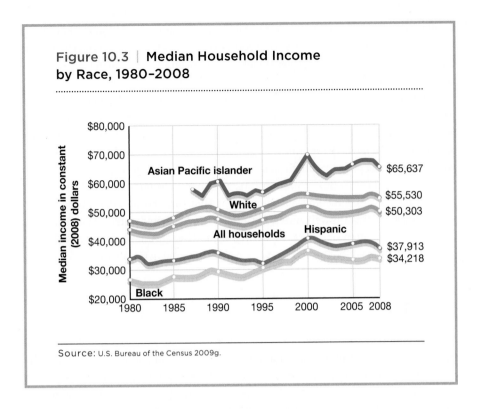

Figure 10.3 | Median Household Income by Race, 1980–2008

Median income in constant (2008) dollars

- Asian Pacific islander — $65,637
- White — $55,530
- All households — $50,303
- Hispanic — $37,913
- Black — $34,218

Source: U.S. Bureau of the Census 2009g.

or professional positions in the United States, whites held about 39.8 million (about 78.9 percent); African Americans, about 4.2 million (about 8.4 percent); and Hispanics, just under 3.3 million (about 6.6 percent) (U.S. Bureau of Labor Statistics 2008a).

The unemployment rate of black and Hispanic men today outstrips that of whites by the same magnitude as in the early 1960s. The total unemployment rate for blacks and Hispanics is higher than that for whites (in 2006, 3.2 percent for whites versus about 6.8 percent for blacks and 4.2 percent for Hispanics) (U.S. Bureau of Labor Statistics 2008a). However this gap is considerably smaller among more educated persons (the unemployment rates with a B.A. degree or more are 2.0, 2.8, and 2.2 for whites, blacks and Hispanics respectively).

There has also been some debate about whether employment opportunities for minorities have improved or worsened, especially in the wake of the 2009 recession. Statistics on unemployment don't adequately measure economic opportunity, since they count only those known to be looking for work. A higher proportion of blacks and Hispanics have simply opted out of the occupational system, neither working nor looking for work. They have become disillusioned by the frustration of searching for employment that is not there. Unemployment figures also do not reflect the increasing numbers of young men from minority groups who have been incarcerated (see also Chapter 6). Finally, although many new jobs were created during the economic boom of the 1990s, most of them either required a college degree or were in lower-paying service occupations. As we just saw, blacks and Hispanics are underrepresented among college graduates.

Nevertheless, the disparities between the earnings of blacks and whites are gradually diminishing. As measured in terms of median weekly income, black men now earn 73.6 percent of the level of pay of white men (U.S. Bureau of Labor Statistics 2009e). In 1959, the proportion was only 49 percent. Black women fare relatively better but still lag behind white women today, earning just 85.1 percent as much. In terms of household family income (adjusted for inflation), blacks are the only social group to have seen an improvement during the 1990s. By 2000, poverty rates for African Americans had fallen to their lowest since the government started tracking the figure in 1955, and they continued to improve for the rest of the decade.

Though the economic status of blacks appears to have improved, prospects for Hispanics have stagnated or worsened over the same time period. Between 2000 and 2005, Hispanic household incomes (adjusted for inflation) decreased significantly. Still, Hispanic household poverty remained very similar to that of blacks. In 2003–2005 the weighted average poverty rate for Hispanics was 20.3 percent, versus 22.4 percent for blacks. The large influx of immigrants, who tend to be poor, has caused some of the decline in average income, but even among Hispanics born in the United States, income levels declined as well. As one Latino group leader commented, "Most Hispanic residents are caught in jobs like gardener, nanny, and restaurant worker that will never pay well and from which they will never advance" (quoted in Goldberg 1997).

HEALTH

Jake Najman recently surveyed the evidence linking health to racial and economic inequalities. After studying data for a number of different countries, including the United States, he concluded that for people in the poorest 20 percent of the income distribution, death rates were 1.5–2.5 times those of the highest 20 percent of income earners. In the United States, the rate of infant mortality for the poorest 20 percent was four times higher than for the wealthiest 20 percent. When differences were measured between the wealthiest whites and the poorest African Americans, the contrast in infant mortality rates was even higher—five times higher for blacks than for whites. The race gap in infant mortality has been increasing rather than decreasing in recent years. The same is true of life expectancy—the average age to which individuals at birth can expect to live. In 2007, whites on average could expect to live 5.3 years longer than African Americans (National Center for Health Statistics 2007b).

How might the influence of poverty and ethnicity on health be countered? Extensive programs of health education and disease prevention are one possibility. But such programs tend to work better among more prosperous, well-educated groups and in any case usually produce only small changes in behavior. Increased accessibility to health services would help, but probably to a limited degree. The only really effective policy option, it is argued, would be to attack poverty itself, so as to reduce the income gap between rich and poor (Najman 1993).

RESIDENTIAL SEGREGATION

Neighborhood segregation seems to have declined little over the past quarter century. Studies show that discriminatory practices toward black and white clients in the housing market continue (Pager and Shepard 2008). Black and white children now attend the same schools in most rural areas of the South and in many of the smaller- and medium-size cities throughout the country. Most black college students now also go to the same colleges and universities as whites, instead of the traditional all-black institutions (Journal of Blacks in Higher Education 2007). Yet in the larger cities a high level of educational segregation persists as a result of the continuing movement of whites to suburbs or rural environs.

In *American Apartheid* (1993), Douglas Massey and Nancy A. Denton argue that the history of racial segregation and its specific urban form, the black ghetto, are responsible for the perpetuation of black poverty and the continued polarization of black and white. The persistence of segregation, they say, is not a result of impersonal market forces. Even many middle-class blacks still find themselves segregated from white society. For them, as for poor blacks, this becomes a self-perpetuating cycle. Affluent blacks who can afford to live in comfortable, predominantly white neighborhoods may deliberately choose not to, because of the struggle for acceptance they know they would face. The black ghetto, the authors conclude, was constructed through a series of well-defined institutional practices of racial discrimination—private behavior and public policies by which whites sought to contain growing urban black populations. Until policy makers, social scientists, and private citizens recognize the crucial role of such institutional discrimination in perpetuating urban poverty and racial injustice, the United States will remain a deeply divided and troubled society.

Barack Obama became the first African American president of the United States in the historic election of 2008.

POLITICAL POWER

Barack Obama made history when he was elected the first black president of the United States in 2008. His election is part of a larger trend of blacks making tremendous gains in holding elective offices; the number of black public officials increased from forty in 1960 to 9,101 in 2000 (Bositis 2001). The numbers of black mayors and judges have increased appreciably. Blacks have been voted into every major political office, including in districts where white voters predominate. In 1992, after congressional districts were reshaped to give minority candidates more opportunity, a record number of African Americans and Latinos were elected to Congress. Yet these changes are still relatively small scale; blacks account for fewer than 2 percent of the elective offices in the country, and most of these are relatively minor local positions (Bositis 2001). The share of representation that Latinos and African Americans have in Congress is not proportional to their overall numbers in American society. Currently there are forty-one black members of the U.S. House of Representatives; but following the defeat of Senator Carol Moseley-Braun in 1998, the U.S. Senate had no black members until Barack Obama was elected to represent Illinois in 2004. Currently, Roland Burris, also from Illinois, is the only black member in the U.S. Senate (Black Americans in Congress 2009). In addition, three Latinos—Ken Salazar from Colorado, Bob Menendez from New Jersey, and Mel Martinez from Florida—serve in the U.S. Senate. These were the first in three decades. And Martinez is the first Cuban American to be elected to the Senate in its history (National Association of Latino Elected and Appointed Officials [NALEO] 2004).

GENDER AND RACE

The status of minority women in the United States is especially plagued by inequalities. Gender and race discrimination combined make it particularly difficult for these women to escape conditions of poverty. They share the legacy of past discrimination against members of minority groups and women in general. Until about twenty-five years ago, most minority women worked in low-paying occupations such as household work, farm work, or low-wage manufacturing jobs. Changes in the law and gains in education have allowed for more minority women to enter white-collar professions, and their economic and occupational status has improved.

Between 1979 and 2006, inflated-adjusted earnings of black women grew by 19 percent, but this increase lagged behind white women, who experienced a 29 percent increase in earnings during the same period (U.S. Bureau of the Census 2007e). Although women have made strides in earnings in the past three decades, stark race and gender earnings disparities persist. In 2009, among full-time workers, white women earned about 79 percent as much as their male counterparts, Hispanic women about 89 percent, and black women had earnings that were about 91.5 percent of their male counterparts'. In actual dollars, black women who worked full time earned just $567 per week in 2009, compared to $666 for white women, $620 for black men, and $842 for white men (U.S. Bureau of Labor Statistics 2009c).

However unequal their status and pay, minority women play a critical role in their communities. They are often the major or sole wage earners in their families. Yet their incomes are not always sufficient to maintain a family. About half of all families headed by African American or Latino women live at poverty levels.

DIVERGENT FORTUNES

When we survey the development and current position of the major ethnic groups in America, one conclusion that emerges is that they have achieved varying levels of success. Whereas successive waves of European immigrants managed to overcome most of the prejudice and discrimination they originally faced and become assimilated into the wider society, other groups have not. These latter groups include two minorities that have lived in North America for centuries, Native Americans and African Americans, as well as Mexicans and Puerto Ricans.

THE ECONOMIC DIVIDE WITHIN
THE AFRICAN AMERICAN COMMUNITY

The situation of blacks is the most conspicuous case of divergent fortunes. A division has opened up between the minority of blacks who have obtained white-collar, managerial, or professional jobs—who form a small black middle class—and the majority whose living conditions have not improved. In 1960, most of the nonmanual-labor jobs open to blacks were those serving the black community—a small proportion of blacks could work as teachers, social workers, or less often, lawyers or doctors. No more than about 13 percent of blacks held white-collar jobs, contrasted to 44 percent of whites. Although there has been significant progress in the fortunes of blacks over the past five decades, pronounced racial differences persist. For example, in 2008, African Americans were still underrepresented in white-collar jobs. Although blacks account for roughly 12.4 percent of the U.S. population, they held 8.3 percent of all managerial, professional or related occupations and 11.2 percent of all sales and office occupations (U.S. Bureau of Labor Statistics 2008a).

THE ASIAN SUCCESS STORY

Unlike African Americans, other minority groups have outlasted the open prejudice and discrimination they once faced. The changing fate of Asians in the United States is especially remarkable. Until about half a century ago, the level of prejudice and discrimination experienced by the Chinese and Japanese in North America was greater than for any other group of nonblack immigrants. Since that time, Asian Americans have achieved a steadily increasing prosperity and no longer face the same levels of antagonism from the white community. The median income of Asian Americans is now actually higher than that of whites.

This statistic conceals some big discrepancies between and within different Asian groups; there are still many Asian Americans, including those whose families have resided in the United States for generations, who live in poverty. For example, in 1999, the overall poverty rate among Asians was 12.6. However, rates varied widely, from just 9.7 percent among Japanese to 37.8 percent among Hmong, an ethnic group from Laos and surrounding areas (Reeves and Bennett 2004). However, the turnaround in the fortunes of Asian Americans is on the whole so impressive that some have referred to the Asian American "success story" as a prime example of what minorities can achieve in the United States.

LATINOS: A TALE OF TWO CITIES

Miami and Los Angeles both have large Latino populations. In Los Angeles, the large majority of Latinos are well down the ladder of privilege and power. But although both cities experience ethnic tensions, in Miami Latinos have achieved a position of economic and political prominence not found elsewhere.

Hundreds of thousands of people marched in Los Angeles on May 1, 2006, to demand basic rights for immigrants.

In Miami, those of Cuban origin have often moved into positions of considerable influence. Some Cubans have become very successful in business and have become more wealthy than the "old" white families that once ran the city. They haven't been assimilated into the white community but maintain their own customs, institutions, and language. Miami is now a place of "parallel structures" existing alongside one another, each including powerful and wealthy people, not integrated into one unified group. There is much tension, but some Anglo and Cuban politicians now speak of Miami as the capital of the Caribbean—a city not only part of the United States, but looking also to the other societies, mostly developing countries, surrounding it.

Los Angeles has been referred to as "the capital of the Third World" because of its large Latino and Asian populations. The city already contained the largest group of Mexicans in the United States in the 1920s. Then, as now, it was Mexicans who performed most of the menial jobs. Then, as now, most Anglos "were at once aware that this was the case," and "yet they would act as if these people, once they had finished working, went home not to the Old Plaza or, as now, to East L.A., but to another planet" (Rieff 1991).

UNDERSTANDING RACIAL INEQUALITY

What distinguishes less fortunate groups such as African Americans and Mexican Americans is not just that they are nonwhite, but that they were originally present in America as colonized peoples rather than willing immigrants. In a classic analysis, Robert Blauner (1972) suggested that a sharp distinction should be drawn between groups who journeyed voluntarily to settle in the new land and those who were incorporated into the society through force or violence. Native Americans are part of American society as a result of military conquest; African Americans were transported in the slave trade; Puerto Rico was colonized as a result of war; and Mexicans were originally incorporated as a result of the conquest of the Southwest by the United States in the nineteenth century. These groups have consistently been the target of racism, which both reflects and perpetuates their separation from other ethnic communities.

But, given that this has been the case for most of American history, what explains the growth of the black middle class? William Julius Wilson (1978; see also Wilson et al. 1987) has argued that race is of diminishing importance in explaining inequalities between whites and blacks. In his view, these inequalities are now based on class rather than skin color. The old racist barriers are crumbling. What remain are inequalities similar to those affecting all lower-class groups.

Are racial inequalities to be explained primarily in terms of class? It is true that racial divisions provide a means of *social closure*, whereby economic resources can be monopolized by privileged class groups. But the argument that racial inequality should be explained primarily in terms of class domination has never been a satisfactory one. Ethnic discrimination, particularly of a racial kind, is partly independent of class differences: The one cannot be separated from the other. This still seems to remain true in the United States today. ✓

CONCEPT CHECKS ✓

1. What are some of the main reasons there is a large gap in educational attainment between Hispanics and blacks in the United States?

2. How do Massey and Denton explain the persistence of residential segregation?

3. Some sociologists argue that racial inequalities should be explained in terms of class rather than race. What are some of the problems associated with social class–based explanations of racial inequalities?

NEED HELP STUDYING?

⊕ **wwnorton.com/studyspace**

Visit StudySpace to access free review materials such as:

- Vocabulary Flashcards
- Diagnostic Review Quizzes
- Study Outlines

REVIEW QUESTIONS

1. What are the similarities and differences between concepts of ethnicity and race? Give an example to illustrate the complexity of these definitions.
2. Describe two examples of racial classification systems. What do these examples tell us about the socially constructed nature of race?
3. Compare and contrast the definitions of prejudice, discrimination, and racism. Give examples of each.
4. What is the relationship between colonialism and contemporary ethnic conflict? How does globalization intensify ethnic conflict?
5. What are some possible strategies for combating racism?
6. What are the key characteristics of a diaspora? Give an example of a diasporic community and show how this fits the characteristics described in the text.
7. Describe two theories that sociologists use to explain racial inequality. What explanation do you find most convincing and why?

THINKING SOCIOLOGICALLY ESSAY QUESTIONS

1. Review the discussion of the assimilation of different American minorities, then write a short essay comparing the different assimilation experiences of Asians and Latinos. In your essay identify the criteria for assimilation and discuss which group has assimilated most readily. Then explain the sociological reasons for the difference in assimilation between these two groups.
2. Does affirmative action still have a future in the United States? On the one hand, increasing numbers of African Americans have joined the middle class by earning college degrees, professional jobs, and new homes. Yet blacks are still far more likely than whites to live in poverty, to attend poor schools, and to lack economic opportunity. Given these differences and other contrasts mentioned in the text, do we still need affirmative action?

11

Families and Intimate Relationships

THE BIG QUESTIONS

HOW DO SOCIOLOGICAL THEORIES CHARACTERIZE FAMILIES?

Review the development of sociological thinking about families and family life.

HOW HAVE FAMILIES CHANGED OVER TIME?

Learn how families have changed over the last three hundred years. See that although a diversity of family forms exist in different societies today, widespread changes are occurring that relate to the spread of globalization.

WHAT DO MARRIAGE AND FAMILY IN THE UNITED STATES LOOK LIKE TODAY?

Learn about patterns of marriage, childbearing, and divorce. Analyze how different these patterns are today compared with other periods.

WHY DOES FAMILY VIOLENCE HAPPEN?

Learn about sexual abuse and violence within families.

HOW DO NEW FAMILY FORMS AFFECT YOUR LIFE?

Learn some alternatives to traditional marriage and family patterns that are becoming more widespread.

Are families around the world in a state of crisis? Or are they simply changing to keep pace with rapid economic, technological, and social changes in the world? In the United States, sociologists David Popenoe and Judith Stacey offer very different perspectives on the future of families. Popenoe, a Rutgers University professor emeritus, argues that families have changed for the worse since 1960. In the last fifty years, divorce, nonmarital births, and cohabitation rates have increased, while marriage and marital fertility rates have decreased. Taken together, these trends are at the root of countless social ills, including child poverty, adolescent pregnancy, substance abuse, and juvenile crime. Increasing rates of divorce and nonmarital births have created millions of female-headed households and have consequently removed men from the child-rearing process. Popenoe (1993, 1996) argues that this is harmful for children.

Stacey, a professor at New York University, counters that the "traditional" American family of the 1950s—praised by Popenoe and conservative politicians as the panacea for all social problems—is an outdated and oppressive institution. According to Stacey (1990, 1993, 1996), the "modern family"—made up of a "breadwinner father and childrearing mother"—perpetuated the "segregation of the sexes by extracting men from, and consigning white married women to, an increasingly privatized domestic domain." The modern family has been replaced by a variety of new family forms, which Stacey calls the "post-modern family." The postmodern family is marked by diversity, flexibility, and change and may include single mothers, *blended families* (remarried families in which both spouses bring children from their prior marriages), cohabiting couples, lesbian and gay partners, and dual-worker families. For Stacey, the relevant question is not whether the postmodern family is superior or inferior to the traditional two-parent family. Rather, she believes this family diversity is partly a sensible adaptation to economic changes and that the "traditional" American family no longer reflects either the cultural or statistical norm of what families look like. Like it or not, according to Stacey, family diversity is here to stay.

Stacey and Popenoe also fail to see eye to eye on which arrangement is best for the kids. Popenoe maintains that "on the whole, two parents—a father and a mother—are better for a child than one parent." Fathers offer a strong male role model to sons; they act as disciplinarian for trouble-prone children; they provide their daughters with a male perspective on heterosexual relationships; and by playing with their children, they teach them about teamwork, competition, independence, self-fulfillment, self-control, and controlling one's emotions. Mothers, alternatively, teach their children about communion, or the feeling of being connected to others. Both needs must be met and can best be achieved through the gender-differential parenting of a mother and father, argues Popenoe.

Stacey retorts that research demonstrates that no single family structure is superior to all the others for raising kids. There is no going back to the modern family, because employment has shifted from jobs in heavy industry to those in nonunionized clerical, service, and new industrial sectors. The loss of union-protected jobs means that many men no longer earn enough to single-handedly support a wife and children. At the same time, employers' need for clerical and service labor, escalating consumption standards, increases in women's educational attainment, and the persistence of high divorce rates have given more and more women reason to seek paid employment outside the home.

Stacey also takes issue with media rhetoric and claims by conservatives such as Popenoe that elevate the married, two-parent family as the ideal family form. The more they elevate marriage, says Stacey, the more they stigmatize and discriminate against the unmarried in every family form. Rather than condemning nontraditional family forms, Stacey reasons that family sociologists and policy makers should instead develop strategies to mitigate the harmful effects of divorce and single parenthood on children. She suggests that restructuring work schedules and benefits policies to accommodate the needs of working parents, reducing unemployment rates, enacting comparable-worth standards of pay equity to enable women as well as men to earn a family wage, providing universal health, prenatal, and child care, and sex education, and rectifying the economic inequities of divorce would be much more admirable and effective efforts. These child-friendly efforts, she argues, are truly pro-family.

Popenoe's policy recommendations are guided by the belief that "marriage must be established as a strong social institution." He argues that employers should reduce the practice of relocating married couples with children and should provide more generous parental leave. He also supports a two-tiered system of divorce law. Marriages without minor children would be relatively easy to dissolve, but marriages with young children would be dissolved only by mutual agreement or on the grounds that clearly involve a wrong by one party against the other. The proposal has been met by skepticism among feminist scholars, who believe that reinstating grounds of fault for divorce will take a toll on children and parents alike.

The changes affecting the personal and emotional spheres go far beyond the borders of any particular country, even one as large as the United States. We find many of the same issues almost everywhere, differing only in degree and according to the cultural context in which they take place. Among all the changes going on today, none are more important than those happening in our personal lives—in sexuality, emotional life, marriage, and family.

Like much of sociology, studies of marriage and family in the United States encompass a range of kinds of scholarship. Some researchers, such as Stacey and Popenoe, draw on their own and others' research to advocate for political, social, and/or economic change—albeit from different perspectives. But a vast majority of researchers restrict themselves to doing descriptive or scientific work that tries to solve some of the most interesting puzzles about marriage and family in the contemporary world. Taken together, the work of these researchers is fascinating and demonstrates that sociology can give us insights that are by no means obvious.

BASIC CONCEPTS

In light of these debates over the changing nature of families, let's define some basic concepts. A **family** is a group of persons directly linked by kin connections, the adult members of which assume responsibility for caring for children. **Kinship** refers to connections between individuals, established either through marriage or through the lines of descent that connect blood relatives (mothers, fathers, offspring, grandparents, etc.). **Marriage** can be defined as a socially and legally acknowledged and approved sexual union between two adult individuals. When two people marry, they become kin to one another; the marriage bond also, however, connects together a wider range of kinspeople. Parents, brothers, sisters, and other blood relatives become relatives of the partner through marriage.

family • A group of individuals related to one another by blood ties, marriage, or adoption, who form an economic unit, the adult members of which are responsible for the upbringing of children. All known societies involve some form of family system, although the nature of family relationships varies widely. While in modern societies the main family form is the nuclear family, extended family relationships are also found.

kinship • A relation that links individuals through blood ties, marriage, or adoption. Kinship relations are by definition part of marriage and the family, but extend much more broadly. While in most modern societies few social obligations are involved in kinship relations extending beyond the immediate family, in other cultures kinship is of vital importance to social life.

marriage • A socially and legally approved relationship between two individuals. Marriage almost always involves two persons of opposite sexes, but in some cultures, types of homosexual marriage are tolerated. Marriage normally forms the basis of a family of procreation—that is, it is expected that the married couple will produce and bring up children. Some societies permit polygamy, in which an individual may have several spouses at the same time.

(a) An extended Kazak family in Mongolia. Kazaks usually live in extended families and collectively herd their livestock. The youngest son will inherit the father's house, and the elder sons will build their own houses close by when they get married. (b) Parents wait for the train with their daughter. How is a nuclear family different from an extended family?

nuclear family • A family group consisting of an adult or adult couple and their dependent children.

extended family • A family group consisting of more than two generations of relatives.

family of orientation • The family into which an individual is born or adopted.

family of procreation • The family an individual initiates through marriage or by having children.

matrilocal family • A family system in which the husband is expected to live near the wife's parents.

patrilocal family • A family system in which the wife is expected to live near the husband's parents.

monogamy • A form of marriage in which each married partner is allowed only one spouse at any given time.

polygamy • A form of marriage in which a person may have two or more spouses simultaneously.

polygyny • A form of marriage in which a man may have two or more wives simultaneously.

polyandry • A form of marriage in which a woman may have two or more husbands simultaneously.

In virtually all societies, sociologists and anthropologists have documented the presence of the **nuclear family**, two adults living together in a household with their own or adopted children. In most traditional societies, the nuclear family was part of a larger kinship network of some type. When close relatives in addition to a married couple and children live either in the same household or in a close and continuous relationship with one another, we speak of an **extended family**. An extended family might, for example, include grandparents, brothers and their wives, sisters and their husbands, aunts, and nephews.

Families also can be divided into **families of orientation** and **families of procreation**. The first is the family into which a person is born; the second is the family into which one enters as an adult and within which a new generation of children is brought up. A further important distinction concerns place of residence. In the United States, when a couple marries, they are usually expected to set up an independent household, separate from either spouse's family of orientation. This can be in the same region in which the bride's or groom's parents live, but may be in some different town or city altogether. In some other societies, however, everyone who marries is expected to live close to or within the same dwelling as the parents of the bride or groom. When the couple lives near or with the bride's parents, the arrangement is called **matrilocal**. In a **patrilocal** pattern, the couple lives near or with the parents of the groom.

In Western societies, marriage, and therefore family, is associated with **monogamy**. It is illegal for a man or woman to be married to more than one individual at any one time. But in many parts of the world, monogamy is far less common than it is in Western nations. In his classic research, George Murdock (1967) compared several hundred societies throughout much of the twentieth century and found that **polygamy**, a marriage that allows a husband or wife to have more than one spouse, was permitted in over 80 percent (see also Gray 1998). There are two types of polygamy: **polygyny**, in which a man may be married to more than one woman at the same time, and **polyandry**, much less common, in which a woman may have two or more husbands simultaneously.

HOW DO SOCIOLOGICAL THEORIES CHARACTERIZE FAMILIES?

Sociologists with diverse theoretical orientations have studied family life. Many of the perspectives that prevailed just a few decades ago now seem much less convincing in the light of recent research and important changes in the social world. Nevertheless it is valuable to trace briefly the evolution of sociological thinking before turning to contemporary approaches to studying families.

FUNCTIONALISM

The functionalist perspective sees society as a set of social institutions that perform specific functions to ensure continuity and consensus. According to this perspective, families perform important tasks that contribute to society's basic needs and helps to perpetuate the existence of major social institutions and practices. Sociologists working in the functionalist tradition have regarded the nuclear family as fulfilling certain specialized roles in modern societies. With the advent of industrialization, families became less important as a unit of economic production and more focused on reproduction, child rearing, and socialization.

According to the American sociologist Talcott Parsons, the family's two main functions are *primary socialization* and *personality stabilization* (Parsons and Bales 1955). **Primary socialization** is the process by which young children learn the cultural norms of the society into which they are born. **Personality stabilization** refers to the role that families play in assisting adult family members emotionally. Marriage between adult men and women is the arrangement through which adult personalities are supported and kept healthy. In industrial society, the role of the family in stabilizing adult personalities is said to be critical. This is because the nuclear family is often distanced from its extended kin and is unable to draw on larger kinship ties as families could before industrialization.

Parsons regarded the nuclear family as the unit best equipped to handle the demands of industrial society. In the "conventional family," one adult can work outside the home while the second adult cares for the home and children. In practical terms, this specialization of roles within the nuclear family involved the husband adopting the "instrumental" role as breadwinner and the wife assuming the "affective," emotional role in domestic settings.

Parsons's view of the family is now widely regarded by sociologists as inadequate and outdated. Functionalist theories of families have come under heavy criticism for justifying the domestic division of labor between men and women as something natural and unproblematic. Yet Parsons's views reflect the historical period in which he was living and working. The immediate post–World War II years saw women returning to their traditional domestic roles and men reassuming positions as sole breadwinners. We can criticize functionalist views of the family on other grounds, however. In emphasizing the importance of families in performing certain functions, Parsons and other functionalist theorists neglect the role that other social institutions—such as government, media, and schools—play in socializing children. Functionalist theories also neglect variations in family forms that do not correspond to the model of the nuclear family. Families that did not conform to the white, suburban, middle-class "ideal" were seen as deviant.

FEMINIST APPROACHES

For many people, families provide a vital source of solace and comfort, love and companionship. Yet the family can also be a locus for exploitation, loneliness, and profound inequality. Feminism has had a great impact on sociology by challenging the vision of the family as a harmonious and egalitarian realm. In the 1960s, one of the first dissenting voices was that of the American feminist Betty Friedan, who wrote of "the problem with no name"—the isolation and boredom that gripped many suburban American housewives, who felt relegated to an endless cycle of child care and housework.

During the 1970s and 1980s, feminist perspectives dominated most debates and research on families. If previously the sociology of family had focused on family structures, the historical development of the nuclear and extended family, and the importance of kinship ties, feminism succeeded in directing attention inside families to examine the experiences of women in the domestic sphere. Many feminist writers have questioned the vision of the family as a cooperative unit based on common interests and mutual support. They have sought to show that the presence of unequal power relationships within families means that certain family members tend to benefit more than others.

primary socialization • The process by which children learn the cultural norms of the society into which they are born. Primary socialization occurs largely in the family.

personality stabilization • According to the theory of functionalism, the family plays a crucial role in assisting its adult members emotionally. Marriage between adult men and women is the arrangement through which adult personalities are supported and kept healthy.

Feminist writings have emphasized a broad spectrum of topics, but three main themes are of particular importance. One of the central concerns is the *domestic division of labor*—the way in which tasks are allocated among members of a household. Feminist sociologists have undertaken studies on the way domestic tasks, such as child care and housework, are shared between men and women. Findings have shown that women continue to bear the main responsibility for domestic tasks and enjoy less leisure time than men, despite the fact that more women are working in paid employment outside the home than ever before (Hochschild and Machung 1989; Gershuny et al. 1994; Sullivan 1997). Pursuing a related theme, some sociologists have examined the contrasting realms of paid and unpaid work, focusing on the contribution that women's unpaid domestic labor makes to the overall economy (Oakley 1974). Others have investigated the way in which resources are distributed among family members and the patterns of access to and control over household finances (Pahl 1989).

Second, feminists have drawn attention to the *unequal power relationships* that exist within many families. One topic that has received increased attention as a result of this is the phenomenon of domestic violence. Wife battering, marital rape, incest, and the sexual abuse of children have all received more public attention as a result of feminists' claims that the violent and abusive sides of family life have long been ignored in both academic contexts and legal and policy circles. Feminist sociologists have sought to understand how families serve as an arena for gender oppression and even physical abuse.

The study of *caring activities* is a third area in which feminists have made important contributions. This is a broad realm that encompasses a variety of processes, from child care to elder care. Sometimes caring means simply being attuned to someone else's psychological well-being—several feminist writers have been interested in "emotion work" within relationships. Not only do women tend to shoulder concrete tasks such as cleaning and child care, but they also invest large amounts of emotional labor in maintaining personal relationships (Duncombe and Marsden 1993). While caring activities are grounded in love and deep emotion, they are also a form of work that demands an ability to listen, perceive, negotiate, and act creatively.

NEW PERSPECTIVES IN THE SOCIOLOGY OF FAMILY

In the past decade, an important body of sociological literature on families has emerged that draws on feminist perspectives but is not strictly informed by them. Of primary concern are the larger transformations that are taking place in family forms—the formation and dissolution of families and households and the evolving expectations within individuals' personal relationships. The rise in divorce and single parenting, the emergence of "reconstituted families" and gay families, and the popularity of cohabitation are all subjects of concern, among conservative political and religious groups. Yet these transformations cannot be understood apart from the larger changes occurring in our society. Attention must be paid to the shifts occurring at the societal, and even global, level if we are to grasp the link between personal transformations and larger patterns of change. ✓

CONCEPT CHECKS ✓

1. According to the functionalist perspective, what are two main functions of families?

2. According to feminist perspectives, what three aspects of family life are sources of concern? Why are these three aspects troubling to feminists?

HOW HAVE FAMILIES CHANGED OVER TIME?

Sociologists once thought that prior to the modern period, the extended family was the predominant form of family in Western Europe. Research has shown this view to be mistaken. The nuclear family seems long to have been preeminent. Premodern household size was larger than it is today, but the difference is not especially great. In the United States, for example, throughout the seventeenth, eighteenth, and nineteenth centuries, the average household size was 4.75 persons. The current average is 2.60 (U.S. Bureau of the Census 2007j). Since the earlier figure includes domestic servants, the difference in family size is small.

"THE WAY WE NEVER WERE": MYTHS OF THE TRADITIONAL FAMILY

Was the family of the past as peaceful and harmonious as many people recall it, or is this simply an idealized fiction? As Stephanie Coontz points out in her book *The Way We Never Were* (1992), as with other visions of a golden age of the past, the rosy light shed on the "traditional family" dissolves when we look back to previous times to see what things really were like.

Popular lore depicts the family of colonial America as disciplined and stable, the ideal arrangement. However, colonial families suffered from the same disintegrative forces as their counterparts in Europe. Especially high death rates meant that the average length of marriages was less than twelve years, and more than half of all children saw the death of at least one parent by the time they were twenty-one. The admired discipline of the colonial family was rooted in the strict authority of parents over their children. The way in which this authority was exercised would be considered exceedingly harsh by today's standards.

In the Victorian period, wives were more or less forcibly confined to the home. According to Victorian morality, women were supposed to be strictly virtuous, while men were sexually licentious: Many visited prostitutes and paid regular visits to brothels. Spouses often had little to do with one another, communicating only through their children. Moreover, domesticity wasn't even an option for poorer groups of this period. African American slaves in the South lived and worked in what were frequently appalling conditions. In the factories and workshops of the North, families worked long hours with little time for home life. Child labor was also rampant in these groups.

Our most recent memory draws us to the 1950s as the time of the ideal American family. This was a period when large numbers of white middle-class women worked only in the home, while men were responsible for earning a family wage. Yet large numbers of women didn't actually want to retreat to a purely domestic role and felt unfulfilled and trapped. Women had held paid jobs during World War II as part of the war effort. They lost these jobs when men returned from the war. Moreover, men were still emotionally removed from their wives and often observed a strong sexual double standard, seeking sexual adventures for themselves but setting strict codes for their spouses.

Betty Friedan's best-selling book *The Feminine Mystique* first appeared in 1963, but its research referred to the 1950s. Friedan struck a chord in the hearts of thousands of women when she spoke of the "problem with no name": the oppressive nature of a

Balancing Family and Work

How many hours each week did your parents spend doing paid work when you were growing up? Did their commitment to work affect the way you or your siblings were raised? One of the ways globalization has affected family life in the United States is by increasing the amount of time that people spend each week at work. While there is some disagreement among researchers as to whether Americans, on average, are putting in more hours at work now than they did in the past, many sociologists give credence to the findings of the economist Juliet Schor, author of the 1992 book *The Overworked American.* Schor argued that workers in the 1980s and 1990s spent on average 164 more hours each year at work than they did twenty years earlier. Recent studies confirm that this high number of work hours persists today. Workers are also taking less vacation time than they did in earlier decades.

Perhaps more significant, the percentage of mothers who are working full time has increased dramatically since the end of World War II. In a comprehensive study of the multiple roles that modern women occupy, Daphne Spain and Suzanne Bianchi (1996) found that the group of women that saw the most dramatic increase in labor force participation in the United States were married women with young children. Taken together, these facts suggest that parents today have less time available to spend with their children than they did in decades past. As a result, there has been a significant increase in the percentage of children enrolled in day-care programs—and, some would argue, a palpable increase in tension and stress

within families as more of the day-to-day parental role is offloaded onto child-care providers.

In her book *The Time Bind* (1997), sociologist Arlie Hochschild suggests that these developments may be related to globalization. Globalization is not, of course, responsible for the gains women have made in securing positions in the paid labor force. Nevertheless, some corporations, according to Hochschild, have responded to the pressures of global competition by encouraging their salaried employees to put in longer hours at work, in order to increase levels of productivity. Why would employees willingly agree to spend so much time at their jobs—often considerably more than forty hours each week—when they are not paid to do so, when they know that such a commitment disrupts their family life, and

domestic life bound up with child care, domestic drudgery, and a husband who only occasionally put in an appearance and with whom little emotional communication was possible.

CHANGES IN FAMILY PATTERNS WORLDWIDE

Just as family structure and family life has shifted over the past three centuries, family life has also been transformed across the globe. In some areas, such as more in an age when computerization has greatly improved workplace efficiency? Shouldn't technological progress allow workers to spend more time with their families rather than less? Hochschild's answer to this question is that some corporations rely on the power of workplace norms to elicit a greater time commitment from their workers. New employees are socialized into a corporate culture in which working long hours is seen as a badge of dedication and professionalism. Employees, seeking status and the approval of their peers and supervisors, become motivated to put as much time into work as possible and to make sure that those around them know precisely how much time they spend working. In some cases, such a corporate culture has arisen unintentionally, as workers respond to the threat of corporate downsizing by redoubling their commitment to the organization. In other cases—as with the corporation Hochschild studied—executives have consciously sought to shape the culture of the organization, reminding employees through handbooks, speeches, and newsletters that working more than forty hours a week is the mark of a "good" worker.

Although globalization has touched all the nations of the world, its effects on work time seem to vary by country. In France and Germany, for example, workers—sometimes acting through unions, sometimes making their power known at the voting booth—have rejected corporate calls for a longer workweek, and are instead pressuring employers to reduce the workweek and to grant longer vacations. Do Europeans simply value family and leisure time more than Americans? Or would American workers be making the same demands if unions were stronger in this country?

remote regions in Asia, Africa, and the Pacific Rim, traditional family systems are little altered. In most developing countries, however, widespread changes are occurring. The origins of these changes are complex, but several factors can be picked out as especially important. One is the spread of Western culture. Western ideals of romantic love, for example, have spread to societies in which they were previously unknown. Another factor is the development of centralized government in areas previously composed of autonomous smaller societies. People's lives become influenced by their involvement in a national political system; moreover, governments make active attempts to alter traditional ways of behaving. Because of the problem of rapidly expanding population growth, states frequently introduce programs advocating smaller families, for example, promoting the use of contraception.

A further influence is the large-scale migration from rural to urban areas. Often men go to work in towns or cities, leaving family members in the home village. Alternatively, a nuclear-family group will move as a unit to the city. In both cases, traditional family forms and kinship systems may become weakened. Finally, and perhaps most important, employment opportunities away from the land and in such organizations as government bureaucracies, mines, plantations, and—where they exist—industrial firms tend to have disruptive consequences for family systems previously centered on landed production in the local community.

In general, these changes are creating a worldwide movement toward the predominance of the nuclear family, breaking down extended-family systems and other types of kinship groups. This was first documented by William J. Goode in his book *World Revolution in Family Patterns* (1963), and subsequent research has shown that these changes continue.

DIRECTIONS OF CHANGE

Families are being transformed throughout the globe today. Sociologists have identified seven important changes that characterize global family change over the past half-century.

1. *Clans,* or small family groups based on shared heredity, and other types of kin groups are declining in their influence.
2. There is a general trend toward the free choice of a spouse.
3. The rights of women are becoming more widely recognized, in respect to both the initiation of marriage and decision making within families.
4. Kin marriages are becoming less common.
5. Higher levels of sexual freedom are developing in societies that were very restrictive.
6. Birth rates are declining, meaning that women are giving birth to fewer babies.
7. There is a general trend toward the extension of children's rights.

In many countries, especially Western industrial societies, the nuclear family has been the preeminent family form. Given the ethnically diverse character of the United States, there are considerable variations in family and marriage within the country, some of the most striking of which are the differences between white and African American family patterns. We will consider the reasons for these differences, and then move on to examine divorce, remarriage, and stepparenting in relation to contemporary patterns of family life. ✓

CONCEPT CHECKS ✓

1. Briefly describe changes in family size over the past three centuries.

2. How has Stephanie Coontz dispelled the myth of the peaceful and harmonious family believed to exist in past decades?

3. Give two examples of problems facing families in past centuries.

4. What are four conditions that have contributed to changing family forms throughout the world?

5. How has migration from rural to urban areas affected family life?

6. What are the six most important changes occurring in families worldwide?

WHAT DO MARRIAGE AND FAMILY IN THE UNITED STATES LOOK LIKE TODAY?

The United States has long been characterized by high marriage rates. Over 96 percent of adults sixty-five years or over are or have previously been married (U.S. Bureau of the Census 2009h). The age at which people first marry has, however, risen over the past half-century. In 1960, the average age of first marriages was 22.8 for men and 20.3 for women. The comparable ages in 2005 were 27 for men and 26 for women (National Marriage Project 2005). Another way of measuring the relation between age and first marriage is to look at the proportion of people who remain unmarried before a certain age (Figure 11.1). Thus, in 1960, just 28 percent of women younger than 24 years had never married. In 2008, that proportion was more than 88 percent.

There are several explanations for this trend in the last several decades toward later marriage. First, increases in cohabitation among younger people account for the decreases (or delays) in marriage among this group. Young people are cohabiting before or instead of marrying. Second, increases in postsecondary school enrollment, especially among women, are partially responsible for delays in marriage. Third, women's increased participation in the labor force often leads to delays in marriage as women work to establish their careers before marrying and starting a family (Oppenheimer 1988). Labor force participation also increases economic independence among women. By earning their own income, many women no longer need a male breadwinner in their home. The flip side of the economic independence argument is the idea that the deterioration of men's economic position since the late 1980s has made them less attractive mates and less ready to marry. Some researchers have used this idea—the "marriageable men" hypothesis—to explain the especially low marriage rates among blacks: Because black men have suffered the worst economic conditions in the last few decades, they might be viewed by black women as particularly poor marriage candidates. Finally, some researchers believe that modernization, changing gender roles,

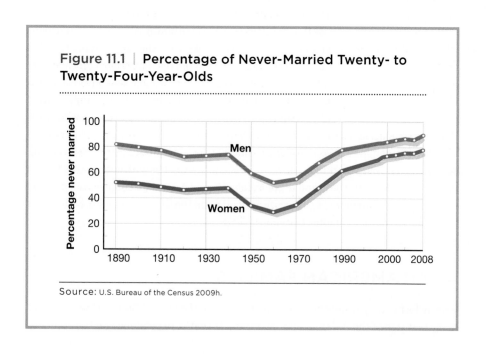

Figure 11.1 | Percentage of Never-Married Twenty- to Twenty-Four-Year-Olds

Source: U.S. Bureau of the Census 2009h.

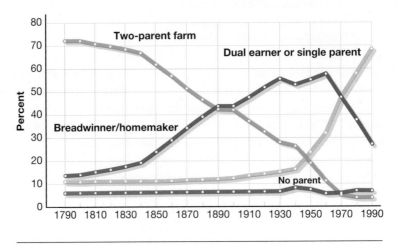

Figure 11.2 | The Changing Structure of American Families with Children

Percentage of American children seventeen and younger living in each of four types of families, 1790–1990.

Source: Hernandez 1993.

and a shift in attitudes that promote individualism make marriage less important than it once was.

An extraordinary increase in the proportion of people living alone in the United States has also taken place over recent years—a phenomenon that partly reflects the high levels of marital separation and divorce. More than one in every four households (28 percent) now consists of one person, a rise of 44 percent since 1960 (U.S. Bureau of the Census 2009i). There has been a particularly sharp rise in the proportion of individuals living alone in the twenty-four-to-forty-four age bracket.

Some people still suppose that the average American family is made up of a husband who works in paid employment and a wife who looks after the home, living together with their two children. This is very different from the real situation: Only about 25 percent of children live in households that fit this picture. One reason is the rising rate of divorce: A substantial proportion of the population live either in single-parent households or in stepfamilies. Another is the high proportion of women who work. Dual-career marriages and single-parent families are now the norm (see Figure 11.2). The majority of married women working outside the home also care for a child or children. Although many working women are concentrated in jobs with poor or nonexistent promotion prospects, the standard of living of many American couples is dependent on the income contributed by the wife, as well as on the unpaid work she undertakes in the home (see also Chapter 13).

ASIAN AMERICAN FAMILIES

Family forms vary widely by race and ethnicity in the United States. One of the primary features of the Asian American family is that of dependence on the extended family. In many Asian cultures, family concerns are often a priority over individual concerns. Family members' interdependence also helps Asian Americans prosper financially. Asian American family and friend networks often pool money to help their members start a business or buy a house. This help is reciprocated as more of the recipients who prosper as a result then contribute to other family members. The result is a median family income for Asian Americans that is higher than that of the median for non-Hispanic whites.

Asian Americans are a heterogeneous group, however, and vary widely in terms of other family patterns. Chinese American and Japanese American women have much lower fertility rates than do any other racial/ethnic group. Chinese, Japanese, and Filipino families have lower levels of nonmarital fertility than all other racial/ethnic groups, including non-Hispanic whites. Low levels of nonmarital fertility combined with low levels of divorce for most Asian American groups demonstrate the emphasis on marriage as the appropriate forum for family formation and maintenance.

NATIVE AMERICAN FAMILIES

Kinship ties are also very important in Native American families. As Cherlin (2005) notes, "kinship networks constitute tribal organization; kinship ties confer identity" for Native Americans. However, fewer than half of all Native Americans live on or near tribal lands, so for those who live in cities or away from reservations, kin ties may be less significant. Furthermore, Native Americans have higher rates of intermarriage than any other racial/ethnic group. In 1990, less than half of all married Native Americans were married to other Native Americans (Sandefur and Liebler 1997).

The Native American fertility experience is similar to that of African Americans. Native American women have a high fertility rate and a high percentage of nonmarital fertility; 64.6 percent of all Native American women giving birth in 2006 were not married (CDC 2009a). Sandefur and Liebler (1997) also report a high divorce rate for Native Americans.

LATINO FAMILIES

Hispanics, like Asian Americans, are very heterogeneous when it comes to family patterns—with particular difference documented between Mexican, Cuban, and Puerto Rican American families. Statistically, Mexican American families are characterized by multigenerational households and a high birthrate. Mexican American families are typically better off financially than Puerto Rican families but less well off than Cuban families. Defying cultural stereotypes of a Mexican American home with a male breadwinner and female homemaker, more than half of all Mexican American women are in the labor force (Ortiz 1995). Still, ethnographic research indicates that this is due to necessity rather than desire. Many Mexican American families say that the breadwinner-homemaker model would be their preference but that they are constrained by finances (Hurtado 1995).

Although Puerto Rico is a U.S. commonwealth, Puerto Ricans are still considered part of the umbrella category of Hispanics. However, because of their status as U.S. citizens, Puerto Ricans can and do move about freely between Puerto Rico and the mainland without the difficulties often encountered by immigrants. Researchers have shown that when barriers to immigration are high, only the most able (physically, financially, and so on) members of a society will be able to leave their homeland

and move to another country. Because Puerto Ricans do not face as many barriers, even the least able can manage the migration process. The economic upshot of unrestricted migration for Puerto Ricans is that they are the most economically disadvantaged of all the major Hispanic groups living in the United States. Puerto Rican American families are also characterized by a higher percentage of children born to unmarried mothers than any other Hispanic group—57.8 percent in 2006 (CDC 2009b); only African Americans (70.2 percent) and Native Americans (64.6 percent) had higher rates of births to unmarried women (CDC 2009a). However, *consensual unions*—cohabiting relationships in which couples consider themselves married but are not legally married—are often the context for births to unmarried mothers. Many Puerto Ricans respond to tough economic times by forming consensual unions as the next best option to what is often a much more expensive legal marriage (Landale and Fennelly 1992).

Cuban American families are the most prosperous of all the Hispanic groups, but are still less prosperous than whites. Most Cuban Americans have settled in the Miami area and have formed immigrant enclaves in which they rely on other Cubans for their business and social needs (e.g., banking, schools, and shopping). The relative wealth of Cuban Americans is driven largely by family business ownership. In terms of childbearing, Cuban Americans have lower levels of fertility than non-Hispanic whites and equally low levels of nonmarital fertility.

AFRICAN AMERICAN FAMILIES

White and black family patterns differ dramatically. Blacks have higher rates of childbearing outside of marriage, they are less likely to ever marry, and they are also less likely to marry after having a nonmarital birth. These differences are of particular interest to sociologists because single parenthood is associated with high rates of poverty in the United States (Harknett and McLanahan 2004).

In 2008, married couples accounted for 79 percent of all white families but just 46.7 percent of black families (Figure 11.3) (U.S. Bureau of the Census 2009j). Throughout most of the twentieth century, black families were more likely than white families to be headed by a female. In 1960, 21 percent of African American families were headed by females; among white families, the proportion was 8 percent. By 2008, the proportion for black families had risen to more than 44.7 percent, while that for white families was 14.8 percent (U.S. Bureau of the Census 2009j). Female-headed families are more prominently represented among poorer blacks. One social condition of the current era that has exacerbated this situation is a shortage of "marriageable" black men. Research shows persuasively that women are most likely to marry—even after the birth of a child—when they live in a labor market that provides suitable employment opportunities for men (Harknett and McLanahan 2004).

But we should not see the situation of African American families purely in a negative light. When white anthropologist Carol Stack (1975) was a young doctoral student, she entered a black ghetto community in Illinois to study the support systems that poor black families form. Living in the community

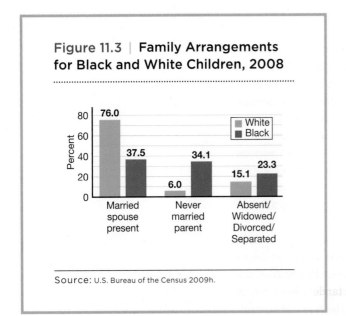

Figure 11.3 | Family Arrangements for Black and White Children, 2008

Source: U.S. Bureau of the Census 2009h.

and getting to know the kinship system from the inside, she demonstrated that families adapted to poverty by forming large, complex support networks. Thus a mother heading a one-parent family is likely to have a close and supportive network of relatives to depend on. A far higher proportion of female-headed families among African Americans have other relatives living with them than do white families headed by females. Social scientists disagree about the implications of this family arrangement, however. Stack suggests that extended family provides important support and assistance to single mothers. Yet more recent data suggests that multigenerational families may pose strains and demands on their members, especially among the economically disadvantaged (Cain and Combs-Orme 2005).

CLASS AND THE AMERICAN FAMILY

While Stack's arguments were specifically geared toward explaining racial differences in the organization of the extended family, contemporary researchers examining similar questions have concluded that "the differences between black and white extended family relationships are mainly due to contemporary differences in social and economic class positions of group members. Cultural differences are less significant" (Sarkisian and Gerstel 2004).

This leads to an interesting question: Are racial differences in family formation primarily due to economic or cultural factors? One of the problems with the culture-class debate is that there is little research on middle-class black families or low-income white families, which makes it difficult to think about whether cultural factors or structural factors are driving racial differences in terms of family formation.

One recent book by Kathryn Edin and Maria Kefalas (2005) offers insightful glimpses into the ways that social class affects the family lives of low-income women. Specifically, the authors conducted interviews with 165 low-income single mothers in black and white neighborhoods, to uncover why low-income women continue to have children out of wedlock, when they can hardly afford to do so. The women of all races whom they interviewed valued and revered marriage, but they believed that if they married their current partners, they might end up divorced or in an unhappy marriage. As one woman told them in an interview, "I'd rather say I had a child out of wedlock than that I married this idiot."

Edin and Kefalas offer three additional explanations for why poor women often have children out of wedlock. First, young women in poor communities feel confident about their ability to raise children, because most were themselves raised in social environments where young people are typically involved in raising the other kids in a family or in one's neighborhood. Second, the poor place an extremely high value on children, perhaps even higher than that of middle-class families, at least in part because they have fewer things to make their lives meaningful. Finally, many women in the study reported that having a child actually saved their lives, bringing order to an otherwise chaotic life.

DIVORCE AND SEPARATION

Divorce rates increased steadily through the latter half of the twentieth century, yet they have plateaued in recent years. Attitudes have changed in tandem, with a stark decline in the proportion of Americans who disapprove of divorce.

Figure 11.4 | Divorce Rates in the United States

Source: U.S. Bureau of the Census 2010a; National Center for Health Statistics 2008e.

Divorce rates, calculated by looking at the number of divorces per thousand married men or women per year, have fluctuated in the United States in different periods (Figure 11.4). They rose, for example, following World War II, then dropped off before climbing to much higher levels. The divorce rate increased steeply from the 1960s to the late 1970s, reaching a peak in 1980 (thereafter declining somewhat). It used to be common for divorced women to move back to their parents' homes after separation; today, most set up their own households.

Divorce exerts a powerful impact on the lives of children, although the vast majority of children of divorce fare well in the years after their parents' divorce. About one half of children born in 1980 became members of a one-parent family at some stage in their lives. Since two thirds of women and three fourths of men who are divorced eventually remarry, most of these children nonetheless grew up in a two-parent family. Less than 4 percent of children under eighteen in the United States today are not living with either parent (U.S. Census 2009k). The remarriage figures are substantially lower for African Americans: Only 32 percent of black women and 55 percent of black men who divorce remarry within ten years (Bramlett and Mosher 2002). Black children are half as likely as white children to be living with both parents or one parent and a stepparent (35 percent versus 74 percent).

The economic well-being of women and children declines in the immediate aftermath of divorce. According to a 1996 study, the living standards of divorced women and their children on average fell by 27 percent in the first year following the divorce settlement. The average standard of living of divorced men, by contrast, rose by 10 percent. Most court judgments left the former husband with a high proportion of his income intact; therefore, he had more to spend on his own needs than while he was married (Peterson 1996). The main reason for the gender gap is that women typically earn less than men and take time out of the labor market to raise children. Many cannot return to work, or cannot easily secure high-paying jobs upon divorcing.

Of special interest to family demographers is the fact that the women with the most resources—especially education—are increasingly following trajectories that provide their children with greater resources, primarily by delaying fertility and being more involved in the labor market. In contrast, women who have the fewest resources—low levels of educational attainment or few economic resources—are increasingly following a trajectory of early fertility and infrequent employment. These different trajectories are problematic because they lead to even higher levels of inequality in the future educational, economic, and health experiences of children (McLanahan 2004).

REASONS FOR DIVORCE

Why did divorce rates increase so steeply in the 1960s and 1970s? First, changes in the law have made divorce easier. Second, except for a small proportion of wealthy people, marriage today no longer has much connection with the desire to perpetuate property and status from generation to generation. Third, as women become more economically independent, marriage is less of a necessary economic partnership. Greater overall prosperity means that it is easier to establish a separate household in case of marital disaffection (Lee 1982). Fourth, the stigma of divorce has declined, thus removing a psychological obstacle to marital dissolution. Fifth, adults now place a great value on personal satisfaction in marriage; few are motivated to remain in a relationship that provides few emotional rewards (Cherlin 1990).

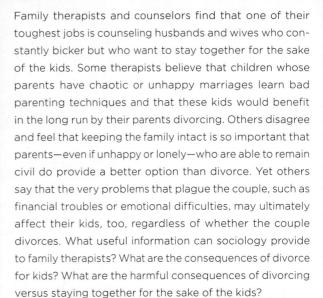

Making Sociology Work
FAMILY THERAPIST

Family therapists and counselors find that one of their toughest jobs is counseling husbands and wives who constantly bicker but who want to stay together for the sake of the kids. Some therapists believe that children whose parents have chaotic or unhappy marriages learn bad parenting techniques and that these kids would benefit in the long run by their parents divorcing. Others disagree and feel that keeping the family intact is so important that parents—even if unhappy or lonely—who are able to remain civil do provide a better option than divorce. Yet others say that the very problems that plague the couple, such as financial troubles or emotional difficulties, may ultimately affect their kids, too, regardless of whether the couple divorces. What useful information can sociology provide to family therapists? What are the consequences of divorce for kids? What are the harmful consequences of divorcing versus staying together for the sake of the kids?

DIVORCE AND CHILDREN

The effects of divorce on children are difficult to gauge. How contentious the relationship is between the parents prior to separation, the age of a child at the time, whether or not there are siblings, the availability of grandparents and other relatives, the child's relationship with her individual parents, and how frequently she continues to see both parents can all affect the process of adjustment. Since children whose parents are unhappy with each other but stay together may also be affected, assessing the consequences of divorce for children is doubly problematic.

Some of the earliest studies of divorce consequences were based on clinical samples, that is, populations of people seeking counseling; these found that children often suffer a period of marked emotional anxiety following the separation of their parents. Judith Wallerstein and Joan Kelly studied 131 children of sixty families in Marin County, California, following the separation of the parents. They contacted the children at the time of the divorce, a year and a half after, and five, ten, and fifteen years later. Almost all the children experienced intense emotional disturbance at the time of the divorce. Preschool-age children were confused and frightened, tending to blame themselves for the separation. Older children were better able to understand their parents' motives for divorce but frequently worried about its effects on their future and expressed sharp

Tomeryl Collier and her mother, Cheryl Ellis, sit on Tomeryl's bed. Cheryl and her husband planned on getting a divorce but stayed together for several years for Tomeryl. They are now divorced.

feelings of anger. At the end of the five-year period, however, the researchers found that two thirds were coping reasonably well with their home lives and their commitments outside. A third remained dissatisfied with their lives, were subject to depression, and expressed feelings of loneliness, even in cases where the parent with whom they were living had remarried (Wallerstein and Kelly 1980).

At the ten- and fifteen-year follow-up interviews, the now–young adult children of divorce said they brought memories and feelings of their parents' divorce into their own romantic relationships. Most hoped for something their parents had failed to achieve—a good, committed marriage based on love and faithfulness. Nearly half the group entered adulthood as "worried, underachieving, self-deprecating, and sometimes angry young men and women." Those who appeared to manage the best were often helped by supportive relationships with one or both parents (Wallerstein and Blakeslee 1988). We cannot say, of course, how the children might have fared if their parents had stayed together. The parents and children studied all came from an affluent white area and might or might not be representative of the wider population. Moreover, they were a clinical sample. Those who actively seek counseling might be less (or more) able to cope with separation than those who do not.

A more recent study found that the majority of persons whose parents had divorced did not have serious mental health problems. They did find small differences in mental health between those whose parents divorced and those whose parents stayed together (favoring those whose parents stayed together), but much of this difference in mental health had been identified in children at age seven, before any of the families experienced divorce (Cherlin et al. 1998). In other words, the purportedly harmful effects of divorce could reflect the harmful experiences for children of living with fighting parents. One of the most prominent family sociologists in the United States, Andrew Cherlin, has argued that these are the general effects of divorce on children:

- Almost all children experience an initial period of intense emotional upset after their parents separate.

DO-IT-YOURSELF SOCIOLOGY

D.I.Y.

When couples marry, they vow to love and support each other "until death do us part." Yet an estimated 35 to 40 percent of couples who marry will ultimately divorce. Sociologists have identified a number of factors that are associated with one's risk of divorce. Of the characteristics listed below, check off those that describe you (or that you expect will be true of you, once you marry). Turn the page to discover whether your risk of divorce is higher or lower than average.

	YES	NO
1. Married at a young age (under age 21)		
2. Have divorced parents		
3. Lived with your romantic partner prior to marrying		
4. Have been divorced at least once		
5. Had a child prior to marrying		
6. Have a childless marriage		
7. Knew your partner for a short time prior to marrying		
8. Experience financial hardship		
9. Have less than a college degree		
10. You and your partner are similar with respect to social class background, age, and religion		
11. You or your partner is depressed		
12. You or your partner frequently drinks alcoholic beverages		
13. You fear disapproval from family and friends		
14. You believe married people should stay together "for the sake of the kids"		

- Most resume normal development without serious problems within about two years after the separation.
- A minority of children experience some long-term problems as a result of the breakup that may persist into adulthood (Cherlin 1999).

REMARRIAGE AND STEPPARENTING

Odd though it might seem, the best way to maximize the chances of marriage, for both sexes, is to have been married previously. People who have been married and divorced are more likely to marry again than single people in similar age groups are to marry for the first time. At all age levels, divorced men are more likely to remarry than divorced

Demographers and family sociologists have documented a number of factors that affect one's likelihood of divorcing (White 1990). These findings are not deterministic: Many children of divorced parents go on to have happy stable marriages. On average, however, their risk of divorce is higher than that of their peers whose parents were stably married. Look below to see which factors increase or decrease divorce risk.

	IF YOU CHECKED YES:
1. Married at a young age (under age 21)	Increase risk
2. Have divorced parents	Increase risk
3. Lived with your romantic partner prior to marrying	Increase risk
4. Have been divorced at least once	Increase risk
5. Had a child prior to marrying	Increase risk
6. Have a childless marriage	Increase risk
7. Knew your partner for a short time prior to marrying	Increase risk
8. Experience financial hardship	Increase risk
9. Have less than a college degree	Increase risk
10. You and your partner are from a similar social class background, age, and religion	Decrease risk
11. You or your partner are depressed	Increase risk
12. You or your partner frequently drinks alcoholic beverages	Increase risk
13. You fear disapproval from family and friends	Decrease risk
14. You believe married people should stay together "for the sake of the kids"	Decrease risk

women. Two in every three divorced women remarry, but three in every four divorced men eventually marry again. Many divorced individuals also choose to cohabit instead of remarry.

A **stepfamily** is a family in which at least one of the adults is a stepparent. Official statistics usually define stepfamilies more specifically as those in which the children *reside* with at least one stepparent; there are many more families in which children regularly visit stepparents. Stepfamilies bring into being kinship ties that resemble those of some traditional societies but that are new in Western countries. Children may now have two "mothers" and two "fathers"—their natural parents and their stepparents, or two same-sex parents in a committed relationship.

Members of stepfamilies are finding their own ways of adjusting to the relatively uncharted circumstances in which they find themselves. Perhaps the most appropriate

stepfamily • A family in which at least one partner has children from a previous marriage.

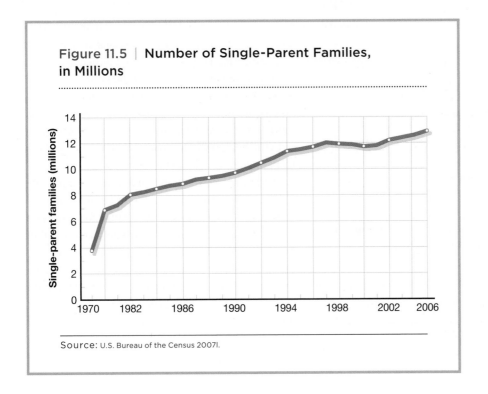

Figure 11.5 | **Number of Single-Parent Families, in Millions**

Source: U.S. Bureau of the Census 2007l.

conclusion to be drawn is that while marriages are broken up by divorce, families on the whole are not. Especially where children are involved, ties persist.

SINGLE-PARENT HOUSEHOLDS

Single-parent households have become increasingly common (Figure 11.5). As a result of the increase in rates of divorce and nonmarital births, about one half of all children spend some time in their lives in a single-parent family (Furstenberg and Cherlin 1991). The vast majority are headed by women, since the mother usually obtains custody of the children following a divorce (in a small proportion of single-parent households, the individual, again almost always a woman, has never been married) There were 11.6 million single-parent households in the United States in 2008, 9.8 million single-mother and 1.8 million single-father families. Such households comprise one in three (34 percent) of all families with dependent children (U.S. Bureau of the Census 2009l).

Most people do not wish to be single parents, but a growing minority choose to become so, setting out to have a child or children without the support of a spouse or partner. "Single mothers by choice" is an apt description of some parents, normally those who possess sufficient resources to manage satisfactorily as a single-parent household. For the majority of unmarried or never-married mothers, however, the reality is different: There is a high correlation between the rate of births outside marriage and indicators of poverty and social deprivation. As we saw earlier, these influences are very important in explaining the high proportion of single-parent households among families of African American background in the United States.

A debate exists among sociologists about the impact on children of growing up with a single parent. The most exhaustive set of studies carried out to date, by Sara McLanahan and Gary Sandefur, rejects the claim that children raised by only one parent do just as well as children raised by both parents. A large part of the reason

Anne Stevenson poses for a portrait with her son Reece in front of her off-campus housing when, as a single parent, she attended Tufts University. She graduated and still heads a group fighting for single parents' rights. Single parents attending college often have trouble finding affordable places to live since most schools do not offer family housing or daycare.

is economic—the sudden drop in income associated with divorce. But about half of the disadvantage comes from inadequate parental attention and lack of social ties. Separation or divorce weakens the connection between child and father, as well as the link between the child and the father's network of friends and acquaintances. On the basis of wide empirical research, the authors conclude that it is a myth that there are usually strong support networks or extended family ties available to single mothers (McLanahan and Sandefur 1994).

Others have been quick to point out that, although children who grow up in a single-parent home are on average disadvantaged, it is better for children's mental health if parents in extremely high-conflict marriages divorce than stay together (Amato et al. 1995). This suggests that divorce may benefit children growing up in high-conflict marriages but may harm children whose parents have relatively low levels of marital conflict before divorcing. ✓

CONCEPT CHECKS ✓

1. Briefly describe changes in family structure in the United States since 1960.

2. Contrast both general and nonmarital fertility rates among whites, blacks, Hispanics, Asians, and Native Americans in the United States.

3. According to Edin and Kefalas, why do many low-income women have babies out of wedlock?

4. What are the main reasons divorce rates increased sharply during the latter half of the twentieth century?

5. How does divorce affect the well-being of children?

WHY DOES FAMILY VIOLENCE HAPPEN?

Family relationships—between wife and husband, parents and children, brothers and sisters, or more distant relatives—can be warm and fulfilling. But they can equally be full of the most extreme tension, driving people to despair or imbuing them with a deep sense of anxiety and guilt. Family discord can take many forms. Among the most devastating in their consequences, however, are the incestuous abuse of children and domestic violence.

FAMILY VIOLENCE

Violence within families is perpetrated primarily by men. The two broad categories of family violence are *child abuse* and *spousal abuse*. Because of the sensitive and private nature of violence within families, it is difficult to obtain national data on levels of domestic violence. Data on child abuse is particularly sparse because of the issues of cognitive development and ethical concerns involved in studying child subjects.

CHILD ABUSE

Definitions of child abuse vary widely, but experts agree that it encompasses serious physical harm (such as physical beatings or severe physical punishment, sexual abuse with injury, or willful malnutrition) with intent to injure. One national study of married or cohabiting adults indicates that about 3 percent of respondent adults abused their children in 1993; cohabiting adults are no more or less likely to abuse their children than married couples (Brown 2004; Sedlak and Broadhurst 1996).

Studies based on parents self-report may underreport the frequency of abuse, as parents may be reluctant to report such problematic behaviors. As a result, most studies of abuse are based on national surveys of child welfare professionals. These surveys may fail to include abused children who are not seen by professionals and thus are not reported to state agencies. Researchers estimate that as many as 50 to 60 percent of child deaths from abuse or neglect are not recorded (U.S. Department of Health and Human Services [DHHS] 2004b). However, studies based on the reports of child welfare professionals remain the most widely used sources of information on child abuse.

The most recent statistics based on the National Child Abuse and Neglect Reporting System, a data resource of the U.S. Department of Health and Human Services, estimate that in 2007 there were about 794,000 reported child victims of abuse or neglect. Of these, 59 percent suffered neglect, 10.8 percent suffered physical abuse, 4.2 percent suffered from emotional maltreatment, and 7.6 percent were sexually abused (DHHS 2009a). Over 80 percent of child abuse or neglect cases are perpetrated by the child's parents, another 4.8 percent by other relatives of the victim.

The highest child victimization rates were for children up to three years old. Researchers concur that child abuse occurs more frequently in low-income families and single-parent families, due in part to high levels of parental stress. Moreover, because economically disadvantaged persons are more likely to live in apartments and densely population neighborhoods, incidences of abuse also are more likely to be noticed and reported by neighbors or social workers.

SPOUSAL ABUSE

A 1988 study by Richard Gelles and Murray Straus found that 16 percent of married persons reported at least one incidence of spousal violence in the prior year, and 28 percent reported that they had at some time in their lives experienced spousal violence. These aggregate statistics do not, however, distinguish between severe acts, such as beating up and threatening with or using a gun or knife, and less severe acts of violence, such as slapping, pushing, grabbing, or shoving one's spouse. When the authors disaggregated this number, they found that approximately 3 percent of all husbands admitted to perpetrating at least one act of severe violence on their spouse in the last year, and this is likely to be an underestimate of actual occurrence.

Straus and his colleagues also reported a finding that has been widely discussed and debated: that equal proportions of women and men reported that they perpetrated spousal abuse. This lies in stark contrast to much of the literature based on crime statistics, hospital records, and shelter administrative records, sources that all indicate that spousal violence is almost exclusively man-on-woman violence.

Michael Johnson (1995) was able to untangle these inconsistencies. Johnson recognized that the data that were generating such conflicting findings were collected from two very different samples. In the shelter samples, respondents are generally women who were severely beaten by their husbands or partners. The severity of their situation drew them to a shelter. On the other hand, those responding to a national survey are generally living in their homes and have the time, energy, or wherewithal to complete a survey. It is unlikely that individuals who are experiencing extreme violence in the home would respond to a national survey. Furthermore, it is unlikely that those who experience less severe kinds of violence (e.g., slapping) will end up in a domestic violence shelter. Therefore, these are two very different groups of people.

CONCEPT CHECKS ✓

1. How do social scientists measure and track patterns of child abuse?

2. Describe gender differences in patterns of spousal abuse.

Johnson argued that the spousal abuse in the two samples was accordingly different in character. He referred to the extreme abuse experienced by many in the shelter samples as "patriarchal terrorism." This type of violence is perpetuated by feelings of power and control. The type of violence reported in national surveys is referred to as "common couple violence." This type of violence is generally reactive to a specific incident and is not rooted in power or control. ✓

HOW DO NEW FAMILY FORMS AFFECT YOUR LIFE?

COHABITATION

cohabitation • Two people living together in a sexual relationship of some permanence, without being married to one another.

If current statistics are any indicator, at least half of all students reading this textbook will live with their romantic partner before marrying. **Cohabitation**—in which a couple lives together in a sexual relationship without being married—has become increasingly widespread in most Western societies. The number of young couples who cohabit has risen steeply (Figure 11.6), from 11 percent in the early 1970s to 44 percent in the early 1980s and probably about 50 percent today (Cherlin 1999; National Center for Health Statistics 2005a). By age thirty about 50 percent of women will have cohabited outside marriage (Bramlett and Mosher 2002).

Cohabitation has become widespread among college and university students, although they were not the initiators of this trend, as many people believe. Bumpass, Sweet, and Cherlin (1991) found that the cohabitation phenomenon started with lower-educated groups in the 1950s because they did not have the economic resources to marry.

While for some cohabitation may be a substitute for marriage, for many it is viewed as a stage in the process of relationship building that precedes marriage. Young people come to live together usually by drifting into it, rather than through calculated planning. A couple who are already having a sexual relationship spend more and more time together, eventually giving up one of their individual homes. The close connection between cohabitation and marriage for many is indicated in Figure 11.7, which shows that the most important reason for cohabiting for both women and men is so that "couples can be sure they are compatible before marriage."

Most cohabiting couples either marry or stop living together, although the chances of a cohabiting union transitioning to a first marriage is related to a number of socioeconomic factors. For instance, the probability that the first

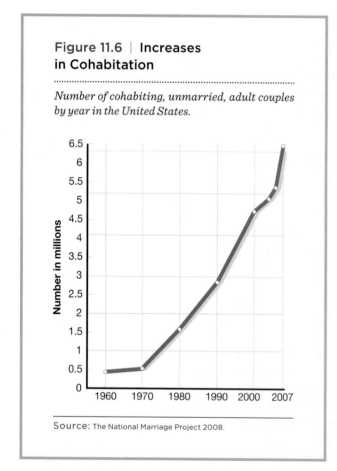

Figure 11.6 | Increases in Cohabitation

Number of cohabiting, unmarried, adult couples by year in the United States.

Source: The National Marriage Project 2008.

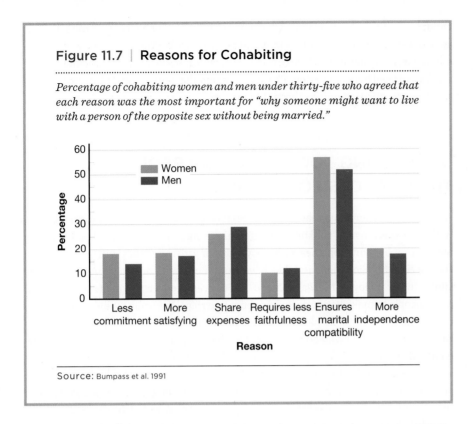

Figure 11.7 | Reasons for Cohabiting

Percentage of cohabiting women and men under thirty-five who agreed that each reason was the most important for "why someone might want to live with a person of the opposite sex without being married."

Source: Bumpass et al. 1991

cohabitation will become a marriage within five years is 75 percent for white women, but only 61 percent for Hispanic women and 48 percent for black women. Similarly, the likelihood of a first marriage resulting from cohabitation is positively associated with higher education, the absence of children during cohabitation, and higher family income. It is also more likely in communities with low male unemployment rates (Bramlett and Mosher 2002). Although many view cohabitation as a precursor to marriage, for a large number of people, it does not end in marriage. Only about 35 percent of cohabitors married their partners within three years of starting to live together. Increasingly, we are seeing evidence that cohabitation is not necessarily a "stage in the process" between dating and marriage, but rather it may be an end in itself for an increasing number of cohabitors.

The United States is certainly not alone in the increasing prevalence of cohabitation. Many European countries are experiencing similar, and in some cases much greater, proportions of unions beginning with cohabitation rather than marriage. The Northern European countries of Denmark, Sweden, and Finland, along with France, show particularly high rates of cohabitation. However, unions in the southern European countries of Spain, Greece, and Italy—along with Ireland and Portugal—still largely begin with marriage.

Just as young adults are more likely than ever before to cohabit prior to marriage, young children are more likely than ever before to live with parents who are cohabiting but who are not legally married to one another. A recent Pew survey finds that about half of all nonmarital births are to cohabiting couples (Taylor et al 2007), although this pattern varies widely by race and ethnicity. In 2002, among first births to Hispanic women, one in five occurred within cohabiting unions, compared with one in ten of first births to white women and one in seven first births to black women (CDC 2006a). Sociologists Larry Bumpass and Hsien-Hen Lu (2000) find that about two fifths of all children spend some time living with their mother and a cohabiting partner and that approximately one third of the time children spend with unmarried mothers is actually spent in cohabitation. Clearly, the lives of children are increasingly embedded in families formed by cohabitation. The effects of this alternative family form on children will become apparent only as these children age.

DOES LIVING TOGETHER HELP REDUCE THE CHANCES FOR DIVORCE?

As we noted earlier, most readers of this textbook will cohabit before marrying. How will this experience of cohabitation affect their marriages? Many college students believe that by living together with a boyfriend or girlfriend, they will learn whether they're right for each other and thus have more successful marriages. As early as the 1960s, anthropologist Margaret Mead (1966) predicted that living together would allow people to make better decisions about marriage. Yet some studies suggest that those who live with their partners before marrying them are more likely to divorce than are individuals who do not cohabit with their partners before marriage. How could this be so?

Sociologists offer two explanations: the *selection explanation* and the *experience of living together* explanation. The selection explanation proposes that people who live together would be more likely to divorce even if they hadn't ever lived together before marriage. That is, the very people who would choose to cohabit differ from those who don't, and the traits that distinguish the two groups are associated with their chances of divorcing. For example, people who cohabit are less religious than those people who refuse to cohabit (Kamp Dush et al. 2003). People who are less religious would be less likely to stay married in any event, whereas people who are more religious would be more likely to stay married.

Although the selection explanation suggests that there is nothing inherent about cohabitation that promotes divorce, there is a competing explanation that suggests that living together is the kind of experience that erodes belief in the permanence of marriage. As people go through their twenties living with various partners, they develop a sense that relationships can be started and ended easily and that they have many options for intimate relations outside of marriage (Teachman 2003).

Which explanation is right? The best evidence seems to indicate that the experience of cohabitation may slightly alter one's beliefs about marriage and the link between cohabitation and divorce is caused by selection factors.

GAY-PARENT FAMILIES

Gay and lesbian college students today can look forward to a much more accepting social world than the one that greeted generations before them. Many homosexuals now live in stable relationships as couples, and there is a swiftly developing movement to legally recognize these unions as marriages. Recent decisions in the United States, Canada, Mexico, and several European nations demonstrate the current pulse of this movement.

In 2001 the Netherlands became the first nation to legalize same-sex marriage. Since that time, Belgium, Spain, Canada, South Africa, Norway, and Sweden have also

Evelyn Rivera's family (her son Mark, nephew Sal, and lesbian partner Debbie Rodriguez) is just one example of the changing idea of the "typical" American family.

legalized such unions. In 2007, Coahuila became the second state in Mexico to legalize civil unions. In 2008, Uruguay became the first nation in Latin America to do so. Between 2005 and 2008, the Czech Republic, Slovenia, Switzerland, and the United Kingdom were among the countries passing laws enabling civil unions, and others are expected to follow suit.

Policies are rapidly changing and are hotly contested in the United States. Vermont was the first state to legalize civil unions: In July 2000, the Vermont legislature voted to allow same-sex partners to register their "civil unions" with town clerks. The move allows same-sex couples access to all the state-granted rights, privileges, and responsibilities of marriage. Though this was a big victory for gay and lesbian marriage advocates, the measure falls short of calling the partnerships "marriage" and instead opts for "civil unions." Marriage is seen as a more desirable arrangement by gay and lesbian couples, because marriages are respected in all 50 states for all purposes, but civil unions are not necessarily recognized as legally binding when a couple leave the state in which they formed the union.

Same-sex couples also can now marry in Massachusetts, Connecticut, and Iowa. From June 2008 until November 2008, California also authorized same-sex marriages, until voters enacted Proposition 8, which banned same-sex marriage, unleashing heated protests. Whether more states follow the lead of Iowa—or of California—remains to be seen. As of November 2008, twenty-nine states had passed constitutional amendments explicitly barring the recognition of same-sex marriage, nineteen of which prohibit the legal recognition of *any* same-sex union. In 1996, the United States Congress passed the Defense of Marriage Act (DOMA) defining marriage as a union between a man and a woman amongst other stipulations. However, President Barack Obama's political platform includes full repeal of the DOMA.

Beyond civil unions or marriages, same-sex couples are forming families with children. Relaxation of previously intolerant attitudes toward homosexuality has been accompanied by a growing tendency for courts to allocate custody of children to mothers living in gay relationships. Techniques of artificial insemination mean that gay women may have children and become gay-parent families without any heterosexual contact. Moreover, only one of the fifty U.S. states—Florida—has laws explicitly preventing lesbians and gay men from adopting children.

Jessica Vandermark-Martinez, left, holds hands with Jodie Vandermark-Martinez at their wedding ceremony outside the Polk County administrative office in Des Moines, Iowa.

STAYING SINGLE

The broad category of "single" encompasses both people who have never married, and those who have married but are now single due to divorce, separation, or widowhood. More people are now "never married" today, and remain in this state for a longer period of time, than in the past due to the delayed age at first marriage. A larger proportion of people in their twenties are unmarried than used to be the case. By their mid-thirties, however, only a small minority of men and women have never been married. The majority of single people aged thirty to fifty are divorced and "in between" marriages. Most single people over fifty are widowed (Federal Interagency Forum on Aging-Related Statistics 2008).

More than ever before, young people are leaving their parents' home simply to start an independent life rather than to get married (which had been one of the most common paths out of their parents' home in the past). Hence it seems that the trend of "staying single" or living on one's own may be part of the societal trend toward valuing independence at the expense of family life. Still, most people (over 90 percent) ultimately marry, including a large majority of these people who originally left home to live independently (Goldscheider and Goldscheider 1999). ✓

CONCEPT CHECKS ✓

1. Why has cohabitation become so common in the United States and worldwide?

2. Does cohabitation lead to divorce? Why or why not?

NEED HELP STUDYING?

⊚ wwnorton.com/studyspace

....

Visit StudySpace to access free review materials such as:

- Vocabulary Flashcards
- Diagnostic Review Quizzes
- Study Outlines

REVIEW QUESTIONS

1. What are the debates about traditional and postmodern families? What are the policies proposed by each side of the debate?
2. What are the two main functions of the family according to Talcott Parsons? What are the critiques of the functionalist perspective?
3. Discuss three main themes studied by feminist theorists of the family.
4. What are the three phases of the development of the family from the 1500s to the 1800s? What does this historical study tell us about current conceptions of the "traditional family"?
5. What are some of the social processes that are changing family structures around the world?
6. Why should racial and class background be considered in research on families? Give an example.
7. What are some of the factors that explain the rise in divorce rates in the United States in the past thirty years?
8. What are the various types of single-parent households? What are some of the potential effects on children from single-parent homes?
9. What are some of the negative aspects of family life? What are some of the social factors involved?
10. Describe alternate forms of the family.

THINKING SOCIOLOGICALLY EXERCISES

1. Using this textbook's presentation, compare the characteristics of contemporary white non-Hispanic, Asian American, Latino, and African American families.
2. Increases in cohabitation and single-parent households suggest that marriage may be beginning to fall by the wayside in our contemporary society. However, this chapter claims that marriage and family remain firmly established institutions in our society. Explain the rising patterns of cohabitation and single-parent households and show how these seemingly paradoxical trends can be reconciled with the claims offered by this textbook.

Education and Religion

THE BIG QUESTIONS

WHY ARE EDUCATION AND LITERACY SO IMPORTANT?

Know how and why systems of mass education emerged in the United States. Know some basic facts about the education system and literacy rates of developing countries.

WHAT IS THE LINKAGE BETWEEN EDUCATION AND INEQUALITY?

Become familiar with the most important research on whether education reduces or perpetuates inequality. Learn the social and cultural influences on educational achievement.

HOW DO SOCIOLOGISTS THINK ABOUT RELIGION?

Learn the elements that make up religion. Know the sociological approaches to religion developed by Marx, Durkheim, and Weber, as well as the religious economy approach.

HOW DOES RELIGION AFFECT LIFE THROUGHOUT THE WORLD?

Learn the various ways religious communities are organized and how they have become institutionalized. Recognize how the globalization of religion is reflected in religious activism in poor countries and the rise of religious nationalist movements.

HOW DOES RELIGION AFFECT YOUR LIFE IN THE UNITED STATES?

Learn about the sociological dimensions of religion in the United States.

D estiny Hatcher, an eighth-grader at Hope Christian School in Milwaukee, Wisconsin, is an A student with dreams of going to college. Just a few years ago, however, she was a failing student who often found herself at the principal's office. Destiny's transformation happened when she started attending a private religious school in her hometown. Wearing a proper tie-and-jacket uniform and her hair neatly pulled back with a headband, she explained, "The school's in a bad neighborhood, but the environment is really loving." The students at Hope are challenged by the school's rigorous curriculum, yet they know that they can call their teachers on their cell phones if they have trouble with their homework and can go to school on some Saturdays (Paulson 2006).

Destiny is able to attend a private school, thanks to a school voucher program that started in Milwaukee in 1990. Voucher programs have sprung up throughout the United States in recent years, with large programs in place in Washington, DC, and Cleveland. Advocates of voucher programs say it gives choices to economically disadvantaged students like Destiny. For example, families with low incomes can get a voucher of up to $6,500 (in 2006) to send their children to one of 125 private schools in the Milwaukee area.

However, these programs are hotly debated; the state of Florida's program was declared unconstitutional by the state's supreme court in January 2006. Opponents of voucher programs say that they take money away from public schools. Others argue that voucher programs challenge the separation of church and state. Roughly 80 percent of all schools participating in the voucher programs are religious schools; that means that federal taxpayers' dollars are going to fund private religious organizations. These sectarian schools often bring religious worship and teachings into the school day, with some taking controversial stands on issues such as gay rights, the role of women in society, and reproductive rights. Critics also say that these schools can be coercive, forcing children to participate in religious practices that they or their parents may disagree with. In response to this concern, Milwaukee requires that charter schools make religious activity in voucher schools voluntary for students.

The school voucher controversy highlights many important themes that are the core of the sociology of education and the sociology of religion. Education is a social institution that teaches individuals how to be members of society. Through education, we become aware of the common characteristics we share with other members of the same society and have at least some sort of knowledge about our society's geographical and political position in the world and its past history. The educational system both directly and indirectly exposes young people to the lessons that they will need to learn to become players in other major social institutions, such as the economy and the family.

Like education, religion is an institution that exercises a socializing influence. However, while education is intended to be universalistic and to expose all children to similar messages, religious institutions vary widely in the values, beliefs, and practices that they impart. Sociologists of religion try to assess under what conditions religion unites communities and under what conditions it divides them. The study of religion is a challenging enterprise that places special demands on the sociological imagination. In analyzing religious beliefs and practices, we must be sensitive to ideals that inspire profound conviction in believers, yet at the same time take a balanced view of them. We must confront ideas that seek the eternal while recognizing that religious groups also promote quite mundane goals, such as acquiring money or followers.

This chapter focuses on the socializing processes of education and religion. To study these issues, we ask how present-day education developed and analyze its socializing influence. We also look at education in relation to social inequality and consider how far the educational system serves to exacerbate or reduce such inequality. Then we move to studying religion and the different forms that religious beliefs and practices take. We also analyze the various types of religious organizations and the effect of social change on the position of religion in the wider world.

WHY ARE EDUCATION AND LITERACY SO IMPORTANT?

The term *school* has its origins in a Greek word meaning "leisure," or "recreation." In premodern societies, schooling existed for the few who had the time and resources available to pursue the cultivation of the arts and philosophy. For some, their engagement with schooling was like taking up a hobby. For others, like religious leaders or priests, schooling was a way of gaining skills and thus increasing their ability to interpret sacred texts. But for the vast majority of people, growing up meant learning by example the same social habits and work skills as their elders. Learning was a family affair—there were no schools at all for the mass of the population. Since children often started to help with domestic duties and farming work at very young ages, they rapidly became full-fledged members of the community.

Education in its modern form, the instruction of pupils within specially constructed school premises, gradually emerged in the first few years of the nineteenth century, when primary schools began to be constructed in Europe and the United States. One main reason for the rise of large educational systems was the process of industrialization, with its ensuing expansion of cities.

EDUCATION AND INDUSTRIALIZATION

Until the first few decades of the nineteenth century, most of the world's population had no schooling whatsoever. But as the industrial economy rapidly expanded, there was a great demand for specialized schooling that could produce an educated, capable workforce. As occupations became more differentiated and were increasingly located away from the home, it was impossible for work skills to be passed on directly from parents to children.

As educational systems became universal, more and more people were exposed to abstract learning (of subjects like math, science, history, and literature), rather than to the practical transmission of specific skills. In a modern society, people have to be furnished with basic skills—such as reading, writing, and calculating—and a general knowledge of their physical, social, and economic environment, but it is also important that they know how to learn, so that they are able to master new, sometimes very technical, forms of information. An advanced society also needs pure research and insights with no immediate practical value, in order to push out the boundaries of knowledge.

In the modern age, education and qualifications became an important stepping-stone into job opportunities and careers. Schools and universities not only broaden people's minds and perspectives but are expected to prepare new generations of citizens

With the spread of industrialization, the demand for educated workers increased. The newly expanded education systems emphasized basic skills like reading, writing, and mathematics instead of specific skills for work.

for participation in economic life. The right balance between a generalist education and specific work skills is a difficult one at which to arrive. Specialized forms of technical, vocational, and professional training often supplement pupils' liberal education and facilitate the transition from school to work. Internships and work experience schemes, for example, allow young people to develop specific knowledge applicable to their future careers.

Although schools and universities seek above all to provide a well-rounded education, policy makers and employers are concerned with ensuring that education and training programs produce a stream of graduates who can meet a country's employment demands. Yet in times of rapid economic and technical change, there is not always a good match between the priorities of the educational system and the availability of professional opportunities. The rapid expansion of a country's health-care system, for example, would dramatically increase the demand for trained health professionals, laboratory technicians, capable administrators, and computer systems analysts familiar with public-health issues. Industry-wide changes in factory-floor production technology would require a workforce with a set of skills that might be in short supply.

SOCIOLOGICAL THEORIES

Sociologists have debated why formal systems of schooling developed in modern societies by studying the social functions that schools provide. For example, some have argued that mass education promotes feelings of nationalism and aided the development of national societies, constituted of citizens from different regions who would know the same history and speak a common language (Ramirez and Boli 1987). Marxist sociologists have argued that the expansion of education was brought about by employers' need for certain personality characteristics in their workers—self-discipline, dependability, punctuality, obedience, and the like—which are all taught in schools (Bowles and Gintis 1976). Another influential perspective comes from the sociologist Randall Collins, who has argued that the primary social function of mass education derives from the need for diplomas and degrees to determine one's credentials for a job, even if the work involved has nothing to do with the education one has received. Over time, the practice of credentialism results in demands for higher credentials, which require higher levels of educational attainment. Jobs that thirty years ago would have required a high school diploma, such as sales representative, now require a college degree. Since educational attainment is closely related to class position, credentialism reinforces the class structure within a society (Collins 1971, 1979).

EDUCATION AND LITERACY IN THE DEVELOPING WORLD

Literacy is the "baseline" of education. Without it, schooling cannot proceed. We take it for granted in the West that the majority of people are literate, but this is only a recent development in Western history. The rise of literacy in Europe was closely tied to sweeping social transformations, particularly the Protestant Reformation, which brought individual study of the Bible, and the development of modern science. Literacy spread during the Reformation and the Renaissance eras due largely to the development of printing from movable type. Compulsory schooling, established in Europe and the United States in the nineteenth century, was perhaps the most important influence on the high rates of literacy in the world today (Barton 2006).

Today, 20.6 percent of the population of developing countries is illiterate (UNESCO 2008a). Although countries have instituted literacy programs, they have made only modest strides in raising the literacy rate. Television, radio, and the other electronic media can be used, where they are available, to skip the stage of learning literacy skills and convey educational programs directly to adults. Although these programs may be more appealing to the general public than formal educational programs, they are typically less effective at improving literacy skills.

During the period of colonialism, colonial governments regarded education with some trepidation. Until the twentieth century, most believed indigenous populations were too primitive to be worth educating. Later, education was seen as a way of making local elites responsive to European ways of life. To some extent, this backfired: The majority of those who led anticolonial and nationalist movements were educated elites who had attended schools in Europe. They were able to compare firsthand the democratic institutions of the European countries with the absence of democracy in their lands of origin.

The education that the colonizers introduced usually focused on issues relevant to Europe, not the colonial areas themselves. Educated Africans in the British colonies knew about the kings and queens of England and read Shakespeare, but knew next to nothing about their own countries' histories or cultural achievements. Policies of educational reform since the end of colonialism have not completely altered the situation even today.

Partly as a result of the legacy of colonial education, which was not directed toward the majority of the population, the educational system in many developing countries is top-heavy: Higher education is disproportionately developed, relative to primary and secondary education. The result is a correspondingly overqualified group who, having attended colleges and universities, cannot find white-collar or professional jobs. Given the low level of industrial development, most of the better-paid positions are in government, and there are not enough of those to go around.

In recent years, some developing countries, recognizing the shortcomings of the curricula inherited from colonialism, have tried to redirect their educational programs toward the rural poor. They have had limited success, because usually there is insufficient funding to pay for the scale of the necessary innovations. As a result, countries such as India have begun programs of self-help education. Communities draw on existing resources without creating demands for high levels of financing. Those who can read and write and who perhaps possess job skills are encouraged to take others on as apprentices, whom they coach in their spare time. ✓

CONCEPT CHECKS ✓

1. Why did schooling become widespread only after the Industrial Revolution?

2. What are some of the functions of formal schooling?

3. What are some of the reasons there are many illiterate people in the developing world?

WHAT IS THE LINKAGE BETWEEN EDUCATION AND INEQUALITY?

The expansion of education in both developing and wealthy nations has always been closely linked to the ideals of democracy. Reformers value education for its own sake—for the opportunity it provides for individuals to develop their capabilities. Yet education has also consistently been seen as a means of promoting equality. Access to universal education, it has been argued, could help reduce disparities of wealth and power. Are educational opportunities truly equal for everyone? Has education in fact proved to be a great equalizer? Much research has been devoted to answering these questions.

"SAVAGE INEQUALITIES"

Between 1988 and 1990, the journalist Jonathan Kozol studied schools in about thirty neighborhoods around the United States. There was no special logic to the way he chose the schools, except that he went where he happened to know teachers, principals, or ministers. What startled him most was the segregation within these schools and the inequalities among them. Kozol brought these terrible conditions to the attention of the American people in his book *Savage Inequalities*, which became a best seller (Kozol 1991).

In his passionate opening chapter, he first took readers to East St. Louis, Illinois, a city that has been roughly 98 percent black for the past several decades. At the time of Kozol's research, the city had no regular trash collection, and few jobs. Three quarters of its residents were living on welfare at the time. City residents were forced to use their backyards as garbage dumps, which attracted a plague of flies and rats during the hot summer months. East St. Louis also had some of the sickest children in the United States, with extremely high rates of infant death, asthma, and poor nutrition and extremely low rates of immunization. Only 55 percent of the children had been fully immunized for polio, diphtheria, measles, and whooping cough. Among the city's other social problems were crime, dilapidated housing, poor health care, and lack of education.

Kozol showed how the problems of the city affected the school on a daily basis. Teachers often had to hold classes without chalk or paper. One teacher commented on these conditions affecting her teaching: "I have no materials with the exception of a single textbook given to each child. If I bring in anything else—books or tapes or magazines—I bring it in myself. The high school has no VCRs. . . . The AV equipment in the school is so old that we are pressured not to use it." Comments from students reflected the same concerns. "I don't go to physics class, because my lab has no equipment," said one student. Only 55 percent of the students in this high school ultimately graduated, about one third of whom went on to college.

Kozol also wrote about the other end of the inequality spectrum, taking readers into a wealthy suburban school in Westchester County outside of New York City. This school had 96 computers for the 546 students. Most studied a foreign language for four or five years. Two thirds of the senior class were enrolled in an advanced placement (AP) class. Kozol visited an AP class to ask students about their perceptions of inequalities within the educational system. Students at this school were well aware of the economic advantages that they enjoyed at both home and school. With regard to their views about students less well-off than themselves, the general consensus was

The problem of schools falling into disrepair is a chronic one in poverty-stricken areas all over the country. Dilapidated schools like this one in the South Bronx lack funding for even the most basic necessities and, once they have fallen into a state of ruin, there is no money to undertake necessary repairs.

that equal spending among schools was a worthy goal but it would probably make little difference, since poor students lacked motivation and would fail because of other problems. These students also realized that equalizing spending could have adverse affects on their school. As one student said, "If you equalize the money, someone's got to be shortchanged. I don't doubt that [poor] children are getting a bad deal. But do we want everyone to get a mediocre education?"

Despite these powerful descriptions of life in East St. Louis and Westchester County, many sociologists have argued that Kozol's book provides an inaccurate view of educational inequality. Why would Kozol's research not be persuasive? There are several reasons, including the unsystematic way that he chose the schools he studied. But in the end, what is most important is that sociologists have proposed a variety of theories and have identified myriad factors contributing to inequality and differential outcomes.

COLEMAN'S STUDY OF "BETWEEN SCHOOL EFFECTS" IN AMERICAN EDUCATION

The study of "between school effects" (or a comparison of how schools differ from one another) has been the focus of sociological research on the educational system for the past three decades. One of the classic investigations of educational inequality was undertaken in the United States in the 1960s. As part of the Civil Rights Act of 1964, the commissioner of education was required to prepare a report on educational inequalities resulting from differences of ethnic background, religion, and national origin. James Coleman, a sociologist, was director of the research program. The outcome was a study, published in 1966, based on one of the most extensive research projects ever carried out in sociology.

Information was collected on more than half a million pupils who were given a range of achievement tests assessing verbal and nonverbal abilities, reading levels, and mathematical skills. Sixty thousand teachers also completed forms providing data for about four thousand schools. The report found that a large majority of children went to schools that effectively segregated black from white. Almost 80 percent of schools attended by white students contained only 10 percent or fewer African American students. White and Asian American students scored higher on achievement tests than did blacks and other ethnic minority students. Coleman had supposed his results would also show schools that were mainly African American to have worse facilities, larger classes, and more inferior buildings than schools that were predominantly white. But surprisingly, the results showed far fewer differences of this type than had been anticipated.

Coleman therefore concluded that the material resources provided in schools made little difference to educational performance; the decisive influence was the children's backgrounds. In Coleman's words, "Inequalities imposed on children by their home, neighborhood, and peer environment are carried along to become the inequalities with which they confront adult life at the end of school" (Coleman et al. 1966). There was, however, some evidence that students from deprived backgrounds who formed close friendships with those from more favorable circumstances were likely to be more successful educationally. The findings of Coleman's study have been replicated many times over the past decades, most notably by Christopher Jencks and colleagues (Jencks et al. 1972; Schofield 1995).

TRACKING AND "WITHIN SCHOOL EFFECTS"

tracking • Dividing students into groups according to ability.

The practice of **tracking**—dividing students into groups that receive different instruction on the basis of assumed similarities in ability or attainment—is common in American schools. In some schools, students are tracked only for certain subjects; in others, for all subjects. Sociologists have long believed that tracking partly explains why schooling seems to have little effect on existing social inequalities, since being placed in a particular track labels a student as either able or otherwise. Children from more privileged backgrounds, in which academic work is encouraged, are likely to find themselves in the higher tracks early on—and by and large stay there.

Jeannie Oakes (1985) studied tracking in twenty-five junior and senior high schools, both large and small and in both urban and rural areas, but concentrating on differences within schools rather than between them. She found that although several schools claimed they did not track students, virtually all of them had mechanisms for sorting students into groups on the basis of purported ability and achievement, to make teaching easier. In other words, they employed tracking but did not choose to use the term *tracking* itself. Oakes found that tracking made both teachers and students label students based on their track—high ability, low achieving, slow, average, and so on. Individual students in these groups came to be defined by teachers, other students, and themselves in terms of such labels. A student in a "high-achieving" group was considered a high-achieving person—smart and quick. Pupils in a "low-achieving" group came to be seen as slow, below average—or, in more colloquial terms, as "dummies," "sweathogs," or "yahoos." What is the impact of tracking on students in the "low" group? A subsequent study by Oakes found that these students received a poorer education in terms of the quality of courses, teachers, and textbooks made available to them (Oakes 1990). Moreover, tracking had a negative impact primarily on students who were poor, and particularly on African American or Latino students.

Despite these negative consequences, school systems typically track students because of the assumption that bright children learn more quickly and effectively in a group of others who are equally able and that clever students are held back if placed in mixed groups. This assumption is partially supported by a path-breaking study by the sociologist Adam Gamoran. Gamoran and his colleagues agreed with Oakes's conclusions that tracking reinforces previously existing inequalities for average or poor students. However, they also found that tracking has positive benefits for "advanced" students (Gamoran et al. 1995). The debate about the effects of tracking is sure to continue as scholars continue to analyze more data.

THE SOCIAL REPRODUCTION OF INEQUALITY

The educational system provides more than formal instruction: It socializes children to get along with each other, teaches basic skills, and transmits elements of culture such as language and values. Sociologists have looked at education as a form of social reproduction, a concept discussed in Chapter 1 and elsewhere. In the context of education, *social reproduction* refers to the ways in which schools help perpetuate social and economic inequalities across the generations. It also directs our attention to the means whereby schools influence the learning of values, attitudes, and habits via the hidden curriculum.

hidden curriculum • Traits of behavior or attitudes that are learned at school but not included within the formal curriculum—for example, gender differences.

The concept of the **hidden curriculum** addresses the fact that much of what is learned in school has nothing directly to do with the formal content of lessons.

The hidden curriculum teaches children that their role in life is "to know their place and to sit still with it" (Illich 1983). Children spend long hours in school, and get an early taste of what the world of work will be like, learning that they are expected to be punctual and apply themselves diligently to the tasks that those in authority set for them.

Another influential theory on the question of how schools reproduce social inequality was introduced by Samuel Bowles and Herbert Gintis. Modern education, they propose, is a response to the economic needs of industrial capitalism. Schools help to provide the technical and social skills required by industrial enterprise, and they instill discipline and respect for authority in the future labor force. Authority relations in school, which are hierarchical and place strong emphasis on obedience, directly parallel those dominating the workplace.

Schooling has not become the "great equalizer"; rather, schools merely produce for many the feelings of powerlessness that continue throughout their experience in industrial settings. Under the current system, schools "are destined to legitimate inequality, limit personal development to forms compatible with submission to arbitrary authority, and aid in the process whereby youth are resigned to their fate" (Bowles and Gintis 1976). If there were greater democracy in the workplace and more equality in society at large, Bowles and Gintis argue, a system of education could be developed that would provide for greater individual fulfillment.

INTELLIGENCE AND INEQUALITY

Suppose differences in educational attainment, and in subsequent occupations and incomes, directly reflected differential intelligence. In such circumstances, it might be argued, there is in fact equality of opportunity in the school system, for people find a level equivalent to their innate potential.

WHAT IS INTELLIGENCE?

For years, psychologists, geneticists, statisticians, and others have debated whether there exists a single human capability that can be called **intelligence** and, if so, whether it rests on innately determined differences. Intelligence is difficult to define because, as the term is usually employed, it covers qualities that may be unrelated to one another. We might suppose, for example, that the "purest" form of intelligence is the ability to solve abstract mathematical puzzles. However, people who are very good at such puzzles sometimes show low capabilities in other areas, such as history or art. Since the concept has proved so resistant to definition, some psychologists have proposed (and many educators have by default accepted) that intelligence should simply be regarded as "what **IQ (intelligence quotient)** tests measure." Most IQ tests consist of a mixture of conceptual and computational problems. The tests are constructed so that the average score is 100 points: Anyone scoring below is thus labeled "below-average intelligence," and anyone scoring above is "above-average intelligence." In spite of the fundamental difficulty in measuring intelligence, IQ tests are widely used in research studies, as well as in schools and businesses.

Scores on IQ tests do in fact correlate highly with academic performance (which is not surprising, since IQ tests were originally developed to predict success at school). They therefore also correlate closely with social, economic, and ethnic differences,

intelligence • Level of intellectual ability, particularly as measured by IQ (intelligence quotient) tests.

IQ (intelligence quotient) • A score attained on tests of symbolic or reasoning abilities.

The Internationalization of Education

How many foreign students are enrolled in your sociology course? How many foreign students are there at your university? In 1943, approximately 8,000 foreign students were enrolled in American colleges and universities. By 2004, this number had skyrocketed to more than 573,000 (U.S. Bureau of the Census 2006a). Although the American university system as a whole grew considerably during this period, such that 573,000 students represented only 3.3 percent of total 2004 student enrollment, it is clear that foreign students are flocking to the United States in record numbers. Most foreign students today come from Asia—China, Japan, Taiwan, India, and South Korea all send sizeable contingents of students abroad.

The United States takes in more foreign students than any other country, and there are six times as many foreign students in the United States as there are American students overseas. What do foreign students in the United States study? At the undergraduate level, more than 18 percent focus on business and management, 16.5 percent study engineering, and 9 percent concentrate on math and computer science (Institute of International Education 2005a). Each of these fields, however, has declined slightly in popularity in recent years, as foreign students increasingly study the physical and life sciences and the health professions (Institute of International Education 2005a). More than 20 percent of foreign graduate students today study engineering, and of the graduate students receiving a doctorate in engineering, 60 percent were foreign students (National Center for Education Statistics 2005).

Some scholars regard the exchange of international students as a vital component of globalization. Foreign students, in addition to serving as global "carriers" of specialized technical and scientific knowledge, have an important cultural role to play in the globalizing process. Cross-national understandings are enhanced and xenophobic and isolationist attitudes are minimized as native students in host countries develop social ties to their foreign classmates and as foreign students return to their country of origin with an appreciation for the cultural mores of the nation in which they have studied.

Yet there is considerable debate in the United States about what is sometimes called the "internationalization of education." On most college campuses, it is not hard to find disgruntled students who complain that given the competitive nature of the U.S. higher education system, the influx of foreign students deprives deserving Americans of educational opportunities. Moreover, although more than two thirds of foreign students receive nothing in the way of scholarships, some top-notch foreign

since these are associated with variations in levels of educational attainment. White students score better, on average, than African Americans or members of other disadvantaged minorities.

The relationship between race and intelligence is best explained by social rather than biological causes, according to a team of Berkeley sociologists in their 1996 book *Inequality by Design: Cracking the Bell Curve Myth* (Fischer et al. 1996). The authors students are given financial inducements to attend American schools. The outcry against this practice has been loudest at public universities, which receive support from tax revenue. Critics charge that U.S. taxpayers should not shoulder the financial burden for educating foreign students whose families have not paid U.S. taxes and who are likely to return home after earning their degrees.

Supporters of international education find such arguments unconvincing. Some Americans may lose out to foreign students in the competition for slots at prestigious universities, but this is a small price to pay for the economic, political, and cultural benefits the United States receives from having educated millions of foreign business executives, policy makers, scientists, and professionals over the years—many of whom became sympathetically disposed to the United States as a result of their experiences here. And although some foreign students receive scholarships from American universities, most are supported by their parents. In fact, it is estimated that foreign students pump hundreds of millions of dollars each year into the U.S. economy—over $13 billion in 2005 alone (Institute of International Education 2005a).

Rather than curtail the number of foreign students admitted to American universities, supporters of international education suggest that even more should be done to encourage the exchange of students. On the one hand, greater effort should be made to recruit foreign students, to help them select the university and program that will best meet their needs, and to provide them with a positive social and educational experience while they are in the United States. On the other hand, more Americans should be encouraged to study abroad. American students are notorious for having poor foreign-language skills and for knowing little about global geography, much less about the cultures of other nations. This ignorance puts the United States at a disadvantage relative to other countries as the world becomes increasingly globalized; encouraging Americans to study overseas may be the best way to inculcate a global worldview.

Should there be a greater focus on international education in American colleges and universities? Should the international exchange of students be expanded? These are among the issues that educational institutions are forced to confront in the context of globalization. Still, more and more U.S. students are studying abroad—191,321 in 2004–2005, nearly a 10 percent increase over the year before (Institute of International Education 2005b).

conducted this research as a way to rigorously evaluate the controversial claims made by Richard J. Herrnstein and Charles Murray in their book *The Bell Curve* (1994), which argued that the black-white gap in IQ was due to in part to genetic differences in intelligence. All societies have oppressed ethnic groups. Low status, often coupled with discrimination and mistreatment, leads to socioeconomic deprivation, group segregation, and a stigma of inferiority. The combination of these forces often prevents racial minorities from obtaining education, and consequently, their scores on standardized intelligence tests are lower.

The average lower IQ score of African Americans in the United States is remarkably similar to that of deprived ethnic minorities in other countries—such as the "untouchables" in India (who are at the very bottom of the caste system), the Maori in New Zealand, and the burakumin of Japan. Children in these groups score an average of 10 to 15 IQ points below children belonging to the ethnic majority. Such observations strongly suggest that the IQ variations between African Americans and whites in the United States result from social, cultural, and economic—rather than genetic—factors.

EDUCATIONAL REFORM IN THE UNITED STATES

Research done by sociologists has played a major role in reforming the educational system. The object of James Coleman's research, commissioned as part of the 1964 Civil Rights Act, was not solely academic; it was undertaken to influence policy. On the basis of the act, it was decided in the courts that segregated schools violated the rights of minority pupils. But rather than attacking the origins of educational inequalities directly, the courts decided that the schools in each district should achieve a similar racial balance. Thus began the practice of busing students to other schools.

Busing provoked a great deal of opposition, particularly from parents and children in white areas. Busing in fact met with a good deal of success, reducing levels of school segregation quite steeply, particularly in the South. But busing has also produced a number of unintended consequences. Some white parents reacted to busing by either putting their children into private schools or moving to mainly white suburbs where busing wasn't practiced. As a result, in the cities, some schools are virtually as segregated as the old schools were in the past. Busing was, however, only one factor prompting the white flight to the suburbs. Whites also left as a reaction to urban decay: to escape city crowding, housing problems, and rising rates of crime.

While busing is less prominent today as an issue, another problem regarding the American educational system has become an important focus of research: functional illiteracy. Most of the population can read and write at a very basic level, but one in every five adults is functionally illiterate—when they leave school, they can't read or write at the fourth-grade level (U.S. Department of Education 1993). Of course, the United States is a country of immigrants, who when they arrive may not be able to read and write and who may also have trouble with English. But this doesn't explain why America lags behind most other industrial countries in terms of its level of functional illiteracy, because many people affected are not recent immigrants at all.

What is to be done? Some educational policy experts have argued that the most important change that needs to be made is to improve the quality of teaching, either by increasing teachers' pay or by introducing performance-related pay scales, with higher salaries going to the teachers who are most effective in the classroom. Others have proposed giving schools more control over their budgets (a reform that has been carried out

Making Sociology Work
SCHOOL ADMINISTRATOR

School administrators often must make difficult decisions. Two of the biggest controversies facing educators today are school tracking and social promotion. **Tracking** is a practice whereby students are assigned to specific groups or classes based on their abilities, talents, or previous achievement. An estimated 60 percent of primary and 80 percent of secondary schools do tracking today. **Social promotion** is the practice of promoting students to the next grade level, despite their poor grades, to keep them with social peers. A number of cities, including Baltimore, Chicago, New York, and Philadelphia, have stopped social promotions. Decisions about school policy require a strong knowledge of sociological research. Drawing on the research of sociologists like Jeannie Oakes, would you maintain the practices of tracking and social promotion in your school? Why or why not?

in Britain). The idea is that more responsibility for and control over budgeting decisions will create a greater drive to improve the school. Further proposals include the re-funding of federal programs such as Head Start to ensure healthy early childhood development and thus save millions of dollars in later costs, and the privatization of public education, a proposal that has gained numerous supporters in recent years.

PRIVATIZATION

Widespread concern about the crisis in education has opened the door for public-private partnerships aimed at injecting private sector know-how into failing public schools. Local school districts can choose to contract out specific educational services—or the entire school administration—to private companies without losing federal funding. In the past decade, a number of U.S. school districts—including large urban systems such as those in Hartford, Baltimore, and Minneapolis—have invited for-profit educational companies to run their school systems.

Supporters of school privatization argue that state and federal education authorities have shown that they are unable to improve the nation's schools. The educational system, they argue, is wasteful and bureaucratic; it spends a disproportionate amount of its funding on noninstructional administrative costs. Because of their top-heavy nature, it is nearly impossible for school systems to be flexible and innovative. Incompetent teachers are difficult to remove because of the strength of teacher unions.

What backers of school privatization claim can solve these problems is a strong dose of private-sector ideology: competition, experimentation, and incentive. For-profit companies can run school systems more efficiently and produce better outcomes by applying private-sector logic. Good teachers would be attracted to teaching—and retained—by performance-based pay schemes, while underperforming teachers could be removed more easily. Competition within and between schools would lead to higher levels of innovation; privatized schools would have more liberty to institutionalize the results of successful experiments.

The crisis in American schools won't be solved in the short term, and it won't be solved by educational reforms alone, no matter how thoroughgoing. The lesson of sociological research is that inequalities and barriers in educational opportunity reflect wider social divisions and tensions. As long as the United States remains wracked by racial tensions and the polarization between decaying cities and affluent suburbs persists, the crisis in the school system is likely to prove difficult to turn around. ✓

In 1970 a U.S. judge in North Carolina ordered that black students be bused to white schools and that white students be bused to black schools. It was hoped that this crosstown "school busing" would end the *de facto* segregation of public schools caused by white students living in predominantly white neighborhoods and black students living in predominantly black neighborhoods.

CONCEPT CHECKS ✓

1. According to Kozol, has education become an equalizer in American society? Why or why not?

2. How do Coleman's findings differ from the results of Kozol's research? Whose theory, in your opinion, can better explain the racial gap in educational achievement?

3. What effect does tracking have on academic achievement?

4. How do schools perpetuate existing inequalities across generations?

5. Explain the relationship between race and intelligence. Do you find the evidence compelling?

HOW DO SOCIOLOGISTS THINK ABOUT RELIGION?

While modern education emerged in the nineteenth century, religion is one of the oldest human institutions. Cave drawings suggest that religious beliefs and practices existed more than forty thousand years ago. According to anthropologists, there have

religion • A set of beliefs adhered to by the members of a community, incorporating symbols regarded with a sense of awe or wonder together with ritual practices. Religions do not universally involve a belief in supernatural entities.

probably been about one hundred thousand religions throughout human history (Hadden 1997a). Sociologists define **religion** as a cultural system of commonly shared beliefs and rituals that provides a sense of meaning and purpose by creating an idea of reality that is sacred, all-encompassing, and supernatural (Durkheim 1965, orig. 1912; Berger 1967; Wuthnow 1988). There are three key elements in this definition:

1. Religion is a form of culture. You will recall from Chapter 2 that culture consists of the shared beliefs, values, norms, and material conditions that create a common identity among a group of people. Religion shares all of these characteristics.
2. Religion involves beliefs that take the form of ritualized practices. All religions have a behavioral aspect—special activities that identify believers as members of the religious community.
3. Perhaps most important, religion provides a sense of purpose—a feeling that life is meaningful. It does so by explaining what transcends or overshadows everyday life, in ways that other aspects of culture (such as an educational system or a belief in democracy) typically cannot (Geertz 1973; Wuthnow 1988).

theism • A belief in one or more supernatural deities.

What is absent from the sociological definition of religion is as important as what is included: Nowhere is there mention of God. We often think of **theism**—a belief in one or more supernatural deities (the term originates from the Greek word for god)—as basic to religion, but this is not necessarily the case. Some religions, such as Buddhism, believe in the existence of spiritual forces rather than a particular god.

Four broad conditions set the stage for the sociological study of religion:

1. **Sociologists are not concerned with whether religious beliefs are true or false.** From a sociological perspective, religions are regarded not as being decreed by God but as being socially constructed by human beings. As a result, sociologists put aside their personal beliefs when they study religion. They are concerned with the human rather than the divine aspects of religion. Sociologists ask: How is the religion organized? How is it related to the larger society? What explains its success or failure in recruiting and retaining believers? The question of whether a particular belief is "good" or "true," however important it may be to the believers of the religion under study, is not something that sociologists are able to address as sociologists. (As individuals, they may have strong opinions, but one hopes that they can keep these opinions from biasing their research.)
2. **Sociologists are especially concerned with the social organization of religion.** Religions are among the most important institutions in society. They are a primary source of the deepest-seated norms and values. At the same time, religions are typically practiced through an enormous variety of social forms. The sociology of religion is concerned with how different religious institutions and organizations actually function. The earliest European religions were often indistinguishable from the larger society, as religious beliefs and practices were incorporated into daily life. This is still true in many parts of the world today. In modern industrial society, however, religions have become established in separate, often bureaucratic, organizations, and so sociologists focus on the organizations through which religions must operate in order to survive (Hammond 1992).
3. **Sociologists often view religions as a major source of social solidarity, because religions often provide their believers with a common set of norms and values.** Religious beliefs, rituals, and bonds help to create a "moral community" in which all members know how to behave toward one another

(Wuthnow 1988). If a single religion dominates a society, the religion may be an important source of social stability. If a society's members adhere to numerous competing religions, however, religious differences may lead to destabilizing social conflicts. Recent examples of religious conflict within a society include struggles among Sikhs, Hindus, and Muslims in India.

4. **Sociologists tend to explain the appeal of religion in terms of social forces rather than purely personal, spiritual, or psychological factors.** For many people, religious beliefs are a deeply personal experience, involving a powerful sense of connection with forces that transcend everyday reality. Sociologists do not question the depth of such feelings and experiences, but they are unlikely to limit themselves to a purely spiritual explanation of religious commitment. Some researchers argue that people often "get religion" when their fundamental sense of a social order is threatened by economic hardship, loneliness, loss or grief, physical suffering, or poor health (Berger 1967; Schwartz 1970; Glock 1976; Stark and Bainbridge 1980). In explaining the appeal of religious movements, sociologists are more likely to focus on the problems of the social order than on the psychological response of the individual.

THEORIES OF RELIGION

Sociological approaches to religion are strongly influenced by the classical theories of Marx, Durkheim, and Weber. None of the three was religious himself, and they all believed that religion would become less and less significant in modern times. Each argued that religion was fundamentally an illusion: The very diversity of religions and their obvious connection to different societies and regions of the world made the claims by their advocates inherently implausible. An individual born into an Australian society of hunters and gatherers would hold different religious beliefs from someone born into the caste system of India or the Catholic Church of medieval Europe.

MARX: RELIGION AND INEQUALITY

In spite of the influence of his views on the subject, Karl Marx never studied religion in any detail. His thinking on religion was derived mostly from the writings of Ludwig Feuerbach, who believed that through a process he called **alienation**, human beings tend to attribute their own culturally created values and norms to divine forces or gods, because they do not understand their own history. Thus, the story of the Ten Commandments given to Moses by God is a mythical version of the origins of the moral precepts that govern the lives of Jewish and Christian believers.

Marx accepted the view that religion represents human self-alienation. In a famous phrase, Marx declared that religion was the "opium of the people." Religion defers happiness and rewards to the afterlife, he said, teaching the resigned acceptance of existing conditions in the earthly life. Attention is thus diverted away from injustices in this world by the promise of what is to come in the next. Religious belief also can provide justifications for those in power. For example, "The meek shall inherit the earth" suggests attitudes of humility and nonresistance to oppression.

DURKHEIM: RELIGION AND FUNCTIONALISM

In contrast to Marx, Émile Durkheim spent a good part of his intellectual career studying religion, concentrating particularly on totemism as practiced by Australian

alienation • The sense that our own abilities as human beings are taken over by other entities. The term was originally used by Karl Marx to refer to the projection of human powers onto gods. Subsequently he used the term to refer to the loss of workers' control over the nature and products of their labor.

aboriginal societies. *The Elementary Forms of the Religious Life*, first published in 1912, is perhaps the most influential single study in the sociology of religion (1965). Durkheim connected religion not with social inequalities or power, but with the overall nature of the institutions of a society. His argument was that totemism represented religion in its most "elementary" form—hence the title of his book.

Durkheim defined religion in terms of a distinction between the sacred and the profane. **Sacred** objects and symbols, he held, are treated as apart from the routine aspects of day-to-day existence—the realm of the **profane**. A totem (an animal or plant believed to have particular symbolic significance), Durkheim argued, is a sacred object, regarded with veneration and surrounded by ritual activities. These ceremonies and rituals, in Durkheim's view, are essential to unifying the members of groups.

Durkheim's theory of religion is a good example of the functionalist tradition in sociology. To analyze the function of a social behavior or social institution like religion is to study the contribution it makes to the continuation of a group, community,

sacred • Describing something that inspires awe or reverence among those who believe in a given set of religious ideas.

profane • That which belongs to the mundane, everyday world.

In his research on the social and economic influence of religions around the world, Max Weber categorized Eastern religions as "other-worldly" and Christianity as a "salvation religion." Weber believed that Hinduism stressed escaping material existence to locate a higher plane of being, which cultivated an attitude of passivity. In contrast, he argued that Christianity and its emphasis on salvation and constant struggle could stimulate revolt against the existing order.

or society. According to Durkheim, religion has the function of cohering a society by ensuring that people meet regularly to affirm common beliefs and values.

WEBER: THE WORLD RELIGIONS AND SOCIAL CHANGE

Whereas Durkheim based his arguments on a restricted range of examples, Max Weber embarked on a massive study of religions worldwide. No scholar before or since has undertaken a task of this scope.

Weber's writings on religion differ from those of Durkheim because they concentrate on the connection between religion and social change, something to which Durkheim gave little direct attention. They also contrast with those of Marx, because Weber argued that religion was not necessarily a conservative force; on the contrary, religiously inspired movements have often produced dramatic social transformations. Thus, Protestantism, particularly Puritanism, according to Weber, was the source of the capitalistic outlook found in the modern West. The early entrepreneurs were mostly Calvinists. Their drive to succeed, which helped initiate Western economic development, was originally prompted by a desire to serve God. Material success was a sign of divine favor.

Weber conceived of his research on the world religions as a single project. His discussion of the impact of Protestantism on the development of the West was connected to a comprehensive attempt to understand the influence of religion on social and economic life in various cultures. After analyzing Eastern religions, Weber concluded that they provided barriers to the development of industrial capitalism such as took place in the West. Eastern civilizations, he observed, were oriented toward different values, such as escape from the toils of the material world.

Weber regarded Christianity as a *salvation religion*. According to such religions, human beings can be "saved" if they are converted to the beliefs of the religion and follow its moral tenets. The notions of "sin" and of being rescued from sinfulness by God's grace are important. They generate a tension and an emotional dynamism essentially absent from the Eastern religions. Salvation religions have a "revolutionary" aspect. Whereas the religions of the East cultivate an attitude of passivity or acceptance within the believer, Christianity demands a constant struggle against sin and so can stimulate revolt against the existing order. Religious leaders—such as Luther or Calvin—have arisen who reinterpret existing doctrines in such a way as to challenge the extant power structure.

CRITICAL ASSESSMENT OF THE CLASSICAL VIEW

Marx, Durkheim, and Weber each identified some important general characteristics of religion, and in some ways their views complement one another. Marx was correct to claim that religion often has ideological implications, serving to justify the interests of ruling groups at the expense of others. There are innumerable instances of this in history. For example, the European missionaries who sought to convert "heathen" peoples to Christian beliefs were no doubt sincere in their efforts. Yet their teachings contributed to the destruction of traditional cultures and the imposition of white domination. Almost all Christian denominations tolerated, or endorsed, slavery in the United States and other parts of the world into the nineteenth century. Doctrines were developed proclaiming slavery to be based on divine law, disobedient slaves being guilty of an offense against God as well as their masters (Stampp 1956).

Yet Weber was certainly correct to emphasize the unsettling and often revolutionary impact of religious ideals on the established social order. In spite of many churches' early support for slavery in the United States, church leaders later played a key role in fighting to abolish the institution. Religious beliefs have prompted social movements seeking to overthrow unjust systems of authority; for instance, religious sentiments played a prominent part in the civil rights movements of the 1960s. Religion has also generated social change through wars fought for religious motives.

These divisive influences of religion, so prominent in history, find little mention in Durkheim's work. Durkheim emphasized the role of religion in promoting social cohesion. Yet it is not difficult to redirect his ideas toward explaining religious division, conflict, and change as well as solidarity. After all, much of the strength of feeling that may be generated against other religious groups derives from the commitment to religious values generated within each community of believers.

Among the most valuable points of Durkheim's writings is his stress on ritual and ceremony. All religions comprise regular assemblies of believers, at which ritual prescriptions are observed. As Durkheim rightly points out, ritual activities also mark the major transitions of life—birth, the transition to adulthood (rituals associated with puberty are found in many cultures), marriage, and death (van Gennep 1977).

Finally, the theories of Marx, Durkheim, and Weber on religion were based on their studies of societies in which a single religion predominated. As a consequence, it seemed reasonable for them to examine the relationship between a predominant religion and the society as a whole. However, in the past fifty years this classical view has been challenged by some U.S. sociologists. Because of their own experience in a society that is highly tolerant of religious diversity, these theorists have focused on religious pluralism rather than on religious domination. Not surprisingly, their conclusions differ substantially from the views of Marx, Durkheim, and Weber, each of whom regarded religion as closely bound up with the larger society. Religion was believed to reflect and reinforce society's values, or at least the values of those who were most powerful; to provide an important source of solidarity and social stability; and to drive social change. According to this view, religion is threatened by the rise of **secular thinking**, particularly as seen in the rise of science, technology, and rational thought in general.

The classical theorists argued that the key problem facing religions in the modern world is **secularization,** or the process by which religious belief and involvement declines and thus results in a weakening of the social and political power of religious organizations. Peter Berger (1967) has described religion in premodern societies as a "sacred canopy" that covers all aspects of life and is therefore seldom questioned. In modern society, however, the sacred canopy is more like a quilt, a patchwork of different religious and secular belief systems. When multiple belief systems coexist, it becomes increasingly difficult to sustain the idea that there is any single true faith. According to this view, secularization is the likely result.

CONTEMPORARY APPROACHES: "RELIGIOUS ECONOMY"

One of the most influential contemporary approaches to the sociology of religion is tailored to societies such as the United States that offer many different faiths from which to pick and choose. Sociologists who favor the **religious economy** approach argue that religions can be thought of as organizations in competition with each other for followers (Stark and Bainbridge 1987; Finke and Stark 1988, 1992; Roof and McKinney 1990; Hammond 1992; Warner 1993; Moore 1994).

secularization • A process of decline in the influence of religion. Although modern societies have become increasingly secularized, tracing the extent of secularization is a complex matter. Secularization can refer to levels of involvement with religious organizations (such as rates of church attendance), the social and material influence wielded by religious organizations, and the degree to which people hold religious beliefs.

secular thinking • Worldly thinking, particularly as seen in the rise of science, technology, and rational thought in general.

religious economy • A theoretical framework within the sociology of religion, which argues that religions can be fruitfully understood as organizations in competition with one another for followers.

Like contemporary economists who study businesses, these sociologists argue that competition is preferable to monopoly when it comes to ensuring religious vitality. This position is exactly opposite to that of the classical theorists. Marx, Durkheim, and Weber assumed that religion weakens when challenged by different religious or secular viewpoints, whereas the religious economists argue that competition increases the overall level of religious involvement in modern society. Religious economists believe this is true for two reasons. First, competition makes each religious group try harder to win followers. Second, the presence of numerous religions means that there is likely to be something for just about everyone. In a culturally diverse society such as the United States, a single religion will probably appeal to only a limited range of followers, whereas the presence of Indian gurus and fundamentalist preachers, in addition to mainline churches, is likely to encourage a high level of religious participation.

A criticism of the religious-economy approach is that overestimates the extent to which people rationally pick and choose among different religions, as if they were shopping for a new car or a pair of shoes. Among deeply committed believers, particularly in societies that lack religious pluralism, it is not obvious that religion is a matter of rational choice. Even when people are allowed to choose among different religions, most are likely to practice their childhood religion without ever questioning whether or not there are more appealing alternatives. Moreover, the spiritual aspects of religion may be overlooked if sociologists simply assume that religious buyers are always on spiritual shopping sprees. Wade Clark Roof's study (1993) of fourteen hundred baby boomers found that a third had remained loyal to their childhood faith, while another third had continued to profess their childhood beliefs although they no longer belonged to a religious organization. Only a third were actively searching for a new religion, making the sorts of choices presumed by the religious economy approach. ✓

CONCEPT CHECKS

1. What are the three main components of religion as a social institution?

2. How do sociologists differ from other scholars, in their approach to studying religion?

3. Why did Karl Marx call religion the "opium of the people"?

4. What are the differences between classical and contemporary approaches to understanding religion?

HOW DOES RELIGION AFFECT LIFE THROUGHOUT THE WORLD?

Religion is one of the most truly global of all social institutions, affecting almost all aspects of social life. In this section, we describe the way religion shapes life throughout the globe. We will begin, however, by briefly describing the different ways that world religions are organized.

TYPES OF RELIGIOUS ORGANIZATIONS

Early theorists such as Max Weber (1963, orig. 1921), Ernst Troeltsch (1931), and Richard Niebuhr (1929) described religious organizations as falling along a continuum, based on the degree to which they are well established and conventional: Churches lie at one end (they are conventional and well established), cults lie at the other (they are neither), and sects fall somewhere in the middle. These distinctions were based on the study of those religions which account for the majority of persons in Europe and the United States. There is much debate over how well they apply to the non-Christian world.

Today, sociologists are aware that the terms *sect* and *cult* have negative connotations, something they wish to avoid. For this reason, contemporary sociologists of religion sometimes use the phrase *new religious movements* to characterize novel religious organizations that have not yet achieved the respectability that comes with being well established for a long period of time (Hexham and Poewe 1997; Hadden 1997b).

CHURCHES AND SECTS

church • A large, established religious body, normally having a formal, bureaucratic structure and a hierarchy of religious officials. The term is also used to refer to the place in which religious ceremonies are carried out.

Churches are large, established religious bodies; one example is the Roman Catholic Church. They normally have a formal, bureaucratic structure, with a hierarchy of religious officials. Churches often represent a traditional face of religion, since they are integrated within the existing institutional order. Most of their adherents are born into and grow up within the church.

sect • A religious movement that breaks away from orthodoxy.

Sects are smaller, less highly organized groups of committed believers, usually set up in protest against an established church. Sects aim to discover or follow the "true way" and either try to change the surrounding society or withdraw from it into communities of their own, a process known as *revival*. Many sects have few or no officials, and all members are regarded as equal participants. For the most part, people are not born into sects, but actively join them in order to further commitments in which they believe.

DENOMINATIONS AND CULTS

denomination • A religious sect that has lost its revivalist dynamism and become an institutionalized body, commanding the adherence of significant numbers of people.

A **denomination** is a sect that has cooled down and become an institutionalized body rather than an activist protest group. Sects that survive over any period of time inevitably become denominations. Denominations are recognized as legitimate by churches and exist alongside them, often cooperating harmoniously with them.

cult • A fragmentary religious grouping to which individuals are loosely affiliated, but which lacks any permanent structure.

Cults, by contrast, are the most loosely knit and transient of all religious organizations. They are composed of individuals who reject what they see as the values of the outside society, unlike sects, which try to revive an established church. They are a form of religious innovation, rather than revival. Their focus is on individual experience, bringing like-minded people together. Like sects, cults often form around the influence of an inspirational leader.

Like sects, cults flourish when there is a breakdown in well-established and widespread societal belief systems. This is happening throughout the world today, in places as diverse as Japan, India, and the United States. When such a breakdown occurs, cults may originate within a society, or they may be "imported" from outside. In the United States, examples of homegrown, or indigenous, cults include New Age religions based on such things as spiritualism, astrology, and religious practices adapted from Asian or Native American cultures. Examples of imported cults include the Reverend Sun Myung Moon's Unification Church ("Moonies"), which originated in South Korea.

GLOBALIZATION AND RELIGION

Nearly half of the world's population follow one of two faiths: Christianity or Islam, religions that have long been unconstrained by national borders. The current globalization of religion is reflected in political activism among religious groups in poor countries and in the rise of religious nationalist movements in opposition to the modern secular state.

THE GLOBAL RISE OF RELIGIOUS NATIONALISM

One of the most important trends in global religion today is the rise of **religious nationalism**, the linking of strongly held religious convictions with beliefs about a people's social and political destiny. In countries around the world, religious nationalist movements reject the notion that religion, government, and politics should be separate and call instead for a revival of traditional religious beliefs that are directly embodied in the nation and its leadership (Beyer 1994). These nationalist movements represent a strong reaction against the impact of technological and economic modernization on local religious beliefs. In particular, religious nationalists oppose what they see as the destructive aspects of "Western" influence on local culture and religion, ranging from U.S. television to the missionary efforts of foreign evangelicals.

Religious nationalist movements accept many aspects of modern life, including modern technology, politics, and economics. For example, Islamic fundamentalists fighting the Russian army in Chechnya have developed Web sites to help promulgate their views. However, at the same time they emphasize a strict interpretation of religious values and completely reject the notion of secularization (Juergensmeyer 1994, 2001). Nationalist movements do not simply revive ancient religious beliefs. Rather, nationalist movements partly "invent" the past, selectively drawing on different traditions and reinterpreting past events to serve their current beliefs and interests. Violent conflicts between religious groups sometimes result from their competing interpretations of the same historical event (Anderson 1991; Juergensmeyer 1994, 2001; van der Veer 1994).

Religious nationalism is on the rise throughout the world perhaps because in times of rapid social change, unshakable ideas have strong appeal. The collapse of the Soviet Union, the end of the cold war, and sweeping global economic and political changes have led many nations to reject the secular solutions offered by the United States and its former socialist enemies and to look instead to their own past and cultures for answers (Juergensmeyer 1995c). In India, for example, Hindus, Muslims, and Sikhs face off against each other. In India's nationwide elections held in early 1998, the religious nationalist Bharatiya Janata Party (BJP) got more votes than the Congress Party, which had dominated Indian politics since independence half a century earlier. (In 2004, the Congress Party regained control of the government.)

RELIGIOUS NATIONALISM AND VIOLENCE

How is it that religious views can give rise to a culture of violence? The sociologist Mark Juergensmeyer (2001) has come to a startling conclusion: Even though virtually all major religious traditions call for compassion and understanding, violence and religion

religious nationalism • The linking of strongly held religious convictions with beliefs about a people's social and political destiny.

nonetheless go hand in hand. Juergensmeyer, who has studied religious violence among Muslims, Sikhs, Jews, Hindus, Christians, and Buddhists, argues that under the right conditions ordinary conflicts can become recast as wars between good and evil that must be won at all costs. He argues that a violent conflict is most likely to seek religious justification as a "sacred war" under three conditions:

- the conflict is regarded as decisive for defending one's basic identity and dignity—for example, when one's culture is seen as threatened; and
- losing the conflict is unthinkable, although
- winning the conflict is unlikely in any realistic sense.

Óscar Romero, Archbishop of El Salvador, led a movement against the repressive political regime.

Under these conditions, the proponents of cosmic or sacred warfare may justify the loss of innocent lives as serving God's larger purpose. According to Juergensmeyer, bin Laden and al Qaeda exemplify such "cosmic warfare." They are seeking to defend Islam against the threat of Westernization. Responding to al Qaeda's violence with still greater violence shows the rest of the Islamic world that the conflict is indeed cosmic, particularly if the most powerful nations on earth become embroiled. Based on his interviews with proponents of terrorism around the world, Juergensmeyer concludes that this is just what Al Qaeda wants—to be elevated from the status of a minor criminal terrorist organization to a worthy opponent in a global war against the West. This, in the view of some of his interviewees, will increase the appeal of Al Qaeda to a wider group of young Islamic men who blame the West for the decline of Islamic influence and the current hardships faced by many Muslims around the world.

ACTIVIST RELIGION AND SOCIAL CHANGE THROUGHOUT THE WORLD

Despite the widespread link between religion and violence, religion has played a critical role in effecting positive social change over the past forty years. In Vietnam in the 1960s, Buddhist priests burned themselves alive to protest the policies of the South Vietnamese government. Their willingness to sacrifice their lives for their beliefs, seen on television sets around the world, contributed to growing U.S. opposition to the war. Buddhist monks in Thailand currently protest deforestation and care for victims of AIDS.

liberation theology •
An activist Catholic religious movement that combines Catholic beliefs with a passion for social justice for the poor.

An activist form of Catholicism, termed **liberation theology**, combines Catholic beliefs with a passion for social justice for the poor, particularly in Central and South America and in Africa. Catholic priests and nuns organize farming cooperatives, build health clinics and schools, and challenge government policies that impoverish the peasantry. A similar role is played by Islamic socialists in Pakistan and Buddhist socialists in Sri Lanka (Berryman 1987; Sigmund 1990; Juergensmeyer 1994). Many religious leaders have paid with their lives for their activism, which government and military leaders often regard as subversive.

In some Central and Eastern European countries once dominated by the former Soviet Union, long-suppressed religious organizations provided an important basis for the overturning of socialist regimes during the early 1990s. In Poland, the Catholic Church was closely allied with the Solidarity movement, which toppled the socialist government in 1989. ✓

CONCEPT CHECKS ✓
....
1. Describe four types of religious organizations.

2. What is religious nationalism? Why can it be viewed as a reaction to economic modernization of local religious beliefs and Westernization?

HOW DOES RELIGION AFFECT YOUR LIFE IN THE UNITED STATES?

In comparison with the citizens of other industrial nations, Americans are highly religious. Indicators such as belief in God, religious membership, and attendance at religious services, found that religiosity reached its highest levels in the 1950s and has been declining ever since—in part because post–World War II "baby boomers" have been less religious than their predecessors (Roof 1999).In one national survey overwhelming majorities of Catholics, liberal Protestants, and conservative Protestants reported attending church on a weekly basis while they were children, but their attendance had dropped sharply by the time they reached their early twenties. Among the three groups, attendance declined the most among liberal Protestants and least among conservative Protestants (Roof 1999).

Another survey of more than fifty thousand adults in 2001 and nearly 114,000 adults in 1990 found that religious identification had declined sharply during the eleven-year period. In 1990, 90 percent of all adults identified with some religious group; in 2001, the figure was only 81 percent. The principal decline was among self-identified Christians (from 86 percent to 77 percent). This decline was not because a growing proportion of adults identified with other religions; rather, it was because the number of adults reporting no religious identification grew from 8 percent to 14 percent of the population. Membership in religious institutions showed a parallel decline (Kosmin, Mayer, and Keysar 2001).

TRENDS IN RELIGIOUS AFFILIATION

It is difficult to estimate reliably the number of people belonging to churches, since the U.S. government does not officially collect such data. Drawing on occasional government surveys, public-opinion polls, and church records, however, sociologists of religion have concluded that church membership has grown steadily in the United States from the eighteenth century to the present. About one in six Americans belonged to a religious organization at the time of the Revolutionary War. That number had grown to about one in three at the time of the Civil War, one in two at the turn of the nineteenth century, and two in three in the 1990s (Finke and Stark 1992).

One reason so many Americans are religiously affiliated is that religious organizations are an important source of social ties and friendship networks. Churches,

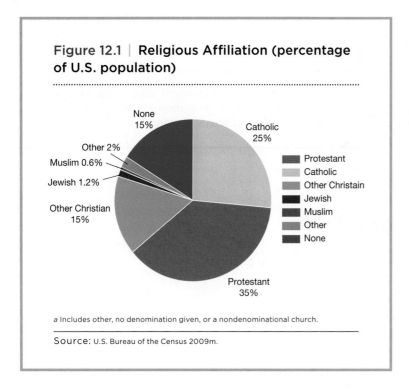

Figure 12.1 | Religious Affiliation (percentage of U.S. population)

- Protestant
- Catholic
- Other Christain
- Jewish
- Muslim
- Other
- None

None 15%
Catholic 25%
Other 2%
Muslim 0.6%
Jewish 1.2%
Other Christian 15%
Protestant 35%

a Includes other, no denomination given, or a nondenominational church.

Source: U.S. Bureau of the Census 2009m.

synagogues, and mosques are communities of people who share the same beliefs and values, and who support one another during times of need. Religious communities thus often play a family-like role, offering help in times of emergency as well as more routine assistance such as child care.

Another reason so many people belong to religious organizations is simply that there are an enormous number of such organizations one can belong to. The United States is the most religiously diverse country in the world, with more than fifteen hundred distinct religions (Melton 1989). Yet the vast majority of people belong to a relatively small number of religious denominations (see Figure 12.1). Fifty-one percent of Americans identify themselves as Protestants, 24 percent as Catholics, 1.7 percent as Jews, and 3 percent as "other," a category that includes Mormons, Seventh-Day Adventists, Buddhists, Hindus, and Muslims and others. Sixteen percent say they have no religious affiliation at all (Pew 2007b).

PROTESTANTS: THE GROWING STRENGTH OF CONSERVATIVE DENOMINATIONS

A more detailed picture of recent trends in American religion can be obtained if we break down the large Protestant category into major subgroups. According to the American Religious Identification Survey (ARIS) of more than fifty-four thousand households in 2008, the largest number of households were Baptist, accounting for 31 percent of all Protestants—over three times the size of the second largest group, Methodists (9.8 percent). There were far fewer Lutherans (7.5 percent), Presbyterians (4 percent), and Episcopalians (2 percent) (ARIS 2008). More than half of all Protestants today describe themselves as "born again" (*Economist* 2003).

These figures are important because they reveal the growing strength of conservative Protestants in the United States. Conservative Protestants, which include denominations such as Baptists and Pentecostals, emphasize a literal interpretation of the Bible, morality in daily life, and conversion through evangelizing. They can be contrasted with the more historically established mainline and liberal Protestants such as Episcopalians and Methodists, who tend to adopt a more flexible, humanistic approach to religious practice.

Although all groups of Protestants showed a growth in membership from the 1920s through the 1960s, a major reversal has since occurred. Both liberal and moderate churches have experienced a decline in membership, whereas the number of conservative Protestants has exploded. Today twice as many people belong to conservative Protestant groups as liberal ones, and conservative Protestants may soon outnumber moderates as well (though if moderates and liberals are combined they still outnumber conservatives) (Green 2004; Roof and McKinney 1990). Since the 1960s, the fastest-growing religious group has been self-identified evangelicals. Although all

How Religious Are You?

As you have learned in this chapter, the United States is one of the most religious nations in the world. How do your religious practices and beliefs compare to people throughout the globe? Answer these questions, and then flip the page to see how you compare.

1. Do you belong to any religious denomination?

2. Do you attend religious services regularly, that is, at least once a week?

3. How important is God in your life (on a scale of 1 to 10, where 10 means very important and 1 means not at all important)?

4. Which of the following statements best describes your views? (a) There exists one and only one true religion. (b) There is truth in many religions. (c) There is no essential truth in any religion. (d) Don't know.

5. Which of the following statements best describes your views? (a) There is a personal God. (b) There is some sort of spirit or life force. (c) I don't really think there is any sort of spirit, God, or force. (d) I don't know what to think.

TURN
PAGE

religious groups lose some converts to other denominations or beliefs, the more conservative religions experienced a net gain in converts during the 1990s, whereas the more liberal religions experienced a net loss (Kosmin, Mayer, and Keysar 2001) (Table 12.1).

CATHOLICISM

Catholics continue to grow in number, yet church attendance declined sharply in the 1960s and 1970s, leveling off in the mid-1970s. One of the main reasons was the papal

How common are your religious views and practices? This chart presents data from the 2000 Gallup International Millennium Survey (Gallup International 2006), which assessed the religious beliefs of men and women in more than 60 nations.

	Total	North America	Latin America	Western Europe	Eastern Europe	West Africa	Southeast Asia
Proportion who…							
belong to a religious denomination	87	91	96	88	84	99	77
attend religious services at least once a week	32	47	35	20	14	82	27
rated God as highly important (scores of 7 to 10)	63	83	87	49	49	97	47
Beliefs about "true religion"							
Only one true religion	31	20	48	21	30	62	31
Truth in many religions	46	71	35	55	34	31	38
No essential truth in any religion	10	6	11	17	11	2	11
Don't know	13	3	7	7	25	5	21
Beliefs about existence of God							
A personal God	45	62	64	35	42	64	27
Some sort of spirit or life force	30	29	24	36	29	31	29
No spirit, God, or life force	8	2	3	15	9	1	11
Don't know	17	7	8	15	21	4	33

Source: Gallup 2006.

Table 12.1 | Changes in Religious Self-Identification in the United States, 1970–2005

RELIGIOUS SELF-IDENTIFICATION	NET GAIN OR LOSS
Evangelical/Born Again	12.8%
No religion	4.5%
Muslim	1.2%
Buddhist	0.8%
Atheist	0.4%
Hindu	0.3%
Jewish	–1.3%
Protestant	–7.5%
Catholic	–1%

Source: Encyclopedia Britannica Online 2006.

encyclical of 1968 that reaffirmed the ban on the use of contraceptives by Catholics. The encyclical offered no leeway for people whose conscience allowed for the use of contraceptives. They were faced with disobeying the Church, and many Catholics did just that. According to one study conducted by the Centers for Disease Control and Prevention, 96 percent of all Catholic women who have had sexual relations report having used contraceptives at one time or another. Similarly, the General Social Survey found that three out of five Catholics say that contraceptives should be available to teens even without parental approval (Catholics for Choice 2004).

The Catholic Church has shown steady increases in membership in recent decades, due largely to the immigration of Catholics from Mexico and Central and South America. Yet the growth in Catholic Church membership has also slowed in recent years, as some followers have drifted away, either ceasing to identify themselves as Catholics or shifting to Protestantism.

OTHER RELIGIOUS GROUPS

The number of Jews has declined in recent years as a result of low birthrates, intermarriage, and assimilation. Yet even assimilated Jews often identify themselves as Jewish, and in recent years, there has been a resurgence of interest among some younger American Jews in rediscovering orthodox practices (Eisen 1983; Goldberg and Rayner 1987; Danzger 1989; Davidman 1991; Bamberger 1992).

Among other denominations, growing immigration from Asia and Africa may somewhat change the U.S. religious profile. For example, estimates of the number of Muslims in the United States run as high as 3 million; many come from Asia or are African refugees from countries like Somalia and Ethiopia (Haddad 1979; Roof and McKinney 1990; Finke and Stark 1992).

RELIGIOUS AFFILIATION AND SOCIOECONOMIC STATUS

The principal religious groupings in the United States vary substantially by region and socioeconomic status. Liberal Protestants tend to be well educated and have jobs and incomes that would classify them as middle or upper class. They are concentrated in the northeastern states, and, to a small extent, in the West as well. Moderate Protestants fall at a somewhat lower level than liberal Protestants in terms of education and income. In fact, they are typical of the national average on these measures. They tend to live in the Midwest, and, to some extent, in the West. Black Protestants are, on average, the least educated and poorest of any of the religious groups. Conservative Protestants have a similar profile, although they fall at a marginally higher level on all these measures.

Catholics strongly resemble moderate Protestants (which is to say, average Americans) in terms of their socioeconomic profile. They are largely concentrated in the Northeast, although many live in the West and the Southwest as well.

Finally, Jews have the most successful socioeconomic profile. Jews tend to be college graduates in middle- or upper-income categories. Whereas the large majority of Jews once lived in the northeastern states, today only half do, since many have moved throughout the United States. One recent study suggests that this high degree of geographical mobility is associated with lowered involvement in Jewish institutions. Jews who move across the country are less likely to belong to synagogues, have Jewish friends, or be married to Jewish spouses (Goldstein and Goldstein 1996).

In sum, Jews and liberal Protestants are the most likely to be middle and upper class; moderate Protestants and Catholics are somewhat in the middle (although the growing number of poor Catholic Latino immigrants may be changing this position); conservative and black Protestants are overwhelmingly lower class. There are political differences across religious groups as well. Jews tend to be the most heavily Democratic of any major religious groups, fundamentalist and evangelical Christians the most Republican. The more moderate Protestant denominations are somewhere in between (Kosmin et al. 2001).

Religion has a subtle yet powerful influence on daily life in the United States and throughout the world. In analyzing religious practices and traditions, we must be sensitive to ideals that inspire profound conviction in believers, yet we must also take a balanced view of them. We must confront ideas that seek the eternal while recognizing that religious groups also promote mundane goals, such as earning money or attracting followers. We need to recognize the diversity of religious beliefs and models of conduct but also the nature of a global phenomenon. ✓

CONCEPT CHECKS ✓

1. What are the reasons so many Americans belong to religious organizations?

2. Describe the main differences between conservative and liberal Protestants.

NEED HELP STUDYING?

⊚ **wwnorton.com/studyspace**

Visit StudySpace to access free review materials such as:

- Vocabulary Flashcards
- Diagnostic Review Quizzes
- Study Outlines

REVIEW QUESTIONS

1. What are school voucher programs? What are pros and cons of such programs?
2. What are several key similarities between the two social institutions of education and religion?
3. Briefly describe the history of formal education in the United States in the twentieth century.
4. What are some of the reasons for the relatively low literacy rates in developing nations?
5. Name several of the pros and cons of school tracking.
6. Do you think that formal schooling perpetuates or eradicates social inequalities? Why?
7. What are the three key characteristics of religion, according to sociological thinkers?
8. Name the main differences in the theories of religion set forth by Marx, Durkheim, and Weber.
9. Contrast the concepts of church, sect, denomination, and cult.
10. What is religious nationalism? Provide two examples of this concept.
11. Describe the socioeconomic and ideological characteristics of Catholic, Protestant and Jewish Americans in the contemporary United States.

THINKING SOCIOLOGICALLY EXERCISES

1. From your reading of this chapter, describe what might be the principal advantages and disadvantages of having children go to private versus public schools in the United States at this time. Assess whether privatization of our public schools would help to improve them.
2. Karl Marx, Émile Durkheim, and Max Weber had different viewpoints on the nature of religion and its social significance. Briefly explain the viewpoints of each. Which theorist's views have the most to offer in explaining the rise of national and international fundamentalism today? Why?

13

Politics and Economic Life

THE BIG QUESTIONS

HOW DID THE STATE DEVELOP?

Learn the basic concepts underlying modern nation-states.

HOW DO DEMOCRACIES FUNCTION?

Learn about different types of democracy, how this form of government has spread around the world, some theories about power in a democracy, and some of the problems associated with modern-day democracy.

WHAT IS TERRORISM?

Learn how social scientists define terrorism and the ways that new-style terrorism is different from the old.

WHAT IS THE SOCIAL SIGNIFICANCE OF WORK?

Assess the sociological ramifications of paid and unpaid work. Understand that modern economies are based on the division of labor and economic interdependence. Learn Marx's theory of alienation. Familiarize yourself with modern systems of economic production.

WHAT ARE KEY ELEMENTS OF THE MODERN ECONOMY?

See the importance of the rise of large corporations; consider particularly the global impact of transnational corporations.

HOW DOES WORK AFFECT EVERYDAY LIFE TODAY?

Learn about the impact of global economic competition on employment. Consider how work will change over the coming years.

On March 20, 2003, the United States launched its "shock and awe" air campaign in Iraq. Intense bombing of strategic targets in the capital city of Baghdad and other Iraqi cities paved the way for the invasion of some 130,000 combat troops, mainly from the United States, with some from Britain, and small numbers from a handful of other countries. Iraq's cities and oil fields were secured with a quickness that surprised many; and by the end of April, Iraq appeared to be securely in American hands.

Although the military objectives had been accomplished in record time, winning the war turned out not to be the same as winning on the battlefield. During the next six years, as Iraqis struggled to build a democracy under the tutelage (and military protection) of the United States, long-suppressed conflicts claimed the lives of over 4,300 American soldiers. Estimates of Iraqi civilian deaths are harder to quantify, with reports ranging anywhere from 45,000 to 223,000 deaths (Altman and Oppel 2008).

The reasons for the invasion of Iraq—and the causes of its bloody aftermath—reveal a great deal about the issues we discuss in this chapter.

One feature of modern politics is that in today's highly globalized world, even a country as powerful as the United States is under considerable pressure to act according to established international procedures before engaging in war. In the case of the Iraq War, one of the principal justifications for the invasion was that Iraq was said to have *weapons of mass destruction* (WMDs)—chemical, biological, and nuclear materials—it was prepared to use against the West and possibly sell to terrorist organizations. The United States accordingly made its case to the United Nations Security Council, providing its best evidence that Iraq was violating the disarmament obligations it had agreed to after its 1991 defeat in the Persian Gulf War. In response to the U.S. presentation, the Security Council unanimously passed Resolution 1441, requiring Iraq to resume inspections and fully disclose its WMD program, and threatening "serious consequences" if these conditions were not met. Although Iraq resumed inspections and issued a twelve-thousand-page declaration of its weapons program, the United States claimed that Iraq was still hiding its WMDs and justified the war on the basis of the UN resolution. Today, for war to be regarded as fully legitimate, it requires some form of international authorization—in this case, that of the United Nations.

The buildup to the war illustrates another feature of modern politics: the importance of the media, including the Internet. President George W. Bush and his administration took their case to the American public, with frequent television appearances by the president and administration officials, emphasizing what they viewed as the threat posed by Iraq's WMDs and Saddam's possible connections to Osama bin Laden and al Qaeda. Opponents of the United States–led invasion also used the media to great effect. They challenged the claims that Iraq had WMDs or posed an immediate threat to the United States, pointing out flaws in the U.S. intelligence reports on which the allegations were based. They also argued that, contrary to the claims of the Bush administration, Saddam Hussein—who had long persecuted religious nationalists such as al Qaeda—was highly unlikely to cooperate with his former enemies. Critics' claims were supported by government leaks, former intelligence officials, and even UN inspectors, and were widely circulated on the Internet.

The critics turned out to be correct: Neither WMDs nor Iraqi connections with Osama bin Laden were ever found. From activist blogs to Internet-based "smart mobs" (mobilizers) such as MoveOn.org, such information circulated around the world. The largest antiwar demonstrations in world history were held on the weekend of February 15, 2003, involving simultaneous protests by an estimated ten million people in eighty countries and eight hundred cities. Such well-coordinated global demonstrations resulted from an international network of *nongovernmental organizations* (NGOs)—an increasing force in global governance.

The violence that followed Saddam's defeat also illustrates another aspect of politics in the modern world—the challenges of building democracy. One of the reasons given for the invasion, apart from ending the threat of WMDs, was the need to foster democracy in the Middle East, a region that is largely ruled by princes, military leaders, and corrupt government officials. Bush administration officials argued that toppling Saddam not only would remove a brutal dictator from power, effectively ending a major source of instability in the Middle East, but would also create ripples throughout the region, showing others that democracy was possible.

The invasion by the United States–led coalition was followed by a military occupation whose purpose was to create democratic institutions, enforce elections, and keep the peace. Such an experiment in nation building proved to be fraught with difficulties.

As we will see later in this chapter, a modern nation-state requires that citizens see themselves as one people under a single government. Previously ruled by the Ottomans and the British, the "state of Iraq" is made up of many different tribal, ethnic, and religious groups, principal among which are the Sunni Turks in the northern region, the Sunni Arab Muslims in the central region (which includes the capital city, Baghdad), and the Shiite Arab Muslims (the large majority) in the southern region. Many experts on the region predicted that the overthrow of Saddam could lead to a civil war, in which Sunnis, Shiites, and Turks fought bitterly over power and resources while settling old scores. Sunni Arabs, who made up less than 15 percent of the total population, had enjoyed a disproportionate share of Iraqi wealth under Saddam—wealth that was largely generated by oil fields in the Kurdish north and the Shiite south. Moreover, the politics of creating a viable democracy were complicated by the presence of *Islamists*, religious nationalists influenced (and perhaps supported) by Osama bin Laden, who sought to create a strict fundamentalist religious state and were willing to engage in widespread suicide bombing to achieve their goals. Furthermore, many Iraqis, whatever their ethnic identity or religious beliefs, resented the invasion itself, the continued presence of occupying forces, and the escalating violence associated with the occupation.

The invasion and its aftermath also have had profound effects on the Iraqi economy. Iraq, the world's third leading producer of oil, saw its oil exports bottom out during the first five years of the war. In 1990, its peak production year, Iraq extracted about 3.5 million barrels a day. From 2003 to 2009, however, this number hovered around 2 million. Iraq's oil system has been damaged repeatedly by insurgent attacks, corruption, theft, and mismanagement of oil production processes. The decline in Iraq's oil production also is creating ripple effects throughout the global economy, with oil prices rising to an all-time high in the summer of 2008.

Democratization and the rise of the global economy are two of the most influential forces in the world. Like so many aspects of contemporary societies, the realms of government, politics, and economic life are undergoing major changes. **Government** refers to the regular enactment of policies, decisions, and matters of state on the part of the officials within a political apparatus; as the example of Iraq shows, creating a stable and successful government can be a challenge in the modern world. **Politics** concerns the means whereby power is used to affect the scope and content of governmental activities. The sphere of the political may range well beyond that of government itself. As in Iraq, it is frequently intertwined with economics. The **economy** consists of institutions that provide for the production and distribution of goods and services. In this chapter, we study the main factors affecting political and economic life today. We begin with a discussion of politics and then turn to work and the economy. The sphere of government is the sphere of political power. All political life is about power: the people who hold it, how they achieve it, and what they do with it.

POWER AND AUTHORITY

As mentioned in Chapter 1, the study of power is of fundamental importance for sociology. **Power** is the ability of individuals or groups to make their own interests or concerns count, even when others resist. It sometimes involves the direct use of force, such as when the United States and its coalition forces invaded Iraq to overthrow Saddam Hussein and create democracy. Power is an element in almost all social relationships, such as that between employer and employee. This chapter focuses on a narrower aspect of power: governmental power. In this form, it is almost always accompanied by

government • The enacting of policies and decisions on the part of officials within a political apparatus. While in the past virtually all governments were headed by monarchs or emperors, in most modern societies governments are run by officials who do not inherit their positions of power but are elected or appointed on the basis of qualifications.

politics • The means by which power is employed to influence the nature and content of governmental activities. The sphere of the political includes the activities of those in government, but also the actions of others. There are many ways in which people outside the governmental apparatus seek to influence it.

economy • The system of production and exchange that provides for the material needs of individuals living in a given society. Economic institutions are of key importance in all social orders. What goes on in the economy usually influences other areas in social life. Modern economies differ substantially from traditional ones, because the majority of the population is no longer engaged in agricultural production.

power • The ability of individuals or the members of a group to achieve aims or further the interests they hold. Power is a pervasive element in all human relationships. Many conflicts in society are struggles over power, because how much power an individual or group is able to achieve governs how far they are able to put their wishes into practice.

ideologies, which are used to justify the actions of the powerful. For example, the U.S. government justified its invasion of Iraq partly on the basis of fostering the ideology of democracy; the escalating violence in that country is justified by its perpetrators in terms of such ideologies as Iraqi nationalism in the face of a foreign occupation, or religious conviction.

authority • A government's legitimate use of power.

Authority is a government's legitimate use of power: Those subject to a government's authority consent to it. Power is thus different from authority. In Iraq, while power is increasingly in the hands of the newly created political institutions, the authority of those institutions remains in doubt. Contrary to what many believe, democracy is not the only type of government people consider legitimate. Dictatorships can have legitimacy as well, as can states governed by religious leaders. But as we shall see later, democracy is presently the most widespread form of government considered legitimate.

HOW DID THE STATE DEVELOP?

state • A political apparatus (government institutions plus civil service officials) ruling over a given territorial order, whose authority is backed by law and the ability to use force. The emergence of the state marked a distinctive transition in human history, because the centralization of political power involved in state formation introduced new dynamics into processes of social change.

A **state** exists where there is a political apparatus of government (institutions like a parliament or congress, plus civil service officials) ruling over a given territory, whose authority is backed by a legal system and by the capacity to use military force to implement its policies. All modern states lay claim to specific territories, possess formalized codes of law, and are backed by the control of military force. **Nation-states** have come into existence at various times in different parts of the world (e.g., the United States in 1776 and the Czech Republic in 1993). Their main characteristics, however, contrast rather sharply with those of states in traditional civilizations.

CHARACTERISTICS OF THE STATE

nation-state • A particular type of state, characteristic of the modern world, in which a government has sovereign power within a defined territorial area, and the population are citizens who know themselves to be part of a single nation. Nation-states developed as part of an emerging nation-state system, originating in Europe; in current times, they span the whole globe.

Sovereignty The territories ruled by traditional states were always poorly defined, the level of control wielded by the central government being quite weak. The notion of **sovereignty**—that a government possesses authority over an area with clear-cut borders, within which it is the supreme power—had little relevance. All nation-states, by contrast, are sovereign states.

sovereignty • The undisputed political rule of a state over a given territorial area.

Citizenship In traditional states, most of the population ruled by the king or emperor showed little awareness of, or interest in, those who governed them. Nor did they have any political rights or influence. Normally only the dominant classes or more affluent groups felt a sense of belonging to an overall political community. In modern societies, by contrast, most people living within the borders of the political system are **citizens**, having common rights and duties and knowing themselves to be members of a national community (Brubaker 1992). Although some people are political refugees or are "stateless," almost everyone in the world today is a member of a definite national political order.

citizen • A member of a political community, having both rights and duties associated with that membership.

nationalism • A set of beliefs and symbols expressing identification with a national community.

Nationalism Nation-states are associated with the rise of **nationalism**, which can be defined as a set of symbols and beliefs providing the sense of being part of a single political community. Thus, individuals feel a sense of pride and belonging in being American, Canadian, or Russian. Probably people have always felt some kind of identity with social groups of one form or another—their family, village, or religious community. Nationalism, however, made its appearance only with the development of the modern state. It is the main expression of feelings of identity with a distinct sovereign community.

Nationalistic loyalties do not always fit the physical borders marking the territories of states in the world today. Virtually all nation-states were built from communities of diverse backgrounds. As a result, **local nationalisms** have frequently arisen in opposition to those fostered by the states. Thus, in Canada, for instance, nationalist feelings among the French-speaking population in Quebec present a challenge to the feeling of "Canadianness." Yet while the relation between the nation-state and nationalism is a complicated one, the two have come into being as part of the same process. (We will return to nationalism later in the chapter as we look at its impact on international politics in the modern world.)

We can now offer a comprehensive definition of the nation-state: It is possessed of a government apparatus that is recognized to have sovereign rights within the borders of a territorial area, it is able to back its claims to sovereignty by the control of military power, and many of its citizens have positive feelings of commitment to its national identity.

local nationalisms • The beliefs that communities that share a cultural identity should have political autonomy, even within smaller units of a nation-state.

CITIZENSHIP RIGHTS

Most nation-states became centralized and effective political systems through the activities of monarchs who successfully concentrated more and more power in their

Global Map 13.1 | Freedom in Global Perspective

The level of freedom is based on the political rights and civil liberties individuals have in each country. And in Africa, a number of previously undemocratic nations—including Benin, Ghana, Mozambique, and South Africa—have come to embrace democratic ideals, while some others have experienced fallbacks—Congo has moved from partly free to not free. Freedom House estimates that 47 percent of the world population lives in free countries, 30 percent in partly free and the remaining 23 percent in countries that are designated as not free (Freedom House 2007a).

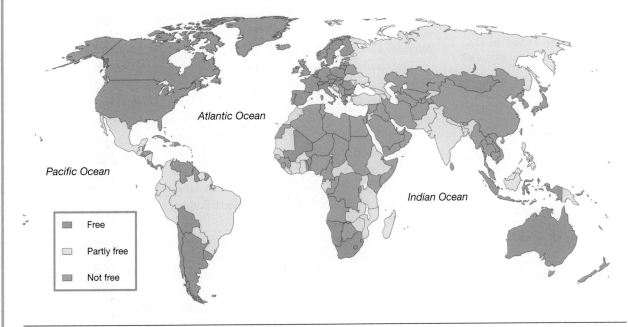

Free
Partly free
Not free

Source: Freedom House 2007a.

A U.S. Border Patrol agent drives along the wall that separates Nogales, Arizona, from Nogales, Sonora, Mexico, on the U.S. and Mexican border. What strategies has the U.S. used to achieve social closure?

civil rights • Legal rights held by all citizens in a given national community.

political rights • Rights of political participation, such as the right to vote in local and national elections, held by citizens of a national community.

social rights • Rights of social and welfare provision held by all citizens in a national community, including, for example, the right to claim unemployment benefits and sickness payments provided by the state.

welfare state • A political system that provides a wide range of welfare benefits for its citizens.

own hands. Citizenship did not originally carry rights of political participation in these states. Such rights were achieved largely through struggles that limited the power of monarchs, as in Britain, or actively overthrew them—sometimes by a process of revolution, as in the cases of the United States and France, followed by a period of negotiation between the new ruling elites and their subjects (Tilly 1996).

Three types of rights are associated with the growth of citizenship (Marshall 1973). **Civil rights** refer to the rights of the individual by law. These include privileges many of us take for granted today but that took a long while to achieve (and are by no means fully recognized in all countries). Examples are the freedom of individuals to live where they choose; freedom of speech and religion; the right to own property; and the right to equal justice before the law. These rights were not fully established in most European countries until the early nineteenth century (see Global Map 13.1). Although the U.S. Constitution granted such rights to Americans well before most European states had them, African Americans were excluded. Even after the Civil War, when blacks were formally given these rights, they were not able to exercise them.

The second type of citizenship rights consists of **political rights**, especially the right to participate in elections and to run for public office. Again, these were not won easily or quickly. Except in the United States, the achievement of full voting rights even for all men is relatively recent and was gained only after a struggle in the face of governments reluctant to admit the principle of the universal vote. In most European countries, the vote was at first limited to male citizens owning a certain amount of property, which effectively limited voting rights to an affluent minority. Universal franchise for men was won in most Western nations by the early years of the twentieth century. Women had to wait longer; in most Western countries, the vote for women was achieved partly as a result of the efforts of women's movements and partly as a consequence of the mobilization of women into the formal economy during World War I.

The third type is **social rights**, the right of every individual to enjoy a certain minimum standard of economic welfare and security. Social rights include such entitlements as sickness benefits, benefits in case of unemployment, and the guarantee of minimum levels of wages. Although in some countries welfare benefits were introduced before legal and political rights were fully established (for example, in nineteenth-century Germany), in most societies social rights have been the last to develop. This is because the establishment of civil and particularly political rights has usually been the basis of the fight for social rights. Social rights have been won largely as a result of the political strength poorer groups have been able to develop after obtaining the vote.

The broadening of social rights is closely connected with the welfare state, which has been firmly established in Western societies only since World War II. A **welfare state** exists where government organizations provide material benefits for those who are unable to support themselves adequately through paid employment—the unemployed, the sick, the disabled, and the elderly. All Western countries today provide extensive welfare benefits. In many poorer countries, these benefits are virtually nonexistent.

Although an extensive welfare state was seen as the culmination of the development of citizenship rights, in recent years welfare states have come under pressure from increasing global economic competition and the movement of people from poor, underdeveloped societies to richer, developed countries. As a result, the United States and some European countries have sought to reduce benefits to noncitizens and to prevent new immigrants from coming. For example, for many years the United States government has patrolled its border with Mexico and constructed walls of concrete and barbed wire in an attempt to keep illegal immigrants out of the country. Citizenship serves as a powerful instrument of *social closure*, whereby prosperous nation-states have attempted to exclude the migrant poor from the status and the benefits that citizenship confers (Brubaker 1992).

Having learned some of the important characteristics of modern states, we now consider the nature of democracy in modern societies. ✓

CONCEPT CHECKS ✓

1. Describe three main characteristics of the state.

2. What is a welfare state? Can the United States be classified as a welfare state? Why?

HOW DO DEMOCRACIES FUNCTION?

The word *democracy* has its roots in the Greek term *demokratia*, the individual parts of which are *demos* ("people") and *kratos* ("rule"), and its basic meaning is therefore a political system in which the people, not monarchs or aristocracies based on blood lines, rule. What does it mean to be ruled by the people? The answer to that question has taken contrasting forms, at varying periods and in different societies. For example, "the people" have been variously understood as owners of property, white men, educated men, men, and adult men and women. In some societies, the officially accepted version of **democracy** is limited to the political sphere, whereas in others, it is extended to other areas of social life.

democracy • A political system that allows the citizens to participate in political decision making or to elect representatives to government bodies.

PARTICIPATORY DEMOCRACY

In **participatory democracy** (or **direct democracy**), decisions are made communally by those affected by them. This was the original type of democracy practiced in ancient Athens, in Greece. Those who were citizens, a small minority of Athenian society, regularly assembled to consider policies and make major decisions. Participatory democracy is of limited importance in modern societies, where the vast majority of the population has political rights and it would be impossible for everyone to participate actively in the making of all the decisions that affect them.

participatory democracy • A system of democracy in which all members of a group or community participate collectively in making major decisions.

direct democracy • A form of participatory democracy that allows citizens to vote directly on laws and policies.

Yet some facets of participatory democracy do play a part in modern societies. The holding of a referendum, for example, whereby the majority express their views on a particular issue, is one form of participatory democracy. Direct consultation of large numbers of people is made possible by simplifying the issue to one or two questions to be answered. Referenda are employed frequently on a state level in the United States to decide controversial issues, such as the legalization of gay marriage.

MONARCHIES AND LIBERAL DEMOCRACIES

Some modern states (e.g., Britain and Belgium) still have monarchs, but these are few and far between. Where traditional rulers of this sort are still found, their real power is usually limited or nonexistent. In a tiny number of countries, such as Saudi Arabia and Jordan, monarchs continue to hold some degree of control over government, but in most cases they are symbols of national identity rather than personages having any direct power in political life. The queen of England, the king of Sweden, and even the emperor of Japan are all **constitutional monarchs**: Their real power is severely restricted by the constitution, which vests authority in the elected representatives of the people. The vast majority of modern states are *republican*—there is no king or queen. Almost every modern state, including constitutional monarchies, professes adherence to democracy.

Countries in which voters can choose between two or more political parties and in which the majority of the adult population has the right to vote are usually called **liberal democracies**. The United States, the Western European countries, Japan, Australia, and New Zealand all fall into this category. Some developing countries, such as India, also have liberal democratic systems.

constitutional monarchs • Kings or queens who are largely figureheads. Real power rests in the hands of other political leaders.

liberal democracies • Systems of democracy based on parliamentary institutions, coupled to the free-market system in the area of economic production.

THE SPREAD OF LIBERAL DEMOCRACY

For much of the twentieth century, the political systems of the world were divided primarily between liberal democracy and communism, as found in the former Soviet Union (and as still exists in China, Cuba, and North Korea). **Communism** was essentially a system of one-party rule. Voters were given a choice not between different parties but between different candidates of the same party—the Communist party; sometimes only one candidate ran. The party controlled the economy as well as the political system.

Since 1989, when the hold of the Soviet Union over Eastern Europe was broken, processes of democratization have swept across the world in a sort of chain reaction. The number of democratic nations almost doubled between 1989 and 2005, from 66 to 119 (Freedom House 2005a). In China, which has about a fifth of the world's population, the communist government is facing strong pressures toward democratization. During the 1990s, thousands of people were held in prison in China for the nonviolent expression of their desire for democracy. Some groups, resisted by the communist government, are still working actively to secure a transition to a democratic system.

The trend toward democracy is hardly irreversible. Electoral democracy does not ensure that liberal democratic governments will be chosen by voters; in recent elections in Palestine, Turkey, and Morocco, the voters chose Islamist parties over more secular, democratic ones.

Why has democracy become so popular? The reasons have to do with the social and economic changes discussed throughout this book. First, democracy tends to be associated with competitive capitalism in the economic system, and capitalism has shown itself to be superior to communism as a wealth-generating system. Second, the more social activity becomes globalized and people's daily lives become influenced by events happening far away, the more they start to push for information about how they are ruled—and therefore for greater democracy (Huntington 1991). Third, with the influence of mass communications, particularly television and the Internet, governments can't maintain control over what their citizens see.

communism • A set of political ideas associated with Marx, as developed particularly by Lenin and institutionalized in the Soviet Union, Eastern Europe, and some Third World countries.

The Barack Obama presidential campaign revolutionized electoral politics with its use of the Internet for fundraising and organizing. What are the implications for grassroots movements in the age of the Internet?

THE INTERNET AND DEMOCRATIZATION

The Internet is a powerful democratizing force. It transcends national and cultural borders, facilitates the spread of ideas around the globe, and allows like-minded people to find one another in the realm of cyberspace. More and more people in countries around the world access the Internet regularly and consider it to be important to their lifestyles.

One prominent example of the political role of the Internet is provided by MoveOn.org, a liberal organization that was originally created by the twenty-two-year-old activist Eli Pariser and software entrepreneurs Wes Boyd and Joan Blades to electronically mobilize opposition to the impeachment of President Bill Clinton. Today MoveOn.org claims five million members. The organization collects millions of dollars through its Web site in support of liberal causes and has attracted some big-money contributors as well: the billionaires George Soros and Peter Lewis together gave the fledgling organization $5 million in late 2003 (Neuman 2003; Brownstein 2003; Menn 2003; Avins 2003).

Yet as we shall see, political indifference and voter apathy are extremely high in the United States, and winning federal elections requires large sums of money that are unlikely to be raised through small online contributions. How "Internet democracy" plays itself out in the national political arena will depend not only on technology, but on the ability of grassroots efforts to make a real difference in political outcomes.

DEMOCRACY IN THE UNITED STATES

POLITICAL PARTIES

A *political party* is an organization of individuals with broadly similar political aims, oriented toward achieving legitimate control of government through an electoral process. Two parties tend to dominate the political system where elections are based on the principle of winner take all, as in the United States. Where elections are based on different principles, as in *proportional representation* (in which seats in a representative assembly are allocated according to the proportions of the vote received), five or six different parties, or even more, may be represented in the assembly. When they lack an overall majority, some of the parties have to form a *coalition*—an alliance with each other to form a government.

In the United States, the system has become effectively a two-party one between the Republicans and Democrats, although no formal restriction is placed on the number of political parties. The nation's founders made no mention of parties in the Constitution because they thought that party conflict might threaten the unity of the new republic.

Two-party systems tend to lead to a concentration on the "middle ground." The parties in these countries often cultivate a moderate image and sometimes come to resemble one another so closely that the choice they offer is relatively slight. Multi-party systems, by contrast, allow divergent interests and points of view to be expressed more directly and provide scope for the representation of radical alternatives. Green party representatives or representatives of far right parties, found in some European parliaments, are cases in point. However, under such systems no one party is likely to achieve an overall majority, and the government by coalition that results can lead to indecision and stalemate if compromises can't be worked out.

POLITICS AND VOTING

Building mass support for a party in the United States is difficult, because the country is so large and includes so many different regional, cultural, and ethnic groups. The parties have each tried to develop their electoral strength by forging broad regional bases of support and by campaigning for very general political ideals.

As measured by their levels of membership, party identification, and voting support, both of the major American parties are in decline (Wattenberg 1996). One study showed that the number of voters declaring themselves to be "independent" of either party grew from 22 percent in 1952 to over 38 percent in 2004 (Pew 2004). This proportion has remained stable, with 39 percent of Americans identifying as "independent" voters in 2009 (Pew 2009c).

In recent years, Democrats have also lost ground to Republicans: Although Democrats held an edge in party identification during the Clinton years, by the end of 2003 roughly the same proportion of Americans (one-third) identified with each party. By April 2009, Democrats had regained a considerable edge in voter identification, with 33 percent of Americans saying that they were Democrats versus 22 percent for Republicans (Pew 2009c). Moreover, Democrats and Republicans have become increasingly polarized in the past few years. For example, Republicans are much more likely to favor an assertive national security strategy, whereas Democrats are increasingly critical of business and more likely to favor stronger government support for the poor (Pew 2009c).

Starting in the early 1960s the proportion of the population that turns out to vote in the United States steadily decreased, to the point where only slightly more than half the electorate voted in presidential elections in the last three decades of the twentieth century. The turnout for congressional elections is lower still—around 40 percent (NES 2003). The presidential election of 2008 bucked this declining trend with voter turnout levels of nearly 59 percent, the highest since the election of 1968. The spike in the number of voters is attributed to campaigns by both parties to mobilize their core constituencies. Youthful voters and African Americans also turned out in unprecedented numbers, inspired by the candidacy of Barack Obama. The 2008 election was an anomaly in comparison to earlier years, however. Political scientists have documented that voter turnout is highest historically among whites and lowest among Hispanics, with blacks and Asian Americans in between. Highly educated persons and those with greater income also are more likely to vote than persons with fewer means. Generally, turnout increases directly with age: Only a little more than a third of all voters in the eighteen-to-twenty-four age group bothered to vote for president in 2000, compared with nearly three-quarters of voters in their sixties. However, in the 2008 presidential election, the number of young voters swelled due to a highly organized voter mobilization campaign. Nearly 52 percent of voters under thirty voted in the election.

Voter turnout in the United States is among the world's lowest. Sweden's International Institute for Democracy and Electoral Assistance tracked voter turnout in all countries that held national elections at any time during the period 2000–2009 by comparing the number of voters with the total voting-age population. According to their study, voter turnout in the United States averaged only 58 percent overall, earning it 112th place (out of 192 countries). By way of comparison, voter turnout in Europe over the same period averaged 61 percent; Asia, 64 percent; South America, 65 percent; Central America and the Caribbean, 61.5 percent; and Africa, 64.5 percent (IDEA 2009).

Why is voter turnout so low in the United States? Many studies have found that countries with high rates of literacy, high average incomes, and well-established political freedoms and civil liberties are likely to have high voter turnouts. Yet the United States ranks high on all of these measures, but still fails to motivate people to vote. Compulsory registration is common throughout Europe, and registration is often made easy. In the United States, where voters are required to register well in advance of elections, many fail to do so and are thus disqualified from voting. In addition to compulsory registration, thirty-three countries have compulsory voting. Even though enforcement is often weak or nonexistent, voter turnout tends to be higher where voting is mandated by law (Pintor and Gratschew 2002).

Another possible reason is that since "winner-take-all" elections discourage the formation of third parties, voters may sometimes feel that they lack effective choices when it comes time to vote. A staunch environmentalist may decide there is no point in voting if the Green party candidate has no real chance of winning a seat in Congress. Finally, the range of elections is much more extensive in the United States than in other Western societies. In no other country are such a variety of offices at all levels—including sheriffs, judges, city treasurers, and many other posts—open to election. Americans are entitled to do about three or four times as much electing as citizens elsewhere. Low rates of voter turnout thus have to be balanced against the wider extent of voter choice.

INTEREST GROUPS

Interest groups and lobbying play a distinctive part in American politics. An **interest group** is any organization that attempts to influence elected officials to consider its aims when deciding on legislation. The American Medical Association, the National Organization for Women, and the National Rifle Association are but three examples. Interest groups vary in size; some are national, others statewide. Some are permanently organized; others are short lived. *Lobbying* is the act of contacting influential officials to present arguments to convince them to vote in favor of a cause or otherwise lend support to the aims of an interest group. The word *lobby* originated in the British parliamentary system: In days past, members of Parliament did not have offices, so their business was conducted in the lobbies of the Parliament buildings.

interest group • A group organized to pursue specific interests in the political arena, operating primarily by lobbying the members of legislative bodies.

To run as a candidate is enormously expensive, and interest groups provide much of the funding at all levels of political office. In the 2008 presidential election, the Obama-Biden campaign spent more than 730 million dollars to win the White House. The McCain-Palin ticket spent roughly 330 million (Center for Responsive Politics 2008). Even to run for the House or Senate costs a small fortune. The most expensive congressional race in history, when Hillary Rodham Clinton (Democrat) beat Rick Lazio (Republican) in the battle to become a senator from New York in 2000, saw total spending of $70.5 million.

Incumbents, or those already in office, have an enormous advantage in soliciting money. Incumbents are favored as fund-raisers partly because they can curry favor with special interests and other contributors, since they are in a position to assure favorable votes on issues of importance to their funders, as well as obtain spending on pet projects and other "pork" for their districts. Incumbency also provides familiarity—a formidable (and costly) obstacle for most challengers to overcome.

Various health care advertisements from interest groups lobbying Congress. The debate over health care reform spurred some mergers of convenience, such as partnerships between drug makers, labor, and the AARP.

About a third of the funding in congressional or senatorial elections comes from *political action committees* (PACs), which are set up by interest groups to raise and distribute campaign funds. Interest groups and PACs not only help elect candidates—they also influence the outcome of votes in Congress. The Medicare Reform Act of 2003, which created a $400 billion program to extend prescription drug benefits to the elderly, was heavily pushed by the pharmaceutical industry, which between 1996 and 2003 had spent more than half a billion dollars to lobby Congress, the White House, and federal regulators, as well as to launch advertising campaigns aimed at the general public (Common Cause 2003). Although the long-run benefit to the elderly was hotly debated by members of Congress, there is no question that drug companies have reaped considerable benefit.

THE POLITICAL PARTICIPATION OF WOMEN

Voting has a special meaning for women, given their long struggle to obtain universal suffrage. The members of the early women's movements saw the vote both as the symbol of political freedom and as the means of achieving greater economic and social equality.

After what was often a long, hard fight, women now can vote in nearly all of the world's nations; however, this has not greatly altered the nature of politics. Women's voting patterns, like those of men, are shaped by party preferences, policy options, and the choice of available candidates. The influence of women on politics cannot be assessed solely through voting patterns, however. Feminist groups have made an impact on political life independently of the franchise, particularly in recent decades. Since the early 1960s, the National Organization for Women (NOW) and other women's groups in the United States have played a significant role in the passing of equal opportunity acts and have pressed for a range of issues directly affecting women to be

One of the most powerful women in United States politics, Speaker of the House Nancy Pelosi (D-Cal).

placed on the political agenda. Such issues include equal rights at work, the availability of abortion, changes in family and divorce laws, and lesbian rights. In 1973, women achieved a legal victory when the Supreme Court ruled in *Roe v. Wade* that women had a legal right to abortion. The 1989 Court ruling in *Webster v. Reproductive Health Services*, which placed restrictions on that right, resulted in a resurgence of involvement in the women's movement.

Although women lag far behind men in the ranks of the political elite, they have made important strides in recent decades. Following the 2008 elections in the United States, there were seventy-five female members in the House of Representatives, making up just over 17 percent of the total membership. This number has tripled since the early 1970s, but it is still not representative of the number of female citizens. In 2008 there were only seventeen women in the Senate, representing 17 percent of those sitting in the upper chamber.

Despite the gender gap in Congress and other elected offices, both the Democratic and Republican parties today are nominally committed to securing equal opportunities for women and men. Since 1990, female candidates for political office have been successful *when they have run for office*. The critical factor seems to be that political parties (which are largely run by men) have not recruited as many women to run for office.

From considering the position of women in politics, we now broaden our scope to look at some basic ideas of political power. First, we take up the issue of who actually holds the reins of power, drawing on comparative materials to help illuminate the discussion. We then consider whether democratic governments around the world are "in crisis."

WHO RULES? THEORIES OF DEMOCRACY

DEMOCRATIC ELITISM

One of the most influential views of the nature and limits of modern democracy was set out by Max Weber and, in rather modified form, by the economist Joseph Schumpeter

Campaign workers have a clear-cut job: to get their candidates elected. Figuring out exactly how to do that isn't quite so simple, though. Campaign managers need to figure out what kind of message to convey, to whom they should convey the message, and—most important—how to get those potential votes out to the polls. In the 2004 presidential election, candidates especially focused their efforts on young people; men and women ages eighteen to twenty-four have lower rates of voter turnout than any other age group. Recognizing that young people could have a powerful effect on the election, campaign workers developed innovative programs to entice young voters. Rap star P. Diddy was enlisted to start the Citizen Change program, urging young adults—particularly African American and Latino young adults—to "Vote or Die!" The nonpartisan group Declare Yourself ran advertisements showing the muzzled mouth of OutKast's Andre 3000, with the motto "Only You Can Silence Yourself." World Wrestling Entertainment initiated the SmackDown Your Vote program, including a Web-based forum where John Kerry and George W. Bush shared their views on jobs, the economy, terrorism, college loans, and other topics of interest to youthful voters. Based on your knowledge of sociological research on politics and voting, which demographic groups would you target for your candidate's campaign? What messages would you convey, and through what medium? Why?

(1983; orig. 1942). The ideas they developed are sometimes referred to as the theory of **democratic elitism**.

Weber began from the assumption that direct democracy is impossible as a means of regular government in large-scale societies. This is not only for the obvious logistical reason that millions of people cannot meet to make political decisions, but because running a complex society demands expertise. Participatory democracy, Weber believed, can only succeed in small organizations in which the work to be carried out is fairly simple and straightforward. Where more complicated decisions have to be made, or policies worked out, even in modest-sized groups—such as a small business firm—specialized knowledge and skills are necessary. Experts have to carry out their jobs on a continuous basis; positions that require expertise cannot be subject to the regular election of people who may only have a vague knowledge of the necessary skills and information. While higher officials, responsible for overall policy decisions, are elected, there must be a large substratum of full-time bureaucratic officials who play a large part in running a country (Weber 1979; orig. 1921).

Weber placed a great deal of emphasis on the importance of *leadership* in democracy—which is why his view is referred to as "democratic elitism." He argued that rule by elites is inevitable; the best we can hope for is that those elites effectively represent our interests and that they do so in an innovative and insightful fashion. Weber valued multiparty democracy more for the quality of leadership it generates than for the mass participation in politics it makes possible.

Joseph Schumpeter fully agreed with Weber about the limits of mass political participation. For Schumpeter, as for Weber, democracy is more important as a method of generating effective and responsible government than as a means of providing significant power for

democratic elitism ● A theory of the limits of democracy, which holds that in large-scale societies democratic participation is necessarily limited to the regular election of political leaders.

the majority. Democracy, Schumpeter stated, is the rule of *the politician*, not *the people*. Politicians are "dealers in votes" much as brokers are dealers in shares on the stock exchange. To achieve voting support, however, politicians must be at least minimally responsive to the demands and interests of the electorate. Only if there is some degree of competition to secure votes can arbitrary rule effectively be avoided.

PLURALIST THEORIES

pluralist theories of modern democracy ● Theories that emphasize the role of diverse and potentially competing interest groups, none of which dominate the political process.

The ideas of Weber and Schumpeter influenced some of the **pluralist theories of modern democracy**, although the pluralists developed their ideas somewhat differently. According to the pluralist view, government policies in a democracy are influenced by continual processes of bargaining among numerous groups representing different interests—business organizations, trade unions, ethnic groups, environmental organizations, religious groups, and so forth. A democratic political order is one in which there is a balance among competing interests, all having some impact on policy but none dominating the actual mechanisms of government. Elections are also influenced by this situation, for to achieve a broad enough base of support to lay claim to government, parties must be responsive to numerous diverse interest groups. The United States, it is held, is the most pluralistic of industrialized societies and, therefore, the most democratic. Competition between diverse interest groups occurs not only at the national level but within the states and in the politics of local communities.

THE POWER ELITE

The view suggested by C. Wright Mills in his celebrated work *The Power Elite* is quite different from pluralist theories (Mills 1956). Mills argues that during the course of the twentieth century a process of institutional centralization occurred in the political order, the economy, and the sphere of the military. Not only did each of these spheres become more centralized, according to Mills, but they became increasingly merged with one another to form a unified system of power. Those who are in the highest positions in all three institutional areas have come from similar social backgrounds, have parallel interests, and often know one another on a personal basis. By the mid-twentieth century they had become a single **power elite** that ran, and continues to run, the country—and, given the international position of the United States, also influences a great deal of the rest of the world.

power elite • Small networks of individuals who, according to C. Wright Mills, hold concentrated power in modern societies.

The power elite, in Mills's portrayal, is composed mainly of white Anglo-Saxon Protestants (WASPs). Many are from wealthy families, have been to the same prestigious universities, belong to the same clubs, and sit on government committees with one another. They have closely connected concerns. Business and political leaders work together, and both have close relationships with the military through weapons contracting and the supply of goods for the armed forces. There is a great deal of movement among top positions in the three spheres. Politicians have business interests; business leaders often run for public office; higher military personnel sit on the boards of the large companies.

Since Mills published his study, numerous other research investigations have analyzed the social background and interconnections of leading figures in the various spheres of American society (Dye 1986). All studies agree on the finding that the social backgrounds of those in leading positions are highly unrepresentative of the population as a whole (Domhoff 1971, 1979, 1983, 1998).

THE ROLE OF THE MILITARY

Mills's argument that the military plays a central role in the power elite was buttressed by a well-known warning from a former military hero and U.S. president, Dwight David Eisenhower. In his farewell presidential speech in 1961, Eisenhower—who was the supreme commander of the Allied forces in Europe in World War II—warned of the dangers of what he termed the "military-industrial complex." As Eisenhower bluntly put it, "The conjunction of an immense military establishment and a large arms industry is new in the American experience. In the councils of government, we must guard against the acquisition of unwarranted influence, whether sought or unsought, by the military-industrial complex. The potential for the disastrous rise of misplaced power exists and will persist" (Eisenhower Library 1961).

With the collapse of the Soviet Union in 1991, the United States has emerged as the world's unrivaled military superpower, accounting for nearly half of total military spending—more than the next fifteen countries combined (Figure 13.1). The global "war on terror," discussed below, has instead triggered yet another cycle of military spending. Eisenhower's dire warning seems no less apt today than when he uttered it some fifty years ago.

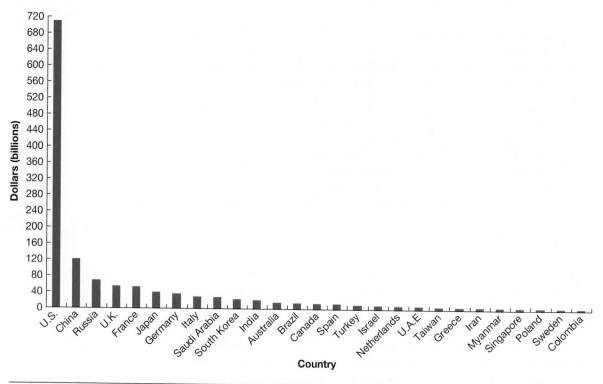

Figure 13.1 | **Military spending in countries that spent at least $5 billion a year on the military, 2008**

Source: Center for Arms Control and Non-Proliferation, 2008.

DEMOCRACY IN TROUBLE?

Democracy almost everywhere is in some difficulty today. Even in the United States, voter turnout is low, and many people tell pollsters that they don't trust politicians. In 1964, confidence in government was fairly high: Nearly four out of five people answered "most of the time" or "just about always" when asked, "How much of the time do you trust the government in Washington to do the right thing?" This level of confidence then dropped steadily for the next twenty years, rising somewhat in the 1980s, then dropping to a low of one in five in 1994. Since that time the level of reported trust has increased steadily. Today—bolstered by an increased confidence in government following the attacks of September 11, 2001—a solid majority of Americans (about three out of every five) report that they trust the government "most of the time" or "just about always" (Public Strategies Inc. 2009).

Of those expressing continuing trust in government, most vote in presidential elections; of those who lack trust, most do not vote. As we have seen, younger people have less interest in electoral politics than older generations have, although the young have a greater interest than their elders in issues like the environment (Nye 1997). Some have argued that trends like these indicate that people are increasingly skeptical of traditional forms of authority. Connected to this has been a shift in political values in democratic

DO-IT-YOURSELF SOCIOLOGY

D.I.Y.

The two main political parties in the United States are Democrats and Republicans. Do you identify as a Republican, Democrat, or Independent? Members of these three groups often have very different political attitudes. Flip the page to see how "typical" your political views are.

For each statement, please indicate how much you agree or disagree on a scale of 0 to 10, with 10 meaning you completely agree and 0 meaning you completely disagree, and 5 meaning you aren't sure whether you agree or disagree.

⟶

**Your score
(0–10)**

1. Government has a responsibility to provide financial support for the poor, the sick, and the elderly.

2. Government must step in to protect the national economy when the market fails.

3. Religious faith should focus more on promoting tolerance, social justice, and peace in society and less on opposing abortion or gay rights.

4. Cultural institutions, the arts, and public broadcasting play an important role in our society and should receive government support.

5. African Americans and other minority groups still lack the same opportunities as whites in this country.

6. Immigrants today are a burden on our country because they take our jobs and abuse government benefits.

7. The federal government should guarantee affordable health coverage for every American.

8. The gap between rich and poor should be reduced even if it means higher taxes for the wealthy.

9. Military force is the most effective way to combat terrorism and make America safe.

10. America must play a leading role in addressing climate change by reducing our own greenhouse gas emissions and complying with international agreements on global warning.

TURN
PAGE

The following chart shows some of the ways that Democrats, Independents, and Republicans differ in their views. These responses are based on a national random sample survey of 1,400 Americans age 18 and older (Halpin and Agne 2009). How might you explain these differences? Can you conclude that there is a causal relationship, such as "being a Republican causes one to oppose national health care"? Or might the relationship be spurious, explained by some other social or demographic factor?

	% who indicated agreement level of 6 or higher		
	Democrat	Independent	Republican
1. Government has a responsibility to provide financial support for the poor, the sick, and the elderly.	84	65	51
2. Government must step in to protect the national economy when the market fails.	75	51	43
3. Religious faith should focus more on promoting tolerance, social justice, and peace in society and less on opposing abortion or gay rights.	71	63	38
4. Cultural institutions, the arts, and public broadcasting play an important role in our society and should receive government support.	65	48	33
5. African Americans and other minority groups still lack the same opportunities as whites in this country.	60	46	36
6. Immigrants today are a burden on our country because they take our jobs and abuse government benefits.	36	36	53
7. The federal government should guarantee affordable health coverage for every American.	86	61	39
8. The gap between rich and poor should be reduced even if it means higher taxes for the wealthy.	80	57	39
9. Military force is the most effective way to combat terrorism and make America safe.	49	46	74
10. America must play a leading role in addressing climate change by reducing our own greenhouse gas emissions and complying with international agreements on global warning.	82	67	48

Source: Halpin and Agne 2009.

nations from "scarcity values" to "post-materialist values" (Inglehart 1997). This means that after a certain level of economic prosperity has been reached, voters become concerned less with economic issues than with the quality of their individual (as opposed to collective) lifestyles, such as whether they have meaningful work. As a result, voters are generally less interested in national politics, except for areas involving personal liberty.

The last few decades have also been a period in which, in several Western countries, the welfare state has come under attack. Rights and benefits, fought for over long periods, have been contested and cut back. One reason for this governmental retrenchment is the decline in revenues available to governments as a result of the general world recession that began in the early 1970s. Yet an increasing skepticism also seems to have developed, shared not only by some governments but by many of their citizens, about the effectiveness of relying on the state for the provision of many essential goods and services. This skepticism is based on the belief that the welfare state is bureaucratic, alienating, and inefficient and that welfare benefits can create perverse consequences that undermine what they were designed to achieve (Giddens 1998).

Why are so many people dissatisfied with the very political system that seems to be sweeping all before it across the world? The answers, curiously, are bound up with the factors that have helped spread democracy—the impact of capitalism and the globalizing of social life. For instance, while capitalist economies have proved to generate more wealth than any other type of economic system, that wealth is unevenly distributed (see Chapter 7). And economic inequalities influence who votes, joins parties, and gets elected. Wealthy individuals and corporations back interest groups that lobby for elected officials to support their aims when deciding on legislation. Not being subject to election, interest groups are not accountable to the majority of the electorate. ✓

CONCEPT CHECKS ✓

1. Why is it problematic for contemporary states to have participatory democracy?

2. Contrast the concepts of democracy and communism.

3. Describe the role interest groups play in American politics.

4. Compare and contrast pluralist theories of modern democracy and the power elite model.

WHAT IS TERRORISM?

Terrorism refers to "any action [by a non-state organization] . . . that is intended to cause death or serious bodily harm to civilians or non-combatants, when the purpose of such an act, by its nature or context, is to intimidate a population, or to compel a Government or an international organization to do or to abstain from doing any act" (Panyarachun et al. 2004). In other words, terrorism concerns attacks on civilians designed to persuade a government to alter its policies, or to damage its standing in the world.

terrorism • Use of attacks on civilians designed to persuade a government to alter its policies, or to damage its standing in the world.

OLD- AND NEW-STYLE TERRORISM

A distinction can be drawn between old- and new-style terrorism. **Old-style terrorism** was dominant for most of the twentieth century and still exists today. It is associated primarily with the rise of nationalism and with the establishment of nations as sovereign, territorially bounded entities, which began in Europe in the late eighteenth century. Most forms of old-style terrorism are linked to nations without states. The

old-style terrorism • A type of terrorism that is local and linked to particular states and has limited objectives, which means that the violence involved is fairly limited.

An example of an old-style terrorist movement, these Basque Nationalists are mostly concerned with territorial control and the formation of states.

point of old-style terrorism is to establish states in areas where nations do not have control of the territory's state apparatus. This is true, for example, of Irish nationalists, such as the Irish Republican Army (IRA), and Basque nationalists, such as ETA, in Spain. The main issues are territorial integrity and identity in the formation of a state. Old-style terrorism is found where there are nations without states and where terrorists are prepared to use violence to achieve their ends. Old-style terrorism is fundamentally local because its ambitions are local. It wants to establish a state in a specific national area.

new-style terrorism • A recent form of terrorism characterized by global ambitions, loose global organizational ties, and a more ruthless attitude toward the violence the terrorists are willing to use.

New-style terrorism, most famously associated with the Islamic fundamentalism of al Qaeda, differs from old-style terrorism in several ways (Tan and Ramakrishna 2002). First, new-style terrorism is different from old-style terrorism in the scope of its claims. One of the distinguishing features of al Qaeda's view of the world, for example, is that it has global geopolitical aims; it seeks to restructure world society. Whereas old-style terrorism is local and linked to particular states, new-style terrorism is global in its ambitions. It seeks to alter the balance world power (Gray 2003).

Second, new-style terrorism differs from old-style terrorism in its organizational structure. There is a lot of autonomy in local cells, and these can reproduce without necessarily having any strong direction from the center. Terrorist organizations also have a global spread of supporters in many countries. New terrorist groups also have some contacts and supports from states; the Libyan involvement in the bombing of a passenger plane that crashed in the Scottish village of Lockerbie in 1988 provides one example of this.

The third and last way in which old-style and new-style terrorism differ is over means. Old-style terrorism had relatively limited objectives, and as a result the violence involved was fairly limited. The new terrorism is much more ruthless in the means it is prepared to use. Al Qaeda Web sites, for example, talk in extremely destructive language of the enemy, which is principally the United States but to some extent the West as a whole. These will often explicitly say that terrorist acts should be carried out that kill as many people as possible. This is very different from the more limited use of violent means, such as bombs or combat, which are characteristic of old-style terrorism.

TERRORISM AND WAR

How should we respond to the threat of new-style terrorism? Terrorism of the kind seen on September 11 raises difficult questions for political sociologists. Can a "war" on terrorism be fought like a conventional war? The coalition that attacked Afghanistan in 2001 did destroy at least some of the al Qaeda terrorist networks. Yet despite some successes against new-style terrorism through conventional warfare, critics are surely right to argue that in many cases the level of violence, aims, and organizational structure of new-style terrorist groups differentiate them from conventional enemies such as hostile nation-states. The debate about whether terrorism can be tackled through conventional warfare raises further difficult questions regarding the relationship between terrorism and nation-states, like Afghanistan, that have supported it. In turn this leads to questions about global governance. In a global age, what international support and proof are needed to act to prevent a perceived threat? And what are the best institutions to deal with a global terrorist threat? ✓

> ### CONCEPT CHECKS ✓
> 1. Compare and contrast old- and new-style terrorism.

WHAT IS THE SOCIAL SIGNIFICANCE OF WORK?

Because politics are inextricably linked with economic life, we now turn our attention to the ways that work and the economy have changed. **Work** refers to carrying out tasks that require mental and physical effort, with the objective of the production of goods and services that cater to human needs. An **occupation**, or job, is work that is done in exchange for a regular wage or salary. In all cultures, work is the basis of the economic system.

The study of economic institutions is of major importance in sociology, because the economy influences all segments of society and therefore social reproduction in general. Hunting and gathering, pastoralism, agriculture, industrialism—these different ways of gaining a livelihood have a fundamental influence on the lives people lead. The distribution of goods and variations in the economic position of those who produce them also strongly influence social inequalities of all kinds. Wealth and power do not inevitably go together, but in general the privileged in terms of wealth are also among the more powerful groups in a society.

In the remainder of this chapter, we will analyze the nature of work in modern societies and look at the major changes affecting economic life today. We will investigate the changing nature of industrial production and of work itself. Modern industry differs in a fundamental way from premodern systems of production, which were based above all on agriculture. Most people worked in the fields or cared for livestock. In modern societies, by contrast, only a tiny fraction of the population works in agriculture, and farming itself has become industrialized—it is carried on largely by means of machines rather than by human hands.

Modern industry is itself always changing—technological change is one of its main features. **Technology** involves the use of science and machinery to achieve greater productive efficiency. The nature of industrial production also changes in relation to wider social and economic influences. We focus on both technological and economic

work • The activity by which people produce from the natural world and so ensure their survival. Work should not be thought of exclusively as paid employment. In traditional cultures, there was only a rudimentary monetary system, and few people worked for money. In modern societies, there remain types of work that do not involve direct payment (e.g., housework).

occupation • Any form of paid employment in which an individual regularly works.

technology • The application of knowledge of the material world to production; the creation of material instruments (such as machines) used in human interaction with nature.

change, showing how these are transforming industry today. We will also see that globalization makes a great deal of difference to our working lives; the nature of the work we do is being changed by forces of global economic competition.

THE IMPORTANCE OF PAID AND UNPAID WORK

We often associate the notion of work with drudgery—with a set of tasks that we want to minimize and, if possible, escape from altogether. You may have this very thought in mind as you set out to read this chapter! Is this most people's attitude toward their work, and if so, why?

Work is more than just drudgery, or people would not feel so lost and disoriented when they become unemployed. How would you feel if you thought you would never get a job? In modern societies, having a job is important for maintaining a sense of purpose. Even where work conditions are relatively unpleasant, and the tasks involved dull, work tends to be a structuring element in people's psychological makeup and the cycle of their daily activities.

Work need not conform to orthodox categories of paid employment. Nonpaid labor (such as repairing one's own car or doing one's own housework) is an important aspect of many people's lives. Much of the work done in the informal economy, for example, is not recorded in official employment statistics. The term **informal economy** refers to transactions outside the sphere of regular employment, sometimes involving the exchange of cash for services provided, but also often involving the direct exchange of goods or services.

informal economy • Economic transactions carried on outside the sphere of orthodox paid employment.

The informal economy includes not only "hidden" cash transactions, but many forms of self-provisioning that people carry on inside and outside the home. Do-it-yourself activities with household appliances and tools, for instance, provide goods and services that would otherwise have to be purchased (Gershuny and Miles 1983). Housework, which has traditionally been carried out mostly by women, is usually unpaid. But it is work, often very hard and exhausting work, nevertheless. Volunteer work, for charities or other organizations, has an important social role. Having a paid job is important—but the category of "work" stretches more widely.

THE IMPORTANCE OF THE DIVISION OF LABOR

division of labor • The specialization of work tasks, by means of which different occupations are combined within a production system. All societies have at least some rudimentary form of division of labor, especially between the tasks allocated to men and those performed by women. With the development of industrialism, the division of labor became vastly more complex than in any prior type of production system. In the modern world, the division of labor is international in scope.

The economic system of modern societies rests on a highly complex **division of labor**: Work is now divided into an enormous number of different occupations in which people specialize. In traditional societies, nonagricultural work entailed the mastery of a specific skill. A worker typically learned craft skills through a lengthy period of apprenticeship, and then carried out all aspects of the production process from beginning to end. For example, a metalworker making a plow would forge the iron, shape it, and assemble the implement itself. With the rise of modern industrial production, most traditional crafts have disappeared altogether, replaced by skills that form part of more large-scale production processes. An electrician working in an industrial setting today, for instance, may inspect and repair only a few parts of one type of machine; different people will deal with the other parts and other machines.

The contrast in the division of labor between traditional and modern societies is truly extraordinary. Even in the largest traditional societies, there usually existed no more than twenty or thirty major craft trades, together with such specialized pursuits as merchant, soldier, and priest. In a modern industrial system, there are literally thousands of distinct occupations. The U.S. Census Bureau lists some twenty thousand distinct jobs in the American economy. In traditional communities, most of the population worked on farms and were economically self-sufficient. They produced their own food, clothes, and other necessities of life. One of the main features of modern societies, by contrast, is an enormous expansion of **economic interdependence**. The vast majority of people in modern societies do not produce the food they eat, or the material goods they consume.

economic interdependence • The fact that in the division of labor, individuals depend on others to produce many or most of the goods they need to sustain their lives.

INDUSTRIAL WORK

Writing some two centuries ago, Adam Smith, one of the founders of modern economics, identified advantages that the division of labor provides in terms of increasing productivity. His most famous work, *The Wealth of Nations*, opens with a description of the division of labor in a pin factory. A person working alone could perhaps make 20 pins per day. By breaking down that worker's task into a number of simple operations, however, ten workers carrying out specialized jobs in collaboration with one another could collectively produce 48,000 pins per day. The rate of production per worker, in other words, is increased from 20 to 4,800 pins, each specialist operator producing 240 times more than when working alone.

More than a century later, these ideas reached their most developed expression in the writings of Frederick Winslow Taylor, an American management consultant. Taylor's approach to what he called "scientific management" involved the detailed study of industrial processes in order to break them down into simple operations that could be precisely timed and organized.

Taylor's principles were appropriated by the industrialist Henry Ford. In 1908, Ford designed his first auto plant at Highland Park, Michigan, to manufacture only one product—the Model T Ford—thereby allowing the introduction of specialized tools and machinery designed for speed, precision, and simplicity of operation. One of Ford's most significant innovations was the introduction of the assembly line, said to have been inspired by Chicago slaughterhouses, in which animals were disassembled section by section on a moving conveyor belt. Each worker on Ford's assembly line was

Factory workers at the Ford Motor Company assemble a Model T automobile.

assigned a specialized task, such as fitting the left-side door handles as the car bodies moved along the line. By 1929, when production of the Model T ceased, over 15 million cars had been assembled.

WORK AND ALIENATION

Karl Marx was one of the first writers to grasp that the development of modern industry would reduce many people's work to dull, uninteresting tasks. According to Marx, the division of labor alienates human beings from their work. **Alienation** refers to feelings of indifference or hostility not only to work, but to the overall framework of industrial production within a capitalist setting.

In traditional societies, Marx pointed out, work was often exhausting—peasant farmers sometimes toiled from dawn to dusk. Yet peasants had control over their work, which required much knowledge and skill. Many industrial workers, by contrast, have little control over their jobs, only contribute a fraction to the creation of the overall product, and have no influence over how or to whom it is eventually sold. Work thus appears as something alien, a task that the worker must carry out in order to earn an income but that is intrinsically unsatisfying.

alienation • The sense that our own abilities as human beings are taken over by other entities. Karl Marx used the term to refer to the loss of workers' control over the nature and products of their labor.

INDUSTRIAL CONFLICT

There have long been conflicts between workers and those with economic and political authority over them. Riots against high taxes and food riots at periods of harvest failure were common in urban areas of Europe in the eighteenth century. These "premodern" forms of labor conflict continued up to the late nineteenth century in some countries. Such traditional forms of confrontation were not just sporadic, irrational outbursts of violence: The threat or use of violence had the effect of lowering the price of grain and other essential foodstuffs (Rudé 1964; Thompson 1971; Booth 1977).

Industrial conflict between workers and employers at first tended to follow these older patterns. In situations of confrontation, workers would quite often leave their places of employment and form crowds in the streets; they would make their grievances known through their unruly behavior or by engaging in acts of violence against the authorities. Workers in some parts of France in the late nineteenth century would threaten disliked employers with hanging (Holton 1978). Use of the strike as a weapon, today commonly associated with organized bargaining between workers and management, developed only slowly and sporadically.

STRIKES

strike • A temporary stoppage of work by a group of employees in order to express a grievance or enforce a demand.

A **strike** is a temporary stoppage of work by a group of employees in order to express a grievance or enforce a demand (Hyman 1984). Workers go on strike for many specific reasons. They may be seeking to gain higher wages, forestall a proposed reduction in their earnings, protest against technological changes that make their work duller or lead to layoffs, or obtain greater job security. However, in all these circumstances the strike is essentially a mechanism of power: a weapon of people who are relatively powerless in the workplace and whose working lives are affected by managerial decisions over which they have little control. Strikes typically occur when other negotiations have failed, because workers on strike either receive no income or depend on union funds, which might be limited (Figure 13.2).

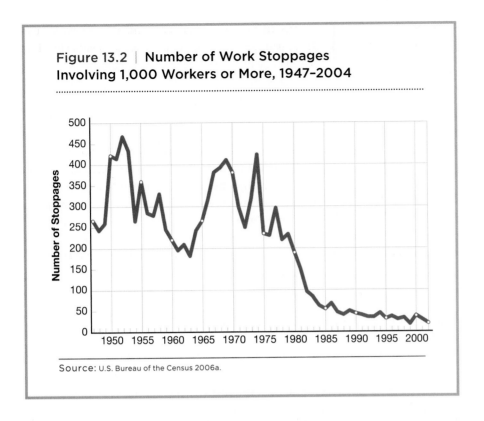

Figure 13.2 | Number of Work Stoppages Involving 1,000 Workers or More, 1947–2004

Source: U.S. Bureau of the Census 2006a.

LABOR UNIONS

Although their levels of membership and the extent of their power vary widely, union organizations exist in all Western countries, which also all legally recognize the right of workers to strike in pursuit of economic objectives. In the early development of modern industry, workers in most countries had no political rights and little influence over their working conditions. Unions developed as a means of redressing the imbalance of power between workers and employers. Whereas workers had virtually no power as individuals, through collective organization their influence was considerably increased. An employer can do without the labor of any particular worker but not without that of all or most of the workers in a factory or plant.

After 1980, unions suffered declines across the advanced industrial countries. In the United States, the share of the workforce belonging to unions declined from 23 percent in 1980 to 12.4 percent in 2008 (Hirsch and Macpherson 2004; U.S. Bureau of the Census 2009n). There are several widely accepted explanations for the difficulties confronted by unions since 1980. Perhaps the most common explanation is the decline of the older manufacturing industries and the rise of the service sector. Bruce Western (1997) has refined this explanation, by documenting that levels of unionization have fallen even within the manufacturing sector.

Writers Guild of America members picket outside Paramount Studios in Los Angeles during their 2008 labor strike.

CONCEPT CHECKS ✓

1. Why is it important for sociologists to study economic institutions?

2. Define and provide an example of an informal economy.

3. Using the concept of division of labor, describe the key differences in the nature of work in traditional versus modern societies.

4. What is a labor union? Why have unions in the United States suffered from a decline in membership since the 1980s?

Other explanations include recession in world economic activity, associated with high levels of unemployment, which weakens the bargaining position of labor; and the increasing intensity of international competition, particularly from East Asian countries, where wages are often lower than in the West. Unions usually become weakened during periods when unemployment is high, as has been the case for a considerable while in many Western countries. Trends toward more flexible production tend to diminish the force of unionism, which flourishes more extensively where many people are working together in large factories. ✓

WHAT ARE KEY ELEMENTS OF THE MODERN ECONOMY?

capitalism • An economic system based on the private ownership of wealth, which is invested and reinvested in order to produce profit.

Modern societies are, in Marx's term, capitalistic. **Capitalism** is a way of organizing economic life that is distinguished by the following important features: private ownership of the means of production; profit as incentive; free competition for markets to sell goods, acquire cheap materials, and utilize cheap labor; and expansion and investment to accumulate capital. Capitalism, which began to spread with the growth of the Industrial Revolution in the early nineteenth century, is a vastly more dynamic economic system than any other that preceded it in history. Although the system has had many critics, such as Marx, it is now the most widespread form of economic organization in the world.

So far, we have been looking at industry mostly from the perspective of occupations and employees. But we also have to concern ourselves with the nature of the business firms in which the workforce is employed. (It should be recognized that many people today are employees of government organizations, although we will not consider these here.) What is happening to business corporations today, and how are they run?

CORPORATIONS AND CORPORATE POWER

corporations • Business firms or companies.

Since the turn of the twentieth century, modern capitalist economies have been increasingly influenced by the rise of large business **corporations**. The share of total manufacturing assets held by the two hundred largest manufacturing firms in the United States has increased by 0.5 percent each year from 1900 to the present day; these corporations now control over half of all manufacturing assets. The two hundred largest financial organizations—banks, building societies, and insurance companies—account for more than half of all financial activity.

entrepreneur • The owner/founder of a business firm.

Of course, there still exist thousands of smaller firms and enterprises within the American economy. In these companies, the image of the **entrepreneur**—the boss who owns and runs the firm—is by no means obsolete. The large corporations are a different matter. Ever since Adolf Berle and Gardiner Means published their celebrated study *The Modern Corporation and Private Property* almost 80 years ago, it has been accepted that most of the largest firms are not run by those who own them (Berle and Means 1982; orig. 1932). In theory, the large corporations are the property of their shareholders, who have the right to make all important decisions. But Berle and Means argued that since share ownership is so dispersed, actual control has passed into the hands of the managers who run firms on a day-to-day basis.

The power of the major corporations is very extensive. Corporations often cooperate in setting prices rather than freely competing with one another. Thus, the giant oil companies normally follow one another's lead in the price charged for gasoline. When one firm occupies a commanding position in a given industry, it is said to be in a **monopoly** position. More common is a situation of **oligopoly**, in which a small group of giant corporations predominate. In situations of oligopoly, firms are able more or less to dictate the terms on which they buy goods and services from the smaller firms that are their suppliers.

monopoly • A situation in which a single firm dominates in a given industry.

oligopoly • The domination of a small number of firms in a given industry.

The emergence of the global economy has contributed to a wave of mergers and acquisitions on an unprecedented scale, which have created oligopolies in industries such as communications and media. In 1999, AT&T acquired the media corporation MediaOne for $5 billion to create the world's largest cable company. Also in 1999, CBS purchased Viacom for $35 billion. In 2000, Time Warner and the Internet service provider America Online announced the largest merger in history—worth over $166 billion (Ross and Hansen 2001). By 2004, the value of cross-border mergers and acquisitions had reached $380.6 trillion. About 83 percent of these mergers and acquisitions occurred between companies in the developed world (United Nations Conference on Trade and Development [UNCTAD] 2005a). In 2008 alone the mergers and acquisitions equaled $673 million (UNCTAD 2009). As the global market becomes increasingly integrated, we are likely to see even more mergers and acquisitions on an even larger scale.

TYPES OF CORPORATE CAPITALISM

There have been three general stages in the development of business corporations, although each overlaps with the others and all continue to coexist today. The first stage, characteristic of the nineteenth and early twentieth centuries, was dominated by **family capitalism**. Large firms were run either by individual entrepreneurs or by members of the same family and then passed on to their descendants. The famous corporate dynasties, such as the Rockefellers and Fords, belong in this category. These individuals and families did not just own a single large corporation, but held a diversity of economic interests and stood at the apex of economic empires.

family capitalism • Capitalistic enterprise owned and administered by entrepreneurial families.

Most of the big firms founded by entrepreneurial families have since become public companies—that is, shares of their stock are traded on the open market—and have passed into managerial control. In the large corporate sector, family capitalism was increasingly succeeded by **managerial capitalism**. As managers came to have more and more influence through the growth of very large firms, the entrepreneurial families were displaced. The result has been described as the replacement of the family in the company by the company itself (Allen 1981).

managerial capitalism • Capitalistic enterprises administered by managerial executives rather than by owners.

Managerial capitalism has left an indelible imprint on modern society. The large corporation drives not only patterns of consumption but also the experience of employment in contemporary society—it is difficult to imagine how different the work lives of many Americans would be in the absence of large factories

welfare capitalism • Practice in which large corporations protect their employees from the vicissitudes of the market.

or corporate bureaucracies. Sociologists have identified another area in which the large corporation has left a mark on modern institutions. **Welfare capitalism** refers to a practice that sought to make the corporation—rather than the state or trade unions—the primary shelter from the uncertainties of the market in modern industrial life. Beginning at the end of the nineteenth century, large firms began to provide certain services to their employees, including child care, recreational facilities, profit-sharing plans, paid vacations, and group life and unemployment insurance. These programs often had a paternalistic bent, such as that sponsoring "home visits" for the "moral education" of employees. Viewed in less benevolent terms, a major objective of welfare capitalism was coercion, as employers deployed all manner of tactics—including violence—to avoid unionization.

institutional capitalism • Capitalistic enterprise organized on the basis of institutional shareholding.

Despite the overwhelming importance of managerial capitalism in shaping the modern economy, many scholars now see the contours of a third, different phase in the evolution of the corporation emerging. They argue that managerial capitalism has today partly ceded place to **institutional capitalism**. This term refers to the emergence of a consolidated network of business leadership, concerned not only with decision making within single firms but also with the development of corporate power beyond them. Institutional capitalism is based on the practice of corporations holding shares in other firms. In effect, interlocking boards of directors exercise control over much of the corporate landscape. This reverses the process of increasing managerial control, since the managers' shareholdings are dwarfed by the large blocks of shares owned by other corporations. Rather than investing directly by buying shares in a business, individuals can now invest in money market, trust, insurance, and pension funds that are controlled by large financial organizations, which in turn invest these grouped savings in industrial corporations. However, in coming decades, Americans may be reluctant to put their resources into pension funds because of the economic crisis of the last few years, a time when many people saw their investments decline if not disappear entirely.

THE TRANSNATIONAL CORPORATIONS

With the intensifying of globalization, most large corporations now operate in an international economic context. When they establish branches in two or more countries, they are referred to as **transnational** or multinational **corporations**.

transnational corporations • Business corporations located in two or more countries.

Transnational is the preferred term, indicating that these companies operate across many different national boundaries. The United Nations Committee on Trade and Development estimated that in 2007 over 79,000 transnational corporations controlled assets outside their home countries (UNCTAD 2008).

The largest transnationals are gigantic; their wealth outstrips that of many countries. The scope of these companies' operations is staggering. The combined sales of these 79,000 transnational corporations totaled $31 trillion in 2007—over half (57 percent) of the value of goods and services produced by the entire world (CIA World Factbook 2007; UNCTAD 2008).

Of the top 500 transnational corporations in the world, 140 are based in the United States. The share of American companies has, however, fallen significantly since 1960, during which time Japanese companies have grown dramatically; only 5 Japanese corporations were included in the top 200 in 1960, as compared with 28 in 2005. Today, 68 Japanese companies are in the top 500 (Fortune 2009).

The reach of the transnationals over the past thirty years would not have been possible without advances in transport and communications. Air travel now allows people to move around the world at a speed that would have seemed inconceivable even sixty

Container ships are cargo ships that carry all of their load in truck-size containers. As this technique greatly accelerates the speed at which goods can be transported to and from ports, these ships now carry the majority of the world's dry cargo.

years ago. Telecommunications technologies now permit more or less instantaneous communication from one part of the world to another. Satellites have been used for commercial telecommunications since 1965. The first satellite could carry 240 telephone conversations at once; current satellites can carry 12,000 simultaneous conversations! The larger transnationals now have their own satellite-based communications systems. The Mitsubishi Corporation, for instance, has a massive network across which 5 million words are transmitted to and from its headquarters in Tokyo each day. ✓

CONCEPT CHECKS ✓

1. What are the main features of capitalism?

2. Compare and contrast four types of corporate capitalism.

HOW DOES WORK AFFECT EVERYDAY LIFE TODAY?

The globalizing of economic production, together with the spread of information technology, is altering the nature of the jobs most people do. As discussed earlier, the proportion of people working in blue-collar jobs in industrial countries has progressively fallen. Fewer and fewer people work in factories. New jobs have been created in offices and in service centers such as supermarkets and airports. Many of these new jobs are filled by women.

WORK AND TECHNOLOGY

The relationship between technology and work has long been of interest to sociologists. How is our experience of work affected by the type of technology that is involved? As industrialization has progressed, technology has assumed an ever greater role at the workplace—from factory automation to the computerization of office work. The current information technology revolution has attracted renewed interest in this question. Technology can lead to greater efficiency and productivity, but how does it affect the way work is experienced by those who carry it out? For sociologists, one of the main questions is how the move to more complex systems influences the nature of work and the institutions in which it is performed.

AUTOMATION AND THE SKILL DEBATE

automation • Production processes monitored and controlled by machines with only minimal supervision from people.

The concept of **automation**, or programmable machinery, was introduced in the mid-1800s, when Christopher Spencer, an American, invented the Automat, a programmable lathe that made screws, nuts, and gears. Automation has thus far affected relatively few industries, but with advances in the design of industrial robots, its impact is certain to become greater. A *robot* is an automatic device that can perform functions ordinarily done by human workers.

The majority of the robots used in industry worldwide are found in automobile manufacture. The usefulness of robots in production thus far is relatively limited, because their capacity to recognize different objects and manipulate awkward shapes is still at a rudimentary level. Yet it is certain that automated production will spread rapidly in coming years; robots are becoming more sophisticated, while their costs are decreasing.

The spread of automation has provoked a heated debate over the impact of the new technology on workers, their skills, and their level of commitment to their work. In his influential *Alienation and Freedom* (1964), Robert Blauner examined the experience of workers in four different industries with varying levels of technology. Blauner measured the extent to which workers in each industry experienced alienation in the form of powerlessness, meaninglessness, isolation, and self-estrangement. He concluded that workers on assembly lines were the most alienated of all, but that levels of alienation were somewhat lower at workplaces using automation. That is, the introduction of automation to factories partly reversed the otherwise steady trend toward increased worker alienation.

A very different thesis was set forth by Harry Braverman in the famous *Labor and Monopoly Capital* (1974). Braverman argued that automation was part of the overall "deskilling" of the industrial labor force. In both industrial settings and modern offices, new technologies have reduced the need for creative human input. Instead, all that is required is an unthinking, unreflective body capable of endlessly carrying out the same unskilled task.

A newer study sheds some more light on this debate. The sociologist Richard Sennett studied the people who worked in a bakery that had been bought by a large food conglomerate and automated with the introduction of high-tech machinery. Instead of using their hands to mix the ingredients and knead the dough and their noses and eyes to judge when the bread was done baking, the bakery's workers had no physical contact with the materials or the loaves of bread. The entire process was controlled and monitored via computer screen. The production process involved little more than pushing buttons on a computer. One time when the computerized machinery broke down, the entire production process was halted because none of the bakery's "skilled" workers were trained or empowered to repair the problem. The workers wanted to be helpful, to make things work again, but they could not, because automation had diminished their autonomy (Sennett 1998). The introduction of computerized technology in the workplace has led to a general increase in all workers' skills, but has also led to a two-tiered workforce composed of a small group of highly skilled professionals with a high degree of flexibility and autonomy in their jobs and a larger group of clerical, service, and production workers who lack autonomy in their jobs.

GLOBAL PRODUCTION

For much of the twentieth century, the most important business organizations were large manufacturing firms that controlled both the production and sale of goods. Giant automobile companies such as Ford and General Motors typify this approach, employing tens of thousands of factory workers making everything from components to the final cars, which are then sold in the manufacturers' showrooms (Figure 13.3). Such *manufacture-dominated production processes* are organized as large bureaucracies, often controlled by a handful of large firms.

During the past quarter century, however, another form of production has become important—one that is controlled by giant retailers. In *retailer-dominated production*, firms such as Wal-Mart and Kmart buy products from manufacturers, who in turn arrange to have their products made by independently owned factories. For example, the sociologists Edna Bonacich and Richard Appelbaum show that in clothing manufacturing, most manufacturers actually employ no garment workers at all. Instead, they rely on thousands of factories around the world to make their apparel, which they then sell in department stores and other retail outlets. Clothing manufacturers do not own any of these factories and therefore are not responsible for the conditions under which the clothing is made.

Two thirds of all clothing sold in the United States is made in factories in other nations, where workers are paid a fraction of U.S. wages. (In China, workers are lucky to make $40 a month.) Bonacich and Appelbaum argue that such competition has resulted in a global "race to the bottom," in which retailers and manufacturers will go anyplace on earth where they can pay the lowest wages possible. One result is that much of the clothing we buy today was made in sweatshops by young workers—most likely teenage girls—who get paid pennies for making clothing or pricy athletic shoes that sell for $100 or even more (Bonacich and Appelbaum 2000).

TRENDS IN THE OCCUPATIONAL STRUCTURE

The occupational structure in all industrialized countries has changed dramatically since the beginning of the twentieth century (see Figure 13.4). In 1900, about three quarters of the employed population was in manual work, either farming or blue-collar work such as manufacturing. White-collar professional and service jobs were much fewer in number. By 1960, however, more people worked in white-collar professional and service jobs than in manual labor. By 1993, the occupational system had nearly reversed its structure from 1900. Almost three quarters of the employed

Figure 13.3 | Where Does Your Car Come From?

Automobile parts are produced in several countries and then sent to a central plant for final production of the car.

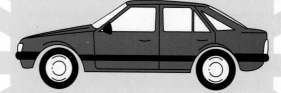

France

Alternator, cylinder head, master cylinder, brakes, underbody coating, weather strips, clutch release bearings, steering shaft and joints, seat pads and frames, transmission cases, clutch cases, tires, suspension bushing, ventilation units, heater, hose clamps, sealers, hardware

Britain

Carburetor, rocker arm, clutch, ignition, exhaust, oil pump, distributor, cylinder bolt, cylinder head, flywheel ring gear, heater, speedometer, battery, rear wheel spindle, intake manifold, fuel tank, switches, lamps, front disc, steering wheel, steering column, glass, weather strips, locks

Germany

Locks, pistons, exhaust, ignition, switches, front disc, distributor, weather strips, rocker arm, speedometer, fuel tank, cylinder bolt, cylinder head gasket, front wheel knuckles, rear wheel spindle, transmission cases, clutch cases, clutch, steering column, battery, glass

The Netherlands

Tires, paints, hardware

Denmark

Fan belt

Canada

Glass, radio

Sweden

Hose clamps, cylinder bolt, exhaust pipes, hardware

Belgium

Tires, tubes, seat pads, brakes, trim

United States

EGR valves, wheel nuts, hydraulic tappet, glass

Austria

Tires, radiator and heater hoses

Spain

Wiring harness, radiator and heater hoses, fork clutch release, air filter, battery, mirrors

Italy

Cylinder head, carburetor, glass, lamps, defroster, grills

Switzerland

Underbody coating, speedometer, gears

Japan

Starter, alternator, cone and roller bearings, windshield-washer pump

Norway

Exhaust flanges, tires

population worked in white-collar professional and service jobs, while the rest worked in blue-collar and farming jobs. In the period May 1999–May 2009, the United States lost 5.3 million manufacturing jobs (Business Week 2009). By 2010, blue-collar work will have declined even further, with most of the increase in new jobs occurring in the service industries.

The reasons for the transformation of the occupational structure seem to be several. One is the introduction of labor-saving machinery, culminating in the spread of information technology and computerization in industry in recent decades. Another is the rise of the manufacturing industry in other parts of the world, primarily Asia. The older industries in Western societies have experienced major job cutbacks because of their inability to compete with the more efficient Asian producers, whose labor costs are lower. As we have seen, this global economic transformation has forced American companies to adopt new forms of production, which in turn has impelled employees to learn new skills and new occupations as manufacturing-related jobs move to other countries. A final important trend is the decline of full-time paid employment with the same employer over a long period of time. Not only has the transformation of the global economy affected the nature of day-to-day work, it has also changed the career patterns of many workers.

THE KNOWLEDGE ECONOMY

Taking these trends into account, some observers suggest that what is occurring today is a transition to a new type of society no longer based primarily on industrialism. We are entering, they claim, a phase of development beyond the industrial era altogether. A variety of terms have been coined to describe this new social order, such as the *postindustrial society,* the *information age,* and the *"new" economy.* The term that has come into most common use, however, is the **knowledge economy**.

A precise definition of the knowledge economy is difficult to formulate, but in general terms, it refers to an economy in which ideas, information, and forms of knowledge underpin innovation and economic growth. Much of the workforce is involved not in the physical production or distribution of material goods, but in their design, development, technology, marketing, sale, and servicing. These employees can be termed "knowledge workers." The knowledge economy is dominated by the

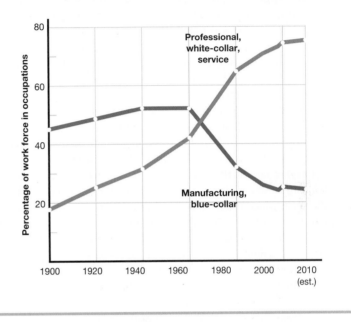

Figure 13.4 | The Changing Occupational Structure

The United States has lost a large number of manufacturing and other blue-collar jobs in the twentieth century. Many new professional/managerial and other white-collar jobs have been created. However, a large proportion entail work in the service industries, and although these can be classified as white-collar, they resemble blue-collar jobs in terms of pay.

knowledge economy •
A society no longer based primarily on the production of material goods but based instead on the production of knowledge. Its emergence has been linked to the development of a broad base of consumers who are technologically literate and have made new advances in computing, entertainment, and telecommunications part of their lives.

Google headquarters. Knowledge-based companies, such as Google, account for more than half of the business output in developed countries.

The iPod: The Global Production of Value

In 2007, Apple reported that it had sold the 100 millionth iPod (Apple Inc. 2007a). Apple's iPod and its online music store have transformed how people in the United States buy and listen to music. Yet the Cupertino, California–based company does not actually manufacture the iPod. Instead, it contracts the entire production process to other firms located in a variety of places outside of the United States. In the first half of 2007, Apple generated $9.6 billion in revenue, more than a third of which came from sales of iPods (Apple Inc. 2007b). So where is the iPod made and how does Apple profit?

Researchers at the University of California–Irvine, sponsored by the Alfred P. Sloan Foundation, studied the way in which the iPod accrues value as it is assembled (Linden et al. 2007). They show how innovation in the electronics industry spreads wealth beyond the firm whose brand name appears on the product and who was the primary actor conceiving, coordinating, and marketing the new item. The mechanism by which wealth gets distributed in the process of manufacturing is called a *value chain.* In a value chain, each producer purchases inputs to make a component and in the process of making it, adds value to it. The difference between the cost of raw materials at each stage and the value of the product at the next stage is called the *value added.* This added value then becomes part of the cost of the next stage of production. The sum of the value added by everyone in the chain plus the cost of materials equals the final wholesale product price, once it has been assembled and delivered to a store for sale.

The iPod is comprised of 451 component parts. Some of these, such as the visual display, are quite complicated,

and are made up of several subcomponents. The retail value of the 30-gigabyte video iPod was $299 when the researchers examined it. They estimated that the cost of all of the components required to make the iPod was about $144. The bulk of that cost was made up by the ten most complicated and expensive parts. The hard drive cost about $73; other expensive parts included the visual display (about $20), the processor chip ($8), and the controller chip ($5). These components are the most likely to incorporate innovative and proprietary knowledge, and they account for the largest share of the cost of assembling the iPod. The rest of the 440 or so parts, plus assembly in China, contributed about $10 to the wholesale cost of the iPod.

The hard drive, provided by the Japanese company Toshiba, was estimated to require about $54 in parts and labor to make. But Toshiba contracts the manufacture of its hard drives to companies located in China and the Philippines. Therefore, some portion of the $54—the cost of parts and labor provided by firms in those two countries—is value created and retained by them. The remaining $19 from the $73 hard drive cost goes to the Japanese economy.

At the other end of the value chain, the difference between the retail price ($299) and the wholesale price ($144) can be divided into retail, distributor, and Apple's profit. For each iPod, Apple makes about $80, which is greater than the cost of any single component. About half of the retail value of the iPod was retained by American firms, with the rest distributed over several countries contributing components to make the iPod. Even though final assembly of the product in China contributed less

constant flow of information and opinions and by the powerful potentials of science and technology.

How widespread is the knowledge economy at the start of the twenty-first century? A mid-1990s study by the Organization for Economic Cooperation and Development has attempted to gauge the extent of the knowledge economy among developed nations by measuring the percentage of each country's overall business output that can be attributed to knowledge-based industries. Knowledge-based industries include high

than 1% of the value, based on the way trade statistics are calculated, each iPod shipped from there to stores in the United States is said to have contributed about $150 to the U.S. trade deficit with China—but adds much less to China's trade surplus. This is because China ships a $150 iPod to the United States, but to do so, imports a substantial part of the components that go into it from other places in Asia.

The iPod is typical of the new global organization of production. In the past, consumer electronics were designed and developed by large companies, which often also produced all components required to make them. In this way, companies created and captured a large share of the value of their products. And because the value was created in-house, it stayed in the home country of the company. But today, value chains have global dimensions, which spread the creation of wealth across several countries. In the case of the iPod, the researchers estimated that there was value created in at least six countries, but it could be much higher if the value chains of components themselves are taken into consideration, since so much of the production of components and subcomponents is outsourced. At the same time, most of the wealth accrues to Apple and other American firms, even though Apple itself does not make the product. Apple profits because it conceptualizes, designs, and markets the iPod, while coordinating the global production process. These are the most profitable parts of the value chain, which demonstrates how profitability is linked to innovation—most profit accrues to those that design and organize rather than those who actually manufacture and assemble.

technology, education and training, research and development, and the financial and investment sector. Among OECD countries as a whole, knowledge-based industries accounted for more than half of all business output in the mid-1990s. Germany had a high figure of 58.6 percent, and the United States, Japan, Britain, Sweden, and France were all at or over 50 percent.

Investments into the knowledge economy—in the form of public education, spending on software development, and research and development—now make up a significant part of many countries' budgets. Sweden, for example, invested 10.6 percent of its overall gross domestic product in the knowledge economy in 1995. France was a close second because of its extensive spending on public education.

THE CONTINGENT WORKFORCE

Another important employment trend of the past decade has been the replacement of full-time workers by part-time workers who are hired and fired on a contingency basis. Most temporary workers are hired for the least-skilled, lowest-paying jobs. Most part-time jobs do not provide the benefits associated with full-time work, such as medical insurance, paid vacation time, or retirement benefits. Because employers can save on the costs of wages and benefits, the use of part-time workers has become increasingly common. Researchers estimate that part-time workers make up between 29 and 33 percent of the American workforce. This is up from 20 to 23 percent just ten years ago. Contingency workers make up approximately 4 percent of the American workforce, or about 5.7 million people (U.S. Bureau of Labor Statistics 2005a).

The temporary employment agency Manpower, Inc., founded in Milwaukee, Wisconsin, in 1948, has become a global leader in the provision of temporary workers. This company employed 4 million temps in eighty-two countries in 2008 and was the 119th largest corporation in the United States and 413th on *Fortune magazine's* list of the Global 500, with a total revenue of $22 billion in 2008 (Manpower Inc. 2009). Manpower provides labor on a "flexible" basis to 95 percent of Fortune 500 companies.

Scholars have debated the psychological effects of part-time work on the workforce. Many temporary workers fulfill their assignments in a prompt and satisfactory manner, but others rebel against their tenuous positions by shirking their responsibilities or sabotaging their results. Some temporary workers have been observed trying to "look busy" or to work longer than necessary on rather simple tasks.

However, some recent surveys of work indicate that part-time workers register higher levels of job satisfaction than those in full-time employment. This may be because most part-time workers are women, who find that part-time work is preferable to full-time employment when trying to juggle work and family demands. Yet men, too, may find that they are able to balance paid part-time work with other activities and enjoy a more varied life. Some people might choose to give full commitment to paid work from their youth to their middle years, then perhaps changing to a second part-time career, which would open up new interests.

UNEMPLOYMENT

The experience of unemployment—being unable to find a job when one wants it—is a perennially important social problem. Yet some contemporary scholars argue that we should think about the relation between being "in work" and "out of work" in a completely different way from the way we did in the recent past.

Rates of unemployment fluctuated considerably over the course of the twentieth century. In Western countries, unemployment reached a peak in the Depression years of the early 1930s, when some 20 percent of the workforce were out of work in the United States. The economist John Maynard Keynes, who strongly influenced public policy in Europe and the United States during the post–World War II period, believed that unemployment results from consumers' lacking sufficient resources to buy goods. Governments can intervene to increase the level of demand in an economy, leading to the creation of new jobs; and the newly employed then have the income with which to buy more goods, thus creating yet more jobs for people who produce them. State management of economic life, most people came to believe, meant that high rates of unemployment belonged to the past. Commitment to full employment became part of government policy in virtually all Western societies. Until the 1970s, these policies seemed successful, and economic growth was more or less continuous.

During the 1970s and 1980s, however, Keynesianism was largely abandoned. In the face of economic globalization, governments lost the capability to control economic life as they once had. One consequence was that unemployment rates shot up in many countries.

Several factors explain the increase in unemployment levels in Western countries at that time. First is the rise of international competition in industries on which Western prosperity used to be founded. In 1947, 60 percent of steel production in the world was carried out in the United States. Today, the figure is only about 6.9 percent, whereas steel production has risen by 300 percent in nations including Japan, Singapore, Taiwan, and Hong Kong (Worldsteel.org 2009). Second is the worldwide economic recession of the late 1980s, which has still not fully abated. Third, the increasing use of microelectronics in industry has reduced the need for labor power. Finally, beginning in the 1970s more women sought paid employment, meaning that more people were chasing a limited number of available jobs.

During this time, rates of unemployment tended to be lower in the United States, for example, than in some European nations. This partly reflects the sheer economic strength of the country, giving it more power in world markets than smaller, more fragile economies. Alternatively, it may be that the exceptionally large service sector in the United States provides a greater source of new jobs than in countries where more of the population has traditionally been employed in manufacturing. And within countries, unemployment is not equally distributed. It varies by race or ethnic background, by age, and by industry and geographic region. Ethnic minorities living in central cities in the United States have much higher rates of long-term unemployment than the rest of the population. A substantial proportion of young people are among the long-term unemployed, again especially among minority groups. These disparities were particularly acute during the economic recession of 2008-2009; in July 2009 the national unemployment rates reached 9.7 percent, but nearly 15 percent for African Americans (National Urban League 2009).

THE FUTURE OF WORK

Over the past twenty years, in all the industrialized countries except the United States, the average length of the working week has become shorter. Workers still undertake long stretches of overtime, but some governments are beginning to introduce new limits on permissible working hours. In France, for example, annual overtime is restricted to a maximum of 130 hours a year. In most countries, there is a general tendency toward shortening the average working career. More people would probably quit the labor force at sixty or earlier if they could afford to do so.

If the amount of time devoted to paid employment continues to shrink, and the need to have a job becomes less central, the nature of working careers might be substantially reorganized. Job sharing or flexible working hours, which arose primarily as a result of the increasing numbers of working parents trying to balance the commitments of workplace and family, might become more common. Some work analysts have suggested that sabbaticals of the university type should be extended to workers in other spheres: People would be entitled to take a year off in order to study or pursue some form of self-improvement. Some might opt to work part time throughout their lives, rather than being forced to because of a lack of full-time employment opportunities.

The nature of the work most people do and the role of work in our lives, like so many other aspects of the societies in which we live, are undergoing major changes. The chief reasons are global economic competition, the widespread introduction of information technology and computerization, and the large-scale entry of women into the workforce.

How will work change in the future? It appears very likely that people will take a more active look at their lives than in the past, moving in and out of paid work at different points. These are only positive options, however, when they are deliberately chosen. The reality for most is that regular paid work remains the key to day-to-day survival and that unemployment is experienced as a hardship rather than an opportunity. ✓

CONCEPT CHECKS

Why does automation lead to worker alienation?

What are some of the changes that occurred in the occupational structure in the twentieth century? How can they be explained?

How did Keynes explain unemployment? What was his solution to high unemployment rates?

In your opinion, how will globalization change the nature of work?

NEED HELP STUDYING?

 wwnorton.com/studyspace

....

Visit StudySpace to access free review materials such as:

- Vocabulary Flashcards
- Diagnostic Review Quizzes
- Study Outlines

REVIEW QUESTIONS

1. What is the difference between power and authority?
2. What are the three types of rights associated with citizenship? What does it mean to say that citizenship has been a "powerful instrument of social closure"?
3. In what ways is the Internet a democratizing force? What are its limitations in promoting democracy?
4. What are some explanations for why voter turnout is so low in the United States compared to other wealthy, literate, and democratic countries?
5. Describe C. Wright Mills's theory of the "power elite." How does it differ from pluralist theories?
6. How is new-style terrorism different from old-style terrorism? Why has new-style terrorism arisen?
7. What is the sociological significance of work? Why is being without work so detrimental to a person's well-being?
8. What is the "division of labor"? How has it changed between traditional and modern societies?

9. Why are transnational corporations important for the international division of labor?
10. What are two global trends shaping the nature of work today as described by the text? Given an example of their impact.

THINKING SOCIOLOGICALLY EXERCISES

1. Discuss the differences between the "pluralistic" and the "power elite" theories of democratic political processes. Which theory do you find most appropriate to describe U.S. politics in recent years?
2. Discuss some of the important ways that the nature of work will change for the contemporary worker as companies apply more automation and larger-scale production processes and as oligopolies become more pervasive. Explain each of these trends and how they affect workers, both now and in the future.

14

The Sociology of the Body: Health, Illness, and Sexuality

THE BIG QUESTIONS

HOW DOES SOCIAL CONTEXT AFFECT THE HUMAN BODY?

Understand how social, cultural, and historical contexts shape attitudes toward "ideal" body forms. Learn about the ways that social context gives rise to two body-related social problems in the United States: eating disorders and the obesity crisis.

HOW DO SOCIOLOGISTS UNDERSTAND HEALTH AND ILLNESS?

Learn about functionalist and symbolic interactionist perspectives on health and illness in contemporary society. Understand the relationship between traditional medicine and complementary and alternative medicine (CAM).

HOW DO SOCIAL FACTORS AFFECT HEALTH AND ILLNESS?

Recognize that health and illness are shaped by cultural and social factors. Learn the social and cultural differences in the distribution of disease.

WHAT CAUSES INFECTIOUS DISEASES IN DEVELOPING NATIONS?

Understand the causes underlying high rates of infectious diseases in developing nations. Learn more about HIV/AIDS as a sociological phenomenon.

HOW DOES SOCIAL CONTEXT SHAPE HUMAN SEXUAL BEHAVIOR?

Learn about the debate over the importance of biological versus social and cultural influences on human sexual behavior. Explore the cultural differences in sexual behavior and patterns of sexual behavior today.

ook at the three photographs on the next page. The first two images of a sunken face and an emaciated body are almost identical. The young girl on the left is Somalian, dying from lack of food. The young woman in the middle is American, dying from anorexia—she chose not to eat or ate too little. The third photograph shows a woman who is severely overweight. Although there are very different social and physical causes of the three women's body shapes and weights, each woman is at risk for major health problems and ultimately a hastened death.

The social dynamics involved in each case are vastly different. Starvation from lack of food is caused by factors outside one's control and afflicts only the very poor. Starvation from anorexia, an illness with no known physical origin, is caused by an obsession with achieving a slim body. Anorexia and other eating disorders are illnesses of the affluent, not of those who have little or no food. **Obesity**, or excessive body weight, is also virtually unknown in impoverished societies where food is scarce and where people work at physically grueling jobs, such as herding or farming. Obesity is caused by a

obesity • Excessive body weight indicated by a body mass index (BMI) over 30.

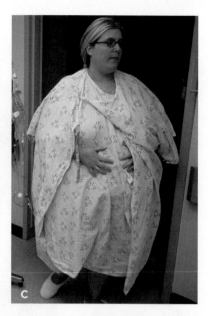

Take a look at the three women above: The first woman (a) is painfully thin as a result of famine and malnutrition, sadly common problems in areas of the world plagued by frequent drought and crop failure. The second (b) has become painfully thin by her own doing; people suffering from anorexia feel compelled by a variety of personal and social pressures to lose weight, and will often continue to view themselves as overweight even when they have reached a state of emaciation. The third woman (c) is severely overweight and is preparing for a dangerous gastric bypass surgery.

high-calorie, high-fat diet, accompanied by a sedentary lifestyle, such as having a desk job, or lacking the time (or money) to maintain a regular exercise regime.

Anorexia and obesity are important social problems in the Western world. Although both are conditions of the body, the causes reflect social factors more than physical or biological factors. If both conditions reflected biology alone, then we would expect that rates would be fairly constant across history—because human physiology has changed little throughout the millennia. However, both are very recent social problems, as we will see later in this chapter. Both conditions also are highly stratified by social factors such as gender, social class, race, and ethnicity. Women are far more likely than men to have anorexia, while economically disadvantaged persons are far more likely than their wealthier counterparts to struggle with obesity today. Both also are shaped by the cultural context. Fashion magazines regularly show images of models who are severely underweight, yet uphold these women as paragons of beauty. The average fashion model today is 23 percent thinner than the average American woman, yet twenty-five years ago that number was 8 percent (Derenne and Beresin 2006). At the same time, our culture also promotes excessive eating; social scientists have observed that we live in an "obesogenic" environment (Brownell and Horgen 2004), where high-fat food and "supersized" meals are plentiful and cheap. A Big Mac is less expensive than a healthy salad in most parts of the country, perpetuating the social class gradient in obesity rates.

sociology of the body • Field that focuses on how our bodies are affected by social influences. Health and illness, for instance, are shaped by social and cultural influences.

The field known as **sociology of the body** investigates how and why our bodies are affected by our social experiences, and the norms and values of the groups to which we belong. Using this framework, we analyze why eating disorders and obesity have become so common in the Western world, study the social dimensions of health and illness, and examine social and cultural influences on our sexual behavior.

HOW DOES SOCIAL CONTEXT AFFECT THE HUMAN BODY?

Let's now turn to two specific social problems facing Americans today: eating disorders and the obesity crisis. Both illustrate the ways that a "personal trouble" such as self-starvation or obesity-related complications such as diabetes reflect "public issues," such as a culture that promotes an unrealistic "thin ideal" for young women or the ways that poverty makes it difficult for individuals to buy costly healthful foods or to reach public parks and other spaces for regular exercise.

ANOREXIA AND EATING DISORDERS

Anorexia is related to the idea of dieting, and it reflects changing views of physical attractiveness in modern society. In most premodern societies, the ideal female shape was a fleshy one. Thinness was not desirable, partly because it was associated with hunger and poverty. The notion of slimness as the desirable feminine shape originated among some middle-class groups in the late nineteenth century, but it became generalized as an ideal for most women only recently.

Anorexia was identified as a disorder in France in 1874, but it remained obscure until the past thirty or forty years (Brown and Jasper 1993). Since then, it has become increasingly common among young women. So has *bulimia*—bingeing on food, followed by self-induced vomiting. Anorexia and bulimia often occur in the same individual. According to the National Institute of Mental Health, an estimated 0.5 percent to 3.7 percent of females have suffered from anorexia at some time during their lives, and an estimated 1.1 percent to 4.2 percent of women have suffered from bulimia. Over 85 percent of those affected are under the age of twenty (National Institute of Mental Health 2008). Women account for more than 90 percent of all persons with eating disorders, so it is difficult for researchers to estimate rates among men. Anorexia has the highest mortality rate of any psychological disorder; 20 percent of anorexics will die from it (Eating Disorder Coalition [EDC] 2003).

The occurrence of eating disorders in the United States has doubled since 1960 (EDC 2003). On any given day, 25 percent of men and 45 percent of women are dieting; Americans spend over $40 billion each year on dieting and dieting-related products (National Eating Disorders Association 2002). About 60 percent of girls age thirteen have already begun to diet; this proportion rises to over 80 percent for young women of eighteen. College men also suffer similar experiences, but to a lesser extent. About 50 percent of American male college students want to lose weight, while about 30 percent are on diets (Hesse-Biber 1997). Over 80 percent of ten-year-old children are afraid of being fat (EDC 2003).

Obsession with slenderness—and the resulting eating disorders—extends beyond the United States and Europe. As Western images of feminine beauty have spread to the rest of the world, so too have associated illnesses. Eating problems also have surfaced among young, primarily affluent women in Hong Kong and Singapore, as well as in urban areas in Taiwan, China, the Philippines, India, and Pakistan (Efron 1997).

The rise of eating disorders in Western societies coincides with the globalization of food production. Since the 1950s, supermarket shelves have been abundant with foods

Making Sociology Work
FASHION MAGAZINE EDITOR

Four months after Christina Kelly was promoted to the position of editor-in-chief of *YM* magazine in 2002, she made a surprising announcement: She was banning dieting stories from the magazine and would feature only "normal" and larger-size models. *YM*, read by more than two million tween- and teenage young women, received bagfuls of appreciative letters from readers who always felt that they were ugly or fat when they flipped through images of ultra-skinny women in other fashion magazines. Not everyone agreed with Kelly's decision, though. One magazine photographer refused to shoot photos of models larger than size 6; *YM* promptly stopped working with her. Kelly recently took a new position, as editor-in-chief of *Elle Girl*. Kelly vows to continue her commitment to girls' healthy body image at her new magazine. What kind of advice would sociologists of the body give to Kelly in her new editorial role? What kind of effect could Kelly's editorial decisions have on the well-being of young women?

socialization of nature • The process by which we control phenomena regarded as "natural," such as reproduction.

from all parts of the world. Most foods are available all the time, not just when they are in season locally. When all foods are available all the time, we must decide what to eat. First, we have to decide what to eat in relation to the new medical information that science bombards us with—for instance, that cholesterol levels contribute to heart disease. Second, we worry about calorie content. The fact that we have much more control over our own bodies than before presents us with positive possibilities as well as new anxieties and problems. All this is part of what sociologists call the **socialization of nature**: Phenomena that used to be "natural," or given in nature, have now become social—they depend on our own social decisions.

Why do eating disorders affect women in particular and young women most acutely? Roughly 10 percent of those with eating disorders are men, but they don't suffer from anorexia or bulimia as often as women—partly because social norms stress the importance of physical attractiveness more for women than for men and partly because desirable body images of men differ from those of women.

Once a young woman starts to diet and exercise compulsively, she can become locked into a pattern of refusing food or vomiting up what she has eaten. As the body loses muscle mass, it loses heart muscle, so the heart gets smaller and weaker, which ultimately leads to heart failure. About half of all anorexics also have low white-blood-cell counts, and about a third are anemic. Both conditions can lower the immune system's resistance to disease, leaving an anorexic vulnerable to infections. However, these harmful patterns may be broken through psychotherapy and medical treatment.

THE OBESITY EPIDEMIC

Obesity is considered the top public health problem facing Americans today. *Obesity* is currently defined as a body mass index (BMI) of 30 or greater (CDC [Center for Disease Control and Prevention] 2008a). (See the "D.I.Y." box for further information on body mass index.) Over the past two decades, there has been a dramatic increase in the obesity rate among adults in the United States. In 1990, ten states had a prevalence of obesity under 10 percent and no states had a prevalence of 15 percent or higher. By 2008, obesity was under 10 percent in only one state (Colorado); in thirty-two states the rate was 25 percent or higher, and six of these states had rates equal to or in excess of 30 percent (CDC 2008a).

Obesity increases an individual's risk for a wide range of health problems, including cardiovascular diseases, diabetes mellitus type 2, sleep apnea, osteoarthritis, and some forms of cancers (Haslam and James 2005). Excessive body weight also may take a severe psychological toll. Overweight and obese Americans are more likely than their thinner peers to experience employment discrimination, discrimination by health-care providers, and daily experiences of teasing, insults, and shame (Carr and Friedman 2005). Negative attitudes toward overweight and obese persons

What Is Your Body Mass Index (BMI)?

As you have read, Americans are grappling with the social problems of both eating disorders that make young women (and to a lesser extent, young men) excessively thin, and a social environment that promotes obesity. What is your body mass index? Flip the page to see how you compare with other Americans.

$$BMI = 703 \times \frac{weight}{height \times height}$$

Note: Weight in pounds, and height in inches.

TURN PAGE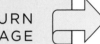

develop as early as elementary school (Latner and Stunkard 2003; Richardson et al. 1961).

Sociologists are fascinated with the persistence of negative attitudes toward overweight and obese persons, especially because these individuals currently make up the statistical majority of all Americans. According to the Centers for Disease Control, roughly 60 to 70 percent of adults are now overweight, and roughly one third are obese (see the "D.I.Y." box for technical definitions of weight categories). An even more troubling trend is the increase in the proportion of American children and adolescents who are overweight. Between 1976 and 1980, an estimated 5 percent of children aged two to five, 6.5 percent of those aged six to eleven, and 5 percent of those aged twelve to nineteen were overweight. By contrast, in 2003–2006, 12.4 percent of young children, 17 percent of children, and 17.6 percent of adolescents were overweight (CDC 2008b).

The reasons behind the obesity crisis are widely debated. Some argue that the apparent increase in the overweight and obese population is a statistical artifact. The proportion of the U.S. population who are middle-aged has increased rapidly during the past two decades, with the aging of the large baby boom cohort. Middle-aged persons, due to slowing metabolism, are at greater risk of excessive body weight. Others attribute the pattern—especially the childhood obesity increase—to shifts in the ethnic makeup of the overall population. The proportion of children today who are black or

The Centers for Disease Control (CDC) classifies adults into one of six body weight categories based on their *body mass index (BMI).* An estimated 60 percent of Americans age 18 and older are now classified as overweight, and one third are obese. The proportion that is obese varies widely by race and gender, with Black and Latino women at the greatest risk of obesity.

Category	BMI Range
Underweight	< 18.5
Normal weight	18.5–24.9
Overweight	25.0–29.9
Obese I	30.0–34.9
Obese II	35.0–39.9
Obese III (Morbidly Obesity)	40.0 +

Source: National Heart, Lung, Blood Institute 1998.

Hispanic is higher than in earlier decades, and these two ethnic groups are at a much greater risk for overweight than their white peers. Still others argue that the measures used to count and classify obese persons have shifted, thus leading to an excessively high count. Finally, some social observers believe that public concern over obesity is blown out of proportion and reflects more of a "moral panic" than a "public health crisis" (Campos et al. 2006).

Most public health experts believe, however, that obesity is a very real problem caused by what Kelly Brownell calls the "obesogenic environment." Among adults, sedentary jobs have replaced physical jobs such as farming. Children are more likely to spend their after-school hours sitting in front of a computer or television than playing tag or riding bikes around the neighborhood. Parents are pressed for time given their hectic work and family schedules and turn to unhealthy fast food rather than home-cooked meals. Restaurants, eager to lure bargain-seeking patrons, provide enormous serving sizes at low prices. The social forces that promote high fat and sugar consumption and that restrict the opportunity to exercise are particularly acute for poor persons and ethnic minorities. Small grocery stores in poor neighborhoods rarely sell fresh or low-cost produce. Large grocery stores are scarce in poor neighborhoods and in predominantly African American neighborhoods (Morland et al. 2002). High

Why do many parents turn to fast food to feed their families? What are the consequences?

crime rates and high levels of traffic in inner-city neighborhoods make exercise in public parks or jogging on city streets potentially harmful (Brownell and Horgen 2004).

Policy makers and public health professionals have proposed a broad range of solutions to the obesity crisis. Some have proposed (unsuccessfully) practices that place the burden directly on the individual. For example, some schools have considered having a "weight report card," where children and parents would be told the child's BMI, in an effort to trigger healthy behaviors at home. Yet most experts endorse solutions that attack the problem at a large-scale level, such as making healthy low-cost produce more widely available; providing safe public places for fitness workouts, free exercise classes, and classes in health and nutrition to poor children and their families; and requiring restaurants and food manufacturers to clearly note the fat and calorie content of their products. Only in attacking the "public issue" of the obesogenic environment will the private trouble of excessive weight be resolved (Brownell and Horgen 2004). ✓

CONCEPT CHECKS ✓

1. Why is anorexia more likely to strike young women than other subgroups?

2. What explanations are offered for the recent increase in obesity rates?

3. What policy solutions have been offered for the obesity crisis?

HOW DO SOCIOLOGISTS UNDERSTAND HEALTH AND ILLNESS?

One of sociologists' main concerns is understanding the experience of illness—how being sick, chronically ill, or disabled is experienced by sick persons and by those with whom they interact. If you have ever been ill, even for a short period, you know that patterns of daily life are temporarily modified and your interactions with others change. This is because the normal functioning of the body is a vital, but often taken for granted, part of our daily lives. Our sense of self is predicated on the expectation that our bodies will facilitate, not impede, our social interactions and daily activities.

Illness has both personal and public dimensions. When we fall ill, others are affected as well. Our friends, families, and coworkers may extend sympathy, care, support, and assistance with practical tasks. They may struggle to understand our illness and its cause, or to adjust the patterns of their own lives to accommodate it. Others' reactions to our illness, in turn, shape our own interpretations and can pose challenges to our sense of self. For instance, a long-time smoker who develops lung disease may be made to feel guilty by family members, who provide constant reminders of the link between smoking and lung disease.

Two sociological perspectives on the experience of illness have been particularly influential. The first, associated with the functionalist school, proposes that "being sick" is a social role, just as "worker" or "mother" is a social role. As such, unhealthy persons are expected to comply with a widely agreed-upon set of behavioral expectations. The second view, favored by symbolic interactionists, explores how the meanings of illness are socially constructed and how these meanings influence people's behavior.

THE SICK ROLE

sick role • A term associated with the functionalist Talcott Parsons to describe the patterns of behavior that a sick person adopts in order to minimize the disruptive impact of his or her illness on others.

The functionalist thinker Talcott Parsons (1951) developed the notion of the **sick role** to describe patterns of behavior that the sick person adopts to minimize the disruptive impact of illness. Functionalist thought holds that society usually operates in a smooth and consensual manner. Illness is, therefore, seen as a dysfunction that can disrupt the flow of this normal state. A sick individual, for example, might be unable to perform standard responsibilities or be less reliable and efficient than usual. Because sick people cannot carry out their normal roles, the lives of people around them are disrupted: Assignments at work go unfinished and cause stress for coworkers, responsibilities at home are not fulfilled, and so forth.

According to Parsons, people learn the sick role through socialization and enact it—with the cooperation of others—when they fall ill. Sick persons face societal expectations for how to behave, yet at the same time other members of society abide by a generally agreed-upon set of expectations for how they will treat the sick individual. The sick role is distinguished by three sets of normative expectations:

1. The sick person is not held personally responsible for his or her poor health.
2. The sick person is entitled to certain rights and privileges, including a release from normal responsibilities.
3. The sick person is expected to take sensible steps to regain his or her health, such as consulting a medical expert and agreeing to become a patient.

EVALUATION

Although the sick-role model reveals how the ill person is an integral part of a larger social context, a number of criticisms can be levied against it. Some argue that the sick-role formula does not adequately capture the *lived experience* of illness. Others point out that it cannot be applied across all contexts, cultures, and historical periods. For example, it does not account for instances in which doctors and patients disagree about a diagnosis or have opposing interests. It also fails to explain illnesses that do not necessarily lead to a suspension of normal activity, such as alcoholism, certain disabilities, and some chronic diseases. Furthermore, assuming the sick role is not always a straightforward process. Some individuals who suffer for years from chronic pain or from misdiagnosed symptoms are denied the sick role until they get a clear diagnosis. Other sick people, such as young women with autoimmune diseases, often appear physically healthy despite constant physical pain and exhaustion; because of their "healthy" outward appearance, they may not be readily granted sick-role status. In other cases, social factors such as race, class, and gender can affect whether and how readily the sick role is granted. The sick role cannot be divorced from the social, cultural, and economic influences that surround it.

The realities of life and illness are more complex than the sick role suggests. The leading causes of death today are heart disease and cancer, two diseases that are associated with unhealthy behaviors such as smoking, a high-fat diet, and a sedentary lifestyle. Given the emphasis on taking control over one's health and lifestyle in our modern age, individuals bear ever-greater responsibility for their own well-being. This contradicts the first premise of the sick role—that the individual is not to blame for his or her illness. Moreover, in modern societies the shift away from acute infectious disease toward chronic illness has made the sick role less applicable. Whereas it might be useful in understanding acute illness, it is less useful in chronic illness because there is no single formula for chronically ill or disabled people to follow. Moreover, the chronically ill often find that their symptoms fluctuate, so that they feel and appear healthy on some days, yet experience disabling symptoms on other days. Living with illness is experienced and interpreted in multiple ways.

ILLNESS AS "LIVED EXPERIENCE"

Symbolic interactionists study the ways people interpret the social world and the meanings they ascribe to it. Many sociologists have applied this approach to health and illness and view this perspective as a partial corrective to the limitations of functionalist approaches to health. Symbolic interactionists are not concerned with identifying risk factors for specific illnesses. Rather, they address questions about the personal experience of illness: How do people react and adjust to news about a serious illness? How does illness shape individuals' daily lives? How does living with a chronic illness affect an individual's self-identity?

One theme that sociologists address is how chronically ill individuals cope with the practical and emotional implications of their illness. Certain illnesses require regular treatments or maintenance that can affect daily routines. Undergoing dialysis or insulin injections, or taking large numbers of pills, requires individuals to adjust their schedules. Other illnesses have unpredictable effects, such as sudden loss of bowel or bladder control or violent nausea. People suffering from such conditions often develop strategies for managing their illness in daily life. These include practical considerations—such as noting the location of the restrooms when in an unfamiliar place—as well as skills for managing interpersonal relations, both intimate and commonplace. Although symptoms can be embarrassing and disruptive, people develop coping strategies to live as normally as possible (Kelly 1992).

At the same time, the experience of illness can pose challenges for individuals to manage their illnesses within the overall context of their lives (Jobling 1988; Williams 1993). Corbin and Strauss (1985) identified three types of "work" incorporated in the everyday strategies of the chronically ill. *Illness work* refers to activities involved in managing the condition, such as treating pain, doing diagnostic tests, or undergoing physical therapy. *Everyday work* pertains to the management of daily life—maintaining relationships with others, running household affairs, and pursuing professional or personal interests. *Biographical work* involves the process of incorporating the illness into one's life, making sense of it, and developing ways of explaining it to others. Such a process can help chronically ill people restore meaning and order to their lives.

Each of these processes of adaptation may be particularly difficult for those who suffer from a stigmatized health condition, such as extreme obesity, alcoholism, AIDS, or even lung cancer. Sociologist Erving Goffman (1963) developed the concept of **stigma**, which refers to any personal characteristic that is devalued in a particular social context. Stigmatized individuals and groups often are treated with suspicion, hostility, or discrimination. Stigmas are, however, rarely based on valid understandings or scientific data. They spring from stereotypes or perceptions that may be false or only partially correct. Further, the nature of a stigma varies widely across sociocultural context: The extent to which a trait is devalued depends on the values and beliefs of those who do the stigmatizing.

stigma • Any physical or social characteristic that is labeled by society as undesirable.

CHANGING CONCEPTIONS OF HEALTH AND ILLNESS

A key theme in the sociological study of health is that cultures and societies differ in what they consider healthy and normal. All cultures have known concepts of physical health and illness, but most of what we now recognize as medicine is a consequence of developments in Western society over the past three centuries. In premodern cultures, the family was the main institution for coping with sickness or affliction. There have always been individuals who specialized as healers, using a mixture of physical and spiritual remedies, and many such traditional systems survive today in non-Western cultures. For instance, traditional Chinese medicine aims to restore harmony among aspects of the personality and bodily systems, involving the use of herbs and acupuncture for treatment.

Modern medicine sees the origins and treatment of disease as physical and explicable in scientific terms. The application of science to medical diagnosis and cure underlay the development of modern health-care systems. Other features were the acceptance of the hospital as the setting within which to treat serious illnesses and the development of the medical profession as a body with codes of ethics and significant social power. The scientific view of disease was linked to the requirement that medical training be systematic and long term; self-taught healers were excluded. Although professional medical practice is not limited to hospitals, the hospital provided an environment in which doctors could treat and study large numbers of patients, in circumstances permitting the concentration of medical technology.

ALTERNATIVE MEDICINE

Alternative therapies, such as herbal remedies, acupuncture, and chiropractic treatments, are being explored by a record high number of adults in the United States today and are slowly gaining acceptance by the mainstream medical community. Physicians increasingly believe that such unorthodox therapies may be an important complement to (although not a substitute for) traditional Western medicine, provided they are upheld to rigorous scientific evaluation. Yet devoted adherents to nontraditional health regimens believe that such practices are effective and that their personal experiences are more meaningful than are the results of controlled trials.

Medical sociologists refer to such unorthodox medical practices as **complementary and alternative medicine (CAM)**. CAM encompasses a diverse set of approaches and therapies for treating illness and promoting well-being that generally fall outside standard medical practices. These approaches are usually not taught in medical schools and not practiced by physicians or other professionals trained in medical programs. However, in recent years a number of medical and nursing schools have started offering courses in alternative medicine (Fenton and Morris 2003; Wetzel et al. 1998). Complementary medicine is distinct from alternative medicine in that the latter is meant to be used in place of standard medical procedures, while the former is meant to be used in conjunction with medical procedures to increase their efficacy or reduce side effects (Saks 1992). Many people use CAM approaches in addition to, rather than in place of, orthodox treatments (although some alternative approaches, such as homeopathy, reject the basis of orthodox medicine entirely).

Industrialized countries have some of the best-developed, best-resourced medical facilities in the world. Why, then, are a growing number of people exploring treatments that have not yet proven effective in controlled clinical trials, such as aromatherapy and hypnotherapy? It has been estimated that as many as ten percent of Americans have consulted an alternative practitioner. An even larger proportion of Americans have sought out CAM treatments on their own. A recent survey found that 62 percent of all Americans said that they had used some form of CAM in 2002, where CAM was broadly defined to include prayer as well as alternative treatments (Pagan and Pauly 2005). The profile of the typical individual who seeks alternative forms of healing is female, young to middle-aged, and middle class.

There are many reasons for seeking the services of an alternative medicine practitioner or pursuing CAM regimens on one's own. Some people perceive orthodox medicine to be deficient or ineffective in relieving chronic pain or symptoms of stress and anxiety. Others are dissatisfied with features of modern health-care systems such as long waits, referrals through chains of specialists, and financial restrictions. Connected to this are concerns about the harmful side effects of medication and the intrusiveness of surgery, both staples of modern Western medicine. The asymmetrical power relationship between doctors and patients also drives some people to seek alternative medicine. Those people feel that the role of the passive patient does not grant them enough input into their own treatment and healing. Finally, some individuals profess religious or philosophical objections to orthodox medicine, which treats the mind and body separately. They believe that orthodox medicine often overlooks the spiritual and psychological dimensions of health and illness. All these concerns are critiques of the **biomedical model of health** (the foundation of the Western medical establishment), which defines disease in objective terms and believes that scientifically based medical treatment can restore the body to health (Beyerstein 1999).

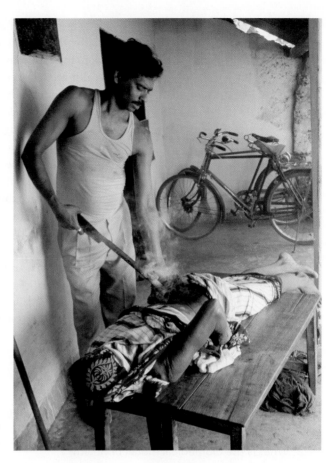

Ayurvedic treatment: Ayurvedic physician Kumar Das uses a hot iron rod and fabric soaked in herbs to heal an arthritic hip.

complementary and alternative medicine (CAM) • A diverse set of approaches and therapies for treating illness and promoting well-being that generally falls outside of standard medical practices.

biomedical model of health • The set of principles underpinning Western medical systems and practices. The biomedical model of health defines diseases objectively, in accordance with the presence of recognized symptoms, and holds that the healthy body can be restored through scientifically based medical treatment. The human body is likened to a machine that can be returned to working order with the proper repairs.

The growth of alternative medicine is a fascinating reflection of the transformations occurring within modern societies. We are living in an age where much more information is available to draw on in making choices. The proliferation of health-related Web sites such as WebMD and MedicineNet provides instant access to information on health symptoms and treatments. Thus individuals are increasingly becoming health consumers, adopting an active stance toward their own health and well-being. Not only are we choosing the type of practitioners to consult, but we are also demanding more involvement in our own care and treatment.

Members of the traditional medical community, once viewed as completely resistant to the notion of alternative medicine, are increasingly taking a more open-minded approach to such therapies. Many now cautiously endorse patients' desires to consult an ever-expanding array of medical information. However, medical leaders believe that CAM should be held to the same level of scientific scrutiny and rigorous scientific evaluation as traditional Western medicine (Angell and Kassirer 1998).

Debates about complementary and alternative medicine also shed light on the changing nature of health and illness over the past two centuries. Many conditions and illnesses for which individuals seek alternative medical treatment seem to be products of the modern age itself. Rates of insomnia, anxiety, stress, depression, fatigue, and chronic pain (caused by arthritis, cancer, and other diseases) are increasing in industrialized societies. Although these conditions have long existed, they are causing greater distress and disruption to people's health than ever before. Ironically, these consequences of modernity are ones that orthodox medicine has difficulty addressing. Alternative medicine is unlikely to overtake mainstream health care altogether, but indications are that its role will continue to grow. ✓

CONCEPT CHECKS ✓

1. How do functionalist theorists and symbolic interactionists differ in their perspectives on health and illness?

2. What is the biomedical model of health?

3. Compare complementary and alternative medicine.

HOW DO SOCIAL FACTORS AFFECT HEALTH AND ILLNESS?

The twentieth century witnessed a significant increase in life expectancy for people living in industrialized countries. Diseases such as polio, scarlet fever, and diphtheria have been all but eradicated. Infant mortality rates have dropped precipitously, leading to an increase in the average age of death in the developed world. Compared with other parts of the world, standards of health and well-being are high. Many advances in public health have been attributed to the power of modern medicine. It is commonly assumed that medical research has been—and will continue to be—successful in uncovering the biological causes of disease and in developing effective treatments.

Although this view has been influential, it is somewhat unsatisfactory for sociologists because it ignores the importance of social and environmental influences on patterns of health and illness. The improvements in overall public health over the past century cannot conceal the fact that health and illness occur unevenly throughout the population. Research has shown that certain groups of people enjoy much better health than others. These *health inequalities* appear to reflect larger socioeconomic patterns.

Dr. Regina Benjamin, a family physician dedicated to serving the working-class families in a small shrimping community on the Gulf Coast, visits one of her patients at home. Working-class women have less access to formal support networks in times of crisis than middle-class women. Formal social support—such as counseling services, hotlines, or home visits—can help patients cope with the effects of stress and illnesses.

SOCIAL CLASS-BASED INEQUALITIES IN HEALTH

In Chapter 7, we defined *social* class as a concept that encompasses education, income, occupation, and assets. In American society, people with better educations, higher incomes, and more prestigious occupations have better health. What is fascinating is that each of these dimensions of social class may be related to health and mortality for different reasons.

Income is the most obvious factor. In countries such as the United States, where medical care is expensive and many people lack insurance, those with more financial resources have better access to physicians and medicine. But inequalities in health also persist in countries like Great Britain that have national health insurance. Differences in occupational status may lead to inequalities in health and illness even when medical care is fairly evenly distributed. One study of health inequalities in Great Britain, the *Black Report* (Townsend and Davidson 1982), found that manual workers had substantially higher mortality rates than professional workers, even though Britain's health service had made great strides in equalizing the distribution of health care. Those who work in offices or in domestic settings have less risk of injury or exposure to hazardous materials.

Differences in education, a third dimension of social class, also are correlated with inequalities in health and illness. Numerous studies find a positive correlation between education and a broad array of preventive health behaviors. Better-educated people are significantly more likely to engage in aerobic exercise and to know their blood pressure (Shea et al. 1991) and are less likely to smoke (Kenkel et al. 2006) or be overweight (Himes 1999). By contrast, poorly educated people engage in more cigarette smoking; they also have more problems with cholesterol and body weight (Winkleby et al. 1992).

RACE-BASED INEQUALITIES IN HEALTH

In the United States, life expectancy at birth in 2006 was about eighty years for white and Hispanic females but seventy-six years for black females. Likewise, life expectancy at birth in 2006 was seventy-six years for white and Hispanic males yet seventy years for black males (CDC 2007).

Racial differences in health reveal the complex interrelations among ethnicity, race, social class, and culture. A powerful example of the multiple ways that race affects health is the Hispanic health paradox: Although Hispanics in the United States have poorer socioeconomic resources than whites, on average, their health—and especially the health of their infants—is just as good as if not better than that of whites. Blacks, by contrast, face economic disadvantages that are similar to those of Hispanics, yet blacks do not enjoy the same health benefits. Experts attribute Hispanics' health advantage relative to blacks' to cultural factors such as social cohesion but also to methodological factors. Studies of Hispanic health in the United States focus on those who successfully migrated to the United States; as such, they are believed to be in better health, or more robust, than those Latinos who remained in their native countries (Franzini et al. 2001).

A close inspection of blacks' health and mortality disadvantage further reveals the multiple ways that race matters for health. One of the main reasons for blacks' health disadvantage is that blacks as a group have less money than whites, as noted in Chapter 7. Yet the differences in black and white health go beyond economic causes and reflect other important aspects of the social and cultural landscape. Consider racial gaps in mortality. The murder rate for young black males is more than six times higher than for their white peers (U.S. Bureau of Justice Statistics 2006). This gap has been attributed to the violent crime that has accompanied the rise of widespread crack cocaine addiction especially in the late 1980 and 1990s, mainly affecting poor African American neighborhoods plagued by high levels of unemployment (Wilson 1996).

Other race-based inequalities in health status, health behaviors, and health care are also stark. There is a higher prevalence of hypertension among blacks than whites, especially black men; this difference may be partly biological. The pattern also may reflect blacks' tendency to eat high-fat foods, a pattern encouraged by the fast food industry's targeting of African Americans as a market (Henderson and Kelly 2005).

Despite the persistence of such inequalities, some progress has been made in eradicating them. According to the National Center for Health Statistics (2007), racial differences in cigarette smoking have decreased. In 1965, half of white men and 60 percent of black men age eighteen and over smoked cigarettes. By 2006, 23.5 percent of white men and 26.1 percent of black men smoked. In 1965, roughly equal proportions of black and white women age eighteen and older smoked (33 to 34 percent). In 2006, a smaller proportion of black women (18.5 percent) smoked than white women (18.8 percent).

Hypertension among blacks also has been greatly reduced. In the early 1970s, half of black adults between ages 20 and 74 suffered from hypertension. By 2006, however, roughly 36 percent of black adults in that age group suffered from hypertension, with black men having a slightly higher risk than women (26.5 to 23.9 percent) (National Center for Health Statistics 2008a).

Patterns of physician visitation, hospitalization, and preventive medicine also have improved, yet racial equity still remains elusive. For example, black women historically have been less likely than white women to receive mammograms. This gap has narrowed in recent years, however. In 2005, roughly 67 percent of white women and 65 percent of black women age 40 and older had received mammograms within the past two years (National Center for Health Statistics 2008b). However, some studies suggest that black women delay receiving mammograms, and thus those with breast cancer have their condition detected at a later—and more dangerous—stage of the disease's progression (Smith-Bindman et al. 2006).

How might the influence of poverty on health be countered? Extensive programs of health education and disease prevention are one possibility. But such programs work better among more prosperous, well-educated groups and in any case usually produce only small changes in behavior. Increased accessibility to health services would help, but probably to a limited degree. The only really effective policy option is to attack poverty itself, so as to reduce the income gap between rich and poor (Najman 1993).

GENDER-BASED INEQUALITIES IN HEALTH

Women in the United States generally live longer than men, and this gender gap increased steadily throughout the twentieth century. In the United States, there was only a two-year difference in female and male life expectancies in 1900. By 1940, this gap had increased to 4.4 years; by 1970, to 7.7 years. The gender gap declined to roughly five years in 2006 (Cleary 1987; National Center for Health Statistics 2009b).

Despite the female advantage in mortality, most large surveys show that women more often report poor health. Women have higher rates of illness from acute conditions and nonfatal chronic conditions, including arthritis, osteoporosis, and depressive and anxiety disorders. They are slightly more likely to report their health as fair or poor, they spend about 40 percent more days sick in bed each year, and their activities are restricted due to health problems about 25 percent more than men. In addition, they make more physician visits each year and undergo twice the number of surgical procedures as do men (National Center for Health Statistics 2003).

There are two main explanations for women's poorer health yet longer lives: (1) Greater life expectancy and age bring poorer health, and (2) women make greater use of medical services, including preventive care (Centers for Disease Control and Prevention [CDC] 2003). Men may experience as many health symptoms as women or more, but may ignore their symptoms, underestimate the extent of their illness, or utilize preventive services less often (Waldron 1986). ✓

CONCEPT CHECKS ✓

1. How do social class and race affect health?

2. Name at least two explanations for the gender gap in health.

WHAT CAUSES INFECTIOUS DISEASES IN DEVELOPING NATIONS?

COLONIALISM AND THE SPREAD OF DISEASE

The hunting and gathering communities of the Americas, before the arrival of the Europeans, were not as susceptible to infectious disease as the European societies of the period. Many infectious organisms thrive only when human populations live above the density level that is characteristic of hunting and gathering life. Permanently settled communities, particularly large cities, risk the contamination of water supplies by waste products. Hunters and gatherers were less vulnerable in this respect because they moved continuously across the countryside.

The Rise of International NGOs and Health Services

In the developing world, the decline of the public sector in the provision of health care services in the 1980s created serious gaps in health care. At the same time, these countries experience greater health problems, including epidemics of preventable and treatable diseases. For example, the World Health Organization (WHO) reported that there were 8.8 million new cases of tuberculosis around the world in 2005, but 7.4 million of these cases were reported in Asia and sub-Saharan Africa (World Health Organization 2007a). In part due to the inability of governments to provide adequate services, health care has been one sector in which the rise of international nongovernmental organizations (INGOs) in the provision of basic social services is most apparent. Development scholars often describe this as the "NGOization" of the developing world. For example, although falling short of its goals, the Global Fund to Fight AIDS, Tuberculosis and Malaria raised 3.7 billion dollars to fight these diseases in 2005, more than the annual gross domestic product of many of the recipient countries. Today, INGOs provide a wide range of health services to citizens of developing nations, including direct health services like disease prevention, training of medical professionals, procuring drugs, research efforts, and patient advocacy, to name a few (Mwabu et al. 2001).

There are advantages to non-state provision of health services. INGOs often have more resources than governments, particularly those in the developing world. Some scholars and practitioners argue that INGOs are more efficient at providing health care than the bureaucratic structure of governments' health care systems. For a government lacking the resources and human capital to deliver basic health services to its citizens, INGOs provide valuable services for public health.

Using INGOs as the primary provider of a nation or region's health services also has its disadvantages:

During the colonial era, efforts to bring Western ideals to developing societies also brought certain diseases into other parts of the world. Smallpox, measles, and typhus, among other major maladies, were unknown to the indigenous populations of Central and South America before the Spanish conquest in the early sixteenth century. The English and French colonists brought the same diseases to North America (Dubos 1959). Some of these illnesses produced epidemics that ravaged or completely wiped out native populations, which had little or no resistance to them.

In Africa and subtropical parts of Asia, infectious diseases have been rife for a long time. Tropical and subtropical conditions are especially conducive to diseases such as malaria, carried by mosquitoes, and sleeping sickness, carried by the tsetse

Namely, the priorities of a given INGO can supersede the improvement of overall societal health. Private organizations are now in positions to dictate the health priorities for poorer regions of the world. A recent article in the *Los Angeles Times* describes the unintended consequences of health programs sponsored by the Bill and Melinda Gates Foundation (Piller and Smith 2007). The Gates Foundation has given 8.5 billion dollars to various organizations that provide vaccines and fight AIDS, tuberculosis, and malaria. However, fighting these high-profile diseases has taken valuable medical staff away from basic care. Basic needs like nutrition and transportation infrastructure are neglected. The article tells the story of Matsepang Nyoba, a woman living with AIDS in Lesotho whose baby died during delivery. Ms. Nyoba's baby did not die of complications due to AIDS. The hospital where she delivered her baby receives funding from the Gates Foundation for HIV/AIDS medications but lacked stethoscope tubes, a basic piece of hospital equipment. These tubes often are used to deliver oxygen to patients; because the hospital lacked these tubes, the baby ultimately died due to lack of oxygen. Ms. Nyoba's story is not uncommon. In fact, WHO reported that the high rates of women who die in pregnancy and childbirth was a major health issue in 2007 (World Health Organization

2007b), but one that is often not a priority among international health-focused NGOs.

The priorities of INGOs are usually shaped by other concerns than the individual needs of a particular hospital or even a particular country. While very important for confronting the spread of disease, INGOs cannot yet replace national health care systems.

fly. Historians believe that risks from infectious diseases were lower in Africa and Asia prior to the time that Europeans tried to colonize these regions—as they often brought with them practices that negatively affected the health of local natives. The threat of epidemics, drought, or natural disaster had always loomed, but colonialism led to major unforeseen changes in the relation between populations and their environments, producing harmful effects on health patterns. The Europeans introduced new farming methods, upsetting the ecology of whole regions. For example, before the Europeans' arrival, Africans successfully maintained large herds of cattle in East Africa. Changes introduced by the intruders allowed the multiplication and uncontrolled spread of the tsetse fly, which carries illnesses that are fatal to both humans and livestock. Today large areas of East Africa are completely devoid of cattle (Kjekshus 1977).

The most significant consequence of the colonial system was its effect on nutrition and, therefore, on levels of resistance to illness as a result of the changed economic conditions involved in producing for world markets. In many parts of Africa, the nutritional quality of native diets became substantially depressed as cash-crop production supplanted the production of native foods.

This was not a one-way process, however. Indeed, early colonialism also radically changed Western diets, having a paradoxical impact in terms of health. On the one hand, Western diets benefited from the addition of new foods, such as bananas, pineapples, and grapefruit. On the other hand, the importation of tobacco and coffee, together with raw sugar (which found uses in all manner of foods), has had harmful consequences. Smoking tobacco, especially, has been linked to cancer and heart disease.

INFECTIOUS DISEASES TODAY IN THE DEVELOPING WORLD

Although major strides have occurred in reducing, and in some cases eliminating, infectious diseases in the developing world, they remain far more common there than in the West. The most important example of a disease that has almost completely disappeared is smallpox, which as recently as the 1960s was a scourge of Europe as well as many other regions. Campaigns against malaria have been much less successful. When the insecticide DDT was first produced, it was hoped that the mosquito, the prime carrier of malaria, could be eradicated. At first, there was considerable progress, but this has slowed because some strains of mosquito have become resistant to DDT. An estimated one million deaths occur due to malaria each year; rates are highest in sub-Saharan Africa, and children are at a particularly high risk (Snow et al. 2005). Recognizing the magnitude of this global health concern, in 2005 President George W. Bush initiated the $1.2 billion, five-year President's Malaria Initiative; its goal is to reduce malaria-related deaths in fifteen African countries by 50 percent.

HUMAN IMMUNODEFICIENCY VIRUS (HIV) AND ACQUIRED IMMUNE DEFICIENCY SYNDROME (AIDS)

A devastating exception to the trend of eliminating infectious diseases in the developing world is HIV/AIDS, which has become a global epidemic. Estimates of the number of people infected with HIV are between 30 million and 36 million worldwide in 2007 (UNAIDS 2008a). In 2007 alone, 32 million people died from AIDS-related illnesses (UNAIDS 2008a). Using middle-range estimates, about 730,000 people are living with HIV/AIDS in Western and Central Europe, 1.2 million in North America, 1.9 million in Latin America and the Caribbean, and 22 million in sub-Saharan Africa (Global Map 14.1). The main effect of the epidemic is still to come, because of the time it takes for HIV infection to develop into full-blown AIDS.

The majority of people affected in the world today are heterosexuals. As of 2005, about half were women. In sub-Saharan Africa, young women are more than twice as

Looking AIDS in the Face: Anonymous (covering face) is a university student at Maputo University in Mozambique. Due to the extreme stigma he might face, he chose not to include any of his clothes in the photograph for fear of being identified. "I can't be identified because it may have a bad impact on my position as a university student. . . . Here in Mozambique there is discrimination promoted by the government. In one of his speeches the prime minister said Mozambique should not invest in educating people with AIDS as there is no hope for them. . . . If my faculty discovered my status . . . they would try all sorts of devious means to get rid of me."

likely as men to be infected. Worldwide, at least four HIV infections are contracted heterosexually for every instance of homosexual spread.

In high-income countries, the rate of new infections has declined, yet the demographics are striking. In the United States, there were almost 37,000 new infections in 2006 and nearly half of these were in southern states (National Center for Health Statistics 2008c; UNAIDS 2005a). Of these, nearly a third were in African Americans. In fact, African American women are eight times more likely to be infected with HIV than white women, and HIV/AIDS is the leading cause of death among African American women age twenty-five to thirty-four in the United States (UNAIDS 2003, 2005b). Although there was a steep drop in AIDS-related deaths after the introduction of antiretroviral therapy, African Americans are not benefiting from such life-prolonging treatments. The United Nations Joint Program on HIV and AIDS reports that African Americans are half as likely as white Americans to be receiving antiretroviral treatment (UNAIDS 2005b).

Stigmatization of people with HIV/AIDS remains a major barrier to successful treatment. The stigma that associates HIV-positive status with sexual promiscuity, homosexuality, and IV drug use results in an avoidance of HIV/AIDS prevention and treatment programs.

In the United States, a quarter of people living with HIV/AIDS do not know that they are infected (UNAIDS 2005b). Part of the reason is the high level of fear and denial associated with being diagnosed as HIV positive. The stigma of having HIV/AIDS and the discrimination against people living with these infections are major barriers to the treatment of the epidemic worldwide. A 2002 survey found that one in ten doctors and nurses in Nigeria have refused treatment to a person because of his or her HIV/AIDS status. In India, 70 percent of people living with HIV/AIDS have reported discrimination by health-care workers (UNAIDS 2003).

Although the spread of AIDS in Western societies has slowed, the opposite has been true in the developing world, where health education is limited and the medical establishment is poor. In low- and middle-income countries, the percentage of pregnant women who receive health-care services aimed at preventing mother-to-child HIV transmission rose from 9 percent in 2004 to 33 percent in 2007 (UNAIDS 2008b). Besides the devastation to individuals who suffer from it, the AIDS epidemic is creating severe social consequences, including sharply rising numbers of orphaned children. Frail older adults are increasingly called on to provide physical care to their adult children who suffer from AIDS (Knodel 2006). Worldwide, the parents of an estimated fifteen million children have died as a result of HIV/AIDS; 11.6 million are in sub-Saharan Africa (Global Map 14.1). In Uganda alone, 77 percent of the population are under the age of eighteen; 30 percent of those are orphans (AIDS Orphans Educational Trust 2003). The decimated population of working adults combined with the surging population of orphans sets the stage for massive social instability; economies break down, and governments cannot provide for the social needs of orphans, who become targets for recruitment into gangs and armies. ✓

CONCEPT CHECKS ✓

1. Why are infectious diseases more common in developing nations than in the United States today?

2. What are three social consequences of the AIDS epidemic in developing nations?

HOW DOES SOCIAL CONTEXT SHAPE HUMAN SEXUAL BEHAVIOR?

As with the study of health and illness, scholars differ over the importance of biological versus social and cultural influences on human sexual behavior, another important facet of the sociology of the body.

THE DIVERSITY OF HUMAN SEXUALITY

Judith Lorber (1994) distinguishes as many as ten different sexual identities: straight (heterosexual) woman, straight man, lesbian woman, gay man, bisexual woman,

Global Map 14.1 | The Number of HIV-Positive People around the World

The effect of HIV/AIDS will be greatest in sub-Saharan Africa. In 2007 alone, there were 1.7 million new HIV infections in sub-Saharan Africa; over three quarters of all AIDS-related deaths occurred there. In Botswana, Namibia, and Swaziland, nearly 40 percent of the population is infected with HIV/AIDS.

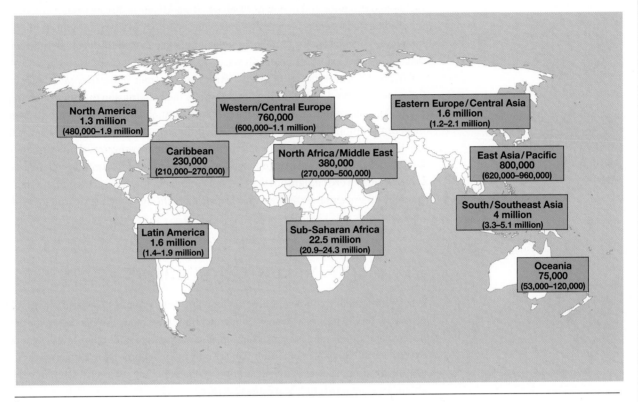

Source: UNAIDS 2007.

bisexual man, transvestite woman (a woman who regularly dresses as a man), transvestite man (a man who regularly dresses as a woman), transsexual woman (a man who becomes a woman), and transsexual man (a woman who becomes a man). Sexual practices themselves are even more diverse. Freud argued that human beings are born with a wide range of sexual tastes that are ordinarily curbed through socialization—although some adults may follow these even when, in a given society, they are regarded as immoral or illegal. Freud began his research during the Victorian period, when many people were sexually prudish; yet his patients still revealed an amazing diversity of sexual pursuits.

Among possible sexual practices are the following: A man or woman can have sexual relations with women, men, or both. This can happen with one partner at a time or with two or more partners participating. One can have sex with oneself (masturbation) or with no one (celibacy). One can have sexual relations with transsexuals or people who erotically cross-dress; use pornography or sexual devices; practice sadomasochism (the erotic use of bondage and the inflicting of pain); and so on (Lorber 1994). In most societies, sexual norms encourage some practices and discourage or condemn others. Such norms, however, vary among cultures. Homosexuality is an example. Among the ancient Greeks, for instance, the love of men for boys was idealized as the highest form of sexual love.

The most extensive cross-cultural study of sexual practices was carried out by Clellan Ford and Frank Beach (1951), using anthropological evidence from more than two hundred societies. Striking variations were found in what was regarded as "natural" sexual behavior and in norms of sexual attractiveness. For example, in some cultures, extended foreplay is desirable and even necessary before intercourse; in others, foreplay is nonexistent. In some societies, it is believed that overly frequent intercourse leads to physical debilitation or illness.

In most cultures, norms of sexual attractiveness (held by both females and males) focus more on physical looks for women than for men, a situation that may be changing in the West as women become active in spheres outside the home. The traits seen as most important in female beauty, however, differ greatly. In the modern West, a slim, small physique is admired, while in other cultures a more generous shape is attractive. Sometimes the breasts are not considered a source of sexual stimulus, whereas some societies attach erotic significance to them. Some societies value the shape of the face, whereas others emphasize the shape and color of the eyes or the size and form of the nose and lips.

SEXUALITY IN WESTERN CULTURE

Western attitudes toward sexual behavior were for nearly two thousand years molded primarily by Christianity, whose dominant view was that all sexual behavior is suspect except that needed for reproduction. During some periods this view produced an extreme prudishness, but at other times many people ignored the church's teachings and engaged in practices such as adultery. The idea that sexual fulfillment can and should be sought through marriage was rare.

In the nineteenth century, religious presumptions about sexuality were partly replaced by medical ones. Most early writings by doctors about sexual behavior, however, were as stern as the views of the church. Some argued that any type of sexual activity unconnected with reproduction would cause serious physical harm. Masturbation was said to cause blindness, insanity, heart disease, and other ailments, while oral sex was claimed to cause cancer. In Victorian times, sexual hypocrisy abounded. Many Victorian men—who appeared to be sober, well-behaved citizens, devoted to their wives—regularly visited prostitutes or kept mistresses. Such behavior was accepted, whereas "respectable" women who took lovers were regarded as scandalous and shunned in polite society. The differing attitudes toward the sexual activities of men and women formed a double standard, which persists today.

Currently, traditional attitudes exist alongside much more permissive attitudes, which developed widely in the 1960s. Some people, particularly those influenced by Christian teachings, believe that premarital sex is wrong; they frown on all forms of sexual behavior except heterosexual activity within marriage—although it is now more commonly accepted that sexual pleasure is an important feature of marriage. Sexual attitudes have undoubtedly become more permissive over recent decades in most Western countries. Movies and plays include scenes that previously would have been unacceptable, and pornographic material is available to most adults who want it. Pornography is reportedly the predominant use for the World Wide Web. By the end of 2004, there were 420 million pages of pornography, and it is believed that the majority of these Web sites are owned by fewer than fifty companies (LaRue 2005).

SEXUAL BEHAVIOR: KINSEY'S STUDY

We can speak more confidently about public values concerning sexuality than we can about private practices, for such practices have gone undocumented for much of history. When Alfred Kinsey began his research in the United States in the 1940s and 1950s, it was the first major investigation of sexual behavior. Kinsey and his co-researchers (1948, 1953) faced condemnation from religious organizations, and his work was denounced as immoral in the newspapers and in Congress. But he persisted, thus making his study the largest rigorous study of sexuality at that time, although his sample was not representative of the overall American population.

Kinsey's results were surprising because they revealed a tremendous discrepancy between prevailing public expectations of sexual behavior and actual sexual conduct. The gap between publicly accepted attitudes and actual behavior was probably especially pronounced just after World War II, the time of Kinsey's study. A phase of sexual liberalization had begun in the 1920s, when many younger people felt freed from the strict moral codes that had governed earlier generations. Sexual behavior probably changed, but issues concerning sexuality were not openly discussed. People participating in sexual activities that were still strongly disapproved of on a public level concealed them, not realizing that others were engaging in similar practices. The more permissive 1960s brought openly declared attitudes more into line with the realities of behavior.

SEXUAL BEHAVIOR SINCE KINSEY

In the 1960s, social movements that challenged the existing order, such as those associated with countercultural lifestyles, also broke with existing sexual norms. These movements preached sexual freedom, and the introduction of the contraceptive pill allowed sexual pleasure to be separated from reproduction. Women's groups also started pressing for greater independence from male sexual values, rejection of the double standard, and the need for women to achieve greater sexual satisfaction in their relationships. Even so, until recently it was unclear to what extent sexual behavior had changed since the time of Kinsey's research.

In the late 1980s, Lillian Rubin (1990) interviewed a thousand Americans between the ages of thirteen and forty-eight to identify changes in sexual behavior and attitudes over the previous thirty years or so. Her findings indicate significant changes. Sexual activity begins at a younger age; moreover, teenagers' sexual practices are as varied and comprehensive as those of adults. There is still a double standard, but it is not as powerful as before. One of the most important changes is that women now expect, and actively pursue, sexual pleasure in relationships—a phenomenon that Rubin argues has major consequences for both sexes.

Women are more sexually available than before, which most men applaud; but women also have a new assertiveness that men find difficult to accept. The men Rubin talked to often said they "felt inadequate," were afraid they could "never do anything right," and found it "impossible to satisfy women these days." Several recent authors concur that masculinity is a burden as much as a source of reward. Much male sexuality, they add, is compulsive rather than satisfying (Kimmel 2003).

In 1994, a team of researchers led by Edward Laumann published *The Social Organization of Sexuality: Sexual Practices in the United States,* the most comprehensive study of sexual behavior since Kinsey. Their findings reflect an essential sexual conservatism among Americans. For instance, 83 percent of their subjects had had only one partner (or no partner at all) in the preceding year, and among married people the figure was 96 percent. Fidelity to one's spouse was also quite common: Only 10 percent of women and less than 25 percent of men reported having an extramarital affair during their lifetime. According to the study, Americans average only three partners during their entire lifetime (Figure 14.1). Despite the apparent ordinariness of sexual behavior, some distinct historical changes were revealed in this study, the most significant being a progressive increase in the level of premarital sexual experience, particularly among women. In fact, over 95 percent of Americans getting married today are sexually experienced.

In addition, sexual experience among young people is much greater today than it was in the 1970s. According to the Centers for Disease Control and Prevention (2008c), in 2007 nearly half (48 percent) of all high school students reported having had sexual intercourse; 15 percent reported having had four or more partners. U.S. rates are far higher than those in most Asian nations (Tang and Zuo 2000; Toufexis 1993). Considering that the General Social Survey in 1997 reported that over 70 percent of American adults believed that teenage sex is "always wrong" and another 16 percent believed it is "almost always wrong," parental beliefs and adolescent behavior are clearly in conflict.

SEXUAL ORIENTATION

Another important aspect of sexuality concerns sexual orientation, the direction of one's sexual or romantic attraction. The term *sexual preference*, which is sometimes incorrectly used instead of sexual orientation, is misleading and is to be avoided because it implies that one's sexual or romantic attraction is entirely a matter of personal choice. As you will see below, sexual orientation results from a complex interplay of biological and social factors not yet fully understood.

The most commonly found sexual orientation in all cultures, including the United States, is *heterosexuality,* a sexual or romantic attraction to persons of the opposite sex. Heterosexuals in the United States are also sometimes referred to as "straight." It is important to note that although heterosexuality may be the prevailing norm in most cultures, it is not "normal" in the sense of being dictated by some universal moral or religious standard. Like all behavior, heterosexual behavior is socially learned within a particular culture.

Homosexuality involves a sexual or romantic attraction to persons of one's own sex. Today, the term gay is used to refer to male homosexuals, *lesbian* for female homosexuals, and bi as shorthand for *bisexuals*, people who experience sexual or romantic attraction to both men and women. Although it is difficult to know for sure because of the stigma attached to homosexuality, which may result in the underreporting of sexuality in demographic surveys, estimates are that from 2 to 5 percent of all women and 3 to 10 percent of all men in the United States are homosexual or bisexual (Burr 1993; General Social Survey [GSS] 1997; Laumann et al. 1994).

The term *homosexual* was first used by the medical community in 1869 to characterize what was then regarded as a personality disorder. The American Psychiatric Association did not remove homosexuality from its list of mental illnesses until 1973 or

Figure 14.1

SEX IN AMERICA

Social Influences on Sexual Behavior

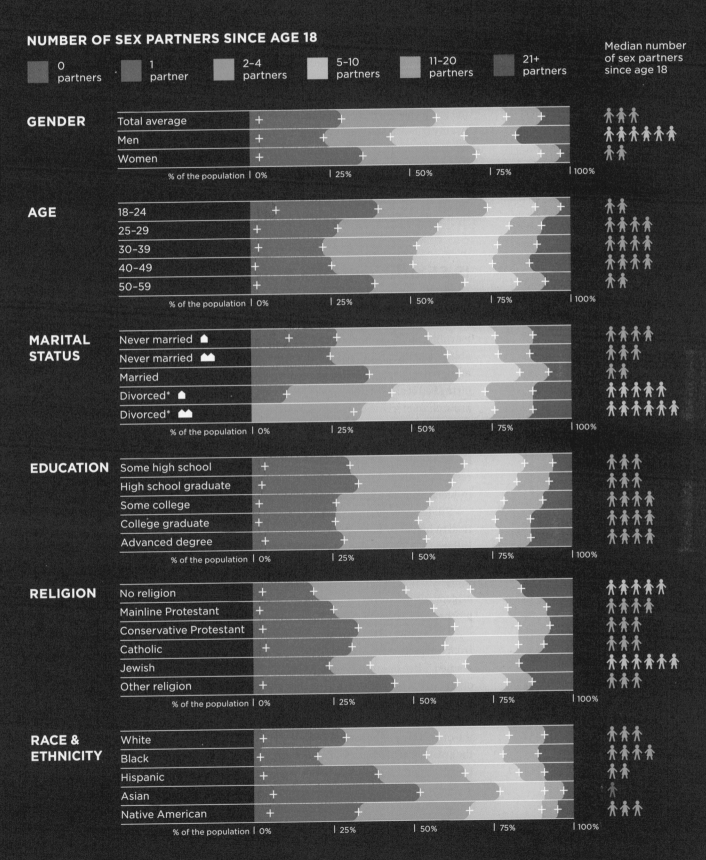

NUMBER OF SEX PARTNERS SINCE AGE 18

- 0 partners
- 1 partner
- 2–4 partners
- 5–10 partners
- 11–20 partners
- 21+ partners

Median number of sex partners since age 18

GENDER
- Total average
- Men
- Women

% of the population   0%   25%   50%   75%   100%

AGE
- 18–24
- 25–29
- 30–39
- 40–49
- 50–59

% of the population   0%   25%   50%   75%   100%

MARITAL STATUS
- Never married 🏠
- Never married ⌂⌂
- Married
- Divorced* 🏠
- Divorced* ⌂⌂

% of the population   0%   25%   50%   75%   100%

EDUCATION
- Some high school
- High school graduate
- Some college
- College graduate
- Advanced degree

% of the population   0%   25%   50%   75%   100%

RELIGION
- No religion
- Mainline Protestant
- Conservative Protestant
- Catholic
- Jewish
- Other religion

% of the population   0%   25%   50%   75%   100%

RACE & ETHNICITY
- White
- Black
- Hispanic
- Asian
- Native American

% of the population   0%   25%   50%   75%   100%

*Divorced, widowed, or separated   🏠 Living alone   ⌂⌂ Living with someone

Source: Laumann et al. 1994.

from its influential *Diagnostic and Statistical Manual of Mental Disorders* (DSM) until 1980. These long-overdue steps were taken only after prolonged lobbying and pressure by homosexual rights organizations. The medical community was belatedly forced to acknowledge that no scientific research had ever found homosexuals as a group to be psychologically unhealthier than heterosexuals (Burr 1993). However, the DSM IV continues to classify other aspects of sexuality as "disorders," including disorders of desire (e.g., low interest in sex), disorders of sexual arousal (e.g., lubrication and erectile problems), and orgasmic disorders (American Psychiatric Association 2000).

In a small number of cultures, same-sex relationships are the norm in certain contexts and do not necessarily signify what today is termed *homosexuality*. For example, the anthropologist Gilbert Herdt (1981, 1984, 1986) reported that among more than twenty tribes in Melanesia and New Guinea, ritually prescribed same-sex encounters among young men and boys were considered necessary for subsequent masculine virility (Herdt and Davidson 1988). Ritualized male-male sexual encounters also occurred among the Azande of Africa's Sudan and Congo (Evans-Pritchard 1970), Japanese samurai warriors in the nineteenth century (Leupp 1995), and highly educated Greek men and boys at the time of Plato (Rouselle 1999).

IS SEXUAL ORIENTATION INBORN OR LEARNED?

Most sociologists believe that sexual orientation—whether homosexual, heterosexual, or bisexual—results from a complex interplay between biological factors and social learning. Since heterosexuality is the norm for most people in U.S. culture, considerable research has focused on why some people become homosexual. Some scholars argue that biological influences predispose certain people to become homosexual from birth (Bell et al. 1981; Green 1987). Biological explanations have included differences in brain characteristics of homosexuals (LeVay 1991) and the effect on fetal development of the mother's *in utero* hormone production during pregnancy (Blanchard and Bogaert 1996; Manning et al. 1997; McFadden and Champlin 2000). Such studies, which are based on small numbers of cases, give highly inconclusive (and highly controversial) results (Healy 2001). It is virtually impossible to separate biological from early social influences in determining a person's sexual orientation.

Studies of twins may shed light on any genetic basis for homosexuality, since identical twins share identical genes. In two related studies, Bailey and Pillard (Bailey and Pillard 1991, Bailey 1993) examined 167 pairs of brothers and 143 pairs of sisters, with each pair of siblings raised in the same family, in which at least one sibling defined himself or herself as homosexual. Some of these pairs were identical twins (who share all genes), some were fraternal twins (who share some genes), and some were adoptive brothers or sisters (who share no genes).

The results offer some support that homosexuality, like heterosexuality, results from a combination of biological and social factors. Among the men and the women studied, when one twin was homosexual, there was about a 50 percent chance that the other twin was homosexual. In other words, a woman or man is five times as likely to be lesbian or gay if her or his identical twin is lesbian or gay than if her or his sibling is lesbian or gay but related only through adoption. These results offer some support for the importance of biological factors, since the higher the percentage of shared genes, the greater the percentage of cases in which both siblings were homosexual. However, because approximately half of the identical twin brothers and sisters of homosexuals were not themselves homosexual, social learning must also be involved; otherwise one would expect all identical twin siblings of homosexuals to be homosexual as well.

HOMOPHOBIA

Homophobia, a term coined in the late 1960s, refers to both attitudes and behaviors marked by an aversion to or hatred of homosexuals, their lifestyles, and their practices. It is a form of prejudice reflected not only in overt acts of hostility and violence toward lesbians and gays but also in forms of verbal abuse that are widespread in American culture, for example, using terms like *fag* or homo to insult heterosexual males or using female-related offensive terms such as *sissy or* pansy to insult gay men.

homophobia • An irrational fear or disdain of homosexuals.

One recent study of homophobia in U.S. schools concluded that the estimated two million lesbian, gay, and bisexual middle and high school students are frequently the targets of humiliating harassment and, sometimes, physical abuse. Interviews with lesbian, gay, and bisexual students, as well as youth service providers, teachers, administrators, counselors, and parents in seven states, found harassment to be a common and painful experience among lesbian, gay, and bisexual students (Bochenek and Brown 2001). The study cited a CBS poll reporting that a third of eleventh-grade students knew about incidents of sexual harassment of gays and lesbians, while more than a quarter admitted to engaging in harassment.

Homophobia is widespread in U.S. culture, although it is slowly starting to erode. In 2007, the Gallup Poll found that 57 percent of Americans viewed homosexuality as an acceptable lifestyle (Saad 2007). Yet social change has been slow. It was only in the very recent past (2003) that the Supreme Court ruled in *Lawrence v. Texas* that the state of Texas's prohibition on homosexual sex was a violation of the constitutional right to privacy.

The Stonewall Inn nightclub raid in 1969 is regarded as the first shot fired in the battle for gay rights in the United States. The twenty-fifth anniversary of the event was commemorated in New York City with a variety of celebrations as well as discussions on the evolution and future of gay rights.

THE MOVEMENT FOR GAY AND LESBIAN CIVIL RIGHTS

Until recently, most gays and lesbians hid their sexual orientation for fear that "coming out of the closet"—publicly revealing one's sexual orientation—would cost them their jobs, families, and friends and leave them open to verbal and physical abuse. Yet, since the late 1960s, many gays and lesbians have acknowledged their homosexuality openly, and in some cities the lives of lesbian and gay Americans have become quite normalized (Seidman et al. 1999). New York City, San Francisco, London, and other large metropolitan areas worldwide have thriving gay and lesbian communities. Coming out may be important not only for the person who does so but also for others in the larger society: Previously closeted lesbians and gays discover they are not alone, while heterosexuals recognize that people whom they admire and respect are homosexual.

The current global wave of gay and lesbian civil rights movements began partly as an outgrowth of the U.S. social movements of the 1960s, which emphasized pride in racial and ethnic identity. One pivotal event was the Stonewall riots in June 1969, when New York City's gay community—angered by continual police harassment—fought the New York Police Department for two days (D'Emilio 1983; Weeks 1977). The Stonewall riots became a symbol of gay pride. In May 2005, the International Day Against Homophobia (IDAHO) was first celebrated, with events held in more than forty countries. Clearly, significant strides have been made, although discrimination and homophobia remain serious problems for many lesbian, gay, and bisexual Americans.

Today there is a growing movement worldwide for the civil rights of gays and lesbians. The International Lesbian and Gay Association (ILGA 2009), which was founded in 1978, has more than 670 member organizations in some 110 countries. It holds international conferences, supports lesbian and gay social movement organizations, and lobbies international organizations. For example, it persuaded the Council of Europe to require all of its member nations to repeal laws banning homosexuality. In general, active lesbian and gay social movements thrive in countries that emphasize individual rights and liberal state policies (Frank and McEneaney 1999).

HOW DOES THE SOCIAL CONTEXT OF SEXUAL BEHAVIOR AFFECT YOUR LIFE?

As we have seen in this section, sexual preferences and practices reflect a complex set of biological, social, cultural, and historical influences. Although most American young adults believe they have freedom to choose whomever they like as their romantic partner (and turn up their nose at the idea of arranged marriage), the gender of whom we choose, what we deem attractive, when and under what circumstances we engage in sexual relationships, and even whether or not we have the legal right to marry our partner is powerfully shaped by laws, norms, and cultural practices. ✓

CONCEPT CHECKS ✓

1. Describe several changes in sexual practices over the past two centuries.

2. What are the most important contributions of Alfred Kinsey's research on sexuality?

3. Name at least three important findings about sexual behavior discovered since Kinsey.

4. What is sexual orientation?

NEED HELP STUDYING?

Visit StudySpace to access free review materials such as:

- Vocabulary Flashcards
- Diagnostic Review Quizzes
- Study Outlines

REVIEW QUESTIONS

1. What are the two body weight issues facing the United States today? Why are these public issues and not just individual problems?
2. Compare and contrast the two main approaches in sociology to thinking about health and illness.
3. Describe some of the differences between traditional and modern approaches to medicine.
4. What is the difference between complementary and alternative medicine? How do sociologists explain widespread use of such therapies?
5. How are the various dimensions of social class related to differences in health and mortality?
6. How does race matter in health inequalities? Give an example.
7. How do biological and social factors explain gender differences in health?
8. What is the relationship between colonialism and health? How has the legacy of colonialism contributed to contemporary health disparities between the developed and developing worlds?
9. What are the sociological debates around Kinsey and Laumann's survey's of sexuality in the United States?
10. What is the difference between *sexual preference* and *sexual orientation?* Why do these differences in terminology matter?

THINKING SOCIOLOGICALLY EXERCISES

1. Statistical studies of our national health show a gap in life expectancies between the rich and the poor. Review all the major factors that would explain why rich people live about eight years longer than poor people.
2. This text discusses the biological and sociocultural factors associated with sexual orientation. Why are twin studies the most promising type of research on the genetic basis of sexual orientation? Summarize the analysis of these studies, and show whether it presently appears that sexual orientation results from genetic differences, sociocultural practices and experiences, or both.

15

Urbanization, Population, and the Environment

THE BIG QUESTIONS

HOW DO CITIES DEVELOP AND EVOLVE?

Learn how cities have changed as a result of industrialization and urbanization. Learn how theories of urbanism have placed increasing emphasis on the influence of socioeconomic factors on city life.

HOW DO RURAL, SUBURBAN, AND URBAN LIFE DIFFER IN THE UNITED STATES?

Learn about the recent key developments affecting American cities, suburbs, and rural communities in the last several decades: suburbanization, urban decay, gentrification, and population loss in rural areas.

HOW DOES URBANIZATION AFFECT LIFE ACROSS THE GLOBE?

See that global economic competition has a profound impact on urbanization and urban life. Recognize the challenges of urbanization in the developing world.

WHAT ARE THE FORCES BEHIND WORLD POPULATION GROWTH?

Learn why the world population has increased dramatically and understand the main consequences of this growth.

HOW DO URBANIZATION AND ENVIRONMENTAL CHANGES AFFECT YOUR LIFE?

See that the environment is a sociological issue related to urbanization and population growth.

H andan, China—When residents of this northern Chinese city hang their clothes out to dry, the black fallout from nearby Handan Iron and Steel often sends them back to the wash.

Half a world away, neighbors of ThyssenKrupp's former steel mill in the Ruhr valley of Germany once had a similar problem. The white shirts men wore to church on Sundays turned gray by the time they got home.

These two steel towns have an unusual kinship, spanning 5,000 miles and a decade of economic upheaval. They have shared the same hulking blast furnace, dismantled and shipped piece by piece from Germany's old industrial heartland to Hebei Province, China's new Ruhr valley.

The transfer, one of dozens since the late 1990s, contributed to a burst in China's steel production, which now exceeds that of Germany, Japan, and the United States combined. Germany was left with lost jobs and a bad case of postindustrial angst.

But steel mills spewing particulates into the air and sucking electricity from China's coal-fired power plants account for a big chunk of the country's surging emissions

A coal miner emerges from a mine after a day's work in Shanxi Province, China.

of sulfur dioxide and carbon dioxide. Germany, in contrast, has cleaned its skies and is now leading the fight against global warming.

In their rush to recreate the industrial revolution that made Western nations rich, Chinese companies—spurred on by strong state support—have become the dominant makers of steel, coal, aluminum, cement, chemicals, leather, and paper. China has become the world's factory, but also its smokestack (Landler and Kahn 2007).

China's rapid rise as an industrial power—with India not far behind—creates enormous environmental challenges, not just for these two countries, but for all of us. Their combined population of 2.4 billion people accounts for one out of every three people on the planet. They contain some of the world's largest and fastest-growing urban areas, whose population is swollen with impoverished rural migrants looking for jobs. They are seeking to achieve the same standard of living achieved by their neighbors in Japan, Europe, the United States, and other industrial countries. But their combination of population growth, urbanization, and industrialization has had toxic environmental results.

China's economy, for example, has grown at nearly 10 percent a year for more than three decades. This rapid industrialization has lifted hundreds of millions of people out of poverty and into the middle class, but at a high environmental cost: Toxic chemical spills have threatened the water supply of millions of people, while the air in major cities has become so polluted that the ultramodern skyscrapers that seemingly go up overnight are often not visible. Sixteen of the most polluted cities in the world are in China.

In its rush to develop, China is building a vast network of highways, like the United States did a half century ago. The nearly 53,000 miles of new roads will connect all major cities in China, supporting (and generating) automobile use that is projected to outstrip that of the United States by the middle of the century—or earlier. For a country where as recently as twenty-five years ago the bicycle and rickshaw were the principal means of transportation, this is an enormous transformation, and one that will contribute to urban traffic congestion, along with increased levels of energy use and pollution. As China makes the transition from rural to urban in record time, its planners call for relocating some four hundred million people—more than the entire U.S. population—to newly built urban centers over the next twenty-five years. If achieved, this will require the construction of half of all the buildings in the world during that time (Economy 2007).

China's booming economy depends on burning coal. Every week or so a new coal-burning power plant is brought on line, most often one using outmoded technology. The sulfur dioxide from these plants is believed to contribute to nearly a half million deaths a year in China, while causing acid rain that poisons lakes, rivers, and farmlands. Climate-changing smoke and soot from China's power plants have been detected across the Pacific Ocean in California. If China continues on its present course, its demand for energy will double over the next quarter century, while its increased production of global warming gases will outstrip that of all other industrial countries combined (Bradsher and Barboza 2007).

The relocation of a polluting steel plant from Germany to China is just one way in which the environmental costs of a global economy have been transferred from wealthy industrial nations to poorer, less developed ones. And China is quick to point out that the United States, the wealthiest industrial nation in the world, is still the world's largest contributor to greenhouse gases.

In this chapter we examine the ways in which population growth, urbanization, and environmental change go hand in hand, against the backdrop of rapid industrialization that is transforming many parts of the world. We begin by studying the origins of cities and the vast growth in the numbers of city dwellers that has occurred over the past century. From there, we review the most influential theories of urban life. We then move on to consider patterns of urban development in North America compared with cities in the developing world. Cities in the developing world are growing at an enormous rate. We consider why this is happening and at the same time look at changes now taking place in world population patterns. We conclude by assessing the connections between urbanization, world population growth, and environmental problems.

HOW DO CITIES DEVELOP AND EVOLVE?

CITIES IN TRADITIONAL SOCIETIES

The world's first cities appeared about 3500 B.C.E., in the river valleys of the Nile in Egypt, the Tigris and Euphrates in what is now Iraq, and the Indus in what is today Pakistan. Cities in traditional societies were very small by modern standards. Babylon, for example, one of the largest ancient Middle Eastern cities, extended over an area of only 3.2 square miles, and at its height, around 2000 B.C.E., probably numbered no more than fifteen to twenty thousand people. Rome under Emperor Augustus in the first century B.C.E. was easily the largest premodern city outside China, with some three hundred thousand inhabitants—the population of Bakersfield, California, or Toledo, Ohio, today.

Most cities of the ancient world shared certain features. They were usually surrounded by walls that served as a military defense and emphasized the separation of the urban community from the countryside. The central area of the city was almost always occupied by a religious temple, a royal palace, government and commercial buildings, and a public square. This ceremonial, commercial, and political center was sometimes enclosed within a second, inner wall and was usually too small to hold more than a minority of the citizens. Although it usually contained a market, the center was different from the business districts found at the core of modern cities, because the main buildings were nearly always religious and political rather than commercial (Fox 1964; Sjoberg 1960, 1963; Wheatley 1971).

The dwellings of the ruling class or elite tended to be concentrated in or near the center. Less privileged groups lived toward the perimeter of the city or outside the walls, moving inside if the city came under attack. Different ethnic and religious communities were often segregated in separate neighborhoods, where their members lived and worked. Sometimes these neighborhoods were also surrounded by walls. Communication among city dwellers was erratic. Lacking any form of printing press, and with very low rates of literacy, public officials had to shout at the tops of their voices to deliver pronouncements. "Streets" were usually strips of land on which no one had yet built. A few traditional civilizations boasted sophisticated road systems linking particular cities, but these existed mainly for military purposes, and transportation for the most part was slow and limited. Merchants and soldiers were the only people who regularly traveled over long distances.

Although cities were the main centers for science, the arts, and cosmopolitan culture, their influence in surrounding areas was always weak. No more than a tiny proportion of the population lived in the cities, and the division between cities and countryside was pronounced. By far the majority of people lived in small rural communities and rarely came into contact with more than the occasional state official or merchant from the towns.

INDUSTRIALIZATION AND URBANIZATION

conurbation • An agglomeration of towns or cities into an unbroken urban environment.

megalopolis • The "city of all cities" in ancient Greece—used in modern times to refer to very large conurbations.

The contrast in size between the largest modern cities today and those of premodern civilizations is extraordinary. The most populous cities in the industrialized countries number over ten million inhabitants. A **conurbation**—a cluster of cities and towns forming a continuous network—may include even larger numbers of people. The peak of urban life today is represented by what is called the **megalopolis**, the "city of cities." The term was originally coined in ancient Greece to refer to a city-state that was planned to be the envy of all civilizations. The current megalopolis, though, bears little relation to that utopia. The term was first applied in modern times to refer to the Northeast Corridor of the United States, an area covering some 450 miles from north of Boston to south of Washington, DC. In this region, about forty-four million people live at a density of over seven hundred persons per square mile. An urban population almost as large and dense is concentrated in the lower Great Lakes region surrounding Chicago.

Britain was the first society to undergo industrialization, beginning in the mid-eighteenth century. The process of industrialization generated increasing **urbanization**—the movement of the population into towns and cities, away from the land. In 1800, fewer than 20 percent of the British population lived in towns or cities with more than 10,000 inhabitants. By 1900, this proportion had risen to 74 percent. London held about 1.1 million people in 1800; by the beginning of the twentieth century, it had increased in size to a population of over 7 million, at that date the largest city ever seen in the world. It was a vast manufacturing, commercial, and financial center at the heart of the still-expanding British Empire.

urbanization • The development of towns and cities.

The urbanization of most other European countries and the United States took place somewhat later. In 1800, the United States was more of a rural society than were the leading European countries. Fewer than 10 percent of Americans lived in communities with populations of more than 2,500 people. Between 1800 and 1900, as industrialization grew in the United States, the population of New York City leapt from 60,000 people to 4.8 million. Today, nearly 80 percent of Americans reside in metropolitan areas.

Urbanization in the twenty-first century is a global process, into which the developing world is being drawn more and more (Kasarda and Crenshaw 1991). From 1900 to 1950, world urbanization increased by 239 percent, compared with a global population growth of 49 percent. The six decades since have seen an even greater acceleration in

Traffic outside of the Bank of England in the financial district of London in 1896. In only one century, the population of London grew from over one million people to over seven million.

urbanization. From 1950 to 1986, urban population growth worldwide was 320 percent, while the total population grew by 54 percent. Most of this growth occurred in cities in developing world societies. In 1975, 39 percent of the world's population lived in urban areas; the figure was around 50 percent in 2000 and is predicted to be 70 percent in 2050. East and South Asia will be home to nearly half of the world's people in 2050. By that date, the urban populations of the developing countries will exceed those of Europe or the United States (UN 2007b).

THEORIES OF URBANISM

THE CHICAGO SCHOOL

Scholars associated with the University of Chicago from the 1920s to the 1940s—especially Robert Park, Ernest Burgess, and Louis Wirth—developed ideas that were for many years the chief basis of theory and research in urban sociology. Two concepts developed by the "Chicago School" are worthy of special attention. One is the so-called **ecological approach** to urban analysis; the other, the characterization of urbanism as a *way of life,* developed by Wirth (Park 1952; Wirth 1938). It is important to understand these ideas as they were initially conceived by the Chicago School and to see how they have been revised and even replaced by sociologists in more recent decades.

ecological approach • A perspective on urban analysis emphasizing the "natural" distribution of city neighborhoods into areas having contrasting characteristics.

URBAN ECOLOGY

Ecology is a term taken from a physical science: the study of the adaptation of plant and animal organisms to their environment. In the natural world, organisms tend to be distributed in systematic ways over the terrain, such that a balance or equilibrium between different species is achieved. The Chicago School believed that the locations of major urban settlements and the distribution of different types of neighborhoods within them can be understood in terms of similar principles. Cities do not grow up at random but in response to advantageous features of the environment. For example, large urban areas in modern societies tend to develop along the shores of rivers, in fertile plains, or at the intersection of trading routes or railways.

According to Park, cities become ordered into "natural areas," through processes of competition, invasion, and succession—all of which also occur in biological ecology. Patterns of location, movement, and relocation in cities, according to the ecological view, have a similar form. Different neighborhoods develop through the adjustments made by inhabitants as they struggle to gain their livelihoods. A city can be pictured as a map of areas with distinct and contrasting social characteristics, in concentric rings, broken up into segments. In the center are the **inner-city** areas, a mixture of big-business prosperity and decaying private homes. Beyond these are older established neighborhoods, housing workers employed in stable manual occupations. Farther out still are the suburbs, in which higher-income groups tend to live. Processes of invasion and succession occur within the segments of the concentric rings. Thus as property decays in a central or near-central area, ethnic minority groups might start to move into it. As they do so, more of the preexisting population start to leave, precipitating movement to neighborhoods elsewhere in the city or out to the suburbs. However, as we will see later in this chapter, these traditional patterns are starting to change—as wealthy persons and the young flood into urban areas, seeking amenities such as arts and entertainment, and suburban areas become more desirable (and affordable) to poor and working-class persons.

Another aspect of the **urban ecology** approach emphasized the *interdependence* of different city areas. Differentiation—the specialization of groups and occupational roles—is the main way human beings adapt to their environment. Groups on which many others depend will have a dominant role, often reflected in their central geographical position. Business groups, for example, such as large banks or insurance companies, provide key services for many in a community and hence are usually to be found in the central areas of settlements (Hawley 1950, 1968).

URBANISM AS A WAY OF LIFE

Wirth's thesis of **urbanism** (1938) outlines the ways that life in cities is different from life elsewhere. In cities, large numbers of people live in close proximity to each other, without knowing most others personally—a fundamental contrast to small, traditional villages. Most contacts between city dwellers are fleeting and partial and are means to other ends rather than being satisfying relationships in themselves. Interactions with sales clerks in stores, baristas at coffee shops, or passengers or ticket collectors on trains are passing encounters, entered into not for their own sake but as means to other aims.

Wirth was among the first to address the "urban interaction problem" (Duneier and Molotch 1999), the necessity for city dwellers to respect social boundaries when so many people are in close physical proximity all the time. Many people walk down the street in cities acting unconcerned about the others near them, often talking on cell phones or listening to iPods that block out the sounds of urban life. Through such appearance of apathy they can avoid unwanted transgression of social boundaries.

Wirth's ideas have deservedly enjoyed wide currency. However, in assessing Wirth's ideas, we should consider that neighborhoods marked by close kinship and personal ties often are actively created by city life; they are not just remnants of a preexisting way of life that survive for a period within the city. Claude Fischer (1984) has put forward an explanation for why large-scale urbanism helps to promote diverse subcultures. Those who live in cities are able to collaborate with others of like background

---

inner city ● The areas composing the central neighborhoods of a city, as distinct from the suburbs. In many modern urban settings in the First World, inner-city areas are subject to dilapidation and decay, the more affluent residents having moved to outlying areas.

urban ecology ● An approach to the study of urban life based on an analogy with the adjustment of plants and organisms to the physical environment. According to ecological theorists, the various neighborhoods and zones within cities are formed as a result of natural processes of adjustment on the part of populations as they compete for resources.

urbanism ● A term used by Louis Wirth to denote distinctive characteristics of urban social life, such as its impersonal or alienating nature.

or interests to develop local connections; and they can join distinctive religious, ethnic, political, and other subcultural groups. A small town or village does not allow the development of such subcultural diversity. For example, some gay and lesbian young people may find more hospitable communities in cities that have large gay subcultures like San Francisco, compared to the small towns where they may have grown up.

A large city is a world of strangers, yet it ultimately supports and creates personal relationships. It may be difficult to meet people when one first moves to a large city. But anyone moving to a small, established rural community may find the friendliness of the inhabitants largely a matter of public politeness—it may take years to become accepted when one is "new" in town. This is not the case in the city, because cities are continually welcoming new, geographically mobile residents. Although one finds a diversity of strangers, each is a potential friend. And once within a group or network, the possibilities for expanding one's personal connections increase considerably.

JANE JACOBS: "EYES AND EARS UPON THE STREET"

Like most sociologists in the twentieth century, the Chicago School researchers were professors who saw their mission as contributing to a scholarly literature and advancing the field of social science. Yet one of the most influential urban scholars of the twentieth century, Jane Jacobs, author *The Death and Life of Great American Cities* (1961), was an architecture critic with a high school education. Through her own independent reading and research in the 1950s, she transformed herself into one of the most learned figures in the emerging field of urban studies.

Like sociologists such as Wirth of the Chicago School before her, Jacobs noted that "cities are, by definition, full of strangers," some of whom are dangerous. She argued that cities are most habitable when they feature a diversity of uses, thereby ensuring that many people will be coming and going on the streets at any time. When enough people are out and about, Jacobs wrote, "respectable" eyes and ears dominate the street and are fixed on strangers, who will thus not get out of hand. The more people are out, or looking from their windows at the people who are out, the more their gazes will safeguard the street.

The "urban interaction problem" is a necessity for city dwellers—respecting social boundaries when so many people are in close physical proximity all the time. Whether listening to music on portable devices or reading magazines or newspapers, many people have strategies for distancing themselves and managing social boundaries in busy urban environments.

The Castro district in San Francisco is not only open to but celebratory about its large and vibrant gay and lesbian population.

created environment •
Constructions established by human beings to serve their needs, derived from the use of man-made technology—including, for example, roads, railways, factories, offices, private homes, and other buildings.

The world has changed a great deal since Jacobs wrote *The Death and Life of Great American Cities.* Most of the people on the sidewalks Jacobs was writing about were more alike in many respects than they are today; now homeless people, drug users, panhandlers, and others representing economic inequalities, cultural differences, and extremes of behavior can make sidewalk life unpredictable (Duneier 1999). Under these conditions, strangers do not necessarily feel the kind of solidarity and mutual assurance she described. Sociologists today must ask, What happens to urban life when "the eyes and ears upon the street" represent vast inequalities and cultural differences? Do the assumptions Jacobs made still hold up? In many cases the answer is yes, but in other cases the answer is no. Nearly five decades after her book was published, Jacobs's ideas remain extremely influential.

URBANISM AND THE CREATED ENVIRONMENT

Whereas the earlier Chicago School of sociology emphasized that the distribution of people in cities occurs naturally, more recent theories of the city have stressed that urbanism is not a natural process but has to be analyzed in relation to major patterns of political and economic change.

According to this view, it is not the stranger on the sidewalk who is most threatening to many urban dwellers, especially the poor; instead, it is the stranger far away, working in a bank or real estate development company, who has the power to make decisions that transform whole blocks or neighborhoods (Logan and Molotch 1987). This focus on the political economy of cities, and on different kinds of strangers, represented a new and critical direction for urban sociology.

HARVEY: THE RESTRUCTURING OF SPACE

Urbanism, David Harvey emphasizes, is one aspect of the **created environment** brought about by the spread of industrial capitalism. In modern urbanism, Harvey points out, space is continually *restructured.* The process is determined by where large firms choose to place their factories, research and development centers, and so forth; the controls that governments maintains over both land and industrial production; and the activities of private investors, buying and selling houses and land.

The activities of private home buyers are strongly influenced by how far, and where, business interests buy up land, as well as by rates of loans and taxes fixed by local and central government. After World War II, for instance, there was vast expansion of suburban development outside major cities in the United States. This was partly due to ethnic discrimination and the tendency of whites to move away from inner-city areas.

However, it was made possible, Harvey argues, because of government decisions to provide tax breaks to home buyers and construction firms and by the setting up of special credit arrangements by financial organizations. These provided the basis for the building and buying of new homes on the peripheries of cities and at the same time promoted demand for industrial products such as the automobile (Harvey 1973, 1982, 1985).

CASTELLS: URBANISM AND SOCIAL MOVEMENTS

Like Harvey, Manuel Castells stresses that the spatial form of a society is closely linked to the overall mechanisms of its development. However, the nature of the created environment is not just the result of the activities of wealthy and powerful people. Castells stresses the importance of the struggles of underprivileged groups to alter their living conditions. Urban problems stimulate a range of social movements, concerned with improving housing conditions, protesting against air pollution, defending parks, and combating building development that changes the nature of an area. For example, Castells has studied the gay movement in San Francisco, which succeeded in restructuring neighborhoods around its own cultural values—allowing many gay organizations, clubs, and bars to flourish—and gained a prominent position in local politics (Castells 1977, 1983). ✓

> ### CONCEPT CHECKS ✓
>
> 1. What are two characteristics of ancient cities?
> 2. What is urbanization? How is it related to globalization?
> 3. How does urban ecology use physical science analogies to explain life in modern cities?
> 4. What is the urban interaction problem?
> 5. According to Jane Jacobs, the more people are on the streets, the more likely the street life will be orderly. Do you agree with Jacobs's hypothesis and her explanation for this pattern?

HOW DO RURAL, SUBURBAN, AND URBAN LIFE DIFFER IN THE UNITED STATES?

What are the main trends that have affected city, suburban, and rural life in the United States over the past several decades? How can we explain patterns including suburban sprawl, the disappearance of traditional rural life, and population declines in central cities and older suburbs? These are questions we will take up in the following sections. One of the major changes in population distribution in the period since World War II is the movement of large parts of city populations to newly constructed suburbs; this movement outward has been a particularly pronounced feature of American cities and is related directly to central-city decay. At the same time, rural populations have continued to decline as young people seek richer professional and personal opportunities in our nation's large and small cities. We therefore begin with a discussion of rural America and suburbia before moving on to look at the inner city.

THE DECLINE OF RURAL AMERICA?

Rural life has long been the focus of romanticized images among Americans: close-knit communities and families, stretches of picturesque cornfields, and isolation from social problems such as poverty. Yet these stereotypes stand in stark contrast to life in many parts of rural America today.

Rural areas of the United States are defined by the Census Bureau as those areas located outside urbanized areas or urban clusters. Rural areas have fewer than 2,500 people and typically are areas where people live in open country. Rural America contains over 75 percent of the nation's land area, yet holds just 17 percent of the total U.S. population (U.S. Bureau of the Census 2004a). For most of the twentieth century, rural communities have experienced significant population losses, despite several modest short-term reversals in the 1970s and the 1990s. Of the 1,346 U.S. counties that shrank in population between 2000 and 2007, 85 percent were located outside metropolitan areas, and 59 percent rely heavily on farming, mining, and manufacturing as their main revenue sources (Mather 2008).

Population losses in rural areas are attributed to declines in farming and other rural industries, high poverty rates, scarce economic opportunities or lifestyle amenities for young people, lack of government services, and—in some regions—a dearth of natural amenities such as forests, lakes, or temperate winters. Population losses are compounded by the fact that most people leaving rural areas are young people, meaning that fewer babies are born to replace the aging population (Johnson 2006). Rural areas now face the difficult challenge of attracting and retaining residents and businesses.

Yet more troubling than the loss of population in rural areas are concerns about social problems including high levels of child poverty, high rates of motor vehicle fatalities and other accidental deaths, and low levels of health and educational services (Mather 2008).

Child poverty is usually perceived as an urban problem, yet 2005 data from the U.S. Census Bureau reveal that of the one hundred counties with the highest child poverty rates, ninety-five are rural. Not all areas are equally likely to be poverty stricken, however. Child poverty rates are highest in the most remote rural counties with the lowest population densities. Race also shapes rural poverty, just as it shapes urban poverty. Rural counties with the highest child poverty rates often are "majority minority" counties, where less than 50 percent of the population are non-Hispanic whites. These areas include black-majority counties in the Mississippi Delta and counties in the Midwest and West that have large Native American populations, often dwelling on Indian reservations (O'Hare and Mather 2008).

Joe Peterson and John Baker have coffee in Chugwater, Wyoming. To attract young families to this small farming and ranching community, the town is offering plots of land for just $100.

Despite the challenges facing rural America, many rural sociologists are guardedly optimistic about the future of nonmetropolitan life. Technological innovations in transportation and telecommunications afford people flexibility to work away from their urban office. A number of government programs offer young people financial incentives to serve as teachers or health-care professionals in remote areas, while not-for-profits like Teach for America place young teachers at schools in rural areas. However, such programs are likely to be effective only in attracting workers and businesses to rural areas that have at least some natural or recreational amenities (Johnson 2006).

SUBURBANIZATION

In the United States, **suburbanization**, the massive development and inhabiting of towns surrounding a city, rapidly increased during the 1950s and 1960s, a time of great economic growth. World War II had absorbed most industrial resources, and any development outside the war effort was restricted. But by the 1950s, war rationing had ended, and the postwar economic boom facilitated moving out of the city. The Federal Housing Administration (FHA) provided assistance in obtaining mortgage loans, making it possible in the early postwar period for families to buy housing in the suburbs for less than they would have paid for rent in the cities. The FHA did not offer financial assistance to improve older homes or to build new homes in the central areas of ethnically mixed cities; its large-scale aid went only to the builders and buyers of suburban housing.

suburbanization • The development of suburbia, areas of housing outside inner cities.

Early in the 1950s, lobbies promoting highway construction launched Project Adequate Roads, aimed at inducing the federal government to support the building of highways. In 1956, the Highway Act was passed, authorizing $32 billion to be used for building such highways. The new highway program led to the establishment of industries and services in suburban areas themselves. Consequently, the movement of businesses from the cities to the suburbs took jobs in the manufacturing and service industries with them. Many suburban towns became essentially separate cities, connected by rapid highways to the other suburbs around them. From the 1960s on, the proportion of people commuting between suburbs increased more steadily than the proportion commuting to cities.

(a) Suburban Levittown, New York, in the 1950s. (b) A new housing development in the exurb, Highland, California.

An important change in suburbs today is that more and more members of racial and ethnic minorities are moving there. Between 1990 and 2000, the suburban population of blacks grew by 14.2 percent, Latinos by 40 percent, Asians by 45 percent, and whites by 7.6 percent (U.S. Bureau of the Census 1999). This steady increase in minority suburban populations was concentrated in so-called *melting-pot metros,* or the metropolitan regions of New York, Los Angeles, Chicago, San Francisco, Miami, and other immigrant gateway cities (Frey 2001a).

Members of minority groups move to the suburbs for reasons similar to those who preceded them: better housing, schools, and amenities. Nevertheless, the suburbs remain mostly white. Minority groups constituted only 25 percent of the total suburban population and 27 percent of suburban populations in the

Americans on the Move

How many times did your parents move from one residence to another while you were growing up? The United States has a high rate of residential mobility. In 1999–2000, 16.1 percent of Americans changed their place of residence at least once. Of these, over half (56 percent) moved to another home within the same county (Schachter 2001). Although this number is no higher than the annual mobility rates of Canada, Australia, and New Zealand, Americans do tend to move more than residents of other industrially developed countries such as France, the United Kingdom, Japan, and Belgium. Yet except for a sharp increase in mobility in the mid-1980s, fueled by recovery from the recession of 1982–1983, mobility rates in the United States are in long-term decline. In the 1950s and 1960s, approximately 20 out of every 100 Americans moved at least once every year. Mobility rates began to fall in the 1970s and, since the late 1980s, have consistently hovered around 17 percent.

Why do people move? According to a 1991 survey, the most commonly cited reason for moving was to improve one's housing situation: to buy a better home, to make the transition from renting to owning, and so on. Many respondents also cited employment factors as a reason for moving (Gober 1993).

Because many Americans move for job-related reasons, migration patterns tend to reflect regional patterns of economic development. For example, the Northeast and Midwest, long home to much of the nation's industrial manufacturing, have suffered what demographers call an "out-migration" as a result of the deindustrialization of the American economy. Much of the growth in service-sector work and high-tech production has occurred in the South and West, and millions of Americans have left the Northeast and Midwest in search of jobs in these areas. The Midwest has slowly been able to recover from this situation, shifting its economic base to more viable forms of production and thus attracting enough new residents from other regions to counter the out-migration to the South and West. But the Northeast continues to lose residents (Schachter 2001).

It is all too easy to view these demographic shifts as the result of natural and inevitable long-term processes: High-tech and service sector work comes to account for a greater share of the GNP, and these industries spring up in the South and West; these regions then become more attractive even for traditional manufacturing firms that wish to relocate, and the Northeast is depopulated.

A better explanation begins with—of all things—globalization. As globalization has proceeded, a number of important transformations have taken place in the economic sector. Changes in the financial

nation's largest metropolitan areas in 2000, although they accounted for 30 percent of the total U.S. population that year. By contrast, whites accounted for three fourths of the suburban population in 2000 but just over half of the population in central cities (U.S. Bureau of the Census 2000a).

While the last several decades saw a movement from the cities to the suburbs, they also witnessed a shift in the regional distribution of the U.S. population from north to south and east to west. As a percentage of the nation's total population, the Northeast dropped from 25 to 18.5 percent and the Midwest from 29 to 22.3 percent. Meanwhile infrastructure have made it easier for investors to put their money into enterprises anywhere on the globe, and corresponding improvements in communications technology, transportation, and managerial practices have made it more practical for businesses to move their production sites to wherever their costs will be minimized. Capital, economists and sociologists say, has become increasingly mobile under the influence of globalization.

Whereas the mobility of capital sometimes translates into American firms shifting the site of their production to the developing world, in other cases it means that firms will open in or relocate to regions of this country where their production costs will be low. All else being equal, if unions are strong in one region and weak in another, firms are more likely to do business in the region with the weak unions, because they will be able to get away with paying lower wages. Firms also prefer to operate in cities and states that are eager for new development and likely to grant substantial tax breaks. In general, state and local governments in the South and West have been more willing than governments in the Northeast to grant tax breaks to firms, and unions tend to be weaker in these regions than in the Northeast. These factors—in addition to cheaper land and energy—have helped pull some firms out of the Northeast and into the South and West, and have encouraged many start-up firms to set up shop in the South and West. Although the dynamics involved are clearly complex, globalization and the mobility of capital appear to lie behind recent trends in regional economic development and therefore underlie key patterns in regional migration.

Should attempts be made to halt these changes? What would migration patterns look like if unions were strong in all regions and if cities and states refused to grant generous tax breaks to corporate America? Is the depopulation of the Northeast a good or bad thing?

the population of the South increased from 30.7 to 36.2 percent and that of the West from 15.6 to 23 percent (U.S. Bureau of the Census 2005d).

URBAN PROBLEMS

Inner-city decay is partially a consequence of the social and economic forces involved in the movement of businesses, jobs, and middle-class residents from major cities

Does gentrification of a run-down inner-city area necessarily result in the dispossession of the existing population, or do renewed interest and an infusion of money in such areas promote a revitalization that works to their advantage? Not long ago, Clinton Street was a grim, graffiti-ridden streetscape (top) but it has evolved into a lively restaurant row on New York's Lower East Side (bottom).

to the outlying suburbs, a trend that began in the 1950s. The manufacturing industries that provided employment for the urban blue-collar class largely vanished and were replaced by white-collar service industries. Millions of blue-collar jobs disappeared, and this affected in particular the poorly educated, drawn mostly from minority groups. Although the overall educational levels of minority groups have improved since the mid-twentieth century, the improvement has not been sufficient to keep up with the demands of an information-based economy (Kasarda 1993). William Julius Wilson (1991, 1996) has argued that the problems of the urban underclass have grown out of this economic transformation (see Chapter 8).

These economic changes also contributed to increased residential segregation of different racial and ethnic groups and social classes, as we saw in Chapter 11. Discriminatory practices by home sellers, real estate agents, and mortgage lending institutions further added to this pattern of segregation (Massey and Denton 1993). In the early 2000s, considering all metropolitan areas, African Americans in the United States lived in neighborhoods, both urban and suburban, that were predominantly black (U.S. Bureau of the Census 2005e). Residential segregation as measured by the dissimilarity index ranging from 0 (complete integration) to 1 (complete segregation) indicated that in the early 2000s, on average, African Americans lived in neighborhoods with an index value of 0.64, down from 0.73 in 1980. That is, neighborhoods have become more racially integrated over the past few decades. The social isolation of minority groups, particularly those in the underclass or "ghetto poor," can escalate urban problems such as crime, lack of economic opportunities, poor health, and family breakdown (Massey 1996).

Adding to these difficulties is the fact that city governments today operate against a background of almost continual financial crisis. As businesses and middle-class residents moved to the suburbs, the cities lost major sources of tax revenue. High rates of crime and unemployment in the city require it to spend more on welfare services, schools, police, and overall upkeep. Yet because of budget constraints, cities are forced to cut back many of these services. A cycle of deterioration develops in which the more suburbia expands, the greater the problems faced by city dwellers become.

URBAN RENEWAL AND GENTRIFICATION

urban renewal • The process of renovating deteriorating neighborhoods by encouraging the renewal of old buildings and the construction of new ones.

gentrification • A process of urban renewal in which older, deteriorated housing is refurbished by affluent people moving into the area.

Urban decay is not wholly a one-way process; it can stimulate countertrends, such as **urban renewal**, or **gentrification**. Dilapidated areas or buildings may be renovated as more affluent groups move back into cities. Such a renewal process is called *gentrification* because those areas or buildings become upgraded and return to the control of the urban "gentry"—high-income dwellers—rather than remaining in the hands of the poor.

In *Streetwise: Race, Class, and Change in an Urban Community* (1990), sociologist Elijah Anderson analyzed the effect of gentrification on cities. Although the renovation of a neighborhood generally increases its value, it rarely improves the living standards of its current low-income residents, who are usually forced to move out. The poor residents who continued to live in the neighborhood receive some benefits in the form of improved schools and police protection, but the resulting increases in taxes and rents also force them to leave for a more affordable neighborhood, most often deeper into the ghetto.

The white newcomers come to the city in search of cheap "antique" housing, closer access to their city-based jobs, and a trendy urban lifestyle. They profess to be "open minded" about racial and ethnic differences; in reality, however, little fraternizing takes place between the new and old residents unless they are of the same social class. Over time, the neighborhood is gradually transformed into a white middle-class enclave. ✓

CONCEPT CHECKS ✓

1. Describe at least two problems facing rural America today.

2. Why did so many Americans move to suburban areas in the 1950s and 1960s?

3. What are two unintended consequences of urbanization? How do they deepen socioeconomic and racial inequalities?

HOW DOES URBANIZATION AFFECT LIFE ACROSS THE GLOBE?

In premodern times, cities were self-contained entities that stood apart from the predominantly rural areas in which they were located. Road systems sometimes linked major urban areas, but travel was a specialized affair for merchants, soldiers, and others who needed to cross distances with any regularity. Communication between cities was limited. The picture at the start of the twenty-first century could hardly be more different. Globalization has had a profound effect on cities by making them more interdependent and encouraging the proliferation of horizontal links between cities across national borders. Physical and virtual ties between cities now abound, and global networks of cities are emerging.

GLOBAL CITIES

The role of cities in the new global order has been attracting a great deal of attention from sociologists. Saskia Sassen has been one of the leading contributors to the debate on cities and globalization. She uses the term **global city** to refer to urban centers that are home to the headquarters of large, transnational corporations and a superabundance of financial, technological, and consulting services. In *The Global City* (1991), Sassen bases her work on the study of three such cities: New York, London, and Tokyo. The contemporary development of the world economy, she argues, has created a novel strategic role for major cities. Most such cities have long been centers of international trade, but they now have four new traits:

global city ● A city—such as London, New York, or Tokyo—that has become an organizing center of the new global economy.

1. They have developed into command posts—centers of direction and policy making—for the global economy.
2. They are the key locations for financial and specialized service firms, which have become more important than manufacturing in influencing economic development.
3. They are the sites of production and innovation in these newly expanded industries.
4. They are markets on which the "products" of financial and service industries are bought, sold, or otherwise disposed of.

Many Americans believe that bigger is better when it comes to housing. That philosophy is the driving force behind a new and potentially troubling trend known as *tearing down*. The National Association of Home Builders estimates about seventy-five thousand houses are being razed each year and replaced with bigger homes (Tarm 2006). Most of the homes being knocked down are located in urban or near-urban areas, and are at least fifty years old. Homebuilders and real estate agents say that the process bolsters the tax base and helps keep families in cities and older suburban neighborhoods. Critics counter that the process is often done without thought to the overall design of the neighborhood, and that neighborhood character is lost when modern cookie-cutter homes replace older residences. For example, a study by the National Trust for Historic Preservation (Moe 2006) found that 1920s bungalows in Denver were being replaced with modern homes three times their size. Denver residents opposed to the teardown process are trying to have older neighborhoods designated as historic, and thus protected from razing. However, it takes two to six years to get this designation. It also costs thousands of dollars and requires that the structures actually be historic. Drawing on your sociological knowledge of suburbanization, urban renewal, and gentrification, what policies and practices would you develop if you were an urban planner? How would you defend your choices?

Within the highly dispersed world economy of today, cities like these provide for central control of crucial operations. Global cities are much more than simply places of coordination, however; they are also contexts of production. What is important here is not the production of material goods, but the production of the specialized services required by business organizations for administering offices and factories scattered across the world, and the production of financial innovations and markets. Services and financial goods are the "things" the global city makes.

INEQUALITY AND THE GLOBAL CITY

The new global economy is highly problematic in many ways. This is seen most clearly in the new dynamics of inequality visible within the global city. It is no coincidence that the central business district adjoins impoverished inner-city areas in many global cities; the business and poverty should be seen as interrelated phenomena, as Sassen and others remind us. The growth sectors of the new economy—financial services, marketing, high technology—are reaping profits far greater than any found within traditional economic sectors. As the salaries and bonuses of the very affluent continue to climb, the wages of those employed to clean and guard their offices are dropping. Sassen (1998) argues that we are witnessing the "valorization" of work located at the forefront of the new global economy and the "devalorization" of work that occurs behind the scenes.

Those who work in finances and global services receive high salaries, and the areas where they live become gentrified. At the same time, orthodox manufacturing jobs are lost, and the very process of gentrification creates a vast supply of low-wage jobs—in restaurants, hotels, and boutiques. Affordable housing is scarce in gentrified areas, forcing an expansion of low-income neighborhoods.

Within global cities, a geography of "centrality and marginality" is taking shape. Alongside resplendent affluence there is acute poverty. Yet although these two worlds exist side by side, the actual contact between them can be surprisingly minimal. As Mike Davis (1990) noted in his study of Los Angeles, there has been a "conscious 'hardening' of the city surface against the poor." Accessible public spaces have been replaced by walled compounds, neighborhoods guarded by electronic surveillance. Benches at bus stops are short or barrel-shaped to prevent people from sleeping on them, the number of public toilets is fewer than in any other North American city, and sprinkler systems have been installed in many parks to deter the homeless from living in them. Police and city planners have attempted to contain the homeless population within certain regions of the city, but in periodically sweeping through and confiscating makeshift shelters, they have effectively created a population of "urban bedouins."

URBANIZATION IN THE DEVELOPING WORLD

In 2007, roughly 3.3 billion people, or about half of the world's population, lived in cities (United Nations Population Division [UNDP] 2008a). The global urban population is expected to increase to more than 6 billion, or roughly 70 percent of the world population, by 2050. Developed nations now have the highest levels of urbanization, surpassing 80 percent in Australia, New Zealand, and North America in 2007. By contrast, Africa and Asia remain mostly rural, with 39 percent and 41 percent of their populations, respectively, living in urban areas. In coming decades, levels of urbanization are expected to rise even higher, with Africa and Asia urbanizing more rapidly than other nations. Experts predict that by 2050, 70 percent of the world's population will live in urban spaces. An estimated 54 percent will be concentrated in Asia, with 19 percent in Africa.

Why is the rate of urban growth in the world's less developed regions so much higher than elsewhere? Two factors in particular must be taken into account. First, rates of population growth are higher in developing countries than they are in industrialized nations. Urban growth is fueled by high fertility rates among people already living in cities. Second, there is widespread *internal migration* from rural areas to urban ones. People are drawn to cities in the developing world either because their traditional systems of rural production have disintegrated or because the urban areas offer superior job opportunities. Rural poverty prompts many people to try their hand at city life. They may intend to migrate to the city only for a short time, aiming to return to their villages once they have earned enough money.

The overcrowded streets of the Hong Kong–Guangdong megacity.

ECONOMIC IMPLICATIONS OF URBANIZATION IN THE DEVELOPING WORLD

As a growing number of unskilled and agricultural workers migrate to urban centers, the formal economy often struggles to absorb the influx into the workforce. In most cities in the developing world, it is the *informal economy* that allows those who cannot find formal work to make ends meet. From casual work in manufacturing and construction to small-scale trading activities, the unregulated informal sector offers earning opportunities to poor or unskilled workers.

The OECD estimates that a billion new jobs will be needed by 2025 to sustain the estimated population growth in cities in the developing world. It is unlikely that all of these jobs will be created within the formal economy. Some development analysts argue that attention should be paid to formalizing or regulating the large informal economy, where much of the excess workforce is likely to cluster in the years to come.

ENVIRONMENTAL CHALLENGES OF URBANIZATION IN THE DEVELOPING WORLD

The rapidly expanding urban areas in developing countries differ dramatically from cities in the industrialized world. Although cities everywhere are faced with environmental problems, those in developing countries are confronted by particularly severe risks. Pollution, housing shortages, inadequate sanitation, and unsafe water supplies are chronic problems for cities in less developed countries. Housing is one of the most acute problems in many urban areas. Cities such as Calcutta and São Paulo are massively congested. In São Paulo, it is estimated that there was a 5.4 million shortfall in habitable homes in 1996; some scholars estimate that the shortage is as high as 20 million, if the definition of "habitable housing" is interpreted more strictly (Barcelona Field Studies Centre 2003).

Congestion and overdevelopment in city centers lead to serious environmental problems in many urban areas. Mexico City is a prime example. About 94 percent of Mexico City consists of built-up areas, with only 6 percent of land being open space. The level of green spaces—parks and open stretches of green land—is far below that found in even the most densely populated U.S. or European cities. Pollution is a major problem, coming mostly from the cars, buses, and trucks that pack the inadequate roads of the city, the rest deriving from industrial pollutants. It has been estimated that living in Mexico City is equivalent to smoking forty cigarettes a day.

SOCIAL EFFECTS OF URBANIZATION IN THE DEVELOPING WORLD

Many urban areas in the developing world are overcrowded, and social programs are underresourced. Poverty is widespread, and existing social services cannot meet the demands for health care, family planning advice, education, and training. The unbalanced age distribution in developing countries adds to their social and economic difficulties. Compared to industrialized countries, a much larger proportion of the

Families sit on the sidewalk with their belongings after being evicted by police from a central São Paulo building. Hundreds of squatters had settled in São Paulo buildings until, facing forced eviction by riot police, they were compelled to leave.

Newspaper salesman Alvarado uses a mask to protect himself from air pollution as he sells papers at a busy crossroad in Mexico City. Behind him a screen indicates the day's pollution levels.

population in the developing world is under the age of fifteen. A youthful population needs a good educational system, but many developing countries lack the resources to provide universal education. When their families are poor, many children must work full time, and others have to eke out a living as street children, begging for whatever they can. When the street children mature, most are unemployed, homeless, or both.

THE FUTURE OF URBANIZATION IN THE DEVELOPING WORLD

In considering the scope of the challenges facing urban areas in developing countries, it can be difficult to see prospects for change and development. Conditions of life in many of the world's largest cities seem likely to decline even further in the years to come. But the picture is not entirely negative.

First, although birthrates remain high in many countries, they are likely to drop in the years to come as urbanization proceeds. (UNDP 2008a). Second, globalization is presenting important opportunities for urban areas in developing countries. With economic integration, cities around the world are able to enter international markets, to promote themselves as locations for investment and development, and to create economic links across the borders of nation-states.

Third, migrants to urban areas are often "positively selected" in terms of traits such as higher levels of educational attainment. Thus, migration may be beneficial to those who find better work opportunities, and for their families, who benefit from *remittances*—the money that the migrant workers send back home. ✓

CONCEPT CHECKS ✓

1. Discuss the effects of globalization on cities.

2. What are the four main characteristics of global cities?

3. Urban growth in the developing world is much higher than elsewhere. Discuss several economic, social, and environmental consequences of such rapid expansion of cities in developing nations.

WHAT ARE THE FORCES BEHIND WORLD POPULATION GROWTH?

There are currently an estimated 6.7 billion people in the world. It was estimated that "baby number 6 billion" was born on October 12, 1999, although of course no one can know when and where this event happened. Paul Ehrlich (Fremlin 1964) calculated in the 1960s that if the rate of population growth at that time continued, nine hundred years from now (not a long period in world history as a whole) there would be 60,000,000,000,000,000 (60 quadrillion) people on the face of the earth. There would be one hundred people for every square yard of the earth's surface, including both land and water.

Such a picture, of course, is nothing more than nightmarish fiction designed to drive home how cataclysmic the consequences of continued population growth would be. The real issue is what will happen over the next thirty or forty years, by which time, if current trends are not reversed, the world's population will already have grown to unsustainable levels. Partly because governments and other agencies heeded the warnings of Ehrlich and others forty years ago by introducing population-control programs, there are grounds for supposing that world population growth is beginning to trail off. Estimates calculated in the 1960s of the likely world population by the year 2000 turned out to be inaccurate. The United Nations (2006) estimated the world population would be 6.7 billion in July 2007, compared with some earlier estimates of over 8 billion. Nevertheless, considering that a century ago there were only 1.5 billion people in the world, this still represents growth of staggering proportions. Moreover, the factors underlying population growth are by no means completely predictable, and all estimates have to be interpreted with caution.

POPULATION ANALYSIS: DEMOGRAPHY

demography • The study of the size, distribution, and composition of populations.

The study of population is referred to as **demography**. The term was invented about a century and a half ago, at a time when nations were beginning to keep official statistics on the nature and distribution of their populations. Demography is concerned with measuring the size of populations, explaining their rise or decline, and documenting the distribution of such populations both within and across continents, nations, states, cities, and even neighborhoods. Population patterns are governed by three factors: births, deaths, and migrations. Demography is customarily treated as a branch of sociology, because the factors that influence the level of births and deaths in a given group or society, as well as migrations of population, are largely social and cultural.

BASIC DEMOGRAPHIC CONCEPTS

crude birthrate • A statistical measure representing the number of births within a given population per year, normally calculated as the number of births per thousand members. Although the crude birthrate is a useful index, it is only a general measure, because it does not specify numbers of births in relation to age distribution.

Among the basic concepts used by demographers, the most important are crude birthrates, fertility, fecundity, and crude death rates. **Crude birthrates** are expressed as the number of live births per year per thousand persons in the population. They are called "crude" rates because of their very general character. Crude birthrates, for example, do not tell us what proportions of a population are male or female, or what the age distribution of a population is (the relative proportions of young and old people in the population). Where statistics are collected that relate birth or death rates to such categories, demographers speak of "specific" rather than "crude" rates. For instance, an age-specific birthrate might specify the number of births per thousand women in the twenty-five- to thirty-four-year-old age group.

If we wish to understand population patterns in any detail, the information provided by specific birthrates is normally necessary. Crude birthrates, however, may be useful for making overall comparisons between different groups, societies, and regions. Thus, the crude birthrate in the United States is almost fourteen per thousand. Other industrialized countries have lower rates: for example, eleven per thousand in Russia, and eight per thousand in Germany and in Italy. In many other parts of the world, crude birthrates are much higher. In India, for instance, the crude birthrate is twenty-two per thousand; in Ethiopia it is forty-four per thousand (CIA World Factbook 2009).

Birthrates are an expression of the fertility of women. **Fertility** refers to how many live-born children the average woman has. A fertility rate is usually calculated as the average number of live births per thousand women of childbearing age.

Fertility is distinguished from **fecundity**, which means the number of children women are biologically capable of bearing. It is physically possible for a normal woman to bear a child every year during the period when she is capable of conception. There are variations in fecundity according to the age at which women reach puberty and menopause, both of which vary among countries as well as among individuals. Although there may be families in which a woman bears twenty or more children, fertility rates in practice are always much lower than fecundity rates, because social and cultural factors limit the actual number of children a woman gives birth to.

Crude death rates (also called "mortality rates") are calculated in the same way as birthrates—the number of deaths per thousand of population per year. Again, there are major variations between countries, but death rates in many societies in the developing world are falling to levels comparable to those of the West. The death rate in the United States in 2009 was eight per thousand. In India it was six per thousand; in Ethiopia it was twelve per thousand. A few countries have much higher death rates. In Sierra Leone, for example, the death rate is twenty-two per thousand due in part to AIDS, warfare, and high infant mortality rates. Like crude birthrates, crude death rates only provide a very general index of **mortality** (the number of deaths in a population). Specific death rates give more precise information. A particularly important specific death rate is the **infant mortality rate**: the number of babies per thousand births in any year who die before reaching age one. One of the key factors underlying the population explosion has been reductions in infant mortality rates.

Declining rates of infant mortality are the most important influence on increasing **life expectancy**—that is, the number of years the average person can expect to live. In 1900, life expectancy at birth in the United States was about forty years. Today it has increased to over seventy-eight years. This does not mean, however, that most people at the turn of the century died when they were about forty years of age. When there is a high infant mortality rate, as there is in many developing nations, the average life expectancy—which is a statistical average—is brought down by deaths that occurred at age 0 or 0.5 years, for example. If we look at the life expectancy of only those people who survive the first year of life, we find that in 1900 the average person could expect to live to age fifty-eight.

Illness, nutrition, and natural disasters are the other factors influencing life expectancy. Life expectancy has to be distinguished from **life span**, which is the maximum number of years that an individual could live. Although life expectancy has increased in most societies in the world over the past century, life span has remained unaltered. Only a small proportion of people live to be one hundred or more.

fertility • The average number of live-born children produced by women of childbearing age in a particular society.

fecundity • A measure of the number of children that it is biologically possible for a woman to produce.

crude death rate • A statistical measure representing the number of deaths that occur annually in a given population per year, normally calculated as the number of deaths per thousand members. Crude death rates give a general indication of the mortality levels of a community or society, but are limited in their usefulness because they do not take into account the age distribution.

mortality • The number of deaths in a population.

infant mortality rate • The number of infants who die during the first year of life, per thousand live births.

life expectancy • The number of years the average person can expect to live.

life span • The maximum length of life that is biologically possible for a member of a given species.

DYNAMICS OF POPULATION CHANGE

Rates of population growth or decline are measured by subtracting the number of deaths per thousand over a given period from the number of births per thousand—this is usually calculated annually. Some European countries have negative growth rates—in other words, their populations are declining. Virtually all of the industrialized countries have growth rates of less than 0.5 percent. Rates of population growth were high in the eighteenth and nineteenth centuries in Europe and the United States but have since leveled off. Many developing countries today have rates of between 2 and 3 percent (Global Map 15.1). These may not seem very different from the rates of the industrialized countries, but in fact, the difference is enormous.

exponential growth ● A geometric, rather than linear, rate of increase. Populations tend to grow exponentially.

The reason is that growth in population is **exponential** rather than arithmetic. An ancient Persian myth helps illustrate this concept. A courtier asked a ruler to reward him for his services by giving him twice as many grains of rice for each service as he had the time before, starting with a single grain on the first square of a chessboard: that is, one grain on the first square, two on the second, four on the third, and so on. By the twenty-first square, over a million grains were needed, more than a trillion (a million million) on the forty-first square (Meadows et al. 1972). This myth conveys an important mathematical principle, that starting with one item and doubling it, doubling the result, and so on rapidly leads to huge numbers. Exactly the same principle applies to population growth. We can measure this effect by means of the **doubling time**, the period of time it takes for the population to double. The formula used to calculate doubling time is 70 divided by the current growth rate. For example, a population growth of 1 percent will produce a doubling of numbers in seventy years. At 2 percent

doubling time ● The time it takes for a particular level of population to double.

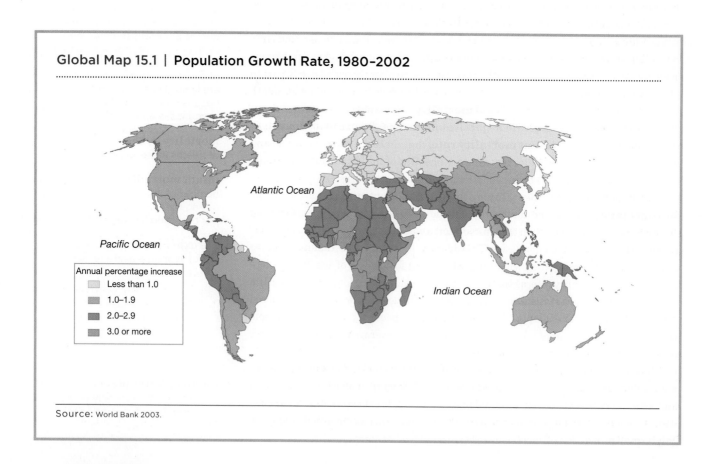

Global Map 15.1 | Population Growth Rate, 1980–2002

Annual percentage increase
- Less than 1.0
- 1.0–1.9
- 2.0–2.9
- 3.0 or more

Atlantic Ocean

Pacific Ocean

Indian Ocean

Source: World Bank 2003.

growth, a population will double in thirty-five years, while at 3 percent it will double in twenty-three years.

MALTHUSIANISM

In premodern societies, birthrates were very high by the standards of the industrialized world today. Nonetheless, population growth remained low until the eighteenth century because there was a rough overall balance between births and deaths. Although there were sometimes periods of marked population increase, these were followed by increases in death rates. In medieval Europe, for example, when harvests were bad, marriages tended to be postponed and the number of conceptions fell, while deaths increased. These complementary trends reduced the number of mouths to be fed. No preindustrial society was able to escape from this self-regulating rhythm (Wrigley 1968).

During the rise of industrialism, many looked forward to a new age in which food scarcity would be a phenomenon of the past. The development of modern industry, it was widely supposed, would create a new era of abundance. In his celebrated work *Essay on the Principle of Population* (2003; orig. 1798), Thomas Malthus criticized these ideas and initiated a debate about the connection between population and food resources that continues to this day. At the time Malthus wrote, the population in Europe was growing rapidly. Malthus pointed out that whereas population increase is exponential, food supply depends on fixed resources that can be expanded only by developing new land for cultivation. Population growth therefore tends to outstrip the means of support available. The inevitable outcome is famine, which, combined with the influence of war and plagues, acts as a natural limit to population increase. Malthus predicted that human beings would always live in circumstances of misery and starvation, unless they practiced what he called "moral restraint." His cure for excessive population growth was for people to delay marriage and to strictly limit their frequency of sexual intercourse. (The use of contraception he proclaimed to be a "vice.")

For a while, **Malthusianism** was ignored, because the population development of the Western countries followed a quite different pattern from that which he had anticipated—as we shall see below. Rates of population growth trailed off in the nineteenth and twentieth centuries. In the 1930s there were major worries about population decline in many industrialized countries, including the United States. Malthus also failed to anticipate the technological developments fostering increases in food production that would develop in the modern era. The upsurge in world population growth in the twentieth century has again lent some credence to Malthus's views, although few support them in their original version. Population expansion in developing countries seems to be outstripping the resources that those countries can generate to feed their citizenry.

THE DEMOGRAPHIC TRANSITION

Demographers often refer to the changes in the ratio of births to deaths in the industrialized countries from the nineteenth century onward as the **demographic transition.** The notion was first worked out by Warren S. Thompson (1929), who described a three-stage process in which one type of population stability would eventually be replaced by another as a society reached an advanced level of economic development.

Malthusianism • A doctrine about population dynamics developed by Thomas Malthus, according to which population increase comes up against "natural limits," represented by famine and war.

demographic transition • An interpretation of population change, which holds that a stable ratio of births to deaths is achieved once a certain level of economic prosperity has been reached. According to this notion, in preindustrial societies there is a rough balance between births and deaths, because population increase is kept in check by a lack of available food, by disease, or by war. In modern societies, by contrast, population equilibrium is achieved because families are moved by economic incentives to limit the number of children.

Stage one refers to the conditions characteristic of most traditional societies, in which both birth and death rates are high and the infant mortality rate is especially large. Population grows little if at all, as the high number of births is more or less balanced by the level of deaths. Stage two, which began in Europe and the United States in the early part of the nineteenth century—with wide regional variations—occurs when death rates fall while fertility remains high. This is, therefore, a phase of marked population growth. It is subsequently replaced by stage three, in which, with industrial development, birthrates drop to a level such that population is again fairly stable.

The theories of demographic transition directly oppose the ideas of Malthus. Whereas for Malthus, increasing prosperity would automatically bring about population increase, the thesis of demographic transition emphasizes that economic development, generated by industrialism, would actually lead to a new equilibrium of population stability.

PROSPECTS FOR CHANGE

Fertility remains high in developing-world societies because traditional attitudes to family size have been maintained. Having large numbers of children is often still regarded as desirable, providing a source of labor on family-run farms. Some religions either are opposed to birth control or affirm the desirability of having many children. Contraception is opposed by Islamic leaders in several countries and by the Catholic Church, whose influence is especially marked in South and Central America.

Yet a decline in fertility levels has at last occurred in some large developing countries. An example is China, which currently has a population of about 1.3 billion people—almost a quarter of the world's population as a whole. In 1979, the Chinese government established one of the most extensive programs of population control that any country has undertaken, with the object of stabilizing the country's numbers at close to their current level. The government instituted incentives (such as better housing and free health care and education) to promote single-child families, whereas families who have more than one child face special hardships (wages are cut for those who have a third child). China's antinatal policies have effectively transformed the Chinese population. During the 1950s, China had a total fertility rate (TFR) of roughly 6 children per woman. TFR refers to the average number of babies a woman will give birth to in her life, if she conforms to current age-specific fertility rates (ASFRs) through her lifetime. China's TFR fell to about 2.4 by 1990, and demographers pin the current TFR at roughly 1.6 to 1.9.

China's program demands a degree of centralized government control that is either unacceptable or unavailable in most other developing countries. The program also has had major unintended consequences. Expectant parents who are eager to have a son have been aborting female fetuses, or putting up their first-born infant daughters for adoption. As a result, social observers fear that a highly skewed sex ratio—where men outnumber women—will lead to low rates of marriage among the least "desirable" men and high levels of antisocial behavior among these socially unconnected men. Furthermore, the policy is at odds with normative beliefs; most young couples in China still view a two-child family as the proper family.

Some claim that the demographic changes that will occur over the next century will be greater than any before in all of human history. It is difficult to predict with any precision the rate at which the world population will rise, but the United Nations has several fertility scenarios. The "high" scenario places the world's population at more than 16 billion people by 2150! The "medium" fertility scenario, which the UN

deems most likely, assumes that fertility levels will stabilize at just over two children per woman, resulting in a world population of 10.8 billion people in 2150 (UN 2003).

This overall population increase conceals two distinct trends. First, most developing countries will undergo the process of demographic transition described above. This will result in a substantial surge in the population, as death rates fall. China is likely to see its population reach 1.5 billion people before growth levels off. Areas in Asia, Africa, and Latin America will similarly experience rapid growth before the population eventually stabilizes.

The second trend concerns the developed countries that have already undergone the demographic transition. These societies will undergo very slight population growth, if any at all. Instead, a process of aging will occur in which the number of young people will decline in absolute terms and the older segment of the population will increase markedly (Figure 15.1). This will have widespread economic and social implications for developed countries. First, there will be an increase in the **dependency ratio**, the ratio of the number of economically dependent members of the population to the number of economically productive members. Economically dependent persons are those considered too young or old to work, typically those under age fifteen and over age sixty-five. Productive members of society are those of working age, typically ages fifteen through sixty-four. As the dependency ratio increases, pressure will mount on health and social services. Yet, as their numbers grow, older people will also have more political weight and may be able to push for higher expenditures on programs and services of importance to them.

What will be the consequences of these demographic changes? Some observers see the makings of widespread social upheaval—particularly in the developing countries

Passengers travel in an overcrowded train in the eastern Indian city of Patna. The Indian railroad, one of the world's largest rail networks, serves over thirteen million people a year and continues to be one of the only forms of affordable transportation available to the majority of Indians.

dependency ratio • The ratio of people of dependent ages (children and the elderly) to people of economically active ages.

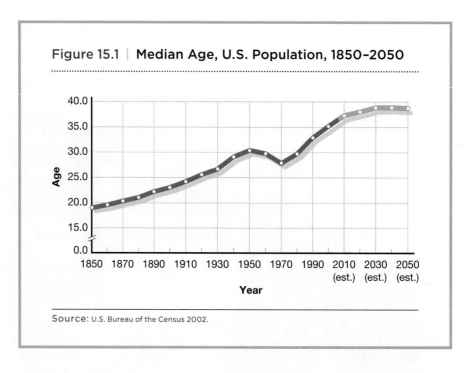

Figure 15.1 | Median Age, U.S. Population, 1850–2050

Source: U.S. Bureau of the Census 2002.

undergoing demographic transition. Changes in the economy and labor markets may prompt widespread internal migration as people in rural areas search for work. The rapid growth of cities will be likely to lead to environmental damage, new public-health risks, overloaded infrastructures, rising crime, and impoverished squatter settlements.

Famine and food shortages are another serious concern. There are already 963 million people in the world who suffer from hunger or undernourishment (United Nations Food and Agriculture Organization [UN FAO] 2008). In some parts of the world, more than a third of the population are undernourished. As the population rises, levels of food output will need to rise accordingly to avoid widespread scarcity. Yet this scenario is unlikely; many of the world's poorest areas are particularly affected by water shortages, shrinking farmland, and soil degradation—processes that reduce, rather than enhance, agricultural productivity. It is almost certain that food production will not occur at a level to ensure self-sufficiency. Large amounts of food and grain will need to be imported from areas where there are surpluses. ✓

CONCEPT CHECKS ✓

1. What is the difference between fertility and fecundity?

2. Explain Malthus's position on the relationship between population growth and the food supply.

3. Describe the stages of the demographic transition.

4. What is life expectancy? How does it differ from life span?

HOW DO URBANIZATION AND ENVIRONMENTAL CHANGES AFFECT YOUR LIFE?

Today the human onslaught on the environment is so intense that few natural processes are uninfluenced by human activity. Nearly all cultivable land is under agricultural production. What used to be almost inaccessible wildernesses are now often nature reserves, visited routinely by thousands of tourists. Modern industry, still expanding worldwide, has led to steeply climbing demands for sources of energy and raw materials. Yet the world's supply of such energy sources and raw materials is limited, and some key resources are bound to run out if global consumption is not restricted. Even the world's climate, as we shall see, has probably been affected by the global development of industry. Nearly every aspect of daily life has been affected, either directly or indirectly, by urbanization, population growth, and climate change.

GLOBAL ENVIRONMENTAL THREATS

One problem we all face concerns **environmental ecology**. The spread of industrial production may already have done irreparable damage to the environment. Ecological questions concern not only how we can best cope with and contain environmental damage but also the very ways of life within industrialized societies. According to one popular Web site, Global Footprint, if all people on earth were to somehow achieve the standard of living of the average American, it would require seven planets to feed, clothe, shelter, and provide the countless consumer items that make up what most of us consider a decent life. If developing countries are to achieve living standards comparable to those currently enjoyed in the West, global readjustments will be necessary.

According to the International Union for Conservation of Nature (IUCN 2009), the most widely accepted authoritative source, nearly 17,000 species are currently threatened with extinction. The loss of biodiversity, in turn, means more to humans than merely the loss of natural habitat. Biodiversity also provides humans with new medicines and sources and varieties of food and plays a role in regulating atmospheric and oceanic chemistry.

Global environmental threats are of several basic sorts: pollution, the creation of waste that cannot be disposed of in the short term or recycled, and the depletion of resources that cannot be replenished. The amount of domestic waste—what goes into our garbage cans—produced each day in the industrialized societies is staggering; these countries have sometimes been called the "throw-away societies" because the volume of items discarded as a matter of course is so large. Food is mostly bought in packages that are thrown away at the end of the day. Some of these can be reprocessed and reused, but most cannot. The disposal of electronic waste—computers, mobile phones, MP3 players, and the host of toys and gadgets that contain electronic circuits—is a growing problem. Discarded electronics, which contain toxins that cause cancer and other illnesses, are routinely "recycled" to landfills in China, India, and other poor countries, where there are few if any safeguards against contaminating local watersheds, farmlands, and communities.

Global green movements and political parties (such as Friends of the Earth, Greenpeace, or Conservation International) have developed in response to the new environmental hazards. Although green philosophies are varied, a common thread concerns taking action to protect the world's environment, conserve rather than exhaust its resources, and protect the remaining animal species.

environmental ecology • A concern with preserving the integrity of the physical environment in the face of the impact of modern industry and technology.

GLOBAL WARMING AND CLIMATE CHANGE

Global warming is thought to happen in the following way. Carbon dioxide and other greenhouse gases are released into the atmosphere by the burning of fuels

Kids play on a merry-go-round near an oil refinery at the Carver Terrace housing project playground in west Port Arthur, Texas. Port Arthur sits squarely on a two-state corridor routinely ranked as one of the country's most polluted regions.

such as oil and coal in cars and power stations and gases released into the air by the use of such things as aerosol cans, material for insulation, and air-conditioning units. This buildup of greenhouse gases in the earth's atmosphere functions like the glass of a greenhouse. It allows the sun's rays to pass through but acts as a barrier to prevent the rays from passing back. The effect is to heat up the earth; global warming is sometimes termed the "greenhouse effect" for this reason.

In 2007 the Intergovernmental Panel on Climate Change (IPCC), a blue-ribbon group of scientists created by the United Nations Environment Program and its World Meteorological Organization in 1988, took the planet's temperature, and found it has risen steadily since the mid-twentieth century. Rising temperatures result in the rapid shrinking of arctic icecaps, along with mountain glaciers; long-term droughts in some regions, with greater rainfall in others; an increase in hurricane activity in the North Atlantic; and in general, more turbulence in global weather. Most significantly, the IPCC report stated unequivocally that human activity is the principal source of global warming, very likely causing most of the temperature increase over the last century.

How does global warming affect our lives? Apart from severe droughts—which will turn once-fertile lands into deserts—global warming will threaten the water supplies of hundreds of millions of people, increase the danger of flooding for others, adversely affect agriculture in parts of the world, and further reduce planetary biodiversity. It will likely have devastating consequences for low-lying areas, as melting polar icecaps—particularly in Greenland and the Antarctic—lead to rising sea levels. Cities that lie near the coasts or in low-lying areas will be flooded and become uninhabitable. The IPCC specifically identified many potential impacts, including:

- *very* likely increase in frequency of hot extremes, heat waves, and heavy precipitation
- *likely* increase in tropical cyclone intensity; less confidence in global decrease of tropical cyclone numbers
- poleward shift of extra-tropical storm tracks with consequent changes in wind, precipitation, and temperature patterns
- *very likely* precipitation increases in high latitudes and *likely* decreases in most subtropical land regions, continuing observed recent trends

The IPCC (2007) suggests ways that the worst consequences of global warming can be mitigated. They include national policies that encourage water, land, and energy conservation, the development of alternative energy sources, and in general incorporating scientific thinking about global climate change into our ways of thinking about everything from tourism to transportation. While the IPCC report addresses government policies, it also stands to reason that individual behavior can make a difference,

DO-IT-YOURSELF SOCIOLOGY

D.I.Y.

Americans consume more resources per capita than residents of nearly every other nation in the world. But there are important steps that we can take to minimize our "carbon footprint," and to slow climate change. Please check off each "green" behavior that you've done.

Y/N

In the past seven days, have you done any of the following?

Turned down the heat or air conditioning in your home to save energy

Bicycled or walked instead of driving

Carpooled

Taken public transit, such as a bus, train, or subway

In the past six months, have you done any of the following?

Bought energy-efficient light bulbs

Bought an appliance or electronic equipment, such as a TV, based on its energy rating

Cut back significantly on how much you drive

Researched or looked into getting a more fuel-efficient or hybrid car

TURN PAGE →

even if that difference is small. Because individuals in the United States and other advanced industrial nations consume far more than the average person in developing nations, their ecological footprint is much larger. Recycling, walking or riding a bicycle rather than driving whenever possible, buying fuel-efficient cars, turning the heat down and the air conditioning off—all of these are small steps that can add up, if practiced by a large enough number of people.

The results below are based on interviews with a random sample of 1,001 adults age 18 and older, in the United States. Interviews were conducted in January 2009. Compare your answers to see how "green" you are relative to other Americans. Are you more, less, or about equally energy-conscious? What do you think explains this difference or similarity?

In the past seven days, have you done any of the following?	Percentage of sample Americans answering "Yes"
Turned down the heat or air conditioning in your home to save energy	75
Bicycled or walked instead of driving	36
Carpooled	26
Taken public transit, such as a bus, train, or subway	14

In the past six months, have you done any of the following?	
Bought energy-efficient light bulbs	76
Bought an appliance or electronic equipment, such as a TV, based on its energy rating	74
Cut back significantly on how much you drive	66
Researched or looked into getting a more fuel-efficient or hybrid car	34

Source: Bittle et al. 2009.

ENERGY

At current rates of use, the known oil resources of the world will be completely consumed by the year 2050. New reserves of oil may be discovered, or alternative sources of cheap energy invented, but there plainly is a point at which some key resources will run out if global consumption is not limited. The United States is the largest consumer of energy in the world, as well as the world's largest producer of greenhouse gases, accounting for perhaps a quarter of the world's total (although as mentioned previously, China is rapidly catching up and may have surpassed the United States by the time you read this). Most of America's energy comes from nonrenewable fossil fuels—mainly petroleum, and to a lesser degree coal and natural gas.

The high level of U.S. consumption is partly due to the fact that, as an advanced industrial economy with a high standard of living, Americans consume more energy from all sources (such as natural gas, coal, and electricity) than persons in all other nations (Figure 15.2). There is an emerging consensus among scientists and policy makers around the world that if economic development is to occur, it has to be concerned increasingly with conservation of scarce resources, as well as reducing the production of greenhouse gases and other pollutants.

SUSTAINABLE DEVELOPMENT

Rather than calling for a reining in of economic growth, more recent policy recommendations turn on the notion of sustainable development. **Sustainable development** means that growth should, at least minimally, be carried on in such a way as to recycle physical resources rather than deplete them and to keep levels of pollution to a minimum. Critics see the notion of sustainable development as too vague and as neglecting the specific needs of poorer countries. According to the critics, the idea of sustainable development tends to focus attention only on the needs of richer countries; it does not consider the ways in which the high levels of consumption in the more affluent countries are satisfied at the expense of other people. For instance, demands on Indonesia to conserve its rain forests could be seen as unfair, because

sustainable development •
The notion that economic growth should proceed only insofar as natural resources are recycled rather than depleted; biodiversity is maintained; and clean air, water, and land are protected.

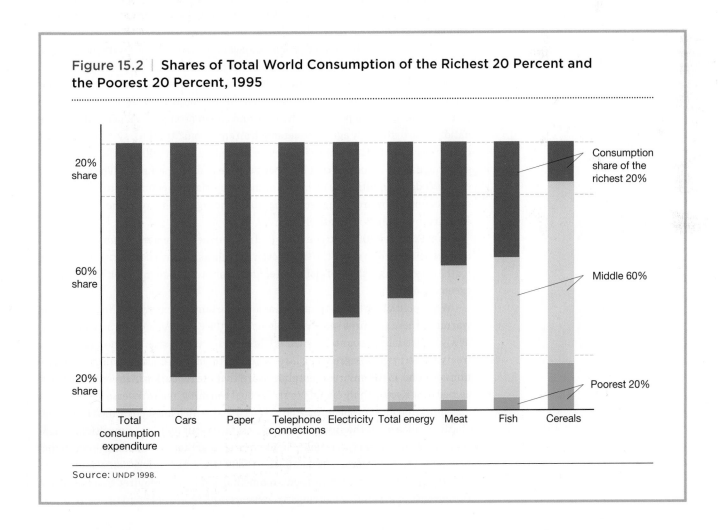

Figure 15.2 | **Shares of Total World Consumption of the Richest 20 Percent and the Poorest 20 Percent, 1995**

Source: UNDP 1998.

Indonesia has a greater need than the industrialized countries for the revenue it must forgo by accepting conservation.

PROSPECTS FOR CHANGE

Of all the environmental problems discussed in this chapter, global warming is arguably the most pressing. Greenhouse gases released in the atmosphere do not simply affect the climate of the country in which they were produced but alter climatic patterns for the entire world. For this reason, many policy makers and scientists believe that any viable solution to the problem must also be global in scale. Yet the political difficulties in negotiating an international treaty to reduce greenhouse gases are enormous and suggest that although globalization has ushered in a new era of international cooperation, the world is still far from being able to speak decisively with a unified political voice about many of the issues that it confronts.

In December 1997, delegates from 166 nations gathered in Kyoto, Japan, in an effort to hammer out an agreement to reduce global warming. The summit was the culmination of two years of informal discussions among the countries. World leaders, faced with mounting scientific evidence that global warming is indeed occurring and under pressure from voters to adopt environmentally friendly policies, clearly recognized that international action of some kind was needed. But faced as well with intense lobbying by industry, which fears it will bear the brunt of the cost for reducing fossil fuel emissions, world leaders felt compelled to balance safeguarding the environment against the threat of economic disruption.

As a result, the pollution reductions agreed to by the countries were meager, and different countries agreed to different specific targets: The United States agreed (upon ratification by the U.S. Congress) to reduce emissions levels by 7 percent from their 1990 levels, during the period 2008–2012. The fifteen countries of the European Union similarly pledged an 8 percent reduction, and Japan promised a 6 percent cut. The nations also tentatively agreed to establish an emissions "trading" system whereby a country that has reduced emissions levels beyond its target will be able to sell emissions "credits" to countries that have been unable to meet their goals. The agreement also includes commitments on behalf of the industrialized countries to assist developing countries by providing technology and funding to help overcome their limited capacity to respond to climate change.

As of February 2009, 183 countries had ratified the agreement. Notably, the United States has refused to ratify the treaty even though, as we have noted, it is responsible for the largest single share of global greenhouse gases of any country, with the possible exception of China.

While politicians hailed the accord as an important first step in dealing with global warming, there are three serious problems with the Kyoto Accord. First, while many newly industrialized countries, such as China, India, and Russia, have now ratified the treaty, the terms of the agreement largely exempt them from making emissions reductions. Second, many environmentalists warn that the reduction in greenhouse gases agreed to at Kyoto is only enough to slow global warming, not to reverse it.

Third, and most problematic, the Kyoto accord, which must be ratified by the legislative bodies of all the signatory countries, faces stiff political opposition. Industry leaders and conservative politicians in the United States, for example, claim that reaching even the 7 percent reduction agreed to by the U.S. delegation would be tremendously expensive and that the environmental regulations required to achieve even this modest goal would hamstring U.S. business and retard economic growth.

A worker at an e-waste recycling company in Bangalore, India, shows shredded pieces of printed circuit boards of obsolete electronic gadgets undergoing the recycling process. E-waste is a growing environmental and public health concern as the world becomes more wired and companies introduce new products at a faster pace.

1. Give two examples of waste materials and their sources.

2. Describe the basic processes that give rise to global warming.

3. Define sustainable development, and provide at least one critique of the concept.

4. What are the three main problems with the Kyoto Accord?

The Intergovernmental Panel on Climate Change's 2007 report has been seen as a wakeup call by many, including the U.S. government, which, as noted above, endorsed the commission's findings. Hopefully the report will lead to actions that will halt and even reverse the worst effects of global climate change. It is clear that modern technology, science, and industry are not exclusively beneficial in their consequences. Sociologists perceive a responsibility to examine closely the social relations and institutions that brought about the current state of affairs, because rectifying the situation will require a profound awareness of human responsibility. ✓

NEED HELP STUDYING?

 wwnorton.com/studyspace

Visit StudySpace to access free review materials such as:

- Vocabulary Flashcards
- Diagnostic Review Quizzes
- Study Outlines

REVIEW QUESTIONS

1. What is the theory of urban ecology?
2. What are the two aspects of Wirth's theory of urbanism as a way of life?
3. How does urban living contribute to the development of subcultures?
4. According to David Harvey, why is geographic space continually restructured?
5. How does population loss affect social problems in rural areas?
6. Why might the distinction between "suburb" and "city" no longer be useful today?
7. What explains higher rates of urbanization in the developing world?
8. How does the theory of demographic transition challenge Malthus's ideas about population growth?
9. What trends are likely to shape world population over the next two centuries? What are the possible implications of this?

THINKING SOCIOLOGICALLY EXERCISES

1. Explain what makes the urbanization now occurring in developing countries, such as Brazil and India, different from and more problematic than the urbanization that took place a century ago in New York, London, Tokyo, and Berlin.

2. Following analysis presented in this chapter, concisely explain how the expanded quest for cheap energy and raw materials and present-day dangers of environmental pollution and resource depletion threaten not only the survival of people in developed countries but also that of people in less developed countries.

16 Globalization in a Changing World

THE BIG QUESTIONS

HOW DOES GLOBALIZATION AFFECT SOCIAL CHANGE?

Recognize that a number of factors influence social change, including the physical environment, political organization, culture, and economic factors.

WHAT COMES AFTER MODERN INDUSTRIAL SOCIETY?

Be able to critically evaluate the notion that social change is leading us into a postindustrial or postmodern stage of social organization.

WHAT ARE SOCIAL MOVEMENTS?

Understand what social movements are, why they occur, and how they affect society.

WHAT FACTORS CONTRIBUTE TO GLOBALIZATION?

Recognize the importance of information flows, political changes, and transnational corporations.

HOW DOES GLOBALIZATION AFFECT YOUR LIFE?

Recognize the ways that large global systems affect local contexts and personal experiences.

The earth's population now tops 6.7 billion people, and will probably increase by half again over the next fifty years. We have spread to every nook and cranny on the planet. Due to modern science and industry, each of us today uses up a vastly greater amount of the planet's limited resources than did our apelike ancestors. Indeed, the combination of population explosion and modern industrial expansion today threatens both our planet and our human civilization.

People are capable of creating massive problems—and finding ways to solve them. Today, more than ever before in the brief span of human history, our problems are global in nature, requiring global solutions. Globalization has contributed to such challenges as global warming, the worldwide spread of AIDS, conflict between nations, terrorism, and global poverty. Yet globalization can also contribute to their solution.

Globalization refers to the fact that we all live in one world, so that individuals, groups, and nations become more interdependent. Such interdependence is

globalization • The development of social and economic relationships stretching worldwide. In current times, we are all influenced by organizations and social networks located thousands of miles away. A key part of the study of globalization is the emergence of a world system—for some purposes, we need to regard the world as forming a single social order.

increasingly at a global scale—that is, what happens halfway across the globe is more likely then ever before to have enormous consequences for our daily lives. In this chapter, we examine these global processes and see what leading sociologists and other social scientists have had to say about them.

Some of these ideas will already be familiar to you, since much of this book has been about the consequences of globalization. In this chapter, we go beyond our earlier discussions, considering why the modern period is associated with especially profound and rapid social change. We examine how globalization has contributed to such rapid social change and offer some thoughts on what the future is likely to bring.

HOW DOES GLOBALIZATION AFFECT SOCIAL CHANGE?

The ways of living and the social institutions characteristic of the modern world are radically different from those of even the recent past. During a period of only two or three centuries—a small sliver of time in the context of human history—human social life has been wrenched away from the types of social order in which people lived for thousands of years. **Social change** can be defined as the transformation over time of the institutions and culture of a society. Globalization has accelerated the pace of social change, bringing virtually all of humanity into the same turbulent seas. As a result, far more than any generations before us, we face an uncertain future. To be sure, conditions of life for previous generations were always insecure: People were at the mercy of natural disasters, plagues, and famines. Yet, although these problems still trouble much of the world, today we must also deal with the social forces that we ourselves have unleashed.

Social theorists have tried for the past two centuries to develop a single grand theory that explains the nature of social change. Marx, for example, emphasized the importance of economic factors in shaping all other aspects of social life, including politics and culture. But no single-factor theory can adequately account for the diversity of human social development from hunting and gathering and pastoral societies to traditional civilizations and finally to the highly complex social systems of today. In analyzing social change, we can at most accomplish two tasks. We can identify a number of major factors that have consistently influenced social change, such as the physical environment, economics, political organization, and culture. We can also develop theories that account for particular periods of change, such as modern times.

social change ● Alteration in basic structures of a social group or society. Social change is an ever-present phenomenon in social life, but has become especially intense in the modern era. The origins of modern sociology can be traced to attempts to understand the dramatic changes shattering the traditional world and promoting new forms of social order.

THE PHYSICAL ENVIRONMENT

The physical environment often has an effect on the development of human social organization. This is clearest in extreme environmental conditions, where people must organize their ways of life in relation to weather conditions. People who live in Alaska, where the winters are long and cold and the days very short, tend to follow different patterns of social life from people who live in the much warmer American South. Most Alaskans spend more of their lives indoors and, except for the summer months, plan outdoor activities carefully, given the frequently inhospitable environment in which they live.

Less extreme physical conditions can also affect society. The native population of Australia has never stopped being hunters and gatherers, since the continent contained hardly any indigenous plants suitable for regular cultivation or animals that could be domesticated to develop pastoral production. The ease of communications across land and the availability of sea routes are also important: Societies cut off from others by mountain ranges, impassable jungles, or deserts often remain relatively unchanged over long periods of time.

A strong case for the importance of environment is made by Jared Diamond (2005) in his widely acclaimed book *Collapse: How Societies Choose to Fail or Succeed*. Diamond, a physiologist, biologist, and geographer, examines more than a dozen past and present societies, some of which collapsed (past examples include Easter Island and the Anasazi of the southwestern United States; more recent candidates include Rwanda and Haiti) and some of which overcame serious challenges to succeed.

Diamond identifies five sets of factors that can contribute to a society's collapse: the presence of hostile neighbors; the absence (or collapse of) trading partners for essential goods; climate change; environmental problems; and an inadequate response to environmental problems. Three of these five factors have to do with environmental conditions. The first four factors are often outside of a society's control and need not always result in collapse. The final factor, however, is always crucial: As the subtitle of his book suggests, success or failure depends on the choices made by a society and its leaders.

The collapse of Rwanda, for example, is typically attributed to ethnic rivalries between Hutu and Tutsi, fueled by Rwanda's colonial past. According to some explanations of the genocide that left more than eight hundred thousand Tutsi dead in the span of a few horrific months in 1994, a large part of the cause lay in the legacy of colonialism. During the first part of the twentieth century, Belgium ran Rwanda through Tutsi administrators because according to the prevailing European racial theories of the time, the Tutsis—who tended on average to be somewhat taller and lighter skinned than the Hutus and, therefore, closer in resemblance to Europeans—were believed by the Belgians to be more civilized. This led to resentments and hatred, which boiled over in 1994, fueled by Hutu demagogues urging the killing of all Tutsi.

Rwandan refugees trying to reach the United Nations camp in Tanzania. Over 800,000 Tutsis and moderate Hutus were killed during a period of 100 days in 1994. Hundreds of thousands of Rwandans fled to neighboring countries to escape the bloodshed.

Diamond does not reject this explanation but shows that it is only part of the story and by itself cannot account for the depth of the violence. Instead, through careful analysis of patterns of landholding, population, and killing, he argues that the root causes are found in overpopulation and resulting environmental destruction. Rwanda, he shows, had one of the fastest-growing populations on earth, with disastrous consequences for its land as well as its people, who had become some of the most impoverished on the planet. Faced with starvation and the absence of land to share among the growing number of (male) children, Rwanda was ripe for violence and collapse. Although ethnic rivalries may have fueled the fires of rage, Diamond shows that in some hard-hit provinces Hutus killed other Hutus, as young men sought to acquire scarce farmland by any means.

Some have criticized Diamond for overemphasizing the importance of the environment, at the expense of other factors. The environment alone does not necessarily determine how a society develops. Today especially, when humans can exert a high degree of control over their immediate living conditions, environment would seem to be less important: Modern cities have sprung up in the arctic cold and the harshest deserts.

POLITICAL ORGANIZATION

A second factor strongly influencing social change is the type of political organization that operates in a society. In hunting and gathering societies, this influence is minimal, since there are no political authorities capable of mobilizing the community. In all other types of society, however, the existence of distinct political agencies—chiefs, lords, monarchs, and governments—strongly affects the course of development a society takes.

How a society and its leaders respond to a crisis can play a decisive role in whether they thrive or fail. A leader capable of pursuing dynamic policies and generating a mass following or radically altering preexisting modes of thought can overturn a previously established order. However, individuals can reach positions of leadership and become effective only if favorable social conditions exist. Mahatma Gandhi, the famous pacifist leader in India, effectively secured his country's independence from Britain because World War II and other events had unsettled the existing colonial institutions in India.

The most important political factor that has helped speed up patterns of change in the modern era is the emergence of the modern state, which has proved a vastly more efficient mechanism of government than the types that existed in premodern societies.

Globalization today may be challenging the ability of national governments to effectively exert leadership. Sociologist William Robinson (2001), for one, claims that as economic power has becoming increasingly deterritorialized, so too has political power: Just as transnational corporations operate across borders, with little or no national allegiance, transnational political organizations are becoming stronger even as national governments are becoming weaker. The World Trade Organization (WTO), for example, has the power to punish countries that violate its principles of free trade (Conti 2003).

Will the twenty-first century see new forms of political organization, better suited to a world in which people, products, knowledge, religious beliefs, MTV, and pollution all cross borders with ever-greater ease? While it is too soon to tell, it seems likely that the most important forms of political organization of the twenty-first century will bear little resemblance to those of the twentieth.

CULTURE

The third main influence on social change is culture, including communication systems, religious and other belief systems, and popular culture. Communication systems, in particular, affect the character and pace of social change. The invention of writing, for instance, allowed for effective record keeping, making possible the development of large-scale organizations. In addition, writing altered people's perception of the relation between past, present, and future. Societies that write keep a record of past events, which then enables them to develop a sense of their society's overall line of evolution. The existence of a written constitution and laws makes it possible for a country to have a legal system based on the interpretation of specific legal precedents—just as written scripture enables religious leaders to justify their beliefs by citing chapter and verse from religious texts like the Bible or the Qur'an.

We have seen in previous chapters how in recent years the Internet has helped change our personal relationships, the nature of politics and social movements, our forms of recreation, the ways in which we learn and work—in fact, almost every aspect of modern life. These changes have been among the most rapid in human history, resulting in what geographer David Harvey (1989) has aptly referred to as "the time-space compression." And they have all occurred within the last quarter century—a single generation.

Religion, as we have seen, may be either a conservative or an innovative force in social life. Some forms of religious belief and practice have acted as a brake on change, emphasizing above all the need to adhere to traditional values and rituals. Yet, as Max Weber emphasized, religious convictions frequently play a mobilizing role in pressures for social change. For instance, American church leaders promote attempts to lessen poverty or diminish inequalities in society. Religious leaders such as Dr. Martin Luther King Jr. were in the forefront of the American civil rights movement.

Yet at the same time, religion today has become one of the driving forces against many of the cultural aspects of globalization. Islamic fundamentalists, fundamentalist Christians, and ultra-orthodox Jewish *haredim* all reject what they regard as the corrupting influences of modern secular culture, now rapidly spreading throughout the world thanks to mass media and the Internet (Juergensmeyer 1994, 2001). Fundamentalist Islamists call this "westoxification"—literally, getting drunk on the temptations of modern Western culture. Although such religious communities are usually willing to embrace modern technology, which they often use effectively to disseminate their ideas, they reject what they view as the "McWorld" corruptions that go along with it.

According to Juergensmeyer (1994), the principal cultural clashes of the twenty-first century will not be between so-called civilizations but rather between those who believe that truthful understanding is derived from religious faith and those whose argue that such understanding is grounded in science, critical thinking, and secular thought.

ECONOMIC FACTORS

Of economic influences, the farthest reaching is industrial capitalism. Capitalism differs in a fundamental way from preexisting production systems because it involves the constant expansion of production and the ever-increasing accumulation of wealth. In traditional production systems, levels of production were fairly stable, since they were geared to habitual, customary needs. Capitalism requires the constant revision of the technology of production, a process into which science is increasingly drawn. The rate of technological innovation fostered in modern industry is vastly greater than in any previous type of economic order. And such technological innovation, as we have seen, has helped create a truly global economy—one whose production lines draw on a worldwide workforce.

Economic changes help shape other changes as well. Science and technology, for example, are driven in part (often in large part) by economic factors. Governments often get into the act, spending far more money than individual businesses can afford in an effort to ensure that their countries don't fall behind technologically, militarily, or economically. For instance, when the Soviet Union launched the world's first satellite (Sputnik) into space in 1957, the United States responded with a massive and costly space program, inspired by fear that the Russians were winning the space race. During the 1960 presidential campaign, John F. Kennedy had effectively stoked that fear by repeatedly accusing the Republicans of being lax on Russian missile technology, suggesting that a growing "missile gap" made us vulnerable to a nuclear attack. The arms race, fueled by government contracts with corporations, provided major economic support for scientific research as well as more general support for the U.S. economy. ✓

CONCEPT CHECKS ✓

1. Name three examples of cultural factors that may influence social change.
2. How does industrial capitalism affect social change?
3. What are the most important political factors that influence social change?

WHAT COMES AFTER MODERN INDUSTRIAL SOCIETY?

Where is social change leading us today? In this section, we examine two competing perspectives: the notion that we are a postindustrial society and the idea that we have reached a postmodern period. In the final section of this chapter, we examine theories that have focused on the dimensions, causes, and consequences of globalization.

TOWARD A POSTINDUSTRIAL SOCIETY?

Some observers have suggested that what is occurring today is a transition to a new society no longer primarily based on industrialism. We are entering, they claim, a phase of development beyond the industrial era altogether. A variety of terms have been coined to describe this new social order, such as **information society, service society,** and **knowledge society**. The term that has come into most common use, however—first employed by Daniel Bell in the United States and Alain Touraine in France—is **postindustrial society** (Touraine 1974; Bell 1976), the *post* (meaning "after") referring to the sense that we are moving beyond the old forms of industrial development.

The diversity of names is one indication of the many ideas put forward to interpret current social changes. But one theme appears consistently: the significance of information or knowledge in the society of the future. Our way of life throughout the nineteenth and twentieth centuries, based in large part on machine power—the

information society • A society no longer based primarily on the production of material goods but on the production of knowledge. The notion of the information society is closely bound up with the rise of information technology.

service society • A concept related to postindustrial society, it refers to a social order distinguished by the growth of service occupations at the expense of industrial jobs that produce material goods.

knowledge society • Another common term for information society—a society based on the production and consumption of knowledge and information.

postindustrial society • A postindustrial society is based on the production of information rather than material goods. According to postindustrialists, we are currently experiencing a series of social changes as profound as those that initiated the industrial era some two hundred years ago.

manufacture of material goods in factories—is being displaced by one in which information is the basis of the production system.

One of the earliest comprehensive portrayals of these changes is provided by Daniel Bell in his now-classic *The Coming of the Post-Industrial Society* (1976). The postindustrial order, Bell argues, is distinguished by a growth of service occupations at the expense of jobs that produce material goods. The blue-collar worker, employed in a factory or workshop, is no longer the most essential type of employee. White-collar (clerical and professional) workers outnumber blue-collar (factory) workers, with professional and technical occupations growing fastest of all.

People working in higher-level white-collar occupations specialize in the production of information and knowledge. The production and control of what Bell calls "codified knowledge"—systematic, coordinated information—is society's main productive resource. Those who create and distribute this knowledge—scientists, computer specialists, economists, engineers, and professionals of all kinds—increasingly become the leading social groups, replacing the industrialists and entrepreneurs of the old system.

The "Geek Squad," a company founded by Robert Stephens in Minneapolis, Minnesota, and later purchased by the Best Buy retail chain, provides consumer computer support and technical repairs. They are an example of the new types of service sector jobs emerging in a postindustrial society.

POSTMODERNITY

Some authors have recently gone as far as saying that the developments now occurring are even more profound than signaling the end of the era of industrialism. They claim that what is happening is nothing short of a movement beyond modernity—the attitudes and ways of life associated with modern societies, such as our belief in progress, the benefits of science, and our capability to control the modern world. An era of **postmodernism** is arriving, or has already arrived.

The advocates of postmodernity claim that modern societies took their inspiration from the idea that history has a shape—it "goes somewhere" and leads to progress—and that now this notion has collapsed. Not only is there no general notion of progress that can be defended, there is no such thing as history. The postmodern world is thus a highly pluralistic and diverse one. In countless films, videos, and TV programs, images circulate around the world. We come into contact with many ideas and values, but these have little connection with the history of the areas in which we live, or indeed with our own personal histories. Everything seems constantly in flux.

Most contemporary social theorists accept that information technology and new communications systems, together with other technological changes, are producing major social transformations for all of us. However, the majority disagree with core ideas of the postmodernists, who argue that our attempts to understand general processes in the social world are doomed, as is the notion that we can change the world for the better. Writers such as Ulrich Beck and one of the authors of this textbook, Anthony Giddens, claim that we need as much as ever to develop general theories of the social world and that such theories can help us intervene to shape it in a positive way. Such theories have focused on how contemporary societies are becoming globalized, while everyday life is breaking free from the hold of tradition and custom. But these changes should not spell the end of attempts at social and political reform. Values such as a belief in the importance of social community, equality, and caring for the weak and vulnerable are still very much alive throughout the world. ✓

postmodernism • The belief that society is no longer governed by history or progress. Postmodern society is highly pluralistic and diverse, with no "grand narrative" guiding its development.

CONCEPT CHECKS ✓

1. What is "postindustrial society"?

2. What is the "postmodern era"? What is the main critique of this concept?

WHAT ARE SOCIAL MOVEMENTS?

In addition to economics, technology, politics, and culture, one of the most common ways social change occurs is through *social movements*, or collective attempts to further a common interest or secure a common goal through action outside the sphere of established institutions. A wide variety of social movements, some enduring, some transient, have existed in modern societies. They are as evident a feature of the contemporary world as are the formal, bureaucratic organizations they often oppose. Many contemporary social movements are international in scope and rely heavily on the use of information technology in linking local social movement participants to global issues.

Making Sociology Work
COMMUNITY ORGANIZER/ SOCIAL ACTIVIST

In July 2006, one of the largest student protests since Tiananmen Square erupted in China. An estimated ten thousand students in Zhengzhou clashed with police, and ransacked classrooms and administrative offices at Shengda Economic, Trade and Management College, which is affiliated with the prestigious Zhengzhou University. What sparked the protest? After paying expensive tuition fees and completing their years of study, graduating students were angered by the college's decision to award diplomas in its own name, rather than in the name of Zhengzhou University, as promised in its advertisements. This seeming bait-and-switch is due to a 2003 government regulation requiring colleges to issue diplomas in their own names rather than those of their higher-prestige affiliates. A diploma from Zhengzhou University Shengda Economic, Trade and Management College will reveal the second-tier character of the students' qualifications to employers. Concern about the prestige of one's alma mater is particularly acute in China today. Given the nation's intensely competitive labor market, even a degree from a well-known university no longer guarantees a job to a new graduate. A 2009 government study predicted that despite the country's annual economic growth of more than 9 percent, as many as 30 percent of China's six million 2009 graduates, including those receiving graduate degrees, would be unlikely to find jobs (University World News 2009). Drawing on the concepts of economic deprivation, relative deprivation, structural strain, and fields of action, do you believe that the students' protests will be effective? Why or why not? If you were a community organizer, what conditions would be necessary to ensure a successful protest?

WHY DO SOCIAL MOVEMENTS OCCUR?

Sociology arose in the late nineteenth century as part of an effort to come to grips with the massive political and economic transformations that Europe experienced on its way from the preindustrial to the modern world (Moore 1966). Perhaps because sociology was founded in this context, sociologists have never lost their fascination with these transformations.

Since mass social movements have been so important in world history over the past two centuries, it is not surprising that a diversity of theories exist to try to account for them. Some theories were formulated early in the history of the social sciences; the most important was that of Karl Marx. Marx, who lived well before any of the social movements undertaken in the name of his ideas took place, intended his views to be taken not just as an analysis of the conditions of revolutionary change but as a means of furthering such change. Whatever their intrinsic validity, Marx's ideas had an immense practical impact on twentieth-century social change.

We shall look at four frameworks for the study of social movements, many of which were developed in the context of revolution: economic deprivation, resource mobilization, structural strain, and fields of action.

ECONOMIC DEPRIVATION

Marx's view of social movements is based on his general interpretation of human history (see Chapter 1). According to Marx, the development of societies is marked by periodic class conflicts that, when they become acute, tend to end in a process of revolutionary change. Class struggles derive from the unresolvable

Relative deprivation between the peasantry and the elite in France led to the overthrow of the monarchy in the late 18th century.

tensions in societies. The main sources of tension can be traced to economic changes, or changes in the *forces of production*. In any stable society, there is a balance between the economic structure, social relationships, and the political system. As the forces of production alter, contradiction is intensified, leading to open clashes between classes—and ultimately to revolution.

Contrary to Marx's expectations, revolutions failed to occur in the advanced industrialized societies of the West. Why? The sociologist James Davies, a critic of Marx, pointed to periods of history when people lived in dire poverty but did not rise up in protest. Constant poverty or deprivation does not make people into revolutionaries; rather, they usually endure such conditions with resignation or silent frustration. Social protest, and ultimately revolution, is more likely to occur when there is an improvement in people's living conditions, according to Davies. Once standards of living have started to rise, people's levels of expectation also go up. If improvement in actual conditions subsequently slows down, propensities to revolt are created because rising expectations are frustrated (Davies 1962). Thus, it is not absolute deprivation that leads to protest but *relative deprivation*—the discrepancy between the lives people are forced to lead and what they think could realistically be achieved.

Davies's theory does not show how and why different groups mobilize to seek revolutionary change, however. Charles Tilly's theory of resource mobilization, by contrast, helps to understand how groups become collectively organized to make effective political challenges.

RESOURCE MOBILIZATION

In *From Mobilization to Revolution*, Charles Tilly analyzed processes of revolutionary change in the context of broader forms of protest and violence (Tilly 1978). He distinguished four main components of *collective action*, action taken to contest or overthrow an existing social order:

1. **The *organization* of the group or groups involved**. Protest movements are organized in many ways, varying from the spontaneous formation of crowds to tightly disciplined revolutionary groups. The Russian Revolution, for example, began as a small group of activists.
2. ***Mobilization*, the ways in which a group acquires sufficient resources to make collective action possible**. Such resources may include material goods, political support, and weaponry. Lenin was able to acquire material and moral support from a sympathetic peasantry.
3. **The *common goals and interests* of those engaging in collective action, what they see as the gains and losses likely to be achieved by their policies**. Lenin managed to weld together a broad coalition of support because many people had a common interest in removing the existing government.
4. ***Opportunity***. Chance events may occur that provide opportunities to pursue revolutionary aims. There was no inevitability to Lenin's success, which depended on a number of contingent factors—including success in battle. If Lenin had been killed, would there have been a revolution?

Collective action itself can simply be defined as people acting together in pursuit of interests they share—for example, gathering to demonstrate in support of their cause. Some of these people may be intensely involved, others may lend more passive or sporadic support. Effective collective action, such as action that culminates in revolution, usually moves through a series of gradual stages.

Typical modes of collective action and protest vary with historical and cultural circumstances. In the United States today, for example, most people are familiar with forms of demonstration like mass marches, large assemblies, and street riots, whether or not they have participated in such activities. Other types of collective protest, however, have become less common or have disappeared altogether in most modern societies (such as fights between villages or lynching). Protesters can also build on strategies adopted elsewhere; for instance, guerrilla movements proliferated in various parts of the world once disaffected groups learned how successful guerrilla actions can be against regular armies.

STRUCTURAL STRAIN

Neil Smelser (1963) distinguished six conditions underlying the origins of collective action in general, and social movements in particular:

1. *Structural conduciveness* refers to the general social conditions promoting or inhibiting the formation of social movements of different types.
2. Just because the conditions are conducive to the development of a social movement does not mean those conditions will bring it into being. There must be *structural strain* or tensions that produce conflicting interests within societies. Uncertainties, anxieties, ambiguities, or direct clashes of goals are expressions of such strains.
3. *Generalized beliefs and ideologies* crystallize grievances and suggest courses of action that might be pursued to remedy them.
4. *Precipitating factors* are events or incidents that actually trigger direct action by those who become involved in the movement.
5. The first four conditions combined might precede minor protests, but they do not lead to the development of social movements unless there is a coordinated group that becomes mobilized for action. *Leadership* and some means of regular *communication* among participants, together with funding and material resources, are necessary for a social movement to exist.

6. The development of a social movement is strongly influenced by *social control forces*. A harsh reaction by governing authorities might encourage further protest and help solidify the movement, whereas divisions within the military can be crucial in deciding the outcome of confrontations with revolutionary movements.

Smelser's model is useful for analyzing the sequences in the development of social movements, and collective action in general. His theory treats social movements as responses to situations, rather than allowing that their members might spontaneously organize to achieve desired social changes. In this respect his ideas contrast with the approach developed by Alain Touraine.

FIELDS OF ACTION

Alain Touraine's (1977, 1981) theory of social movements is based on four main ideas. The first, which he called *historicity*, explains why there are so many more movements in the modern world than there were in earlier times. In modern societies, individuals and groups know that social activism can be used to achieve social goals and reshape society.

Second, social movements typically have *rational objectives*; they develop from specific views and rational strategies as to how injustices can be overcome.

Third, social movements are shaped by *social interaction*. They do not develop in isolation; instead, they develop in deliberate antagonism with established organizations and sometimes with other rival social movements.

Fourth, social movements and change occur in the context of what Touraine called "fields of action." A *field of action* refers to the connections between a social movement and the forces or influences opposing it. The process of mutual negotiation among antagonists in a field of action may lead to the social changes sought by the movement as well as to changes in the social movement itself and in its antagonists. In either circumstance, the movement may evaporate—or become institutionalized as a permanent organization.

GLOBALIZATION AND SOCIAL MOVEMENTS

Social movements come in all shapes and sizes. Some are very small, numbering fewer than a dozen members; others include thousands or even millions of people. Some social movements carry on their activities within the laws of the society, while others operate as illegal or underground groups. However, most protest movements operate near the margins of what is defined as legally permissible by governments at any particular time or place.

Social movements often arise with the aim of bringing about a major change, such as expanding civil rights for a segment of the population. In response, countermovements sometimes arise in defense of the status quo. The campaign for women's right to legal abortion, for example, has been vociferously challenged by antiabortion ("pro-life") activists, who believe that abortion should be illegal.

Often, laws or policies are altered as a result of the action of social movements. These changes in legislation can have far-ranging effects. For example, it used to be illegal for groups of workers to call their members out on strike, and striking was punished with varying degrees of severity in different countries. Eventually, however, the laws were amended, making the strike a permissible tactic of industrial conflict.

NEW SOCIAL MOVEMENTS

The last three decades have seen an explosion of social movements in countries around the globe. These movements—ranging from the civil rights and feminist movements of the 1960s and 1970s to the antinuclear and ecological movements of the 1980s to the gay rights campaign of the 1990s—are often referred to by commentators as *new social movements*. This description seeks to differentiate contemporary social movements from those that preceded them in earlier decades. They are often concerned with the quality of private life as much as with political and economic issues, calling for large-scale changes in the way people think and act.

In other words, what makes new social movements "new" is that—unlike conventional social movements—they are not based on single-issue objectives that typically involve changes in the distribution of economic resources or power. Rather, they involve the creation of collective identities based around entire lifestyles, often calling for sweeping cultural changes. New social movements have emerged in recent years around issues such as ecology, peace, gender and sexual identity, gay and lesbian rights, women's rights, alternative medicine, and opposition to globalization.

Participation in new social movements often is viewed as a moral obligation (and even a pleasure), rather than a calculated effort to achieve some specific goal. Moreover, the forms of protest chosen by new social movements are a form of "expressive logic" whereby participants make a statement about who they are: Protest is an end in itself, a way of affirming one's identity, as well as a means to achieving concrete objectives (Polletta and Jasper 2001).

The rise of new social movements in recent years is a reflection of the changing risks facing human societies. The conditions are ripe for social movements—increasingly traditional political institutions are unable to cope with the challenges before them. Existing democratic political institutions cannot hope to fix sweeping problems like climate change and the dangers of nuclear energy. As a result, these unfolding challenges are frequently ignored or avoided until it is too late and a full-blown crisis is at hand.

The cumulative effect of these new challenges and risks is a sense that people are losing control of their lives in the midst of rapid change. Individuals feel less secure and more isolated—a combination that leads to a sense of powerlessness. By contrast, corporations, governments, and the media appear to be dominating more and more aspects of people's lives, heightening the sensation of a runaway world. There is a growing sense that left to its own logic, globalization will present ever-greater risks to citizens' lives.

Although faith in traditional politics seems to be waning, the growth of new social movements is evidence that citizens in late modern societies are not apathetic or uninterested in politics, as is sometimes claimed. Rather, there is a belief that direct action and participation is more useful than reliance on politicians and political systems. New social movements are helping to revitalize democracy in many countries. They are at the heart of a strong civic culture or **civil society**—the sphere between the state and the marketplace occupied by family, community associations, and other noneconomic institutions.

civil society • The realm of activity that lies between the state and the market, including the family, schools, community associations, and other noneconomic institutions. Civil society, or civic culture, is essential to vibrant democratic societies.

TECHNOLOGY AND SOCIAL MOVEMENTS

In recent years, two of the most influential forces in late modern societies—information technology and social movements—have come together, with astonishing results. In our current information age, social movements around the globe are able to join together in huge regional and international networks comprising nongovernmental organizations, religious and humanitarian groups, human rights associations, consumer protection advocates, environmental activists, and others who campaign in the public interest. These electronic networks now have the unprecedented ability to respond immediately to events as they occur, to gain access to and share sources of information, and to put pressure on corporations, governments, and international bodies as part of their campaigning strategies. As we saw earlier, Web-based organizations such as MoveOn.org played an influential role in the anti–Iraq War movement.

The Internet has been at the forefront of these changes, although Twitter, mobile phones, fax machines, and satellite broadcasting have also hastened their evolution. With the press of a button, local stories are disseminated internationally. The ability of citizens to coordinate international protests is highly worrisome for governments. For example, young people protesting the alleged election fraud in the June 2009 presidential election in Iran found that the government had blocked access to the Internet by lowering the bandwidth, and blocking access to sites like YouTube.

From global protests in favor of canceling Third World debt to the international campaign to ban land mines (which culminated in a Nobel Peace Prize), the Internet has the potential to unite campaigners across national and cultural borders. Some observers argue that the information age is witnessing a migration of power away from nation-states into new nongovernmental alliances and coalitions. ✓

CONCEPT CHECKS ✓

1. Compare and contrast four theoretical approaches to the study of social movements.

2. What distinguishes new social movements from their precursors?

WHAT FACTORS CONTRIBUTE TO GLOBALIZATION?

Globalization is often portrayed solely as an economic phenomenon. Some make much of the role of transnational corporations whose massive operations stretch across national borders, influencing global production processes and the international distribution of labor. Others point to the electronic integration of global financial markets and the enormous volume of global capital flows. Still others focus on the unprecedented scope of world trade, involving a much broader range of goods and services than ever before.

Although economic forces are an integral part of globalization, it would be wrong to suggest that they alone produce it. Globalization is created by the coming together of technological, political, and economic factors. It has been driven forward above all by the development of information and communications technologies that have intensified the speed and scope of interaction between people all over the world.

INFORMATION FLOWS

The explosion in global communications has been facilitated by some important advances in technology and the world's telecommunications infrastructure. In the post–World War II era, there has been a profound transformation in the scope and intensity of telecommunications flows. Traditional telephone communication, which depended on analog signals sent through wires and cables, has been replaced by integrated systems in which vast amounts of information are compressed and transferred digitally. Cable technology and the spread of communications satellites, beginning in the 1960s, have been significant in expanding international communications. Today a network of more than two hundred satellites is in place to facilitate the transfer of information around the globe.

The impact of these communications systems has been staggering. In countries with highly developed telecommunications infrastructures, homes and offices now have multiple links to the outside world, including telephones (both landlines and mobile phones), fax machines, digital and cable television, electronic mail, and the Internet. The Internet has emerged as the fastest-growing communication tool ever developed—nearly 1.7 billion people worldwide (almost one fifth of the world population) were estimated to be using the Internet at the end of June 2009, nearly twice the number of only five years earlier and over four times as many as in 2000 (Internet World Stats 2009d).

As we noted earlier, these forms of technology facilitate the compression of time and space: Two individuals located on opposite sides of the planet—in Tokyo and London, for example—not only can hold a conversation in real time, but can also send documents and images to one another with the help of satellite technology. Widespread use of the Internet and mobile phones is deepening and accelerating processes of globalization; more and more people are becoming interconnected through the use of these technologies and are doing so in places that have previously been isolated or poorly served by traditional communications. Although the telecommunications infrastructure is not evenly developed around the world (Table 16.1), a growing number of countries now have access to international communications networks in a way that was previously impossible.

Table 16.1 | Global Unevenness of Telecommunications Infrastructure and Use

COUNTRY	POPULATION (MILLIONS)	TELEPHONE MAINLINES (PER 1,000)[a]	FIXED LINE AND MOBILE PHONE SUBSCRIBERS (PER 1,000)[b]	PERSONAL COMPUTERS (PER 1,000)[b]
China	1,319.98	280	690	41
France	61.71	550	1,390	575
Germany	82.27	650	1,830	545
India	123.32	30	240	16
Japan	127.77	360	1,150	542
Sweden	9.15	590	1,650	763
United Kingdom	61.03	550	1,730	600
United States	301.62	540	1.390	762

[a] In 2006.
[b] In 2005.

Source: World Bank 2008d.

A call center in Gurgaon, India.

Globalization is also being driven forward by the electronic integration of the world economy. The global economy is increasingly dominated by activity that is weightless and intangible (Quah 1999). This *weightless economy* is one in which products have their base in information, as is the case with computer software, media and entertainment products, and Internet-based services. The emergence of the *knowledge society* has been linked to the development of a broad base of consumers who are technologically literate and eagerly integrate new advances in computing, entertainment, and telecommunications into their everyday lives.

The very operation of the global economy reflects the changes that have occurred in the information age. Many aspects of the economy now work through networks that cross national boundaries, rather than stopping at them (Castells 1996). In order to be competitive in globalizing conditions, businesses and corporations have restructured themselves to be more flexible and less hierarchical in nature. Production practices and organizational patterns have become more flexible, partnering arrangements with other firms have become commonplace, and participation in worldwide distribution networks has become essential for doing business in a rapidly changing global market.

Whether a job is in a factory or a call center, it can be done more cheaply in China, India, or some other developing country than in countries like the United States. This is increasingly true for the work of software engineers, graphic designers, and financial consultants as well. Of course, to the extent that global competition for labor reduces the cost of goods and services, it also provides for a wealth of cheaper products (Roach 2005). As consumers we all benefit from low-cost flat-panel TVs made in China and inexpensive computer games programmed in India. It is an open question, however, whether the declining cost of consumption will balance out wage and job losses due to globalization.

POLITICAL CHANGES

A number of political changes are driving forces behind contemporary globalization. One of the most significant of these is the collapse of Soviet-style communism, which occurred in a series of dramatic revolutions in Eastern Europe in 1989 and culminated in the dissolution of the Soviet Union itself in 1991. Since the fall of Soviet-style communism, countries in the former Soviet bloc—including Russia, Ukraine, Poland, Hungary, the Czech Republic, the Baltic states, the states of the Caucasus and Central Asia, and many others—are moving toward Western-style political and economic systems. They are no longer isolated from the global community, but are becoming integrated within it. The collapse of communism has hastened processes of globalization but should also be seen as a result of globalization itself. The centrally planned communist economies and the ideological and cultural control of communist political authority were ultimately unable to survive in an era of global media and an electronically integrated world economy.

A second important political factor leading to intensifying globalization is the growth of international and regional mechanisms of government. The United Nations and the European Union are the two most prominent examples of international organizations that bring together nation-states in a common political forum. Whereas the UN does this as an association of individual nation-states, the EU is a more pioneering form of transnational governance in which a certain degree of national sovereignty is relinquished by its member states. The governments of individual EU states are bound by directives, regulations, and court judgments from common EU bodies, but they also reap economic, social, and political benefits from their participation in the regional union.

A third important political factor is the growing importance of *international governmental organizations (IGOs)* and *international nongovernmental organizations (INGOs*; see also Chapter 6). An *international governmental organization* is a body that is established by participating governments and given responsibility for regulating or overseeing a particular domain of activity that is transnational in scope. The first such body, the International Telegraph Union, was founded in 1865. Since that time, a great number of similar bodies have been created to regulate a range of business activities ranging from civil aviation to broadcasting to the disposal of hazardous waste. In 1909, there were thirty-seven IGOs in existence to regulate transnational affairs; by 2005, there were estimated to be more than seven thousand (Union of International Organizations 2005). As the name suggests, *INGOs* differ from international governmental organizations in that they are not affiliated with government institutions. Rather, they are independent organizations that work alongside governmental bodies in making policy decisions and addressing international issues. Some of the best-known INGOs—Greenpeace, Médecins Sans Frontières (Doctors without Borders), the Red Cross, and Amnesty International—are involved in environmental protection and humanitarian relief efforts. But the activities of the nearly fifty-nine thousand lesser-known groups also link together countries and communities.

Finally, the spread of information technology has expanded the possibilities for contact between people around the globe. Every day, the global media bring news, images, and information into people's homes, linking them directly and continuously to the outside world. Some of the most gripping events of the past three decades—such as the fall of the Berlin Wall, the violent crackdown on democratic protesters in Beijing's Tiananmen Square, and the terrorist attacks of September 11, 2001—have unfolded through the media before a truly global audience. Such events, along with thousands of less dramatic ones, have resulted in a reorientation in people's thinking from the level of the nation-state to the global stage. Individuals are now more aware of their interconnectedness with others and more likely to identify with global issues and processes than in times past.

DO-IT-YOURSELF SOCIOLOGY

An important theme of this chapter is that globalization touches every aspect of our daily lives. You may not even recognize how interconnected you are with people who live half-way across the world. Think about the products and services you use every day. You may be surprised to know that on a daily basis, you are interacting with objects and people from around the globe. Look around your dorm room or apartment. How many of the following items do you use regularly? Turn the page to see how much you are linked into the global economy.

1. IKEA furniture _____
2. Wii games _____
3. H&M fashions _____
4. L'Oreal shampoos or beauty products _____
5. Samsung cell phone or PDA _____
6. Molson beer _____
7. Birkenstock sandals _____
8. Diesel jeans _____
9. Apple iPhone _____
10. American Express credit card _____

TURN PAGE

1. *IKEA furniture.* The discount furniture store IKEA was founded in 1943 by Ingvar Kamprad in Sweden and is currently owned by a Dutch-registered foundation controlled by the Kamprad family.

2. *Wii games.* Wii is manufactured by Nintendo, a multinational corporation located in Kyoto, Japan. Nintendo was founded in 1889 by Fusajiro Yamauchi, and was originally a playing card company. The company expanded to electronic toys in the 1960s, before moving into videogame design and production in the 1970s.

3. *H&M fashions.* H&M, or Hennes & Mauritz AB, is a Swedish clothing company. The company began as a women's clothing store in 1947 and was originally called Hennes (Swedish for "hers"). In 1968, Erling Persson, the company's founder, acquired a Stockholm hunting equipment store named Mauritz Widforss. He renamed the company, and transformed it into a men's and women's clothing chain.

4. *L'Oreal shampoos or beauty products.* L'Oreal is the world's largest cosmetics and beauty company and is headquartered in the Paris suburb of Clichy, Hauts-de-Seine, France. In 1907, Eugène Schueller, a young French chemist, developed a new formula for hair coloring. He called his product *Auréole*. The company eventually expanded to produce other beauty products, and currently markets over 500 brands.

5. *Samsung cell phone or PDA* Samsung Electronics is the one of the world's largest electronics company, and is headquartered in Seoul, South Korea. Samsung Electronics was founded in 1969 and originally manufactured electronic appliances such as TVs. In 1988, it merged with Samsung Semiconductor & Communications.

6. *Molson beer.* Founded by John Molson in Montreal, Canada in 1786, Molson brewery is the second oldest company in Canada. In 2005, Molson merged with U.S.-based Coors to form Molson Coors Brewing Company.

7. *Birkenstock sandals.* Birkenstock is a German-made brand of sandal. The company was founded by German Johann Adam Birkenstock in 1774. In 1897 the founder's grandson, Konrad Birkenstock, developed the first contoured insole, and in 1902 he developed the first flexible arch support to be inserted in factory-made shoes.

8. *Diesel jeans.* Diesel is an Italian design company, best known for its jeans. The company was founded in 1978 by Renzo Rosso, and is based in Molvena in northern Italy.

9. *Apple iPhone.* The iPhone was developed by Apple Inc., an American multinational corporation that designs and manufactures consumer electronics and software products. Apple was established as Apple Computer Inc. in Cupertino, California in 1976. Despite its American roots, many components of the iPhone are manufactured by companies in China.

10. *American Express credit card.* American Express, also known as Amex, is a diversified global financial services company that is headquartered in New York City. It was founded in Albany, New York, in 1850, as an express mail business. American Express, along with dozens of other banks, credit card companies, airlines, and computer manufacturers, has its telephone support staff located in India.

This shift to a global outlook has two significant dimensions. First, as members of a global community, people increasingly perceive that social responsibility does not stop at national borders but instead extends beyond them. There is a growing assumption that the international community has an obligation to act in crisis situations to protect the physical well-being or human rights of people whose lives are under threat. In the case of natural disasters, such interventions take the form of humanitarian relief and technical assistance. In recent years, earthquakes in Armenia, Turkey, and Haiti, floods in Mozambique, famine in Africa, hurricanes in Central America, and the tsunami that hit Asia and Africa have been rallying points for global assistance.

Second, a global outlook means that people are increasingly looking to sources other than the nation-state in formulating their own sense of identity. Local cultural identities in various parts of the world are experiencing powerful revivals at a time when the traditional hold of the nation-state is undergoing profound transformation. In Europe, for example, inhabitants of Scotland and the Basque region of Spain might be more likely to identify themselves as Scottish or Basque—or simply as Europeans—rather than as British or Spanish. The nation-state as a source of identity is waning in many areas as political shifts at the regional and global level loosen people's orientations toward the states in which they live.

TRANSNATIONAL CORPORATIONS

Among the many economic factors driving globalization, the role of transnational corporations is particularly important. **Transnational corporations** are companies that produce goods or market services in more than one country. These may be relatively small firms with one or two factories outside the country in which they are based, or gigantic international ventures whose operations crisscross the globe.

Transnational corporations account for two thirds of all world trade, they are instrumental in the diffusion of new technology around the globe, and they are major actors in international financial markets. As one observer has noted, they are "the linchpins of the contemporary world economy" (Held et al. 1999). Nearly 500

transnational corporations •
Business corporations located in two or more countries.

Transnational corporations such as Coca-Cola are eager to tap growing markets in countries like China and India. Corporate leaders break ground on a new plant in the Gansu province of China. The plant will be the twenty-fifth bottling plant Coca-Cola has opened in mainland China since it entered the market twenty-five years ago.

transnational corporations had annual sales of more than $15 billion in 2007, whereas only 110 countries (over half of all countries in the world) could boast gross domestic products (GDPs) of at least that amount; the world's leading transnational corporations are larger economically than most of the world's countries. Walmart, the world's largest corporation in terms of sales, had sales revenues that surpassed the GDPs of all but twenty-seven countries. Among the world's largest fifty economies, eight are transnational corporations.

The "electronic economy" is another factor that underpins economic globalization. Banks, corporations, fund managers, and individual investors are able to shift funds internationally with the click of a mouse. This new ability to move "electronic money" instantaneously carries with it great risks, however. Transfers of vast amounts of capital can destabilize economies, triggering international financial crises such as the ones that spread from the Asian "tiger economies" to Russia and beyond in 1998. As the global economy becomes increasingly integrated, a financial collapse in one part of the world can have an enormous effect on distant economies.

The political, economic, social, and technological factors described above are joining together to produce a phenomenon that lacks any earlier parallel in terms of its intensity and scope. The consequences of globalization are many and far-reaching, as we will see later in this chapter. But first we will turn our attention to the main views about globalization that have been expressed in recent years.

THE GLOBALIZATION DEBATE

In recent years, globalization has become a hotly debated topic. Most people accept that important transformations are occurring around us, but the extent to which it is valid to explain these as "globalization" is contested. As an unpredictable and turbulent process, globalization is seen and understood very differently by observers. David Held and his colleagues (1999) have surveyed the controversy and divided its participants into three schools of thought: *skeptics, hyperglobalizers*, and *transformationalists*. These three tendencies within the globalization debate are summarized in Table 16.2.

THE SKEPTICS

Some thinkers argue that the idea of globalization is overrated—that the debate over globalization is a lot of talk about something that is not new. The skeptics in the globalization controversy believe that present levels of economic interdependence are not unprecedented. Pointing to nineteenth-century statistics on world trade and investment, they contend that modern globalization differs from the past only in the intensity of interaction between nations.

The skeptics agree that there may now be more contact between countries than in previous eras, but in their eyes the current world economy is not sufficiently integrated to constitute a truly globalized economy. This is because the bulk of trade occurs within three regional groups—Europe, Asia-Pacific, and North America (Hirst 1997).

Many skeptics focus on processes of regionalization within the world economy such as the emergence of major financial and trading blocs. To skeptics, the growth of regionalization is evidence that the world economy has become less integrated rather than more (Boyer and Drache 1996; Hirst and Thompson 1999). Compared with the patterns of trade that prevailed a century ago, they argue, the world economy is less global in its geographical scope and more concentrated on intense pockets of activity.

Table 16.2 | Conceptualizing Globalization: Three Tendencies

CHARACTERISTIC	SKEPTICS	TRANSFORMATIONALISTS	HYPERGLOBALIZERS
What's new?	Trading blocs, weaker geogovernance than in earlier periods	Historically unprecedented levels of global interconnectedness	A global age
Dominant features	World less interdependent than in 1890s	"Thick" (intensive and extensive) globalization	Global capitalism, global governance, global civil society
Power of national governments	Reinforced or enhanced	Reconstituted, restructured	Declining or eroding
Driving forces of globalization	Governments and markets	Combined forces of modernity	Capitalism and technology
Pattern of stratification	Increased marginalization of global south	New architecture of world order	Erosion of old hierarchies
Dominant motif	National interest	Transformation of political community	McDonald's, Britney Spears, etc.
Conceptualization of globalization	As internationalization and regionalization	As the reordering of interregional relations and action at a distance	As a reordering of the framework of human action
Historical trajectory	Regional blocs/clash of civilizations	Indeterminate: global integration and fragmentation	Global civilization
Summary argument	Internationalization depends on government acquiescence and support	Globalization transforming government power and world politics	The end of the nation-state

Source: Adapted from Held et al. 1999

According to the skeptics, national governments continue to be key players because of their involvement in regulating and coordinating economic activity. For example, they are the driving force behind many trade agreements and policies of economic liberalization.

THE HYPERGLOBALIZERS

The hyperglobalizers take an opposing position to that of the skeptics. They argue that globalization is a very real phenomenon whose consequences can be felt almost everywhere. They see globalization as a process that is indifferent to national borders. It is producing a new global order, swept along by powerful flows of cross-border trade and production. One of the best-known popularizers of the idea of hyperglobalization is the Japanese writer Kenichi Ohmae (1990, 1995), who sees globalization as leading to a "borderless world"—a world in which market forces are more powerful than national governments. Another is journalist Thomas Friedman, whose pair of best-selling books—*The Lexus and the Olive Tree* (2000) and *The World Is Flat* (2005)—paint a picture of globalization as a juggernaut that sweeps up everything in its path, sometimes with unfortunate short-term results but ultimately with enormous benefit for everyone.

Much of the analysis of globalization offered by hyperglobalizers focuses on the changing role of the nation-state. It is argued that individual countries no longer control their economies because of the vast growth in world trade. Some hyperglobalizers believe that the power of national governments is also being challenged from above—by new regional and international institutions, such as the European Union. Taken together, these shifts signal to the hyperglobalizers the dawning of a global age (Albrow 1997) in which national governments decline in importance and influence.

Social scientists endorsing the "strong globalization" position include sociologists such as William Robinson (2001, 2004, 2005a, 2005b), Leslie Sklair (2002a, 2002b, 2003), and Saskia Sassen (1996, 2005). These scholars do not see themselves as hyperglobalists, yet they argue that transnational economic actors and political institutions are challenging the dominance of national ones. Robinson, one of the strongest proponents of this position, has studied these changes throughout the world, with special focus on Latin America. He argues that the most powerful economic actors on the world scene today are not bound by national boundaries; they are, instead, transnational in nature. For example, he argues that nation-states are being transformed into "component elements" of a transnational state—exemplified by the World Trade Organization, whose purpose is to serve the interests of global businesses as a whole by ensuring that individual countries adhere to the principles of free trade. Robinson (2001) concludes that "the nation-state is a historically-specific form of world social organization in the process of becoming transcended by globalization."

THE TRANSFORMATIONALISTS

The transformationalists take more of a middle position. Writers such as David Held (Held et al. 1999) and one of the authors of this textbook, Anthony Giddens (1990), see globalization as the central force behind a broad spectrum of changes that are currently shaping modern societies. In this view, the global order is being transformed, but many of the old patterns still remain. Governments, for instance, still retain a good deal of power in spite of the advance of global interdependence. These transformations are not restricted to economics alone, but are equally prominent within the realms of politics, culture, and personal life. Transformationalists contend that the current level of globalization is breaking down established boundaries between internal and external, international and domestic. In trying to adjust to this new order, societies, institutions, and individuals are being forced to navigate contexts where previous structures have been shaken up.

Unlike hyperglobalizers, transformationalists see globalization as a dynamic and open process that is subject to influence and change. Globalization is not a one-way process, as some claim, but a two-way flow of images, information, and influences. Global migration, media, and telecommunications are contributing to the diffusion of cultural influences. The world's vibrant "global cities" are thoroughly multicultural, with ethnic groups and cultures intersecting and living side by side. According to transformationalists, globalization is a decentered and self-aware process characterized by links and cultural flows that work in a multidirectional way. Because globalization is the product of numerous intertwined global networks, it cannot be seen as being driven from one particular part of the world.

Rather than losing sovereignty, as the hyperglobalizers argue, countries are seen by transformationalists as restructuring in response to new forms of economic and social organization that are nonterritorial in basis (e.g., corporations, social movements, and international bodies). They argue that we are no longer living in a state-centric world; governments are being forced to adopt a more active, outward-looking stance toward governance under the complex conditions of globalization (Rosenau 1997).

Whose view is most nearly correct? There are elements of truth in all three views, although the view of the transformationalists is perhaps the most balanced. The skeptics underestimate how far the world is changing; world finance markets, for example, are organized on a global level much more than they ever were before. Yet, at the same time, the world has undergone periods of intense globalization before, only to withdraw into periods in which countries sought to protect their markets and closed their borders to trade. While the march of globalization today often seems inevitable, it is by no means certain that it will continue unabated: Countries that find themselves losing out may attempt to stem the tide.

The hyperglobalizers are correct in pointing to the current strength of globalization as dissolving many national barriers, changing the nature of state power, and creating new and powerful transnational social classes. On the other hand, they often see globalization too much in economic terms and as too much of a one-way process. In reality, globalization is much more complex. National governments will neither dissolve under the weight of a globalized economy (as some hyperglobalizers argue) nor reassert themselves as the dominant political force (as some skeptics argue) but rather will seek to steer global capitalism to their own advantage. The world economy of the future may be much more globalized than today's, with multinational corporations and global institutions such as the World Trade Organization playing increasingly important roles. But some countries in the world economy may still be more powerful than even the most powerful transnational actors. ✓

CONCEPT CHECKS ✓

1. Compare and contrast how skeptics, hyperglobalizers, and transformationalists explain the phenomenon of globalization.

2. How might skeptics, hyperglobalizers, and transformationalists differently interpret the growing global prominence of China?

HOW DOES GLOBALIZATION AFFECT YOUR LIFE?

Although globalization is often associated with changes within big systems—such as the world financial markets, production and trade, and telecommunications—the effects of globalization are felt equally strongly in the private realm.

Globalization is fundamentally changing the nature of our everyday experiences. As societies undergo profound transformations, the established institutions that used to underpin them have become outmoded. This is forcing a redefinition of intimate and personal aspects of our lives, such as the family, gender roles, sexuality, personal identity, our interactions with others, and our relationships to work.

THE RISE OF INDIVIDUALISM

In our current age, individuals have much more opportunity to shape their own lives than once was the case. At one time, tradition and custom exercised a very strong influence on the path of people's lives. Factors such as social class, gender, ethnicity, and even religious affiliation could close off certain avenues for individuals or open up others. In times past, individuals' personal identities were formed in the context of the community into which they were born. The values, lifestyles, and ethics prevailing in that community provided relatively fixed guidelines according to which people lived their lives.

Under conditions of globalization, however, we are faced with a move toward a new individualism in which people have actively to construct their own identities. The weight of tradition and established values is diminishing as local communities interact with a new global order. We are constantly responding and adjusting to the changing environment around us; as individuals, we evolve with and within the larger context in which we live. Even the small choices we make in our daily lives—what we wear, how we spend our leisure time, and how we take care of our health—are part of an ongoing process of creating and recreating our self-identities.

WORK PATTERNS

Globalization has unleashed profound transformations within the world of work. New patterns of international trade and the move to a knowledge economy have had a significant impact on long-standing employment patterns. Many traditional industries have been made obsolete by new technological advances or are losing their share of the market to competitors abroad whose labor costs are lower than in industrialized countries. Global trade and new forms of technology have had a strong effect on traditional manufacturing communities, where industrial workers have been left unemployed and without the types of skills needed to enter the new knowledge-based economy. These communities are facing a new set of social problems, including long-term unemployment and rising crime rates, as a result of economic globalization.

If at one time people's working lives were dominated by employment with one employer over the course of several decades—the so-called job-for-life framework—today many more individuals create their own career paths, pursuing individual goals and exercising choice in attaining them. Often this involves changing jobs several times over the course of a career, building up new skills and abilities, and transferring them to diverse work contexts. Standard patterns of full-time work are being dissolved into more flexible arrangements: working from home with the help of information technology, job sharing, short-term consulting projects, flextime, and so forth (Beck 1992). While this affords new opportunities for some, for most it means far greater uncertainty. Job security—and the health and retirement benefits that went with it—have largely become things of the past.

Women have entered the workforce in large numbers, a fact that has strongly affected the personal lives of people of both sexes. Expanded professional and educational opportunities have led many women to delay marriage and children until after they have begun a career. These changes have also meant that many working women return to work shortly after having children, instead of remaining at home with young children as was once the case. These shifts have required important adjustments within families, in the nature of the domestic division of labor, in the role of men in child rearing, and with the emergence of more family-friendly working policies to accommodate the needs of dual-earner couples.

POPULAR CULTURE

The cultural impacts of globalization have received much attention. Images, ideas, goods, and styles are now disseminated around the world more rapidly than ever before.

Trade, new information technologies, the international media, and global migration have all contributed to the free movement of culture across national borders. Many people believe that we now live in a single information order—a massive global network where information is shared quickly and in great volumes. Films like *King Kong, Harry Potter and the Goblet of Fire*, and *Star Wars: Episode III—Revenge of the Sith* have enjoyed worldwide popularity. The film *Titanic*, the most popular film of all time, has grossed more than $1.8 billion in fifty-five countries since its release in 1997—two thirds of it outside of the United States. What can account for the enormous popularity of a film like *Titanic*? And what does its success tell us about globalization?

Sociologists argue that one reason for *Titanic*'s popularity is that it reflected a particular set of ideas and values that resonated with audiences worldwide. One of the film's central themes is the possibility of romantic love prevailing over class differences and family traditions. While such ideas are generally accepted in most Western countries, they are still taking hold in many other areas of the world. The success of a film like *Titanic* reflects the changing attitudes toward personal relationships and marriage, for example, in parts of the world where more traditional values have been favored. Yet *Titanic,* along with many other Western films, can also be said to *contribute* to this shift in values. Western-made films and television programs, which dominate the global media, tend to advance a set of political, social, and economic agendas that reflect a specifically Western worldview.

Some people worry that globalization is leading to the creation of a global culture in which the values of the most powerful and affluent—in this instance, Hollywood filmmakers—overwhelm the strength of local customs and tradition. According to this view, globalization is a form of cultural imperialism in which the values, styles, and outlooks of the Western world are being spread so aggressively that they smother individual national cultures.

Others, by contrast, claim that global society is now characterized by an enormous diversity of cultures existing side by side. Local traditions are joined by a host of additional cultural forms from abroad, presenting people with a bewildering array of lifestyle options from which to choose. Rather than a unified global culture, what we are witnessing is the fragmentation of cultural forms (Baudrillard 1988). Established identities and

A Chinese woman buys a ticket to see *Titanic* at a Beijing theater. *Titanic* is one of the most commercially successful films ever made.

ways of life grounded in local communities and cultures are giving way to new forms of hybrid identity composed of elements from contrasting cultural sources (Hall 1992).

GLOBALIZATION AND RISK

The consequences of globalization are far-reaching, affecting virtually all aspects of the social world. Yet because globalization is an open-ended and internally contradictory process, it produces outcomes that are difficult to predict and control. Another way of thinking of this dynamic is in terms of risk. Many of the changes wrought by globalization are presenting us with new forms of risk that differ greatly from those that existed in previous eras. Unlike risks from the past, which had established causes and known effects, today's risks are incalculable in origin and indeterminate in their consequences.

THE SPREAD OF "MANUFACTURED RISK"

Humans have always had to face risks of one kind or another, but today's risks are qualitatively different from those of earlier times. Until quite recently, human societies were threatened by **external risk**—dangers such as drought, earthquakes, famines, and storms that spring from the natural world and are unrelated to the actions of humans. Today, however, we are increasingly confronted with various types of **manufactured risk**—risks that are created by the impact of our own knowledge and technology on the natural world. As we shall see, many environmental and health risks facing contemporary societies are instances of manufactured risk—they are the outcomes of our own interventions into nature.

One of the clearest illustrations of manufactured risk can be found in threats currently posed by the natural environment (see Chapter 15). One of the consequences of accelerating industrial and technological development is that few aspects of the natural world remain untouched by humans. Urbanization, industrial production and pollution, large-scale agricultural projects, the construction of dams and hydroelectric plants, and nuclear power are just some of the ways in which human beings have had an impact on their natural surroundings. The collective outcome of such processes has been the creation of widespread environmental destruction whose precise cause is indeterminate and whose consequences are similarly difficult to calculate.

In our globalizing world, ecological risk confronts us in many guises. Concern over global warming has been mounting in the scientific community for some years. Most scientists now accept that the earth's temperature has been increasing due to a rising concentration of greenhouse gases—a byproduct of manmade processes such as deforestation and fossil fuel burning.

The potential consequences of global warming are devastating: If polar icecaps continue to melt at the current rate, sea levels will rise and may threaten low-lying land masses and their human populations. Changes in climate patterns have been cited as possible causes of the severe floods that afflicted Mozambique in 2000 and the record number of hurricanes (including the one that devastated New Orleans) that swept through the Atlantic and the Gulf of Mexico in the fall of 2005.

In the past decade, the dangers posed to human health by manufactured risks have attracted great attention. For example, in recent years, sun exposure has been linked to a heightened risk of skin cancer in many parts of the world. This is thought to be related to the depletion of the ozone layer—the layer of the earth's atmosphere that normally filters out ultraviolet light. Due to the high volume of chemical emissions

external risk • Dangers that spring from the natural world and are unrelated to the actions of humans. Examples of external risk include droughts, earthquakes, famines, and storms.

manufactured risk • Dangers that are created by the impact of human knowledge and technology on the natural world. Examples of manufactured risk include global warming and genetically modified foods.

A dairy farmer uses rBST (bovine growth hormone) to increase his herd's milk production.

that are produced by human activities and industry, the concentration of ozone in the atmosphere has been diminishing and, in some cases, ozone holes have opened up.

There are many examples of manufactured risk that are linked to food. For example, chemical pesticides and herbicides are widely used in commercial agriculture, and many animals (such as chickens and pigs) are pumped full of hormones and antibiotics. Some people have suggested that farming techniques such as these compromise food safety and could have an adverse effect on humans.

THE GLOBAL "RISK SOCIETY"

Manufactured risks have presented individuals with new choices and challenges in their everyday lives. Because there is no roadmap to these new dangers, individuals, countries, and transnational organizations must negotiate risks as they make choices about how lives are to be lived. The German sociologist Ulrich Beck sees these risks contributing to the formation of a global *risk society* (1992). As technological change progresses more and more rapidly and produces new forms of risk, we must constantly respond and adjust to these changes. The risk society, he argues, is not limited to environmental and health risks alone; it includes a whole series of interrelated changes within contemporary social life: shifting employment patterns, heightened job insecurity, the erosion of traditional family patterns, and the democratization of personal relationships. Because personal futures are much less fixed than they were in traditional societies, decisions of all kinds present risks for individuals. According to Beck, an important aspect of the risk society is that its hazards are not restricted spatially,

The Manufactured Risks of Electronic Viruses and World Climate Change

Globalization comes with many unfamiliar, manufactured risks. Among them are two that may have had a direct impact on you. On May 4, 2000, chaos engulfed the electronic world when a virus nicknamed the "Love Bug" succeeded in overloading computer systems worldwide. Launched from a personal computer in Manila, the capital of the Philippines, the "Love Bug" spread rapidly across the globe and forced almost a tenth of the world's e-mail servers to shut down. The virus was carried worldwide through an e-mail message with the subject heading "I Love You." When recipients opened the file that was attached to the message, they unknowingly activated the virus in their own computer. The "Love Bug" would then replicate itself and automatically send itself to all the e-mail addresses listed in the computerized address book, before attacking information and files stored on the computer's hard drive. The virus spread westward around the globe as employees, first in Asia, then in Europe and North America, arrived to work in the morning and checked their e-mail. By the end of day, the "Love Bug" was estimated to have caused more than $1.5 billion of damage worldwide.

The "Love Bug" was a particularly fast-spreading virus, but it was not the first of its kind. Electronic viruses have become more common—and more dangerous—as computers and electronic forms of communication have grown in importance and sophistication. Viruses such as the "Love Bug" demonstrate how interconnected the world has become with the advance of globalization. You might think that in this particular instance global interconnectedness proved to be quite a disadvantage, since a harmful virus was able to spread so rapidly around the globe. Yet many positive aspects of globalization are reflected in this case as well. As soon as the virus was detected, computer and security experts from around

temporally, or socially (1995). Today's risks affect all countries and all social classes; they have global, not merely personal, consequences.

GLOBALIZATION AND INEQUALITY

Beck and other scholars have drawn attention to risk as one of the main outcomes of globalization and technological advance. New forms of risk present complex challenges for both individuals and whole societies that are forced to navigate through unknown terrain. Yet globalization is generating other important challenges as well.

Globalization is proceeding in an uneven way. The impact of globalization is experienced differentially, and some of its consequences are far from benign. Next to mounting

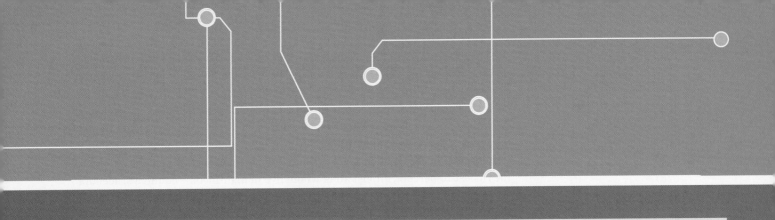

the world worked together to prevent its spread, protect national computer systems, and share intelligence about the virus's origins.

Another aspect of manufactured risk, and one you likely have noticed—or been directly affected by—is the unusual weather in recent years. Scientists and disaster experts have pointed out that extreme weather events—such as unseasonably hot temperatures, droughts, floods, and cyclones—have been occurring

with increasing frequency. In 1998 alone, for example, eighty separate natural catastrophes were recorded at points around the globe, including devastating floods in China, hurricanes in Latin America, wildfires in Indonesia, and severe ice storms in North America. Since that time, drought has gripped regions as diverse as Ethiopia, southern Afghanistan, and the midwestern United States; floods have ravaged Venezuela and Mozambique; violent windstorms have battered parts of Europe; and a plague of locusts has swarmed through the Australian outback.

Although no one can be certain, many people believe that these natural disasters are caused in part by *global warming* (the heating up of the earth's atmosphere). If carbon dioxide emissions that contribute to global warming continue unchecked, it seems likely that the earth's climate will be irreversibly harmed. Who is to blame for global warming, and what can be done to slow its progress? As with so many aspects of our changing world, the risks associated with global warming are experienced worldwide, yet its precise causes are nearly impossible to pinpoint. In an age of globalization, we are constantly reminded of our interdependence with others: The actions of individuals or institutions in one part of the world can, and do, have significant consequences for people everywhere.

ecological problems, the expansion of inequalities within and between societies is one of the most serious challenges facing the world at the start of the twenty-first century.

INEQUALITY AND GLOBAL DIVISIONS

As we learned in our discussions of types of societies (Chapter 2) and of global inequality (Chapter 8), the vast majority of the world's wealth is concentrated in the industrialized or developed countries of the world, whereas the nations of the developing world suffer from widespread poverty, overpopulation, inadequate educational and health care systems, and crippling foreign debt. The disparity between the developed and the developing world widened steadily over the course of the twentieth century and is now the largest it has ever been.

The 1999 Human Development Report, published by the United Nations, revealed that the average income of the fifth of the world's population living in the richest countries was 74 times greater than the average income of the fifth living in the poorest. The poorest 20 percent of the world's population account for 1.5 percent of the world's income. The combined income of the world's richest 500 people is greater than that of the poorest 416 million. The poorest 40 percent of the world's population, who live on less than $2 a day, account for 5 percent of global income, whereas the richest 10 percent, almost all of whom live in high-income countries, account for 54 percent of global income (UNDP 2006). The United Nations estimates that if wealthy countries were to stop growing and poor countries were to continue growing at their current rate, it would take over two hundred years for the poorest to catch up (UNDP 2005).

In much of the developing world, levels of economic growth and output over the past century have not kept up with the rate of population growth, whereas the level of economic development in industrialized countries has far outpaced it. These opposing tendencies have led to a marked divergence between the richest and poorest countries of the world. The world's richest country had a GDP approximately three times that of the poorest country in 1820, 11 times as wealthy in 1913, 35 in 1950, 72 in 1992, and 173 times as wealthy in 2001 (see Figure 16.1). The figure for 2008 using GNI per capita (ATLAS Method) is 622 to 1 (World Bank 2009d). Over the past century, among the richest quarter of the world's population, per capita income has increased almost sixfold, while among the poorest quarter, the increase has been less than threefold.

Globalization is exacerbating these trends by further concentrating income, wealth, and resources within a small core of countries. As we have seen in this chapter, the global economy is growing and integrating at an extremely rapid rate. The expansion of global trade has been central to this process. The volume of merchandise exports and imports in 2008 exceeded $30 trillion or 51 percent of total global output, up from 44 percent in 1980 (Monthly Bulletin of Statistics 2009; World Bank 2008c). Only a handful of developing countries have managed to benefit from that rapid growth, and the process of integration into the global economy has been uneven. Some countries—such as the East Asian economies, Chile, India, and Poland—have fared well, with growth in exports of over 5 percent. Other countries—such as Russia, Venezuela, and Algeria—have seen few benefits from expanding trade and globalization (UNDP 1999). Findings from the World Bank support this picture: Among ninety-three nations in the developing world, only twenty-three can be said to be "rapid integrators." There is a danger that many of the countries most in need of economic growth will be left even further behind as globalization progresses (World Bank 2000).

Free trade is seen by many as the key to economic development and poverty relief. Organizations such as the World Trade Organization (WTO) work to liberalize trade regulations and to reduce barriers to trade between the countries of the world. Free trade across borders is viewed as a win-win proposition for both developed and developing countries alike. While the industrialized economies are able to export their products to markets around the world, it is claimed that developing countries will also benefit by gaining access to world markets. This, in turn, is supposed to improve their prospects for integration into the global economy.

THE CAMPAIGN FOR GLOBAL JUSTICE

Not everyone agrees that free trade is the solution to poverty and global inequality. In fact, many critics argue that free trade is a rather one-sided affair that benefits those

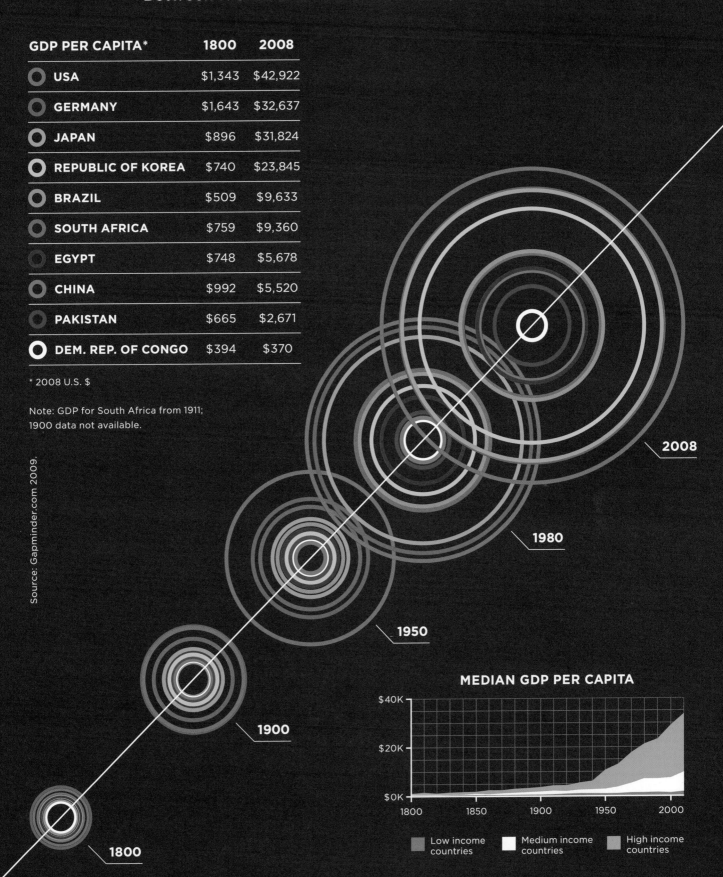

Figure 16.3

THE WIDENING GAP

Between Richer and Poorer Countries, 1800 to 2008

GDP PER CAPITA*	1800	2008
USA	$1,343	$42,922
GERMANY	$1,643	$32,637
JAPAN	$896	$31,824
REPUBLIC OF KOREA	$740	$23,845
BRAZIL	$509	$9,633
SOUTH AFRICA	$759	$9,360
EGYPT	$748	$5,678
CHINA	$992	$5,520
PAKISTAN	$665	$2,671
DEM. REP. OF CONGO	$394	$370

* 2008 U.S. $

Note: GDP for South Africa from 1911;
1900 data not available.

Source: Gapminder.com 2009.

2008

1980

1950

1900

1800

MEDIAN GDP PER CAPITA

$40K

$20K

$0K

1800   1850   1900   1950   2000

Low income countries   Medium income countries   High income countries who are already well off and exacerbates existing patterns of poverty and dependency within the developing world. Recently, much of this criticism has focused on the activities and policies of the World Trade Organization (WTO), which is at the forefront of efforts to increase global trade.

In December 1999, more than fifty thousand people from around the world took to the streets of Seattle to protest during the WTO's "Millennium Round" of trade talks. Negotiators from the WTO's 134 member states (the number of members has since risen to 153) had come together to discuss and agree on measures to liberalize conditions for global trade and investment in agriculture and forest products, among other issues. Yet the talks broke off early with no agreements reached. The trade unionists, environmentalists, human rights activists, farmers, and representatives from hundreds of NGOs were triumphant—not only had the demonstrations succeeded in disrupting the talks, but internal disputes among delegates had also risen to the surface. The Seattle protests were heralded as the biggest victory to date for campaigners for "global justice." Since that time, every ministerial meeting of the WTO has been met by massive demonstrations by those excluded from the processes of setting the rules for global trade.

But what is this campaign about, and does it represent the emergence of a powerful antiglobalization movement, as some commentators have suggested? In the months following the Seattle protests, similar demonstrations were held in other cities around the world, such as London and Washington, DC. These events were much smaller than those that took place in Seattle, but they were organized around similar themes. Protesters argued that free trade and economic globalization succeed in further concentrating wealth in the hands of a few, while increasing poverty for the majority of the world's population. Most of these activists agree that global trade is necessary and potentially beneficial for national economies, but they claim that it needs to be regulated by different rules from those favored by the WTO. They argue that trade rules should be oriented, first and foremost, to protecting human rights, the environment, labor rights, and local economies—not to ensuring larger profits for already rich corporations.

The protesters claim that the WTO is an undemocratic organization that is dominated by the interests of the world's richest nations—particularly the United States. Such imbalances have very real consequences. For example, although the WTO has insisted that developing nations open their markets to imports from industrialized countries, it has allowed developed countries to maintain high barriers to agricultural imports and provide vast subsidies for their domestic agriculture production in order to protect their own agricultural sectors. Between 1995 and 2006, the United States government spent $177 billion to subsidize the income of crop and livestock farmers (Environmental Working Group 2008). This has meant that the world's poorest countries, many of which remain predominantly agricultural, do not have access to the large markets for agricultural goods in developed countries.

Protesters against the WTO and other international financial institutions such as the World Bank and the International Monetary Fund argue that exuberance over global economic integration and free trade is forcing people to live in an economy rather than a society. Many are convinced that such moves will further weaken the economic position of poor societies by allowing transnational corporations to operate with few or no safety and environmental

CONCEPT CHECKS

1. How has technology facilitated the compression of time and space?

2. What are the three causes of increasing globalization?

3. What effects does globalization have on our everyday lives?

4. Why is globalization associated with new forms of risks? What are they?

regulations. Commercial interests, they claim, are increasingly taking precedence over concern for human well-being. Not only within developing nations but in industrialized ones as well, there needs to be more investment in "human capital"—public health, education, and training—if global divisions are not to deepen even further. The key challenge for the twenty-first century is to ensure that globalization works for people everywhere, not only for those who are already well placed to benefit from it. ✓

NEED HELP STUDYING?

 wwnorton.com/studyspace

Visit StudySpace to access free review materials such as:

- Vocabulary Flashcards
- Diagnostic Review Quizzes
- Study Outlines

REVIEW QUESTIONS

1. What is social change? What do sociologists hope to learn by studying it?
2. What are the five factors that lead to societal collapse, according to Jared Diamond?
3. What are three ways that political organization shapes social change?
4. What is the idea of postmodernity as it relates to history? What is the critique of this argument?
5. Describe three political changes that have contributed to increasing globalization.
6. How has the spread of information technology challenged ideas about the nation-state?
7. Describe the transformationalist perspective on globalization.
8. How is globalization challenging traditional frameworks of identity?
9. What is the difference between external and manufactured risk? Which poses a greater threat?
10. What is the goal of the World Trade Organization (WTO)? What do critics have to say about it, according to the text?

THINKING SOCIOLOGICALLY EXERCISES

1. Discuss the many influences on social change: environmental, political, and cultural factors. Summarize how each element can contribute to social change.
2. According to this chapter, we now live in a society where we are increasingly confronted by various types of manufactured risks. Briefly explain what these risks consist of. Do you think the last decade has brought us any closer to or further away from confronting the challenges of manufactured risks? Explain.

glossary

Words in **bold** type within entries refer to terms found elsewhere in the glossary.

absolute poverty: The minimal requirements necessary to sustain a healthy existence.

activity theory: A functionalist theory of aging which holds that busy, engaged people are more likely to lead fulfilling and productive lives.

age-grades: The system found in small traditional cultures by which people belonging to a similar age group are categorized together and hold similar rights and obligations.

ageism: Discrimination or prejudice against a person on the grounds of age.

agents of socialization: Groups or social contexts within which processes of socialization take place.

aging: The combination of biological, psychological, and social processes that affect people as they grow older.

agrarian societies: Societies whose means of subsistence are based on agricultural production (crop growing).

alienation: The sense that our own abilities as human beings are taken over by other entities. The term was originally used by Karl Marx to refer to the projection of human powers onto gods. Subsequently he used the term to refer to the loss of workers' control over the nature and products of their labor.

anomie: A concept first brought into wide usage in sociology by Durkheim, referring to a situation in which social norms lose their hold over individual behavior.

assimilation: The acceptance of a minority group by a majority population, in which the new group takes on the values and norms of the dominant culture.

authority: A government's legitimate use of power.

automation: Production processes monitored and controlled by machines with only minimal supervision from people.

biomedical model of health: The set of principles underpinning Western medical systems and practices. The biomedical model of health defines diseases objectively, in accordance with the presence of recognized symptoms, and holds that the healthy body can be restored through scientifically based medical treatment. The human body is likened to a machine that can be returned to working order with the proper repairs.

black feminism: A strand of feminist theory that highlights the multiple disadvantages of gender, class, and race that shape the experiences of nonwhite women. Black feminists reject the idea of a single, unified gender oppression that is experienced evenly by all women and argue that early feminist analysis reflected the specific concerns of white, middle-class women.

bureaucracy: A type of organization marked by a clear hierarchy of authority and the existence of written rules of procedure and staffed by full-time, salaried officials.

capitalism: An economic system based on the private ownership of wealth, which is invested and reinvested in order to produce profit.

capitalists: People who own companies, land, or stocks (shares) and use these to generate economic returns.

caste society: A society in which different social levels are closed, so that all individuals must remain at the social level of their birth throughout life.

caste system: A social system in which one's social status is given for life.

church: A large, established religious body, normally having a formal, bureaucratic structure and a hierarchy of religious officials. The term is also used to refer to the place in which religious ceremonies are carried out.

citizen: A member of a political community, having both rights and duties associated with that membership.

civil inattention: The process whereby individuals in the same physical setting demonstrate to one another that they are aware of each other's presence.

civil rights: Legal rights held by all citizens in a given national community.

civil society: The realm of activity that lies between the state and the market, including the family, schools, community associations, and other noneconomic institutions. Civil society, or civic culture, is essential to vibrant democratic societies.

class: Although it is one of the most frequently used concepts in sociology, there is no clear agreement about how the notion should be defined. Most sociologists use the term to refer to socioeconomic variations between groups of individuals that create variations in their material prosperity and power.

clock time: Time as measured by the clock, in terms of hours, minutes, and seconds. Before the invention of clocks, time reckoning was based on events in the natural world, such as the rising and setting of the sun.

cognition: Human thought processes involving perception, reasoning, and remembering.

cohabitation: Two people living together in a sexual relationship of some permanence, without being married to one another.

colonialism: The process whereby Western nations established their rule in parts of the world away from their home territories.

communism: A set of political ideas associated with Marx, as developed particularly by Lenin and institutionalized in the Soviet Union, Eastern Europe, and some Third World countries.

community policing: A renewed emphasis on crime prevention rather than law enforcement to reintegrate policing within the community.

comparable worth: Policies that attempt to remedy the gender pay gap by adjusting pay so that those in female-dominated jobs are not paid less for equivalent work.

comparative questions: Questions concerned with drawing comparisons between different human societies for the purposes of sociological theory or research.

comparative research: Research that compares one set of findings on one society with the same type of findings on other societies.

complementary and alternative medicine (CAM): A diverse set of approaches and therapies for treating illness and promoting well-being that generally falls outside of standard medical practices.

compulsion of proximity: People's need to interact with others in their presence.

concrete operational stage: A stage of human cognitive development, as formulated by Jean Piaget, in which the child's thinking is based primarily on physical perception of the world. In this phase, the child is not yet capable of dealing with abstract concepts or hypothetical situations.

conflict theory: Argument that deviance is deliberately chosen and often political in nature.

conflict theories of aging: Arguments that emphasize the ways in which the larger social structure helps to shape the opportunities available to the elderly. Unequal opportunities are seen as creating the potential for conflict.

constitutional monarchs: Kings or queens who are largely figureheads. Real power rests in the hands of other political leaders.

control theory: A theory that views crime as the outcome of an imbalance between impulses toward criminal activity and controls that deter it. Control theorists hold that criminals are rational beings who will act to maximize their own reward unless they are rendered unable to do so through either social or physical controls.

conurbation: An agglomeration of towns or cities into an unbroken urban environment.

conversational analysis: The empirical study of conversations, employing techniques drawn from ethnomethodology. Conversation analysis examines details of naturally occurring conversations to reveal the organizational principles of talk and its role in the production and reproduction of social order.

core countries: According to world-systems theory, the most advanced industrial countries, which take the lion's share of profits in the world economic system.

corporate crime: Offenses committed by large corporations in society. Examples of corporate crime include pollution, false advertising, and violations of health and safety regulations.

corporate culture: An organizational culture involving rituals, events, or traditions that are unique to a specific company.

corporations: Business firms or companies.

correlation coefficient: A measure of the degree of correlation between variables.

created environment: Constructions established by human beings to serve their needs, derived from the use of man-made technology—including, for example, roads, railways, factories, offices, private homes, and other buildings.

crime: Any action that contravenes the laws established by a political authority. Although we may think of criminals as a distinct subsection of the population, there are few people who have not broken the law in one way or another during their lives. While laws are formulated by state authorities, it is not unknown for those authorities to engage in criminal behavior in certain situations.

crude birthrate: A statistical measure representing the number of births within a given population per year, normally calculated as the number of births per thousand members. Although the crude birthrate is a useful index, it is only a general measure, because it does not specify numbers of births in relation to age distribution.

crude death rate: A statistical measure representing the number of deaths that occur annually in a given population per year, normally calculated as the number of deaths per thousand members. Crude death rates give a general indication of the mortality levels of a community or society, but are limited in their usefulness because they do not take into account the age distribution.

cult: A fragmentary religious grouping to which individuals are loosely affiliated, but which lacks any permanent structure.

cultural relativism: The practice of judging a society by its own standards.

cultural universals: Values or modes of behavior shared by all human cultures.

culture: The values, norms, and material goods characteristic of a given group. Like the concept of society, the notion of culture is widely used in sociology and the other social sciences (particularly anthropology). Culture is one of the most distinctive properties of human social association.

culture of poverty: The thesis, popularized by Oscar Lewis, that poverty is not a result of individual inadequacies but is instead the outcome of a larger social and cultural atmosphere into which successive generations of children are socialized. The culture of poverty refers to the values, beliefs, lifestyles, habits, and traditions that are common among people living under conditions of material deprivation.

data: Factual information used as a basis for reasoning, discussion, or calculation. Social science data often refers to individuals' responses to survey questions.

debriefing: Following a research study, the investigator will inform study participants about the true purpose of the study, and will reveal any deception that happened during the study.

degree of dispersal: The range or distribution of a set of figures.

democracy: A political system that allows the citizens to participate in political decision making or to elect representatives to government bodies.

democratic elitism: A theory of the limits of democracy, which holds that in large-scale societies democratic participation is necessarily limited to the regular election of political leaders.

demographic transition: An interpretation of population change, which holds that a stable ratio of births to deaths is achieved once a certain level of economic prosperity has been reached. According to this notion, in preindustrial societies there is a rough balance between births and deaths, because population increase is kept in check by a lack of available food, by disease, or by war. In modern societies, by contrast, population equilibrium is achieved because families are moved by economic incentives to limit the number of children.

demography: The study of the size, distribution, and composition of populations.

denomination: A religious sect that has lost its revivalist dynamism and become an institutionalized body, commanding the adherence of significant numbers of people.

dependency culture: A term popularized by Charles Murray to describe individuals who rely on state welfare provision rather than entering the labor market. The dependency culture is seen as the outcome of the "paternalistic" welfare state that undermines individual ambition and people's capacity for self-help.

dependency ratio: The ratio of people of dependent ages (children and the elderly) to people of economically active ages.

dependency theories: Marxist theories of economic development arguing that the poverty of low-income countries stems directly from their exploitation by wealthy countries and the multinational corporations that are based in wealthy countries.

developing world: The less-developed societies, in which industrial production is either virtually nonexistent or only developed to a limited degree. The majority of the world's population live in less-developed countries.

developmental questions: Questions that sociologists pose when looking at the origins and path of development of social institutions from the past to the present.

deviance: Modes of action that do not conform to the norms or values held by most members of a group or society. What is regarded as deviant is as variable as the norms and values that distinguish different cultures and subcultures from one another. Forms of behavior that are highly esteemed by one group are regarded negatively by others.

deviant subculture: A subculture whose members hold values that differ substantially from those of the majority.

diaspora: The dispersal of an ethnic population from an original homeland into foreign areas, often in a forced manner or under traumatic circumstances.

differential association: An interpretation of the development of criminal behavior proposed by Edwin H. Sutherland, according to whom criminal behavior is learned through association with others who regularly engage in crime.

direct democracy: A form of participatory democracy that allows citizens to vote directly on laws and policies.

discrimination: Behavior that denies the members of a particular group resources or rewards that can be obtained by others. Discrimination must be distinguished from prejudice: Individuals who are prejudiced against others may not engage in discriminatory practices against them; conversely, people may act in a discriminatory fashion toward a group even though they are not prejudiced against that group.

disengagement theory: A functionalist theory of aging that holds that it is functional for society to remove people from their traditional roles when they become elderly, thereby freeing up those roles for others.

displacement: The transferring of ideas or emotions from their true source to another object.

division of labor: The specialization of work tasks, by means of which different occupations are combined within a production system. All societies have at least some rudimentary form of division of labor, especially between the tasks allocated to men and those performed by women. With the development of industrialism, the division of labor became vastly more complex than in

any prior type of production system. In the modern world, the division of labor is international in scope.

dominant group: The opposite of a minority group; the dominant group possesses more wealth, power, and prestige in a society.

doubling time: The time it takes for a particular level of population to double.

downward mobility: Social mobility in which individuals' wealth, income, or status is lower than what they or their parents once had.

dyad: A group consisting of two persons.

ecological approach: A perspective on urban analysis emphasizing the "natural" distribution of city neighborhoods into areas having contrasting characteristics.

economic interdependence: The fact that in the division of labor, individuals depend on others to produce many or most of the goods they need to sustain their lives.

economy: The system of production and exchange that provides for the material needs of individuals living in a given society. Economic institutions are of key importance in all social orders. What goes on in the economy usually influences other areas in social life. Modern economies differ substantially from traditional ones, because the majority of the population is no longer engaged in agricultural production.

egocentric: According to Jean Piaget, the characteristic quality of a child during the early years of her life. Egocentric thinking involves understanding objects and events in the environment solely in terms of the child's own position.

emigration: The movement of people out of one country in order to settle in another.

empirical investigation: Factual inquiry carried out in any area of sociological study.

encounter: A meeting between two or more people in a situation of face-to-face interaction. Our daily lives can be seen as a series of different encounters strung out across the course of the day. In modern societies, many of these encounters are with strangers rather than people we know.

endogamy: The forbidding of marriage or sexual relations outside one's social group.

entrepreneur: The owner/founder of a business firm.

environmental ecology: A concern with preserving the integrity of the physical

environment in the face of the impact of modern industry and technology.

ethnicity: Cultural values and norms that distinguish the members of a given group from others. An ethnic group is one whose members share a distinct awareness of a common cultural identity, separating them from other groups. In virtually all societies, ethnic differences are associated with variations in power and material wealth. Where ethnic differences are also racial, such divisions are sometimes especially pronounced.

ethnocentrism: The tendency to look at other cultures through the eyes of one's own culture, and thereby misrepresent them.

ethnography: The firsthand study of people using participant observation or interviewing.

ethnomethodology: The study of how people make sense of what others say and do in the course of day-to-day social interaction. Ethnomethodology is concerned with the "ethnomethods" by which people sustain meaningful interchanges with one another

experiment: A research method in which variables can be analyzed in a controlled and systematic way, either in an artificial situation constructed by the researcher or in naturally occurring settings.

exponential growth: A geometric, rather than linear, rate of increase. Populations tend to grow exponentially.

extended family: A family group consisting of more than two generations of relatives.

external risk: Dangers that spring from the natural world and are unrelated to the actions of humans. Examples of external risk include droughts, earthquakes, famines, and storms.

factual questions: Questions that raise issues concerning matters of fact (rather than theoretical or moral issues).

family: A group of individuals related to one another by blood ties, marriage, or adoption, who form an economic unit, the adult members of which are responsible for the upbringing of children. All known societies involve some form of family system, although the nature of family relationships varies widely. While in modern societies the main family form is the nuclear family, extended family relationships are also found.

family capitalism: Capitalistic enterprise owned and administered by entrepreneurial families.

family of orientation: The family into which an individual is born or adopted.

family of procreation: The family an individual initiates through marriage or by having children.

fecundity: A measure of the number of children that it is biologically possible for a woman to produce.

feminism: Advocacy of the rights of women to be equal with men in all spheres of life. Feminism dates from the late eighteenth century in Europe, and feminist movements exist in most countries today.

feminist theory: A sociological perspective that emphasizes the centrality of gender in analyzing the social world and particularly the experiences of women. There are many strands of feminist theory, but they all share the intention to explain gender inequalities in society and to work to overcome them.

feminization of poverty: An increase in the proportion of the poor who are female.

fertility: The average number of live-born children produced by women of childbearing age in a particular society.

focused interaction: Interaction between individuals engaged in a common activity or in direct conversation with one another.

formal operational stage: According to Jean Piaget, a stage of human cognitive development at which the growing child becomes capable of handling abstract concepts and hypothetical situations.

formal organization: Means by which a group is rationally designed to achieve its objectives, often using explicit rules, regulations, and procedures.

formal relations: Relations that exist in groups and organizations, laid down by the norms, or rules, of the official system of authority.

functionalism: A theoretical perspective based on the notion that social events can best be explained in terms of the functions they perform—that is, the contributions they make to the continuity of a society.

gender: Social expectations about behavior regarded as appropriate for the members of each sex. Gender refers not to the physical attributes distinguishing men and women but to socially formed traits of masculinity and femininity. The study of gender relations has become one of the most important areas of sociology in recent years.

gender inequality: The inequality between men and women in terms of wealth, income, and status.

gender socialization: The learning of gender roles through social factors such as schooling, the media, and family.

gender typing: Designation of occupations as male or female, with "women's" occupations, such as secretarial and retail positions, having lower status and pay, and men's occupations, such as managerial and professional positions, having higher status and pay.

generalized other: A concept in the theory of George Herbert Mead, according to which the individual takes over the general values of a given group or society during the socialization process.

genocide: The systematic, planned destruction of a racial, political, or cultural group.

gentrification: A process of urban renewal in which older, deteriorated housing is refurbished by affluent people moving into the area.

glass ceiling: A promotion barrier that prevents a woman's upward mobility within an organization.

glass escalator: The process by which men in traditionally female professions benefit from an unfair rapid rise within an organization.

global city: A city—such as London, New York, or Tokyo—that has become an organizing center of the new global economy.

global commodity chain: A worldwide network of labor and production processes yielding a finished product.

global inequality: The systematic differences in wealth and power between countries.

globalization: The development of social and economic relationships stretching worldwide. In current times, we are all influenced by organizations and social networks located thousands of miles away. A key part of the study of globalization is the emergence of a world system—for some purposes, we need to regard the world as forming a single social order.

government: The enacting of policies and decisions on the part of officials within a political apparatus. We can speak of government as a process, or the government as the officialdom responsible for making binding political decisions. While in the past virtually all governments were headed by monarchs or emperors, in most modern societies governments are run by officials who do not inherit their positions of power but are elected or appointed on the basis of qualifications.

groupthink: A process by which the members of a group ignore ways of thinking and plans of action that go against the group consensus.

hidden curriculum: Traits of behavior or attitudes that are learned at school but not included within the formal curriculum—for example, gender differences.

homeless: People who have no place to sleep and either stay in free shelters or sleep in public places not meant for habitation.

homophobia: An irrational fear or disdain of homosexuals.

housework: Unpaid work carried on in the home, usually by women; domestic chores such as cooking, cleaning, and shopping. Also called domestic labor.

human resource management: A style of management that regards a company's workforce as vital to its economic competitiveness.

hypothesis: An idea or a guess about a given state of affairs, put forward as a basis for empirical testing.

ideal type: A "pure type," constructed by emphasizing certain traits of a social item that do not necessarily exist in reality. An example is Max Weber's ideal type of bureaucratic organization.

ideology: Shared ideas or beliefs that serve to justify the interests of dominant groups. Ideologies are found in all societies in which there are systematic and ingrained inequalities between groups. The concept of ideology connects closely with that of power, since ideological systems serve to legitimize the power that groups hold.

immigration: The movement of people into one country from another for the purpose of settlement.

impression management: Preparing for the presentation of one's social role.

income: Payment, usually derived from wages, salaries, or investments.

industrialization: The emergence of machine production, based on the use of inanimate power resources (such as steam or electricity).

industrialized societies: Highly developed nation-states in which the majority of the population work in factories or offices rather than in agriculture, and most people live in urban areas.

infant mortality rate: The number of infants who die during the first year of life, per thousand live births.

informal economy: Economic transactions carried on outside the sphere of orthodox paid employment.

informal networks: Relations that exist in groups and organizations developed on the basis of personal connections; ways of doing things that depart from formally recognized modes of procedure.

information society: A society no longer based primarily on the production of material goods but on the production of knowledge. The notion of the information society is closely bound up with the rise of information technology.

information technology: Forms of technology based on information processing and requiring microelectronic circuitry.

informed consent: The process whereby the study investigator informs potential participants about the risks and benefits involved in the research study. Informed consent must be obtained before an individual participates in a study.

in-group: A group toward which one feels particular loyalty and respect—the group to which "we" belong.

inner city: The areas composing the central neighborhoods of a city, as distinct from the suburbs. In many modern urban settings in the First World, inner-city areas are subject to dilapidation and decay, the more affluent residents having moved to outlying areas.

instinct: A fixed pattern of behavior that has genetic origins and that appears in all normal animals within a given species.

institutional capitalism: Capitalistic enterprise organized on the basis of institutional shareholding.

institutional racism: Patterns of discrimination based on ethnicity that have become structured into existing social institutions.

intelligence: Level of intellectual ability, particularly as measured by IQ (intelligence quotient) tests.

IQ (intelligence quotient): A score attained on tests of symbolic or reasoning abilities.

interest group: A group organized to pursue specific interests in the political arena, operating primarily by lobbying the members of legislative bodies.

intragenerational mobility: Movement up or down a social stratification hierarchy within the course of a personal career.

intergenerational mobility: Movement up or down a social stratification hierarchy from one generation to another.

interactional vandalism: The deliberate subversion of the tacit rules of conversation.

iron law of oligarchy: A term coined by Weber's student Robert Michels meaning that large organizations tend toward centralization of power, making democracy difficult.

kinship: A relation that links individuals through blood ties, marriage, or adoption. Kinship relations are by definition part of marriage and the family, but extend much more broadly. While in most modern societies few social obligations are involved in kinship relations extending beyond the immediate family, in other cultures kinship is of vital importance to social life.

knowledge economy: A society no longer based primarily on the production of material goods but based instead on the production of knowledge. Its emergence has been linked to the development of a broad base of consumers who are technologically literate and have made new advances in computing, entertainment, and telecommunications part of their lives.

knowledge society: Another common term for information society—a society based on the production and consumption of knowledge and information.

labeling theory: An approach to the study of deviance that suggests that people become "deviant" because certain labels are attached to their behavior by political authorities and others.

language: The primary vehicle of meaning and communication in a society, language is a system of symbols that represent objects and abstract thoughts.

latent functions: Functional consequences that are not intended or recognized by the members of a social system in which they occur.

law: A rule of behavior established by a political authority and backed by state power.

leader: A person who is able to influence the behavior of other members of a group.

liberal democracies: Systems of democracy based on parliamentary institutions, coupled to the free-market system in the area of economic production.

liberal feminism: Form of feminist theory that believes that gender inequality is produced by unequal access to civil rights and certain social resources, such as education and employment, based on sex. Liberal feminists tend to seek solutions through changes in legislation that ensure that the rights of individuals are protected.

liberation theology: An activist Catholic religious movement that combines Catholic beliefs with a passion for social justice for the poor.

life chances: A term introduced by Max Weber to signify a person's opportunities for achieving economic prosperity.

life course: The various transitions and stages people experience during their lives.

life expectancy: The number of years the average person can expect to live.

life span: The maximum length of life that is biologically possible for a member of a given species.

linguistic relativity hypothesis: A hypothesis, based on the theories of Edward Sapir and Benjamin Lee Whorf, that perceptions are relative to language.

local nationalisms: The beliefs that communities that share a cultural identity should have political autonomy, even within smaller units of a nation-state.

lower class: A social class comprised of those who work part time or not at all and whose household income is typically low.

macrosociology: The study of large-scale groups, organizations, or social systems.

Malthusianism: A doctrine about population dynamics developed by Thomas Malthus, according to which population increase comes up against "natural limits," represented by famine and war.

managerial capitalism: Capitalistic enterprises administered by managerial executives rather than by owners.

manifest functions: The functions of a particular social activity that are known to and intended by the individuals involved in the activity.

manufactured risk: Dangers that are created by the impact of human knowledge and technology on the natural world. Examples of manufactured risk include global warming and genetically modified foods.

market-oriented theories: Theories about economic development that assume that the best possible economic consequences will result if individuals are free to make their own economic decisions, uninhibited by governmental constraint.

marriage: A socially approved sexual relationship between two individuals. Marriage almost always involves two persons of opposite sexes, but in some cultures, types of homosexual marriage are tolerated. Marriage normally forms the basis of a family of procreation—that is, it is expected that the married couple will produce and bring up children. Some societies permit polygamy, in which an individual may have several spouses at the same time.

Marxism: A body of thought deriving its main elements from Karl Marx's ideas.

material goods: The physical objects that a society creates; these influence the ways in which people live.

materialist conception of history: The view developed by Marx, according to which material, or economic, factors have a prime role in determining historical change.

matrilocal family: A family system in which the husband is expected to live near the wife's parents.

mean: A statistical measure of central tendency, or average, based on dividing a total by the number of individual cases.

means of production: The means whereby the production of material goods is carried on in a society, including not just technology but the social relations between producers.

measures of central tendency: The ways of calculating averages.

median: The number that falls halfway in a range of numbers—a way of calculating central tendency that is sometimes more useful than calculating a mean.

Medicare: A program under the U.S. Social Security Administration that reimburses hospitals and physicians for medical care provided to qualifying people over sixty-five years old.

megalopolis: The "city of all cities" in ancient Greece—used in modern times to refer to very large conurbations.

melting pot: The idea that ethnic differences can be combined to create new patterns of behavior drawing on diverse cultural sources.

microsociology: The study of human behavior in contexts of face-to-face interaction.

middle class: A social class composed broadly of those working in white-collar and lower managerial occupations.

minority group: A group of people who are in a minority in a given society and who, because of their distinct physical or cultural characteristics, find themselves in situations of inequality within that society. Also known as *ethnic minority*.

mode: The number that appears most often in a given set of data. This can sometimes be a helpful way of portraying central tendency.

modernization theory: A version of market-oriented development theory that argues that low-income societies develop economically only if they give up their traditional ways and adopt modern economic institutions, technologies, and cultural values that emphasize savings and productive investment.

monogamy: A form of marriage in which each married partner is allowed only one spouse at any given time.

monopoly: A situation in which a single firm dominates in a given industry.

mortality: The number of deaths in a population.

multiculturalism: The viewpoint according to which ethnic groups can exist separately and share equally in economic and political life.

multinational corporations: Business corporations located in two or more countries.

nationalism: A set of beliefs and symbols expressing identification with a national community.

nation-state: A particular type of state, characteristic of the modern world, in which a government has sovereign power within a defined territorial area, and the population are citizens who know themselves to be part of a single nation. Nation-states are closely associated with the rise of nationalism, although nationalist loyalties do not always conform to the boundaries of specific states. Nation-states developed as part of an emerging nation-state system, originating in Europe; in current times, they span the whole globe.

neoliberalism: The economic belief that free market forces, achieved by minimizing government restrictions on business, provide the only route to economic growth.

network: A set of informal and formal social ties that links people to each other.

new criminology: A branch of criminological thought, prominent in Great Britain in the 1970s, that regarded deviance as deliberately chosen and often political in nature. The new criminologists argued that crime and deviance could only be understood in the context of power and inequality within society.

newly industrializing economies (NIEs): Developing countries that over the past two or three decades have begun to develop a strong industrial base, such as Singapore and Hong Kong.

new-style terrorism: A recent form of terrorism characterized by global ambitions, loose global organizational ties, and a more ruthless attitude toward the violence the terrorists are willing to use.

nonverbal communication: Communication between individuals based on facial expression or bodily gestures rather than on language.

norms: Rules of conduct that specify appropriate behavior in a given range of social situations. A norm either prescribes a given type of behavior or forbids it. All human groups follow definite norms, which are always backed by sanctions of one kind or another—varying from informal disapproval to physical punishment.

nuclear family: A family group consisting of an adult or adult couple and their dependent children.

obesity: Excessive body weight indicated by a body mass index (BMI) over 30.

occupation: Any form of paid employment in which an individual regularly works.

oldest old: Sociological term for persons aged eighty-five and older.

old old: Sociological term for persons aged seventy-five to eighty-four.

old-style terrorism: A type of terrorism that is local and linked to particular states and has limited objectives, which means that the violence involved is fairly limited.

oligarchy: Rule by a small minority within an organization or society.

oligopoly: The domination of a small number of firms in a given industry.

oral history: Interviews with people about events they witnessed or experienced at some point earlier in their lives.

organic solidarity: According to Émile Durkheim, the social cohesion that results from the various parts of a society functioning as an integrated whole.

organization: A large group of individuals with a definite set of authority relations. Many types of organizations exist in industrialized societies, influencing most aspects of our lives. While not all organizations are bureaucratic, there are close links between the development of organizations and bureaucratic tendencies.

organized crime: Criminal activities carried out by organizations established as businesses.

out-group: A group toward which one feels antagonism and contempt—"those people."

pariah groups: Groups who suffer from negative status discrimination—they are looked down on by most other members of society. The Jews, for example, have been a pariah group throughout much of European history.

participant observation: A method of research widely used in sociology and anthropology, in which the researcher takes part in the activities of the group or community being studied. Also called *fieldwork*.

participatory democracy: A system of democracy in which all members of a group or community participate collectively in making major decisions.

pastoral societies: Societies whose subsistence derives from the rearing of domesticated animals.

patriarchy: The dominance of men over women. All known societies are patriarchal, although there are variations in the degree and nature of the power men exercise, as compared with women. One of the prime objectives of women's movements in modern societies is to combat existing patriarchal institutions.

patrilocal family: A family system in which the wife is expected to live near the husband's parents.

peer group: A friendship group composed of individuals of similar age and social status.

peripheral countries: Countries that have a marginal role in the world economy and are thus dependent on the core producing societies for their trading relationships.

personality stabilization: According to the theory of functionalism, the family plays a crucial role in assisting its adult members emotionally. Marriage between adult men and women is the arrangement through which adult personalities are supported and kept healthy.

personal space: The physical space individuals maintain between themselves and others.

pilot study: A trial run in survey research.

pluralism: A model for ethnic relations in which all ethnic groups in a society retain their independent and separate identities, yet share equally in the rights and powers of citizenship.

pluralist theories of modern democracy: Theories that emphasize the role of diverse and potentially competing interest groups, none of which dominate the political process.

political rights: Rights of political participation, such as the right to vote in local and national elections, held by citizens of a national community.

politics: The means by which power is employed to influence the nature and content of governmental activities. The sphere of the political includes the activities of those in government, but also the actions of others. There are many ways in which people outside the governmental apparatus seek to influence it.

polyandry: A form of marriage in which a woman may have two or more husbands simultaneously.

polygamy: A form of marriage in which a person may have two or more spouses simultaneously.

polygyny: A form of marriage in which a man may have two or more wives simultaneously.

postindustrial society: A postindustrial society is based on the production of information rather than material goods. According to postindustrialists, we are currently experiencing a series of social changes as profound as those that initiated the industrial era some two hundred years ago.

postmodernism: The belief that society is no longer governed by history or progress. Postmodern society is highly pluralistic and diverse, with no "grand narrative" guiding its development.

poverty line: An official government measure to define those living in poverty in the United States.

power: The ability of individuals or the members of a group to achieve aims or further the interests they hold. Power is a pervasive element in all human relationships. Many conflicts in society are struggles over power, because how much power an individual or group is able to achieve governs how far they are able to put their wishes into practice.

power elite: Small networks of individuals who, according to C. Wright Mills, hold concentrated power in modern societies.

prejudice: The holding of preconceived ideas about an individual or group, ideas that are resistant to change even in the face of new information. Prejudice may be either positive or negative.

preoperational stage: According to Jean Piaget, a stage of human cognitive development, in which the child has advanced sufficiently to master basic modes of logical thought.

primary deviance: According to Edwin Lemert, the actions that cause others to label one as a deviant.

primary group: A group that is characterized by intense emotional ties, face-to-face interaction, intimacy, and a strong, enduring sense of commitment.

primary socialization: The process by which children learn the cultural norms of the society into which they are born. Primary socialization occurs largely in the family.

profane: That which belongs to the mundane, everyday world.

psychopath: A specific personality type; such individuals lack the moral sense and concern for others held by most normal people.

race: Differences in human physical characteristics used to categorize large numbers of individuals.

racialization: The process by which understandings of race are used to classify individuals or groups of people. Racial

distinctions are more than ways of describing human differences; they are also important factors in the reproduction of patterns of power and inequality.

racism: The attribution of characteristics of superiority or inferiority to a population sharing certain physically inherited characteristics. Racism is a form of prejudice focusing on physical variations between people. Racist attitudes became entrenched during the period of Western colonial expansion, but also rest on mechanisms of prejudice and discrimination found in human societies today.

radical feminism: Form of feminist theory that believes that gender inequality is the result of male domination in all aspects of social and economic life.

random sampling: Sampling method in which a sample is chosen so that every member of the population has the same probability of being included.

rape: The forcing of nonconsensual vaginal, oral, or anal intercourse.

reference group: A group that provides a standard for judging one's attitudes or behaviors.

regionalization: The division of social life into different regional settings or zones.

relative poverty: Poverty defined according to the living standards of the majority in any given society.

religion: A set of beliefs adhered to by the members of a community, incorporating symbols regarded with a sense of awe or wonder together with ritual practices. Religions do not universally involve a belief in supernatural entities.

religious economy: A theoretical framework within the sociology of religion, which argues that religions can be fruitfully understood as organizations in competition with one another for followers.

religious nationalism: The linking of strongly held religious convictions with beliefs about a people's social and political destiny.

representative sample: A sample from a larger population that is statistically typical of that population.

response cries: Seemingly involuntary exclamations individuals make when, for example, being taken by surprise, dropping something inadvertently, or expressing pleasure.

sacred: Describing something that inspires awe or reverence among those who believe in a given set of religious ideas.

sample: A small proportion of a larger population.

sampling: Studying a proportion of individuals or cases from a larger population as representative of that population as a whole.

sanction: A mode of reward or punishment that reinforces socially expected forms of behavior.

scapegoat: An individual or group blamed for wrongs that were not of their doing.

science: The disciplined marshaling of empirical data, combined with theoretical approaches and theories that illuminate or explain those data. Scientific activity combines the creation of new modes of thought with the careful testing of hypotheses and ideas. One major feature that helps distinguish science from other idea systems (such as religion) is the assumption that all scientific ideas are open to criticism and revision.

secondary deviance: According to Edwin Lemert, following the act of primary deviance, secondary deviance occurs when an individual accepts the label of deviant and acts accordingly.

sect: A religious movement that breaks away from orthodoxy.

secondary group: A group characterized by its large size and by impersonal, fleeting relationships.

secularization: A process of decline in the influence of religion. Although modern societies have become increasingly secularized, tracing the extent of secularization is a complex matter. Secularization can refer to levels of involvement with religious organizations (such as rates of church attendance), the social and material influence wielded by religious organizations, and the degree to which people hold religious beliefs.

secular thinking: Worldly thinking, particularly as seen in the rise of science, technology, and rational thought in general.

segregation: The practices of keeping racial and ethnic groups physically separate, thereby maintaining the superior position of the dominant group.

self-consciousness: Awareness of one's distinct social identity as a person separate from others. Human beings are not born with self-consciousness but acquire an awareness of self as a result of early socialization. The learning of language is of vital importance to the processes by which the child learns to become a self-conscious being.

self-identity: The ongoing process of self-development and definition of our personal identity through which we formulate a unique sense of ourselves and our relationship to the world around us.

semiotics: The study of the ways in which linguistic and nonlinguistic phenomena can generate meaning.

semiperipheral countries: Countries that supply sources of labor and raw materials to the core industrial countries and the world economy but are not themselves fully industrialized societies.

sensorimotor stage: According to Jean Piaget, a stage of human cognitive development in which the child's awareness of its environment is dominated by perception and touch.

service society: A concept related to postindustrial society, it refers to a social order distinguished by the growth of service occupations at the expense of industrial jobs that produce material goods.

sex: The biological and anatomical differences distinguishing females from males.

sexual harassment: The making of unwanted sexual advances by one individual toward another, in which the first person persists even though it is clear that the other party is resistant.

shaming: A way of punishing criminal and deviant behavior based on rituals of public disapproval rather than incarceration. The goal of shaming is to maintain the ties of the offender to the community.

short-range downward mobility: Social mobility that occurs when an individual moves from one position in the class structure to another of nearly equal status.

sick role: A term associated with the functionalist Talcott Parsons to describe the patterns of behavior that a sick person adopts in order to minimize the disruptive impact of his or her illness on others.

signifier: Any vehicle of meaning and communication.

slavery: A form of social stratification in which some people are owned by others as their property.

social aggregate: A collection of people who happen to be together in a particular place but do not significantly interact or identify with one another.

social capital: The social knowledge and connections that enable people to accomplish their goals and extend their influence.

social category: People who share a common characteristic (such as gender or occupation) but do not necessarily interact or identify with one another.

social change: Alteration in basic structures of a social group or society. Social change is an ever-present phenomenon in social life, but has become especially intense in the modern era. The origins of modern sociology can be traced to attempts to understand the dramatic

changes shattering the traditional world and promoting new forms of social order.

social constraint: The conditioning influence on our behavior of the groups and societies of which we are members. Social constraint was regarded by Émile Durkheim as one of the distinctive properties of social facts.

social construction of gender: The learning of gender roles through socialization and interaction with others.

social exclusion: The outcome of multiple deprivations that prevent individuals or groups from participating fully in the economic, social, and political life of the society in which they live.

social facts: According to Émile Durkheim, the aspects of social life that shape our actions as individuals. Durkheim believed that social facts could be studied scientifically.

social gerontologists: Those who study aging and the elderly.

social group: A collection of people who regularly interact with one another on the basis of shared expectations concerning behavior and who share a sense of common identity.

social interaction: The process by which we act and react to those around us.

socialization: The social processes through which we develop an awareness of social norms and values and achieve a distinct sense of self. Although socialization processes are particularly significant in infancy and childhood, they continue to some degree throughout life. None of us are immune from the reactions of others around us, which influence and modify our behavior at all phases of our life course.

social mobility: Movement of individuals or groups between different social positions.

social position: The social identity an individual has in a given group or society. Social positions may be general in nature (those associated with gender roles) or may be more specific (occupational positions).

social reproduction: The process whereby societies have structural continuity over time. Social reproduction is an important pathway through which parents transmit or produce values, norms, and social practices among their children.

social rights: Rights of social and welfare provision held by all citizens in a national community, including, for example, the right to claim unemployment benefits and sickness payments provided by the state.

social role: The expected behavior of a person occupying a particular social position. The idea of social role originally comes from the theater, referring to the parts that actors play in a stage production. In every society, individuals play a number of social roles.

social roles: Socially defined expectations of an individual in a given status, or social position.

Social Security: A government program that provides economic assistance to persons faced with unemployment, disability, or old age.

social self: The basis of self-consciousness in human individuals, according to the theory of G. H. Mead. The social self is the identity conferred upon an individual by the reactions of others. A person achieves self-consciousness by becoming aware of this social identity.

social stratification: The existence of structured inequalities between groups in society, in terms of their access to material or symbolic rewards. While all societies involve some forms of stratification, only with the development of state-based systems did wide differences in wealth and power arise. The most distinctive form of stratification in modern societies is class divisions.

socialization of nature: The process by which we control phenomena regarded as "natural," such as reproduction.

society: A group of people who live in a particular territory, are subject to a common system of political authority, and are aware of having a distinct identity from other groups. Some societies, like hunting and gathering societies, are small, numbering no more than a few dozen people. Others are large, numbering millions—modern Chinese society, for instance, has a population of more than a billion people.

sociobiology: An approach that attempts to explain the behavior of both animals and human beings in terms of biological principles.

sociological imagination: The application of imaginative thought to the asking and answering of sociological questions. Someone using the sociological imagination "thinks himself away" from the familiar routines of daily life.

sociology: The study of human groups and societies, giving particular emphasis to analysis of the industrialized world. Sociology is one of a group of social sciences, which include anthropology, economics, political science, and human geography. The divisions between the various social sciences are not clear-cut, and all share a certain range of common interests, concepts, and methods.

sociology of the body: Field that focuses on how our bodies are affected by social influences. Health and illness, for instance, are determined by social and cultural influences.

sovereignty: The undisputed political rule of a state over a given territorial area.

standard deviation: A way of calculating the spread of a group of figures.

state: A political apparatus (government institutions plus civil service officials) ruling over a given territorial order, whose authority is backed by law and the ability to use force. The emergence of the state marked a distinctive transition in human history, because the centralization of political power involved in state formation introduced new dynamics into processes of social change.

state-centered theories: Development theories that argue that appropriate government policies do not interfere with economic development, but rather can play a key role in bringing it about.

status: The social honor or prestige that a particular group is accorded by other members of a society. Status groups normally display distinct styles of life—patterns of behavior that the members of a group follow. Status privilege may be positive or negative. Pariah status groups are regarded with disdain or treated as outcasts by the majority of the population.

stepfamily: A family in which at least one partner has children from a previous marriage, living either in the home or nearby.

stereotype: A fixed and inflexible category.

stigma: Any physical or social characteristic that is labeled by society as undesirable.

strike: A temporary stoppage of work by a group of employees in order to express a grievance or enforce a demand.

structuration: The two-way process by which we shape our social world through our individual actions and by which we are reshaped by society.

subculture: Values and norms distinct from those of the majority, held by a group within a wider society.

suburbanization: The development of suburbia, areas of housing outside inner cities.

suffragettes: Members of early women's movements who pressed for equal voting rights for women and men.

surplus value: The value of a worker's labor power, in Marxist theory, left over when an employer has repaid the cost of hiring the worker.

survey: A method of sociological research in which questionnaires are administered to the population being studied.

sustainable development: The notion that economic growth should proceed only insofar as natural resources are recycled rather than depleted; biodiversity is maintained; and clean air, water, and land are protected.

symbol: One item used to stand for or represent another—as in the case of a flag, which symbolizes a nation.

symbolic interactionism: A theoretical approach in sociology developed by George Herbert Mead, which emphasizes the role of symbols and language as core elements of all human interaction.

target hardening: Practical measures used to limit a criminal's ability to commit crime, such as community policing and use of house alarms.

technology: The application of knowledge of the material world to production; the creation of material instruments (such as machines) used in human interaction with nature.

terrorism: Use of attacks on civilians designed to persuade a government to alter its policies, or to damage its standing in the world.

theoretical questions: Questions posed by sociologists when seeking to explain a particular range of observed events. The asking of theoretical questions is crucial to allowing us to generalize about the nature of social life.

theism: A belief in one or more supernatural deities.

time-space: When and where events occur.

tracking: Dividing students into groups according to ability.

transactional leader: A leader who is concerned with accomplishing the group's tasks, getting group members to do their jobs, and making certain that the group achieves its goals.

transformational leader: A leader who is able to instill in the members of a group a sense of mission or higher purpose, thereby changing the nature of the group itself.

transnational corporations: Business corporations located in two or more countries.

triad: A group consisting of three persons.

triangulation: The use of multiple research methods as a way of producing more reliable empirical data than is available from any single method.

underclass: A class of individuals situated at the bottom of the class system, normally composed of people from ethnic minority backgrounds.

unfocused interaction: Interaction occurring among people present in a particular setting but not engaged in direct face-to-face communication.

Uniform Crime Reports (UCR): Documents that contain official data on crime that is reported to law enforcement agencies who then provide the data to the FBI.

upper class: A social class broadly composed of the more affluent members of society, especially those who have inherited wealth, own businesses, or hold large numbers of stocks (shares).

urban ecology: An approach to the study of urban life based on an analogy with the adjustment of plants and organisms to the physical environment. According to ecological theorists, the various neighborhoods and zones within cities are formed as a result of natural processes of adjustment on the part of populations as they compete for resources.

urbanism: A term used by Louis Wirth to denote distinctive characteristics of urban social life, such as its impersonal or alienating nature.

urbanization: The development of towns and cities.

urban renewal: The process of renovating deteriorating neighborhoods by encouraging the renewal of old buildings and the construction of new ones.

values: Ideas held by individuals or groups about what is desirable, proper, good, and bad. What individuals value is strongly influenced by the specific culture in which they happen to live.

wealth: Money and material possessions held by an individual or group.

welfare capitalism: Practice in which large corporations protect their employees from the vicissitudes of the market.

welfare state: A political system that provides a wide range of welfare benefits for its citizens.

white-collar crime: Criminal activities carried out by those in white-collar, or professional, jobs.

work: The activity by which people produce from the natural world and so ensure their survival. Work should not be thought of exclusively as paid employment. In traditional cultures, there was only a rudimentary monetary system, and few people worked for money. In modern societies, there remain types of work that do not involve direct payment (e.g., housework).

working class: A social class broadly composed of people working in blue-collar, or manual, occupations.

working poor: People who work, but whose earnings are not enough to lift them above the poverty line.

world-systems theory: Pioneered by Immanuel Wallerstein, this theory emphasizes the interconnections among countries based on the expansion of a capitalist world economy. This economy is made up of core countries, semiperipheral countries, and peripheral countries.

young old: Sociological term for persons aged sixty-five to seventy-four.

bibliography

ABC News/Washington Post Poll. (2006). Which punishment do you prefer for people convicted of murder: the death penalty or life in prison with no chance of parole? Retrieved fall 2007, from http://www.pollingreport.com/crime.htm

Abeles and Riley. (1987). Longevity, social structure, and cognitive aging in Carmi Schooler and K. Warner Schaie, eds., *Cognitive Functioning and Social Structure over the Life Course*. Norwood, NJ: Ablex.

Accad, E. (1991). Contradictions for contemporary women in the Middle East, in Chandra Talpade Mohanty, Ann Russo, and Lourdes Torres, eds., *Third World Women and the Politics of Feminism*. Bloomington: Indiana University Press.

Achen and Stafford. (2005). *Data Quality of Housework Hours in the Panel Study of Income Dynamics: Who Really Does the Dishes*. Panel Study of Income Dynamics report. http://psidonline.isr.umich.edu/Publications/Papers/achenproxyreports04.pdf, accessed December 10, 2010.

AIDS Orphans Educational Trust. (2003). *AIDS Orphans Educational Trust–Uganda*. www.orphanseducation.org, accessed 12/28/04.

Albrow, M. (1997). *The Global Age: State and Society beyond Modernity*. Stanford, CA: Stanford University Press.

Aldrich and Marsden. (1988). *Environments and organizations, in Neil J. Smelser, ed., Handbook of Sociology*. Newbury Park, CA: Sage.

Allen, M. P. (1981). *Managerial power and tenure in the large corporation*. Social Forces, vol. 60.

Altman and Oppel. (2008, January 10). W.H.O. says Iraq civilian death toll higher than cited. *New York Times*. www.nytimes.com/2008/01/10/world/middleeast/10casualties.html?_r=1&oref=slogin, accessed fall 2008.

Alvarez, et al. (1996). Women in the professions: Assessing progress, in Paula J. Dubeck and Kathryn Borman, eds., *Women and Work: A Handbook*. New York: Garland.

Amato, et al. (1995). Parental divorce, marital conflict, and offspring well-being during early Adulthood. *Social Forces*, 73: 895–915.

American Association for the Advancement of Retired People (AARP). (1997). "Report of Social Security Advisory Council." www.aarp.org/focus/ssecure/part2/advisory.htm, accessed 11/24/03.

American Association of University Women (AAUW). (1992). How Schools Shortchange Girls. Washington, DC: American Association of University Women Educational Foundation.

American Council on Education, (ACE). (2001). The American Freshman: National Norms for Fall 2000. Los Angeles, California: UCLA Higher Education Research Institute and ACE. Results also published in "This year's freshmen at 4-year colleges: Their opinions, activities, and goals." Chronicle of Higher Education, January 26.

American Psychiatric Association. (2000). Diagnostic and statistical manual of mental disorders (4th ed., Text rev.). Washington, DC: American Psychiatric Association.

American Religious Identification Survey ARIS. (2008). Part 1A: Belonging. http://b27.cc.trincoll.edu/weblogs/AmericanReligionSurvey-ARIS/reports/p1a_belong.html, accessed August 2009.

Amin, S. (1974). *Accumulation on a World Scale*. New York: Monthly Review Press.

Ammons and Markham. (2004). Working at home: Experiences of skilled white collar workers, *Sociological Spectrum*, 24(2): 191–238.

Amsden, A. H. (1989). *Asia's Next Giant: South Korea and Late Industrialization*. New York: Oxford University Press.

Amsden, Kochanowicz and Taylor. (1994). *The Market Meets Its Match: Restructuring the Economies of Eastern Europe*. Cambridge, MA: Harvard University Press.

Anderson, B. (1991). *Imagined Communities: Reflections on the Origin and Spread of Nationalism*. Rev. ed. New York: Routledge.

Anderson, E. (1990). *Streetwise: Race, Class, and Change in an Urban Community*. Chicago: University of Chicago Press.

Angell and Kassirer. (1998). *Alternative medicine—the risks of untested and unregulated remedies*. New England Journal of Medicine, 339, 839.

Angier, N. (1995). If you're really ancient, you may be better off. *New York Times*, June 11.

Anzaldua, G. (1990). *Making Face, Making Soul: Haciendo Caras: Creative and Cultural Perspectives by Feminists of Color*. San Francisco: Aunt Lute Foundation.

Appadurai, A. (1986). *Introduction: commodities and the politics of value*, in A. Appadurai, ed., The Social Life of Things. Cambridge: Cambridge University Press.

Appelbaum, R. P. (1990). *Counting the homeless*, in J. A. Momeni, ed., Homeless in the United States, vol. 2. New York: Praeger.

Appelbaum and Christerson. (1997). Cheap labor strategies and export-oriented industrialization: Some lessons from the East Asia/Los Angeles apparel connection. *International Journal of Urban and Regional Research*, vol. 21, no. 2.

Appelbaum and Henderson, eds. (1992). States and Development in the Asian Pacific Rim. Newbury Park, CA: Sage.

Apple Inc. (2007a). *100 Million iPods Sold*. Press release. http://www.apple.com/pr/library/2007/04/09ipod.html, accessed 12/23/07.

Apple, Inc. (2007b). *Unaudited Second Quarter 2007 Summary Data*. http://images.apple.com/pr/pdf/q207data_sum.pdf, accessed 12/23/07.

Ariès, P. (1965). *Centuries of Childhood*. New York: Random House.

Asch, S. (1952). *Social Psychology*. Englewood Cliffs, NJ: Prentice-Hall.

Ashworth, A. E. (1980). *Trench Warfare: 1914–1918*. London: Macmillan.

Atchley, R. C. (2000). *Social Forces and Aging: An Introduction to Social Gerontology*. 9th ed. Belmont, CA: Wadsworth.

Attaran, M. (2004). Exploring the relationship between information technology and business process reengineering, *Information & Management*, 41(5): 585–596.

Avery and Canner. (2005). New information reported under HMDA and its application in fair lending enforcement. *Federal Reserve Bulletin*. Summer 2005. www.federalreserve.gov/pubs/bulletin/2005/3-05hmda.pdf, accessed spring 2006.

Avins, M. (2003). MoveOn redefines party politics, *Los Angeles Times*. December 9, p. A-1.

Bailey, J. M. (1993). Heritable factors influence sexual orientation in women. *Archives of General Psychiatry*, vol. 50.

Bailey and Pillard. (1991). A genetic study of male sexual orientation. *Archives of General Psychiatry*, vol. 48.

Bales, K. (1999). *Disposable People: New Slavery in the Global Economy*. Berkeley, CA: University of California Press.

Bales, R. F. (1953). *The egalitarian problem in small groups*, in Talcott Parsons, ed., Working Papers in the Theory of Action. Glencoe, IL: Free Press.

Bales, R. F. (1970). Personality and Interpersonal Behavior. New York: Holt, Rinehart, and Winston.

Baltic 21 Secretariat. (2006). *Passenger Car Density*. www.baltic21.org/reports/indicators/re08.atm, accessed spring 2009.

Bamberger, B. J. (1992). *Judaism*. In the American Academic Encyclopedia (online edition). Danbury, CT: Grolier Electronic.

Barcelona Field Studies Centre. (2003). *Sao Paulo Growth and Management*. www.geographyfieldwork.com/SaoPauloManagement.htm, accessed 12/28/04.

Barras, C. (2009, May 1). *Unknown Internet 3: How Big is the Net?* New Scientist. http://newscientist.com/data/images/archive/2706/27062201.jpg

David B. (2006). *Literacy: An Introduction to the Ecology of Written Language*. 2nd ed Blackwell.

Basu, A., ed. (1995). *The Challenge of Local Feminisms: Women's Movements in Global Perspective*. Boulder, CO: Westview.

Baudrillard, J. (1988). *Jean Baudrillard: Selected Writings*. Stanford, CA: Stanford University Press.

Bean, et al. (1994). *Illegal Mexican Migration and the U.S./Mexico Border*. Washington, DC: U.S. Commission on Immigration Reform.

Beck, U. (1992). *Risk Society*. London: Sage. 1995. Ecological Politics in an Age of Risk. Cambridge, UK: Polity Press.

Becker, H. S. (1963). *Outsiders: Studies in the Sociology of Deviance*. New York: Macmillan.

Bell, Weinberg, and Hammersmith. (1981). *Sexual Preference: Its Development in Men and Women*. Bloomington: Indiana University Press.

Bell, D. (1976). *The Coming of Post-Industrial Society: A Venture in Social Forecasting*. New York: Basic Books.

Bellah, Madsen, Sullivan, Swidler, and Tipton. (1985). *Habits of the Heart: Individualism and Commitment in American Life*. New York: Harper & Row.

Bem, S. L. (1974). The Measurement of Psychological Androgyny, *Journal of Consulting and Clinical Psychology* 42: 155–62.

Bennett, J. W. (1976). *The Ecological Transition: Cultural Anthropology and Human Adaptation*. New York: Pergamon Press.

Berger, P. L. (1967). *The Sacred Canopy: Elements of a Sociological Theory of Religion*. Garden City, NY: Anchor Books.

Berger, P. L. (1986). *The Capitalist Revolution: Fifty Propositions about Prosperity, Equality, and Liberty*. New York: Basic Books.

Berger and Hsiao. (1988). *In Search of an East Asian Development Model*. New Brunswick, NJ: Transaction.

Berle and Means. (1982; orig. 1932). *The Modern Corporation and Private Property*. Buffalo, NY: Heim.

Bernstein and Mishel. (1997). Has Wage Inequality Stopped Growing? *Monthly Labor Review* (December): 3–16.

Berryman, P. (1987). *Liberation Theology: Essential Facts About the Revolutionary Movement in Central America and Beyond*. Philadelphia: Temple University Press.

Bertram, et al. (1996). *Drug War Politics*. Berkeley, CA: University of California Press.

Beyer, P. (1994). *Religion and Globalization*. Thousand Oaks, California: Sage.

Beyerstein, B. L. (1999, Fall/Winter). Psychology and "'alternative medicine": social and judgmental biases that make inert treatments seem to work. The Scientific Review of Alternative Medicine, 3(2).

Birren and Bengston, eds. (1988). *Emerging Theories of Aging*. New York: Springer.

Bittle, Rochkind, and Ott. (2009). *The Energy Learning Curve: A Report for the Public Agenda*. San Francisco, CA: Public Agenda. http://www.publicagenda.org/pages/energy-index-2009-topline, accessed June 15, 2009.

Black Americans in Congress (2009). Black-American Representatives and Senators by Congress, 1870–Present, 111th Congress. http://baic.house.gov/historical-data/representatives-senators-by-congress.html?congress=111, accessed July 2009.

Blanchard and Bogaert. (1996). Homosexuality in men and number of older brothers. *American Journal of Psychiatry*, vol. 153.

Blau, Duncan, and Dudley. (1967). *The American Occupational Structure*. New York: Wiley.

Blauner, R. (1964). *Alienation and Freedom*. Chicago: University of Chicago Press.

Blauner, R. (1972). Racial Oppression in America. New York: Harper and Row.

Blondet, C. (1995). *Out of the kitchen and onto the streets: Women's activism in Peru*, in Amrita Basu, ed., The Challenge of Local Feminisms. Boulder, CO: Westview.

Blum, L. M. (1991). *Between Feminism and Labor: The Significance of the Comparable Worth Movement*. Berkeley, CA: University of California Press.

Bobak, L. (1996). India's Tiny Slaves, *Ottawa Sun*, October 23.

Bochenek and Brown. (2001). *Hatred in the Hallways: Violence and Discrimination against Lesbian, Gay, Bisexual, and Transgender Students in U.S. Schools*. New York: Human Rights Watch, www.hrw.org/reports/2001/uslgbt/toc.htm, accessed 12/28/04.

Boden and Molotch. (1994). *The compulsion of proximity*, in Deirdre Boden and Roger Friedland, eds., Nowhere: Space, Time, and Modernity. Berkeley, CA: University of California Press.

Bogardus, E. (1967). *A Forty-Year Racial Distance Study*. Los Angeles: University of Southern California.

Bonacich and Appelbaum. (2000). *Behind the Label: Inequality in the Los Angeles Garment Industry*. Berkeley, CA: University of California Press.

Booth, A. (1977). Food riots in the northwest of England, 1770–1801. *Past and Present*, no. 77.

Bositis, D. (2001). Black Elected Officials. Joint Center for Political and Economic Studies. www.jointcenter.org/publications1/publication-PDFs/BEO-pdfs/2001-BEO.pdf, accessed 1/27/06.

Bosse, et al. (1987). Mental health differences among retirees and workers: Findings from the normative aging study. *Psychology and Aging*, vol. 2.

Bouma et al. (2004). Conference on Human Factors in Computing Systems. CHI '04 extended abstracts on Human factors in computing systems. New York: ACM Press.

Bourdieu, P. (1984). *Distinction: A Social Critique of Judgement of Taste*. Cambridge, MA: Harvard University Press.

Bourdieu, P. (1988). *Language and Symbolic Power*. Cambridge, UK: Polity Press.

Bourdieu, P. (1990). *The Logic of Practice*. Palo Alto, CA: Stanford University Press.

Bowles and Gintis. (1976). *Schooling in Capitalist America*. New York: Basic Books.

Boyer and Drache, eds. (1996). *States against Markets: The Limits of Globalization*. New York: Routledge.

Bradsher and David. (2007): Hong Kong and Shanghai vie to be China's financial centre, *International Herald Tribune*, 15 January.

Braithwaite, J. (1996). *Crime, shame, and reintegration*, in P. Cordella and L. Siegal, eds., Readings in Contemporary Criminological Theory. Boston: Northeastern University Press.

Bramlett and Mosher. (2002). Cohabitation, marriage, divorce, and remarriage in the United States. *Vital Health Stat* vol. 23, no. 22. Washington, DC: National Center for Health Statistics. www.cdc.gov/nchs/data/series/sr_23/sr23_022.pdf, accessed 1/9/07.

Brass, D. J. (1985). Men's and women's networks: A study of interaction patterns and influence in an organization. *Academy of Management Journal*, vol. 28.

Braverman, H. (1974). *Labor and Monopoly Capital*. New York: Monthly Review Press.

Bresnahan, Brynjolfsson, and Lorin. (2002). Information technology, workplace organization, and the demand for skilled labor: firm-level evidence. *Quarterly Journal of Economics*, vol. 117(1), pp. 33976.

Brewer, R. M. (1993). Theorizing race, class and gender: The new scholarship of black feminist intellectuals and black women's labor, in Stanlie M. James and Abena P. A. Busia, eds., *Theorizing Black Feminisms: The Visionary Pragmatism of Black Women*. New York: Routledge.

Bricout, J. C. (2004). Using telework to enhance return to work outcomes for individuals with spinal cord injuries. *Neurorehabilitation*, 19(2): 147–159.

Brown and Jasper., eds. (1993). *Consuming Passions: Feminist Approaches to Eating Disorders and Weight Preoccupations*. Toronto: Second Story Press.

Brown, D. E. (1991). *Human Universals*. New York: McGraw-Hill.

Brown, Judith K. (1977). A note on the division of labor by sex, in Nona Glazer and Helen Y. Waehrer, eds., *Woman in a Man-Made World*. 2nd ed. Chicago: Rand McNally.

Brown, S. L. (2004). Family Structure and Child Well-being: the Significance of Parental cohabitation. *Journal of Marriage and Family* 66 (May): 351–367.

Brownmiller, S. (1986). *Against Our Will: Men, Women, and Rape*. Rev. ed. New York: Bantam.

Brownell and Horgen. (2004). *Food fight: The inside story of the food industry, America's obesity crisis, and what we can do about it*. New York: McGraw-Hill.

Brownstein, R. (2003). Liberal group flexes online muscle in its very own primary. *Los Angeles Times*, June 23, p. A-9.

Brubaker, R. (1992). *The Politics of Citizenship*. Cambridge, MA: Harvard University Press.

Bull, P. (1983). *Body Movement and Interpersonal Communication*. New York: Wiley.

Bumpass and Lu. (2000). Trends in cohabitation and implications for children's family context in the United States. *Population Studies*, vol. 54.

Bumpass, Sweet, and Cherlin. (1991). The role of cohabitation in declining rates of marriage. *Journal of Marriage and the Family*, vol. 53 (November).

Burr, C. (1993). Homosexuality and biology. *Atlantic Monthly*, March.

Burris, B. H. (1993). *Technocracy at Work*. Albany: State University of New York Press.

Burris, B. H. (1998). Computerization of the workplace. in *Annual Review of Sociology*, vol. 24. Palo Alto, CA: Annual Reviews.

Business Week. (1997). Good News on Wage Inequality December 15.

Business Week (2009). A Lost Decade for Jobs. http://www.businessweek.com/the_thread/economicsunbound/archives/2009/06/a_lost_decade_f.html, accessed September 2009.

Butler, J. (1989). *Gender Trouble: Feminism and the Subversion of Identity*. New York: Routledge.

Butterfield, F. (1998). Decline of violent crimes is linked to crack market. *New York Times*, December 28, p. A18.

Cain, and Combs-Orme. (2005). Family structure effects on parenting stress and practices in the African-American family. *Journal of Sociology and Social Welfare*, XXXII (2), 19–40.

Cairncross, F. (1997). The Death of Distance: How the Communications Revolution Will Change Our Lives. Boston: *Harvard Business School Press*.

Campos, Saguy, Ernsberger, Oliver, and Gaesser. (2006). The epidemiology of overweight and obesity: Public health crisis or moral panic? *International Journal of Epidemiology*, 35, 55–60.

Carr and Friedman. (2005). Is obesity stigmatizing? Body weight, perceived discrimination and psychological well-being in the United States. *Journal of Health and Social Behavior*, 46, 244–259.

Castells, M. (1977). *The Urban Question: A Marxist Approach*. Cambridge, MA: MIT Press.

Castells, M. (1983). The City and the Grass Roots: A Cross-Cultural Theory of Urban Social Movements. Berkeley, CA: University of California Press.

Castells, M. (1992). Four Asian tigers with a dragon head: A comparative analysis of the state, economy, and society in the Asian Pacific Rim, in Richard P. Appelbaum and Jeffrey Henderson, eds., *States and Development in the Asian Pacific Rim*. Newbury Park, CA: Sage.

Castells, M. (1996). *The Rise of the Network Society*. Malden, MA: Blackwell.

Castells, M. (1998). *End of Millennium*. Malden, MA: Blackwell.

Castells, M. (2000). *The Rise of the Network Society*. Oxford: Oxford University Press.

Castells, M. (2001). *The Internet Galaxy*. Oxford: Oxford University Press.

Castles and Miller. (1993). *The Age of Migration: International Population Movements in the Modern World*. London: Macmillan.

Catalano, S. M. (2005). Criminal Victimization, 2004. *National Crime Victimization Survey*, Table 2. www.ojp.usdoj.gov/bjs/pub/pdf/cv04.pdf, accessed 10/5/05.

Catholics for Choice. (2004). Catholic Attitudes on Sexual Behavior & Reproductive Health. Washington, DC: Author. http://www.catholicsforchoice.org/topics/international/documents/2004worldview.pdf

Center for Arms Control and Non-Proliferation. (2008). *U.S. Military Spending vs. the World*. February 22.

Center for Responsive Politics (CRP). (2008). Banking on becoming president. http://www.opensecrets.org/pres08/index.php, accessed November 2008.

Centers for Disease Control and Prevention (CDC). (2003). "National ambulatory care survey, 2001 summary." Advanced Data From Vital and Health Statistics, Number 337 (August 11), www.cdc.gov/nchs/data/ad/ad337.pdf, accessed 12/29/04.

Centers for Disease Control and Prevention (CDC). (2006a). Morbidity and mortality weekly report: QuickStats: Percentage of parents who were married or cohabitating at birth of first child, by race/ethnicity and sex. http://www.cdc.gov/MMWR/preview/mmwrhtml/mm5536a8.htm, accessed January 2008.

Centers for Disease Control and Prevention (CDC). (2006b, July 21). Births, marriages, divorces, and deaths—Provisional data for 2005. National vital statistics report, 54, 20. http://www.cdc.gov/nchs/data/nvsr/nvsr54/nvsr54_20.pdf, accessed spring 2008.

Centers for Disease Control and Prevention (CDC). (2007a). Adult cigarette smoking in the United States: Current estimates. www.cdc.gov/tobacco/data_statistics/fact_sheets/adult_data/adult_cig_smoking.htm, accessed 9/19/08.

Centers for Disease Control and Prevention (CDC). (2007b). Deaths: Final Data for 2005. National Vital Statistics Reports 55:19. Washington, DC: CDC. http://www.cdc.gov/nchs/data/nvsr/nvsr55/nvsr55_19.pdf, accessed 3/6/10.

Centers for Disease Control and Prevention (CDC). (2008a). Childhood Overweight and Obesity. http://www.cdc.gov/obesity/childhood, accessed August 2009.

Centers for Disease Control and Prevention (CDC). (2008b). Obesity Trends among U.S. Adults. http://www.cdc.gov/obesity/downloads/obesity_trends_2008.pdf, accessed August 2009.

Centers for Disease Control and Prevention (CDC). (2008c). Healthy Youth: Sexual

Risk Behavior. http://www.cdc.gov/ HealthyYouth/sexualbehaviors/index. htm, accessed August 2009.

Centers for Disease Control and Prevention (CDC). (2009a). Unmarried Childbearing. Table 18 from http://www.cdc.gov/ nchs/data/nvsr/nvsr57/nvsr57_07.pdf

Centers for Disease Control and Prevention (CDC). (2009b). Unmarried Childbearing. Table 20 from http://www.cdc.gov/ nchs/data/nvsr/nvsr57/nvsr57_07.pdf

Central Intelligence Agency (CIA). (2000). CIA World Fact book. www.cia.gov/ cia/publications/factbook/geos/ rs.html#Econ, accessed 12/29/04.

CIA World Fact Book. (2007). http://www. google.com/search?hl=en&safe= off&rls=com. microsoft%3A*&q=world+ GDP+2007& aq=f&oq=&aqi=g-m1, accessed September 2009.

CIA World Fact Book. (2009). United States Data. https://www.cia.gov/library/ publications/the-world-factbook/ geos/us.html, accessed August 2009.

Chafetz, J. S. (1990). *Gender Equity: An Integrated Theory of Stability and Change.* Newbury Park, CA: Sage.

Chambliss, W. J. (1988). *On the Take: From Petty Crooks to Presidents.* Bloomington: Indiana University Press.

Chase-Dunn, C. (1989). *Global Formation: Structures of the World Economy.* Cambridge, MA: Basil Blackwell.

Chepesiuk, R. (1998). *Hard Target: The United States War against International Drug Trafficking, 1982–1997.* Jefferson, NC: McFarland and Company.

Cherlin, A. (1990). Recent changes in American fertility, marriage, and divorce. *Annals of the American Academy of Political and Social Science,* vol. 510 (July).

Cherlin, A. (1999). *Public and Private Families: An Introduction.* 2nd ed. New York: McGraw-Hill.

Cherlin, A. (2005). "American Marriage in the Early Twenty-First Century," *The Future of Children* 15 (no. 2): 33–55.

Cherlin, et al. (1998). Effects of parental divorce on mental health throughout the life course. *American Sociological Review,* vol. 63.

Chua, A. (2003). *World on Fire: How Exporting Free Market Democracy Breeds Ethnic Hatred and Global Instability.* New York: Doubleday.

Cleary, P. D. (1987). Gender Differences in Stress-Related Disorders, in Rosalind C. Barnett, ed., *Gender and Stress.* New York: Free Press.

Cloward and Ohlin. (1960). *Delinquency and Opportunity.* New York: Free Press.

CNN. (2003). INS: 7 million Illegal Immigrants in United States. February 1. www.cnn.com/2003/US/01/31/illegal. immigration, accessed 1/27/06.

Coate, J. (1994). Cyberspace innkeeping: Building online community. Online paper, www.well.com:70/0/Community/ innkeeping, accessed 12/29/04.

Cohen, A. (1955). *Delinquent Boys: The Culture of the Gang.* Glencoe, IL: Free Press.

Cohen, Broschak, and Haveman. (1998). And then there were more? The effect of organizational sex composition on the hiring and promotion of managers. *American Sociological Review,* vol. 63, no. 5.

Coleman, J. S. (1988). Social capital in the creation of human capital. *American Journal of Sociology,* supplement, vol. 94.

Coleman, J. S. (1990). *The Foundations of Social Theory.* Cambridge, MA: Harvard University Press.

Coleman, et al. (1966). *Equality of Educational Opportunity.* Washington, DC: U.S. Government Printing Office.

Collins, R. (1971). Functional and conflict theories of educational stratification. *American Sociological Review,* vol. 36.

Collins, R. (1979). *The Credential Society: An Historical Sociology of Education.* New York: Academic Press.

Coltrane, S. (1992). The micropolitics of gender in non-industrial societies. *Gender and Society,* vol. 6.

Common Cause. (2002). Campaign finance reform: Election 2002—incumbent advantage. www.commoncause.org/ news/ default.cfm?ArtID538, accessed 11/6/02.

Coleman, J. S. (2003). Spending more than a half billion on political contributions, lobbying and ad campaigns, Pharma wins big on Medicare. www.commoncause. org/action/070103_phrma_report.pdf, accessed 7/1/03.

Conley, D. (1999). *Being Black, Living in the Red: Race, Wealth, and Social Policy in America.* Berkeley and Los Angeles: University of California Press.

Conley, D. (2003). The cost of slavery. *New York Times,* February 15.

Connell, R. W. (1987). *Gender and Power: Society, the Person, and Sexual Politics.* Boston: Allen and Unwin.

Conner, Dorfman, and Tompkins. (1985). Life satisfaction of retired professors: The contribution of work, health, income, and length of retirement. *Educational Gerontology,* vol. 11.

Cooley, C. H. (1964). (orig. 1902). *Human Nature and the Social Order. i.* New York: Schocken Books.

Coontz, S. (1992). *The Way We Never Were: American Families and the Nostalgia Trap.* New York: Basic Books.

Corbin and Strauss. (1985). Managing chronic illness at home: Three lines of work. *Qualitative Sociology,* vol. 8.

Corsaro, W. (1997). *The Sociology of Childhood.* Thousand Oaks, CA: Pine Forge Press.

Cosmides and Tooby. (1997). Evolutionary psychology: A primer. University of California at Santa Barbara: Institute for Social, Behavioral, and Economic Research Center for Evolutionary Psychology, available at www.psych.ucsb. edu/research/cep/primer.htm, accessed 1/11/05.

Cumings, B. (1987). The origins and development of the northeast Asian political economy: Industrial sectors, product cycles, and political consequences, in F. C. Deyo, ed., *The Political Economy of the New Asian Industrialism.* Ithaca, NY: Cornell University Press.

Cumings, B. (1997). *Korea's Place in the Sun: A Modern History.* New York: Norton.

Cumming, E. (1963). Further thoughts on the theory of disengagement. *International Social Science Journal,* vol. 15.

Cumming, E. (1975). Engagement with an old theory. *International Journal of Aging and Human Development,* vol. 6.

Cumming and Henry. (1961). *Growing Old: The Process of Disengagement.* New York: Basic.

Dahlburg, J. (1995). Sweatshop case dismays few in Thailand. *Los Angeles Times,* August 27, p. A-4.

Dannefer, D. (1989). Human action and its place in theories of aging. *Journal of Aging Studies,* vol. 3.

Danzger. (1989). *Returning to Tradition.* New Haven, CT: Yale University Press.

Danziger and Gottschalk. (1995). *America Unequal.* Cambridge, MA: Harvard University Press.

David, R. (2007). Indian middle class slowly changing its ways. http://www.forbes. com/facesinthenews/2007/11/10/ india-middleclass-survey-face-markets-cx_rd_1108autofacescan01.html, accessed fall 2007.

Davidman, J. (1991). Tradition in a Rootless World: Women Turn to Orthodox Judaism. Berkeley: University of California Press.

Davies, B. (1991). *Frogs and Snails and Feminist Tales.* Sydney: Allen and Unwin.

Davies, J. (1962). Towards a theory of revolution. *American Sociological Review,* vol. 27.

Davis and Polonko. (2001). Telework in the United States: Telework American Research Study 2001. Washington, DC: International Telework Association & Council.

Davis, K. (1937). The Sociology of Prostitution. *American Sociological Review 11:* 744–55.

Davis and Moore. (1945). Some principles of stratification. *American Sociological Review,* vol. 10 (April).

Davis, Mike. (1990). *City of Quartz: Excavating the Future in Los Angeles.* New York: Verso.

Davis, S. (1987). *Future Perfect.* Reading, MA: Addison-Wesley.

Davis, S. (1988). *2001 Management: Managing the Future Now*. New York: Simon and Schuster.

Deacon, T. (1998). *The Symbolic Species: The Co-Evolution of Language and the Brain*. New York: Norton.

Death Penalty Information Center. (2009). www.deathpenaltyinfo.org/documents/FactSheet.pdf, accessed July 2009.

D'Emilio. (1983). *Sexual Politics, Sexual Communities: The Making of a Homosexual Minority in the United States, 1940–1970*. Chicago: University of Chicago Press.

DeNavas-Walt, Proctor and Lee. (2005). U.S. Census Bureau, Current Population Reports, P60-229, *Income, Poverty, and Health Insurance Coverage in the United States: 2004*, U.S. Government Printing Office, Washington, DC. www.census.gov/ prod/2005pubs/p60-229.pdf, accessed spring 2006.

DeNavas-Walt, Proctor, and Smith. (2008). Income, Poverty, and Health Insurance Coverage in the United States: 2007. *U.S. Census Bureau*. http://www.census.gov/prod/2008pubs/p60-235.pdf, accessed July 2009.

Derenne and Beresin. (2006). Body image, media, and eating disorders. *Academic Psychiatry*, 30, 257–261.

Deyo, F. (1987). *The Political Economy of the New Asian Industrialism*. Ithaca, NY: Cornell University Press.

Deyo, F. (1989). *Beneath the Miracle: Labor Subordination in the New Asian Industrialism*. Berkeley, CA: University of California Press.

Diamond, J. (2005). *Collapse: How Societies Choose to Fail or Succeed*. New York: Penguin.

Dicum and Luttinger. (1999). *The Coffee Book: Anatomy of an Industry from Crop to the Last Drop*. New York: New Press.

Dimitrova, D. (2003). Controlling teleworkers: supervision and flexibility revisited. *New Technology Work and Employment*, 18(3): 181–195.

Dolbeare, C. (1995). *Out of Reach: Why Everyday People Can't Find Affordable Housing*. Washington, DC: Low Income Housing Information.

Domhoff, W. (1971). *The Higher Circles: The Governing Class in America*. New York: Vintage Books.

Domhoff, W. (1979). *The Powers That Be: Processes of Ruling Class Domination in America*. New York: Vintage Books

Domhoff, W. (1983). *Who Rules America Now? A View for the '80s*. New York: Prentice-Hall.

Domhoff, W. (1998). Who Rules America?: Power and Politics in the Year 2000. Belmont, CA: Mayfield.

Dreier and Appelbaum. (1992). The housing crisis enters the 1990s. *New England Journal of Public Policy*, spring–summer.

DrugWarFacts.org. (2005). "Drug War Facts: Economics." www.drugwarfacts.org/economi.htm, accessed spring 2006.

Du Bois, W. E. B. (1903). *The Souls of Black Folk*. New York: Dover.

Dubos, R. (1959). *Mirage of Health*. New York: Doubleday/Anchor.

Duignan and Gann, eds. (1998). *The Debate in the United States over Immigration*. Stanford, CA: Hoover Institution Press.

Duncan, Brooks-Gunn, Yeung, and Smith. (1998). How much does childhood poverty affect the life chances of children? *American Sociological Review*, vol. 63, no. 3 (June): 406–23.

Duncombe and Marsden. (1993). Love and intimacy: The gender division of emotion and emotion work: A neglected aspect of sociological discussion of heterosexual relationships. *Sociology*, vol. 27.

Duneier, M. (1999). *Sidewalk*. New York: Farrar, Straus, and Giroux.

Duneier, M. (2000). Questions for Jane Jacobs. *The New York Times Magazine* (April 9).

Duneier and Molotch. (1999). Talking city trouble: Interactional vandalism, social inequality, and the urban interaction problem. *American Journal of Sociology*, vol. 104.

Durkheim, É. (1964). *The Division of Labor in Society*. Originally published 1893. New York: Free Press.

Durkheim, É. (1965). *The Elementary Forms of the Religious Life*. Originally published 1912. New York: Free Press.

Durkheim, É. (1966). *Suicide*. Originally published 1897. New York: Free Press.

Dutt, M. (1996). Some reflections on U.S. women of color and the United Nations fourth world conference on women and NGO forum in Beijing, China. *Feminist Studies*, vol. 22.

Dworkin, A. (1981). *Pornography: Men Possessing Women*. New York: Pedigree.

Dworkin, A. (1987). *Intercourse*. New York: Free Press.

Dye, T. (1986). *Who's Running America?* 4th ed. Englewood Cliffs, NJ: Prentice Hall.

Eating Disorder Coalition (EDC). (2003). "Statistics." www.eatingdisorderscoalition.org/reports/statistics.html, accessed 12/29/04.

Ebomoyi, E. (1987). The prevalence of female circumcision in two Nigerian communities. *Sex Roles*, vol. 17, nos. 3–4.

Economic and Social Research Council. ESRC. (2007). Immigration Statistics: Where Lies the Truth? http://www.esrc.ac.uk/ESRCInfoCentre/about/CI/CP/Our_Society_Today/Spotlights_2006/immigration.aspx, accessed 2/3/100.

The Economist. (1996). Pocket World in Figures. London: Profile Books.

The Economist. (2003). "A Nation Apart," May 6, www. economist.com/surveys/showsurvey.cfm?issue520031108, accessed 12/29/04.

Economy, E. (2007). "The Great Leap Backward?" *Foreign Affairs* Vol. 86, No. 5 (September/October), http://www.foreignaffairs.org/20070901faessay86503/elizabeth-c-economy/the-great-leap-backward.html.

E-Crime Watch. (2007). 2007 E-Crime watch survey: Survey results. www.cert.org/archive/pdf/ecrimesummary07.pdf, accessed 11/3/07.

Edin and Kefalas. (2005). *Promises I Can Keep: Why Poor Women Put Motherhood before Marriage*. Berkeley, CA: University of California Press.

Efron, S. (1997). Eating disorders go global, *Los Angeles Times*, October 18, p. A-1.

Eibl-Eibesfeldt, I. (1972). Similarities and differences between cultures in expressive movements, in Robert A. Hinde, ed., *Nonverbal Communication*. New York: Cambridge University Press.

Eisen, A. (1983). *The Chosen People in America: A Study in Jewish Religious Ideology*. Bloomington, Indiana: Indiana University Press.

Eisenhower Library. (1961). Farewell Address, Abilene, Kansas: The Dwight D. Eisenhower Presidential Library. www.eisenhower.utexas.edu/farewell.htm, accessed 12/29/04.

Ekman and Friesen. (1978). *Facial Action Coding System*. New York: Consulting Psychologists Press.

El Dareer, A. (1982). *Woman, Why Do You Weep? Circumcision and Its Consequences*. Westport, CT: Zed.

Elias, N. (1987). *Involvement and Detachment*. London: Oxford University Press.

Elias and Dunning. (1987). *Quest for Excitement: Sport and Leisure in the Civilizing Process*. Oxford, UK: Blackwell.

Elshtain, J. (1981). *Public Man: Private Woman*. Princeton, NJ: Princeton University Press.

Emmanuel, A. (1972). *Unequal Exchange: A Study of the Imperialism of Trade*. New York: Monthly Review Press.

Encyclopedia Britannica. (2006). "Religion:" Britannica Book of the Year, 2005. Encyclopedia Britannica Online http://search.eb.com/eb/article-9398490, accessed 1/23/06.

Environmental Working Group. (2008). Farm Subsidy Database Update. Washington, DC: EWG. http://farm.ewg.org/farm/index.php?key=nosign

Epstein, G. (2003). More women advance, but sexism persists, *Barron's*. www.collegejournal.com/successwork/workplacediversity/20030605=Epstein.html, accessed spring 2006.

ERGD. (2009). http://www.ergd.org/ Governors.htm, accessed July 2009.

Ericson and Haggerty. (1997). *Policing the Risk Society*. Toronto: University of Toronto Press.

Estes, C. (1986). The politics of aging in America. *Aging and Society*, vol. 6.

Estes, C. (1991). The Reagan legacy: Privatization, the welfare state, and aging, in J. Myles and J. Quadagno, eds., *States, Labor Markets, and the Future of Old Age Policy*. Philadelphia: Temple University Press.

Estes, Binney, and Culbertson. (1992). The gerontological imagination: Social influences on the development of gerontology, 1945–present. *Aging and Human Development*, vol. 35.

Estes, Swan, and Gerard. (1982). Dominant and competing paradigms in gerontology: Toward a political economy of aging. *Aging and Society*, vol. 2.

Estes, et al. (1984). *Political Economy, Health, and Aging*. Boston: Little, Brown.

Evans, P. (1987). Class, state, and dependence in East Asia: Some lessons for Latin Americanists, in F. C. Deyo, ed., *The Political Economy of the New Asian Industrialism*. Ithaca, NY: Cornell University Press.

Evans, P. (1995). *Embedded Autonomy: States and Industrial Transformation*. Princeton, NJ: Princeton University Press.

Evans-Pritchard, E. (1970). Sexual inversion among the Azande. *American Anthropologist*, vol. 72.

Fallows, D. (2007). China's Online Population Explosion What It May Mean for the Internet Globally . . . and for U.S. Users. Washington, DC: Pew Internet and American Life Project. www.pewinternet.org/~/media//Files/Reports/2007/China_Internet_July_2007.pdf.pdf

Federal Bureau of Investigation (FBI). (2005a). "Crime in the United States, 2004." The Uniform Crime Report. Table 38. www.fbi.gov/ucr/cius_04/index.html

Federal Bureau of Investigation (FBI). (2007a). Crime in the United States, 2006. Table 38, Arrests, by Age, 2006. www.fbi.gov/ucr/cius2006/data/table_38.html, accessed fall 2007.

Federal Bureau of Investigation (FBI). (2009a). Crime in the United States, 2008. Table 1: Crime in the United States by Volume and Rate per 100,000 Inhabitants, 1989–2008. www.fbi.gov/ucr/cius2008/data/table_01.html

Federal Bureau of Investigation (FBI). (2009b). Crime in the United States, 2008. Expanded Homicide Data Table 1: Murder Victims by Race and Sex, 2008. http://www.fbi.gov/ucr/cius2008/offenses/expanded_information/data/shrtable_01.html

Federal Interagency Forum on Aging-Related Statistics. (2004a). "Older Americans 2004: Key Indicators of Well-Being." Federal Interagency Forum on Aging-Related Statistics, Washington, DC: U.S. Government Printing Office. November. www.agingstats.gov, accessed 1/9/07.

Federal Interagency Forum on Aging-Related Statistics. (2008). Key indicators of well-being. www.agingstats.gov/Agingstatsdotnet/Main_Site/Data/2008_Documents/OA_2008.pdf, accessed June 2009.

Federal Register 2009. (2009). Federal Poverty Guidelines. www.atdn.org/access/poverty.html, accessed July 2009.

Fenton and Morris. (2003). The integration of holistic nursing practices and complementary and alternative modalities into curricula of schools of nursing. *Alternative Therapies in Health and Medicine*, 9(4):62–67.

Finke and Stark. (1988). Religious economies and sacred canopies: Religious mobilization in American cities, 1906. *American Sociological Review*, vol. 53.

Finke and Stark. (1992). *The Churching of America, 1776–1990: Winners and Losers in Our Religious Economy*. New Brunswick, NJ: Rutgers University Press.

Finley, Roberts, and Banahan. (1988). Motivators and Inhibitors of Attitudes of Filial Obligation Toward Aging Parents. *The Gerontologist*, 28:73–78.

Fischer, C. (1984). *The Urban Experience*. 2nd ed. New York: Harcourt Brace Jovanovich.

Fischer, et al. (1996). *Inequality by Design: Cracking the Bell Curve Myth*. Princeton, NJ: Princeton University Press.

Fisher, Cullen, and Turner. (2000). The Sexual Victimization of College Women. Washington, DC: U.S. Department of Justice, National Institute of Justice, Bureau of Justice Statistics (December), NJJ 182369, www.ncjrs.org/pdffiles1/nij/182369.pdf, accessed 12/29/04.

Forbes. (2009). www.forbes.com/2009/03/11/worlds-richest-people-billionaires-2009-billionaires-intro.html, accessed July 2009.

Ford and Beach. (1951). *Patterns of Sexual Behavior*. New York: Harper and Row.

Fortune. (2009). Global 500 Rankings 2009. money.cnn.com/magazines/fortune/global500/2009/countries/Japan.html {AND?} http://money.cnn.com/magazines/fortune/global500/2009/countries/US.html, accessed September 2009.

Foucault, M. (1979). *Discipline and Punish: The Birth of the Prison*. New York: Random House.

Foucault, M. (1988). Technologies of the self, in Luther H. Martin, Huck Gutman, and Patrick H. Hutton, eds., *Technologies of the Self: A Seminar with Michel Foucault*. Amherst, MA: University of Massachusetts Press.

Fox, O. (1964). The pre-industrial city reconsidered. *Sociological Quarterly*, vol. 5.

Frank, A. (1966). The development of underdevelopment. *Monthly Review*, vol. 18.

Frank, A. (1969a). *Latin America: Underdevelopment or Revolution*. New York: Monthly Review Press.

Frank, A. (1969b). *Capitalism and Underdevelopment in Latin America: Historical Studies of Chile and Brazil*. New York: Monthly Review Press.

Frank, A. (1979). *Dependent Accumulation and Underdevelopment*. London: Macmillan.

Frank and McEneaney. (1999). The individualization of society and the liberalization of state policies on same-sex sexual relations, 1984–1995. *Social Forces*, vol. 7, no. 3.

Franzini, Ribble, and Keddie. (2001). Understanding the Hispanic paradox. *Ethnicity & Disease*, 11(3): 496–518.

Freedom House. (2005a). "Electoral Democracies, 2005" www.freedomhouse.org/template.cfm?page=205&year=2005, accessed 1/9/06.

Freedom House. (2007a). Map of freedom 2007. www.freedomhouse.org/template.cfm?page=363&year=2007, accessed January 2008.

Freeman, R. (1999). *The New Inequality: Creating Solutions for Poor America*. Boston: Beacon Press.

Fremlin, J. (1964). How many people can the world support? *New Scientist*, (October 19).

French, H. (2001a). Diploma at hand, Japanese women find glass ceiling reinforced with iron. *New York Times*, January 1, p. A1.

French, H. (2001b). Japan's new premier picks precedent-setting cabinet. *New York Times*, April 27, p. A1.

Frey and Liaw. (1998). The impact of recent immigration on population redistribution in the United States, in James Smith and Barry Edmonston, eds., *The Immigration Debate*. Washington, DC: National Academy Press.

Frey, W. (2001). Melting Pot Suburbs: A Census 2000 Study of Suburban Diversity. Washington, DC: *The Brookings Institution, Census 2000 Series*, 2001.

Friedman and Currall. (2003). Conflict Escalation: Dispute Exacerbating Elements of E-mail Communication. *Human Relations* 56(11): 1325–1347.

Friedman, T. (2000). *The Lexus and the Olive Tree: Understanding Globalization*. New York: Anchor.

Friedman, T. (2005). *The World is Flat: A Brief History of the Twenty-First Century.* New York: Farrar, Straus and Giroux.

Furstenberg and Cherlin. (1991). *Divided Families.* Cambridge, MA: Harvard University Press.

Gallup Organization. (1998). *Have and Have-Nots: Perceptions of Fairness and Opportunity – 1998.* www.gallup.com/poll/9877/havenots-perceptions-fairness-opportunity-1998.aspx, accessed 2/3/10.

Gallup. (2006). Of the People, 2006: What the World Thinks on Today's Global Issues. Washington, DC: Gallup International. www.gallup-international.com/ContentFiles/pdf/VoP.pdf

Gallup. (2008). Trust In Government Remains Low (Published September 2008). www.gallup.com/poll/110458/trust-government-remains-low.aspx, accessed June 2009.

Gamoran, et al. (1995). An organizational analysis of the effects of ability grouping. *American Educational Research Journal,* vol. 32, no. 4.

Gans, H. (1979). Symbolic ethnicity: The future of ethnic groups and cultures in America. *Ethnic and Racial Studies,* vol. 2 (January).

Gapminder.com. (2009). Historical Income per person. http://graphs.gapminder.org/world/#$majorMode=chart$is;shi=t;ly=2003;lb=f;il=t;fs=11;al=30;stl=t;st=t;nsl=t;se=t$wst;tts=C$ts;sp=6;ti=2007$zpv;v=0$inc_x;mmid=XCOORDS;iid=ti;by=ind$inc_y;mmid=YCOORDS;iid=phAwcNAVuyj1jiMAkmq1iMg;by=ind$inc_s;uniValue=8.21;iid=phAwcNAVuyj0XOoBL_n5tAQ;by=ind$inc_c;uniValue=255;gid=CATID0;by=grp$map_x;scale=lin;dataMin=1700;dataMax=2007$map_y;scale=log;dataMin=269;dataMax=119849$map_s;sma=49;smi=2.65$cd;bd=0$inds=

Gardner, C. (1995). *Passing By: Gender and Public Harassment.* Berkeley and Los Angeles: University of California Press.

Garfinkel, H. (1963). A conception of, and experiments with, 'trust' as a condition of stable concerted actions, in O. J. Harvey, ed., *Motivation and Social Interaction.* New York: Ronald Press.

Garfinkel, H. (1967). *Studies in Ethnomethodology.* Englewood Cliffs, NJ: Prentice-Hall.

Garland, D. (2002). *The Culture of Control: Crime and Social Order in Contemporary Society.* Chicago: University of Chicago Press.

Geertz, C. (1973). *The Interpretation of Cultures.* New York: Basic Books.

Geertz, C. (1983). *Local Knowledge: Further Essays in Interpretive Anthropology.* New York: Basic Books.

Gelb, I. (1952). *A Study of Writing.* Chicago: University of Chicago Press.

Gelles and Cornell. (1990). *Intimate Violence in Families.* 2nd ed. Newbury Park, CA: Sage.

General Social Survey (GSS). (1997). General Social Surveys, 1972–1994: [Cumulative File]. Accessed and analyzed online through the *University of Michigan Interuniversity Consortium for Political and Social Research* (ICPSR), http:webapp. icpsr.umich.edu/cocoon/ICPSR-StUDY/03728.xml, accessed 1/10/05.

Genworth. (2009). Cost of Care Survey, 2009. www.genworth.com/content/etc/medialib/genworth_v2/pdf/ltc_cost_of_care.Par.41652.File.dat/Cost%20of%20Care%20Maps_gnw.pdf, accessed June 2009.

Gereffi, G. (1995). Contending paradigms for cross-regional comparison: Development strategies and commodity chains in East Asia and Latin America, in Peter H. Smith, ed., *Latin America in Comparative Perspective: New Approaches to Methods and Analysis.* Boulder, CO: Westview Press.

Gereffi, G. (1996). Commodity chains and regional divisions of labor in East Asia. *Journal of Asian Business,* vol. 12, no. 1.

Gershuny, et al. (1994). The domestic labor revolution: A process of lagged adaptation, in Michael Anderson, Frank Bechofer, and Jonathan Gershuny, eds., *The Social and Political Economy of the Household.* Oxford, UK: Oxford University Press.

Gershuny and Miles. (1983). *The New Service Economy: The Transformation of Employment in Industrial Societies.* London: Francis Pinter.

Giddens, A. (1984). *The Constitution of Society.* Cambridge, UK: Polity Press.

Giddens, A. (1990). *The Consequences of Modernity.* Cambridge, UK: Polity Press.

Giddens, A. (1998). *The Third Way: The Renewal of Social Democracy.* Cambridge, UK: Polity Press.

Global Issues. (2006). Poverty Facts and Stats. www.globalissues.org/article/26/poverty-facts-and-stats, accessed 2/4/10.

Glock, C. (1976). On the origin and evolution of religious groups, in Charles Y. Glock and Robert N. Bellah, eds., *The New Religious Consciousness.* Berkeley, CA: University of California Press.

Glueck and Glueck. (1956). *Physique and Delinquency.* New York: Harper and Row.

Gober, P. (1993). *Americans on the Move.* Washington, DC: Population Reference Bureau.

Goffman, E. (1963). *Stigma: Notes on the Management of Spoiled Identity.* Englewood Cliffs, NJ: Prentice-Hall.

Goffman, E. (1967). *Interaction Ritual.* New York: Doubleday/Anchor.

Goffman, E. (1971). *Relations in Public: Microstudies of the Public Order.* New York: Basic Books.

Goffman, E. (1973). *The Presentation of Self in Everyday Life.* New York: Overlook Press.

Goffman, E. (1981). *Forms of Talk.* Philadelphia: University of Pennsylvania Press.

Gold, T. (1986). *State and Society in the Taiwan Miracle.* Armonk, NY: M. E. Sharpe.

Goldberg, C. (1997). Hispanic Households Struggle Amid Broad Decline in Income. *New York Times,* January 30, pp. A1, A16.

Goldberg and Rayner. (1987). *The Jewish People: Their History and Their Religion.* New York: Penguin Books.

Goldscheider, F. (1990). The aging of the gender revolution: What do we know and what do we need to know? *Research on Aging,* vol. 12.

Goldscheider and Goldscheider. (1999). *The Changing Transition to Adulthood: Leaving and Returning Home.* Thousand Oaks, California: Sage.

Goldscheider and Waite. (1991). *New Families, No Families? The Transformation of the American Home.* Berkeley, CA: University of California Press.

Goldstein and Morning. (2000). The Multiple-Race Population of the United States: Issues and Estimates. *Proceedings of the National Academy of Sciences* 97(11): 6230–6235.

Goldstein and Goldstein. (1996). *Jews on the Move: Implications for Jewish Identity.* Albany, NY: SUNY Press.

Gonnerman, J. (2004). *Life on the Outside: The Prison Odyssey of Elaine Bartlett.* New York: Farrar Straus and Giroux.

Goode, W. (1963). *World Revolution in Family Patterns.* New York: Free Press.

Gottfredson and Hirschi. (1990). *A General Theory of Crime.* Stanford, CA: Stanford University Press.

Granovetter, M. (1973). The strength of weak ties. *American Journal of Sociology,* vol. 78.

Gray, J. (1998). Ethnographic Atlas Codebook. *World Cultures* 10(1):86–136

Gray, J. (2003). *Al Qaeda and What It Means to be Modern.* Chatham, UK: Faber and Faber.

Green, F. (1987). *The "Sissy Boy" Syndrome and the Development of Homosexuality.* New Haven, CT: Yale University Press.

Green, J. (2004). The American Religious Landscape and Political Attitudes: A Baseline for 2004. *The Pew Forum on Religion & Public Life.* Table 1 http://pewforum.org/publications/surveys/green-full.pdf, accessed 1/23/06.

Greenfield, P. (1993). Representational competence in shared symbol systems. In R. R. Cocking & K. A. Renninger (Eds) *The Development and Meaning of Psychological Distance*. Hillsdale, NJ: Erlbaum.

Gubrium, J. (1986). *Oldtimers and Alzheimer's: The Descriptive Organization of Senility*. Greenwich, CT: JAI Press.

Gubrium, J. (1991). *The Mosaic of Care: Frail Elderly and Their Families in the Real World*. New York: Springer.

Gubrium, J. (1993). *Speaking of Life: Horizons of Meaning for Nursing Home Residents*. Hawthorne, NY: Aldine de Gruyter.

Gubrium and Sankar, eds. (1994). *Qualitative Methods in Aging Research*. Newbury Park, CA: Sage.

Haddad, Y. (1979). The Muslim Experience in the United States. *The Link*, September–October, Vol. 12, issue 4.

Haddad, Y. (1997a). The concepts 'cult' and 'sect' in scholarly research and public discourse. *New Religious Movements* website, http://religiousmovements. lib.virginia.edu/cultsect/concult.htm, accessed 1/10/05.

Haddad, Y. (1997b). New religious movements mission statement. *New Religious Movements* website, http://religous movements.lib.virginia.edu/welcome/ mission.htm, accessed 1/10/05.

Hagan and McCarthy. (1992). Mean streets: The theoretical significance of situational delinquency among homeless youth. *American Sociological Review*, vol. 98.

Haggard, S. (1990). *Pathways from the Periphery: The Politics of Growth in Newly Industrializing Countries*. Ithaca, NY: Cornell University Press.

Hall, E. (1969). *The Hidden Dimension*. New York: Doubleday.

Hall, E. (1973). *The Silent Language*. New York: Doubleday.

Hall, Stuart. (1992). The question of cultural identity, in Stuart Hall, David Held, and Tony McGrew, eds., *Modernity and Its Futures*. Cambridge, UK: Polity Press.

Halpin and Agne. (2009). *State of American Political Ideology, 2009: A National Study of Political Values and Beliefs*. Washington, DC: Center for American Progress.

Hammond, P. (1992). *Religion and Personal Autonomy: The Third Disestablishment in America*. Columbia, SC: University of South Carolina Press.

Hare, Borgatta, and Bales. (1965). *Small Groups: Studies in Social Interaction*. New York: Knopf.

Harknett and McLanahan. (2004). Racial and Ethnic Differences in Marriage after the Birth of a Child. *American Sociological Review*, 69: 790–811.

Harris, D. (2003). Racial classification and the 2000 census. Commissioned paper, Panel to Review the 2000 Census. *Committee on National Statistics*. University of Michigan, Ann Arbor.

Harris and Sim. (2000). An Empirical Look at the Social Construction of Race: The Case of Mixed-Race Adolescents. *Population Studies Center Research Report* 00-452, University of Michigan.

Harris. (1998). *The Nurture Assumption: Why Children Turn Out the Way They Do*. New York: Free Press.

Harris, M. (1975). *Cows, Pigs, Wars, and Riches: The Riddles of Culture*. New York: Random House.

Harris, M. (1978). *Cannibals and Kings: The Origins of Cultures*. New York: Random House.

Harris, M. (1980). *Cultural Materialism: The Struggle for a Science of Culture*. New York: Vintage Books.

Harris Poll. (2008). www.pollingreport.com/ crime.htm, accessed July 2009.

Hartig, Johansson, and Kylin. (2003). Residence in the Social Ecology of Stress and Restoration, *Journal of Social Issues*, 59(3), 611–636.

Hartmann, et al. (1985). An agenda for basic research on comparable worth, in H. I. Hartmann et al., eds., *Comparable Worth: New Directions for Research*. Washington, DC: National Academy Press.

Harvard Magazine. (2000). The world's poor: A Harvard Magazine roundtable. Harvard Magazine, vol. 103, no. 2. www. harvard-magazine.com/on-line/1100134. html, accessed 1/11/03.

Harvey, D. (1973). *Social Justice and the City*. Oxford, UK: Blackwell.

Harvey, D. (1982). *The Limits to Capital*. Oxford, UK: Blackwell.

Harvey, D. (1985). *Consciousness and the Urban Experience: Studies in the History and Theory of Capitalist Urbanization*. Oxford, UK: Blackwell.

Harvey, D. (1989). *The Condition of Postmodernity: An Enquiry into the Origins of Cultural Change*. Cambridge, MA: Blackwell.

Haslam and James. (2005). *Obesity*. Lancet, 366(9492): 1197–1209.

Hathaway. (1997). Marijuana and tolerance: Revisiting Becker's sources of control. *Deviant Behavior*, vol. 18, no. 2.

Haugen, E. (1977). Linguistic relativity: Myths and methods, in William C. McCormack and Stephen A. Wurm, eds., *Language and Thought: Anthropological Issues*. The Hague: Mouton.

Hawkes, T. (1977). *Structuralism and Semiotics*. Berkeley, CA: University of California Press.

Hawley, A. (1950). *Human Ecology: A Theory of Community Structure*. New York: Ronald Press Company.

Hawley, A. (1968). Human ecology, in *International Encyclopedia of Social Science*, vol. 4. New York: Free Press.

Healy, M. (2001). Pieces of the puzzle. *Los Angeles Times*, http://pqasb. pqarchiver. com/latimes/results.html?RQT=511&sid= 1&firstIndex=460&PQACnt=1, accessed 1/10/05.

Held, McGrew, Goldblatt, and Perraton. (1999). *Global Transformations: Politics, Economics, and Culture*. Cambridge, UK: Polity Press.

Helm, L. (1992). Debt puts squeeze on Japanese. *Los Angeles Times*, November 21.

Henderson, J. (1989). *The Globalization of High Technology Production: Society, Space, and Semiconductors in the Restructuring of the Modern World*. London: Routledge.

Henderson and Appelbaum. (1992). Situating the state in the Asian development process, in Richard P. Appelbaum and Jeffrey Henderson, eds., *States and Development in the Asian Pacific Rim*. Newbury Park, CA: Sage.

Henderson and Kelly. (2005). Food advertising in the age of obesity: content analysis of food advertising on general market and African American television. *Journal of Nutrition Education and Behavior*; 37:191–196

Hendricks and Hatch. (1993). Federal policy and family life of older Americans. In J. Hendricks & C.J. Rosenthal, eds., *The Remainder of Their Days: Impact of Public Policy on Older Families*. New York: Greenwood.

Hendricks, J. (1992). Generation and the generation of theory in social gerontology. *Aging and Human Development*, vol. 35.

Hendricks and Hendricks. (1986). *Aging in Mass Society: Myths and Realities*. Boston: Little, Brown.

Henry, W. (1965). *Growing Older: The Process of Disengagement*. New York: Basic Books.

Herdt, G. (1981). *Guardians of the Flutes: Idioms of Masculinity*. New York: McGraw-Hill.

Herdt, G. (1984). *Ritualized Homosexuality in Melanesia*. Berkeley, CA: University of California Press.

Herdt, G. (1986). *The Sambia: Ritual and Gender in New Guinea*. New York: Holt, Rinehart and Winston.

Herdt and Davidson. (1988). The Sambia 'urnim-man': Sociocultural and clinical aspects of gender formation in Papua, New Guinea. *Archives of Sexual Behavior*, vol. 17.

Heritage, J. (1985). *Garfinkel and Ethnomethodology*. New York: Basil Blackwell.

Hernandez, D. (1993). *America's Children: Resources from Family, Government, and Economy*. New York: Russell Sage Foundation.

Herrnstein and Murray. (1994). *The Bell Curve: Intelligence and Class Structure in American Life*. New York: Free Press.

Hesse-Biber, S. (1997). *Am I Thin Enough Yet?: The Cult of Thinness and the Commercialization of Identity*. New York: Oxford University Press.

Hexham and Poewe. (1997). *New Religions as Global Cultures*. Boulder, CO: Westview Press.

Higher Education Research Institute. (2008). *The American Freshman: National Norms*. Los Angeles: University of California.

Hirsch and Macpherson. (2004). Wages, Sorting on Skill, and the Racial Composition of Jobs. *Journal of Labor Economics*, University of Chicago Press, vol. 22(1), pages 189-210, January.

Himes, C. (1999). Racial differences in education, obesity, and health in later life. In N. E. Adler, M. Marmot, B. S. McEwen, & J. Stewart, eds., Socioeconomic status and health in industrial nations: Social, psychological, and biological pathways. *Annals of the New York Academy of Sciences*, 896, 370–372.

Hirschi, T. (1969). *Causes of Delinquency*. Berkeley, CA: University of California Press.

Hirst, P. (1997). The global economy: Myths and realities. *International Affairs*, vol. 73.

Hirst and Thompson. (1992). The problem of 'globalization': International economic relations, national economic management, and the formation of trading blocs. *Economy and Society*, vol. 24.

Hirst, P. (1999). *Globalization in Question: The International Economy and the Possibilities of Governance*. Rev. ed. Cambridge, UK: Polity Press.

Hochschild, A. (1975). Disengagement theory: A critique and proposal. *American Sociological Review*, vol. 40.

Hochschild, A. (1997). *The Time Bind*. New York: Metropolitan Books.

Hochschild and Machung. (1989). *The Second Shift: Working Parents and the Revolution at Home*. New York: Viking.

Hofstede, G. (1997). *Cultures and organizations: Software of the Mind*. New York: McGraw Hill.

Hogan, B. (2000). U.N.: Women's conference presses for political parity. *Radio Free Europe*, June.

Hogan, B. (1997). New reports say minorities benefit in fiscal recovery. *New York Times*, September 30, p. A1.

Holton, R. (1978). The crowds in history: Some problems of theory and method. *Social History*, vol. 3.

Homans, G. (1950). *The Human Group*. New York: Harcourt, Brace.

Homans, H. (1987). Man-made myth: The reality of being a woman scientist in the NHS, in Anne Spencer and David Podmore, eds., *In a Man's World: Essays on Women in Male-Dominated Professions*. London: Tavistock.

Hood, J. (2002). More Abuse Seen as Elder Population Grows. *Caregiver USA News*. December 16. www.andthoushalthonor.org/news/abuse.html, accessed 12/7/05.

Hopkins and Wallerstein. (1996). *The Age of Transition: Trajectory of the World-System, 1945–2025*. London: Zed Books.

Human Rights Watch. (1995). The global report on women's human rights. www.hrw.org/about/projects/womrep/, accessed 1/3/05.

Humphreys, L. (1970). *Tearoom Trade: Impersonal Sex in Public Places*. Chicago: Aldine.

Huntington, S. (1991). *The Third Wave: Democratization in the Late Twentieth Century*. Norman, OK: University of Oklahoma Press.

Hurtado, A. (1995). Variation, combinations, and evolutions: Latino families in the United States, in R. Zambrana, ed., *Understanding Latino Families*. Thousand Oaks, CA: Sage.

Hyman and Singer. (1968). *Readings in Reference Group Theory and Research*. New York: Free Press.

Hyman, R. (1984). *Strikes*. 2nd ed. London: Fontana.

IDEA. (2009). Voter Turnout 2009. www.idea.int/vt/view_data.cfm, accessed September 2009.

Illegems and Verbeke. (2004). Telework: What does it mean for management? *Long Range Planning*, 37(4): 319–334.

Illich, I. (1983). *Deschooling Society*. New York: Harper & Row.

Inglehart, R. (1997). *Modernization and Postmodernization: Cultural, Economic and Political Change in 43 Societies*. Princeton, NJ: Princeton University Press.

Institute of International Education. (2005a). Open Doors Online: Report on International Educational Exchange. http://opendoors.iienetwork.org/?p=69736, accessed 1/20/06.

Institute of International Education. (2005b). U.S. Study Abroad Increases by 9.6%, Continues Record Growth. November 14. www.iie.org/Content/NavigationMenu/Pressroom/PressReleases/U_S__STUDY_ABROAD_INCREASES_BY_9_6_CONTINUES_RECORD_GROWTH.htm, accessed spring 2006.

International Labor Organization. (1995). Women work more, but are still paid less. Press release. www.ilo.org/public/english/bureau/pr/1995/22.htm, accessed 1/11/05.

International Labor Organization. (1999). C182 Worst Forms of Child Labour Convention, www.ilo.org/public/english/standards/ipec/ratification/convention/text.htm, accessed 1/11/05.

International Labor Organization. (2000). Statistical information and monitoring programme on child labour (SIMPOC): Overview and strategic plan 2000–2002. Prepared by the International Program on the Elimination of Child Labour (IPEC) and Bureau of Statistics (STAT), January.

International Labor Organization. (2003). Identification of Economic Opportunities for Women's Groups and Communities. Geneva: ILO.

International Labor Organization. (2004a). More Women are Entering the Global Labor Force Than Ever Before, But Job Equality, Poverty Reduction Remain Elusive. www.ilo.org/public/english/bureau/inf/pr/2004/9.htm, accessed 12/4/05.

International Labor Organization. (2004b). Breaking the Glass Ceiling: Women in Management. www.ilo.org/dyn/gender/docs/RES/292/F267981337/Breaking%20Glass%20PDF%20English.pdf, accessed 12/4/05.

International Labor Organization. (2006). Key Indicators of the Labor Market Programme. www.ilo.org/public/english/employment/strat/kilm/download/kilm01.pdf, accessed July 2009.

ILGA. (2009). About ILGA. www.ilga.org/aboutilga.asp, accessed August 2009.

International Money Fund. (2005). World Economic Lookout. www.imf.org/external/pubs/ft/weo/2005/01/pdf/chapter4.pdf, accessed spring 2006.

International Road Federation. (1987). United Nations Annual Bulletin of Transport Statistics, cited in Social Trends London: HMSO.

International Telework Association & Council. (2004). Telework Facts and Figures. www.telecommute.org/resources/abouttelework.htm, accessed 1/20/05.

International Telework Association & Council. (2009). Telework Trendlines 2009. www.workingfromanywhere.org/news/Trendlines_2009.pdf, accessed June 2009.

Internet Society (ISOC). (1997). Web Languages Hit Parade. http://alis.isoc.org/palmares.en.html, accessed 1/11/05.

IUCN 2009. {International Union for Conservation of Nature} Summary Statistics for Globally Threatened Species. www.iucnredlist.org/documents/2008RL_stats_table_1_v1223294385.pdf, accessed August 2009.

Internet World Stats (2009a). Internet Usage and Population in North America. www.internetworldstats.com/stats14.htm, accessed May 2009.

Internet World Stats (2009b). Asia Internet Usage and Population. www.internetworldstats.com/stats3.htm#asia, accessed May 2009.

Internet World Stats (2009c). Top Ten Languages Used in the Web. www.internetworldstats.com/stats7.htm, accessed May 2009.

Internet World Stats (2009d). World Usage Stats. www.internetworldstats.com/pr/edi008.htm

Jacobs, J. (1961). *The Death and Life of Great American Cities*. New York: Random House.

Jaher, ed. (1973). *The Rich, the Well Born, and the Powerful*. Urbana, IL: University of Illinois Press.

Janis, I. (1972). *Victims of Groupthink*. Boston: Houghton Mifflin.

Janis, I. (1989). *Crucial Decisions: Leadership in Policy Making and Crisis Management*. New York: Free Press.

Janis, I. and Mann, Leon. (1977). *Decision Making: A Psychological Analysis of Conflict, Choice, and Commitment*. New York: Free Press.

Jencks, et al. (1972). *Inequality: A Reassessment of the Effects of Family and School in America*. New York: Basic Books.

Jin, G. (2006). Chinese gold farmers in the game world. Consumers, Commodities and Consumption: A Newsletter of the Consumer Studies Research Network, 7(2). https://etfiles.uiuc.edu/dtcook/www/CCC newsletter/7-2/jin.htm, accessed 10/26/08.

Jobling, R. (1988). The experience of psoriasis under treatment, in Michael Bury and Robert Anderson, eds., *Living with Chronic Illness: The Experience of Patients and Their Families*. London: Unwin Hyman.

Johnson and Morton. (1991). *Biology and Cognitive Development: The Case of Face Recognition*. Oxford, UK: Blackwell.

Johnson, K. (2006). *Demographic Trends in Rural and Small town America*. Carsey Institute Reports on Rural America: 1.

Johnson, M. (1995). Patriarchal terrorism and common couple violence: Two forms of violence against women in U.S. families. *Journal of Marriage and the Family*, vol. 57.

Johnson, O. (1991). Common themes, different contexts: Third World women and feminism, in Chandra Mohanty, et al., eds., *Third World Women and the Politics of Feminism*. Bloomington, IN: Indiana University Press.

Joint Center for Housing Studies of Harvard University. (2005). The State of the Nation's Housing, 2005. www.jchs.harvard.edu/publications/markets/son2005/son2005. pdf, accessed spring 2006.

Jones, S. (1995). Understanding community in the information age. in S. G. Jones, ed., *CyberSociety: Computer-Mediated Communication and Community*. Thousand Oaks, CA: Sage.

The Journal of Blacks in Higher Education. (2007). Black Student College Graduation Rates Inch Higher But a Large Racial Gap Persists. www.jbhe.com/preview/winter07preview.html

Juergensmeyer, M. (1994). *The New Cold War? Religious Nationalism Confronts the Secular State (Comparative Studies in Religion and Society)*. Berkeley: University of California Press.

Juergensmeyer, M. (2001). *Terror in the Mind of God: The Global Rise of Religious Violence*. Berkeley, California: University of California Press.

Kamp, Cohan, and Amato. (2003). The Relationship between Cohabitation and Marital Quality and Stability: Change across Cohorts? *Journal of Marriage and the Family*, 65:539–549.

Kanter, R. (1983). *The Change Masters: Innovation for Productivity in the American Corporation*. New York: Simon and Schuster.

Kanter, R. (1991). The future of bureaucracy and hierarchy in organizational theory, in Pierre Bourdieu and James Coleman, eds., *Social Theory for a Changing Society*. Boulder, CO: Westview.

Kasarda, J. (1993). Urban industrial transition and the underclass, in William Julius Wilson, ed., *The Ghetto Underclass*. Newbury Park, CA: Sage.

Kasarda and Crenshaw. (1991). Third World urbanization: Dimensions, theories, and determinants, in *Annual Review of Sociology*, 1991, vol. 17. Palo Alto, CA: Annual Reviews.

Kautsky, J. (1982). *The Politics of Aristocratic Empires*. Chapel Hill: University of North Carolina Press.

Kelling and Coles. (1997). *Fixing Broken Windows: Restoring Order and Reducing Crime in Our Communities*. New York: The Free Press.

Kelley and Evans. (1995). Class and class conflict in six western nations. *American Review of Sociology*, vol. 60, no. 2.

Kelly, L. (1987). The continuum of sexual violence, in Jala Hanmer and Mary Maynard, eds., *Women, Violence, and Social Control*. Atlantic Highlands, NJ: Humanities Press.

Kelly, M. (1992). *Colitis: The Experience of Illness*. London: Routledge.

Kemp, et al. (1995). The dawn of a new day: Redefining South African feminism, in Amrita Basu, ed., *The Challenge of Local Feminisms*. Boulder, CO: Westview.

Kenkel, Lillard, and Mathios. (2006). The roles of high school completion and GED receipt in smoking and obesity. *Journal of Labor Economics*, 24(3): 635–660.

Kimmel, M. (2003). *The Gender of Desire: Essays on Male Sexuality*. Albany: State University of New York Press.

King, N. (1984). Exploitation and abuse of older family members: An overview of the problem, in J. J. Cosa, ed., *Abuse of the Elderly*. Lexington, MA: Lexington Books.

Kinsey, et al. (1948). *Sexual Behavior in the Human Male*. Philadelphia: Saunders.

Kinsey, et al. (1953). *Sexual Behavior in the Human Female*. Philadelphia: Saunders.

Kjekshus, H. (1977). *Ecology, Control, and Economic Development in East African History*. Berkeley, CA: University of California Press.

Kling, R. (1996). Computerization at work, in R. Kling, ed., *Computers and Controversy*. 2nd ed. New York: Academic Press.

Kluckhohn, C. (1949). *Mirror for Man*. Tucson: University of Arizona Press.

Knodel, J. (2006, August). Parents of persons with AIDS: Unrecognized contributions and unmet needs. *Journal of Global Ageing*, 4, 46–55.

Knoke, D. (1990). *Political Networks: The Structural Perspective*. New York: Cambridge University Press.

Knorr-Cetina and Cicourel, eds. (1981). *Advances in Social Theory and Methodology: Towards an Integration of Micro- and Macro-Sociologies*. Boston: Routledge and Kegan Paul.

Kobrin, S. (1997). Electronic Cash and the End of National Markets, *Foreign Policy* 107 (Summer): 65–77.

Kohn, M. (1977). *Class and Conformity*. 2nd ed. Homewood, IL: Dorsey Press.

Kollock and Smith. (1996). Managing the virtual commons: Cooperation and conflict in computer communities, in S. Herring, ed., *Computer-Mediated Communication*. Amsterdam: John Benjamins.

Kosmin, Mayer, and Keysar. (2001). American Religious Identification Survey (ARIS). New York: *CUNY Graduate Center* (December 19). www.gc.cuny.edu/studies/aris.pdf, accessed 1/3/05.

Kozol, J. (1991). *Savage Inequalities: Children in America's Schools*. New York: Crown.

Krueger, C. (1995). Retirees with company health plans on decline. *Los Angeles Times*, September 22.

Lacayo, R. (1994). Lock 'em up! *Time*, February 7.

Landale and Fennelly. (1992). Informal unions among mainland Puerto Ricans: Cohabitation or an alternative to legal marriage? *Journal of Marriage and the Family*, vol. 54.

Landler and Barbaro. (2006). No, Not Always. Wal-Mart Discovers that its Formula Doesn't Fit Every Culture. *New York Times*, C1, 4 (August 2).

Lander and Kahn. (2007). China Grabs West's Smoke Spewing Factories, *New York Times*. www.nytimes.com/2007/12/21/world/asia/21transfer.html?_r=1&oref=slogin.

Lappe, et al. (1998). *World Hunger: 12 Myths*. 2nd ed. New York: Grove Press.

LaRue, J. (2005). *Obscenity and the First Amendment. Summit on Pornography*. Rayburn House Office Building, Room 2322.

Latner and Stunkard. (2003). Getting worse: The stigmatization of obese children. *Obesity Research*, 11, 452–456.

Laumann, et al. (1994). *The Social Organization of Sexuality: Sexual Practices in the United States*. Chicago: University of Chicago Press.

Leach, E. (1976). *Culture and Communication: The Logic by Which Symbols Are Connected*. New York: Cambridge University Press.

Lee, G. (1982). *Family Structure and Interaction: A Comparative Analysis*. 2nd ed. Minneapolis: University of Minnesota Press.

Lemert, E. (1972). *Human Deviance, Social Problems, and Social Control*. Englewood Cliffs, NJ: Prentice-Hall.

Leupp, G. (1995). *Male Colors, the Construction of Homosexuality in Tokugawa Japan*. Berkeley, CA: University of California Press.

LeVay, S. (1991). A Difference in Hypothalamic Structure between Heterosexual and Homosexual Men. *Science* 253(5023): 1034–1037.

Levin, W. (1988). Age stereotyping: College student evaluations. *Research on Aging*, vol. 10.

Lewis, O. (1968). The culture of poverty, in Daniel P. Moyhihan, ed., *On Understanding Poverty: Perspectives from the Social Sciences*. New York: Basic Books.

Lightfoot-Klein. (1989). *Prisoners of Ritual: An Odyssey into Female Genital Circumcision in Africa*. New York: Haworth.

Lin and Rogerson. (1995). Elderly parents and the geographic availability of their adult children. *Research on Aging*, 17, 303–331.

Linden, Kraemer, and Dedrick. (2007). Who captures value in a global innovation system? The case of Apple's iPod. Alfred P. *Sloan Foundation: Personal Computing Industry Center*. pcic.merage.uci.edu/papers/2007/AppleiPod.pdf, accessed fall 2007.

Lipsky, D. (2003a). *Absolutely American: Four Years at West Point*. Boston, MA: Houghton Mifflin.

Lipsky, D. (2003b). After Four Years at West Point, David Lipsky Still Wants More, *Powell's Author Interviews*, August 6. www.powells.com/authors/lipsky.html, accessed spring 2006.

Liptak, A. (2008). U.S. Prison Population Dwarfs That of Other Nations. *New York Times* (April 23, 2008).

Logan and Molotch. (1987). *Urban Fortunes: The Political Economy of Place*. Berkeley, California: University of California Press.

Lopez, Levine, Both, Kiesa, Kirby, and Marcelo. (2006). *The 2006 Civic and Political Health of the Nation: A Detailed Look at How Youth Participate in Politics and Communities*. College Park, MD: Center for Information and Research on Civic Learning and Engagement (CIRCLE).

Lorber, J. (1994). *Paradoxes of Gender*. New Haven, CT: Yale University Press.

Loury, G. (1987). Why should we care about group inequality? *Social Philosophy and Policy*, vol. 5.

Lyotard, J. (1985). *The Post-Modern Condition: A Report on Knowledge*. Minneapolis: University of Minnesota Press.

Maddox, G. (1965). Fact and artifact: Evidence bearing on disengagement from the Duke Geriatrics Project. *Human Development*, vol. 8.

Maddox, G. (1970). Themes and issues in sociological theories of human aging. *Human Development*, vol. 13.

Maharidge, D. (1996). *The Coming White Minority*. New York: Times Books.

Malotki, E. (1983). *Hopi Time: A Linguistic Analysis of the Temporal Concepts in the Hopi Language*. Berlin: Mouton.

Malthus, T. (2003; orig. 1798). *Essay on the Principle of Population: A Norton Critical Edition, Revised Edition*. Ed. Philip Appleman. New York: Norton.

Manning, Koukourakis, and Brodie. (1997). Fluctuating asymmetry, metabolic rate and sexual selection in human males. *Evolution and Human Behavior*, vol. 18, no. 1.

Manpower Inc. (2009). About Manpower. www.manpower.com/about/about.cfm, accessed September 2009.

Manton, Corder, and Stallard. (1993). Estimates of change in chronic disability and institutional incidence and prevalence rates in the U.S. elderly population from the 1982, 1984, and 1989 national long term care survey. *Journal of Gerontology*, vol. 48, no. 466.

Mare, R. (1991). Five decades of educational assortative mating. *American Sociological Review*, vol. 56, no. 1.

Marsden and Lin. (1982). *Social Structure and Network Analysis*. Beverly Hills, California: Sage.

Marshall, T. (1973). *Class, Citizenship, and Social Development: Essays by T. H. Marshall*. Westport, CT: Greenwood Press.

Martineau, H. (2009) *Society in America*. 3 volumes. Saunders and Otley, 1837; Reissued by Cambridge University Press.

Marx, K. (1977). *Capital: A Critique of Political Economy*. Vol. 1. Originally published 1864. New York: Random House.

Massey, D. (1996). The age of extremes: Concentrated affluence and poverty in the twenty-first century. *Demography*, vol. 33, no. 4.

Massey and Denton. (1993). *American apartheid: Segregation and the making of the underclass*. Cambridge, MA: Harvard University Press.

Massey, Denton, and Durand. (1993). *American Apartheid: Segregation and the Making of the Underclass*. Cambridge, MA: Harvard University Press.

Mather, M. (2008). *Population Losses Mount in U.S. Rural Areas*. Washington, DC: Population Reference Bureau.

Matsueda, R. (1992). Reflected appraisals, parental labeling, and delinquency: Specifying a symbolic interactionist theory. *American Journal of Sociology*, vol. 97.

Mauer, M. (2004). Hispanic Prisoners in the United States. *The Sentencing Project*. www.sentencingproject.org/Admin%5CDocuments%5Cpublications%5Cinc_hispanicprisoners.pdf, accessed spring 2006.

McDonough, S. (2005). U.S. Prison Population Soars in 2003, '04. *ABCNews*. com. April 25. http://abcnews.go.com/US/LegalCenter/wireStory?id=699808&CMP=OTC-RSSFeeds0312, accessed spring 2006.

McFadden and Champlin. (2000). Comparison of auditory evoked potentials in heterosexual, homosexual, and bisexual males and females. *Journal of the Association for Research in Otolaryngology*, vol. 1.

McKinlay, J. (1975). A case for refocusing downstream: The political economy of illness, in P. Conrad and R. Kern, eds., *The Sociology of Health and Illness: Critical Perspectives*. New York: St. Martin's Press.

McLanahan, S. (2004). Diverging Destinies: How Children Are Faring under the Second Demographic Transition. *Demography*, 41:607–627.

McLanahan and Sandefur. (1994). *Growing Up with a Single Parent: What Hurts, What Helps*. Cambridge, MA: Harvard University Press.

Mead, M. (1963). *Sex and Temperament in Three Primitive Societies*. Originally published 1935. New York: William Morrow.

Mead, M. (1966). Marriage in Two Steps. *Redbook Magazine*, 48–49, 84–86.

Mead, M. (1972). *Blackberry Winter: My Earlier Years*. New York: William Morrow.

Meadows, et al. (1972). *The Limits to Growth.* New York: Universe Books.

Meatto, K. (2000). Real reformers, real results: Our seventh annual roundup of student protest. *Mojo Wire Magazine,* September–October, www.mojones.com/mother_jones/SO00/activist_campuses.html, accessed 1/3/05.

Melton, J. (1989). *The Encyclopedia of American Religions.* 3rd ed. Detroit, MI: Gale Research Co.

Menn, J. (2003). The 'geeks' who once shunned activism amid the digital revolution are using their money and savvy to influence public policy, *Los Angeles Times,* August 11, p. A-1.

Merton, R. (1957). *Social Theory and Social Structure.* Rev. ed. New York: Free Press.

Merton, R. (1968). Social structure and anomie. Originally published 1938. *American Sociological Review,* vol. 3.

Meyer and Rowan. (1977). Institutionalized organizations: Formal structure as myth and ceremony. *American Journal of Sociology,* vol. 83.

Michels, R. (1967). *Political Parties.* Originally published 1911. New York: Free Press.

Milgram, S. (1963). Behavioral studies in obedience. *Journal of Abnormal Psychology,* vol. 67.

Mills, C. (1956). *The Power Elite.* New York: Oxford University Press.

Mills, C. (1959). *The Sociological Imagination.* New York: Oxford University Press.

Mills, T. (1967). *The Sociology of Small Groups.* Englewood, NJ: Prentice-Hall.

Milner Jr., M. (2004). *Freaks, Geeks, and Cool Kids: American Teenagers, Schools, and the Culture of Consumption.* New York: Routledge.

Mirza, H. (1986). *Multinationals and the Growth of the Singapore Economy.* New York: St. Martin's Press.

Moe, R. (2006). Presidential Address. National Trust for Historic Preservation. *Commonwealth Club,* San Francisco, Calif. (June 28). www.nationaltrust.org/news/2006/20060628_speech_sf.html, accessed 1/8/07.

Moffitt, T. (1996). The neuropsychology of conduct disorder, in P. Cordella and L. Siegel, eds., *Readings in Contemporary Criminological Theory.* Boston: Northeastern University Press.

Mohanty, C. (1991). Under Western eyes: Feminist scholarship and colonial discourse, in Chandra Talpade Mohanty, Ann Russo, and Lourdes Torres, eds., *Third World Women and the Politics of Feminism.* Bloomington, IN: Indiana University Press.

Monthly Bulletin of Statistics. (2009). Total Imports and Exports – *World.* http://unstats.un.org/unsd/mbs/app/DataView.aspx?tid=34&cid=1&yearfrom=1997&yearto=2009&p=Y, accessed August 2009.

Moore Jr., B. (1966). *Social Origins of Dictatorship and Democracy: Lord and Peasant in the Making of the Modern World.* Boston: Beacon Press.

Moore, L. (1994). *Selling God: American Religion in the Marketplace of Culture.* New York: Oxford University Press.

Mor-Barak, et al. (1992). Employment, social networks, and health in the retirement years. *International Journal of Aging and Human Development,* vol. 35.

Morland, Wing, Diez-Roux, and Poole. (2002). Neighborhood characteristics associated with the location of food stores and food service places. *American Journal of Preventive Medicine,* 22(1): 23–29.

Morris, J. (1974). *Conundrum.* New York: Harcourt Brace Jovanovich.

Mumford, L. (1973). *Interpretations and Forecasts.* New York: Harcourt Brace Jovanovich.

Muncie, J. (1999). *Youth and Crime: A Critical Introduction.* London: Sage.

Murdock, G. (1967). *Ethnographic Atlas.* Pittsburgh: Pittsburgh University Press.

Murray, C. (1984). *Losing Ground: American Social Policy, 1950–1980.* New York: Basic Books.

Mwabu, Ugaz, and White. (2001). *Social Provision in Low-income Countries: New Patterns and Emerging Trends.* Oxford: Oxford University Press.

Najman, J. (1993). Health and poverty: past, present, and prospects for the future. *Social Science and Medicine,* vol. 36, no. 2.

Narayan, D. (1999). *Can Anyone Hear Us? Voices From 47 Countries.* Washington, DC: World Bank Poverty Group, PREM, December.

National Assessment Center. (2006). At Risk Online: National Assessment of Youth on the Internet and the Effectiveness of i-SAFE Internet Safety Education. www.isafe.org/imgs/pdf/NAC_summary.pdf, accessed June 2009.

National Center for Education Statistics. (2005). Digest of Education Statistics, 2004. http://nces.ed.gov/programs/digest/d04/tables/dt04_298.asp, accessed 1/20/06.

National Center for Health Statistics. (2008e). National Marriage and Divorce Rate Trends. www.cdc.gov/nchs/nvss/mardiv_tables.htm

National Center for Health Statistics. (2003). Women's health. www.cdc.gov/nchs/fastats/womens_health.htm, accessed 1/11/05.

National Center for Health Statistics. (2005a). Health, United States, 2005. www.cdc.gov/nchs/data/hus/ hus05.pdf, accessed spring 2006.

National Center for Health Statistics. (2007). Percent of adults 18 years of age and over who currently smoke. www.cdc.gov/nchs/data/hus/hus08.pdf#data06, accessed August 2009.

National Center for Health Statistics. (2007b). *Health, United States, 2007, with Chartbook on Trends in the Health of Americans.* Washington, DC: NCHS. www.cdc.gov/nchs/data/hus/hus07.pdf, accessed 2/23/10.

National Center for Health Statistics. (2008a). Percent of women 40 years of age and over who had a mammogram within the past 2 years. www.cdc.gov/nchs/data/hus/hus08.pdf#089, accessed August 2009.

National Center for Health Statistics. (2008b). AIDS cases by year of diagnosis and selected characteristics (table 51). www.cdc.gov/nchs/data/hus/hus08.pdf#051, accessed August 2009.

National Center for Health Statistics. (2008c). Hypertension Data. www.cdc.gov/nchs/data/hus/hus08.pdf#071, accessed August 2009.

National Center for Health Statistics. (2008d). Percent of women 40 years of age and over who had a mammogram within the past 2 years. www.cdc.gov/nchs/data/hus/hus08.pdf#089, accessed August 2009.

National Center on Elder Abuse. (2005). Fact Sheet: Elder Abuse Prevalence and Incidence. www.elderabusecenter.org/pdf/publication/FinalStatistics050331.pdf, accessed 12/7/05.

National Coalition of Homeless Veterans. (2007). Background and statistics. www.nchv.org/background.cfm, accessed fall 2007.

National Eating Disorders Association. (2002). Statistics: Eating Disorders and their Precursors. www.nationaleatingdisorders.org/p.asp?WebPage_ID=286&Profile_ID=41138, accessed 1/29/06

National Heart, Lung, Blood Institute. (1998). *Clinical Guidelines on the Identification, Evaluation, and Treatment of Overweight and Obesity in Adults.* Bethesda, MD.

National Immigration Forum. (2006). Facts on Immigration. January 26. www.immigrationforum.org/DesktopDefault.aspx?tabid=790, accessed 1/27/06.

National Law Center on Homelessness and Poverty. (2004). Key Data Concerning Homeless Persons in America. July. www.nlchp.org/FA_HAPIA/HomelessPersonsinAmerica.pdf, accessed spring 2006.

National Law Center on Homelessness and Poverty. (2009). *Indicators of Increasing Homelessness Due to the Foreclosure and Economic Crises.* www.nlchp.org/content/pubs/

Foreclosure_effects_on_homelessness. pdf, accessed 12/09/09.

National Low Income Housing Coalition (NLIHC). (2000). Out of Reach: The Growing Gap between Housing Costs and Income of Poor People in the United States. (September) Washington, DC: The National Low Income Housing Coalition/Low Income Housing Information Service, www.nlihc.org/oor2000/index.htm, accessed 1/3/05.

National Marriage Project. (2005). The State of Our Unions: The Social Health of Marriage in America. http://marriage.rutgers.edu/Publications/SOOU/SOOU2005.pdf, accessed 1/13/06.

National Marriage Project. (2008). The State of Our Unions: The Social Health of Marriage in America. www.virginia.edu/marriageproject/pdfs/2008update.pdf

National Urban League. (2009). July 2009 Monthly Employment Report (August 7, 2009). Washington, DC: National Urban League. www.nul.org/publications/policyinstitute/monthlyemployment-stats/2009_July_Employment_Report. pdf, accessed 9/2/09.

NCSL. (2009). Women in State Legislatures: 2009 Legislative Session. www.ncsl.org/LegislaturesElections/WomensNetwork/WomeninStateLegislatures2009/tabid/15398/Default.aspx, accessed July 2009.

Nelson and Dannefer. (1992). Aged heterogeneity: Fact or fiction? The fate of diversity in gerontological research. *Gerontologist*, vol. 32.

NES. (2003). The NES Guide to Public Opinion and Electoral Behavior, The National Election Studies, Graph 5A.1.2, Center for Political Studies, University of Michigan. Ann Arbor, MI: University of Michigan, *Center for Political Studies*. www.umich.edu/nes/nesguide/graphs/g5a_1_2.htm, accessed 1/3/05.

Neuman, J. (2003). Liberals take a cue from Republicans and turn to big donors to set up think tanks and media outlets to counter the conservative message. *Los Angeles Times*, November 30, p. A-20.

Newman, K. (2000). *No Shame in My Game: The Working Poor in the Inner City*. New York: Vintage.

Nie, Simpser, Stepanikova, and Zheng. (2004). Ten Years After the Birth of the Internet, How do Americans use the Internet in their Daily Lives? Draft Report. *Stanford University*. www.stanford.edu/group/siqss/SIQSS_Time_Study_04.pdf, accessed 9/23/05.

Niebuhr, H. (1929). *The Social Sources of Denominationalism*. New York: Holt.

Nielsen Media Research. (2001a). Internet access for blue collar workers spikes 52 percent, according to Nielsen/

Net-ratings, http://209.249.142.22/press_releases/PDF/pr_010412.pdf, accessed 5/3/01.

Nielsen Media Research. (2001b). Lower income surfers are the fastest growing group on the web, according to Nielsen/Netratings. http://209.249.142.22/press_releases/PDF/pr_010313.pdf, accessed 5/3/01.

Nielsen, Francois. (1994). Income inequality and industrial development: Dualism revisited. *American Sociological Review*, vol. 59 (October).

Nonprofit Voter Engagement Network. (2009). America Goes to the Polls: A Report on Voter Turnout in the 2008 Election. St. Paul, MN: NVEN. www.nonprofitvote.org/Voter-Turnout-2008.html, accessed 2/3/10.

NPD. (2009). Total game console sales, May 2009. www.digital-digest.com/blog/DVDGuy/2009/06/13/game-consoles-may-2009-npd-sales-figure-analysis/, accessed June 2009.

Nua.com. (2000). www.nua.ie/surveys/how_many_online/ index.html, accessed 1/3/05.

Oakes, J. (1985). *Keeping Track: How Schools Structure Inequality*. New Haven, CT: Yale University Press.

Oakes, J. (1990). *Multiplying Inequalities: The Effects of Race, Social Class, and Tracking on Opportunities to Learn Mathematics and Science*. Santa Monica, CA: Rand.

Oakley, A. (1974). *The Sociology of Housework*. New York: Pantheon.

Office of National Drug Control Policy. (2005). Drug Control Funding Tables. *The White House*. www.whitehousedrugpolicy. gov/publications/policy/06budget/funding_tbls.pdf, accessed spring 2006.

O'Hare and Mather. (2008). Child poverty is highest in rural counties in U.S. Population Reference Bureau. Retrieved February 15, 2008. www.prb.org.

Ohmae, K. (1990). *The Borderless World: Power and Strategy in the Industrial Economy*. New York: HarperCollins.

Ohmae, K. (1995). *The End of the Nation Sate: How Region States Harness the Prosperity of the Global Economy*. New York: Free Press.

Oliver and Shapiro. (1995). *Black Wealth/White Wealth: A New Perspective on Racial Inequality*. New York: Routledge.

Olson and Sophia. (1984). Working at home with computers. *Journal of Social Issues*, 40(3): 97–112.

Oppenheimer, V. (1970). *The Female Labor Force in the United States*. Westport, CT: Greenwood Press.

Oppenheimer, V. (1988). A theory of marriage timing. *American Journal of Sociology*, vol. 94.

Organization for Economic Co-operation and Development. (2005a). Fact book: Economic, Environmental, and Social Statistics. www.oecd.org/site/0,2865, en_21571361_34374092_1_1_1_1,00/html, accessed spring 2006.

Organization for Economic Co-operation and Development. (2005b). OECD Science, Technology, and Industry Scoreboard 2005—Towards a Knowledge-based Economy. Section C.11. http://lysander.sourceoecd.org/vl=11306884/cl=28/nw=1/rpsv/scoreboard/c11.htm, accessed 12/1/05.

Ortiz, V. (1995). Families, in R. Zambrana, ed., *Understanding Latino Families*. Thousand Oaks, CA: Sage.

Pagan and Pauly. (2005). Access to conventional medical care and the use of complementary and alternative medicine. *Health Affairs*, 24, 255–263.

Pager, D. (2003). The mark of a criminal record, *American Journal of Psychology* vol. 108, no. 5: 937–75.

Pager, Devah and Hana Shepard. (2008). The Sociology of Discrimination: Racial Discrimination in Employment, Housing, Credit and Consumer Markets. *Annual Review of Sociology* 34: 181–209.

Pahl, J. (1989). *Money and Marriage*. London: Macmillan.

Paludi and Barickman. (1991). *Academic and Workplace Sexual Harassment: A Resource Manual*. Albany, NY: SUNY Press.

Panyarachun, et al. (2004). A More Secure World: Our Shared Responsibility: report of the high-level panel on threats, challenges and change. New York: *United Nations*. www.un.org/secureworld, accessed spring 2006.

Parents Television Council, (2006). Dying to Entertain. www.parentstv.org/ptc/publications/reports/violencestudy/exsummary.asp, accessed June 2009.

Parillo and Donaghue. (2005). Updating the Borgardus Social Distance Studies: A New National Survey. *Social Science Journal* 42: 257–271.

Park, R. (1952). *Human Communities: The City and Human Ecology*. New York: Free Press.

Parsons, T. (1951). *The Social System*. Glencoe, IL: Free Press.

Parsons, T. (1960). Towards a healthy maturity. *Journal of Health and Social Behavior*, vol. 1.

Parsons, T. (1964). *The Social System*. New York: Free Press.

Parsons and Bales. (1955). *Family, Socialization, and Interaction Process*. Glencoe, IL: Free Press.

Pascoe, Eva. (2000). Can a sense of community flourish in cyberspace? *The Guardian* (March 11).

Paulson, A. (2006). Milwaukee's Lessons on School Vouchers. *Christian Science Monitor* (May 23).

Pearce, F. (1976). *Crimes of the Powerful: Marxism, Crime, and Deviance*. London: Pluto Press.

Pennenberg, A. (2004). Voter Polls Don't Count for Much. Wired (10/27). www.wired.com/culture/lifestyle/news/2004/10/65481

Peterson, R. (1996). A re-evaluation of the economic consequences of divorce. *American Sociological Review*, vol. 61.

Pew Center on the States. (2008). *One in 100: Behind Bars in America 2008*. Washington, DC: Pew Charitable Trusts., accessed November 25, 2008.

Pew Research Center for the People and the Press. (2002). Public Opinion Six Months Later. March 7. http://people-press. org/commentary/display.php3?AnalysisID=44, accessed 9/25/05.

Pew Research Center for the People and the Press. (2004). Democrats Gain Edge in Party Identification. http://people-press.org/commentary/display.php3?AnalysisID=95, accessed 1/9/06.

Pew Research Center for the People and the Press. (2005). Internet: The Mainstreaming of On-line Life. www.pewinternet.org/ pdfs/Internet_Status_2005.pdf, accessed 9/25/05.

Pew Research Center for the People and the Press. (2007). *World Publics Welcome Global Trade but Not Immigration. 47-Nation Pew Global Attitudes Survey*. Washington, DC: The Pew Global Attitudes Project. http://pewglobal. org/reports/display.php?ReportID=258, accessed 5/25/09.

PEW (2007b). Key Findings and Statistics on Religion in America. http://religions .pewforum.org/reports, accessed August 2009.

Pew Research Center for the People and the Press. (2009a). Generations *Online in 2009*. Washington, DC: Pew Internet and American Life Project. www. pewinternet.org/PPF/r/275/report_display.asp, accessed 3/13/09.

Pew (2009b). Daily Internet Activities. Pew Internet and American Life Project. www.pewinternet.org/Static-Pages/Trend-Data/Online-Activities-Daily. aspx, accessed June 2009.

Pew (2009c). Independents Take Center Stage in Obama Era: Trends in Political Values and Core Attitudes: 1987-2009. http://people-press.org/report/517/political-values-and-core-attitudes, accessed September 2009.

Pfizer (2007). Pfizer Public Policy: Price Controls. www.pfizer.com/about/public_policy/price_controls.jsp, accessed 2/4/10.

Pillemer, K. (1985). The dangers of dependency: New findings in domestic violence against the elderly. Social Problems, vol. 33.

Pillemer and Finkelhor. (1988). The prevalence of elder abuse: A random sample survey. *Gerontologist*, vol. 28.

Piller and Smith. (2007). Unintended Victims: The Gates Foundation's generous gifts to fight AIDS, TB and malaria have inadvertently put many of those with other healthcare needs at risk. *Los Angeles Times* (December 16).

Pintor and Gratschew. (2002). Voter Turnout Since 1945: A Global Report. Stockholm, Sweden: International Institute for Democracy and Electoral Assistance (International IDEA). www.idea.int/publications/turnout/ VT_screenopt_2002.pdf, accessed 1/3/05.

Pollak, O. (1950). *The Criminality of Women*. Philadelphia: University of Pennsylvania Press.

Polletta and Jasper. (2001). Collective Identity and Social Movements, *Annual Review of Sociology* vol. 27: 283-305.

Popenoe, D. (1993). American family decline, 1960-1990: A review and appraisal. *Journal of Marriage and Family*, 55: 527-42.

Popenoe, D. (1996). *Life Without Father: Compelling New Evidence That Fatherhood and Marriage Are Indispensable for the Good of Children and Society*. New York: Martin Kessler Books.

Prebisch, R. (1967). *Hacia una dinamica del desarollo Latinoamericano*. Montevideo, Uruguay: Ediciones de la Banda Oriental.

Prebisch, R. (1971). *Change and Development— Latin America's Great Task: Report Submitted to the Inter-American Bank*. New York: Praeger.

President's Commission on Organized Crime. (1986). Records of Hearings, June 24–26, 1985. Washington, DC: U.S. Government Printing Office.

Provenzo Jr., E. (1991). *Video Kids: Making Sense of Nintendo*. Cambridge, MA: Harvard University Press.

Public Strategies Inc. (2009). 2009 Public Trust Monitor, Q1. Washington, DC: Author. www.politico.com/static/PPM41_publictrust.html

Purnell and Paulanka. (2005). *Guide to Culturally Competent Health Care*. Philadelphia: F. A. Davis, Co.

Putnam, R. (1993). The prosperous community: Social capital and public life. *American Prospect*, vol. 13.

Putnam, R. (1995). Bowling alone: America's declining social capital. *Journal of Democracy*, vol. 6.

Putnam, R. (2000). *Bowling Alone: The Collapse and Revival of American Community*. New York: Simon & Schuster.

Quah, D. (1999). *The Weightless Economy in Economic Development*. London: Centre for Economic Performance.

Raghuram and Wiesenfeld. (2004). Work-nonwork conflict and job stress among virtual workers, *Human Resource Management*, 43(2–3): 259–277.

Ramirez and Boli. (1987). The political construction of mass schooling: European origins and worldwide institutionalism. *Sociology of Education*, vol. 60.

Ranis, G. (1996). *Will Latin America now put a stop to 'stop-and-go?'* New Haven, CT: Yale University, Economic Growth Center.

Ranis and Mahmood. (1992). *The Political Economy of Development Policy Change*. Cambridge, MA: Blackwell.

Redding, S. (1990). *The Spirit of Chinese Capitalism*. Berlin: De Gruyter.

Reeves and Claudette. (2004). *We the People: Asians in the United States*. Washington, D.C.: U.S. Census Bureau.

Renzetti and Curran. (1995). *Women, Men, and Society*. 3rd ed. Needham Heights, MA: Allyn and Bacon.

Renzetti and Curran. (2000). *Social Problems: Society in Crisis*. 5th ed. Needham Heights, MA: Allyn & Bacon.

Richardson, Goodman, Hastorf, and Dornbusch. (1961). Cultural uniformity in reaction to physical disabilities. *American Sociological Review*, 26, 241–247.

Riddick, C. (1985). Life satisfaction for older female homemakers, retirees, and workers. *Research on Aging*, vol. 7.

Rieff, D. (1991). *Los Angeles: Capital of the Third World*. New York: Simon and Schuster.

Riley, Foner, and Waring. (1988). Sociology of age, in Neil J. Smelser, ed., *Handbook of Sociology*. Newbury Park, CA: Sage.

Ritzer, G. (1993). *The McDonaldization of Society*. Newbury Park, CA: Pine Forge Press.

Roach, S. (2005). The New Macro of Globalization, *Global: Daily Economic Comment*, June 6.

Roberts, S. (1995). Women's Work: What's New, What Isn't. *New York Times*, April 27, p. B6.

Robinson, W. (2001). Social Theory and Globalization: The Rise of a transnational State, *Theory and Society* 30:2 (April): 157–200.

Robinson, W. (2004). *A Theory of Global Capitalism: Production, Class and State in a Transnational World*. Baltimore: Johns Hopkins University Press.

Robinson, W. (2005a). Gramsci and Globalisation: From Nation-State to Transnational Hegemony, *Critical Review of International Social and Political Philosophy* 8: 4 (December): 1–16.

Robinson, W. (2005b). Global Capitalism: The New Transnationalism and the Folly of Conventional Thinking, *Science and Society* 69: 3 (July): 316–328.

Roof, W. (1993). *A Generation of Seekers: The Spiritual Journeys of the Baby Boom Generation.* San Francisco: Harper San Francisco.

Roof, W. (1999). *Spiritual Marketplace: Baby Boomers and the Remaking of American Religion.* Princeton, NJ: Princeton University Press.

Roof and McKinney. (1990). *American Mainline Religion: Its Changing Shape and Future Prospects.* New Brunswick, NJ: Rutgers University Press.

Roscoe, W. (1991). *The Zuni Man-Woman.* Albuquerque, NM: University of New Mexico Press.

Rosenau, J. (1997). *Along the Domestic-Foreign Frontier: Exploring Governance in a Turbulent World.* Cambridge, UK: Cambridge University Press.

Ross and Hansen (2001). AOL, Time Warner complete merger with FCC blessing. *CNET News.com.* http://news.cnet. com/2100-1023-250781.html, accessed 12/16/09.

Rossi, A. (1973). The first woman sociologist: Harriett Martineau, in *The Feminist Papers: From Adams to de Beauvoir.* New York: Columbia University Press.

Rostow, W. (1961). *The Stages of Economic Growth.* Cambridge, UK: Cambridge University Press.

Rousselle, R. (1999). Defining ancient Greek sexuality. *Digital Archives of Psychohistory,* vol. 26, no. 4, www.geocities.com/ kidhistory/ja/defining.htm, accessed 1/11/05.

Rowe and Kahn. (1987). Human aging: Usual and successful. *Science* (July 10).

Rowling, J. (1998). *Harry Potter and the Sorcerer's Stone.* New York: Scholastic.

Rubin, L. (1990). *Erotic Wars: What Happened to the Sexual Revolution?* New York: Farrar, Straus, and Giroux.

Rubinstein, W. (1986). *Wealth and Inequality in Britain.* Winchester, MA: Faber and Faber.

Rudé, G. (1964). *The Crowd in History: A Study of Popular Disturbances in France and England, 1730–1848.* New York: Wiley.

Rutter and Giller. (1984). *Juvenile Delinquency: Trends and Perspectives.* New York: Guilford Press.

Ryan, T. (1985). The roots of masculinity, in Andy Metcalf and Martin Humphries, eds., *Sexuality of Men.* London: Pluto.

Saad, L. (2007). Tolerance for gay rights at high-water mark. *Gallup News Service.* http://www.gallup.com/poll/27694/ Tolerance-Gay-Rights-HighWater-Mark. aspx, accessed 2/17/08.

Sachs, J. (2000). A new map of the world. *The Economist* (June 22).

Sadker and Sadker. (1994). *Failing at Fairness.* New York: Scribner.

Saks, M., ed. (1992). *Alternative Medicine in Britain.* Oxford, UK: Clarendon.

Salganik, Dodds, and Watts. (2006). Experimental study of inequality and unpredictability in an artificial cultural market. *Science* 311:854-856.

Sampson and Cohen. (1988). Deterrent effects of the police on crime: A replication and theoretical extension. *Law and Society Review,* vol. 22, no. 1.

Sandefur and Liebler. (1997). The demography of American Indian families. *Population Research and Policy Review,* vol. 16.

Sarkisian and Gerstel. (2004). Kin Support among Blacks and Whites: Race and Family Organization. *American Sociological Review,* 69:812–837.

Sartre, J. (1965). *Anti-Semite and Jew.* Originally published 1948. New York: Schocken Books.

Sassen, S. (1991). *The Global City: New York, London, Tokyo.* Princeton, NJ: Princeton University Press.

Sassen, S. (1996). *Losing Control: Sovereignty in the Age of Globalization.* New York: Columbia University Press.

Sassen, S. (1998). *Globalization and Its Discontents.* New York: New Press.

Sassen, S. (2005). *Denationalization: Territory, Authority and Rights.* Princeton, NJ: Princeton University Press.

Sax, Lindholm, Astin, Korn, and Mahoney. (2001). The American freshman: National norms for fall 2001. *Higher Education Research Institute,* UCLA Graduate School of Education & Information Studies. www.gseis.ucla.edu/heri/ norms_pr_01. html, accessed 1/3/05.

Schachter, J. (2001). *Why People Move: Exploring the 2000 Current Population Survey (Special Studies).* Washington, DC: U.S. Census Bureau.

Schaie, K. (1983). *Longitudinal Studies of Adult Psychological Development.* New York: Guilford Press.

Schaie and Hendricks, eds. (2000). *The Evolution of the Aging Self: The Societal Impact on the Aging Process.* New York: Springer.

Scheff, T. (1966). *Being Mentally Ill.* Chicago: Aldine.

Schofield, J. (1995) Review for Research on school desegregation's impact on elementary and secondary school students. In J.A. Banks and C.A.M. Banks, eds., *Handbook on Research on Multicultural Education.* New York, NY: Simon & Schuster.

Schumpeter, J. (1983). *Capitalism, Socialism, and Democracy.* Originally published 1942. Magnolia, MA: Peter Smith.

Schwartz, G. (1970). *Sect Ideologies and Social Status.* Chicago: University of Chicago Press.

Scottand Morgan. (1993). Bodies in a social landscape, in Sue Scott and David Morgan, eds., *Body Matters: Essays on the Sociology of the Body.* Washington, DC: Falmer Press.

Sedlak and Broadhurst. (1996). *Third National Incidence Study of Child Abuse and Neglect.* Washington, DC: U.S. Department of Health and Human Services.

Seidman, Meeks, and Traschen. (1999). Beyond the closet? The changing social meaning of homosexuality in the United States. *Sexualities,* vol. 2, no. 1.

Sennett, R. (1998). *The Corrosion of Character: The Personal Consequences of Work in the New Capitalism.* New York: Norton.

Seville Statement on Violence. (1990). *American Psychologist,* vol. 45, no. 10, www.lrainc.com/swtaboo/taboos/ seville1. html, accessed 1/3/05.

Sewell, Sewell, and Hauser. (1980). The Wisconsin longitudinal study of social and psychological factors in aspirations and achievements. *Research in Sociology of Education and Socialization,* vol. 1.

Shea, Stein, Basch, Lantigua, Maylahn, Strogatz, and Novick. (1991). Independent associations of educational attainment and ethnicity with behavioral risk factors for cardiovascular disease. *American Journal of Epidemiology,* vol. 134, no. 6.

Sheldon, et al. (1949). *Varieties of Delinquent Youth.* New York: Harper and Row.

Sigmund, P. (1990). *Liberation Theology at the Crossroads: Democracy or Revolution?* New York: Oxford University Press.

Simmel, G. (1955). *Conflict and the Web of Group Affiliations.* Trans. Kurt Wolff. Glencoe, IL: Free Press.

Simpson, Stark, and Jackson. (1988). Class identification processes. *American Sociological Review,* vol. 53.

Sjoberg, G. (1960). *The Pre-Industrial City: Past and Present.* New York: Free Press.

Sjoberg, G. (1963). The rise and fall of cities: A theoretical perspective. *International Journal of Comparative Sociology,* vol. 4.

Sklair, L. (2002a). Democracy and the Transnational Capitalist Class, *Annals of the American Academy of Political and Social Science,* 581: 144–157.

Sklair, L. (2002b). *Globalization: Capitalism and its Alternatives.* 3rd ed. New York: Oxford University Press.

Sklair, L. (2003). Transnational Practices and the Analysis of the Global System, pp. 15–32 in Axel Hulsemeyer, *Globalization in the Twenty-First Century.* New York: Palgrave Macmillan.

Slapper and Tombs. (1999). *Corporate Crime.* Essex, UK: Longman.

Slevin, P. (2005). Prison Experts See Opportunity for Improvement. *Washington Post.* (July 26). www.washingtonpost.com/ wpdyn/content/article/2005/07/25/ AR2005072501484.html, accessed spring 2006.

Smedley, A. (1993). *Race in North America: Origin and Evolution of a World View.* Boulder, CO: Westview Press.

Smeeding, T. (2000). Changing income inequality in OECD countries: Updated results from the Luxembourg income study (LIS). *Luxembourg Income Study Working Paper #252*, March. Syracuse, New York: Maxwell School of Citizenship and Public Affairs, Syracuse University, www.lisproject.org/ publications/ liswps/252.pdf, accessed 1/11/05.

Smeeding, Rainwater, and Burtless. (2000). United States poverty in a cross-national context. *Luxembourg Income Study Working Paper #244*, September. Syracuse, New York: Maxwell School of Citizenship and Public Affairs, Syracuse University, www.lisproject.org/publications/ liswps/244.pdf, accessed 1/11/05.

Smelser, N. (1963). *Theory of Collective Behavior.* New York: Free Press.

Smith, D. (2003). The Older Population in the United States: March 2002. *U.S. Census Bureau Current Population Reports*, P20-546. Washington, DC. www.census. gov/prod/2003pubs/p20-546.pdf, accessed spring 2006.

Smith-Bindman, R., et. al. (2006). Does utilization of screening mammography explain racial and ethnic differences in breast cancer? *Annals of Internal Medicine*, 144(8): 541–553.

Snow, Guerra, Noor, Myint, and Hay. (2005). The global distribution of clinical episodes of Plasmodium falciparum malaria. *Nature*, 434(7030): 214–217.

So, A. (1990). *Social Change and Development: Modernization, Dependency, and World-Systems Theories.* Newbury Park, CA: Sage.

Soumerai, and Avorn. (1983). Perceived health, life satisfaction, and activity in urban elderly: A controlled study of the impact of part-time work. *Journal of Gerontology*, vol. 38.

Southwick, S. (1996). Liszt: Searchable Directory of E-Mail Discussion Groups. www.liszt.com, accessed 1/3/05.

Spain, and Bianchi. (1996). *Balancing Act: Motherhood, Marriage, and Employment among American Women.* New York: Russell Sage Foundation.

Spectrem Group (2009). Affluent Market Insights 2009. Retrieved July 2009 from http://www.luxist.com/2009/03/11/ number-of-u-s-millionaires-falls-steeply/

Spinks, and Wood. (1996). Office-Based Telecommuting: An International Comparison of Satellite Offices in Japan and North America, in *Proceedings of SIGCPR/SIGMIS '96*. Denver, CO: ACM.

Stacey, J. (1990). *Brave New Families: Stories of Domestic Upheaval in Late-Twentieth-Century America.* New York: Basic Books.

Stacey, J. (1993). Good Riddance to 'The Family': A response to David Popenoe. *Journal of Marriage and Family*, vol. 55.

Stacey, J. (1996). *In the Name of the Family: Rethinking Family Values in a Postmodern Age.* Boston: Beacon Press.

Stack, C. (1975). *All Our Kin: Strategies For Survival In A Black Community.* New York: Harper Calophon.

Stampp, K. (1956). *The Peculiar Institution.* New York: Knopf.

Stark, and Bainbridge. (1980). Towards a theory of religious commitment. *Journal for the Scientific Study of Religion*, vol. 19.

Stark, and Bainbridge. (1987). *A Theory of Religion.* New Brunswick, NJ: Rutgers University Press.

Starrs, P. (1997). The sacred, the regional, and the digital. *Geographical Review*, vol. 87, no. 2.

Statistical Office of the European Communities. (1991). *Basic Statistics of the Community.* Luxembourg: European Union.

Steinberg, R. (1990). Social construction of skill: Gender, power, and comparable worth. *Work and Occupations*, vol. 17.

Steinmetz, S. (1983). Family violence toward elders, in Susan Saunders, Ann Anderson, and Cynthia Hart, eds., *Violent Individuals and Families: A Practitioner's Handbook.* Springfield, IL: Charles C. Thomas.

Stillwagon, E. (2001). AIDS and poverty in Africa. *The Nation* (May 21).

Stockholm International Peace Research Institute. (2009). *SIPRI 2009 Yearbook*, Appendix 5A. Military expenditure data, 1999–2008. www.sipri.org/ yearbook/2009/05/05A

Stryker, R. (1996). Comparable worth and the labor market, in Paula J. Dubeck and Kathryn Borman, eds., *Women and Work: A Handbook.* New York: Garland.

Sullivan, O. (1997). Time waits for no (wo) man: An investigation of the gendered experience of domestic time. *Sociology*, vol. 31.

Survey of Consumer Finances. (2009). www. federalreserve.gov/pubs/bulletin/2009/ pdf/scf09.pdf, accessed July 2009.

Sutherland, E. (1949). *Principles of Criminology.* Chicago: Lippincott.

Swidler, A. (1986). Culture in action: Symbols and strategies. *American Sociological Review*, vol. 51.

Tan and Ramakrishna., eds. (2002). *The New Terrorism.* Singapore: Eastern Universities Press.

Tang and Zuo. (2000). Dating Attitudes and Behaviors of American and Chinese College Students. *Social Science Journal*, vol. 37, no. 1.

Tarm, M. (2006). Old Houses Spared by Slow Market: Decade-long Teardown Tide Turns as Preservationists Gain Influence. *Chicago Sun-Times* (December 22). www.suntimes.com/classifieds/homes/ homelife/181875,HOF-News-oldhouses22. article, accessed 1/8/07.

Taylor, Funk, and Clark. (2007). As marriage and parenthood drift apart, public is concerned about social impact. *A social and demographic trends report.* Retrieved January 2008 from http://pewresearch. org/assets/social/pdf/Marriage.pdf

Teachman, J. (2003). Premarital Sex, Premarital Cohabitation, and the Risk of Subsequent Marital Dissolution among Women. *Journal of Marriage and the Family*, 65:444–455.

Telework Coalition. (2004). Telework Facts. www.telcoa.org/id33.htm, accessed 9/23/05.

Thompson, E. (1971). The moral economy of the English crowd in the eighteenth century. *Past and Present*, vol. 50.

Thompson, W. (1929). Population. *American Journal of Sociology*, vol. 34.

Tilly, C. (1978). From Mobilization to Revolution. Reading, MA: Addison-Wesley.

Tilly, C. (1996). The emergence of citizenship in France and elsewhere, in Charles Tilly, ed., *Citizenship, Identity, and Social History.* Cambridge, UK: Cambridge University Press.

Totti, X. (1987). The making of a Latino ethnic identity. *Dissent*, vol. 34 (Fall).

Toufexis, A. (1993). Sex has many accents. *Time.* (May 24).

Touraine, A. (1974). *The Post-Industrial Society.* London: Wildwood.

Touraine, A. (1977). *The Self-Production of Society.* Chicago: University of Chicago Press.

Touraine, A. (1981). *The Voice and the Eye: An Analysis of Social Movements.* New York: Cambridge University Press.

Townsend and Davidson, eds. (1982). *Inequalities in Health: The Black Report.* Harmondsworth, UK: Penguin.

Toyota Corporation. (2001). 2001 Number and Diffusion Rate for Motor Vehicles in Major Countries. www.toyota.co.jp/ IRweb/corp_info/and_the_word/ pdf/2003_c07.pdf, accessed spring 2006.

Treas, J. (1995). Older Americans in the 1990s and beyond. *Population Bulletin 50.* Washington, DC: Population Reference Bureau.

Treiman, D. (1977). *Occupational Prestige in Comparative Perspective.* New York: Academic Press.

Troeltsch, E. (1931). *The Social Teaching of the Christian Churches*. 2 vols. New York: Macmillan.

Turnbull, C. (1983). *The Human Cycle*. New York: Simon and Schuster.

U.K. Statistics Authority. (2001). *Ethnicity and identity: Inter-Ethnic Marriage*. www.statistics.gov.uk/CCI/nugget.asp?ID=1090&Pos=1&ColRank=2&Rank=416, accessed spring 2008.

UNAIDS. (2003). AIDS Epidemic Update, December 2003. *Joint United Nations Program on HIV/AIDS*. www.unaids.org/ html/pub/publications/irc_pubOb/jc943-epiupdate2003_en_pdf.htm, accessed 1/10/05.

UNAIDS. (2005a). AIDS Epidemic Update, December 2005: Sub-Saharan Africa. www.unaids.org/epi/2005/doc/EPIupdate2005_pdf_en/Epi05_05_en.pdf, accessed spring 2006.

UNAIDS. (2005b). AIDS Epidemic Update, December 2005: North America, Western and Central Europe. www.unaids.org/epi/2005/doc/EPIupdate2005_pdf_en/Epi05_10_en.pdf, accessed spring 2006.

UNAIDS (2008a). Report on the Global AIDS Epidemic: Executive Summary. http://data.unaids.org/pub/GlobalReport/2008/JC1511_GR08_ExecutiveSummary_en.pdf, accessed August 2009.

UNAIDS (2008b). Report on the Global AIDS Epidemic: Executive Summary. http://data.unaids.org/pub/GlobalReport/2008/JC1511_GR08_ExecutiveSummary_en.pdf, accessed August 2009

United Nations Chronicle. (1995). vol. 32, no. 4: 29.

UNICEF. (1997). *The State of the World's Children, 1997*. New York: Oxford University Press.

UNICEF. (2000). *The State of the World's Children, 2000*. New York: United Nations Children's Fund.

UNICEF (2009). *The State of the World's Children 2009*. New York: United Nations Children's Fund. www.unicef.org/sowc09/docs/SOWC09-FullReport-EN.pdf, accessed 2/4/2010.

United Nations Joint Programme on HIV/AIDS (UNAIDS). (2007). Press release: Global HIV prevalence has leveled off; AIDS is among the leading causes of death globally and remains the primary cause of death in Africa. http://data.unaids.org/pub/EPISlides/2007/071119_epi_pressrelease_en.pdf, accessed fall 2007.

United Nations Joint Programme on HIV/AIDS (UNAIDS). (2007a). Press release: Global HIV prevalence has leveled off; AIDS is among the leading causes of death globally and remains the primary cause of death in Africa. http://data.

unaids.org/pub/EPISlides/2007/071119_epi_pressrelease_en.pdf, accessed fall 2009.

Union of International Organizations. (2005). Yearbook of International Organizations—Guide to Global Civil Society. 42nd ed. Vol. 1B, appendix 3, table 1. Munich: K.G. Saur.

United Nations. (1995). Human Development Report, Gender and Human Development—Overview. http://hdr.undp.org/reports/global/1995/en/pdf/hdr_1995_overview.pdf, accessed 1/3/05.

United Nations. (2003). Table 26. United Nations Human Development Report, 2003. www.undp.org/hdr2003/pdf/hdr03_HDI.pdf, accessed 1/3/05.

United Nations. (2006). World population prospects: The 2006 revision. www.un.org/esa/population/publications/wpp2006/wpp2006.htm, accessed 9/18/08.

United Nations (2007a). World Urbanization Prospects: The 2007 Revision Population Database. http://esa.un.org/unup/p2k-0data.asp, accessed July 2009.

United Nations. (2007b). World Urbanization Prospects. http://esa.un.org/unup/, accesses August 2009.

United Nations. (2008a). Human development report 2007/2008. www.weforum.org/pdf/gendergap/report2007.pdf, accessed fall 2008.

United Nations Conference on Trade and Development (UNCTAD). (2005a). World Investment Report, 2005 pp. 325 Annex table B4.

UNCTAD (2008). Largest transnational corporations pursued further expansion abroad in 2007, Report says. www.unctad.org/Templates/webflyer.asp?docid=10509&intItemID=4697&lang=1, accessed September 2009.

UNCTAD (2009). Press Release. www.unctad.org/Templates/webflyer.asp?docid=11666&intItemID=1528, accessed September 2009.

United Nations Development Programme (UNDP). (1998). *Human Development Report 1998*. New York: Oxford University Press.

United Nations Development Programme (UNDP). (1999). *Human Development Report 1999*. New York: Oxford University Press.

United Nations Development Programme (UNDP). (2005). Human Development Report, 2005. http://hdr.undp.org/reports/global/2005/, accessed 9/28/05.

United Nations Development Programme (UNDP). (2006). Human Development Indicators. http://hdr.undp.org/en/media/Human_development_indicators.pdf, accessed August 2009.

United Nations Development Programme (UNDP). (2007). Human development

report: Inequality in income or expenditure, Table 15. http://hdrstats.undp.org/indicators/146.html, accessed full 2007.

United Nations Development Programme (UNDP). (2008a). World Population Highlights. www.prb.org/pdf08/63.3highlights.pdf, accessed August 2009.

United Nations Development Programme (UNDP). (2009a). Human development report. Overcoming barriers: Human mobility and development. http://hdr.undp.org/en/reports/global/hdr2009/

United Nations Economic Commission for Europe. (2003). Ireland, www.unece.org/stats/trend/irl.pdf, accessed spring 2006.

United Nations Educational, Scientific, and Cultural Organization (UNESCO). (2008a). Regional Literacy Rates for Youths and Adults. http://stats.uis.unesco.org/unesco/TableViewer/tableView.aspx?ReportId=201, accessed August 2009

United Nations Food and Agriculture Organization (UN FAO). (2001). The impact of HIV/AIDS on food security. *United Nations Food and Agriculture Organization, Conference on World Food Security*, May 28–June 1.

UN FAO. (2004). The State of Food Insecurity, 2004. *United Nations Food and Agriculture Organization*. www.fao.org/documents/show_cdr.asp?url_file=/docrep/ 007/y5650e/y5650e00.htm, accessed 11/30/05.

UN FAO. (2005). Armed Conflicts Leading Cause of World Hunger Emergencies. *United Nations Food and Agriculture Organization*. www.fao.org/newsroom/en/news/2005/102562/index.html, accessed 12/1/05.

UN FAO. (2008). FAO Newsroom. Number of hungry people rises to 963 million. www.fao.org/news/story/en/item/8836/, accessed August 2009.

UN FAO. (2009). http://esa.un.org/unup/p2k0data.asp, accessed July 2009.

United Nations Intergovernmental Panel on Climate Change (IPCC). (2007). Climate Change 200&: *Policy Report, Summary for Policy Makers*. www.ipcc.ch/pdf/assessment-report/ar4/syr/ar4_syr_spm.pdf, accessed 3/6/07.

United Nations Office on Drugs and Crime. (2005). World Drug Report, 2005. www.unodc.org/unodc/en/world_drug_report.html, accessed spring 2006.

United Nations Population Division. (2005a). Violence Against Women Fact Sheet. www.unfpa.org/swp/2005/presskit/factsheets/facts_vaw.htm, accessed 12/4/05.

United Nations Population Division. (2005b). Gender-Based Violence: A Price too High. State of the World Population,

2005. www.unfpa.org/swp/ 2005/english/ ch7/index.htm, accessed 12/4/05

United Nations World Food Program (UN WFP). (2001). News release: WFP head releases world hunger map and warns of hunger 'hot spots' in 2001. (January 8) New York: UNWFP.

(UN WFP). (2004). Paying the Price of Hunger: The Impact of Malnutrition on Women and Children. *United Nations World Food Program*. http://documents. wfp. org/stellent/groups/public/ documents/newsroom/wfp076313. pdf, accessed 12/1/05.

Urban Institute. (2005). Low-Income Working Families: Facts and Figures. August 25. www.urban.org/Uploaded-PDF/900832.pdf, accessed spring 2006.

U.S. Bureau of Justice Statistics (2006). Homicide Trends by Race. www.ojp. usdoj.gov/bjs/homicide/race.htm, accessed August 2009.

U.S. Bureau of Justice Statistics. (2008a). Victim Characteristics. U.S. Department of Justice. www.ojp.usdoj.gov/bjs/ cvict_v.htm, accessed 11/12/08.

U.S. Bureau of Justice Statistics. (2008b). Jail Populations by Age and Gender 1998-2008. www.ojp.usdoj.gov/bjs/ glance/tables/jailagtab.htm, accessed July 2009.

U.S. Bureau of Justice Statistics. (2008c). Prison Statistics. www.ojp.usdoj.gov/bjs/ prisons.htm, accessed July 2009.

U.S. Bureau of Justice Statistics. (2008d). Direct Expenditure by Level of Government. www.ojp.usdoj.gov/bjs/glance/d_ expgov.htm, accessed July 2009.

U.S. Bureau of Justice Statistics. (2009a). Prisoners in 2008. http://bjs.ojp.usdoj. gov/content/pub/pdf/p08.pdf

U.S. Bureau of Labor Statistics. (2005a). Women in the Labor Force: a Databook. Table 6. www.bls.gov/cps/wlf-databook2005.htm, accessed 12/3/05.

U.S. Bureau of Labor Statistics. (2007a). Women in the Labor Force: A Databook (2007 Edition). Table 7. www.bls.gov/ cps/wlf-table7-2007.pdf, accessed July 2009.

U.S. Bureau of Labor Statistics. (2008a). Employed persons by detailed occupation, sex, race, and Hispanic or Latino ethnicity. ftp://ftp.bls.gov/pub/special. requests/lf/aat11.txt, accessed July 2009.

U.S. Bureau of Labor Statistics. (2009a). A Profile of the Working Poor 2007. www.bls.gov/cps/cpswp2007.pdf, accessed July 2009.

U.S. Bureau of Labor Statistics. (2009b). Current Population Survey Table 2. www.bls.gov/cps/wlf-table2-2009.pdf

U.S. Bureau of Labor Statistics. (2009c). Current Population Survey

Table 11. www.bls.gov/cps/wlf-table11-2009.pdf

U.S. Bureau of Labor Statistics. (2009d). Current Population Survey Table 16. www.bls.gov/cps/wlf-table16-2009.pdf

U.S. Bureau of Labor Statistics. (2009e). Usual Weekly Earnings Summary. www.bls.gov/news.release/wkyeng.nr0. htm, accessed July 2009.

U.S. Bureau of the Census. (1996). P23-190 Current Population Reports: Special Studies—651 in the United States, by Frank B. Hobbs with Bonnie L. Damon. Washington, DC: U.S. Government Printing Office.

U.S. Bureau of the Census. (1999). Population profile of the United States, chapter 2." www.census. gov/population/pop-profile/1999/chap02. pdf, accessed 1/4/05.

U.S. Bureau of the Census. (2000a). The changing shape of the nation's income distribution. www. census.gov/prod/ 2000pubs/p60-204.pdf, accessed 1/4/05.

U.S. Bureau of the Census. (2001). Asset ownership of households: 1995. www. census.gov/hhes/ www/wealth/ 1995/ wlth95-1.html, accessed 1/4/05.

U.S. Bureau of the Census. (2002). Geographical mobility, population characteristics. Current Population Reports, PS20–538. www. census.gov/prod/2001pubs/ p20-538.pdf, accessed 1/4/05.

U.S. Bureau of the Census. (2003a). Statistical Abstract of the United States 2000. Washington, DC: U.S. Government Printing Office. www.census. gov/prod/2004pubs/03statab/pop.pdf, accessed 1/4/05.

U.S. Bureau of the Census. (2003b). Characteristics of the Foreign Born by World Region of Birth. Table 3.1. www.census. gov/population/www/socdemo/foreign/ ppl-174.html#reg, accessed spring 2006.

U.S. Bureau of the Census. (2004a). American community survey: Selected social characteristics, 2004. Table DP-2. Retrieved December 7, 2005, from http:// factfinder.census.gov/servlet/ADPTable?_ bm=y&-geo_id=01000US&-qr_name= ACS_2004_EST_G00_DP2&-ds_name= ACS_2004_EST_G00_&-redoLog= false&-_scrollToRow=46&-format

U.S. Bureau of the Census. (2005a). Number, Timing, and Duration of Marriages and Divorces: 2001. Current Population Reports (P70-97) by Rose Krieder. www. census.gov/ prod/2005pubs/p70-97.pdf, accessed 9/5/2005.

U.S. Bureau of the Census. (2005b). Historical Income Table H-1: Income Limits for Each Fifth and Top 5 Percent of Households, All Races, 1967 to 2004. www. census.gov/hhes/www/ income/histinc/ h01ar.html, accessed spring 2006.

U.S. Bureau of the Census. (2005c). Table H-9. Race of Head of household by Median and Mean Income, 1980-2004. www.census. gov/hhes/www/ income/histinc/h09w. html, accessed spring 2006.

U.S. Bureau of the Census. (2005d). America's families living arrangements: 2004. Current population survey. www.census. gov/population/www.socdemo/hh-fam/ cps2004.html, accessed 1/12/06.

U.S. Bureau of the Census. (2005d). Hispanic Population Passes 40 Million, Census Bureau Reports. Table 2. www.census. gov/Press-Release/ www/releases/ archives/population/ 005164.html, accessed 12/6/05.

U.S. Bureau of the Census. (2006a). Statistical abstract of the United States. www. census.gov/statab/, accessed 1/9/06.

U.S. Bureau of the Census. (2007a). Historical income inequality tables. Table H-2. www.census.gov/hhes/www/ income/histinc/h02ar.html, accessed fall 2007.

U.S. Census Bureau (2007b). 2007 American Consumer Survey. http://factfinder. census.gov/servlet/DatasetMainPageSe-Frvlet?_program=ACS&_submenuId=&_ lang=en&_ts=, accessed July 2009.

U.S. Census Bureau (2007c). Current Population Survey. www.census.gov/ hhes/www/macro/032008/hhinc/ new05_000.htm, accessed July 2009.

U.S. Bureau of the Census. (2007d). Historical income inequality tables. Table H-3. www.census.gov/hhes/www/income/ histinc/h03ar.html, accessed fall 2007.

U.S. Bureau of the Census. (2007e). Income, poverty, and health insurance coverage in the United States: 2006. www.census. gov/prod/2007pubs/p60–233.pdf, accessed fall 2007.

U.S. Bureau of the Census. (2007f). Historical poverty tables, Table 4. www.census. gov/hhes/www/poverty/histpov/hst-pov4.html, accessed fall 2007

U.S. Census Bureau. (2007g). Hispanic or Latino Origin by Specific Origin. http:// factfinder. census.gov/servlet/DTTa-ble?_bm=y&-ds_name=ACS_2007_1YR_ G00_&-_geoSkip=0&-CONTEXT= dt&-mt_name=ACS_2007_1YR_G2000_ B03001&-redoLog=false&-_skip= 0&-geo_id=01000US&-_showChild= Y&-format=&-_lang=en&-_toggle=ACS_ 2007_1YR_G2000_B03001, accessed July 2009.

U.S. Census Bureau. (2007h). Race - Total Population. http://factfinder. census.gov/servlet/DTTable?_ bm=y&-geo_id=01000US&-ds_ name=ACS_2007_1YR_G00_&-_lang =en&-redoLog=false&-mt_name =ACS_2007_1YR_G2000_C02003

&-format=&-CONTEXT=dt, accessed July 2009.

U.S. Census Bureau. (2007i). Table B15002B. Sex by Educational Attainment for Population 25 years and over (Black or African-American alone). http://factfinder.census.gov/servlet/DTTable?_bm=y&-ds_name=ACS_2007_1YR_G00_&-_geoSkip=0&-CONTEXT=dt&-mt_name=ACS_2007_1YR_G2000_C15002B&-redoLog=false&-_skip=0&-geo_id=01000US&-_showChild=Y&-format=&-_lang=en&-_toggle=ACS_2007_1YR_G2000_C15002B, accessed July 2009.

U.S. Census Bureau. (2007j) American Community Survey Estimates. http://factfinder.census.gov/servlet/ACSSAFFFacts?_event=&geo_id=01000US&-geoContext=01000US&_street=&_county=&_cityTown=&_state=&_zip=&_lang=en&_sse=on&ActiveGeoDiv=&_useEV=&pctxt=fph&pgsl=010&_submenuId=factsheet_1&ds_name=DEC_2000_SAFF&_ci_nbr=null&qr_name=null&reg=&_keyword=&_industry=, accessed August 2009.

U.S. Bureau of the Census. (2007k). Historical income inequality tables. Table H-13. www.census.gov/hhes/www/income/histinc/h13.html, accessed fall 2007.

U.S. Bureau of the Census. (2007l). America's families and living arrangements: 2006. U.S. Census Bureau, Housing and Household Economic Statistics Division, Fertility & Family Statistics Branch. www.census.gov/population/www/socdemo/hh-fam/cps2006.html, accessed January 2008.

U.S. Bureau of the Census. (2008a). Current Population Survey. Income, Poverty and Health Insurance in the United States: 2007. www.census.gov/prod/2008pubs/p60-235.pdf, accessed July 2009.

U.S. Bureau of the Census. (2008b). Race. 2006-2008 American Community Survey. http://factfinder.census.gov/servlet/ADPTable?_bm=y&-geo_id=01000US&-qr_name=ACS_2008_3YR_G00_DP3YR5&-ds_name=&-_lang=en&-redoLog=false&-format=

U.S. Bureau of the Census. (2008c). Hispanic Heritage Month 2008: Facts for Features. Washington, D.C. Census News Bureau. www.census.gov/PressRelease/www/releases/pdf/cb08ff-15_hispherit.pdf

U.S. Bureau of the Census. (2009a). Population Estimates. www.census.gov/popest/national/asrh/

U.S. Bureau of the Census. (2009b). National Population Projections. www.census.gov/population/www/projections/summary-tables.html, accessed June 2009.

U.S. Bureau of the Census. (2009c). American Community Survey 2007. http://factfinder.census.gov/servlet/DatasetMainPageServlet?_program=ACS&_submenuId=&_lang=en&_ts=, accessed June 2009.

U.S. Bureau of the Census. (2009d). American Community Survey 2007, 1-year estimate. Table B01001, Sex by Age-Universe. http://factfinder.census.gov/servlet/DTTable?_bm=y&-geo_id=01000US&-ds_name=ACS_2007_1YR_G00_&-_lang=en&-mt_name=ACS_2007_1YR_G2000_B01001&-format=&-CONTEXT=dt, accessed June 2009.

U.S. Bureau of the Census. (2009e). Income, Poverty, and Health Insurance Coverage in the United States: 2008. www.census.gov/prod/2009pubs/p60-236.pdf

U.S. Bureau of the Census. (2009f). Educational Attainment in the United States: 2008. www.census.gov/population/www/socdemo/education/cps2008.html

U.S. Census Bureau. (2009g). Current Population Survey, 1968 to 2009 Annual Social and Economic Supplements. www.census.gov/prod/2009pubs/p60-236.pdf

U.S. Bureau of the Census. (2009h). America's Families and Living Arrangements: 2008. Marital Status of People 15 Years and Over, by Age, Sex, Personal Earnings, Race, and Hispanic Origin, 2008 (All Races). www.census.gov/population/www/socdemo/hh-fam/cps2008.html, accessed August 2009.

U.S. Bureau of the Census. (2009i). Unmarried and Single Americans Week Press Release. www.census.gov/Press-Release/www/releases/archives/facts_for_features_special_editions/014004.html, accessed August 2009.

U.S. Bureau of the Census. (2009j). Family Households, by Type, Age of Own Children, Age of Family Members, and Age, Race and Hispanic Origin of Householder: 2008. www.census.gov/population/www/socdemo/hh-fam/cps2008.html (table F1), accessed August 2009.

U.S. Bureau of the Census. (2009k). Living Arrangements of Children Under 18 Years and Marital Status of Parents, by Age, Gender, Race, and Hispanic Origin of the Child for All Children: 2008. www.census.gov/population/www/socdemo/hh-fam/cps2008.html (table C3), accessed August 2009.

U.S. Bureau of the Census. (2009l). Table FG10. Family Groups: 2008. www.census.gov/population/www/socdemo/hh-fam/cps2008.html, accessed August 2009.

U.S. Bureau of the Census. (2009m). Statistical Abstract. Table 75. Self-Described Religious Identification of Adult Population: 1990 to 2008. www.census.gov/compendia/statab/2010/tables/10s0075.pdf

U.S. Bureau of the Census. (2009n). Economic News Release: Union Members 2008. www.bls.gov/news.release/union2.nr0.htm, accessed September 2009.

U.S. Bureau of the Census. (2010a). The 2010 Statistical Abstract: Births, Deaths, Marriages, & Divorces: Marriages and Divorces. Table 126. www.census.gov/compendia/statab/cats/births_deaths_marriages_divorces/marriages_and_divorces.html

U.S. Courts. (2008). Costs of Imprisonment Far Exceed Supervision Costs. www.uscourts.gov/newsroom/2009/costsOfImprisonment.cfm, accessed July 2009.

U.S. Department of Education, National Center for Education Statistics. (1993). Adult Literacy in America: A First Look at the Results of the National Adult Literacy Survey. Washington, DC: U.S. Government Printing Office.

U. S. Department of Health and Human Services. (2004). Indicators of Welfare Dependence: Annual Report to Congress, 2004, Table 2. http://aspe.hhs.gov/hsp/indicators04, accessed spring 2006.

U. S. Department of Health and Human Services. (2004b). Child Abuse and Neglect Fatalities: Statistics and Interventions. *National Clearinghouse on Child Abuse and Neglect Information*. http://nccanch.acf.hhs.gov/pubs/factsheets/fatality.cfm, accessed spring 2006.

U. S. Department of Health and Human Services. (2005a). National Survey of Drug Use and Health, 2004. *Department of Health and Human Services, Substance Abuse and Mental Health Services*. Tables A. 3 and A.8. www.drugabusestatistics.samhsa.gov/nsduh/2k4nsduh/2k4overview/2k4overview.htm#toc, accessed spring 2006.

U.S. Department of Health and Human Services. (2007a). Health, United States, 2006. Table 27: Life expectancy at birth, at 65 years of age, and at 75 years of age, by race and sex: United States, selected years, 1900–2004. www.cdc.gov/nchs/data/hus/hus06.pdf#027, accessed January 2008.

U.S. Department of Health and Human Services. (2007b). National Survey on Drug Use and Health. (2007). www.oas.samhsa.gov/nsduhLatest.htm, accessed July 2009.

U.S. Department of Health and Human Services DHHS. (2009a). Child Maltreatment

U.S. Department of Housing and Human Services. (2009). 2008 Annual Homeless

Assessment Report to Congress. www.
hudhre.info/documents/4thHomeless
AssessmentReport.pdf, accessed July
2009.

U.S. Department of Labor. (2008). Quick
Stats on Women Workers 2008. www.
dol.gov/wb/stats/main.htm, accessed
July 2009.

U.S. Federal Reserve Board. (2009). 2007
Survey of Consumer Finances. www.
federalreserve.gov/pubs/oss/oss2/
2007/2007%20SCF%20Chartbook.pdf

U.S. House of Representatives. (2009). www.
senate.gov/artandhistory/history/
common/briefing/women_senators.htm,
accessed July 2009.

University World News. (2009). China:
Graduate Unemployment on the Rise.
www.universityworldnews.com/article.
php?story=20090409203634912,
accessed August 2009.

van Gennep, A. (1977). *The Rites of Passage.*
Originally published 1908. London:
Routledge and Kegan Paul.

Vanneman and Cannon. (1987). *The American Perception of Class.* Philadelphia:
Temple University Press.

Wacquant, L. (1993). Redrawing the urban
color line: The state of the ghetto in the
1980s, in Craig Calhoun and George
Ritzer, eds., *Social Problems.* New York:
McGraw-Hill.

Wacquant, L. (1996). The rise of advanced
marginality: Notes on its nature and
implications. *Acta Sociologica,* vol. 39,
no. 2.

Wacquant, L. (2002). Scrutinizing the
street: poverty, morality, and the pit-
falls of urban ethnography, *American
Journal of Sociology,* vol. 107 (May):
1468–1532.

Wacquant and Wilson. (1993). The cost of
racial and class exclusion in the inner
city, in William Julius Wilson, ed., *The
Ghetto Underclass: Social Science Perspectives.* Newbury Park, CA: Sage.

Wagar, W. (1992). *A Short History of the
Future.* Chicago: University of Chicago
Press.

Wagner-Wright. (2006). *Birth, Marriage,
Honor & Poverty: Ramifications Of
Traditional Hindu Culture & Custom On
Modern Indian Women.* Forum on Public
Policy: Oxford, England.

Waldron, I. (1986). Why do women live longer
than men? in Peter Conrad and Rachelle
Kern, eds., *The Sociology of Health and
Illness.* New York: St. Martin's.

Wallerstein, I. (1974a). *Capitalist Agricul-
ture and the Origins of the European
World-Economy in the Sixteenth Century.*
New York: Academic Press.

Wallerstein, I. (1974b). *The Modern World-
System.* New York: Academic Press.

Wallerstein, I. (1979). *The Capitalist World
Economy.* Cambridge, UK: Cambridge
University Press.

Wallerstein, I. (1990). *The Modern World-
System II.* New York: Academic Press.

Wallerstein, I. (1996a). *Historical Capitalism with Capitalist Civilization.* New
York: Norton.

Wallerstein, I, ed. (1996b). *World Inequality.*
St. Paul, MN: Consortium Books.

Wallerstein and Berlin. (1980). *Surviving
the Break-Up: How Children and Parents
Cope with Divorce.* New York: Basic
Books.

Wallerstein and Blakeslee. (1988) *Second
Chances: Men, Women and Children a
Decade After Divorce Who Wins, Who
Loses—and Why.* Ticknor and Fields.

Wallraff, B. (2000). What global language?
Atlantic Monthly

Walmsley, R. (2009). World Prison Population List, 8th Edition. *International
Centre for Prison Studies,* Kings College
London. www.kcl.ac.uk/depsta/law/
research/icps/downloads/wppl-8th_
41.pdf

Warner, St. (1993). Work in progress toward
a new paradigm for the sociological study
of religion in the United States. *American
Journal of Sociology,* vol. 98.

Warren, B. (1980). *Imperialism: Pioneer of
Capitalism.* London: Verso.

Waters, M. (1990). *Ethnic Options: Choosing Identities in America.* Berkeley, CA:
University of California Press.

Wattenberg, Martin P. (1996). *The Decline of
American Political Parties, 1952–1994.*
Rev. ed. Cambridge, MA: Harvard
University Press.

Watts, D. (2007). Is Justin Timberlake the
Product of Cumulative Advantage? *New
York Times Magazine,* April 15, 2007.

Waxman and Hinderliter. (1996). *A Status
Report on Hunger and Homelessness in
America's Cities.* Washington, DC: U.S.
Conference of Mayors.

Weber, M. (1947). *The Theory of Social and
Economic Organization.* New York: Free
Press.

Weber, M. (1963) (orig. 1921). *The Sociology
of Religion.* Boston: Beacon Press.

Weber, M. (1977) (orig. 1904). *The Protestant
Ethic and the Spirit of Capitalism.* New
York: Macmillan.

Weber, M. (1979) (orig. 1921). *Economy and
Society: An Outline of Interpretive Sociol-
ogy.* 2 vols. Berkeley, CA: University of
California Press.

Weeks, J. (1977). *Coming Out: Homosexual
Politics in Britain, from the Nineteenth
Century to the Present.* New York:
Quartet.

Weeks, J. (1986). *Sexuality.* New York: Routledge, Chapman and Hall.

Weitzman, L., et al. (1972). Sexual socialization in picture books for preschool

children. *American Journal of Sociology,*
vol. 77.

Wellman, B. (2008). What is the Internet
Doing to Community – and Vice-Versa?
pp. 239–42 in *New Urbanism and Beyond,*
edited by Tigran Haas. Milan: Rizzoli.

Wellman, Carrington, and Hall. (1988). Net-
works as personal communities, in Barry
Wellman and S. D. Berkowitz, eds., *Social
Structures: A Network Approach.* New
York: Cambridge University Press.

Wellman, B., et al. (1996). Computer networks as social networks: Collaborative
work, telework, and virtual community.
Annual Review of Sociology, vol. 22.

West and Fenstermaker. (1995). Doing difference. *Gender and Society,* vol. 9, no. 1.

West and Fenstermaker and Zimmerman.
(1987). Doing gender. *Gender and Society,*
vol. 1 (June).

Western, B. (1997). *Between Class and
Market: Postwar Unionization in the
Capitalist Democracies.* Princeton, NJ:
Princeton University Press.

Western and Beckett. (1999). How unregulated
is the U.S. labor market?: The penal system
as a labor market institution. *American
Journal of Sociology,* vol. 104, no. 4.

Wetzel, Eisenberg and Kaptchuk. (1998).
Courses involving complementary and
alternative medicine at US medical
schools. *JAMA,* 280(9): 784–787.

Wheatley, P. (1971). *The Pivot of the Four
Quarters.* Edinburgh: Edinburgh
University Press.

Wheeler, D. (1998). Global culture or culture
clash: New information technologies in
the Islamic world—a view from Kuwait.
Communication Research, vol. 25, no. 4.

White, L. (1990). Determinants of divorce:
A review of research in the Eighties.
Journal of Marriage and the Family,
52, 904–912.

White, M. (1993). *The Material Child: Coming of Age in Japan and America.* New
York: Free Press.

Widom and Newman. (1985). Characteristics of non-institutionalized psychopaths, in David P. Farrington and John
Gunn, eds., *Aggression and Dangerous-
ness.* Chichester, UK: Wiley.

Will and Datan. (1976). Maternal behavior
and perceived sex of infant. *American
Journal of Orthopsychiatry,* vol. 46.

Williams, C. (1992). The glass escalator: Hidden advantages for men in the 'female'
professions. *Social Problems,* vol. 39.

Williams, S. (1993). *Chronic Respiratory
Illness.* London: Routledge.

Wilson, E. (1975). *Sociobiology: The New
Synthesis.* Cambridge, MA: Harvard
University Press.

Wilson and Kelling. (1982). Broken windows,
Atlantic Monthly (March).

Wilson, W. (1978). *The Declining Significance
of Race: Blacks and Changing American*

Institutions. Chicago: University of Chicago Press.

Wilson, W. (1991). Studying inner-city social dislocations: The challenge of public agenda research. *American Sociological Review,* vol. 56 (February).

Wilson, W. (1996). *When Work Disappears: The World of the New Urban Poor.* New York: Knopf.

Wilson, W., et al. (1987). The changing structure of urban poverty. Paper presented at the annual meeting of the *American Sociological Association.*

Winkleby, M., et al. (1992). Socioeconomic status and health: How education, income, and occupation contribute to risk factors for cardiovascular disease. *American Journal of Public Health,* vol. 82.

Wirth, L. (1938). Urbanism as a way of life. *American Sociological Review,* vol. 44 (July).

Witkowski and Brown. (1982). Whorf and universals of number nomenclature. *Journal of Anthropological Research,* vol. 38.

Women in National Parliaments (WNP). (2009). www.ipu.org/wmn-e/classif.htm, accessed July 2009.

Wong, S. (1986). Modernization and Chinese culture in Hong Kong. *Chinese Quarterly,* vol. 106.

World Bank. (1997). World development report 1997: The state in a changing world. New York: Oxford University Press. 1998. World Development Indicators. Washington, DC: World Bank.

World Bank. (1999). International Bank for Reconstruction and Development, World Development Indicators 1999. Washington, DC: World Bank.

World Bank. (2000). World Development Report. New York: Oxford University Press.

World Bank. (2000–2001). World development indicators, in *World Development Report 2000–2001: Attacking Poverty.* http://poverty.worldbank.org/library/topic/3389/, accessed 1/4/05.

World Bank. (2001). PovertyNet: Topics relevant to social capital.

World Bank. (2003). World development indicators 2003. www.worldbank.org/data/onlinedatabases/onlinedatabases.html, accessed 1/4/05.

World Bank. (2005). World Development Indicators 2005. http://devdata.worldbank.org/wdi2005/cover.ht, accessed spring 2006.

World Bank. (2007a). Key Development Data and Statistics. http://web.worldbank.org/WBSITE/EXTERNAL/DATASTATISTICS/0,,contentMDK:20535285-menuPK:1192694-pagePK:64133150-piPK:64133175-theSitePK:239419,00.html, accessed July 2009.

World Bank. (2007b). Gross national income per capita, 2007. http://siteresources.worldbank.org/DATASTATISTICS/Resources/GNIPC.pdf, accessed fall 2007.

World Bank. (2008a). New Data Show 1.4 Billion Live On Less Than US$1.25 A Day, But Progress Against Poverty Remains Strong. http://web.worldbank.org/WBSITE/EXTERNAL/TOPICS/EXTPOVERTY/0,,contentMDK:21883042-menuPK:2643747-pagePK:64020865-piPK:149114-theSitePK:336992,00.html, accessed May 2009.

World Bank. (2008b). Country Classification by Income. http://web.worldbank.org/WBSITE/EXTERNAL/DATASTATISTICS/0,,contentMDK:20420458-menuPK:64133156-pagePK:64133150-piPK:64133175-theSitePK:239419,00.html, accessed July 2009.

World Bank. (2008c). Global Output Totals $59 trillion. http://web.worldbank.org/WBSITE/EXTERNAL/NEWS/0,,contentMDK:21726167-pagePK:64257043-piPK:437376-theSitePK:4607,00.html, accessed August 2009.

World Bank. (2008d). World development indicators, 2007. http://go.worldbank.org/1SF48T40L0, accessed fall 2008.

World Bank. (2009a). Country Classification. http://go.worldbank.org/K2CKM78CC0

World Bank. (2009b). Key Development Data and Statistics. http://go.worldbank.org/1SF48T40L0

World Bank. (2009c). World Development Indicators, 2009. http://go.worldbank.org/U0FSM7AQ40

World Bank. (2009d). GNI per capita 2008 (ATLAS Method). http://siteresources.worldbank.org/DATASTATISTICS/Resources/GNIPC.pdf, accessed August 2009.

World Health Organization. (2000). What is Female Genital Mutilation? www.who.int/mediacentre/factsheets/fs241/en/print.html, accessed 12/4/05.

World Health Organization. (2007a). World Health Statistics 2007. http://www.who.int/whosis/whostat2007.pdf, accessed 12/16/09.

World Health Organization. (2007b). 2007: A review of notable health issues, http://www.who.int/features/2007/year_review/en/index.html, accessed 12/30/07.

Worldsteel.org. (2009). World Steel in Figures 2009. www.worldsteel.org/pictures/publicationfiles/WSIF09.pdf, accessed September 2009.

World Trade Organization (WTO). (2008). Merchandize Trade by Export. www.wto.org/english/res_e/statis_e/its2008_e/its08_merch_trade_product_e.pdf, accessed July 2009.

Worrall, A. (1990). *Offending Women: Female Lawbreakers and the Criminal Justice System.* London: Routledge.

Wrigley, E. (1968). *Population and History.* New York: McGraw-Hill.

Wuthnow, R. (1988). Sociology of religion, in Neil J. Smelser, ed., *Handbook of Sociology.* Newbury Park, CA: Sage.

Zammuner, V. (1986). Children's sex-role stereotypes: A cross-cultural analysis, in Phillip Shaver and Clyde Hendrick, eds., *Sex and Gender.* Beverly Hills, CA: Sage.

Zee News. (2007). www.zeenews.com/news414869.html, accessed July 2009.

Zernike, K. (2009). To Keep Students, Colleges Cut Anything but Aid. *New York Times* (February 27). www.nytimes.com/2009/02/28/education/28college.html?_r=1, accessed 2/3/10.

Zerubavel, E. (1979). *Patterns of Time in Hospital Life.* Chicago: University of Chicago Press.

Zerubavel, E. (1982). The standardization of time: A sociohistorical perspective. *American Journal of Sociology,* vol. 88.

Zhang and Wu. (1995). Discovering the positive within the negative: The women's movement in a changing China, in Amrita Basu, ed., *The Challenge of Local Feminisms.* Boulder, CO: Westview.

Zimbardo, P. (1969). The human choice: Individuation, reason, and order versus deindividuation, impulse, and chaos, in W. J. Arnold and D. Levine, eds., *Nebraska Symposium on Motivation.* Vol. 17. Lincoln, NE: University of Nebraska Press.

Zerubavel, E. (1972). Pathology of imprisonment. *Society,* vol. 9.

Zerubavel, Ebbesen, and Maslach. (1977). *Influencing Attitudes and Changing Behavior.* Reading, MA: Addison-Wesley.

Zuboff, S. (1988). *In the Age of the Smart Machine: The Future of Work and Power.* New York: Basic Books.

credits

Chapter 1: p. 3: Ed Kashhi/Corbis; p. 5: Ricco Torres/Epsilon/20th Century Fox /The Kobal Collection/WireImage.com /Getty Images; p. 7: The New Yorker Collection 1969 Dana Fradon from HYPERLINK "http://www.cartoonbank.com" www .cartoonbank.com; p. 8: Pablo Corral V /Corbis; p. 9: Radius Images/Alamy; p. 12: Anderson Ross/Blend Images/Corbis; p. 13: Corbis; p. 14: Bettmann/Corbis; p. 15: (top) Bettmann/Corbis; (bottom) Granger Collection; p. 16: Bettmann/Corbis; p. 17: Warder Collection; p. 21: Photorush/Stock Connection/IPNstock; p. 26: Bildarchiv Preussischer Kulturbesitz/Art Resource, NY; p. 30: Philip G. Zimbardo/Stanford Prison Experiment

Chapter 2: p. 39: AP Photo; p. 42: Getty Images; p. 43: (left): Peter Simon/IPN Stock; (right): Steven Vidler/Eurasia Press/Corbis; p. 48: Bob Krist/Corbis; p. 49: Phil Schermeister/Corbis; p. 50: Bruno Morandi /Hemis/Corbis; p. 51: (top) Othala Images /Alamy; (bottom) J&L Images /Getty Images; p. 56: Andre Jenny/Stock Connection/IPNstock; p. 59: Nora Bibel/laif/Redux; p. 61: Alamy; p. 65: AP Photo

Chapter 3: p. 69: Photofest; p. 71: Courtesy of Dan Bartell; p. 75: Reed Kaestner/Corbis; p. 76: Jacques Langevin/Corbis; p. 78: © JeongMee Yoon; p. 80: Alinari Archives /Corbis; p. 82: Thinkstock Images /Getty Images; p. 83: Datacraft - Sozaijiten / Alamy

Chapter 4: p. 95: Alex di Suvero/The New York Times/Redux; p. 97: Richard Perry/The New York Times/Redux; p. 98: Paul Ekman; p. 103: Courtesy Marion Goodman Gallery, New York; p. 104: Courtesy Stacy Snyder; p. 108: Solus-Veer/Corbis; p. 111: Natalie Behring/The New York Times/Redux; p. 112: Getty Images; p. 114: Jetta Productions /Getty Images

Chapter 5: p. 117: Tim Fadek/Polaris; p. 119: (both) Peter Turnley/Corbis; p. 121: Dung Vo Trung/Coup D'Etat Productions /Corbis; p. 123: Peter Turnley/Corbis; p. 125: Courtesy of Alexandra Milgram; p. 128: Ed Kashi/Corbis; p. 131: John Zich/zrImages /Corbis; p. 135: Librado Romero /The New York Times/Redux; p. 136: Courtesy Matthew Salganik; p. 139: Getty Images

Chapter 6: p. 145: Ovie Carter; p. 148: AP Photo; p. 153: Christian Poveda /Agence VU /Aurora Photos; p. 155: Randy Tepper /© Showtime / Courtesy: Everett Collection; p. 166: Hiroko Masuike/Getty Images; p. 168: AP Photo; p. 170: Owen Franken/Corbis; p. 171: Tom Nebia/Corbis

Chapter 7: p. 179: Ruth Fremson/The New York Times/Redux; p. 180: CW Network / The Kobal Collection; p. 183: Johnston /Sipa; p. 194: AP Photo; p. 195: Vince Streano/Corbis; p. 200 (top): Damon Winter/ The New York Times/ Redux; p. 200 (bottom): Reuters/ Corbis; p. 204: Q. Sakamaki/Redux; p. 209: Juan Carlos Ulate/Reuters/Landov

Chapter 8: p. 213: AP Photo; p. 214: Luis Acosta/AFP/Getty Images; p. 220: David Lewis / Reuters /Landov; p. 223: Gavin Hellier/JAI/Corbis; p. 226: Dean Conger /Corbis; p. 227: Danny Lehman/Corbis; p. 228: George Esiri/Reuters/Corbis; p. 229: AP Photo; p. 233: (both) Peter Menzel Photography

Chapter 9: p. 239: Monica Almeida/The New York Times/ Redux; p. 241: Tatiana Markow/Corbis/Sygma; p. 243: (both) Bettmann/Corbis; p. 244: National Anthropological Archives /Smithsonian Institution; p. 251: Justin Guariglia/Corbis; p. 252: AP Photo; p. 254: Nadia Borowski Scott/ Zuma Press; p. 261: Karen Kasmauski/ Corbis; p. 262: Bettmann /Corbis; p. 264: Henry Romero/Reuters /Landov; p. 265: AP Photo

Chapter 10: p. 269: Courtesy of France Winddance Twine. Photo by Michael Smyth; p. 271: Peter Marshall www .mylondondiary.co.uk; p. 272: Alain Nogues /Corbis Sygma; p. 276: Mark Peterson/ Corbis; p. 279: AP Photo; p. 285: Bettmann/ Corbis; p. 286: AP Photo; p. 287: Adam Woolfitt/Corbis; p. 288: Hulton-Deutsch/ Corbis; p. 290: Corbis; p. 295: Chip Somodevilla/Getty Images; p. 297: Getty Images

Chapter 11: p. 301: Micah Walter/Reuters; p. 303: (left) Hamid Sardar/Corbis; (right) Kazuhiro Nogi/AFP/Getty Images; p. 308: Katja Heinemann/Aurora; p. 309: Pat Greenhouse/Boston Globe /Landov; p. 318: Newscom; p. 321: Melanie Stetson

Freeman/ The Christian Science Monitor /Getty Images; p. 327: Najlah Feanny/Corbis; p. 328: AP Photo

Chapter 12: p. 331: Nancy Borowick; p. 333: Bettmann/Corbis; p. 336: J.A. Giordano/Corbis; p. 340: Gary Connor /PhotoEdit/PNI; p. 341: Matt Eich/ The New York Times/Redux; p. 343: Ted Streshinsky /Corbis; p. 346: Bennett Dean, Eye Ubiquitous/Corbis; p. 352: Leif Skoogfors/Corbis

Chapter 13: p. 361: Reuters/Corbis; p. 365: Jeff Topping /Reuters/Landov; p. 369: John Anderson/UPI/ Landov; p. 372: AP Photo; p. 373: Rod Lamkey Jr/The Washington Times/Landov; p. 380: Reuters/Corbis; p. 383: Bettmann/Corbis; p. 385: AP Photo; p. 389: Justin Guariglia/Corbis; p. 393: Eros Hoagland/The New York Times/Redux; p. 395: AP Photo

Chapter 14: p. 401: Howard Schatz /IPN Stock; p. 402: (left) C. Steele Perkins /Magnum Photos; (center) Ed Quinn/Corbis; (right) Karen Kasmauski/Corbis; p. 407: Mark Peterson/Corbis; p. 411: Lindsay Hebberd/Corbis; p. 413: Jeffrey Allan Salter /Corbis; p. 417: Gideon Mendel/Corbis; p. 419: Fredrik Renander/Redux; p. 421: AP Images/James Nachtwey/VII; p. 427: New York Daily News

Chapter 15: p. 431: Wu Hong/epa/Corbis; p. 432: Natalie Behring/Bloomberg News /Landov; p. 435: Getty Images; p. 437: David Brabyn/Sipa; p. 438: Kat Wade/Corbis; p. 440: AP Photo; p. 441: (top) Hulton Archive/Getty Images; (botttom) David McNew/Getty Images; p. 442: Philippa Lewis/Edifice/Corbis; p. 443: AP Photo; p. 444: Daniel/Corbis Sygma; p. 447: AP Photo; p. 448: AP Photo; p. 449: Krishna Murari Kishan/Reuters; p. 455: AP Photo; p. 458: Manjunath Kiran/epa/Corbis

Chapter 16: p. 467: David Butow/Redux; p. 469: Getty Images; p. 471: Getty Images; p. 473: Réunion des Musées Nationaux /Art Resourcec; p. 475: Zach Canepari/The New York Times/Redux; p. 481: (both) AP Photo; p. 483: AP Photo; p. 485: AP Photo; p. 491: Jim Richardson/Corbis; p. 493: AFP/Getty Images; p. 494: AP Photo

index

Page numbers in *italics* refer to illustrations, figures, and tables.

street talk and, 113–14
violence against women, 258–60
in the workplace, *see* women, in the
workplace
gender roles, 77
gender socialization, 77–79, 243
defined, 77
gender learning, 77–79
parental role in, 77, 242
from storybooks, 79
from television, 79
gender typing of occupations, 249
gene-environment interaction, 150
generalized other, 71
General Motors, 391
General Social Survey, 357, 424
"genital mutilation," 50, 258
genocide, 275, 276–77, 278, 469–70
gentrification, 444–45, *444*, 446
Gerbner, George, 74
Germany, 257
industrialization in, 431, 433
knowledge-based industries in, 395
length of workweek in, 309
gestures, 97, 99, 100, 102
Ghana, 60
ghettos, 294–95
Giddens, Anthony, 473, 488
Gintis, Herbert, 339
glass ceiling, 251, 252
glass escalator, 251
global cities, 445–46
inequality and, 446–47
global citizens, 63
Global City, The (Sassen), 445
global commodity chains, 230–31
Global Footprint, 457
Global Fund to Fight AIDS, Tuberculosis
and Malaria, 416
global inequality, 213–36, 494–98
defined, 215
differences among countries, 215–22
high-income countries, 215–16, 218–19
low-income countries, 215, 216–19
middle-income countries, 216, 218–19
future of, 235–36
globalization and, 235–36, 494–99
growing, 218–19
in health, 220
in hunger, malnutrition, and famine,
221–22
newly industrializing economies,
advancement of, 222–24
theories of, 224–32, 233
dependency, 228–29, 232
evaluation of, 232
market-oriented, 224–25, 228, 232
state-centered, 231, 232
world-systems, 229–31, 232
globalization, 111, 467–99
antiglobalization protests, 498–99
corporate mergers and acquisitions
and, 387

of crime, 166
debate, 486–89
the hyperglobalizers, 487–88, 489
the skeptics, 486–87, 489
the transformationalists, 488–89
defined, 467–68
drug trafficking and, 171
economic inequality and, 194–95
factors contributing to, 479–89
"electronic economy," 486
information flows, 479–81
political changes, 481–85
transnational corporations,
485–86, *485*
of food production, 403–4
global culture
forces creating a, 63
Internet and, 63–65, *65*
global inequality and, 235–36, 494–99
global justice, campaign for, 498–99
HIV/AIDS and, 416–17, 467
impact on contemporary culture, 62–67
impact on everyday life, 489–99
popular culture, 490–92
rise of individualism, 489–90
work patterns, 490
inequality and the global city, 446–47
interdependence and, 467–68
local cultures and, 65–66
resurgence of, 491
local impact of, 7–8
of material culture, 41
migration and, 195, 286–87
postindustrial society, 472–73
production of value and, 394–95
religion and, 351–53
residential mobility and, 442–43
rise of INGOs and health services, 416–17
risk and, 492–94
the global "risk society," 493–94
manufactured risk, 492–95
social change and, 468–72
culture and, 471
economic factors, 471–72
the physical environment, 468–70
political organization, 470
social movements and, 477–78
urbanism and, 445–47, 449
wealth accumulation by individuals
and, 192–93, 214, 215
worker rights and computerization of
the workplace, 392–93
work time and, 308–9
global migration, 274, 278–80
global perspective, developing a, 7–10
global warming, 432, 433, 457–59, 462,
464, 467, 492, 495
Goffman, Erving, 96, 100, 102–3, 107,
108, 114, 410
gold farms, 110–11
Goode, William J., 310
Google, *393*
Gore, Al, 29

government:
defined, 363
level of confidence, 376, 379
Granovetter, Mark, 126
Greece, ancient, 367, 434
homosexuality in, 422, 426
slavery in, 182
Greenfield, Patricia, 75
Greenland, global warming and, 458
Green Party, 370, 371
Greenpeace, 482
groups, social, *see* social groups
groupthink, 125–26
Guangdong, China, *447*
guerrilla movements, 476
guidance counselors, 202
*Guide to Cultural Competent
Health Care* (Paulanka and
Purnell), 54
Guinea, hunger, malnutrition, and
famine in, 221
guns, violent crime and availability
of, 159, 163

hackers, 148, *148*
Haiti, 60
Hall, Edward T., 108
Hamilton, Charles, 272
Handan, China, 431
Handan Iron and Steel, 431
H&M fashions, 484
Harry Potter series, 69–70
Harvey, David, 438–39, 471
Hatcher Destiny, 331–32
Hauser, Robert M., 200, 202
headings, table, 34
Head Start, 343
health and illness, 403–20
aging and, 91–93
alternative medicine, 410–12
biomedical model of health, 411
changing conceptions of, 410–12
in the developing world, 415–20
global inequality, 220
health-care providers and cultural
diversity, 54
international NGOs and health
services, 416–17
manufactured risk, 492, 493
obesity epidemic and, 404–7
racial and ethnic inequality, 294,
413–15
social factors and, 412–15
gender-based inequalities, 415
race-based inequalities, 413–15
social-class based inequalities,
413, *413*
sociological perspectives of, 407–12
illness as "lived experience," 409–10
sick role, 408–9
stigmas of, 410, *419*, 420
health inequalities, 412–15
health insurance, 92

heart disease, 418
Heaven's Gate, 148, 153
Held, David, 486, 488
Helu, Carlos Slim, 214, *214*
Herdt, Gilbert, 426
Herrnstein, Richard, 341
heterosexuality, 424
hidden curriculum, 338–39
high-income countries, 215–16, 217,
    218–19
Highland, Calif., *441*
Highway Act of 1956, 441
highways, construction of interstate, 441
Hinduism, 351, 352, 357
Hirschi, Travis, 155, 156
Hispanics/Latinos, *see* Latinos/Hispanics
historical analysis, 30–31
historicity, 477
HIV/AIDS, 352, 416–17, 418–20, *419*,
    421, 467
    in Africa, 220, 418–20, 421
Hmong, 297
Hochschild, Arlie, 308–9
Holocaust, 135, 276
homeless, the, 446–47
    as deviants and conformists, 147, 149
    reasons for becoming, 209
    social exclusion of, 208–9
homeownership, *see* housing
homicide, 159, 160
    mass, *see* mass murder
homicide rates, race and, 414
homophobia, 427
homosexuality, 420–22, 424–26
    gay marriage, 326–27, *328*
    homophobia, 427
    sexual norms and, 421–22
    see also gays and lesbians
Hong Kong, 61, 62, *447*
    eating disorders in, 403
    as high-income country, 215
    as newly industrializing economy (NIE),
        222, *223*, 224
    steel production in, 397
hospitals, *128*
House of Representatives, U.S., 295
    female representatives, 255, 373
    voting turnout in congressional races, 370
housework, 254–55, 382
housing:
    homeless, *see* homeless, the
    mortgages, discrimination in
        financing, 188, 444
    net worth and, 187
    residential mobility in the U.S., 442–43
    residential segregation, 291, 294–95,
        444–45
    tearing down, 446
    in urban areas of the developing world,
        220, 448
    wealth and homeownership, 187–88
Human Development Report (UNDP),
    266, 496

human resource management, 133
human sexuality, *see* sexuality
Humphreys, Laud, 31–35
Hungary, women in the workplace, 253
hunger, malnutrition, and famine, global,
    221–22, 401, 456
hunting and gathering societies, 57–58,
    181, 470
Hurricane Katrina, 492
Hussein, Saddam, 362, 363
hyperglobalists, 487–88, 489
hypertension, 414
hypotheses, 25

ideal types, 129
identity, 76–77, *76*
ideology, 19
Ikea, 484
illiteracy, *see* education and literacy
illness, *see* health and illness
illness work, 409–10
imagination, sociological, 5–8
imitation, learning through, 71
immigration, 279, 282–85
    demographic structure of the
        U.S. and, 286–87
        port-of-entry settlement,
        286–87
    discrimination and, 282, 285, *285*
    functional illiteracy in the U.S. and,
        342–43
    illegal, 286, 287, 290, 367
    of Latinos/Hispanics, 289–90
    quotas, 285
    U.S. policy, 290, 291
    welfare state and, 367
    see also migration
impression management, 100–102,
    103–5, 108
incarceration, *see* prisons
incest prohibition as cultural
    universal, 53
income:
    defined, 186
    inequality
        global, *see* global inequality
        health and, 413, 414
        in industrialized countries, 197, 198
        in the U.S., 186–87, 189, 197–99, 210
    real, 186
incumbents, 372
index crimes, 158
India, 60, 235, 420, 432, 451, *455*, 462, 481,
    485, 496
    caste system in, 182–83, *183*
    eating disorders in, 403
    independence from Britain, 470
    as low-income country, 215
    marriage in, 184
    poverty in, 61
    religion in, 351
    self-rule, 61
    violence against women in, 258

individualism, 489–90
    cultures valuing, 41, 43
Indonesia, 461–62
    hunger, malnutrition, and famine in, 221
    as newly industrializing economy
        (NIE), 222
Indus, 433
industrial conflicts, 384
industrialization, 59
    education and, 333–34, *333*, 393
    environment and, 431, 432–33, 448,
        456–64
    urbanization and, 431, 432, 433
    see also capitalism
industrialized societies, 59–60
    key features of, 59–60
    social stratification in, 181
Industrial Revolution, 13, 386
inequality:
    in consumption, 461
    education and, *see* education and literacy,
        inequality and
    gender, *see* gender inequality
    global, *see* global inequality
    globalization and
        economic inequality, 194–95
        the global city, 446–47
    in health and illness, 294, 412–15
    racial and ethnic, 291–98, 397, 413–15
    social stratification and, *see* social
        stratification
    in the U.S., gap between rich and poor,
        186–87, 189, 197–99, 210
*Inequality by Design: Cracking the Bell Curve
    Myth* (Fischer, et al.), 340–41
infanticide, 47, 258
infant mortality, 220, 294, 412, 451, 454
infectious disease, 415–20
    in the developing world today, 418
informal economy, 382, 447
informal relations within organizations, 130
information age, 393
information society, 472
information technology:
    computerization and the workplace,
        134–37
    electronic communications,
        see electronic communications
    global inequality and, 235–36
    globalization and, 482
    hackers, 148, *148*
    organizational structures, influence
        on, 134–37
    social movements and, 478–79
informed consent, 35–36
in-groups, 120
inner-city areas, 436
innovators, Merton's theory of deviance
    and, 152–53
instincts, 41, 46
institutional capitalism, 388
institutional racism, 272
instrumental roles, 260

Merton, Robert K., 18–19, 21, 130
  on deviance, 152–53, 154
  on reference groups, 121
Methodists, 354
Mexican Americans, 289–90, 298
  families, 313
Mexico, 62, 279, 367
  same-sex marriage in, 326, 327
  U.S. immigration policy and, 290
Mexico City, Mexico, 448, *449*
Meyer, John, 130
Miami, Florida, 297–98, 314
Michels, Robert, 131
Michigan, University of, Law School of, 296
microsociology, 22, 96
  linking of macrosociology and, 107, 113–15
  see also social interaction
middle age, 81
middle class in the U.S., 193–94, 210
Middle East, 276, 433
  personal space in the, 108, *112*
  women in politics in, 256
middle-income countries, 215, 216, 217,
      218–19
middle-range theories, 21
migration:
  from developing countries to the U.S., 61
  global, 274, 278–80, 449
  globalization and, 195, 286–87
  internal, in the developing world, 447, 456
  see also emigration; immigration
Milgram, Stanley, 124–25, *125*, 135
military:
  budgets, 376
  military-industrial complex, 375
Military Academy, U.S. (West Point),
      117–18
Miller, Mark, 279
Mills, C. Wright, 6
  The Power Elite, 375
Milner, Murray, 179–80
minimum wage, 203, 207
Mink, Michael, *254*
minority groups, 273–74
  endogamy and, 274
  incarceration of, 146
  poverty rates and, 204, 205
  wealth and income gaps, 198–99
  see also individual groups
"missile gap," 472
Mitnick, Kevin, 148, *148*
Mitsubishi Corporation, 389
mode, defined, 32
Model T Ford, 383, *383*, 384
Modern Corporation and Private Property,
      The (Berle and Means), 387
modernization theory, 225
modern societies, 59–62
Molotch, Harvey, 113, *114*
Molson Coors Brewing Company, 484
monarchies:
  constitutional, 368
  liberal democracy and, 368

money laundering, 171
monogamy, 41, 304
monopoly, 387
Moon, Reverend Sun Myung, 350
morality, child development and, 71
Morocco, 368
Morris, Jan (James), 243–44
Morrison, Toni, 289
mortality, 451
mortality rates, 451, 455
Moseley-Braun, Carol, 295
MoveOn.org, 362, 369, 479
moving and residential mobility in the U.S.,
      442–43
Mozambique, *419*, 492
multiculturalism, 48, 274, 278
multinational corporations, 388–89
multiparty systems, 370
Mundugumor tribe, 244
Murdock, George, 304
Murray, Charles, 208, 341
music:
  rave, 75
  Reggae, 48–49
music taste, 134–35
Muslims, 277, 351, 352
Myanmar (Burma), 61

NAACP, 17, 288
Najman, Jake, 294
Namibia, 421
National Association for the
      Advancement of Colored People
      (NAACP), 17, 288
National Association of Home Builders, 446
National Center for Education
      Statistics, 202
National Center for Health Statistics, 414
National Child Abuse and Neglect Reporting
      System, 323
National College Women Sexual
      Victimization Study, 259
National Crime Victimization Survey, 159
National Institute of Mental Health, 403
National Institutes of Health, 32
nationalism, 364–65
  defined, 364
  education and, 334
  local, 54, 365, 485
  religious, 351–52
  resurgence of, 66
National Law Center on Homelessness and
      Poverty, 208
National Organization for Women (NOW),
      141, 372
National Science Foundation, 32
National Survey of Drug Use and Health,
      163–64, 170
National Trust for Historic Preservation,
      446
National Urban League, 288
National Women's Conference, *262*
nation-states, 60, 488, 489

citizenship in, 364
  defined, 364, 365
  globalization and, 470, 482, 485, 488, 489
  sovereignty of, 364
Native Americans, 282, 286, 296, 298
  child poverty among, 440
  families, 313
  homeless, 208
"natural difference," theories of, 242
nature:
  interaction of nurture and, 46
  nurture debate, 45–46, 240, 241–46
  sexual orientation, 426
  socialization of, 404
Navajos and eye contact, cultural norm
      for, 41
Nazi Germany, 125
neoliberalism, 228
Netherlandish Proverbs (Brueghel), *26*
Netherlands, 326
  women in politics in, 256
  women in the workforce in the, 253
networks:
  informal, within organizations, 130
  social, 126–27
    Internet as, 127
    music taste and, 134–35
New Age religions, 350
new criminology, 156
new economy, 393
New Guinea:
  gender roles in, 244
  same-sex encounters in, 426
newly industrializing economies (NIEs),
      62, 222–24, 235
  "Asian meltdown" of 1998, 224
New Orleans, Hurricane Katrina and, 492
new religious movements, 350
new social movements, 478
new-style terrorism, 380, 381
New York City, New York, *21*, 445
  population growth in, 434
New York City Police Department,
      institutional racism and, 272
New Zealand, 256, 275, 368
Niebuhr, Richard, 349
Nigeria, 60, 61, *228*, 420
Nintendo, 74–75, 484
Nobel Peace Prize, 288
nongovernmental organizations
      (NGOs), 362
  international (INGOs), 416–17, 482
nonverbal communication, 97–100, 106
  bodily posture, 99, 102
  facial expression, 98–100, *98*, 102, 103
  gestures, 97, 99, 100, 102
  Internet interactions and, 99–100
norms, 41–42, 44, 146, 149
  change over time, 42
North Korea, 368
Norway, women in politics in, 257
nuclear family, 73, 301–2, 303, *303*, 304,
      305, 307, 310, 312

smoking, 418
   racial differences in, 414
   social norms of, changes in, 42
Snyder, Stacy, *104*
social activists, 474
social aggregate, 119
social aging, 84
social capital, 138–41
social category, 119–20
social change, 10, 15, 17
   defined, 468
   globalization and, 468–72
      culture, 471
      economic factors, 471–72
      the physical environment, 468–70
      political organizations, 470
   religion and, 347, 352–53, 471
   see also sexuality; *specific areas of social*
      change, e.g. health and illness
social class, *see* class
social closure, *365,* 367
social conflict theories of aging, 87–88
social constraint, 14, 16
social construction of gender, 243
   evidence from other cultures, 244–46
social control, 44, 477
social distance, 108
social exclusion, 207–9
   agency and, 207–8
   crime and, 207
   the homeless and, 208–9
social facts, 14, 16
social gerontology, 84
   explanation of aging, 85–88
social groups, 119–26
   characteristics of, 120–23
   conformity within, 117–18, 123–24,
      125–26
   defined, 119
   deviance and, 149
   in-groups, 120
   leadership in, 123
   out-groups, 120
   primary, 120
   reference groups, 121, *121*
   secondary, 120–21
   size of, effects of, 121–23
   variety of, 119–21
social identity, 76–77, *76*
social interaction, 477
   electronic communication and, 97,
      99–100, 103–5, 108, 110–13, *114*
   time-space, 109–13
social interaction and everyday life,
   95–115
   encounters, 103
   front and back regions, 104, 107, 109
   impression management, 100–102,
      103–5, 108
   linking macrosociology and
      microsociology, 107, 113–15
   nonverbal communication,
      see nonverbal communication

personal space, 108–9
reasons for studying, 96–97
response cries, 108
social rules and talk, 106–9
in time and space, *see* time-space social
   interaction
socialism, 20
social isolation and aging, 90
socialization, 44, 46
   agents of, 72–75
      the family, 73
      mass media, 74–75, *75*
      peer relationships, 72, 74
      schools, 72, 73
      work, 75
   defined, 70
   gender, *see* gender socialization
   identity, 76–77, *76*
   life course stages, 80–84
      childhood, 80
      midlife or "middle age," 81
      old age, 82–84, 93
      teenagers, 80–81
   primary, 72, 305
   secondary, 72–73
   social roles, 76, 100, 101
socialization of nature, 404
social mobility, 199–201
   defined, 199, 201
   downward, 201, 210
   education and, 200–201
   intergenerational, 199, 200, 201
   intragenerational, 199, 201
   opportunities for, 200–201
social movements, 474–79
   feminism, *see* feminism and feminist
      theory
   frameworks for studying
      economic deprivation, 474–75, *475*
      fields of action, 477
      resource mobilization, 475–77
      structural strain, 476–77
   globalization and, 477–78
   new, 478
   technology and, 478–79
   urbanism and, 439
social networks, 126–27
   Internet as, 97, 103, 110, 127
   music taste and, 134–35
Social Organization of Sexuality: Sexual
   Practices in the United States,
   The (Laumann), 424
social position, 73, 100
social promotion, 342
social reproduction, 70, 338–39
social rights, 366
social roles, 76, 100, 101, 104
Social Security, 93, 206
social self, 71
social status, 100
   defined, 180
   education and, 200
   occupation and, 190

status power, 180
teenagers and, 179–80
Weber's theory of, 185
social stratification, 179–210
   class and, *see* class
   defined, 181
   poverty, *see* poverty
   social exclusion and, *see* social exclusion
   social mobility and, *see* social mobility
   systems of, 181–84
      caste systems, 182–83, 184
      characteristics of, 181
      class, *see* class
      slavery, 182
   theories of, in modern societies,
      184–86
      of Marx, 184–85
      of Weber, 185
   in the U.S., gap between rich and poor,
      186–87, 189, 197–99, 210
social structure, 7
society:
   culture and, 42–44
   defined, 42–43
Society in America (Martineau), 16
sociobiology, 45–46
Sociobiology: The New Synthesis
   (Wilson), 45
sociological imagination, 5–8
sociological questions, 23
sociological thinking, development of,
   13–17
sociology:
   defined, 4
   as a science, 13–14, 23
   the word, Comte's invention of, 13
sociology of the body, *see* body, sociology
   of the
sodomy laws, 428
Solidarity movement, 353
Soros, George, 369
South Africa, 275
   African National Congress, 123
   apartheid in, 123, 271, 272, 277, 278
   "racial scale" in, *272*
   women's movement in, 264
South America, 275, 289, 371
   colonialism in, 61
   developing societies of, 60
South Korea, as newly industrializing
   economy (NIE), 62, 222, *223,* 235
sovereignty, 364
Soviet Union, 351, 352, 368
   space race with the, 472
Soviet Union, former:
   collapse of, 375, 481–82
   economic future of, 236
   middle-income countries, 216
space race, 472
space-time social interaction, *see*
   time-space social interaction
Spain, 380
   as colonial power, 61